CW01509059

A history of the French in London

liberty, equality, opportunity

A history of the French in London

liberty, equality, opportunity

Edited by
Debra Kelly and Martyn Cornick

LONDON
INSTITUTE OF HISTORICAL RESEARCH

Published by

UNIVERSITY OF LONDON
SCHOOL OF ADVANCED STUDY
INSTITUTE OF HISTORICAL RESEARCH
Senate House, Malet Street, London WC1E 7HU

ISBN 978 1 905165 86 5

Contents

List of contributors

CONSTANCE BANTMAN is a lecturer in French at the University of Surrey. Her research focuses on Anglo-French cultural and political exchanges in the long nineteenth century as well as the methodology of transnational history. She is the author of *The French Anarchists in London, 1880-1914: Exile and Transnationalism in the First Globalisation* (Liverpool, 2013).

FABRICE BENSIMON is professor of British civilization at the Université Paris-Sorbonne. His research focuses on the history of Victorian Britain and in particular on Franco-British exchanges in the mid nineteenth century. He is the author of *Les Britanniques face à la révolution française de 1848* (Paris, 2000) and, more recently, 'British workers in France, 1815–48' (*Past & Present*, ccxiii (2011), 147–89).

PAUL BOUCHER has been a performing musician since spending 1967 singing with Benjamin Britten and the English Opera Group. He studied violin in London and Moscow and was active internationally as a chamber musician, ran a music festival in France and a music charity for state primary schoolchildren in London before becoming research and artistic director of the Montagu music collection at Boughton House.

KIRSTY CARPENTER is senior lecturer in history, Massey University, Palmerston North, New Zealand. She has worked on the French Revolution since she completed her doctorate on the French émigrés at the Institut d'Histoire de la Révolution Française at the Sorbonne in 1993. Her research focuses on émigrés and their connections to French and European politics and literature. She has written *Refugees of the French Revolution: Emigrés in London 1789–1802* (Basingstoke, 1999), and edited *The French Emigrés in Europe and the Struggle against Revolution 1789–1814* (Basingstoke, 1999). Her most recent book, *The Novels of Madame de Souza in Social and Political Perspective* (Oxford and New York, 2007), looks at one émigré woman's fiction and the influence that the revolutionary wars had upon her work.

MARTYN CORNICK is professor of French cultural history at the University of Birmingham. His principal research areas are twentieth-century cultural history (Jean Paulhan and the *Nouvelle Revue Française*), the life and intellectual biography of Armand Petitjean, and Franco-British intercultural studies, with a particular focus on the French presence in London during the Second World War. He has published widely in both these fields, most recently the edition of the correspondence between Paulhan and Petitjean with the Gallimard publishing house.

Máire Cross is head of French at Newcastle University and an international scholar and leading authority on Flora Tristan. Her publications include: *The Letter in Flora Tristan's Politics* (Basingstoke, 2004), and an edited book entitled *Gender and Fraternal Orders* (Basingstoke, 2010). She is currently president of the Association for the Study of Modern and Contemporary France and a member of the Franco-British Council.

David Drake is an independent scholar who formerly taught at Middlesex University and in the Institut d'Etudes Européennes at Université Paris VIII. He has lectured and written widely on French intellectuals and politics, notably producing two monographs, both published by Palgrave. He is a former president of the UK Society for Sartre Studies and his biography of Sartre was published by Haus in 2005. He is a regular contributor to the *Times Educational Supplement* and is currently writing an account of life in Paris 1939–44, to be published by Harvard University Press.

Helen Drake is professor of French and European studies at Loughborough University, and has been chair of UACES (University Association of Contemporary European Studies) since September 2012. Her research centres on contemporary French politics and on France's relationship with the European Union. Her most recent book, *Contemporary France* (Basingstoke, 2011), is the culmination of many years spent teaching British students about France; and her 2000 volume published by Routledge, *Jacques Delors: Perspectives on a European Leader*, is a study of contemporary political leadership.

Charlotte Faucher is a PhD student at Queen Mary, University of London. She has been awarded a Collaborative Doctoral Award by the Arts and Humanities Research Council and her work focuses on the history of the Institut Français du Royaume-Uni.

Saskia Huc-Hepher is a lecturer in French at the University of Westminster, where she specializes in applied language transfer skills. Recently, she has worked as researcher and co-author on several major projects, including a HEFCE-funded qualitative investigation into language policy at major events such as the Olympic Games, which culminated in a publication entitled *Languages and International Events: Are We Ready to Talk to the World in 2012?* Huc-Hepher is currently conducting doctoral research on the digital presence of London's French diaspora, as represented in a special collection she is curating for the UK Web Archive. Her particular research interests include community and identity, multimodal ethnography or 'ethnosemiotics', cultural dynamics and display, linguistic accessibility and translation theory.

THOMAS JONES completed his PhD on French republican exiles in Britain at the University of Cambridge in 2010. He is a lecturer in history at the University of Buckingham, holds a visiting lecturer post at Queen Mary, University of London, and has taught at Roehampton University. He is interested in British and French political and intellectual history, and his publications include 'The memory of the First Republic in Ledru-Rollin's political thought', in *Historicising the French Revolution*, ed. C. Armenteros and others (Newcastle-upon-Tyne, 2008), pp. 124–45; and 'Louis Blanc's *Historical Revelations* and the memory of 1848 in France and Britain' (forthcoming).

DEBRA KELLY is professor of French and Francophone literary and cultural studies, University of Westminster, London. Her main research interests are in war and culture studies, the relationship between literature and cultural memory, text and image studies (with a focus on the twentieth-century avant-garde), and Franco-British cultural relations. Her major publications are *Pierre Albert-Birot: a Poetics in Movement, Poetics of Movement* (Madison, NJ, 1997) and *Autobiography and Independence: Selfhood and Creativity in North African Postcolonial Writing in French* (Liverpool, 2005). She is director of the Group for War and Culture Studies, an international network of researchers established in 1995, and has edited and co-edited volumes of essays in this field, and is the founding editor of the *Journal of War and Culture Studies* (Maney).

PHILIPPE LANE has been professor of French linguistics at the Université de Rouen, and vice-president of the same University, visiting professor at the University of Cambridge, and attaché de coopération universitaire at the French Embassy in London (Service Culturel). He is now conseiller de coopération et d'action culturelle at the French Embassy in Jordan. His most recent major work is *Présence française dans le monde: l'action culturelle et scientifique* (Paris, 2011; published in English in 2013 by Liverpool University Press) with a preface by M. Laurent Fabius.

PHILIP MANSEL is the author of several books on French history, including lives of Louis XVIII (1981) and the prince de Ligne (2003), and histories of the French court from 1789 to 1830; and of *Paris between Empires: Monarchy and Revolution 1814-1852* (New York, 2001). All have been translated into French. He is currently writing a life of Louis XIV. He is editor of *The Court Historian*, the journal of the Society for Court Studies, and a member of the committee of the Centre de Recherche du Chateau de Versailles.

VALERIE MARS is a senior research associate in the Department of Anthropology at University College London. Her PhD 'Ordering dinner: Victorian celebratory dining in London', and twelve of her twenty-two papers, are on nineteenth-century food-ways in their social context, and on their material culture.

TESSA MURDOCH is the acting keeper of the Department of Sculpture, Metalwork, Ceramics & Glass at the V&A. She specializes in the metalwork collections and silver. Permanent displays she has curated at the V&A include the Sacred Silver and Stained Glass Galleries (2005) and the Rosalinde and Arthur Gilbert Galleries (2009). Previously, she was senior assistant keeper of the Tudor and Stuart Department at the Museum of London where she organized the exhibitions Treasures and Trinkets: Jewellery in London from Pre-history to 1914, London Silver 1680–1780 and The Quiet Conquest: the Huguenots 1685–1985. Tessa has edited and contributed to numerous publications including *Noble Households: Eighteenth-Century Inventories of Great English Houses. A Tribute to John Cornforth* (Cambridge, 2006), and the forthcoming *Going for Gold: the Craftsmanship and Collecting of Gold Boxes* (2013). She also co-edited, with Olga Dmitrieva, the publication *Treasures of the Royal Courts: Tudors, Stuarts and the Russian Tsars* (2013).

ELIZABETH RANDALL is general editor of the publications of the Huguenot Society of Great Britain and Ireland. A former teacher, with a Master's degrees in Renaissance studies and in French and English early modern history, she is currently interested in the extent to which seventeenth-century innovation and change were due to the influence of Protestant rulers and their courts.

MICHEL RAPOPORT is honorary professor of modern history at the Université Paris Est Créteil and also has given lectures at l'Ecole Pratique des Hautes Etudes (5ème section). He is a specialist in the modern history of Great Britain and the history of Franco-British cultural relations. His publications include *L'Entente Cordiale: cent ans de relations culturelles franco-britanniques*, ed. with D. Cooper Richet (Paris, 2006); *Le Débat sur l'abolition de l'esclavage, Grande-Bretagne 1787–1840*, ed. with E. Dziembowski (Paris, 2009); *Le Monde Britannique 1815–1931*, ed. with S. Aprile (Paris, 2010); and *Affirmations de foi: etudes d'histoire religieuse et culturelle*, ed. with F. Bourillon and R. Fabre (Bordeaux, 2012).

ROBERT TOMBS is professor of French history at the University of Cambridge and a fellow of St. John's College. He specializes in nineteenth-century France, and is co-author of *That Sweet Enemy: the French and the British from the Sun King to the Present* (2007).

List of abbreviations

AN	Paris, Archives Nationales
BL	British Library
HSP	Proceedings of the Huguenot Society of Great Britain and Ireland
HSQS	Huguenot Society Quarto Series
IWM	Imperial War Museum
ODNB	*Oxford Dictionary of National Biography* (Oxford, 2004) <http://www.oxforddnb.com> [accessed 1 Oct. 2012]
TNA	The National Archives of the UK

List of figures

List of tables

List of maps

Please note that the maps are not drawn to scale. While every attempt has been made to make them as accurate as possible, they are primarily intended to be indicative.

Acknowledgements

The editors wish gratefully to acknowledge the financial support of the British Academy (grant RRBS15375) without which this project would not have been feasible. Our special thanks go to Saskia Huc-Hepher, the project's appointed research assistant, as well as to M. Philippe Lane, former attaché for higher education at the Cultural Service of the French Embassy, for his constant encouragement and generous welcome at the French Institute in London.

We are grateful too for the assistance of the staff of the French Institute and for the support and encouragement of M. Edouard Braine, former consul-general at the French Consulate in London.

Our heartfelt thanks go to Helena Scott, of the University of Westminster, for her vigilance and patience, and for deploying her incomparable copy-editing skills in the preparation of the typescript.

Thanks also to the IHR Publications Team, especially Jane Winters, for their encouragement of the book project and for readily accepting the idea of creating maps for many of the chapters. We are especially grateful to Olwen Myhill for her work in making the maps a reality.

Finally, we should like to express our warm gratitude to all the contributors to this book. It has been a pleasure to work with you all.

Introduction
The French in London: a study in time and space

Martyn Cornick

'London has always been a city of immigrants'. Thus Peter Ackroyd, in his 'biography' of London, opens a chapter on the long history of immigrant influx to the city. London was once widely known as 'the city of nations'. Of Joseph Addison's remark – 'when I consider this great city, in its several quarters, or divisions, I look upon it as an aggregate of various nations, distinguished from each other by their respective customs, manners, and interests' – Ackroyd comments that 'the same observation could have been applied in any period over the last 250 years'.[1] We believe he is right in this assertion. It is a very long history too, and one which, no doubt, over the *longue durée*, helped to prepare London's 'secret of successful assimilation':

> Fresh generations, with their songs and customs, arrived at least as early as the time of the Roman settlement, when London was opened up as a European marketplace. The working inhabitants of the city might have come from Gaul, from Greece, from Germany, from Italy, from North Africa, a polyglot community speaking a variety of rough or demotic Latin … By the tenth century the city was populated by Cymric Brythons and Belgae, by the remnants of the Gaulish legions, by East Saxons and Mercians, by Danes, Norwegians and Swedes, by Franks and Jutes and Angles, all mingled and mingling together to form a distinct tribe of 'Londoners'.[2]

This book takes as its specific focus the *French* presence in London. It is the result of a series of workshops and seminars attended by most of the contributors, beginning in the spring of 2011.[3] The 'French' presence in London is one whose roots may indeed be traced back to Gallo-Roman times. This book surveys the 'London French' from the seventeenth century, as it is from this time onwards that their presence, their impact on the developing city are most clearly marked. In doing so, its intention is to respond in some measure to a remark made by Jerry White, that

---

[1] P. Ackroyd, *London: the Biography* (2000), p. 701.
[2] Ackroyd, *London*, pp. 701–2.
[3] See the acknowledgements above, p. xxv.

indefatigable historian of London, hidden away in an endnote in his book *London in the Eighteenth Century*: 'The wider French community in modern London has yet to find its historian'.[4]

This book aims, then, to explore and provide elements toward a history of the social, cultural, political and – to some extent – economic presence of the French in London, and to examine the many ways in which this presence has contributed to the life of the British capital. Using both a historical and a contemporary focus, the varied exchanges that characterize the relationship between French 'exile', 'migrant', 'visitor' and host city are surveyed. As implied in Ackroyd's remarks on the population of London, the British capital has often provided a place of refuge and/or opportunity to very different French men and women from across the political spectrum, of differing religious and social beliefs, and from different social classes. The chapters of the book examine in detail some of the well-known and less well-known stories in the history of these disparate French incomers.

Elizabeth Randall, in her opening chapter on 'London's French Protestants', offers a summary overview of the extraordinarily rich historiography on the 65,000 or so French-speaking Protestants who arrived in the English capital in roughly 200 years between 1550 and 1759. By the 1630s, the number of French-speaking residents had risen to over 1,000, but partly because of upheavals on the continent, as many as 25,000 came between 1680 and 1700. These were the 'Huguenots', whose nickname, we learn, may derive from the Hugon gate, in Tours, where Protestants would congregate. In the important year of 1685, when France annulled the Edict of Nantes, the British king Charles II died, leaving his Catholic brother James the task of dealing with the sudden influx of 13,500 French people. Despite the hostility of the House of Commons, their presence also met with favourable reactions as their contribution was seen as beneficial for London's future economic standing. Thus the Huguenots brought with them the refined and exquisite artisanal and artistic skills which have long since been associated with them: silk-weaving, book-binding and stationery, lace-, glove- and periwig-making, tailoring, jewellery and shoemaking. Nicaise Le Fèvre, professor of chemistry and royal apothecary, became one of the very first French members of the Royal Society. Their invaluable contribution to the British Enlightenment, between 1680 and 1720, is reflected in the fact that sixteen Huguenots were elected to the Royal Society in that time. Such artistic and intellectual skills could not help but make a major impact on London life, and so well did they assimilate that by the end of the eighteenth century most of the Huguenots had ceased speaking French.

[4] J. White, *London in the 18th Century: a Great and Monstrous Thing* (2012), p. 573.

In chapter two, Paul Boucher and Tessa Murdoch provide a tantalizing glimpse into the life and interior of Montagu House, in Bloomsbury. This 'French household in London, 1673–1733', belonged to Ralph Montagu, who had the good fortune to be appointed ambassador to the court of Louis XIV. While in France, Montagu acquired a liking for *le goût français*, a taste and style which he brought back to London, some of which was manifest in the 200 trunks of luxury goods and artefacts he imported. The Montagus had established an estate in Bloomsbury, on the site of the current British Museum. He furnished this house in the French taste with contributions from artists and artisans whom Ralph Montagu had encouraged to cross to London, among whom were Daniel Marot and Baptiste Monnoyer. Boucher and Murdoch base their account mainly on the incomparable archive collection of account books and other documents affording a breath-taking insight into Montagu's influence over taste. Several of the Montagu artists and craftsmen – many of whom were Huguenot in origin – were recommended to work in London's royal palaces. Later, some artefacts and many of the fittings and furnishings from Bloomsbury were transferred to Boughton House, in Northamptonshire, where they may be seen today. Montagu had a French doctor, Pierre Silvestre, who would travel to Boughton from London when required; and the archives show that French suppliers continued to submit bills drafted in French until the 1750s. Another of the treasures described by Boucher and Murdoch are the notes of the French master of dance, Anthony L'Abbé, whose meticulous choreographer's notations survive in the Montagu music collection.

In chapter three, Kirsty Carpenter reveals the 'novelty value' of French émigrés to London in the 1790s. She reminds us of the closeness of the cultural exchange and mutual influences which obtained in a volatile political context dominated by the French Revolution, and when, in London, fashion and taste were French. Armed with the Abbé Tardy's guide, émigrés came to a thriving city, the largest in Europe at the time, and some, via Soho and Marylebone, eventually settled in Somers Town, located around present-day St. Pancras. This developing suburb attracted French people escaping the Revolution. Carpenter shows how these new immigrants often arrived in a precarious state: through the good offices of such as the Abbé Carron, French schools, a hospice and a home for elderly priests were founded. Somers Town also saw the construction, in 1799, of a French chapel dedicated to St. Aloysius. Homage was paid to this French area of London by the poet Jacques Delille: 'Salutations O Somers Town, shelter dear to France'. The difference between the Huguenots, and this wave of émigrés, was that the Huguenots gradually became assimilated completely into London life and society, whereas many of the 1790s émigrés would return to France after 1814. In the end, Carpenter draws the conclusion that the 'vast majority of émigrés represented no political threat, and their gratitude and endorsement of what they considered the essential goodness of the British character did much to bring the two nations closer together'.[5]

This sense of common cause paved the way for the solace found in London by French courts in exile, as examined by Philip Mansel in chapter four. Contrary to the view that relations between France and Britain were antagonistic, London was convenient, congenial and attractive to those French royalists who sought exile. Despite the obstacle of the Channel, in the early years of the nineteenth century London was only thirty hours from Paris. Here we are on the threshold of the modern era of easier travel between France and Britain: passenger traffic between French and British ports rose from 12,000 per annum in 1815 to around 30,000 in 1830; the railway era beginning in 1830–5 quickly expanded possibilities still further.[6] Indeed, British innovations in applying the power of steam to transport meant that by the mid nineteenth century 'the journey Paris-London was all steam-powered; the route Paris-Rouen resembled an English railway, with an English driver, with English railway architecture, English-style uniforms', not to mention 'the 15,000 English workers on the extensions of the line to Le Havre and to Dieppe.' And by 1939, the writer Bernard Faÿ noted, simply: 'On the platform at the Gare du Nord it's as though I'm already in London'.[7]

Mansel traces the lives and experience of a succession of royal and imperial exiles and pretenders in and around the British capital: in particular, Philippe Egalité; the comte d'Artois and the Bourbons; Louis-Napoléon and the Bonapartes; and finally the House of Orléans, who became 'permanent exiles'. Philippe Egalité came to London as a pleasure-seeker, and already

---

[5] This chapter is followed by some notes on French Catholics in London after 1789, extracted with permission from Douglas Newton's 1950 book on the topic.

[6] Figures from P. Gerbod, *Les Voyageurs Français à la découverte des Iles Britanniques du XVIIIe siècle à nos jours* (Paris, 1995), p. 29. On the growth of rail travel and the concomitant improvement and expansion of the entry ports of Dover and Folkestone, see R. Bucknall, *Boat Trains and Channel Packets: the English Short Sea Routes* (1957), esp. ch. 2, a source that remains essential reading. For a useful anthology of French travellers' accounts to Britain, see J. Gury, *Le Voyage outre-manche: anthologie de voyageurs français de Voltaire à Mac Orlan* (Paris, 1999), esp. pts. i and ii, respectively on the Channel crossing itself, and on the experience of contending with London.

[7] 'Par le railway de Paris à Rouen, on peut déjà se croire en Angleterre depuis la rue Saint-Lazare. C'est un railway anglais; l'ingénieur est anglais ... les entrées et les sorties des tunnels et les stations sont d'architecture anglaise; les inspecteurs ont l'uniforme anglais ... enfin les travaux ... projetés de Rouen au Havre et à Dieppe emploient plus de quinze mille ouvriers anglais' (quoted in Gury, *Le Voyage outre-manche*, p. 67 (the source dates from 1830); and B. Faÿ, 'Londres en guerre', *La Revue de Paris* (15 Dec. 1939), pp. 1107–15 (quoted at p. 1107)).

in 1782 was renting a house in Portland Place. This set a trend which then extended through the coming nineteenth century: the history recounted by Mansel draws a surprising and vivid portrait of London-French life for this class. Such was the impact of their presence that already in 1811, French royalists were in receipt of pensions from the British government totalling over £150,000 per annum, a staggering sum. By 1840, London had become a springboard for Bonapartist plots, much as it had for royalist plots in the years between 1799 and 1814. When the prince imperial ('Napoleon IV') was killed in the Zulu Wars in 1879, his funeral at Chislehurst on 12 July that year brought together a huge assembly of people: the Bonaparte family, officers of the imperial crown, other court officials; 'many British came, because of his popularity and his tragic death fighting in the British army'. In all around 30,000 people attended, many of whom were transported in the thirty-two special trains which had been laid on.

In chapter five, in a study offering an intriguing counterpoint to Mansel's, Máire Cross explores the 'multidimensional occupancy' of French visitors to London in the mid nineteenth century. On the continent this was a period of intense interest in London and Britain, nowhere more so than in France. Industrialized Britain was fast becoming a global power, and therefore attracted a succession of French observers keen to learn from this experience. Conscious of the gendered perspective too, Cross points to the paucity of comparative studies on French and British travelogue literature. She reviews successively the experiences of the great historian and republican enthusiast Jules Michelet; the liberal political theorist and traveller Alexis de Tocqueville; and finally, the socialist and feminist activist and traveller Flora Tristan. In contrast to Michelet and Tocqueville, who, relatively speaking, left only brief traces of their impressions of London within posthumously published works, Tristan made her interpretation of London life the central focus of one of her most arresting, even innovative, works, *Promenades dans Londres*. Prefiguring – from a French perspective of course – the work of Henry Mayhew (*London Labour and the London Poor*), women's emancipation and London's slums were of particular interest to her; and while her representation of London was not always accurate, her study subsequently gained her recognition as an original thinker among socialists. Although London – 'the monster city' – was for Tristan a megalopolis of striking contrasts, her experience there provided her with fruitful inspiration, as Cross reveals.

Chapter six consists of an introductory exposition by Fabrice Bensimon on 'French republicans and communists in exile to 1848'. In chapter seven, Thomas Jones and Robert Tombs provide a survey of the 'French left in exile' during the remaining decades of the nineteenth century. Because of upheavals in France in 1830, 1848 and 1870–1 – to mention only the most memorable years – London became home to hundreds if not thousands of revolutionary-republican and socialist exiles. Their influence made a lasting imprint on the physiognomy of the city in certain areas. The year of European revolutions 1848 brought many French exiles, but the biggest wave arrived in the winter of 1851–2. According to the Home Office, in 1853 there were at least 800 refugees who would stay on until the amnesty of 1859. After the Commune (May 1871), 1,500 adult males, 600 spouses and 1,200 children arrived. Most stayed on until the 1880 amnesty, whereupon there was a general return to France. Such political exiles settled in London because of its size (compare Flora Tristan's 'monster city'), its economic importance and the opportunities which flowed from that. It is this settlement, in and around Soho, Fitzrovia and the West End around Leicester Square, which would eventually gain purchase as a permanent colony, many of whose sites continue in French occupancy or filiation to this day. Strikingly – and Jones and Tombs illustrate this with multiple examples – exiles' reactions to their predicament as 'London-French' ranged from alienation to real elation at the opportunities and challenges that the megalopolis afforded. They deployed their talents as best they could, among other things entering the service industries and becoming school and university teachers. There was, eventually, a reciprocal ideological process at work here too: the returning Blanquist Communards who knew Karl Marx in London played an appreciable role in the introduction of Marxism into France.

Constance Bantman, in chapter eight, surveys the fascinating history of the French anarchist presence in London between the late 1870s and the outbreak of the war in 1914. As such, and following on from the previous chapters, we see the drawing to a close of cross-Channel revolutionary exile in the long nineteenth century. In the 1890s a wave of anarchist outrages in Paris provoked a clampdown by the French police, leading to another influx of political refugees seeking relative safety in London. The Franco-Italian journalist and activist Charles Malato paid his own homage to the 'monster-city' in the first page of his memoir: 'O Albion's big metropolis, of you I shall not speak a bad word because, for three years, you gave me hospitality'. It is fascinating to note, too, that Malato provides a 'Practical guide for the refugee in London', going so far as to outline the details of the train connections and ferry times to the British capital.[8] Coincidentally, this information finds a cross-reference in the popular *Guide instantané de Londres* (*Instant Guide to London*) produced by Guides Nilsson, as shown

---

[8] C. Malato, *Les Joyeusetés de l'exil* (1897; Paris, 1985), pp. 160–1. We are grateful to Constance Bantman for providing details from this chapter.

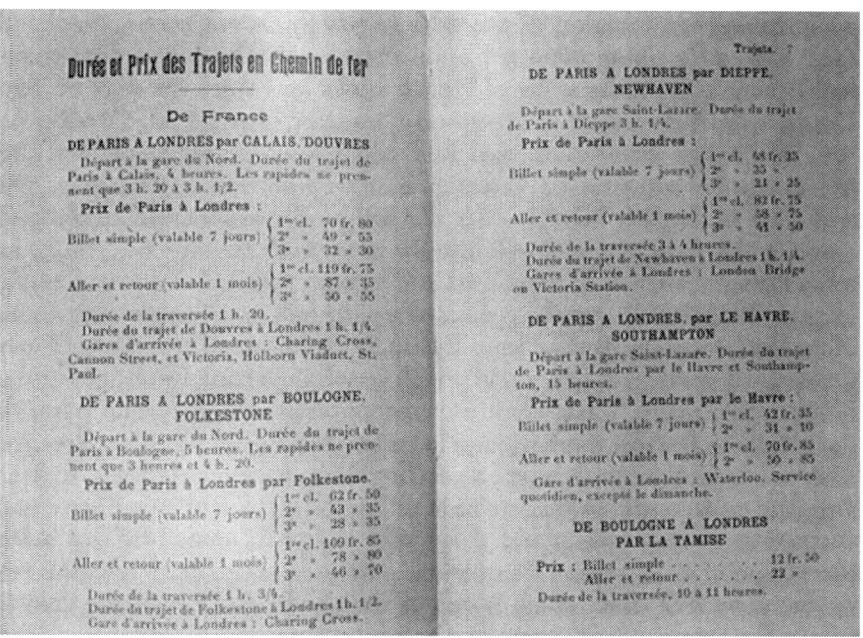

Figure 0.1. Routes to London and fares from *Guide instantané de Londres* (Guides Nilsson, Paris and London, n.d. [1908?]), pp. 6–7.

in Figure 0.1.[9] Baedeker's guide from the same period gives similar advice in much greater detail, and reflects identical concerns to those of the anarchist Malato: the advantages of the short sea route (for avoiding sea-sickness in a journey of just over an hour) come at greater cost to the passenger, so if one has a natural resistance to the 'mal de mer', there is certainly a pecuniary interest to be had in taking a longer sea crossing, via Newhaven or Southampton.[10] Having put the discomfort of the Channel crossing behind them, the anarchists headed towards Soho and Fitzrovia, as numerous of their predecessors had done. Charlotte Street and Goodge Street were at the heart of the anarchist presence, providing the location for the famous Autonomie Club, set up at 32 Charlotte Street in 1886.

One tangible and lasting result of the settlement of French political refugees in London was the founding of catering businesses, such as the Maison Bertaux patisserie in Soho. The chapter by Valerie Mars provides

[9] *Guide instantané de Londres* (Guides Nilsson, Paris and London, n.d. [1908?]).
[10] Compare Malato, *Les Joyeusetés*, p. 161, with K. Baedeker, *Londres et ses environs: manuel du voyageur* (Leipzig and Paris, 1907), introduction, p. xiii.

a captivating examination of the ways in which French cooks, chefs and their styles of cooking impacted upon the capital. The rich and powerful had benefited from the skills of French cooks ever since the days of Pero Doulx, who had worked at Hampton Court for Henry VIII. Cookbooks too, in English translation, also laid down long-lasting guidelines and influences: for instance, La Varenne's book – published in France in 1651 and then in English in 1653 – set the recipes for foundation stocks and sauces which then persisted well into the nineteenth century. Fashion, as in other domains such as literature, art and interior design, led the way, and it became de rigueur in certain sections of society to have a French cook, more often than not male. And we learn that male cooks earned around five times the wage of women, a differential which certainly persisted throughout the nineteenth century. Travel made a contribution as well, for when travel to the continent became more widespread after 1860 British travellers returned with tastes acquired for bourgeois cooking. French standard dishes, such as *bœuf à la mode*, underwent adaptation to English tastes and ingredients: one description from the 1850s and 1860s talks of an à la mode beef that 'with the exception of its bovine foundation, presented no culinary resemblance to that *bœuf à la mode* which is one of the standing dishes of the French *cuisine bourgeoise*'. With the expansion of the hotel and restaurant trade in and beyond the late nineteenth century, French cooks continued to prosper. By the 1890s grand hotels were being established that required the means to serve haute cuisine to large numbers.

It is, finally, interesting to compare visitors' guides regarding the food to be consumed in London: the upper middle-class Baedeker offered the opinion that 'first rank restaurants have good French cuisine', and discreetly referenced another page for its description of English cooking, 'which leaves a lot to be desired. Too often it lacks seasoning, everything being boiled without salt'; the Guide Nilsson – aimed at more modest travelling classes – also called English fare 'dull' ('fade'), but it did recommend oxtail and mock-turtle soup, and was clearly impressed by the quality and value of the London tea-rooms. Interestingly, both noted that English 'beefsteaks' were superior to the French.[11]

In chapter ten Michel Rapoport offers a detailed and thorough survey of the French presence in London from the late nineteenth century until the end of the inter-war period. Rapoport bases his analysis on two distinct,

---

[11] 'les hôtels de premier ordre sont bons mais chers … mais la cuisine anglaise laisse à désirer. Elle manque trop souvent d'assaisonnement, tout étant cuit sans sel' (Baedeker, *Londres et ses environs*, pp. 10, 2); 'Les viandes sont excellentes: le roastbeef bien saignant, les mutton chops … les beefsteaks grillés sont supérieurs aux viandes que l'on a en France' (*Guide instantané de Londres*, p. 30).

if broad, categories: the permanent French 'colony', as it had come to be known in the inter-war period, and visitors, whether occasional or frequent. It is estimated here (based on census information) that at the peak of the French colony there were some 18,000 French people residing in London. In other words, among the incomers to London, the French contingent was third after the Russians and the Germans, with women outnumbering men, and with mainly younger cohorts rather than older. Although this period has, relatively speaking, been under-researched, Rapoport reconstructs a detailed picture of the nature of French businesses, and their location: for instance, immediately after the Great War there used to be a Galeries Lafayette in Regent Street. There are numerous portraits drawn too of some of the better-known political exiles in London: we meet General Boulanger, Henri de Rochefort and Emile Zola, the hero par excellence of the Dreyfus affair, to whom one might add the arch-villain Ferdinand Walsin-Esterhazy, to be seen in the library of the British Museum researching for the profoundly Anglophobic articles he sent for publication in the Paris right-wing press.[12] Particularly impressive is Rapoport's analysis of the contribution of the London-French labour force to the capital's commerce and industry: by the 1920s, the major areas of activity included food, fashion, shoes, furniture and, of course, the service sector, including its seamier side, in and around Soho, infamous as the centre of the sex industry. In the mid 1880s, of the 4,200 prostitutes arrested in the West End, 769 were French.[13] In addition, the burgeoning number of French societies is examined in this rich and dense chapter.

In chapter eleven Philippe Lane and Charlotte Faucher review the contribution of French cultural diplomacy to France's development of 'soft power'. This effort derives from that very French ideal that humanity may be perfected or at least improved by the projection and exploitation of culture. In London there was a ready and highly articulate Francophile audience: it just remained to create a French Institute in London, when others were being founded in the decade or so before the outbreak of the First World War in other European cities, such as Florence, Athens, Madrid and St. Petersburg. Lane and Faucher explore the precursor institutions out of which the French Institute emerged, such as the Université des Lettres Françaises. The importance of promoting culture and civilization by means of international exhibitions is also reviewed, such as the 1908 Franco-British Exhibition held at the White City, in Shepherd's Bush, West London, when

---

[12] See M. Cornick, 'Esterhazy, Charles-Marie-Ferdinand Walsin- (1847–1923)', *ODNB*.

[13] For a well-documented further study, see S. Slater, 'Pimps, police and *filles de joie*: foreign prostitution in interwar London', *London Journal*, xxxii (2007), 53–74.

a purpose-built site was constructed to showcase French and British goods and culture in a spirit of international co-operation: it was this event which 'sealed the Entente Cordiale'.

There follows a sequence of three chapters on the presence in London of those now broadly known as the 'Free French', after the outbreak of the Second World War in September 1939. In chapter twelve Debra Kelly reminds us that there were a good number of French refugees and exiles who, while they certainly chose to fight Nazism and the Occupation of France, did not necessarily all or always wholeheartedly embrace the Gaullist vision. Her study is based upon rarely used and unusual sources, including papers and diaries contained in the Imperial War Museum in London. In addition to this, she is interested in 'mapping' the traces and places associated with these people, who are often not found among the usual subjects of academic historical scrutiny. Particularly fruitful here is the mapping of people's experiences of real places and spaces alongside the imaginary, if not mythical, space(s) of London, spaces which were of crucial importance during the war. One of the most engaging sources unearthed here is the series of 'war novels' by Mrs. Robert Henrey (Madeleine Henrey), who transposed her lived experience as a Frenchwoman in pre-war and wartime London.

Martyn Cornick, in chapter thirteen, follows on from this in an effort to reveal how, first of all, Denis Saurat (director of the French Institute in London) placed the Institute at the service of the Free French cause, leading to its characterization by one of the men who spent time there as the 'first bastion of the Resistance'. Through the numerous French journalists who frequented it, the Institute had close ties with the BBC, and the study reviews some of the ways in which London radio helped to support the Free French cause, especially through some of the members of the BBC's French Service. The chapter draws, moreover, on an interview with Stéphane Hessel, one of the last surviving witnesses of this period. Cornick reveals the presence in London of a forgotten French novelist, Ignace Legrand, who composed a special issue of a French-language review, *Aguedal*, based in Rabat, Morocco, to promote and celebrate the contribution to the war effort of a wide range of anglophone authors, including T. S. Eliot and Rosamond Lehmann. The French Institute and its inhabitants were engaged in fighting an intense propaganda war, and freely and effectively mobilized cultural production to further this end.

David Drake, in chapter fourteen, focuses more closely on Raymond Aron's often underestimated contribution to the high-quality monthly review, *La France Libre*. Aron escaped from France in June 1940 in one of the last transports to leave Bordeaux. Once in London, André Labarthe contacted him and proposed that he should collaborate on *La France Libre* as it was being set up in the summer of 1940. Its primary mission was to keep alive the beacon of French civilization, in contrast to the way that cultural activity in Occupied France was entirely under the thrall of the Nazis. The review's print runs were highly impressive, with some of the early issues needing reprints. David Drake makes the point that even if some of the material in the review smacks of sentimentality today, at that time Anglo-French amity was very real, that emotional bonds between the two countries were sometimes raw and often close, and that Occupied France would never be the true France.

To bring the book up to date, the extraordinary influx of the contemporary French to London is the subject of Helen Drake and Saskia Huc-Hepher's joint chapter, 'From the 16ème to South Ken: a study of the contemporary French population in London'. This chapter aims to explore why it is that so many contemporary French people are driven to come and settle in London. Compared to the historical experience we have already evoked, they are no longer seeking political exile, neither do they come as refugees from persecution by authoritarian forces in France, nor still are they fleeing from war or occupation. Today it is explained rather by the quest for personal independence and the search for opportunity. Figures vary, of course, but there are certainly between 200,000 and 400,000 French people residing in the whole of Greater London and the south-east. The results of the 2011 census should reveal more. French economic investment in Britain represents an appreciable proportion of the economy: 35 per cent of French overseas investment, amounting to some thirteen billion euros, comes to the UK. The study draws on data collected from interviews and two focus groups, one at a state-funded sixth-form college in Newham and the other at the Lycée Français in South Kensington. Their survey reveals some surprising facts about the London French; the highest proportion of French speakers in the metropolis is not to be found in South Kensington, as might be expected, but in Lambeth. Indeed, Drake and Huc-Hepher reveal that a shift is under way from the stereotypical notion that South Kensington is the most populous French 'ghetto' in London: the shift is towards the east of the city. Apart from the appeal of 'Cool Britannia', or at least 'Cool London' (an idea which, of course, goes back to the 'Swinging 60s'),[14] the draw of the British capital is multiple. London is seen as a place of opportunity, very different from the comparatively rigid structures of employment in France: there is the English language, the perception of

---

[14] See A. Tachin, *Amie et rivale: la Grande-Bretagne dans l'imaginaire français à l'époque Gaullienne* (Brussels, 2009).

London as a 'melting pot' – and one is instantly reminded of the comment on the 'city of nations' quoted at the beginning of this introduction – the green spaces, the nature of the housing, the attitudes of the English, the existence of the Channel Tunnel for ease of return to one's relatives and families; all these reasons come together to explain the draw of London for the French.

1. A special case? London's French Protestants

Elizabeth Randall

Between 1550, when a French Reformed church was first established in London, and the beginning of the 1789 Revolution in France, an estimated 65,000 French-speaking Europeans moved into England, bringing with them their skills and knowledge, and over half of them settled in what is now the Greater London area.[1] The principal reason for this migration, which lasted for over 200 years, was the search by French Protestants for the freedom to practise their religion without intimidation and persecution by Roman Catholic rulers who regarded the Reformation as heretical. In Protestant England, it was understood, where papal authority had been replaced by that of a Protestant monarch, liberty of conscience was available to those French citizens who had chosen to follow the Reformed faith.

The movement reached its peak in the last two decades of the seventeenth century, when, following Louis XIV's decision that France should become an exclusively Catholic kingdom, approximately 25,000 French Protestant refugees arrived in London. The English capital was still relatively small at that time, its population being about 400,000 in 1650,[2] and it barely extended beyond the twin heartlands of the City, centre of trade and industry, and Westminster, the seat of government. Its suburbs were little more than hamlets or villages and, until as late as 1750, there was only one bridge across the River Thames. However, its position as an international sea-port had always made London particularly attractive to overseas 'strangers', and there had been a French presence there since the middle ages. Men and women of all social backgrounds had traditionally crossed the Channel in search of patronage and employment, and London was well adjusted to receiving them.[3] Before the Reformation, a good deal of business had been carried out on behalf of the universal Catholic Church, and certain French religious houses had acquired land in the English capital, an example being

---

[1] R. D. Gwynn, *Huguenot Heritage: the History and Contribution of the Huguenots in Britain* (2nd edn., Brighton, 2001), pp. 37–9, 44–7.

[2] D. C. Coleman, *The Economy of England, 1450–1750* (Oxford, 1977), p. 97.

[3] I. Scouloudi, 'The stranger community in the metropolis, 1558–1640', in *Huguenots in Britain and their French Background*, ed. I. Scouloudi (1987), p. 42.

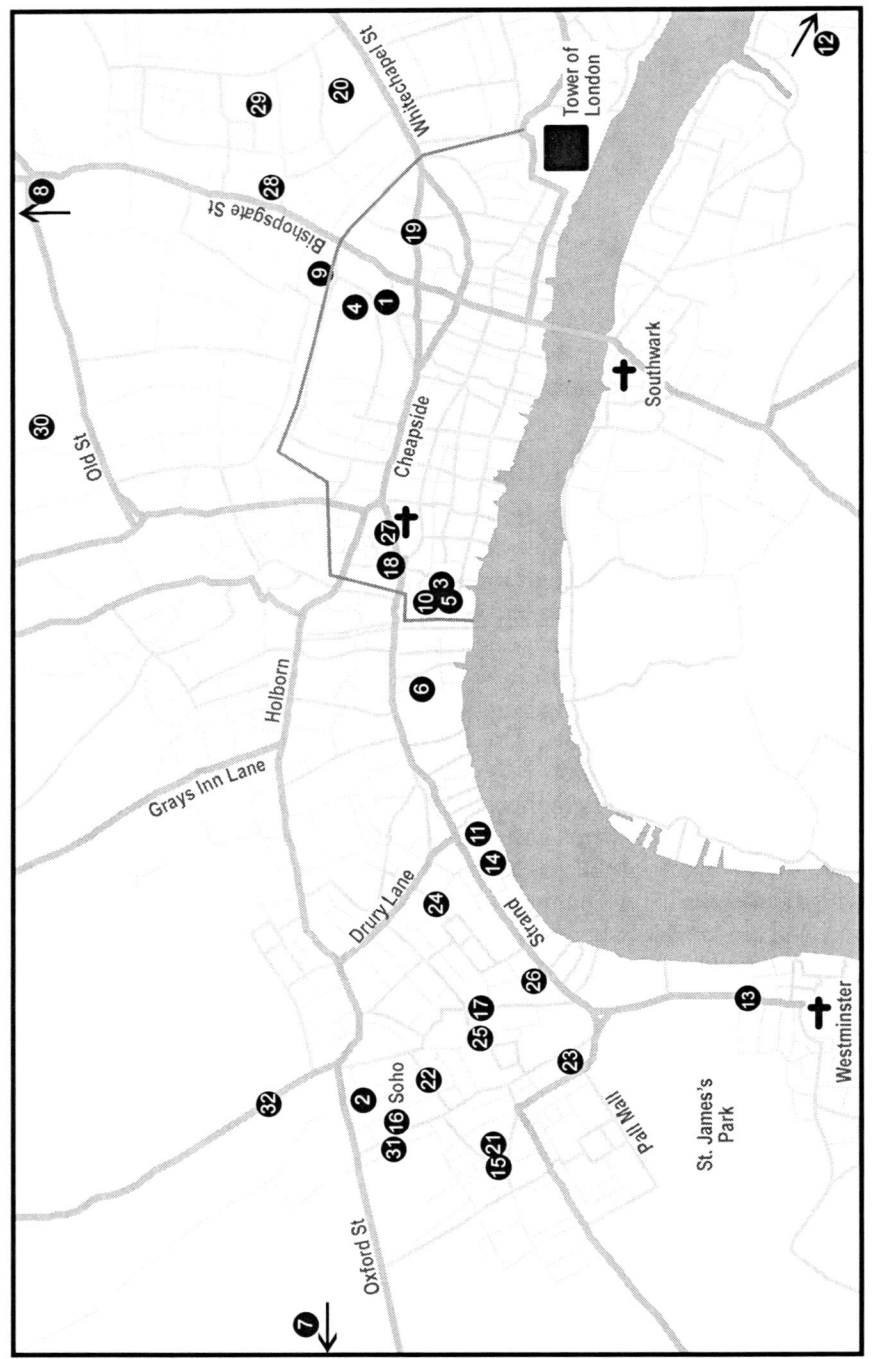

Map 1.1. Places mentioned in the text (Base map: London c.1700)

Key to Map 1.1

1. The French church, Threadneedle Street (formerly St. Anthony's Hospital)
2. French Protestant church of London, Soho Square
3. Blackfriars
4. The Dutch church, Austin Friars
5. Vautrollier, Blackfriars
6. Bouverie Street
7. Bouverie Place (W2, off map c.1.5 miles)
8. Bouverie Road (N16, off map c.3 miles)
9. Petty Fraunce
10. Apothecaries' Hall
11. Somerset House
12. Croom's Hill, Greenwich (off map c.3.5 miles)
13. King Street, Westminster
14. Palace of the Savoy
15. Foubert's 'royal' Academy
16. St. Anne's church, Wardour Street
17. Old Slaughter's coffee-house, St. Martin's Lane
18. Black Boy coffee-house, Ave Maria Lane
19. Motteux, Leadenhall Street
20. La Patente church, Spitalfields
21. Paul de Lamerie, Windmill Street
22. Paul Crespin, Old Compton Street
23. Paul Daniel Chenevix, Suffolk Street
24. David Grignion, Russell Street
25. Nicholas Massy, Cranbourn Street
26. David Lestourgeon, Church Lane, St. Martin in the Fields
27. Paternoster Row
28. Artillery Lane
29. Christ Church Spitalfields
30. La Providence hospital, Bath Street
31. Joseph Duffour, Berwick Street
32. Pierre Langlois, Tottenham Court Road

15

the congregation of St. Antoine de Vienne from the Dauphiné, to whom Henry III (reigned 1216–72) granted a plot on Threadneedle Street in the City. Henry's son Edward I invited French Dominicans to establish a large priory in Blackfriars where, under royal protection, they provided alien craftsmen and merchants with shelter from the jurisdiction of the City and its guilds.[4] Although the religious character of this precinct disappeared in the sixteenth century, Blackfriars would remain an important location for immigrants from France.

The Tudor monarchy encourages French settlement

Henry VIII's ambitions to establish his kingdom as a power in Europe, and to rival the prestige of the court of France's François I, led him to call on the services of an increasing number of artisans from overseas.[5] During Henry's reign (1509–47), the majority of these were Flemish or German-speaking, but there was a significant Norman contribution to glass and iron production, and the king, who employed a Norman printer, favoured French culture, the French language, and French clothes and food.[6] Yet, in spite of his break with Rome in 1534, Henry continued to regard Protestants as heretics, and gave orders for them to be severely punished, so that few French migrants would claim to be entering England for sanctuary until after the accession of Edward VI.[7]

Henry's 'Great Pillage' of the medieval monasteries, in which twenty-three Catholic foundations in London were destroyed, had beneficial results for the stranger communities who adopted Protestantism under his son Edward. Although most Church property fell into lay hands, some surviving chapels were made available for Protestant services, which were held in the vernacular after 1549. It was soon appreciated that both 'Dutch' and French strangers would need churches of their own, where they could follow their Reformed liturgy in their own language, and Edward granted leases to each of them under royal charter. Initially, both groups were accommodated in the same Augustinian priory close to Bishopsgate,[8] but the francophone contingent was later moved to the Threadneedle Street premises that had once belonged to the hospital of St. Antoine de Vienne.

[4] Citizens of London did not always welcome the presence of strangers or their industries (see N. G. Brett-James, *The Growth of Stuart London* (1935), pp. 48–9).

[5] C. Giry-Deloison, 'A diplomatic revolution? Anglo-French relations and the treaties of 1527', in *Henry VIII: a European Court in England*, ed. D. Starkey (1991), p. 77.

[6] S. Thurley, *Whitehall Palace* (2008), p. 25.

[7] See Gwynn, *Huguenot Heritage*, p. 37.

[8] The Dutch church in Austin Friars was destroyed in the Second World War but has been reconstructed.

The church on Threadneedle Street was to become the English headquarters of French Reformed worship for the next 300 years, apart from a brief interruption in Mary Tudor's reign (1553–8).[9] When Elizabeth replaced Mary on the throne, London's stranger congregations would discover that their Calvinist discipline and doctrine was not the same as that of the re-established Anglican Church, but they were nevertheless allowed to keep the religious liberties that they had been given under Edward, and, in spite of the Act of Uniformity of 1559, they retained their own system of government by a consistory of elders, and their own liturgy. Although a new requirement since Edward's time was that both Dutch and French churches should submit to the overall control of the bishop of London, it seems that, in the case of Edmund Grindal, bishop from 1559 to 1570, there was 'a fraternal rather than a political connexion'.[10]

This favourable treatment could be explained by the difficulties of enforcing uniformity on worshippers who spoke another language, and by the primary importance the English administration attached to the care and supervision that the churches gave to alien communities. As the church bodies depended on the crown for their legal privileges, they could be expected to show it their loyalty, both by acting as useful agents and by keeping a watch for undesirable influences. The Threadneedle Street congregation therefore continued to keep its confessional independence and to enjoy the direct personal protection of successive English monarchs, even when, as sometimes happened, this was given grudgingly.

There was, in fact, another good reason for treating the London stranger churches as a special case. England was still economically and technically backward in the late sixteenth century and looked towards her nearest neighbours for more sophisticated methods of production.[11] William Cecil, Elizabeth's secretary of state, wanted to attract a limited number of workers from the continent to teach crafts to the native English, who could then supply the domestic market with the luxury goods that were currently imported, such as hats, gloves, white paper, the lighter 'new draperies' and the fine silk material woven at Lille.[12] However, whereas these potential settlers would almost certainly have been Roman Catholic in the past, it was now essential, in view of the turbulent events of the Reformation, that

---

[9] During Mary's unsuccessful attempt to restore Roman Catholicism in England, strangers who had been previously granted denization were not required to leave the country.

[10] P. Collinson, *Archbishop Grindal, 1519–83: the Struggle for a Reformed Church* (1978), p. 128.

[11] J. R. Black, *The Reign of Elizabeth 1558–1603* (2nd edn., Oxford, 1959), p. 236.

[12] Lille, formerly within the duchy of Burgundy, had become part of the Habsburg Empire through inheritance. After 1555 it was ruled from Madrid.

they should be Protestants. If hard-working Calvinists from France and the Netherlands were offered the opportunity to worship under their own rite, it was thought, they might be expected to choose England as their destination and the country could benefit from their skills. A comparison of a London 'return of aliens' of 1593 with the records of the 1630s suggests that this theory was probably correct, for the 352 French-speaking residents recorded at the earlier date had risen to well over 1,000 during the later period.[13]

Not all Protestant migrants were refugees 'for religion', and intermittent inquiries revealed that many claimed to have come to seek their living. Yet better opportunities to practise a profession were often associated with greater freedom of thought and ideas. This applied to the production of books, for, in its efforts to prevent the spread of the new religion, the Sorbonne in Paris had imposed a restrictive censorship on the publication of what it regarded as subversive material.[14] Robert Estienne, the Parisian scholar-printer, was obliged to move his press to Geneva as early as 1552 and, ten years later, Thomas Vautrollier, a Protestant from Troyes in Champagne, transferred his printing equipment from France to the more favourable climate of London. Soon after his arrival, Vautrollier was naturalized and became a brother of the Stationers' Company, opening a business in Blackfriars where he acted as an agent for the Antwerp printer Christopher Plantin.[15] He imported advanced typefaces, some made in the French Protestant citadel of La Rochelle, and undertook the entire book production process from manuscript to binding and selling, examples being the first edition of Sir Thomas North's *Plutarch* and the English text of Calvin's *Institutes of the Christian Religion*, as well as music. Enterprise on such a scale had not previously been seen in England and set a new high standard of craftsmanship.[16]

Among those with whom Vautrollier worked in London were fellow French Protestants Jean de Beauchesne, whose book on calligraphy was, in itself, an innovation, and Claudius Hollyband or Holyband, a refugee teacher from Moulins in the Bourbonnais. Holyband, who had anglicized his name from Claude de Saintliens, supplied schoolbooks to King James I. He seems to have ignored Threadneedle Street's admonitions against taking English wives, having married two in succession, and this may have helped him in the successful composition of *The French Littleton*; 'an apt and easy

[13] Scouloudi, 'The stranger community', p. 44.

[14] The Sorbonne was the faculty of religion at Paris University.

[15] Blackfriars retained its privileges, in spite of the City's objections (see J. Strype, *A Survey of the Cities of London and Westminster* (2 vols., 1720), i, bk. 3, pp. 177–80).

[16] W. R. LeFanu, 'Thomas Vautrollier, printer and bookseller', *HSP*, xx (1958–64), 12–25.

way to learn an understanding of French language', which was an advance in modern-language teaching. Holyband also pioneered the first bilingual French-English dictionaries.[17]

Had Holyband not made his escape to London, he might have suffered a less pleasant fate. By 1562, Protestants in France were being described by their enemies as 'Huguenots', and violent civil disturbances were taking place.[18] The French Wars of Religion, fuelled by the findings of the Council of Trent (1545–63), lasted until the end of the century and caused widespread suffering and displacement. Meanwhile, in the neighbouring Netherlands, the Spanish Habsburg king, Philip II, had declared war on his Calvinist subjects, many of whom took flight for England. These included a number of French-speaking, or 'Walloon', master weavers from Lille like the des Bouveries, a family whose resources enabled them to set up their own silk-weaving business in London. Proof of the prosperity and respect acquired by the des Bouveries is shown in the presence of their name among several London addresses – Bouverie Street, EC4, Bouverie Place, W2, and Bouverie Road, N16 – and by the eventual ennoblement of their family as earls of Radnor. Other successful refugees from Lille were the de la Forteries, whose descendant Samuel Fortrey designed Kew Palace, and the Houblons, ancestors of Sir John Houblon, first governor of the Bank of England.[19] These Walloon settlers joined the French Reformed church in Threadneedle Street and placed themselves at the centre of the infant London silk industry, supplying, by 1600, the taffetas, velvets, satins and silk mixtures that were then coming into fashion, and providing the industrial base on which seventeenth-century Huguenot master weavers would found their Spitalfields businesses.[20]

The 1571 return of aliens shows that weavers were also arriving from France and, indeed, the part of east London lying beyond St. Botolph's without Bishopsgate became known as 'Petty Fraunce' soon after this date.[21] As in the case of Blackfriars, it was an area outside the control of the

[17] M. C. Cormier and A. Francoeur, 'Claudius Holyband: pioneer Huguenot lexicographer in England', *HSP*, xviii (2003–7), 160–75.

[18] The Revd. Francis Tallents, visiting France in 1671, asserted that the name 'Huguenot' came from the Hugon gate at Tours, where local Protestants met at the beginning of the Reformation (see *The Travels of Francis Tallents in France and Switzerland, 1671–3*, ed. J. V. Cox (2011), p. 68).

[19] Samuel Fortrey published a treatise recommending further immigration to enrich the kingdom (see S. Fortrey, *England's Interest and Improvement* (1663), p. 1). Of the first 24 governors of the Bank of England (1694), seven were of Walloon or Huguenot descent.

[20] L. B. Luu, 'French-speaking refugees and the foundation of the London silk industry in the 16th century', *HSP*, xxvi (1994–7), 564–75.

[21] Brett-James, *Growth of Stuart London*, p. 490.

City guilds, although the Weavers' Company agreed to admit trained and experienced foreign weavers, provided they employed English journeymen.[22] More French immigrants were now claiming to be religious refugees, and stories of exceptional horror began to reach London of the events of St. Bartholomew's Day, 1572, which, starting in Paris, had led to the murder of some 10,000 Huguenots country-wide. In Rouen, where the Protestant population had been as high as 16,500, it suddenly shrank to 3,000, partly because those who were unable to leave the city agreed to become Catholics out of fear for their lives.[23] The limited confessional and legal rights which Henri IV eventually gave to his Huguenot subjects under the Edict of Nantes of 1598 did have the effect of guaranteeing them some protection, but the spectre of the St. Bartholomew's massacre was not easily erased from the collective memory of Protestants in either France or England. When Henri was himself assassinated in 1610, a new era of insecurity set in and London was once again viewed as a potential place of exile.

The protection and patronage of the early Stuarts

James VI of Scotland, who became James I of England in 1603, was the grandson of Mary of Guise and his mother had been briefly married to Francis II of France. Although baptized as a Catholic, he was educated as a Protestant, and his favourite poet was the Huguenot Guillaume de Sallust du Bartas. James disliked the Calvinism of the London Reformed church, but he preserved the English crown's special understanding with the Threadneedle Street consistory and he hoped to involve them in his schemes for a united Protestant Europe. One of James's early actions was to engage the services of Maximilien Colt, a Protestant sculptor from Arras who had married the daughter of Marcus Gheeraerts the Elder. James gave Colt the prestigious commission of creating a monument for Elizabeth I in Westminster Abbey and, later, of adding memorials to the king's daughters Mary and Sophia, who had died in infancy. Having completed his task in good time, Colt was named master sculptor to the king in 1608, the first in a series of Huguenot artists who would serve the Stuart dynasty in London. He went on to carry out decorative work in the royal palaces, producing carvings in wood, as well as in marble and stone, and made heavily ornate chimney-pieces for James and for his secretary of state Robert Cecil.[24]

---

[22] D. Statt, *Foreigners and Englishmen: the Controversy over Immigration and Population, 1660–1760* (Newark, Del., 1995), p. 182.

[23] H. H. Leonard, 'The Huguenots and the St Bartholomew's massacre', in *The Huguenots: History and Memory in Transitional Context*, ed. D. J. B. Trim (Leiden, 2011), p. 58.

[24] A. White, 'Maximilien Colt: master sculptor to James I', *HSP*, xxvii (1998–2002), 36–47.

Two important Huguenots who had worked for Henri IV were invited to England by James after the French king's death: Isaac Casaubon had been Henri's librarian, and Theodore Turquet de Mayerne one of his three physicians. Casaubon, reputed to have one of the most brilliant minds in Europe, was the son of a pastor at Crest in the Dauphiné, and had been sent to study in Geneva, where he met and married the sister of the refugee Protestant printer Robert Estienne. James granted Casaubon an annual pension of £300 in return for his advice, which included the opinion that the Anglican Church followed the doctrine most closely in accordance with early Christianity. Casaubon's tomb can be found in Westminster Abbey, but neither he nor his wife enjoyed London and it was left to their son Meric to become anglicized, after winning a scholarship to Eton.[25]

Theodore Mayerne's family were silk manufacturers from Lyons, and had taken refuge in Geneva following the St. Bartholomew's Day massacre. Theodore was sent to Montpellier to study at the large international medical school where most French physicians were trained, and where the majority of teachers and students were Protestants. Although the smaller Paris faculty followed the ancient classical teachings of Galen, Montpellier believed in more 'up-to-date' treatments and a practical approach.[26] Mayerne was condemned as a quack by the Paris faculty, but in London he became immensely popular and was made a fellow of the College of Physicians. Some of his cures sound curious by modern standards and he was unable to save the life of the heir to the throne, Prince Henry, yet his work did much to further the good name of French Protestant medicine. He was useful to the English sovereign in other ways, serving as James's confidential agent on the continent, and bringing to London the Huguenot miniaturist Jean Petitot and the medallist and engraver Nicholas Briot, as well as carrying out research into silk dyes and leather gilding.[27]

The first Huguenot surgeons to appear in London were the Chamberlen brothers, whose father had arrived in England in 1569. Like Mayerne, Peter Chamberlen the elder was patronized by the Stuart court, and he attended James's wife Anne in 1605 and 1606, and was present at Charles II's birth in 1630. The Chamberlens were greatly interested in obstetrics, and Peter's brother (also named Peter) is thought to have been the pioneer of delivery by forceps, a closely guarded secret of the family.[28] He married Sarah, sister

    [25] E. J. Lefroy, 'Isaac Casaubon, 1559–1614', *HSP*, xx (1958–64), 586–603.

    [26] L. Brockliss, 'The rise and fall of the Huguenot physician in early modern France', *HSP*, xxviii (1958–64), 36–55.

    [27] H. Trevor-Roper, *Europe's Physician: the Various Life of Sir Theodore de Mayerne* (New Haven, Conn., 2006), pp. 63–4, 331–48.

    [28] W. H. Prioleau, 'The Chamberlen family and the introduction of obstetrical

Figure 1.1. Gideon Delaune (1564/5–1659), attrib. Cornelius Jansen, 1640.
By kind permission of The Worshipful Society of Apothecaries of London.
This portrait now hangs in the Apothecaries' Hall, Blackfriars.

of the Huguenot apothecary Gideon Delaune, and their eldest son (yet another Peter), born in Blackfriars and baptized at the French church in Threadneedle Street, was physician-in-ordinary to Charles I. Of the third Peter's own fourteen sons, four went into medicine and the eldest, Hugh, treated the sick during the London plague of 1665 and survived to become physician-in-ordinary to Charles II from 1673 to 1682.

Gideon Delaune's father, a Norman physician and Protestant minister, brought him to London soon after the St. Bartholomew's Day massacre. Like Thomas Vautrollier, the Delaunes settled in Blackfriars, and Gideon was a successful apothecary by 1590. He was given a royal appointment, granted a coat-of-arms and made a freeman of the City of London, assimilating early

instruments', *HSP*, xxvii (1998–2002), 705–14.

into English society by marrying his daughter to a Yorkshire baronet and his son to the daughter of Sir Edwin Sandys. Delaune made an important contribution to English medicine by helping to compile the *Pharmacopoeia Londinensis*, an early attempt to prescribe the ingredients sold for medicinal purposes, and by taking a lead in the creation of an Apothecaries' Hall. Although the first hall, like the Threadneedle Street church, was destroyed by fire in 1666, it was rapidly replaced and is now one of the oldest buildings in the capital.

Charles I's relationship with the London Huguenots suffered through the actions of his archbishop of Canterbury, William Laud, who attempted to ride rough-shod over the 'special case' understanding of eighty years by forcing the Threadneedle Street congregation to accept full government by the Anglican Church.[29] This threatened breaking of trust by the crown may have persuaded the Walloon and Huguenot elders to support parliamentary opposition to the king during the English civil wars. Charles also appeared to have permitted some resurgence of Roman Catholicism following his marriage with the French princess Henrietta Maria, god-daughter of Pope Urban VIII. Henrietta Maria's marriage contract had granted her the same liberty that the Huguenots had been given in England, namely the free practice of her religion, but this was not appreciated in a country still unwilling to tolerate Catholicism.[30] When it was observed that the new queen, who arrived in 1625 and was lodged at the palace of Somerset House, was accompanied by twelve priests of the Oratory, a Parisian congregation founded by Pierre Bérulle to fight Protestant heresy, and that her confessor was Father Bérulle himself, there were fears of a French plot to reintroduce 'popery'. On this occasion Charles acted firmly, and the priests and a large section of Henrietta's household were sent back to France, including her friend and first lady of the bedchamber 'Mamie' St. George, but the Oratorians were soon replaced by an equal number of Capuchin observant friars, destined to staff the personal chapel that Henrietta had been promised. Designed by Inigo Jones and opened in 1636, this chapel would become a magnet for English Catholics.[31]

Somerset House, between the Strand and the river, was the royal court's centre of fashion, and it was here that Henrietta Maria introduced the painted ceilings and panelling of French decorative and furnishing taste, as well as a new style in dress.[32] During Charles's personal rule in the 1630s,

[29] I. Scouloudi, *Returns of Strangers in the Metropolis, 1593, 1627, 1635, 1639* (HSQS, lvii, 1985), p. 85.
[30] J. Miller, *Popery and Politics in England, 1660–88* (Cambridge, 1973), p. 55.
[31] S. Thurley, *Somerset House 1551–1692* (2009), p. 53.
[32] A. Strickland, *The Queens of England* (6 vols., 1888), iv. 333.

the queen helped to arouse an English interest in French art and design, and in this she was assisted by Inigo Jones, who had travelled and studied in continental Europe, and who collaborated with her in the production of court masques, recalling the theatrical activities of the French court during her childhood.[33] Like her mother Marie de Médicis, Henrietta Maria showed no aversion to employing the talents of French Protestants. The Huguenot Laniers, musicians to the English court since Elizabeth's day, lived on Crooms Hill near the Queen's House in Greenwich and enjoyed Henrietta's patronage, with all six sons holding salaried posts as musicians in the queen's service.[34] Nicholas Lanier was an art expert who advised Charles on the purchase of some of the paintings for his collection; others were chosen by another Huguenot immigrant, Balthazar Gerbier, who negotiated directly with Peter Paul Rubens.

Although Elizabeth and James had both tried to prevent further building in the capital, restrictions were relaxed under Charles, and London began to spread westwards, partly due to the ambitious development plans of Francis, fourth earl of Bedford. He engaged Inigo Jones to lay out the Covent Garden piazza, north of the Strand, with the assistance of the Huguenot architect Isaac de Caus. De Caus, who specialized in garden design, worked with the Huguenot sculptor Hubert Le Sueur on Henrietta Maria's garden at Somerset House.[35] 'Praxiteles Le Sueur', as he liked to be known, had helped to erect Henri IV's statue on the Pont Neuf in Paris and came to London in 1625. He and his family were members of the Threadneedle Street congregation, and in 1634 he cast the bronze equestrian statue of Charles I which now faces down Whitehall from Trafalgar Square. More of Le Sueur's work can be seen in Westminster Abbey, where he was responsible for the effigies of the duke of Buckingham and the duke of Richmond and Lennox in Henry VII's chapel.

The French Protestant church in Westminster

As England's capital spread west, so too did its Huguenot population, and a privy council census of London, made between 1638 and 1639, shows 641 French residents of Westminster, as opposed to a French-speaking population of 558 in or near the City, which included 330 Walloons. Most of these City-dwellers were occupied in the weaving industry, but the French in Westminster had more varied kinds of work, being described as painters,

[33] Thurley, *Somerset House*, p. 45.

[34] L. Cust, 'Foreign artists of the Reformed religion working in London from about 1560 to 1660', *HSP*, vii (1901–4), 79.

[35] D. Duggan, 'Isaac de Caus, Nicholas Stone and the Woburn Abbey grotto', *Apollo* (Aug. 2003), p. 55.

picture drawers, limners, engravers, musicians and silverworkers.[36] Twenty-three out of the twenty-seven tailors listed for Westminster were French, and there are details of French servants who waited on the court and the nobility, and of individuals such as Henrietta Maria's French surgeon, Maurice Aubert, who lived in King Street and was unfortunate enough to have his house wrecked by an anti-Catholic mob in 1641.[37]

An unwelcome visitor for Charles in 1638, just as his financial difficulties were leading him towards a clash with Parliament, was his mother-in-law Marie de Médicis, homeless and penniless since the death of her cousin the Archduchess Isabella Clara in Brussels.[38] Accompanied by a host of Catholic followers, Marie was housed in St. James's Palace, at the cost to the crown, it was said, of £100 per day. She stayed in England for almost three years, attempting to negotiate her return to France, and is recorded as having forty-five French employees, presumably Catholic. Other prominent French malcontents in London were the duchesse de Chevreuse and the duc de Valette, not forgetting the duc de Soubise, the brother of Charles's godfather Henri de Rohan and a French Huguenot exile of long standing.[39] Soubise lived in some style in the parish of St. Clement Danes, and employed as his chaplain a certain Jean d'Espagne, whose presence would ultimately lead to the opening of a second French Protestant church in the capital. D'Espagne had applied for an appointment at Threadneedle Street but had not been accepted, although his sermons evidently attracted members of the English aristocracy because, when Soubise died in 1642, Philip, fourth earl of Pembroke, arranged for d'Espagne to hold services in the chapel of Durham House.

With the outbreak of the English civil wars, Charles and Henrietta Maria left London and the Capuchin missionaries were expelled from Somerset House. Under the Cromwellian Protectorate, Jean d'Espagne was permitted to use their former chapel for preaching, sometimes to audiences as large as 600,[40] but the arrangement presented a problem when Henrietta wished to reclaim her property after the Stuart Restoration for, although d'Espagne was already in his grave, the numerous Huguenots of the Strand and Charing Cross areas argued that they had no other convenient place of worship. It

---

[36] Brett-James, *Growth of Stuart London*, p. 141.

[37] E. L. Furdell, *The Royal Doctors, 1485–1714: Medical Personnel at the Tudor and Stuart Courts* (Rochester, NY, 2001), p.124.

[38] Scouloudi, *Returns of Strangers*, pp. 104–5.

[39] Soubise was a living reproach to England's failure to relieve the Huguenot citadel of La Rochelle in 1628.

[40] R. Vareilles, 'A controversial Calvinist minister: from Dauphiné to Somerset House', *HSP*, xxix (2008–12), 220–6.

was in answer to their pleas, and over the heads of the Threadneedle Street consistory, that Charles II decided to offer them alternative accommodation in a chapel in the grounds of the neighbouring palace of the Savoy.[41] However, although Threadneedle Street was allowed to keep its historic privileges and – in spite of its fleeting disloyalty to the Stuarts – its special position stayed unchanged, the French church of the Savoy was required to adopt the English Book of Common Prayer, translated into French, and to accept a royalist minister, John Durel, who had been ordained as an Anglican. This obvious move to draw the Huguenot community closer to established English Protestantism did not please all of the Savoy church's members, but was acceptable to the majority because a place of worship so close to the court at Whitehall was seen to have certain advantages.[42]

The ending of Interregnum austerity brought rising demand for the kind of goods that Huguenot artisans and craftsmen habitually made and sold. A market soon appeared for the lace, gloves, embroidery, periwigs, perfumery and elegant shoes then fashionable in Paris, and French tailoring and silk patterns once again became popular. Huguenot master weavers were responsible for much of the organization of the silk industry, and new workshops were set up in 'Petty Fraunce' and beyond, with retail outlets appearing in the Charing Cross area. Among the successful Huguenot City merchants was Thomas Papillon, whose father David had come from Dijon as a child refugee and had designed the fortifications of Gloucester during the first English civil war. With the return of peace, Thomas, a keen investor in the East India Company, was made master of the Mercers' Company on no fewer than four occasions.

When Henrietta Maria resumed possession of Somerset House, her costly programme of renovation did much to reawaken English interest in French decorative arts. After spending sixteen years in exile in *la région parisienne*, Henrietta wanted her dowager court to mirror the splendour of the French capital and its surrounding palaces. Her innovations, which included parquetry flooring, were much admired by the diarist Samuel Pepys, who acknowledged that she had quite eclipsed her daughter-in-law Catherine of Braganza.[43] Unfortunately, Henrietta and her spiritual adviser, the Abbé 'Wat' Montagu, were determined to obtain greater toleration for Catholics in England, and their activities, together with the reappearance of the Capuchin missionaries, drew attention to the fact that, since the

---

[41] Not to be confused with the modern Savoy Chapel. It was too small from the first, and in a state of bad repair, and had to be closed in 1730. Its remains lie hidden under the approach road to Waterloo Bridge.

[42] Gwynn, *Huguenot Heritage*, pp. 122–3.

[43] *The Diary of Samuel Pepys*, ed. R. Latham and W. Matthews (1970), iii. 299.

queen's return, 'popery' was once again on the increase.[44] In 1665 the queen mother left for France, allegedly on a visit, and never returned, although she left behind her a growing suspicion that the French community in London included Catholic spies.[45]

Charles II would have recognized the folly of inviting too many French Roman Catholics into a country still prone to spells of anti-papal hysteria, but the years he had spent in continental Europe had given him a taste for French culture and a wish to rival his cousin, Louis XIV. In 1665 he sent Christopher Wren to Paris to see the Louvre and meet François Mansart and Gianlorenzo Bernini;[46] he also brought in French upholsterers and ordered state beds, aiming to improve the comforts of living and to organize his court along sophisticated French lines. Anxious to introduce new ideas, Charles appointed the Huguenot Nicaise Le Fèvre, demonstrator of chemical experiments at the Paris 'Jardin du Roi', as royal apothecary and professor of chemistry, and Le Fèvre became one of the first French members of the Royal Society.[47] Another early member was Denis Papin from Blois, who had studied at the Protestant Academy of Saumur and qualified as a physician at Angers, but whose interests had taken him in the direction of mechanical science. In 1675 Papin gave a demonstration to the Royal Society of his 'New Digester of Bones', a prototype for the modern pressure-cooker, and went on to develop an early version of the steam engine. He was assistant to Robert Boyle, whose works he translated into French, and a herald of the fresh talent that would soon arrive in England from France.

French religious policies provoke le grand refuge

Louis XIV took over the reins of French government on the death of Jules Mazarin (1602–61) and almost immediately began to pursue policies that would make life difficult for his Protestant subjects. A total of 2,200 Huguenots were ordered to leave La Rochelle because they had been living there 'illegally' since 1628. In 1669, a decree banning Protestants from membership of artisanal corporations effectively excluded Huguenot surgeons and apothecaries from practising in French towns.[48] When Francis

---

[44] Miller, *Popery and Politics*, pp. 40–1.

[45] This seemed to be confirmed when a deranged watchmaker from Rouen claimed to have started the Great Fire of 1666 (see Cox, *Travels of Francis Tallents*, p. 19).

[46] P. Thornton, *Seventeenth-Century Interior Decoration in England, France and Holland* (1978), p. 25.

[47] The 'Jardin du Roi' was established in 1635 by Gui de la Brosse, Louis XIII's physician, a converted Huguenot.

[48] Brockliss, 'Rise and fall of the Huguenot physician', p. 43.

DIONYSIUS PAPIN M.D.
FAIR PROF ORD AU REG. SOC LOND SOCIUS.
ANNO 1689.

Figure 1.2. Denis Papin, after a painting at Marburg University.
Papin is holding a diagram of his 1689 invention of a steam
engine with piston. Wellcome Library, London.

Tallents visited France in 1671, he found much evidence of Huguenot
temples destroyed, or threatened with destruction, indicating that
Protestant ministers were losing their jobs.[49] Although Henri IV's Edict
of Nantes had granted eight learned academies to the Huguenots, funding
for these had been withdrawn by Cardinal Richelieu in 1632, and Louis
was now presiding over the steady closure of all Protestant colleges and

[49] Cox, *Travels of Francis Tallents*, pp. 23, 64, 73, 85, 88.

academies.[50] It would have been surprising if the Huguenot intelligentsia were not already looking for opportunities abroad.

In 1679 French academies of equitation were brought under central control and Protestants forbidden to teach in them, causing Solomon Foubert to move his famous Paris academy to London.[51] Here he was made supernumerary equerry to the king and opened a 'royal' academy near the modern Foubert's Place off Regent Street, where young English gentlemen were taught modern languages, drawing, fencing and dancing. Under 'Major Foubert', his son, this enterprise became a manège and dressage school where aspiring British army officers were given instruction in military science and manoeuvres.[52]

The French king's next move was the suppression of Henri IV's special Huguenot legal courts, making it plain that Louis had no respect for his grandfather's promises, and Henry Savile, Charles II's envoy extraordinary in Paris, urged Charles to invite as many Huguenots as possible to England.[53] Savile had been unsuccessful in getting a naturalization bill through the English Parliament in 1676, and he was concerned that there would be a brain drain to countries offering more attractive terms. But it was not until 1681 that Charles agreed to act, after news began to arrive of the French government's use of *dragonnades*, or aggressive billeting, in its attempts to force Protestant households to convert to Catholicism. Faced with the prospect of large numbers of Huguenots leaving their French homes, the two London French Protestant churches appealed to the English crown for help, and Charles, motivated by 'honour and conscience', issued an order in council which offered free letters of denization to Huguenot refugees and guaranteed them privileges and immunities, as well as the unimpeded exercise of trades and handicrafts.[54] By the time the Edict of Fontainebleau of 1685 had finally annulled Henri IV's Edict of Nantes, together with its original guarantee of Huguenot rights and liberties, the English crown had remembered its special relationship with French Protestants and was raising funds for the refugees' relief.

Charles II died in the spring of 1685 and his Catholic brother James was left to deal with the 13,500 immigrants who arrived in the Greater London area that year.[55] Although he did not like the Huguenots, and attempted

---

[50] K. Maag, 'The Huguenot academies: an uncertain future', in *Society and Culture in the Huguenot World*, ed. R. A. Mentzer and A. Spicer (Cambridge, 2002), pp. 151–2.

[51] Cox, *Travels of Francis Tallents*, p. 175.

[52] W. H. Manchee, 'The Fouberts and their royal academy', *HSP*, xvi (1937–41), 77–97.

[53] *Savile Correspondence*, ed. W. D. Cooper (Camden Society, 1858), pp. 209–11.

[54] Brett-James, *Growth of Stuart London*, p. 487.

[55] Brett-James, *Growth of Stuart London*, p. 488.

to deny the extent of their persecution, James had little choice but to continue the policy of public collections and 'royal bounty' state support. His Declaration of Indulgence of 1687, designed to give more freedom to English Roman Catholics, actually encouraged Huguenot refugees to make their way to England.

It was to be expected that the arrival of a wave of foreign refugees would bring about a protest from certain Londoners, and especially from members of the guilds attempting to control economic enterprise. Some of these organizations dated from a much earlier period, but the comparatively recent formation of the Worshipful Company of Clockmakers (1631) was proof that local anxieties about competition were never far away. The plague of 1665 and the fire that followed it, in which 1,300 houses and eighty-one churches were destroyed, had disrupted trade and caused hardship, for which the presence of foreigners was frequently blamed. In 1675 London weavers had rioted, declaring that their livelihoods were threatened, and contemporary petitions from other industries alleged that French craftsmen were failing to observe such regulations as the length of apprenticeships.

The Goldsmiths' Company, which wanted skilled work to be reserved for native-born subjects, had already complained to the king that numerous migrants without qualifications were being given equal rights, something that became a particularly sensitive issue after Peter Harache obtained favourable terms of entry to the London market in 1681.[56] Yet, in spite of this evident hostility to new arrivals, the crown continued to give its support to Huguenot settlement during the *grand refuge* and, together with the bishop of London, assisted the French churches in providing help.

In spite of the concerns about employment, and others about housing and the potential burden on the poor rate, most Londoners appear to have had sympathy for the sufferings of the Huguenot refugees and, writing a generation later, John Strype gave his opinion that the latter's arrival had set a good example to the neighbourhoods, brought God's blessing on the parishes, and was of 'great advantage to the whole nation'.[57] But that was not the way it was regarded by the House of Commons of the time, which continued to throw out naturalization bills until well past the end of the century, and to encourage the circulation of hostile pamphlets.[58] The *Rights and Liberties of Englishmen Asserted* (1701) condemned the admission of French immigrants, who, it was maintained, would pay no taxes and would undersell English goods. Far from being of benefit to the country, they were

[56] H. Tait, 'London Huguenot silver', in Scouloudi, *Huguenots in Britain*, pp. 98–9.

[57] Strype, *Survey*, ii, bk. 4, p. 48.

[58] 'The mercantile jealousy of the trading companies and London authorities was the principal reason' (Gwynn, *Huguenot Heritage*, p. 153).

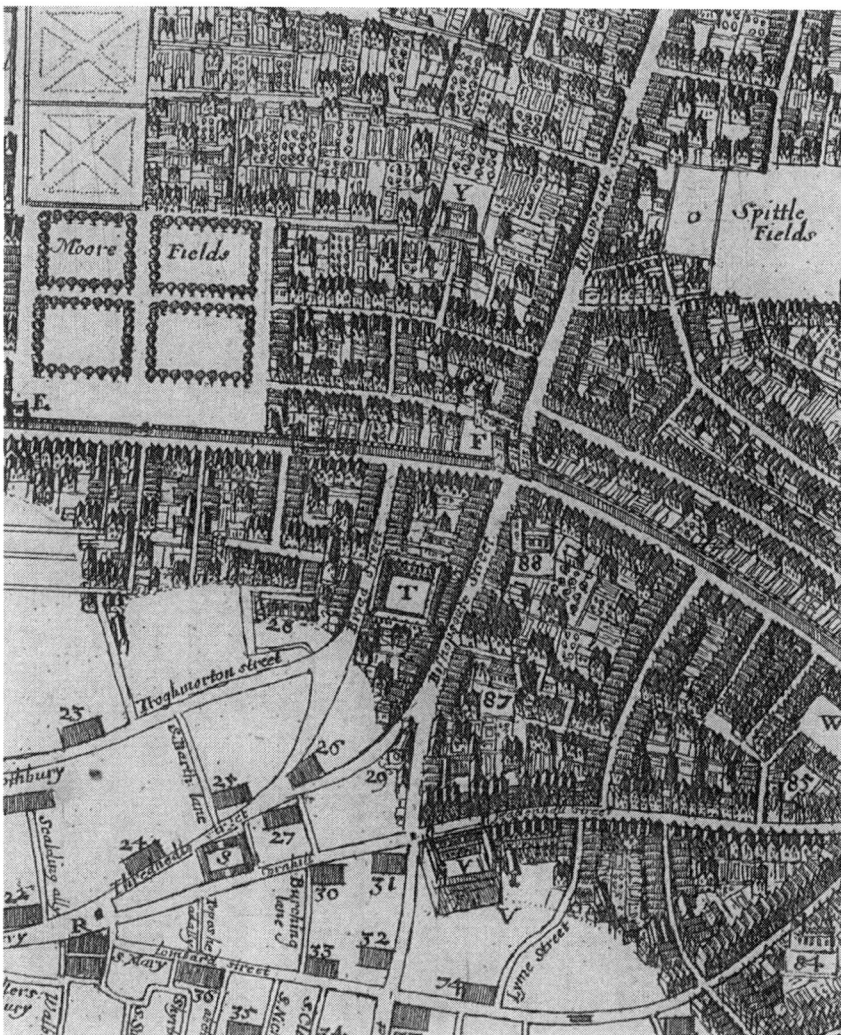

Figure 1.3. The north-east of the City after the Great Fire, from Wenceslas Hollar's 'map or groundplot' of 1666. Reproduced by permission of the British Library, Maps Crace Port. II.54. Spitalfields lies beyond Bishopsgate, and the French church (26) just inside the walls and the area of destruction.

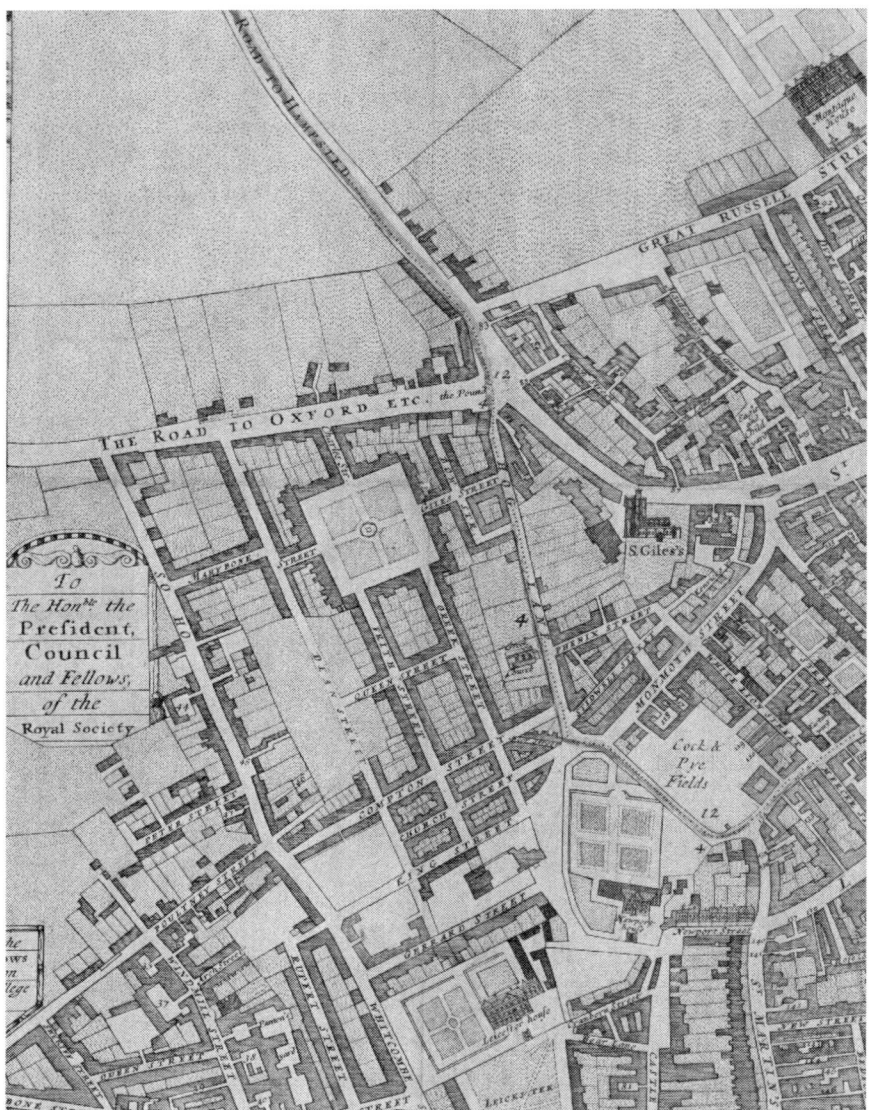

Figure 1.4. Soho in the 1680s, from Wm. Morgan's map of Westminster. Reproduced by permission of the British Library, Maps Crace Port. 11.58. It shows open country north of Oxford 'Road' and west of the future Wardour Street, and modern Charing Cross Road as 'Hog Lane'.

coming to exchange their poverty for English prosperity.[59]

However, Samuel Fortrey's opposite argument, published in his *England's Interest and Improvement* (1663), had been that an increase in population would actually enrich the kingdom, and these recommendations had influenced the prevailing government policy. In any case, London's French Protestants soon demonstrated that they were prepared to do a great deal to help themselves. They opened twenty-six new churches, organized their own poor relief and schooling, and took advantage of the opportunities offered through existing Huguenot networks. Some who had not previously woven silk moved into the Spitalfields area, where the contemporary boom had induced firms like the Walloon Lekeux to move up from Canterbury. Other recent events were also in their favour. The rapid housing development that followed the Great Fire of 1666 had resulted in an over-expansion of building and, particularly in the Soho area, property was standing empty. The 1711 vestry records of St. Anne's church in Wardour Street, first consecrated in 1686, show that 40 per cent of contemporary parish residents were Huguenots.[60]

William III came to the throne in 1688 with the support of three French Protestant regiments, and had strong sympathies with the Huguenots. He and his wife Mary Stuart demonstrated these feelings between 1689 and 1693, when they made personal gifts to the refugees amounting to £39,000 from the Civil List.[61] Some Huguenots who accompanied William to London were French army officers who had migrated to the Dutch Republic, but others were Protestant artists like Daniel Marot (1661–1732), the Parisian designer whose father was engraver and architect to the French court. In the course of his work at Het Loo Palace, Marot introduced William and Mary to the Louis XIV court style, and the ideas that he took to England through his own engravings included novel concepts on the decoration of interiors. His great versatility in being able to turn his capabilities to garden design, as well as to silver, fabric and porcelain, would influence the work of William Kent and others. The state coach created by Marot for William III is still used today by the speaker of the House of Commons.[62]

London's Huguenots and the spread of international knowledge
Nearly all European capitals were eager at that time to reflect the prestige of Paris and Versailles, but London was particularly well placed to do so

[59] Statt, *Foreigners and Englishmen*, p. 117.
[60] *Survey of London*, xxxiii: *the Parish of St Anne's Soho*, ed. F. H. W. Sheppard (1966), p. 7.
[61] Gwynn, *Huguenot Heritage*, pp. 71–2.
[62] *The Quiet Conquest: the Huguenots 1685–1985*, comp. T. Murdoch (Museum of London catalogue, 1985), pp. 183–6.

because of its stock of Huguenot craftsmen and artists and the number of recently arrived French Protestant intellectuals. Graham Gibbs has calculated that, between 1680 and 1720, no fewer than sixteen Huguenot immigrants were elected fellows of the Royal Society, and has shown how Huguenot writers helped England to share in the contemporary international exchange of ideas.[63] Old Slaughter's coffee-house in St. Martin's Lane was frequented by Westminster's French Protestant community, and was renowned as a place where persons of all languages and nations were free to meet 'gentry, artists, and others'. Journalism naturally benefited and, operating from the Black Boy coffee-house off Ludgate Hill, Pierre Motteux, a Huguenot from Rouen, founded a monthly magazine called the *Gentleman's Journal*. Modelled on the *Mercure Galant*, this publication anticipated *The Spectator* in its attempts to woo women readers. In a remarkable display of French (or perhaps Norman) immigrant energy and resourcefulness, Motteux established a second and less precarious source of income by apprenticing himself to the Huguenot apothecary Paul Franjoux and setting up a business selling East India goods in Leadenhall Street.[64] Another influential literary figure was Abel Boyer from Castres, who followed in Claudius Holyband's sixteenth-century footsteps by writing *The Compleat French Master for Ladies and Gentlemen* (1694); he also wrote a history of William III and Queen Anne and published a periodical with reports of parliamentary debates. Boyer had arrived as a penniless refugee in 1685 and received assistance to train as a Protestant minister, yet succeeded in living by his pen alone and died in comfort in fashionable Chelsea.

Matthieu Maty (1718–76) came to London with his father, who had first left the Dauphiné for Utrecht but then moved to England. In the tradition of European erudite journalism, Maty started the *Journal Britannique* from London, helping to familiarize French readers with English literature. His abilities were acknowledged when he was elected to the Royal Society and was made under-librarian at the newly formed British Museum. Yet energetic Huguenot intellectuals like Maty and Boyer were often regarded with prejudice by the English literary establishment, as seems clear from Samuel Johnson's alleged description of Maty as a 'little black dog', whom he would have liked to throw in the Thames, and from Jonathan Swift's similarly insulting references to Boyer.[65]

[63] G. C. Gibbs, 'Huguenot contributors to intellectual life', in Scouloudi, *Huguenots in Britain*, p. 27.

[64] E. Grist, 'Pierre Motteux (1663–1718): writer, translator, entrepreneur', *HSP*, xxviii (2003–7), 377–87.

[65] See G. C. Gibbs's series of articles in *HSP*, xxviii–xxix.

Figure 1.5. Abraham de Moivre (1667–1754), by Joseph Highmore, 1736. © The Royal Society. De Moivre was elected a fellow of the Royal Society in 1697.

Three other Huguenots who helped to spread knowledge from London were Pierre Coste, Abraham de Moivre and Jean-Theophile Desaguliers. Pierre Coste, one of several immigrant writers obliged to work as tutor in an English family, translated Newton's *Optics* into French and contributed to France's 'enlightenment' by translating the philosophy of John Locke. De Moivre and Desaguliers were other translators of Sir Isaac Newton's work, and de Moivre, a gifted mathematician, helped to launch the insurance business in London by introducing probability theory. Apart from his scientific researches, Desaguliers, born in La Rochelle, was an important figure in English freemasonry, and Desaguliers' Huguenot assistant Charles

Labelye, another freemason, drew plans for a bridge across the Thames at Westminster. Labelye's bridge, the second in the capital, was eventually completed in 1750, the Huguenot watchmaker James Valoué having designed the pile-driver that enabled the construction of its supporting piers.[66] This was the first London bridge to be built according to scientific calculation, and looked forward to the nineteenth-century achievements of other French engineers: the Brunels, whose Rotherhithe tunnel was the first to be built under a river, and Joseph Bazalgette, grandson of an immigrant tailor, whose extensive improvements to London's sewers made the city fit for modern living.

The influence of French design and craftsmanship

Some of the valuable effects of 1680s French Protestant settlement did not begin to become apparent until the next century was well on its way and businesses were occupying the newly developed areas between the Tottenham Court Road and St. James's Palace. Following Louis XIV's Edict of Fontainebleau, a second piece of legislation pushing Huguenots towards London had been the French king's 1689 decree that silver plate must be melted down for coin in order to assist the financing of France's war effort. The king set a good example by ordering the destruction of silver furniture at his palace at Versailles,[67] but after a ban was placed on all new work many craftsmen faced ruin, and looked towards other European opportunities. Some French Protestant goldsmiths had already begun to serve their apprenticeships in London, and marriage into one of the growing Huguenot craft dynasties could often help in setting up a successful business, as the career of Louis Mettayer, son of the minister of La Patente church in Spitalfields, demonstrates.[68]

The Mettayers had originated in the Ile de Ré, close to La Rochelle, and became English denizens in 1687. Thus they were already in London when the French ban on goldsmiths was announced, and young Louis (or Lewis) was in a favourable position to start his career. He became apprenticed to the successful immigrant goldsmith and banker David Willaume I in 1693, and entered his first mark in 1700 from an address in Pall Mall. One of Lewis's sisters married David Willaume and another married the silver engraver Simon Gribelin; Mettayer himself married the sister-in-law of Pierre Harache II, who had premises in Suffolk Street, close to the Haymarket.

---

[66] A. T. Carpenter, *John Theophilus Desaguliers* (2011), pp. 133, 146, 147.

[67] R. Pillorget and S. Pillorget, *France baroque, France classique, 1589–1715* (Paris, 1995), p. 1080.

[68] I. Hutchinson, 'Two studies in Huguenot silver, ii: a Louis Mettayer sideboard dish', *HSP*, xxix (2008–12), 489–98.

The leading Huguenot goldsmith Paul de la Merie, or de Lamerie, was brought to England as a child in 1691 and apprenticed to Pierre Platel, who had learned his craft in France. During the first half of the eighteenth century, de Lamerie ran a workshop in Windmill Street, where he employed thirteen apprentices and became the acknowledged leader in silver in the English rococo style, elaborately French in concept but with modifications to suit the more subdued English taste. He supplied the English aristocracy, the French regency and the Czarina Anna. The Crespin family had also moved to London, where their son Paul was brought up. He opened a workshop in Old Compton Street, Soho, in 1720, from which he kept in close touch with the latest fashions in France and supplied silverware to wealthy clients in England. He also supplied a silver bath to the king of Portugal, and part of a dinner service to Catherine the Great. From 1700 onwards, Huguenot imagination and skill played an essential role in introducing new forms and new techniques to English silver: Pierre Harache II's cut-cardwork is one example and piercework is another.[69]

Not all London Huguenots chose to stay within their traditional craft, as the history of the Courtauld family illustrates. Although Augustin Courtauld was a successful goldsmith, his son Samuel married into the Ogier family of weavers and his grandson invested in textiles, leading to the family becoming the foremost manufacturers of mourning crape in the world.[70] Similarly, Peter Dollond, who began his career as a master weaver, developed an interest in optics and set up in business with his son 'At the Spectacles and Sea Quadrant in the Strand' in 1752. The superior telescopes that their achromatic lens made possible were an advantage to British commanders during the Napoleonic wars. Nicholas Sprimont was

[69] P. Mincio, 'Fantastic piercework by the unknown "stencil master"', *Apollo* (Jan. 2003), p. 23.

[70] R. W. Dixon, 'Some account of the French refugee family of Courtauld', *HSP*, xi (1915–17), 138–48. The money for the Courtauld Gallery's collection of French late 19th-century paintings (housed at Somerset House, Strand, London, WC2), and for the French Impressionist and Post-Impressionist works acquired for the nation by the National Gallery with the Courtauld Fund, came from Courtaulds Ltd., the highly successful Courtauld family textiles firm, as arranged by Samuel Courtauld IV (1876–1947), who was determined that French Impressionist art should be amply represented in collections in England. The Courtauld Gallery has paintings, sculptures, drawings and prints by Pierre Bonnard, Rodolphe-Théophile Bosshard, Eugène Boudin, Paul Cézanne, Honoré Daumier, Edgar Degas, Raoul Dufy, Jean-Louis Forain, Emile Othon Friesz, Paul Gauguin, Vincent Van Gogh, Constantin Guys, Edouard Manet, Jean Hippolyte Marchand, Amedeo Modigliani, Claude Monet, Pablo Picasso, Camille Pissarro, Pierre-Auguste Renoir, Auguste Rodin, Henri Rousseau, Pierre Roy, Georges Seurat, Paul Signac, Alfred Sisley, Paul Tchelitchew, Henri de Toulouse-Lautrec, Maurice Utrillo, Edouard Vuillard, and more. It is thus a major international source for the study of French art and artists.

another versatile character; having been apprenticed to his uncle in Liège, he started to work as a goldsmith from Compton Street, then set up a factory in Chelsea where he made fine hard-paste porcelain in the Meissen style, which he later sold in St. James's Street, Westminster.[71]

Artists with a Huguenot background were particularly skilled in the fine detail associated with engraving, or the ivory carvings produced in Dieppe. An immigrant carver of note, Jean Cavalier, who trained in Paris under Michael Mollet, created a relief of Charles II in 1684, and one of Samuel Pepys in 1688. His striking ivory medallion portrait of William III is on show at the Victoria and Albert Museum, and work by David le Marchand, another Huguenot ivory carver, can be seen both there and at the British Museum. Small articles made from ivory or tortoiseshell, together with gold and silver items and clocks and watches, were on sale at French Huguenot 'toyshops' in the Charing Cross and Soho areas, an example being Paul Daniel Chenevix's Suffolk Street premises, first recorded in 1731. His family was from Picardy and his father, killed at the Battle of Blenheim, had been a major in the Carabiniers. David Grignion, who came to London from Poitou at the age of four, was connected to the Harache family of goldsmiths and had a shop in Russell Street, on the Bedford Estate, where he cleaned and mended watches from 1730 until his death in 1763.[72]

French clock-making skills had been valued since the days of Henry VIII, and the early Protestant watchmakers settled in Blackfriars, followed by a movement towards Holborn and Covent Garden in the 1630s. Nicholas Massy, from Blois, had a business in Cranbourn Street until his death in 1698. A member of an extensive clock-making fraternity from Rouen, David Lestourgeon, a freeman of the London guild of clockmakers in 1698, is thought to have had a goldsmith's business in Church Lane, St. Martin-in-the-Fields, in the early eighteenth century. Another family of Norman clockmakers, the Jourdains from Dieppe, arrived in 1686 and settled in Spitalfields, where they were also involved in the silk industry. The clock business was run from an address in Paternoster Row for the next 100 years, and at the same time the family traded as mercers at No. 58 Artillery Lane. They appear to have been prominent members of the local Huguenot community, which they presented with a clock for the tower of Christ Church Spitalfields. Nicholas Jourdain was governor of the Spitalfields workhouse in 1754, and a director of the French hospital known as 'La Providence'.[73]

[71] *Victoria History of Middlesex*, xii. 158–9.
[72] Murdoch, *Quiet Conquest*, p. 250.
[73] B. de Save, 'The Jourdain family of Spitalfields', *HSP*, xxix (2008–12), 105–6.

Figure 1.6. Jacques de Gastigny (d. 1708), circle of Pierre Mignard,
by permission of the French Hospital. Gastigny's bequest led to the
founding of a hospital for poor French Protestants. FHR 419646. © The
French Hospital, Rochester, Kent / The Bridgeman Art Library.

'La Providence' is an early eighteenth-century institution that is still with
us today. It began as one man's charitable wish to help sick Huguenots too
poor to afford treatment at home, and the example it set helped to inspire
English philanthropy. Jacques de Gastigny came to England with William
III and, having fought for him at the Battle of the Boyne, served him as
master of the royal buckhounds. When Gastigny died in 1708 he left in
his will the sum of £1,000 towards the establishment of a hospital, and this

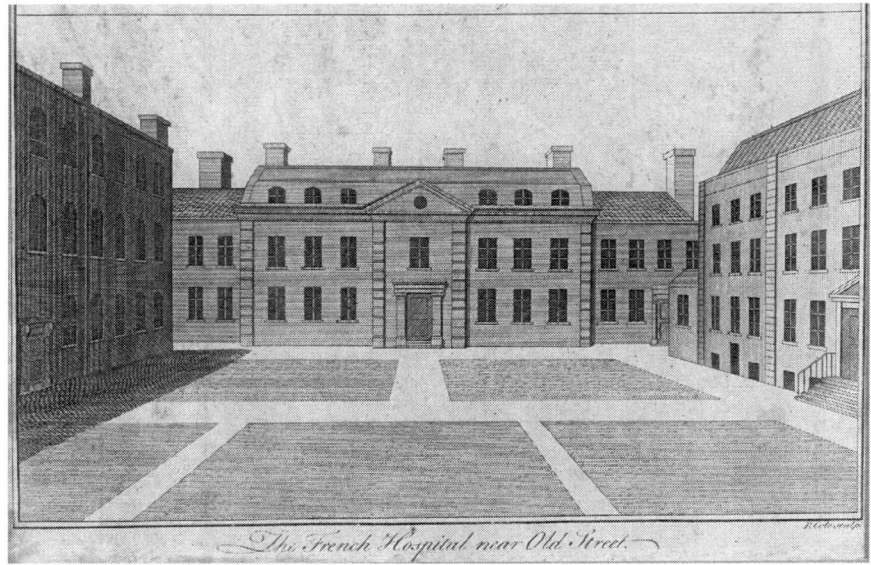

The French Hospital near Old Street.

Figure 1.7. The French Hospital, Old Street, Finsbury, artist unknown,
by permission of the French Hospital. The hospital, which opened in
1718, became known as 'La Providence'. FHR 419645. © The French
Hospital, Rochester, Kent / The Bridgeman Art Library.

finally opened its doors ten years later.[74] A new building designed for it
in 1865 by Robert Louis Roumieu, an architect of Huguenot descent, was
expropriated after the Second World War and, since then, 'La Providence'
has moved out of London to Rochester, in Kent, where it now provides
sheltered accommodation to those of Huguenot ancestry.

London's Huguenot legacy

As confessional passions began to cool in the years following William III's
'glorious revolution', it became less important that the French craftsmen,
artists and writers who lived and worked in England should hold Protestant
beliefs. Although Ralph, first duke of Montagu, was noted for his patronage
of Huguenots, and had brought the Protestant painter Louis Chéron to
London, he also employed Catholic talent in his decorative schemes. A
fashionable demand for French furniture caused the Catholic carver
and gilder Joseph Duffour to open a shop in Berwick Street, and Pierre
Langlois, probably a co-religionist, ran a very successful business in the

[74] T. Murdoch and R. Vigne, *The French Hospital in England* (Cambridge, 2009), pp.
9–12.

Tottenham Court Road. Hubert Gravelot, the renowned Catholic engraver and illustrator from Paris, stayed in London from 1732 to 1745 and taught drawing in the rococo style to pupils who included Thomas Gainsborough. He was friendly with the London Huguenot sculptor Louis François Roubiliac, who taught at the St. Martin's Lane Academy, and with William Hogarth. In the world of theatre, too, there was a move towards greater toleration.

Thomas Betterton had travelled to France soon after the Restoration to study the French stage; in 1698 he invited Anthony L'Abbé and other French Catholic dancers to perform at his Lincoln's Inn theatre. L'Abbé stayed in England for another thirty years, and became dancing-master to George I's grand-daughter.[75] David Garrick (1717–79), whose Huguenot grandfather came from Bordeaux, employed the composer François Hippolyte Barthélémon, also from Bordeaux, to write music for his productions at the Theatre Royal and Barthélémon eventually settled in England. Garrick's management at Drury Lane is legendary, and he died a rich man; his personal life may be glimpsed through the pair of paintings he commissioned from Johann Zoffany in 1762, recently sold at auction for almost £7,000,000, which are now hanging, appropriately, at the Garrick Club.

The Treaty of Ryswick of 1697 and the 1713 Peace of Utrecht both failed to extract concessions from Louis XIV over the treatment of his Protestant minority, whose full rights were ignored until 1789, when the Declaration of the Rights of Man finally recognized the fundamental importance of liberty of conscience. London French Protestants, meanwhile, had become resigned to their surroundings and, by the second half of the eighteenth century, most of them had ceased to speak French. The special position of the French church in Threadneedle Street became less significant as the capital's Huguenot population began to assimilate into its host society and to desert the churches opened during the height of the *grand refuge.* Once their members had shown a preference for Anglicanism, or English Nonconformism, all these smaller churches closed down. Threadneedle Street itself was forced by building development to give up the ancient site of St. Antoine and to move to its present position in Soho Square.

Did the original Huguenot migrants find the life they sought in London? On the whole, the answer is probably 'yes'. The greater confessional freedom that England offered suited their needs and, apart from bouts of civil war, plague, fire and riot, they had the opportunity to follow their occupations undisturbed. Complete equality with all their fellow citizens they would not

---

[75] J. Thorp, 'L'Abbé, Anthony (b. 1666/7, d. in or after 1753)', *ODNB.*

have expected, living as they did when society was still ordered by status and degree, and when gender equality was not foreseen. Voltaire, in his *Lettres sur les anglais* (1734), found equality to be present in the English tax system and because the same laws applied to everyone, in contrast to France's *taille* and the sovereign's powers of arbitrary arrest and imprisonment.

Huguenots' sentiments about their land of adoption are frequently expressed in their wills, as in that of the Reverend Peter Allix, who, in his preface, 'full of gratitude for the kindness of that good king', declared his loyalty to George I and offered his prayers to God that the monarch might have a long and happy reign. Magdalen Amyot's will of 1743, written at St. James's, Westminster, gave simple thanks to God for causing her to be received 'into this country of liberty'.[76] Her testimony echoes, to some extent, that of Voltaire, who praised the liberty of Englishmen to think what they pleased and publish what they thought. It also anticipates that of Jean Deschamps, whose 1756 letter to his friend Jean Henri Samuel Formey in Berlin stated his satisfaction with London and described its atmosphere of liberty and peace.[77]

This sense of comparative liberty may still be attractive to the French who come to London today. In a secular and ecumenical age disagreement over religious confessions has lost its significance, but even at a sub-conscious level French visitors will be aware that the Huguenots, despite sometimes modest beginnings, found opportunities in the British capital denied to them in their land of origin, and were 'unusually well-received' there in the sixteenth and seventeenth centuries.[78] In City circles, there is a continuing recognition of the part played by successful French Protestants in the setting up of Great Britain's financial services, and of the contribution that their loyalty made to national stability. Huguenots are also well remembered in Spitalfields, both for the industriousness of their lives and for their perceived virtues of honesty and compassion. However, it is to their many descendants, a large number of whom are now scattered across the globe, that we must look for a true appreciation of London's French Protestants. The consciousness of their origins, and the extraordinary interest that this arouses, has not only encouraged them to research their own genealogy; it has also led to the exchange and publication of the extensive knowledge that has been gained through the study of a rich and varied fund of historical records.

[76] R. Vigne, 'Testaments of faith: wills of Huguenot refugees in England as a window on their past', in Trim, *The Huguenots*, pp. 280–1.

[77] *Lettres de l'Angleterre à Jean Henri Samuel Formey à Berlin*, ed. U. Janssens and J. Schillings (Paris, 2006), pp. 59–60.

[78] Gwynn, *Huguenot Heritage*, p. 141.

2. Montagu House, Bloomsbury: a French household in London, 1673–1733

Paul Boucher and Tessa Murdoch[1]

'The Duke of Montagu lived with a greater Splendour and Magnificence in his Family, than any man of Quality perhaps in Great Britain', wrote the duke's contemporary, the Huguenot historian Abel Boyer. It was at the court of Louis XIV that 'his Grace formed his Ideas in his own Mind of Buildings and Gardening'. As Charles II's highly ambitious and political ambassador to France, Ralph Montagu maintained the most lavish ambassadorial style in order to support the reputation of his monarch abroad, making his formal entry 'with a vast Equipage … in a most splendid manner'.[2] It was during these formative years that Montagu developed his taste for refined French artistic connoisseurship, shared by his close friend Henriette-Anne d'Orléans, Charles II's sister and Louis XIV's sister-in-law, who then lived in ostentatious luxury at the palace of St. Cloud. Ralph Montagu was forced to retreat from Paris in 1678 after affairs with both the duchess of Cleveland, one of Charles II's mistresses, and her daughter Lady Sussex. He returned to London with more than 200 trunks of luxury goods, including much silver.[3]

After his marriage to Elizabeth Wriothesley, daughter of the fourth earl of Southampton, Montagu obtained land from his father-in-law's estate in Bloomsbury and commissioned the design of a new house from the architect and experimental philosopher Robert Hooke (1635–1703). This was built 'after the French pavilion way', with a gateway and stable courtyard, on the site now occupied by the British Museum.[4] Montagu's portrait by the Italian artist Benedetto Gennari, painted in London in 1678–9 (Figure 2.1), shows his informal dress. The links in his shirt cuffs demonstrate his attention to

---

[1] Tessa Murdoch's contribution is built on 'The dukes of Montagu as patrons of the Huguenots', *HSP*, xxv (1992), 340–55.

[2] A. Boyer, *History of the Life and Reign of Queen Anne* (1722), p. 374.

[3] H. Jacobsen, *Luxury and Power: the Material World of the Stuart Diplomat 1660–1714* (Oxford, 2011), p. 99. See TNA, PRO 30/32/48 fo. 7 (1672); PRO 30/32/50 fo. 109 (27 Oct. 1674); PRO 30/32/39 fos. 45v–51.

[4] *The Diary of John Evelyn*, ed. E. S. De Beer (6 vols., 1955), iv. 345.

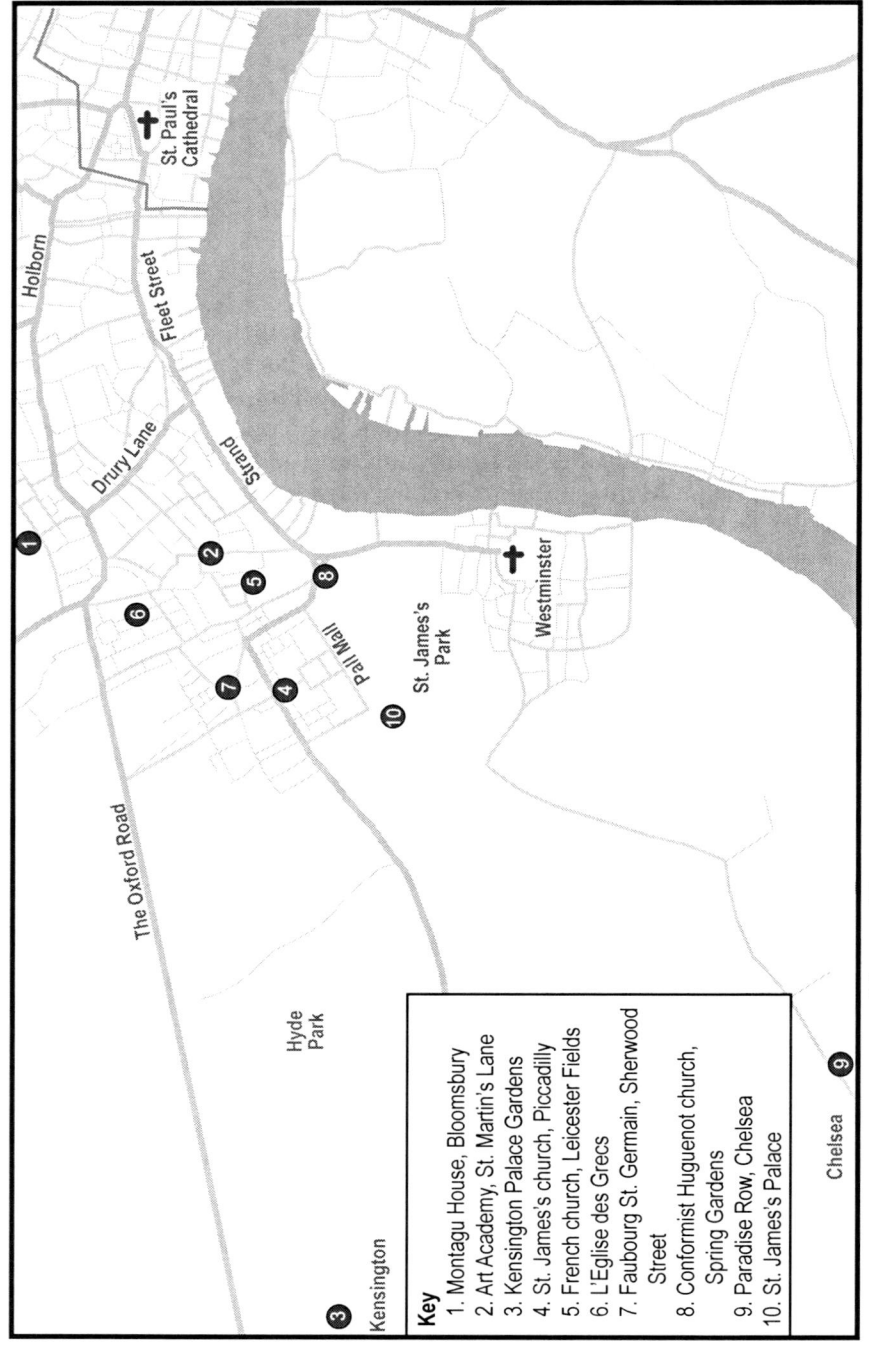

Map 2.1. Places mentioned in the text (Base map: London c.1700)

Key
1. Montagu House, Bloomsbury
2. Art Academy, St. Martin's Lane
3. Kensington Palace Gardens
4. St. James's church, Piccadilly
5. French church, Leicester Fields
6. L'Eglise des Grecs
7. Faubourg St. Germain, Sherwood Street
8. Conformist Huguenot church, Spring Gardens
9. Paradise Row, Chelsea
10. St. James's Palace

Figure 2.1. Ralph Montagu, oil on canvas, Benedetto Gennari,
1679. Northamptonshire, Boughton House.

detail, which characterized his patronage of architects, designers, artists and
craftsmen both for his own family use and in his official capacity as master
of the king's wardrobe – a role Montagu enjoyed during the reign of Charles
II and again under William III.

Montagu spent several years in political exile in Montpellier in the 1680s
and while abroad rented Montagu House to the fourth earl of Devonshire.
Early in 1686 Montagu's London home was effectively destroyed by fire
and was rebuilt on his return from France, after an unsuccessful lawsuit, to
the designs of a French architect identified by contemporaries as Monsieur

Figure 2.2. The north prospect of Montagu House, engraving by
J. Simon, c.1714. Northamptonshire, Boughton House.

Puget (Figure 2.2).[5] The architect may be François Puget, the son of the
better known French sculptor Pierre Puget, who was then based in Marseilles
not far from Montpellier. On his return to London, Montagu encouraged
a group of artists to come to London from Paris. They included Charles de
Lafosse, who arrived in 1689. A pupil of Charles Le Brun, Lafosse won the
Prix de Rome in 1658 and subsequently spent three years in Italy; on his
return to France in 1670 he painted three ceilings at the Tuileries and two at
Versailles. At Montagu House, Lafosse painted the staircase, the north wall
with 'Diana and Actaeon' and the ceiling with the story of 'Phaeton'. He
also painted the first floor saloon ceiling with the 'Assembly of the Gods' and
in different compartments, the 'Fall of the giants', 'Ceres', 'Pan', 'Neptune
and Amphitrite', 'Mercury as the messenger of the gods' and 'Phaeton
in the chariot of the sun, preceded by Aurora'. Lafosse was paid £2,000
for his work at Montagu House, 'besides £500 allowed for diet and other

[5] G. Jackson-Stops, 'Daniel Marot and the 1st duke of Montagu', *Nederlands
Kunsthistorisch Jaarboek*, xxxi (1980), 244–62.

STAIRCASE OF THE OLD BRITISH MUSEUM, MONTAGUE HOUSE

Figure 2.3. The staircase, Montagu House, Bloomsbury,
watercolour by George Scharf, *c.*1830. British Museum.

expenses'. He returned to Paris to paint the dome of Les Invalides for the
architect Jules Hardouin-Mansart (1646–1708), but his assistants remained
in London to complete the work. On 9 May 1690 the housekeeper Madame
de Rit wrote to her husband Elias, then in Geneva: 'We drank your health
this morning with Monsieur de la Fosse and Monsieur Rousseau. They
have almost finished the salon and will begin the staircase soon'.[6] Jacques
Rousseau painted landscape backgrounds and the *trompe-l'œil* architecture
of the staircase.[7] In watercolours recording the interiors of Montagu House,
painted by George Scharf in the 1830s when the house was occupied by

---

[6] 'Nous avons bu ce matin à votre santé avec M. de la Fosse et M. Rousseau. Ils ont
presque achevé le Salon et commenceront bientôt l'escalier' (Northamptonshire Record
Office, A.13/11, French letters to the Montagu family, vol. 2, 1678–1735, fo. 157, letter from
Madame de Rit to Elias de Rit in Geneva).

[7] For Jacques Rousseau, see E. Evans, 'Jacques Rousseau: a Huguenot decorative artist at
the courts of Louis XIV and William III', *HSP*, xxii (1972), 142–61.

Figure 2.4. Jean Baptiste Monnoyer, mezzotint after Sir
Godfrey Kneller. British Museum, *c.*1690.

the British Museum, it is difficult to distinguish between the real and the simulated architecture (Figure 2.3).

Montagu House was decorated with over fifty flower paintings by Louis XIV's former flower painter Jean Baptiste Monnoyer, known as Baptiste; there were five in the stone hall, and others positioned above chimney-pieces and over doors in several of the reception rooms on the ground floor. Both Rousseau and Baptiste had previously worked for Louis XIV. Baptiste was of Franco-Flemish origin, born at Lille in 1634 and trained at Antwerp; he presented his reception piece at the French Academy in Paris when he was twenty-seven. He produced more than sixty paintings for Versailles and the royal palaces at Vincennes, Meudon and Marly. As Baptiste also designed flowers and floral borders for the Gobelins and Beauvais tapestries, Montagu may have intended to employ him in designing for the Mortlake tapestry manufactory which he had acquired in the 1670s. In London, Baptiste sat to Sir Godfrey Kneller for his portrait, and although the oil is lost, a preparatory sketch and mezzotint survive (Figure 2.4). Montagu settled on Rousseau a pension of £200 a year, and the artist died in December 1693. In that same year Louis Chéron, another artist trained at the French Academy in Paris and Rome, is first recorded in London (Figure 2.5). Like Rousseau and Baptiste, Chéron was attracted to London as a Protestant, because practice of that faith in France was banned following Louis XIV's revocation of the Edict of Nantes in October 1685. Chéron was accepted by the French Protestant church of the Savoy in 1693[8] and subsequently worked for Montagu at Montagu House, where he painted the ceilings of two rooms 'below stairs', and at Boughton House, Northamptonshire, the country home which Ralph Montagu inherited on his father's death in 1684. Louis Chéron later taught at the art academy in St. Martin's Lane, where 'he soon distinguish'd his talent in delineating … being very assiduous, he was much imitated by the Young people & indeed on that account by all lovers of Art much esteem'd & from thence raised his reputation'.[9] On the duke's death in 1709, Chéron provided a valuation of the paintings in his patron's cabinet at Montagu House.

The decorative paintings by Baptiste were mounted in gilded frames provided by the London workshop of Jean Pelletier and his two sons Thomas and René, carvers and gilders who came from Paris via Amsterdam. Detailed accounts of their work for Montagu survive in three volumes assembled

[8] *Le Livre des conversions et des reconnoissances faites à l'église française de la Savoye, 1684–1702*, ed. W. Minet and S. Minet (HSQS, xxii, 1914), entry dated 1 Oct. 1693 as 'Le Sieur Louis Cheron. Pintre 30 ans de Paris' (see previous chapter, for more details on the Huguenots).

[9] G. Vertue, 'Note books III', *The Walpole Society*, xxii (1933–4), 22.

Figure 2.5. Louis Chéron, engraving. National Portrait Gallery.

by the duke's executors after his death. The Pelletiers gilded fixtures and fittings, as well as freestanding looking-glass and picture frames. A typical entry in Montagu's accounts records a payment of £3 10*s* 'for gilding a large frame with corners & middles for a flower piece of Baptists' (July 1700) or £9 12*s* 'for carving & gilding a large frame for one of Baptist's pieces for the chimney'.[10] Both Baptiste and the Pelletiers also worked for the royal palaces. Baptiste was a favourite with Queen Mary II, who sat and watched him paint a mirror for her apartment at Kensington Palace. Baptiste's paintings incorporated flowers which bloomed at different times of the year, and were built up from his studies. A series of prints based on

---

[10] Northamptonshire, Boughton House, 'Accounts of the executors of Ralph, 1st duke of Montagu, 1712' (hereafter Boughton House, executors' accounts), vol. 2, fos. 819–31, at fo. 825; for the Pelletier workshop, see T. Murdoch, 'Jean, René and Thomas Pelletier, a Huguenot family of carvers and gilders in England 1682–1726, pts. i and ii ', *Burlington Magazine*, cxxxix (1997), 732–42, cxl (1998), 363–74.

Figure 2.6. Daniel Marot, engraving, Jacob Gole. Rijksmuseum.

his work was produced by John Smith. Baptiste died in 1699 and was buried in St. James's, Piccadilly.

After Lafosse returned to Paris in 1691, Montagu called in an outside designer on at least two occasions to advise him on aspects of interior decoration. This was Daniel Marot, trained at the court of Louis XIV at Versailles under Jean Berain (Figure 2.6). As a Protestant, Marot took refuge in Amsterdam and worked for the court of William and Mary at The Hague. In 1689 he provided a design for the layout of the parterre at the royal palace of Hampton Court. In 1694 Marot came to London – his marriage in that year and the baptism of his two children, in June 1695 and June 1696, were recorded at the French church of Leicester Fields. Drawings in Marot's hand of painted panels thought to originate from a closet at Montagu House provide documentary evidence for the colours used but may be record drawings of the panels rather than preparatory designs. The panels, which illustrate the 'Loves of the gods, Apollo and

Daphne, Diana and Endymion, Venus and Adonis, Jupiter and Io and the triumph of Galatea', now hang in a small boudoir at the south-west corner of Boughton House.[11] They may have been brought back to London from Paris by Ralph Montagu. An inscription on the Marot drawings refers to a Monsieur Loir – probably the French designer Nicholas Loir. An entry in the 1709 inventory of Ditton, Montagu's Buckinghamshire home inherited through his mother's family the Winwoods, refers to 'Five Large Pannells painted by Louvois'.[12] Another series of carved panels given to the Victoria and Albert Museum in 1918 by the sixth duke of Buccleuch may be the work of the French carvers Gedeon du Chesne and Henri Nadauld, both recorded as working at Montagu House in the 1690s.[13]

Furnishings were often transported from the London house to Montagu's country residences: Ditton, and the Montagu seat at Boughton, Northamptonshire. In 1705, the London upholsterer Francis Lapierre was paid for 'taking a Crimson & gold damask bed all to pieces & new making it up again to go to Boughton'. In 1706, Lapierre charged £14 'for a fine large wainscot Bedstead lath Bottom & molding cornishes & a fine carved Tester & Headboard for making a bed of fine tapestry needlework, curtains, valence, bases, canton & Tester head cloth, case post & counterpane'. A further £3 paid for '4 carved cups & covering them' and another £3 was paid to 'Marot' for drawing the 'Cornishes and the Cupps'.[14] As Daniel Marot was back in Amsterdam, this must refer to his brother Isaac, who is described in 1707 as 'dessinateur' in the registers of the Huguenot Savoy church and can also be identified as the Isaac Marot who stood godfather to Isaac, the baby son of Thomas Renard, Montagu's gardener in 1704.[15]

In 1694, Francis Lapierre made Montagu a trustee of a £500 marriage portion for his daughter Frances, an indication of Montagu's close involvement with the craftsmen he employed. Frances Lapierre had married the tailor Joseph Boucher, whose name recurs in Montagu's accounts as providing suits of clothing for members of the family. The evidence for this is preserved in the legal documents collected by Ralph, duke of Montagu's executors after his death. Francis Lapierre acted as a witness for his son-in-law and recorded:

[11] Jackson-Stops, 'Daniel Marot', pp. 244–62.
[12] *Noble Households: 18th-Century Inventories of Great English Houses. A Tribute to John Cornforth*, ed. T. Murdoch (Cambridge, 2006), p. 84.
[13] Victoria and Albert Museum, museum no. W.184-1923.
[14] Boughton House, executors' accounts, 1712, vol. 2, fo. 581.
[15] *Registers of the French Churches of the Savoy, Spring Gardens, and Les Grecs, London*, ed. W. Minet and S. Minet (HSQS, xxvi, 1922).

Some short time before the 4th of June 1705 the late Duke told him that he was indebted to Jos: Boucher in £500 for Cloth & other Taylor's goods & work done & provided for the Duke & his family & that if Boucher would release the £500 Debt he would settle the same by a further portion for this Defendant's daughter then Boucher's wife which proposal the Duke made known to Boucher who approved it & Boucher accordingly released to the Duke the £500 the Duke did on or abt the 4th June 1705 with Boucher & his wife, Dr Silvester & this Dft execute the indenture shewed him dated 4th June 1705.[16]

The accounts kept by Ralph Montagu's steward record the high cost of furnishings and furniture for the interiors of his London house. 'Two little white India cabinets' provided a note of exoticism in the 'Corner Room at the West End' of Montagu House 'below stairs'. This room had five windows hung with white damask curtains trimmed with green lace; the walls were hung with green figured velvet and there were flower paintings by Baptiste; there was a large looking-glass in a glass frame, a white marble table edged with black, with two matching carved gilt stands, and eight chairs were upholstered in matching velvet fringed with gold.[17] The two looking-glasses with inlaid frames and matching tables may be identified with the set in the low pavilion anteroom at Boughton today which have been attributed to Gerrit Jensen but may be the work of Daniel Marot's cousin Cornelius Gole, the son of Louis XIV's cabinet-maker Pierre Gole. A payment to 'Corneille Gole upon acct of mending the frame of a looking-glass and scrutoire £3' in July 1702 and earlier payments to Gole for a 'scrutoire' (desk) in 1700–1 demonstrate that he was certainly supplying Montagu with carcase furniture.[18] Furnishing fabrics were acquired through John Noguier, David Bosanquet and Simon Beranger at enormous cost to provide an appropriate setting and coverings for such luxurious furniture.[19] Details of the contents of the reception rooms are recorded in the inventory taken on Montagu's death in 1709 and a later inventory of 1733 taken when Montagu's eldest son, the second duke, moved to a new house in Whitehall overlooking the Thames, built for him by the architect Henry Flitcroft.[20]

A reference in the executors' accounts refers to 'mending the table that was bought of the French Ambassador'.[21] Was this perhaps the most

[16] Boughton House, legal examinations of Ralph Montagu's creditors, 1712.
[17] The 1709 inventory of the contents of Montagu House is published in full in Murdoch, *Noble Households*, pp. 11–26.
[18] A. Bowett, *English Furniture from Charles II to Queen Anne* (New York, 2002), pp. 190–1; Boughton House, Mr. de Rit's accounts, 1698–1705.
[19] Boughton House, Mr. de Rit's accounts, 1698–1705.
[20] Both these inventories are published in Murdoch, *Noble Households*.
[21] Boughton House, executors' accounts, 1712, vol. 2, fo. 646.

exceptional piece of French furniture to remain at Boughton today? A bureau of marquetry of brass and pewter, with borders of ebony inlaid with mother-of-pearl and gilt bronze mounts on a gilded console stand, is attributed to Pierre Gole. By family tradition this is said to have been a personal gift from Louis XIV to Ralph Montagu and is linked with a similar piece supplied by Gole for the use of Louis XIV at a cost of 1,800 livres in 1672. The stand consists of winged putti which may originally have had contrasting gilded and silvered surfaces to complement the pewter and brass inlay of the bureau. These consoles are linked by cross pieces with a double fleur de lis in the centre; a second fleur de lis in the centre of the gradin confirms its French origin.[22] Another potential gift from Louis XIV is the pendulum clock in Boulle case which is known as the *pendule à parques* – named after the three Fates who spin the thread of life which is then cut short. The carcase of this clock case, like the Gole bureau, is of oak, veneered with pewter and brass, and bears Ralph Montagu's cipher 'RM' beneath a ducal coronet; the movement has been replaced at a later date and is signed by the English clockmaker William Allan.[23]

Certainly the architecture, furnishings and furniture of the rebuilt Montagu House, Bloomsbury, were inspired by the latest French fashions, and support the thesis that Montagu may indeed have benefited from a pension from Louis XIV, on condition that Montagu only employed French architects and artists in the reconstruction of his great London house.[24] By 1689, three years after the fire, rebuilding was sufficiently complete for William III to dine there in order to admire the newly completed decorative schemes. As a result, many of the artists and craftsmen employed by Montagu on his own home were recommended to assist in the decoration and furnishing of the royal palaces during the 1690s.[25]

Montagu leaned heavily on his French household in supervising the rebuilding and refurnishing and in providing the maintenance and service that such a large establishment required. The 1709 inventory lists various members of the household. Mr. Portal was responsible for the stables and carriages; Dr. Pierre Silvestre (1662–1718), Montagu's personal physician,

---

[22] P. Hughes, 'The French furniture', in *Boughton House: the English Versailles*, ed. T. Murdoch (1992), pp. 119–20, plate 70.

[23] Hughes, 'The French furniture', p. 120, plate 71.

[24] L. E. Dussieux, *Les Artistes Français à l'étranger* (Paris, 1876), p. 267, quoting Paris, Bibliothèque Nationale de France, MS. 1846, writes 'Louis XIV s'engagea à supporter les moitiés des frais de la reconstruction à la condition que les architectes et des peintres français y seraient seuls employés'.

[25] Murdoch, *The English Versailles*, p. 33; Boughton House, executors' accounts, vol. 2, fo. 666.

also doubled as his inspector of building works and gardens; other French members of the household included Mr. Falaizeau and Mr. Mirande, a wig-maker. Even the gardeners Francis Dursau and Thomas Renard were members of the London Huguenot community. The London house was set in seven acres with a garden to the north with views towards the hills of Highgate and Hampstead. The garden was a miniature version of Montagu's country seat at Boughton, which was particularly remarkable for its parterres, in particular 'the Water Parterre: wherein is an Octagon Basin whose circumference is 216 Yards, which in the middle of it has a "Jet d'Eau" whose height is above 50 feet, surrounded by other smaller Jets d'Eau's'.[26] In London, the formal planting of yews, hollies, laurels and evergreens could be enjoyed in winter as well as summer.[27] Here the gardens were tended by Thomas Renard – payments are recorded to him in Montagu's accounts for 1700 and he is also documented as 'Gardener for Lord Montagu' in the registers of the French church of the Savoy.[28]

Montagu's household accounts demonstrate that many of the tradesmen he patronized were French. Household pewter was supplied by Jonas Durand and James Taudin (Tahourdin). This expenditure was vouched for by Nicholas Bernardeau, who had served Jonas Durand as his servant and bookkeeper and witnessed that 'the late Duke did bespeak in 1704 & 1705 of his Master severall parcels of Pewter delivered by his Master to the Duke on order at Montagu House & that he went along with & saw the parcels delivered to the Duke's Butler'.[29]

The low pavilion anteroom at Boughton House still contains some of this treasured furniture acquired by Ralph Montagu. Needlework chair covers were supplied by Marie Pariselle, Esther Regneaux and Madame Justell. Their names are all recorded in Ralph Montagu's accounts: Marie Pariselle was paid, in December 1703, £10 on account for tapestry chairs and again for the same in August 1704 and July 1705; Esther Regneaux was paid £8 in March 1704 for two tapestry chairs; and in August 1705 Madame Justell was paid £20 for three silk and needlework chairs. Appropriately Montagu's portrait by Michael Dahl is displayed between a matching pair of mirrors and tables which imitate the technique of metal marquetry developed in Paris by André Charles Boulle. The Dahl portrait probably

[26] For a full description of the Boughton gardens in 1712, see Murdoch, *The English Versailles*, p. 25.

[27] T. Murdoch, 'London gardens and the decorative arts', in *London's Pride: the Glorious History of the Capital's Gardens*, ed. M. Galinou (1990), p. 136.

[28] 'Jardinier chez my lord Montaigu' (Minet and Minet, *Registers of the French Churches of the Savoy*) (for 1704).

[29] Boughton House, legal examinations of Ralph Montagu's creditors, 1712.

dates from August 1704 when Thomas Pelletier was asked to pay 'Mr Doll' £32 5s for two pictures.[30] The centre table in the low pavilion anteroom has a monogram of the letters 'C' and 'M' which may record Ralph Montagu's second marriage to Elizabeth Cavendish, duchess of Albemarle. The marquetry decoration is thought to have formed a central motif in the parquet flooring at Montagu House, the work of the Huguenot joiner Peter Rieusset of St. Anne's, Westminster, who was also responsible for the parquet flooring in the state apartments at Boughton. The elaborate wooden parquet flooring on the upper landing, which continues through the state apartments, was also the work of Rieusset, who was paid nearly £5,000 for his combined work at Montagu House and Boughton. It was laid in 1706 when Rieusset was paid £24 18s to 'go to Boughton with my man 8 days work 27 1/2 yds of Parkett at 18s per yard for the Gt stairs'. In 1706 Rieusset supplied Montagu with a 'large wainscot Desk 8 foot in length 4 foot 6 inches in breadth & 2 foot 4 inches in height, with several partitions: hinges, locks and keys, covering it with green cloth & garnishing it with galloone & brass nails'; this was for his official role as master of the wardrobe. Rieusset was also responsible for supplying billiard tables for Boughton House and Ditton in Buckinghamshire. The table at Boughton survives with at least one of its original cues – it is shown today in the unfinished wing but is recorded in the 1709 inventory on the death of Duke Ralph as in the attics, where it was set up by Rieusset between March and May 1697. Here it was used by the staff who managed the house during the long winter months – the house was only used as a residence by the family in the summer. The billiard table which Rieusset supplied in 1702 for Ditton cost £22.[31]

Between the windows in the Boughton drawing room are the two remarkable oval looking-glass sconces which came from a closet at Montagu House, Bloomsbury, but may originally have come from Queen Mary II's gallery at Kensington Palace. The carving is attributed to Robert Derignée, a French carver working in London, whose name occurs both in the lord chamberlain's accounts and in Mr. de Rit's accounts for Ralph Montagu. The gilding may be the work of Jean Pelletier, who, with his two sons Thomas and René, provided the giltwood furniture for Montagu's houses and through Montagu for the royal palaces – the giltwood tables and stands provided for the king's state apartments at Hampton Court Palace can still be seen in the Royal Collection today.[32]

[30] Boughton House, Mr. de Rit's accounts, 1698–1705.
[31] Boughton House, executors' accounts, 1712.
[32] Murdoch, 'Jean, René and Thomas Pelletier, pt. i'.

Picture frames were provided by Mr. Tabary (one of the Tabary brothers who had worked at the Royal Hospital Kilmainham, outside Dublin, in the 1680s), Robert Derigneé and René Cousin. Samuel Marc the locksmith supplied 'a button to the lock at the Pew in the French Church' in 1697, providing evidence that Montagu and members of his household attended services in the local Huguenot church, known as L'Eglise des Grecs, from its former Greek congregation.[33] This was an annexe of the Savoy Chapel used by the London Huguenot community from 1661 for services which conformed to the Anglican liturgy, although translated into French. Such attendance provided educational opportunities for improving knowledge of the French language.

Montagu's accounts also record the specialists employed in the education of his eldest surviving son Monthermer, who travelled to Aix-La-Chapelle in the company of a Huguenot tutor, Germaine Colladon, in 1699, and again with Pierre Silvestre from 1700. A portrait of Monthermer, attributed to the French artist François de Troy (possibly painted while visiting the continent with his tutor), was reframed in a white and gilt neo-Palladian Vitruvian scroll border, probably for the new house at Whitehall to which the sitter moved as second duke in 1733. In February 1703 Dr. Silvestre paid ten guineas to Mr. Haylst for another portrait of Monthermer. By 1703 Monthermer was sufficiently mature to receive a sword with gilded hilt provided by Mr. Coliveaux, and a silver watch by Henry Massy, both Huguenot craftsmen.[34]

Elias de Rit's accounts for Ralph Montagu record payments for Monthermer's education. The latter benefited from drawing lessons given by François Gasselin in 1700 and René Pelletier in 1706, and prints supplied by Thomas Pelletier. He had singing lessons from Margaret Rambour, presumably with music provided by Mr. Dupré, a London bookseller; music lessons from Mr. Nicolas Colin (between 1708 and 1713) and dancing by Mr. Isaac Thorpe; and geometry lessons from the famous French mathematician Abraham de Moivre.[35] A book for instruction in architecture was purchased through Mr. William Portal; a case of instruments and two books of geometry were purchased in 1704; and in October 1705 John Rowley was paid for a large surveying instrument with a level case and chain for Lord Monthermer's use. Monthermer had handwriting lessons from Mr. Camberupon. For fencing and riding lessons, he attended Major Foubert's

---

[33] Boughton house, executors' accounts, 1712.

[34] Boughton House, Mr. de Rit's accounts, 1698–1705.

[35] See previous chapter, under 'London's Huguenots and the spread of international knowledge', for more on De Moivre in London.

academy, which has given its name to Foubert's Place, Soho.[36] Solomon Foubert, a military émigré, recreated his Parisian military academy from the Faubourg St. Germain in Sherwood Street, off London's Piccadilly, in 1679 and was succeeded by his son Henry in 1700. 'This academy, as it is called, had become very fashionable, and was frequented by the sons of many of the leading men of the day. The curricula consisted chiefly of what we should call accomplishments, such as riding, fencing, dancing, the handling of arms, and finally mathematics.'[37]

Henry Foubert was paid on several occasions for horses for his use. As second duke, Montagu became celebrated for his horsemanship; the dedication copy of *Twenty-Five Actions of the Manage Horse* (1729), engraved by Joseph Sympson from original drawings by John Vanderbank, remains in the library at Boughton. The second duke's horsemanship is celebrated at the house in the painting by John Wootton, 'Breaking cover', which shows the duke shedding his coat. It has been suggested that the figures were painted by William Hogarth.

Ralph Montagu depended on French expertise for his medical needs. His physician was Dr. Pierre Silvestre, who lived at Montagu House and travelled to Boughton when required. He was paid an annual salary of £50. Silvestre supplied catarrh pills, purging syrups and powders, and arranged for Mr. Gerrard, the French oculist, to come to London from Holland to treat Ralph Montagu's eyes. Silvestre also advised other members of the household: Mr. Verdier was paid for 'bathing and cupping some of His Grace's servants'; Mr. Bussière performed several unspecified surgical procedures.[38]

The day-to-day running of the household is recorded in the household accounts books, compiled in various elegant hands on crisp, thick paper which bears a fleur de lis watermark. These provide details of the artists, craftsmen, employees and suppliers, English and French, who played an essential role in the maintenance of Montagu House. Many French names were anglicized; the Montagu archives preserved at Boughton and Beaulieu demonstrate that other French suppliers continued to submit their bills in French as late as the 1750s. A bill from Jeanne Lavorne adressed to Lady Mary Cardigan, Ralph Montagu's granddaughter, records 'Item: for Lady Cardigan: pair of satin slippers embroidered in silver'.[39] Lady Cardigan ordered large numbers of French books from the London booksellers

---

[36] W. H. Manchée, 'The Fouberts and their Royal Academy', *HSP*, xvi (1937–41), 77–97.
[37] *Manuscripts of His Grace the Duke of Portland, K.G., preserved at Welbeck Abbey* (10 vols., 1901), iii (see also previous chapter, for more on Foubert's academy).
[38] Boughton House, executors' accounts, 1712.
[39] 'Mémoire pour Miledy Cartaiguene – paire de souliers satin brodé en argant'.

François Changuin, Paul Vaillant and P. Fouvencel, including Gabriel Daniel's *Voyage du monde de Descartes*, *Dictionnaire de Bayle*, *Lettres de Ciceron*, *Nouveaux contes de fée*, Ovid's *Imitation de l'art d'aimer*, and Jean Galli De Bibiena's *Le Petit Touton: mémoire d'une fille de France* and *Lettres de Mazarin*. She was also supplied with a diamond necklace and rows of pearls by Charles Gouyn, an Indian cabinet by Daniel Barbier, wigs and powder by L. Chamfort, china and porcelain by Paul Chenevix and haberdashery by David Régnier.[40]

The household accounts recorded under the beady eye of Mark Antonie provide a glimpse of the daily running of the kitchens at Montagu House in the first decade of the eighteenth century. Montagu had developed sophisticated tastes in food and wine during his stay in France, and much French wine was consumed, supplied by a long list of French wine merchants. The inventory of the contents of his wine cellar in 1709 includes 'Bordeaux, Burgundy, Hermitage, White wine, Sack, Frontinmark, ordinary claret and Rhenish'. Mr. Hattanville was the most regular supplier; in 1708 he provided 'one bottle of French white wine and one flask of florance red wine for a taste'. Other suppliers included Anthony Reilhan, Mr. de Grave 'for Burgundy', Mr. John Gachon 'for Bordeaux', Mr. Godin, Charles and Elias Dupuy, Mr. Maudet, Daniel Minet, Mr. Sabatier 'for wine and anchovies' and Joseph Soulard. These names recur in the registers of the conformist London Huguenot churches of the Savoy, Spring Gardens and Les Grecs.

Judging by the amounts of sugar consumed, there was a predilection for confectionery and desserts. Mr. Biron, a member of the household, took responsibility for ordering hams and other general groceries. Peter Lavigne supplied salt, sugar, 'moist sugar for coffee', cinnamon, nutmeg, cloves, almonds, vinegar, rose water, 'flanders candy' and sweet wafers, as well as writing paper, candles and 'yellow wax flamboys'. Anthony Reilhan supplied sugar, various teas and coffee; Mrs. Ivinée le Bonot, fresh herbs; and Anthony Gayon, anchovies and olives. Chocolate was an expensive and highly taxed luxury but that did not discourage regular repeat orders with Mr. Baptiste, the chocolate-maker, the most spectacular being a bumper order for 290 pounds of chocolate recorded just before Christmas 1698.[41]

Montagu enjoyed French society and surrounded himself with French friends – they included, until her death, Hortense Mancini, duchesse de Mazarin, the niece of Cardinal Mazarin and erstwhile mistress of Charles II. Montagu had himself introduced her to the king in 1675. After Charles

[40] Hampshire, Beaulieu, Montagu Archives, M/M 33, book of vouchers, Mary, countess of Cardigan, later duchess of Montagu, 1740s–*c*.1750.
[41] Boughton House, Montagu House kitchen accounts.

Ortance Manchini Duchesse of Mazarin &c.

Figure 2.7. Hortense Mancini, duchesse de Mazarin, line engraving by Gerard Valck, after Sir Peter Lely, 1678. Boughton House/National Portrait Gallery.

II's death she stayed in England, living in St. James's and then in Paradise Row, Chelsea, where she died in 1699. She remained the charming and witty heart of the exiled French society that often gathered at Montagu House on Sundays and Wednesdays (Figure 2.7). Her close friendship with Montagu is evident from the fact that her portrait hung in his bedroom at Montagu House. This survives today at Boughton in its original Pelletier frame. Hortense Mancini benefited from Ralph Montagu's generosity in many ways and he even paid for her body to be transported back to France for burial after her death. Other regular visitors at Montagu House were the military Huguenot Henri de Massue, marquis de Ruvigny, later first earl of Galway and lord justice of Ireland, a protector of the Huguenot refugee communities in England and Ireland; Michael Le Vassor (1648–1718), a Protestant convert, theologian and historian; and the great intellectual and savant Henri Justel (1620–93), a Huguenot who had been at the heart of the French establishment. He had been driven from office in France, but once settled in Piccadilly he was unanimously elected a member of the Royal Society and became royal librarian at St. James's Palace, where, according to John Evelyn, he 'put those MSS (which were great in number) into excellent order, they having lain neglected for many years'.[42] Finally, there was Charles de St.-Evremond, the exiled Catholic essayist and letter writer. St.-Evremond, who received an annuity of £100 from Ralph Montagu until his death aged ninety in 1703, has left the most eloquent account of Montagu's patronage in a letter to Pierre Silvestre, evoking the duke's taste and company: 'I never desired anything so earnestly as to go to Boughton to see my Lord, the good Company and Learning in its full lustre'.[43] He went on to remind Silvestre:

> Let but a thing please my Lord Montagu, and don't trouble your head any further: whatever expense is to be made: whatever care, whatever industry is to be employed to have it, you will be sure not to go without it. These are the very words of the late Duchesse Mazarin, which are as good as Oracles, and which were never more just than on this occasion.

St.-Evremond regretted that:

> if my new infirmities, or rather my old ones which are very much grown upon me, had not hindered me from going to Boughton, I should have been happy as a man almost a hundred years of age can be. I lose a thousand pleasures which are all to my taste. That of seeing the fine House, the fine WaterWorks, the fine Ducks, would have pleased me extreamly, altho' I be but an indifferent Inspector. But you will easily guess the greatest of all, and that is being with my Lord Montagu, to enjoy his conversation twice a day, before and after the best cheer in the world. No person ever merited to be more magnificently receiv'd and more handsomely entertain'd, than my Lady Sandwich:[44] no man was ever more proper to receive and entertain her will than my Lord Montagu. I hope that the Cascade, the Octagon, the Water-Sheafs, and the Water-Spouts, shall have made my Lady Sandwich forget France. And as my Lord is very happy in inspiring his taste and his designs as to Buildings and Gardens, I don't question but she will soon undertake some new Work at Hinchinbrooke, which will not be behind those of Boughton. I must make up the loss of so many advantages by the Sundays and Wednesdays of Montagu House.

[42] *Diary of John Evelyn*, v. 44.

[43] C. de St.-Evremond, *Works*, trans. P. des Maizeux (2 vols., 1728), ii. 259.

[44] Lady Sandwich was the daughter of Wilmot, earl of Rochester. She abandoned her husband the earl of Sandwich at Hinchinbrooke, and established a salon in Paris; she was a frequent visitor to Boughton.

In England, although consoled by his friendship with the duchesse de Mazarin – 'That miracle of beauty which I formerly saw at Bourbon is the same miracle of Beauty which I daily see at London' – St.-Evremond sorely missed hearing the music of his favourite composer Jean-Baptiste Lully, whom he admired 'as well for the diversion of Dances, as for what concerns the voices and instruments'. To indulge this passion he and Hortense de Mazarin organized private concerts at Paradise Row, Chelsea, with the help of the emigré composer and recorder player Jacques Paisible (James Peasable), a member of the Drury Lane Theatre band, who arranged Lully's music for whatever musical instruments were available and helped to create intimate musical scenes for Hortense's drawing room, such as 'Idylle,' 'Les opéras,' 'Les noces d'Isabelle' and 'Concert de Chelsey'.[45]

While ambassador, Ralph Montagu must also have witnessed the sumptuous entertainments enjoyed by Louis XIV, who, as a keen dancer himself, had founded the Académie Royale de Danse in 1661. The operas, or 'tragédies en musique', by Lully and the 'comédie-ballet' plays of Molière have come down to us with their choreographies intact, meticulously notated in the system devised by Pierre Beauchamp and published by Raoul-Auger Feuillet. Beauchamp was court dancer to Louis XIV, director of the Académie Royale de Danse, principal choreographer to Molière's Troupe du Roy, ballet-master at the Académie Royale de Musique and compositeur des ballets du roi. He taught Louis XIV for over twenty-two years and was highly influential in the development of French dance. His system of codifying and notating the steps, arm and hand movements of classical ballet allowed the spread of court dance and manners far beyond the borders of France. Feuillet published a description of Beauchamp's dance notation system in Paris in 1700 as *Chorégraphie, ou l'art de décrire la dance* [sic] *par caractères*. This system was used in Europe throughout the eighteenth century.

On the restoration of the monarchy in England in 1660, the numbers of French dancers increased to meet the growing requirements of the royal court. Many French dancers settled permanently in London and became an established part of the cultural life of the capital. Probably the most important 'London French' dancer was Anthony L'Abbé (1666–1753) who became a friend and dancing-master to the family of the second duke of Montagu and, despite his Catholic faith, to successive members of the royal family. He arrived in London straight from the Paris Opéra in 1698 and became the foremost choreographer of his day, creating some of the

---

[45] D. Lasocki, *A Biographical Dictionary of Court Musicians, 1485–1714* (Farnham, 1998).

Figure 2.8. François le Rousseau, *A New Collection of Ball and Stage Dances*
(1720). Northamptonshire, Boughton House, Montagu music collection, 448.

most beautiful (and still extant) dances for the London stage.[46] To English
audiences his elegant, almost Watteau-like, conversational style of dance
was the epitome of 'French' *galant* taste. He successfully passed on the
tradition of dance from Louis XIV's France to the England of King William
III, Queen Anne and the Hanoverian Georges, not just by performing and
teaching, but also by his meticulous dance notations, which allowed French
dance to put down roots and eventually take on its own English character.

[46] J. Thorp, 'Monsieur L'Abbé and Le Palais des Plaisirs: a new source for a London
spectacle' (paper given at the Society of Dance History Scholars, Guildford, 2010).

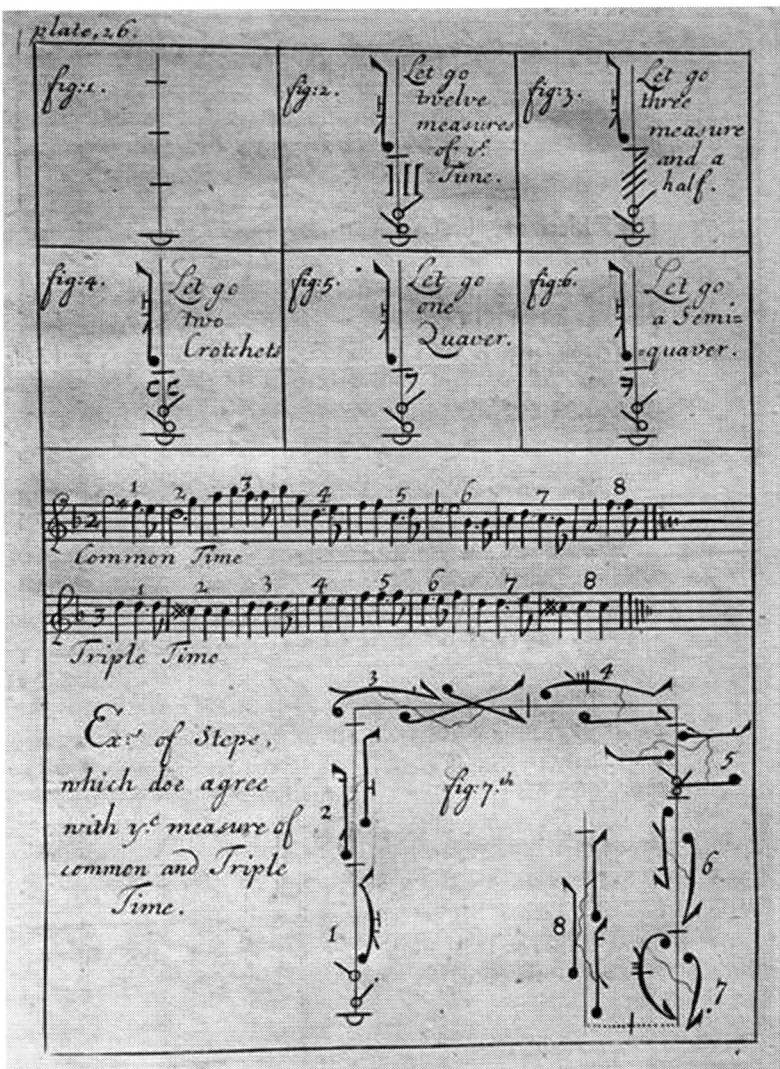

Figure 2.9. R.-A. Feuillet, *The Art of Dancing Demonstrated by Character and Figure*, trans. P. Siris (1706). Northamptonshire, Boughton House, Montagu music collection, 461.

An original book of dances by L'Abbé, using the Beauchamp Feuillet system, survives today in the Montagu music collection,[47] along with the English translation of Feuillet's *Chorégraphie* which was published by the French emigré dancing-master P. Siris in London in 1706, and which allows reconstruction of all the intricacies of the original dances.[48]

Another dancing-master keen perhaps to gain Montagu's patronage in London was François le Rousseau, a noted harlequin dancer, who choreographed an entire dance, a duet for a man and a woman, using the letters of the name MONTAIGU to trace out the complex steps. The dance survives thanks again to the Beauchamp Feuillet system but one wonders whether the sense of the steps could possibly have been understood visually by the audience, or whether its impact was simply the pun on the printed page to impress the duke.[49]

For a visual impression of French dance of the period we can turn to the Huguenot artist Marcellus Laroon (Lauron), whose small painting 'Dancers and musicians' depicts a tiny stage, with simple, almost improvised scenery and a couple performing perhaps a gigue, flanked by Watteau-like musicians. The presence of Harlequin could be a reference to the Little Theatre in the Haymarket, described in the *Weekly Journal and British Gazetteer* of 3 December 1720 as 'the new French theatre in the Hay-Market'. The theatre had a very small stage where Francisque Moylin's French *commedia* pantomime troupe, under the patronage of the second duke of Montagu (who inherited his father's love of French culture), gave regular performances. Referred to by resentful contemporaries as the 'Duke of Montagu's French vermin', it is most likely that they also joined with other dancers brought in from the Paris Opéra by Anthony L'Abbé for Handel's 1720 opera season in the King's Theatre,[50] which was supported by Montagu in his role as member of the board of directors.

For a lady, dancing was an indispensable social skill, as was music, and the second duke encouraged his daughters, Mary and Isabella, to play the harpsichord. The instrument with barley-twist legs which figures in some

[47] Boughton House, Montagu music collection, 448, F. le Rousseau, 'A new collection of dances'.

[48] Montagu music collection, 461, R.-A. Feuillet, *The Art of Dancing, Demonstrated by Characters and Figures*, trans. P. Siris (1706).

[49] See also J. Thorp, 'Harlequin dancing-master, the career of F. Le Rousseau', in *Annales de l'Association pour un Centre de Recherche sur les Arts du Spectacle aux XVIIe et XVIIIe siècles: Arlequin danseur au tournant du XVIIIe siècle (atelier-rencontre et recherche, Nantes, 14 et 15 mai 2004)*, ed. J.-N. Laurenti (2005), p. 77.

[50] J. Thorp, '"To come to a resolution about the dancers": Anthony L'Abbé and the staging of opera at the King's Theatre, London, 1719–21' (paper given at the Royal Musical Association Conference, Oxford, 2009).

of Marcellus Laroon's retrospective depictions of music parties held at Montagu House[51] is typically French, and it is likely to have been made by the Huguenot emigré Joseph Tisseran, who arrived in London around 1700, one of the very few French keyboard instrument-makers working in the capital at the time. If so, he may have provided only plain wooden casework, for an entry in the first duke's executors' accounts lists a payment due to Jean Pelletier 'for varnishing a Harpsichal and the frame belonging to it and for painting the inside thereof'.

This instrument is probably the one passed down in 1733 from the second duke to his daughter Mary, countess of Cardigan, who had harpsichord lessons with Johann Ernst Galliard, son of a Huguenot wig-maker and one of Handel's key theatre musicians. Her flute teacher was Raphael Courtiville (Ralph Cortiville), originally a psalmodist, who had become another useful musician in London's burgeoning music theatre culture. Memories of these musical passions have been preserved in the exceptional Montagu music collection at Boughton House, where many rare volumes of music are housed along with accounts and receipts for music lessons and the purchase and maintenance of keyboard instruments spanning the entire century. French musicians had been respected in England since the arrival of Nicolas Lanier in 1561 during earlier Protestant persecutions. Three generations of this remarkable family subsequently served British royalty as court musicians, with Nicholas the younger becoming the first to hold the title 'Master of the King's Musick', a position he retained from the Restoration until his death in 1666.

The return of the Stuart monarchy opened the doors for fresh continental ideas, which London certainly welcomed after the years under Cromwell. Huguenot exiles and economic migrants alike were streaming out of France, and Ralph Montagu was ready with deep pockets and unrestrained flair to receive and provide employment for these talented and displaced workers and artists. As we have seen, his own taste for French luxury was firmly set by the time of his arrival in Paris for his 1669 embassy, which he achieved in a style not seen since the duke of Buckingham went to France to claim the hand of Henrietta Maria for Charles I.[52] An upholsterer was paid the staggering sum of £326 'for an Estate of crimson damask richly embroidered with our Armes and Supporters and trimd with gold and silver ffringe with a Chair of Estate and two stooles and a footstoole and two

---

[51] J. Miller and P. Boucher, 'The Music Party': Paintings Drawings and Prints by Marcellus Laroon (a catalogue of the exhibition at Boughton House and Handel House Museum, 2011).

[52] Anon., The Court in Mourning. Being the Life and Worthy Actions of Ralph, Duke of Mountague (1709).

cushions all suitable', along with a 'rich altar cloth and a foot carpet'.[53] For his second embassy in 1676 he rented one of the best houses in Paris, here he maintained fifty-two servants. Back in London he continued in the same vein, living literally a gilded life in his reincarnation of a Paris *hôtel*, complete with gardens reminiscent of Versailles and its fountains, and employing a largely French household staff along with artists, some of whom had worked for Louis XIV himself.

The influence of the French dance style and aesthetic, known as 'la danse noble', also held sway through the eighteenth century. In the ballroom a knowledge of the etiquette and form of French-inspired dances like the formal minuet was considered essential to the education of a gentleman and his family, taught by a French or at least a French-trained dancing-master. London theatres had seen a particular influx of the best dancers from the Paris Opéra, who could earn phenomenal sums of money during their brief visits and did much to influence the way that English dancers trained and performed. Indeed, the duke of Montagu's own dancing-master and friend Mr. L'Abbé adapted many of his choreographic ideas specifically for English dancers and audiences.

These French dancers remained a significant presence in London theatres through most of the century, and by the 1780s were again making an enormous impact, partly through the virtuosic skills of the celebrated dancer Auguste Vestris. The King's Theatre in the Haymarket, patronized by successive members of the Montagu family, was remodelled to cater for the demand for full-length ballets danced between the acts of Italian operas. The carefully constructed narrative ballets of Jean Dauberval and his former pupil from Paris, Charles-Louis Didelot, keenly observed and noted down by the second duke of Montagu's granddaughter Elizabeth from the family box, led the way towards the later era of romantic ballet.[54]

Ralph Montagu's second marriage, in 1692, to the hugely wealthy widow of the duke of Albemarle, had enabled him further to indulge his lavish patronage of the decorative arts, which helped to change the look of London. It did not stop with him, but echoed down the next century, with second- and third-generation migrants continuing to be employed by the family both in London and at Boughton, where many elements of this early imported French taste – *parquet de Versailles*, wall and ceiling *trompe-l'œil* painting, gilded furniture and frames, woodwork, tapestries and flower paintings from Montagu House – survive untouched by time.

[53] TNA, LC 5/41 fo. 84v.
[54] J. Thorp, 'The French in London with particular reference to dance 1660–1800' (unpublished paper).

The French had given a spectacular boost to fashions in domestic design and decoration, setting new standards which home-grown English artists eventually surpassed.

3. The novelty of the French émigrés in London in the 1790s

Kirsty Carpenter

They are clever beings those French, they are, always playing fools' tricks, like so many monkeys, yet always lighting right upon their feet, like so many cats!
Fanny Burney, *The Wanderer*[1]

From the outset emigration during the French Revolution had an aspect of novelty in Britain. It brought a cross-section of now famous French men and women from Parisian society – writers Madame de Staël, Madame de Flahaut (Souza), Antoine, comte de Rivarol, François-René de Chateaubriand, poets Abbé Jacques Delille and Louis-Marcelin the marquis de Fontanes, painter Pierre Henri Danloux, and musicians vicomte de Marin and Sébastien Erard (harp- and piano-maker). Even if only for a short time, as the émigrés in general did not stay in Britain, these people both enriched London society and added their Frenchness to the capital's streets.

From the first priests who arrived on the south coast saying Mass in the local pubs, to the eccentric old men who stayed on to teach in schools, the British were given a sense of the difference of cultures in their midst; and, one could strongly argue, a heightened appreciation of their own by comparison. Who better placed than Frances Burney,[2] married to French émigré General Alexandre d'Arblay, to put this reflection in the mouth of a British sea captain? 'For my part, Madam, I hope the compliment you make our country in coming to it, is that of preferring good people to bad;

---

[1] F. Burney, *The Wanderer* (Oxford 1991), p. 17.

[2] Fanny Burney was already a published author when she met her husband, who had come to live at Juniper Hall in Mickleham with a group of émigrés that included Madame de Staël and the comte de Narbonne. Her diary from these years recounts stories of the French émigrés whom she met in England, and her life in Paris when she returned to France with d'Arblay in 1802. She assumed a truly Franco-British culture that is perhaps best expressed in her novel *The Wanderer* (see J. Farrar Thaddeus, *Frances Burney: a Literary Life* (Basingstoke, 2000), chs. 6–8).

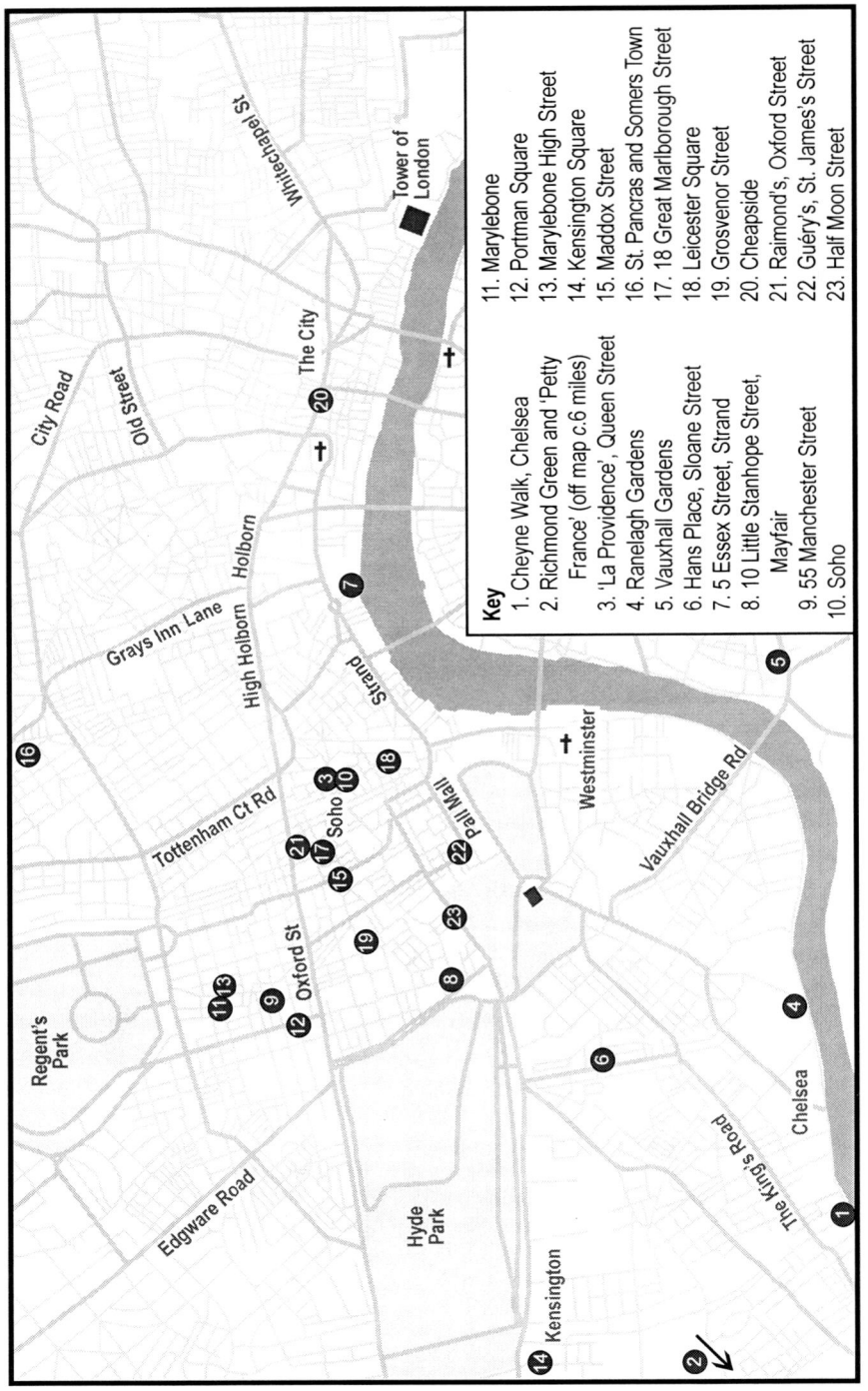

Key

1. Cheyne Walk, Chelsea
2. Richmond Green and 'Petty France' (off map c.6 miles)
3. 'La Providence', Queen Street
4. Ranelagh Gardens
5. Vauxhall Gardens
6. Hans Place, Sloane Street
7. 5 Essex Street, Strand
8. 10 Little Stanhope Street, Mayfair
9. 55 Manchester Street
10. Soho
11. Marylebone
12. Portman Square
13. Marylebone High Street
14. Kensington Square
15. Maddox Street
16. St. Pancras and Somers Town
17. 18 Great Marlborough Street
18. Leicester Square
19. Grosvenor Street
20. Cheapside
21. Raimond's, Oxford Street
22. Guéry's, St. James's Street
23. Half Moon Street

Map 3.1. Places mentioned in the text (Base map: London c.1850)

in which case every Englishman should honour and welcome you'.[3] The comparing of cultures during the French Revolution was the culmination of the scrutiny that had gone on throughout the eighteenth century.

From the publication of Burke's *Reflections on the Revolution in France* in 1790, the British were quick to congratulate themselves on their superiority of political culture while vying to wear the latest French fashions and to read their latest novels.[4] What becomes increasingly apparent in Burney's writing is that what the French brought with them to Britain was perhaps the most valuable legacy of the Revolution. They provided the British with a living example of deep-rooted similarities between their two cultures that were in many ways more powerful and persuasive than the superficial differences suggested by dress and language. At the end of Burney's novel *The Wanderer*, we find 'an honest Englishman, sitting cheek by jowl, beside a Frenchman; as lovingly as if they were both a couple of Christians coming off the same shore'.[5] The incongruity of friendship between a French bishop and an English admiral was as ironic as the British Admiral Lord Keith's daughter Margaret Mercer marrying Napoleon's former aide-de-camp Charles de Flahaut in 1817 (Keith objected to his daughter's French marriage on the grounds that 'the General is a foreigner and of a different religion from that of this country and yourself, that of course all his natural feelings must be adverse to this country').[6] But these Franco-British marriages, exceptions though they were, worked remarkably well and produced some stunning commercial successes. Sir Marc Isambard Brunel had by the end of the French wars married a British woman and settled in Cheyne Walk, Chelsea, close to his Battersea mill and engineering plant. His son Isambard Kingdom Brunel was born a French Londoner, son of an émigré. Augustus Northmore Welby Pugin was similarly the son of a Franco-British marriage between his émigré father Augustus Pugin and a British woman of the Anglican faith, Catherine Welby; and he later became responsible for the refurbishment of the interior of the Palace of Westminster.[7]

The London to which the émigrés came was a thriving city of one million inhabitants, the largest in Europe. To the arriving stranger or foreigner it

---

[3] Burney, *Wanderer*, p. 17.

[4] This appetite for each other's literature was mutual. Gouverneur Morris wrote of being asked by Madame de Staël to bring back a novel from London 'if any good one comes out' (*The Diary and Letters of Gouverneur Morris*, ed. A. Cary Morris (2 vols., 1889), i. 295).

[5] Burney, *Wanderer*, p. 864. This expresses a wish as much as a reality on the part of the author.

[6] AN, 565 AP dos 20 pièce 4: 'That so far as I have been able to learn his habits of life have not been satisfactory nor such as to induce me to suppose he is calculated to make a good husband and render you happy according to the notions of this country which differ widely from those of others'.

[7] A. Pugin, *Recollections of A. N. Welby Pugin and his Father* (1861), p. 1.

was also the political and economic hub of Europe and the wider world.[8] The path the French took to get to London from the south coast brought them to Soho, Bloomsbury and Marylebone in the first instance, and then took them further out to the poorer suburbs of Highgate, St. Pancras and Somers Town north of the river, and St. George's Fields in Southwark south of the river. The main stopping-off point was Soho, and there many émigrés remained throughout their time in London. Travelling around London was easy from Soho, and guides like the Abbé Tardy's *Manuel d'un voyageur à Londres* were indispensible.[9] It listed the chapels, the French bookshops, the markets and theatres as well as other information about the gardens at Ranelagh and Vauxhall. The French travelled mainly on foot, and that decided their choice of residence. Other determining factors were what rent they could afford to pay, and, even more important, a landlord who was not hostile to French food habits. By April 1799, living in George Street off Portman Square, Thomas Moore wrote to his mother of his fondness for this French area of London: 'I dine at the traiteur's like a prince, for eightpence or ninepence. The other day I had soup, bouilli, rice pudding, and porter, for ninepence halfpenny; if that be not cheap, the deuce is in it'.[10]

The first wave of emigrants to arrive in London were among the most colourful. They stood out for reasons of their peculiarity (and ridiculousness) in British eyes. The men habitually wore hair-powder or wigs, and Paris fashions out of French society or court context provided amusement.[11] One of the first examples was a caricature dating from August 1789 entitled 'La France se purge petit à petit' (Figure 3.1). Walpole's correspondence with Mary Berry describes the swarms of émigrés to be found at the French ambassador's. George Selwyn, another informer of the fashionable world, had no idea who they all were but he was fully informed about one whom he called 'the queen of the aristocratic refugees in England', Madame de Boufflers. With her was her step-daughter the duchesse de Biron, her

[8] *London World City 1800–40*, ed. C. Fox (1992), esp. the introduction, 'A visitor's guide to the London world city', pp. 11–13.

[9] This guide, undoubtedly the most important of the emigration period, went through several editions and gave important addresses: the French chapels, the French markets, the theatres and the amusements (Abbé Tardy, *Manuel du voyageur à Londres, ou recueuil [sic] de toutes les instructions nécessaires aux étrangers qui arrivent dans cette capitale, précédé du grand plan de Londres, par l'Abbé Tardy, auteur du dictionnaire de prononciation française à l'usage des Anglois* (1800)).

[10] *Thomas Moore: Memoirs, Journal and Correspondence, 1793–1813*, ed. J. Russell (1853), p. 82.

[11] Vicomte de Broc, *Dix ans de la vie d'une femme pendant l'émigration, Adélaide de Kerjean, marquise de Falaiseau* (Paris, 1893), p. 138.

Figure 3.1. 'Salus in fugâ: la France se purge petit a petit'. Isaac Cruikshank, artist, 1764–1811; S. W. Fores, publisher, 1761–1838. © The Fitzwilliam Museum, Cambridge, P.4-2002.

daughter-in-law the comtesse Emilie de Boufflers, and Madame de Cambis. These were the most fashionable of Frenchwomen – Madame de Boufflers mixed with the most fashionable and wealthy in British society and was received by Mrs. Fitzherbert.[12] They settled in Richmond on the Green and the Hill behind the Green that was described as a Petty France.[13]

Until mid 1791, the French émigrés were not refugees or asylum seekers, but simply travellers. They came to London by their own means and were welcomed as friends, relatives and visitors. Most importantly, they were not at that point prevented from returning to France. They made no demands on the local population and for the most part settled their debts. While it is impossible to know in any exact detail how much wealth these émigrés brought with them to London, mentions of deliveries of money can be traced. The *Gentleman's Magazine* records a shipment of cash that was 'brought by Dover coach under strong guard, and deposited at the White Horse Cellar … for the use of some great personages of that Kingdom who have taken asylum in this country'.[14] There was certainly the impression given that these émigrés did not lack means and were relatively carefree – an impression that was hard to erase when later émigrés needed assistance. Not much time had elapsed until diamonds were sold at low prices because of the glut.[15] The *St James's Chronicle* reported on 'A magnificent pair of brilliant ear-rings, which once decorated the person of the unfortunate Marie Antoinette now in the possession of an eminent jeweller on Ludgate Hill'.[16]

However, before August 1792 there were the signs of an overflow of French in London that looked increasingly unlikely to subside. As early as July 1791 Lady Malmesbury wrote to Lady Elliott: 'you must take to studying French as the whole island will be full of them soon'.[17] That not only suggested the *chic* that the newcomers added to the season, but the fact that conversation took place in French more often than in English. This might also explain some negative reactions to the influx. Lord Sackville

---

[12] Gouverneur Morris tells of being introduced at dinner with his brother to 'the Ladies Hays, who are very handsome, Lady Tancred and her sister, and Miss Byron' as well as 'Mr and Mrs Montresor' (*Diary and Letters*, i. 318).

[13] Horace Walpole to Miss Berry, 3 Aug. 1791 (*Extracts from the Journal and Correspondence of Miss Berry*, ed. Lady T. Lewis (3 vols., 1865), i. 322). On the émigrés in Richmond, see T. H. R. Cashmore, *The Orleans Family in Twickenham 1800–32* (1982).

[14] *Gentleman's Magazine*, xvi (March 1791), 265.

[15] Vicomte de Walsh, *Souvenirs de cinquante ans* (Brussels, 1845), p. 139, mentions 'les plus brillantes parures' selling for a song.

[16] *St James's Chronicle*, 20 Oct. 1792.

[17] Lady Malmesbury to Lady Elliott, 19 July 1791 (Countess of Minto, *The Life and Letters of Sir Gilbert Elliott, 1st Earl of Minto, 1751–1806* (3 vols., 1874), i. 389).

declined an invitation to meet all the great foreigners, replying to Lady Sheffield that 'He hated France and the French and she might say he was sick; he did not like such people'.[18] The American Gouverneur Morris, a great admirer and supporter of the French, returned the compliment on his travels to London, finding the British (compared to the Parisians) vastly dull.[19] Antoine, comte de Rivarol, was even more unflattering, describing British women as having two left arms.[20] Madame de Boigne, in a rare moment of objectivity about the English, remarked: 'What society doesn't present striking anomalies for the observer who is not accustomed?'[21] For many French men and women it was difficult to understand the appeal of separate sexual spheres after dinner, when both men and women were often content with being silent.[22] A letter on England printed in *L'Ambigu* lamented that 'Conversation in England has not that grace, that finesse that the presence of women necessarily inspires'.[23] Abbé Delille, enamoured among others of the duchess of Devonshire, for whom he was regularly invited to read, disagreed, and was one Frenchman who wrote high praise of British women and their ways:

> Your laws are Reason, your customs Wisdom,
> Your women Beauty, their discourse Discretion,
> Their behaviour is Decency, and their complexion Modesty.[24]

---

[18] Lady Sheffield to M. J. Holroyd, 30 Apr. 1791 (*Girlhood of Maria Josepha Holroyd (Lady Stanley of Alderley) Recorded in Letters of a Hundred Years Ago*, ed. J. H. Adeane (1896), p. 29.

[19] Morris, *Diary and Letters*, p. 370, describing an evening at the duchess of Gordon's: 'Here in one room the young are dancing, and in another the old are gambling at a faro-table. I stay but a little while, for the party is to me vastly dull. The male dancers are very indifferent'.

[20] 'Rivarol ne se plut pas en Angleterre, dont les femmes, suivant lui, ont deux bras gauches, et ne fit que passer dans un pays où, en fait de fruits murs, on ne trouve que des pommes cuites' (Baron Roger Portalis, *Henri-Pierre Danloux et son journal durant l'émigration* (Paris, 1910), p. 160).

[21] 'Quelle société ne présente pas des anomalies choquantes pour l'observateur qui n'y est pas accoutumé?' (C.-L. de Boigne, *Mémoires de la comtesse de Boigne, née d'Osmond, du règne de Louis XVI à 1820* (4 vols., Paris, 1921), i. 389).

[22] 'Après le diner, on se réunissait dans une belle galérie, où les femmes sont à part, occupées de broder, à faire de la tapisserie, et sans dire un seul mot. De leur côté les hommes prennent des livres et gardent le même silence' (E. Vigée Le Brun, *Mémoires d'une portraitiste 1755–1842*, préface de Jean Chalon (Paris, 1989), p. 198).

[23] 'La conversation, en Angleterre, n'a donc jamais cette grâce, cette finesse que la présence des femmes excite nécessairement' (J. Fiévée, *Lettres sur l'Angleterre, et réflexions sur la philosophie du XVIIIe siècle* (Paris, 1802), p. 204).

[24] 'Tes lois sont la raison, tes mœurs sont la sagesse, / Tes femmes la beauté, leurs discours la candeur, / Leur maintien la décence, et leur teint la pudeur' (J. Delille, *Malheur et pitié* (1805), chant quatrième, ll. 414–16).

Even the way the day was divided up and visits made differed significantly between Europe's two largest capital cities. At least one émigré blamed British drunkenness on the withdrawal of a civilizing female influence in the evening hours:

> The thing that makes life so sad in London for a foreigner is that when he has no invitation, and he does not wish to go to the theatre there is nothing to fill the evening with. No walk in the town, no house open, there is absolutely no diversion. Women receive in the morning, never the evening, a habit caused by the state of drunkenness that British men normally find themselves in at this time of day.[25]

This very clearly reflects the degree of scrutiny being indulged in by both cultures.

In early 1792 the French Catholic clergy began to arrive in numbers that increased with every month (Figure 3.2). They were perhaps the most contentious and visible manifestation of the emigration in Britain, because of the status of Catholics in Britain:[26] 'It is impossible to walk a hundred yards in any public street here in the middle of the day without meeting two or three French priests'.[27] Even more than the lay French, the clergy were responsible for paving the way for the demystification of 'popery', and the eventual repeal of the laws preventing Catholic emancipation. They were model citizens in Britain, led by Jean-François de la Marche, the bishop of St. Pol de Léon. He and his landlady, Mrs. Dorothy Silburn, from her house in Queen Street, Soho – which the French clergy christened 'La Providence' – began the relief effort that lasted until the general return to France in 1814.[28] Mrs. Silburn, wrote the Abbé Barruel, was one Londoner who 'doesn't understand their language [French], everyone understands hers'.[29] 'Her house was filled from morn till night and ... was more like an hospital than a decent lodging'.[30] Perhaps the stories about Dorothy Silburn

---

[25] 'C'est ce qui rend la vie de Londres si triste pour un étranger: lorsqu'il n'a pas d'invitation, et qu'il ne veut pas aller au spectacle il ne sait comment passer la soirée. Pas de promenade dans la ville, nulle maison ouverte, absolument aucune dissipation. Les femmes reçoivent le matin, jamais le soir, usage qui doit son origine à l'état d'ivresse dans lequel sont ordinairement plongés les Anglais à cette partie de la journée' (Fiévée, *Lettres sur l'Angleterre*, p. 160).

[26] A. Bellenger, *The French Exiled Clergy in the British Isles after 1789* (Bath, 1986), remains the best work on the ecclesiastical emigration in Britain and contains a list of priests.

[27] Samuel Romilly to M. Dumont, 15 Sept. 1792 (S. Romilly, *Memoirs of the Life of Sir Samuel Romilly* (3 vols., 1840), ii. 11).

[28] A. C. Kerr, *What England Owed to France, 1791–1802* (1928), p. 6.

[29] 'Elle n'entend pas leur langage, tous entendent le sien' (A. Barruel, *Histoire du clergé pendant la Révolution Française* (1800), p. 572).

[30] 'Biographical memoirs of the late Bishop of Leon', *Gentleman's Magazine*, lxxvii (March 1807), 195–7, at p. 197.

Figure 3.2. 'Emigrant clergy reading the late Decree, that all who returns shall be put to Death'. Isaac Cruikshank. The private collection of the abbot of Downside. Reproduced with permission.

were exaggerated because of the intense gratitude of the French clergy who experienced her kindness. The account in the *Gentleman's Magazine* goes on to relate that she died in France in 1820, ruined as a result of her unstinting charity, but accorded a pension by Louis XVIII in recognition of her dedication and service to the French clergy.

The initial period of independence and self-sufficiency among the émigrés ended relatively quickly. The new arrivals were penalized by property confiscations in France cutting off their incomes, and these increased with the beginning of the war. After 10 August and the September Massacres, persecuted priests were commonplace in London, and there was an ever-increasing cross-section of the former second estate, and a growing complement of the third.[31]

---

[31] On 10 Aug. 1792 the French monarchy was overthrown and the king's powers suspended, ending any hopes of a re-establishment of the *ancien régime*, and thus of the financial pensions upon which many émigrés had depended. The September Massacres that took place 2–6 Sept. broke out when news of the siege and impending fall of Verdun reached Paris. Over 1,000 inmates of Paris prisons were murdered, with the connivance of the Commune's Comité de Surveillance. Many of the inmates were priests waiting for deportation and the lack of justice encouraged other refractory priests to emigrate without further ado. This

By 1792 the *Public Advertiser* was able to report that 'the lower class of people act with much barbarity to those poor Frenchmen who have taken refuge in this land of liberty'.[32] While this was not universally true, sporadic outbursts of very hostile behaviour were not uncommon. The émigrés presented a target for radical criticism, and, before the Seditious Meetings Act (1793), it was not a crime to admire the French government or to hold those who did not support it accountable for impeding the most modern of political systems. The very great popularity of the writings of Tom Paine meant that opinion about the French Revolution was divided.[33] And some émigrés found solace in the accusations that they felt were, at least to some extent, merited. Madame de la Ferronnays said: 'How much I prefer these English salons where people say much that is unflattering about us and where I feel so rightly humiliated by my own insufficiency'.[34]

Whether the novelty value of the French in the 1790s in London was about the émigrés themselves or Revolution politics more generally, there was no question that the French stood out as much for their oddness of dress as for their politics.[35] There was a high level of interest in French politics in the London papers, and continuity between the political challenges that the two countries faced. The émigrés represented a spectrum of right-wing politics from the moderate centre to the *purs* on the radical right. It was not quite accurate to write, as Jean-Gabriel Peltier did, of 'London enclosing in its bosom at the same time the victims and the executioners'[36] (he referred here to the disgruntled magistrates who found emigration preferable to presiding over the reformed national bodies of the judiciary after 1792), but it does give a sense of the wide political spectrum that existed in London.

The émigrés had their favourite places in their temporary home. The gardens at Ranelagh and Vauxhall provided them with pleasure and

---

resulted in their crossing the Channel in a variety of more or less unseaworthy vessels in the wintry conditions of Sept. and Oct. to arrive on the south coast of Britain (see W. Doyle, *The Oxford History of the French Revolution* (Oxford, 2002), pp. 189–92).

[32] *Public Advertiser*, 17 Sept. 1792.

[33] Part I of Paine's *The Rights of Man* appeared in Feb. 1791 and sold 50,000 copies at 3*s*, and Part II appeared a year later, when both sold for 6*d*. The criticism of corruption that Paine levelled at the monarchy could be construed as being given living example by the émigrés – because they were once the beneficiaries of court pensions and subsidies.

[34] 'Combien je préfère ces salons anglais où l'on dit tant de mal de nous, et où je me sens si utilement humilié de mon insuffisance' (Marquis de Costa de Beauregard, *Souvenirs tirés des papiers du Comte A. de la Ferronnays, 1777–1814* (Paris, 1900), p. 231).

[35] Vicomte de Broc, *Dix ans de la vie*, p. 138.

[36] 'Londres renfermant à la fois dans son sein les victimes et les bourreaux' (J.-G. Peltier, *Dernier tableau de Paris ou récit historique de la Révolution du 10 août* (2 vols., 1794), i. 240). See H. Maspero-Clerc, *Un Journaliste Contre-Révolutionnaire, J.-G. Peltier* (Paris, 1793), p. 65.

distraction.[37] What was interesting was the diversity of people who found themselves at Ranelagh. Gouverneur Morris visited on 24 May 1790 and commented: 'We do not arrive until after twelve. The room is filled, and it is an immense one. The amusement here is to walk around until one is tired, and then sit down to tea and rolls'.[38] The walk to and from the gardens was also often described in memoirs because it took time and created entertainment in itself. The abbé de Calonne, brother of the ex-finance minister and editor of the émigré newspaper the *Courrier de Londres* from 1792 to 1797, lived close by in leafy Sloane Street, Chelsea.[39] There were many streets that the French found pleasant. In January of 1794 Capitaine d'Auvergne, the prince de Bouillon, lived at 5 Essex Street, Strand, and then at 10 Little Stanhope Street, Mayfair, Piccadilly.[40] The Comte Auguste de la Ferronnays lived at 56 Manchester Street. His wife found the house charming; it had four windows on each floor and three bedrooms.[41] Modern-day Soho accounted for 32 per cent of the addresses of the émigrés receiving British aid in 1796, and Marylebone, further north-west, for 29 per cent.[42] The area of Portman Square and Marylebone High Street was a hive of French émigré activity.

Hyde Park represented all that was ecologically green and healthy about London. It was a favoured destination for walks close to Soho and Mayfair, the green of the park breaking the gloom of the narrow streets. Talleyrand lived at nearby Kensington Square when not enjoying the hospitality of the Landsdownes or life at Juniper Hall.[43] Madame de Gontaut lived near Golden Square and wrote: 'I understand so well what the French feel upon arriving on a Sunday in London – the silence, the lack of movement surprises, and one gets an attack of spleen that dissipates on Monday with a bright sunshine in Hyde Park'.[44] Sundays in London were noted particularly

---

[37] Tardy, *Manuel du voyageur à Londres*, pp. 248–50, was dedicated to a detailed description of Ranelagh, and pp. 250–1 to Vauxhall.

[38] Morris, *Diary and Letters*, p. 332.

[39] Hans Place, No. 4, Sloane Square (addresses mentioned in letters conserved in the papers of Christian de Parrel (see AN, ABXIX-3790 VI/3, letter from Charles Alexandre de Calonne to Pitt, June 1795); and see also Maspero-Clerc, *Un Journaliste*, p. 92; and Burrows, *French Exile Journalism*).

[40] His London address appears in the Bouillon papers conserved in the privy council archives series 115, containing letters to the prince from different émigrés (TNA, PC 1/115/402).

[41] Costa de Beauregard, *Souvenirs*, p. 208.

[42] K. Carpenter, *Refugees of the French Revolution: Emigrés in London, 1789–1802* (Basingstoke, 1999), p. 197.

[43] E. de Waresquiel, *Talleyrand, le prince immobile* (Paris, 2003), p. 170.

[44] M. J. Gontaut, *Mémoires de madame la duchesse de Gontaut, gouvernante des enfants de France pendant la restauration, 1773–1836* (Paris, 1897), p. 23.

by Frenchwomen. Elisabeth Vigée Le Brun, who lived in Maddox Street, wrote:

> Sundays in London are as sad as the climate. No shop is open, there are no theatres, balls or concerts. A general silence reigns everywhere and as on that day no one can work, nor even play music without risk of having their windows broken by the crowd, there is no other way to make the time pass than walks which are often taken.[45]

The painter Danloux was another frequent visitor who appreciated the changing light:

> After the departure of the Abbé de Saint-Far I went to take a turn about Hyde Park where I saw not without pleasure two horses running at a very great speed. I drew some of the pretty effects of the sun that seduced me in the gardens of Kensington, in particular on the little lake where the trees were reflected in the water.[46]

Many émigrés took pleasure in the openness of central London that almost represented political and economic freedom by comparison with their own capital city in the clutches of the Jacobins.[47] There was also great admiration for the countryside: 'One can see [other] streets that resemble those of London, but I do not think that there is another country that can give you an idea of the English countryside'.[48]

In the north-east, St. Pancras and Somers Town attracted émigrés mainly from 1796 onwards. Somers Town (to the north of present-day St. Pancras) was an area that opened up to the French after 1796 when the émigrés from Jersey were repatriated to the mainland. Very quickly this area of London developed and became very French, with schools and lending libraries opening to cater to their needs. The Abbé Carron, described as the St.

---

[45] 'Les dimanches à Londres sont aussi tristes que le climat. Aucune boutique n'est ouverte, il n'y a point de spectacles, de bals, de concerts. Un silence général règne partout; et comme ce jour-là nul peut travailler, pas même faire de la musique, sans courir le risque de voir ses vitres cassées par le peuple, on n'a d'autre ressource, pour passer le temps, que les promenades, qui sont très fréquentées' (Vigée Le Brun, *Mémoires d'une portraitiste*, p. 189).

[46] 'Après son départ [de l'abbé de Saint-Far] je vais faire un tour à Hyde Park où je vis non sans plaisir courir deux chevaux avec une vitesse très grande. Je dessinai dans les jardins de Kensington quelques jolis effets de soleil qui me séduisirent, l'un surtout sur le petit lac dans les eaux duquel les arbres se réfléchissaient' (Danloux, *Journal*, p. 109).

[47] D. George, *London Life in the 18th Century* (repr., 1992), p. 312. She underscores that 'this sense of personal liberty had a real importance in the social life of the time'.

[48] 'On a pu voir des rues que ressemblent à celles de Londres, mais je ne crois pas qu'aucun autre pays puisse donner l'idée de la campagne en Angleterre' (Boigne, *Mémoires*, i. 373). She described the city a few lines before as 'composée de petites maisons parailles et de larges rues tirées au cordeau, toutes semblables les unes aux autres … frappée de monotonie et d'ennui'.

Vincent de Paul of the Emigration, was a particular figure associated with this extension of émigré London.[49] He was endlessly energetic in finding funding from rich patrons to alleviate émigré problems, work that, after the intense supervision and scrutiny of the relief payments in 1797, was ever more necessary. It was the first time that this village really became part of London, so one could almost say it was French before it was truly urban British – Delille hailed it in his famous poem *Malheur et pitié*: 'Salutations O Somers Town, shelter dear to France'.[50] It was certainly one of the areas of London where the French were most visible, with schools, a hospice and a home for elderly priests who could no longer look after themselves. It was also, in 1799, the site of a French chapel dedicated to St. Aloysius. This provided one visible legacy of the French sojourn in London, but the chapel did not survive long into the nineteenth century. The district became:

> a living mosaic of old officers and magistrates, of wives of ex-representatives from the provincial parliaments and wives of chevaliers de St. Louis, young men and women, widows, and old priests, as well as domestic servants, some of whom had remained with their masters out of attachment and served them in their poverty.[51]

The commercial impact of the French in London was minimal by measurement against any economic innovation of the time, and there was little that could really be said to have been invented by the émigré French. This migration has historically been compared with that of the Huguenot refugees, who brought many artistic and artisanal skills with them, including silk-making and the latest gunpowder techniques. It must certainly be remembered that the French of this earlier emigration settled for the rest of their lives in London, whereas the vast majority of the émigrés after 1789 were concerned only with their financial survival until their return to France.[52]

Yet the emigration was significant because this influx of French men and women cultivated niche markets and provided services, as opposed to engaging in trade and manufacturing. They attempted to benefit financially from what they were familiar with, and this provided both entertainment for others at a profit, and solace for themselves – this in a century where psychological trauma and its effects went undiagnosed and untreated. They immersed themselves in the day-to-day tasks they most liked. It was no surprise that the clergy coped well, or at least better than some of the other

---

[49] For Abbé Guy Toussaint Julien Carron, see Bellenger, *The French Exiled Clergy*, pp. 104–8; and Carpenter, *Refugees*, pp. 98–9.

[50] 'Salut ô Sommerstown, abri cher à la France' (Delille, *Malheur et pitié*, chant deuxième).

[51] Walsh, *Souvenirs*, p. 66.

[52] This point is made clear in ch. 1 above.

émigrés. But the skills upon which the émigrés relied to get them through their time of emigration, whether clergy or laity, were teaching, publishing, small business, art and music. Madame de Boigne teasingly observed that 'The émigrés in Britain were accustomed to thinking of English money as their legitimate prey by any means'.[53] And there was fun, in return, poked by and at the British for being so gullible:

> However it hap't John surmounted his woes, …
> Now the French in confusion to England came over,
> Some landed at Brighton and others at Dover.
> Come open your purse, John, they cry, for d'ye see
> We can't live at home, so come over to Thee.[54]

The émigrés certainly brought to London a new awareness of French music forms as opposed to Italian – the nationality of most musicians in London. Musical talents were much sought after and Madame de Boigne describes how the difference of rank could be bridged by a recognized artist: 'At this time I played music often with Mme de Grassini. She was the first singer in London whose art elevated her to the position of a person of society'.[55] This was corroborated by Elisabeth Vigée Le Brun, who gave soirées at which Madame Grassini and Mrs. Billington (the first two cantatrices of the London Opera) sang duets for her guests accompanied by the violin of Giovanni Battista Viotti.[56]

The most successful commercial venture of the emigration period was the harp sales of Sébastien Erard, who lived in London from late 1792 and returned to Paris in 1811, having opened a business in London that survived into the last quarter of the nineteenth century.[57] One of his harps, dating from 1794 and made at 18 Great Marlborough Street, is permanently on display in the Musée de la Musique at La Villette. Erard sold £25,000-worth of harps in 1811 alone, having invented the double action harp before returning to France in 1815 (see Figures 3.3a and 3.3b).[58]

---

[53] 'Les émigrés, en Angleterre, s'étaient accoutumés à regarder l'argent anglais comme de légitime prise, par tous les moyens' (Boigne, *Mémoires*, i. 131).

[54] 'On the emigration of the French into England and John Bull's liberality', *Public Advertiser*, 15 Sept. 1792.

[55] 'J'ai fait dans ce même temps bien souvent de la musique avec madame Grassini. C'est la première chanteuse qui ait été reçue à Londres précisément comme une personne de la société' (Boigne, *Mémoires*, i. 134).

[56] 'Les deux premières cantatrices de l'opéra de Londres' (Vigée Le Brun, *Mémoires d'une portraitiste*, p. 191).

[57] It survived as the firm of Morley Brothers.

[58] A. Grangier, *A Genius of France: a Short Sketch of the Famous Inventor Sébastien Erard and the Firm he Founded in Paris 1780*, trans. J. Fouqueville (Paris, 1924), p. 3.

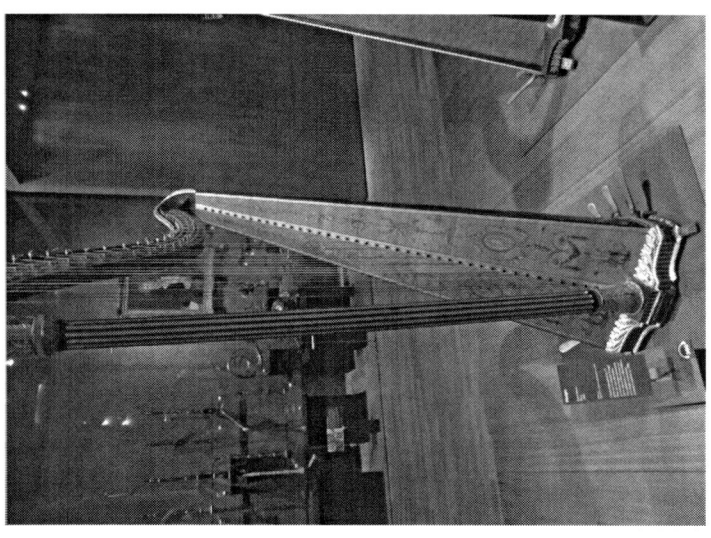

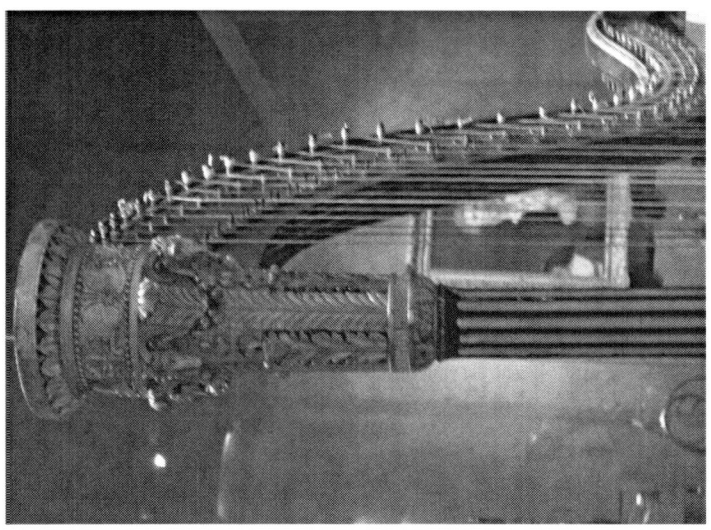

Figures 3.3a and 3.3b. Erard's double action harp. 'E981.6.1 Legs de Madame Marcotte de Quivières en 1981. L'instrument porte le No. 7 gravé sur la console. Il s'agit donc d'un des toutes premières harpes construites par la maison Érard pourvue d'un système dit 'à fourchettes' et à simple mouvement, breveté à Londres en 1794'. Collection Musée de la Musique, Paris. Author's photographs.

Erard, unlike his colleague, the painter Pierre Henri Danloux, was not in competition with British instrument-makers and had his own established name as a piano-maker before coming to Britain. Music moved easily around the European continent, and music masters were much sought after. The guitar (classical, but back then known as the Romantic guitar) was taught by émigrés, and not only to earn money.[59] Lessons were offered out of gratitude in an advertisement in the *Courrier de Londres* as a way that one émigré could return the favours rendered to him.[60] The appeal of this gesture of thanks from the French émigré master of the instrument also signals the popularity of the guitar among the French in London.[61] Music teaching was a staple of the émigré survival repertoire. While subscription concerts were attempted (usually singing, although occasionally violin and other single-instrument concerts), they were often not well enough subscribed to encourage repeat offerings, and venues were frequently poorly heated, creating problems for performers and audience alike. Many examples of subscription performances with singing and reading were tried with differing degrees of success. One of those that did succeed was the violin of the vicomte de Marin, who captivated London audiences. As a violin master he was so sought after that he returned to France with money to spare.[62] Other less able musicians found work copying scores. Michael Kelly, the manager of the Opera House and musical director of Drury Lane, left an account of giving work to the duc d'Aiguillon, who came to him reduced to his last shilling and begged him to be allowed to copy music for his theatres 'upon the same terms that you would give to any common copyist'. No one ever suspected this former aristocrat of copying music for a shilling a sheet.[63] Closely related to music teaching was the teaching of dance. Mary Russell Mitford remembered her lessons with 'a Marquis of

---

[59] Not only in London. Antoine de Lhoyer, a former member of the Armée de Condé, taught guitar in Hamburg, Vienna and St. Petersburg, where the Empress Elizabeth gave him a post for 10 years from 1804 (see A. de Lhoyer, *Douze romances avec accompagnement de guitare, Opus 24* (Paris, 2003)).

[60] Carpenter, *Refugees*, p. 72. 'Monsieur B. [Brillaud de Lonjac, 103 Marylebone High Street] has the honour to offer his humble talents to all the respectable French families exiled in this city. He proposes to offer, three days a week, to a limited number of people group lessons in singing, the English guitar and accompaniment' (*Courrier de Londres*, 17 May 1793).

[61] A. Miteran, *Histoire de la guitare* (Bourg-la-Reine, 1997), p.117. The emigration corresponds to the time when the six-string guitar became the norm, compared to the previous five-string standard of the 18th century. Emigrés who played and taught the guitar played a six-string instrument.

[62] *Le Chevalier de Pradel de Lamase, nouvelles notes intimes d'un émigré*, ed. P. and M. Pradel de Lamase (Paris, 1914–20), p. 70.

[63] M. Kelly, *Reminiscences of Michael Kelly of the King's Theatre* (2 vols., 1826), ii. 86–7.

the ancient regime ... slim and long, and pale ... who seemed so at home with his Terpsichorean vocation, that one could hardly fancy him fit for any other'.[64]

Artwork painted and created by the émigrés was sold in shops in Soho and was bought as gifts and keepsakes. Many émigrés turned to the hobbies of their youth to make a little money. The most famous artist of the emigration, Danloux, found that he was at a loss to compete with Reynolds despite living in the same part of London and offering cut-price rates.[65] The British preferred to have their family portraits painted by British artists. His diary is nevertheless an incomparable account of French life in London. His life was one of convivial company and encroaching poverty. He describes the amateurs and the out of work, as well as the rare serious clients who peopled his studio in Leicester Square, giving a list of elegant or formerly elegant members of French society and clergy, some 'much tempted to have their portrait painted', and the beauties who accompanied them, both English and French, and whom the artist used as his models.[66]

Business was hard to establish for the émigrés and in many cases embarrassing, as it required them to admit, even to parade, their impoverishment in front of the British. This feeling of acute embarrassment at having to ask for money for their goods is described again and again in the memoirs and novels of emigration.[67] It was a necessary evil if the goods were to be sold. However, with the generosity of British friends such as the duchess of Buccleuch, with the support of the marchioness of Buckingham and the duchess of York, premises were acquired in Grosvenor Street. Emigré ladies were invited to send to this depot all the work they wished to sell, marked with the price, and private customers and traders could buy from there.[68] This shop sold all manner of 'French rags' ('chiffonage à la française'): handbags made from scraps of silk and velvet, toys, beaded boxes and fancy boxes, pin cushions, painted note-books, as well as tatting and appliqué work.

---

[64] M. Russell Mitford, *Recollections of a Literary Life* (3 vols., 1852), ii. 89–90.

[65] See A. Goodden, 'Danloux in England (1792–1802)', in *The Emigrés in Europe and the Struggle against Revolution 1789–1815*, ed. K. Carpenter and P. Mansel (1999), p. 165.

[66] 'bien tenté de se faire peindre' (Danloux, *Journal*, p. 106). 'Et les amateurs, les désœuvrés, des clients sérieux parfois, de peupler l'atelier de Leicester Fields amenés, qui par les pensionnaires de Brice, qui par les Greenwood: ... L'abbé de Saint-Far et son frère l'abbé de Saint-Albin, hommes de plaisir, n'ayant d'ecclésiastique que l'étiquette, s'empressent escortés qu'ils sont des courtisanes à la mode. Séduisantes, encore qu'un peu trop respirées, ces filles-fleurs de l'exil, les Duthé, les Nauzières, les Roussée, les Mérelle, sans oublier de belles anglaises, vont devenir les modèles de l'artiste'.

[67] E.g., Madame de Souza's *Eugénie et Mathilde*, ch. lxii.

[68] *Courrier de Londres*, 22 Apr. 1794.

Straw hats and millinery made by the French émigrés were highly fashionable and sought after in the 1790s. Muslin dresses and straw hats of the sort described and worn in Jane Austen's novels were made by the émigré ladies in London and Richmond, because the embroidery could be done at home and in the company of other émigré women and men, and the products sold without fuss. The men made themselves useful sourcing the straw for the hats at the markets in Holborn. This gave both sexes gainful employment. An émigré woman ran a warehouse in Cheapside, and the comte de Guerchy, a former ambassador to the Court of St. James's, with his comtesse, ran a haberdashery business under an assumed name.[69] This was not an unusual choice of occupation, considering that sourcing material and accessories for clothing went on in private both before and after the emigration.[70]

As pastrycooks and confectioners too, émigrés made their mark in London. Raimond's in Oxford Street, famed for its ices, became one of the chosen resorts of fashionable society, and Guéry's in St. James's Street was patronized by the prince regent and his brothers.[71] Salad seasoning made its mark. The Abbé Baston, describing an English dish, wrote in horror: 'but a salad so seasoned, and chopped up as thinly as sorrel or spinach that was going to be cooked'.[72] No surprise, then, that an enterprising émigré turned an invitation to toss a salad for his British host into a job and went around doing it for a fee – making by one account 80,000 francs![73]

Teaching French and other subjects like Latin, history and geography was also a staple choice of occupation. French abbés became tutors in middle-class British homes and schools.[74] British schools, too, like Rugby, advertised in the French émigré newspapers for London émigré children to be sent boarding in Warwickshire.[75] Setting up a school was a popular choice for those qualified to relay their own education to English children. There were, however, not many émigrés who had the funds to finance a

---

[69] *Bon Ton Magazine*, ii (Dec. 1792), 394.

[70] Madame de Souza's correspondence with her daughter-in-law Margaret Mercer often mentioned sending or obtaining fashion accessories and clothes (see AN, 565 AP 25 dos 2 pièce 2, Madame de Souza to Margaret Mercer wife of Charles de Flahaut).

[71] M. Weiner, *The French Exiles, 1789–1815* (1960), p. 113.

[72] 'Mais une salade tout assaisonnée et hachée aussi menu que de l'oseille ou des épinards qu'on va faire cuire' (*Mémoires de L'Abbé Baston, chanoine de Rouen 1741–92* (2 vols., Paris, 1897), i. 102).

[73] Duc de Castries, *La Vie Quotidienne des émigrés* (Paris, 1966), p. 145.

[74] Boigne, *Mémoires*, i. 104.

[75] E.g., *Courrier de Londres*, 19 July 1793, carried an offering of board and instruction in the English language to émigré children for 100 guineas per year.

school. Schools were private affairs and patronage could be gained through contacts, but was equally easy to lose, so it was hard to remain in business. The *St James's Chronicle* predicted in September 1792 that 'we shall now have a swarm of seminaries in the neighbourhood of London cheaply and promptly supplied with teachers … where … the knack of chattering bad French shall be happily obtained'.[76]

To those hatching unsuccessful plots to overthrow the Revolution, writing books was perhaps even more important than publishing them. Writing provided solace, and editing required a degree of concentration that left no room for the contemplation of the sadder realities of life. It was an engrossing hobby, and many intellectual émigrés had need of that protection from the grim reality of daily life, as well as their fears for the future.[77]

Jane Austen in *Northanger Abbey* put these words in the mouth of Mr. Thorpe:

> 'I was thinking of that other stupid book, written by that woman they make such a fuss about; she who married the French emigrant.' 'I suppose you mean "Camilla"?' 'Yes; that's the book; such unnatural stuff! An old man playing at see-saw; I took up the first volume once, and looked it over, but I soon found it would not do; indeed, I guessed what sort of stuff it must be before I saw it, as soon as I heard she had married an emigrant, I was sure I should never be able to get through it.'[78]

But in fact Londoners and the British elite got through a varied diet of French and English reading material, ranging from the much celebrated *Adèle de Sénange* (published by Deboffe in 1794) by Madame de Flahaut, who lived in Half Moon Street, Soho, to the more serious works of political and religious commentary and criticism embarked upon by Lally Tolendal, François-René de Chateaubriand (the first edition of the *Génie du Christianisme* appeared in London) and others. Cox and Baylis specialized in printing French scripts, and Dulau and Deboffe, the French bookshops in Soho, operated as a central meeting-point where the French émigré community habitually gathered to read the newspaper reports of events in France.[79] Londoners cried over the accounts of Louis XVI in the Temple

---

[76] *St James's Chronicle*, 22 Sept. 1792.

[77] See S. Burrows, 'The émigrés and conspiracy in the French Revolution 1789–99', in *Conspiracy in the French Revolution*, ed. P. R. Campbell (Manchester, 2007).

[78] *Complete Novels of Jane Austen* (Collins Classics edn., Glasgow, 1993), p. 997.

[79] There were a number of newspapers in French: the *Courrier de Londres*, previously the *Courrier de l'Europe*; the *Mercure Britannique*; and the *Actes des Apôtres*; all edited by émigrés and printed in London (see Maspero-Clerc, *Un Journaliste*; and also Burrows, *French Exile Journalism*).

Prison written by his escaped servant Jean-Baptiste Cléry, and went into raptures over the Abbé Delille's poem *Malheur et pitié* (1803). On a more scurrilous note, the émigré newspapers, edited by former leading political figures like Calonne and Comte François Dominique de Reynaud de Montlosier, poked fun at the Republican French government from a safe distance. London throughout the period of the post-1789 emigration was a centre for counter-revolutionary plot-hatching, much of it time-consuming and entertaining rather than effective. These activities took up otherwise idle émigré time, and produced two newspapers that even the first consul could not prevail on his British connections to shut down.

There was division among the English about just how dangerous the French émigrés were. Burke believed that 'The last importation of Frenchmen are of that kind from whom little danger is to be expected. Distress and famine have worn them down so that they can be objects of envy only to a lecturer in anatomy'.[80] To Londoners, the French were simply eccentric. They regretted their country, their customs and their salons. They were in every way typical of *dépaysement*, another phenomenon that would not get psychological recognition until the twentieth century: 'London is above all an industrial and egoistical town and refined people and delicate hearts find it more bitter, sad and isolated there than anywhere else'.[81] Emigration was lonely and psychologically challenging. Those who survived and returned to France were strong characters. Balzac's hero of *Le Lys dans la vallée* was typical of the émigré who withdrew to his properties (those he managed to save) and lived apart from the world, rejecting its hypocrisy and political corruption.

The émigrés had made a stand against the Republic, sometimes very much at their own cost, and at the cost of their children's future prospects. Children who grew up in emigration in London faced uncertain and very different lives from those their parents had envisaged for them. The luckier ones, like Charles de Flahaut, continued their education in British and German schools, and some managed to be included on the roll of the émigré school at Penn in Buckinghamshire set up by Edmund Burke for the education of sons of those killed in the service of the French royalist cause. They were truly European citizens at the beginning of the nineteenth century, as we talk of children being global citizens in the twenty-first century.

---

[80] *Public Advertiser*, 9 Jan. 1793.

[81] 'London – la ville mercantile et égoiste par excellence et les esprits et les cœurs délicats … y trouvent plus amers que partout ailleurs la tristesse et l'isolement' (M. de Lescure, *Rivarol et la société française pendant la Révolution et l'émigration, 1753–1801* (Paris, 1883), p. 415).

Those children were the elite of the old regime, what was left of it, to whom, along with other surviving moderates of the revolutionary regimes, would fall the task of remaking France in the nineteenth century. Perhaps it is no surprise that diplomatic relations between Britain and France were generally good throughout the nineteenth century. The French and the British believed that they understood each other, or at least their mutual eccentricities. 'It does not necessarily follow that the total absence of conversation makes it impossible to communicate with amiability. I know many Englishmen and women who are refined. I would even add that I have not met one that is an idiot', wrote Madame Vigée Le Brun.[82]

Both nationalities provided verbal sport for each other, but William Windham wrote in 1796: 'We abuse the emigrants for their hospitality to one another. What sort of charity shall I feel for the Dukes of Bedford, the Plumbers or the Cokes and other large lists that I could name, when we meet in exile and beggary in some town on the Continent?'[83] This underscores the point made by David Bindman that 'To a large extent the story of the British response to the French Revolution was about British rather than French politics'.[84] And the British knew that they themselves faced many of the same issues that had led to revolution in France, so this was a reflection of their own concerns lived out in the experience of their neighbours – neighbours who were by the mid 1790s in their midst in central London.

The vast majority of émigrés represented no political threat, and their gratitude and endorsement of what they considered the essential goodness of the British character did much to bring the two nations closer together. While it is too much to claim that the London émigrés ensured peace in Europe in the nineteenth century, the diplomats who negotiated the peace settlements were well known in émigré circles, and they were, like William Windham, well aware of the threat of exile. Those accustomed to the creature comforts of London and Paris shared an urbanity, a cosmopolitanism and an artistic culture that both nations valued. The realization and acknowledgement of their common cultural values and the demystification of French (Catholic) novelty was without doubt the most lasting legacy of émigrés who arrived in

---

[82] 'Il est pourtant de fait que l'absence totale de conversation ne tient pas en Angleterre à l'impossibilité de causer avec agrément; je connais beaucoup d'Anglais qui sont fort spirituels; j'ajouterai même que je n'en ai pas rencontré un seul qui fût un sot' (Vigée Le Brun, *Mémoires d'une portraitiste*, p. 199).

[83] Quoted by Weiner, *The French Exiles*, p. 100. Windham goes on: 'When England becomes too vile or too dangerous to live in and we meet in Siberia we shall at least have the satisfaction of thinking that we are not the authors of our own calamities'.

[84] D. Bindman, *The Shadow of the Guillotine: Britain and the French Revolution* (1989), p. 27.

London in the early 1790s and remained until 1802 or, in smaller numbers, until the wars ended in 1815.

Note on French Catholics in London after 1789

The first chapter of this volume dealt with the French Protestants who took refuge in London. Having expelled the Huguenots, after the 1789 Revolution it was French Catholics' turn to be forced into exile, many of them also fleeing to London. The following account is adapted, by courtesy of the publishers Robert Hale Limited, from Douglas Newton's book *Catholic London* (1950), pp. 276–80, 286, 288, 295–7. It is included here specifically for its references to the Catholic religious exile and to numerous named London places in the period. Compiled by Helena Scott.

In the late eighteenth century Drury Lane ended at the point where Holborn touched Broad Street (now High Street), St. Giles-in-the-Fields, and was continued into the heart of Bloomsbury (there was then no New Oxford Street) by Bow Street, Peter Street and Queen Street (approximately Museum Street) to Great Russell Street. In Queen Street (often called Little Queen Street, no doubt to distinguish it from Great Queen Street, connecting Drury Lane with Lincoln's Inn Fields) was situated the bureau for assisting the refugee priests who crowded into England during the French Revolution.

This influx of French began in the spring of 1791, when Mgr. Jean-François de la Marche, bishop of Saint-Pol-de-Léon (d. 1806), and others who had early stood out against the French Republican government, made their escape to England in smugglers' vessels. By 1792 there were already 3,000 French priests in England, 1,500 of these being in London, many of the others being in Winchester, Jersey and other parts of the 'London district' – that is, under Bishop Douglass (1743–1812; Roman Catholic vicar apostolic of the London district from 1790 onwards). By 1801 the figures had risen to 5,600 clergy and 4,000 laymen in England, independent of the large numbers in Jersey. Among the clergy were thirty French bishops and fifty vicars-general.

Bishop Douglass himself reported that he had five French archbishops, twenty-seven bishops and thirteen vicars-general employed by him. The most notable of these was Mgr. de la Marche of Pol-de-Léon. He took up his residence at 10, Little Queen Street, and, assisted by Abbé Floch (the exiled curé of the church of Saint Louis, Brest) and other priests, provided assistance for his fellow countrymen with an extraordinary energy. He had the help of an English widow, Dorothy Silburn, who spent every day at the

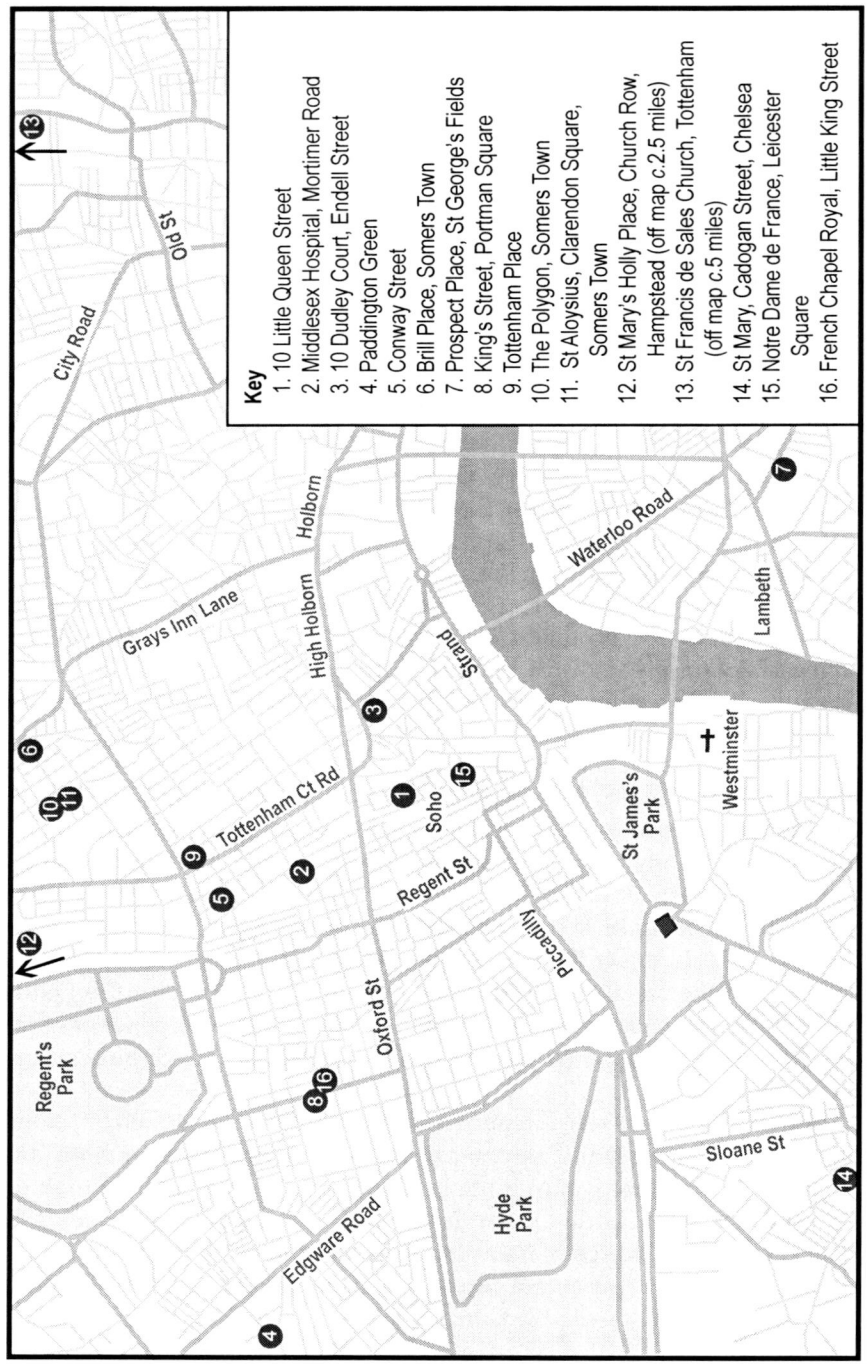

Key
1. 10 Little Queen Street
2. Middlesex Hospital, Mortimer Road
3. 10 Dudley Court, Endell Street
4. Paddington Green
5. Conway Street
6. Brill Place, Somers Town
7. Prospect Place, St George's Fields
8. King's Street, Portman Square
9. Tottenham Place
10. The Polygon, Somers Town
11. St Aloysius, Clarendon Square, Somers Town
12. St Mary's Holly Place, Church Row, Hampstead (off map c.2.5 miles)
13. St Francis de Sales Church, Tottenham (off map c.5 miles)
14. St Mary, Cadogan Street, Chelsea
15. Notre Dame de France, Leicester Square
16. French Chapel Royal, Little King Street

Map 3.2. Places mentioned in the text (Base map: London c.1850)

bureau, and with such tireless efforts and sympathy that she became known as 'La Mère des Prêtres exilés'. When, in 1815, she went to live in France, Louis XVIII gave her a pension out of the Civil List and, on her death five years later, aged sixty-seven, the French government put up a memorial to her honour in Roscoff (N.-E. Dionne, *Les Ecclésiastiques et les royalistes français réfugiés au Canada à l'époque de la revolution – 1791–1802* (Quebec, 1905), pp. 19–20).

The need of the exiles was indeed desperate. The priests in particular were often utterly destitute, and many of the laity were in little better case. According to Bishop Ward (Bernard Ward, 1857–1920, the first bishop of Brentwood, a president of St. Edmund's College, Ware, and a historian of pre-emancipation English Catholicism), the Protestant English received these émigrés not only with hospitality but with open-hearted generosity. The king himself exempted them from the operations of the Aliens Act, while all classes showed kindliness, subscribing large sums for their support, the Treasury alone making grants of over £450,000. Oxford University first printed a Latin version of the New Testament for the use of the priests, and later the four parts of the Roman Breviary, both being gifts.

With such co-operation Bishop Douglass, the bishop of Pol-de-Léon, Dorothy Silburn and others were able to provide clothes, means and living accommodation for the refugees, even fitting up large schoolrooms as dormitories when necessary. A wing of the Middlesex Hospital was given over to house the sick priests, and a chapel put into it for those well enough to say or hear Mass. Two English doctors, Vaughan and Oliphant, gave their services, and many Englishwomen, among them the duchess of Buckingham, visited and carried comforts to them (J. H. Harting, *Catholic London Missions from the Reformation to the Year 1850* (1903), p. 223).

The English on their part were impressed by the conduct of the French clergy, who showed themselves to be ready to do all they could, by teaching and other occupations, to provide for themselves; and the same could be said of the laity. As to the spiritual zeal of the priests, it was such that Pitt declared in the House of Commons that it had not been equalled since the earliest ages of Christianity. This behaviour of the clergy, together with the sight of so many of them about the London streets, did much at the critical time of the Relief Bills to break down prejudices as well as familiarize the public with Catholic services, chapels and ways of life.

One of the deepest needs of these exiles was the provision of places to say daily Mass. The bishop of Pol-de-Léon was perturbed at the fact that many celebrated Mass in improper places, such as their own bedrooms, which were sometimes small and dirty, or without lights or vestments; some even used paper vestments, which, says Ward, Bishop Douglass forbade in the London district. All this led to the opening up of many chapels, and permission to erect chapels in private houses.

St. Patrick's, Soho, was the first chapel to be used, Bishop Douglass paying the expense of the priests' wax and wine; but presently the bishop of Pol-de-Léon opened a church at 10, Dudley Court, Soho, close to St. Patrick's, dedicating it to La Sainte Croix, the Abbé Floch being the director. It carried on from 1793 to 1802. The French bishop also opened a little chapel in Paddington Green for the Abbé Romain of Rouen, who had come to London with about seventy priests, and around whom gathered many more Catholics (Harting, *Catholic London Missions*, pp. 222–3).

At the same time the Abbé Guy Carron, who had arrived in England quite penniless, took two large houses in Conway Street, Fitzroy Square, off Tottenham Court Road, and turned them into a chapel; then, starting without any resources at all, added successful free schools for boys and girls. By 1800 he and others such as he had founded eight French chapels in the London district, the three already named and others at Brill Place, Somers Town; Prospect Place, St. George's Fields; King's Street, Portman Square; Tottenham Place; and the Polygon, Somers Town, as recorded by Bishop Douglass in his diary.

Of these chapels the only survivors are the two Somers Town chapels which have merged into the church of St. Aloysius, Clarendon Square. This district, which occupies a brick-hemmed area behind Euston and St. Pancras stations, was in those days beginning to change hedges into terraces. Drawn perhaps by the semi-rural atmosphere, the Abbé Chantral had established a colony of French émigrés from Jersey, with workshops where French ladies found employment in making vestments and altar linen for their priests. About thirty of these priests were housed in what became No. 32, The Polygon. It was, of course, a Mass centre, but the chapel of the colony was at 6, Garden Gate, at the corner of Brill Place, Skinner Street, and had the charming dedication of 'Our Lady of the Garden Gate' (Harting, *Catholic London Missions*, p. 244).

The Abbé Carron (1760–1821) came from Fitzroy Square to take charge of the mission in 1799. He doubled the existing schools for boys and girls and built others; he supported two hospitals and an ecclesiastical seminary, an orphanage and a providence – which is a night shelter and hostel. He also built the present church in 1808. At the Restoration, when many French priests returned to their country, the Abbé Carron was among them. He left the Somers Town mission in charge of Abbé Jean Nérinckx, a Belgian Capuchin, who was actually ordained at Somers Town by the emigrant bishop of Avranches. During the ministry of this priest a convent school adjoining the church was established by Madame Bonnault d'Houet, the foundress of the Society of the Faithful Companions of Jesus (Harting, *Catholic London Missions*, p. 246).

The memory of the Abbé Carron is preserved by a memorial tablet and a bust, while some of the vestments used in this church at least until 1950 were his. There is also a memorial to Jean-François de la Marche, bishop and comte de Léon, who was buried in old St. Pancras churchyard.

A number of other chapels were built later by French priests, and some survive, like St. Mary's, Holly Place, Church Row, Hampstead, where a mission was established in 1796 by Abbé Morel (1766–1852) for French families in the neighbourhood. His first Mass was said over a stable in Rosslyn Park, but in 1816 the present little chapel was built and opened by Dr. Poynter, vicar-apostolic. Another of their churches is St. Francis of Sales, Tottenham, established in 1793 by Abbé Cheverus (Jean-Louis Lefebvre de Cheverus, 1768–1836, afterwards cardinal archbishop of Bordeaux; B. W. Kelly, *Historical Notes on English Catholic Missions* (1907), p. 396, where however the name is misspelt Cheireux). St. Mary, Cadogan Street, Chelsea, also seems to have arisen out of the work of several French abbés who cared for their countrymen in the 'village of Chelsea'. Their mission was continued by the remarkable Abbé Voyaux de Franous, who built a church in Cadogan Terrace in 1812; this remained in use until the present St. Mary's was opened in 1879.[1] Abbé Jean Nicolas Voyaux de Franous arrived in London in 1793. By 1832, he had been appointed honorary canon of the Chapter of St. Denis by Louis XVIII (see *Almanach Royal et National* (Paris, 1832), p. 769). He worked as chaplain of the church in Cadogan Terrace until his death in 1840. The French also used the Moorfield and Virginia Street chapels, and many smaller Mass centres.

For Douglas Newton, writing in 1950, the Soho district had for long years been London's French quarter, and he notes that in the parish of St. Patrick's, but south of it in Leicester Square, French Catholics have their own church, Notre Dame de France. It is not an old church as London churches go, having been opened on 8 December 1868, by Père Faure, a Bordeaux priest. It stands on ground once covered by Leicester House, built in 1632 by the family which gave its name to the square. The house was pulled down in 1791, and one of the large circular panoramas so popular at that time replaced it. It proceeded through several failures to the day when Père Faure acquired it and two neighbouring houses in 1865. The panorama building was adapted to worship in a most ingenious way, making the church one of the most interesting in London. It is entirely French and

---

[1] For fuller details, see *A History of the County of Middlesex*, xii: *Chelsea*, ed. P. E. C. Croot (2004), p. 259.

meets the needs of a large population not only in the neighbourhood but in London, and links with its own French schools and hospitals. It has been served from its beginning to the present by French Marist Fathers, one of whom is Catholic chaplain to the French Lycée in South Kensington.

The church of Notre Dame was a rallying centre for the French in the two World Wars, the Free French, whose headquarters were in London, using it in the last, when it was damaged by bombing. Not only did the Free French help to repair it with their own hands, but, its notable statue of Notre Dame des Victoires having been smashed, a French officer, often dropped in France by aeroplane to act as liaison with the French underground, got in touch with Henri Vallette, a Parisian sculptor, on one of his secret trips. The head of the statue was parachuted into France and brought to Vallette, who secretly made a replica of the statue based on the dimensions of the head. In 1945 the new statue was taken to England and erected in the church to replace the broken one. The rich collection of artworks in the church stems from the 1950s restoration of the church after the bombing and includes the famous murals by Jean Cocteau; these are dedicated to the Virgin Mary and divided into three panels: the Annunciation, the Crucifixion and the Assumption. The murals are simplified line drawings with muted colours, and Cocteau included a self-portrait within the Crucifixion scene on the left side of the altar.

To return to the end of the eighteenth century: near Portman Square, in a turning called Little George Street, the French émigrés erected with their own hands the remarkable little church that once carried the brave name of the Chapel Royal of France. It arose from the imperative need of supplying the ever-growing numbers of refugee priests with a definite central church of their own. The mission was begun under the direction of the bishop of Pol-de-Léon and Bishop Douglass, by a Sulpician, Abbé Bourret, a professor of theology of the Seminary of Orléans. He first set up a temporary chapel in a sort of half cellar, half poulterer's shop in an alley called Dorset Mews East: here Mass and marriages were celebrated, until the Sulpicians of Montreal sent a sum of money, which the Abbé Bourret was able to use for the immediate building of the church in Little King Street (now Carlton Street, near Portman Square).

Funds were short and all were anxious to have a church of their own, and quickly; so the exiled priests themselves set to work on it, digging the foundations, sawing the wood and carrying the bricks. The sight of them working in their shovel hats and white bands made Londoners stop and gape; with them worked lay exiles, some of royal blood. They also gave what money they could towards the building, and there they were helped by English Catholics and non-Catholics too.

The chapel was finished in 1799, dedicated to 'Notre Dame de l'Annonciation', and consecrated on 25 March by the bishop of Aix-en-Provence. He was one of sixteen mitred bishops at the ceremony, together with a mass of clergy, regular and secular, and princes and princesses of the royal blood, all exiles.

Once the church was in use, it was quite a common experience to see from fifteen to twenty bishops seated on the left side of the altar at High Mass, with half of the royal house of France sitting on a similar bench to the right. When retreats were given, French clergy could be seen approaching the altar in hundreds to receive communion from the hands of their bishops. The English who came to share such occasions were reportedly much edified by the behaviour of the priests. In return the French clergy facilitated the restoration of old practices among Catholics, and marked great occurrences with great ceremonials. His Eminence Cardinal Alexandre de Talleyrand-Périgord, archbishop of Rheims, grand almoner of France, officiated at the requiem of Marie-Josephine of Savoy, wife of Louis XVIII, who died in 1810, with all the high ritual of St. Denis, amid a huge gathering of the French and English aristocracy. It was royal and Catholic France transposed for a space to London soil, and when the émigrés were able to return to their own country, the restored king in gratitude bestowed upon the church the title of Chapel Royal of France and granted it an annuity for its upkeep.

It continued to exist almost to our time, serving, it is true, a dwindling French congregation. The comte de Paris made his first communion there in 1850; the prince imperial went to confession before starting on his fateful journey to Africa; Princesse Hélène d'Orléans was confirmed at the altar by Cardinal Manning. The Republican regime caused the name to be changed again to St. Louis of France. Then difficulties arose, financial and connected with the lease, and ultimately this shrine of many memories was closed.

Among those seeking refuge in England were the Benedictine nuns from Montargis, who landed at Shoreham, Sussex, in a state of total destitution. Hearing of this, the prince regent's morganatic wife Mrs. Fitzherbert immediately collected money and went to meet them. Some of the nuns were from old English families, and one, Sister Catherine Dillon, proved to be a friend of Mrs. Fitzherbert's. She carried them all to Brighton and lodged them at the 'Ship', where they were visited by the prince regent, who welcomed them and discussed plans for their future, courteously insisting on their sitting while he was standing. On going to London they found that the prince had furnished a house for them in Duke Street. Here they opened a school, going later to Princethorpe, near Rugby, where in another school they were able to take up their community life once more (A. Leslie, *Mrs Fitzherbert: a Biography* (New York, 1960), p. 84). Many other small groups and individuals spent a relatively short time in London, and it would be enlightening to be able to trace them all.[2]

[2] For further details, see K. Carpenter, *Refugees of the French Revolution: Émigrés in London, 1789–1802* (1999); A. Bellenger, *The French Exiled Clergy in the British Isles after 1789: an Historical Introduction and Working List* (Bath, 1986); P. Emery and K. Wooldridge, *St Pancras Burial Ground: Excavations for St Pancras International, the London Terminus of High Speed 1, 2002–3* (2011); J. H. Harting, *Catholic London Missions from the Reformation to the Year 1850* (1903); B. W. Kelly, *Historical Notes on English Catholic Missions* (1907); *Catholicism in Britain and France since 1789*, ed. F. Tallett and N. Atrin (1996); and B. Ward, *The Dawn of the Catholic Revival in England, 1781–1803* (2 vols., 1909), and *The Eve of Catholic Emancipation, being the History of the English Catholics during the First 30 Years of the 19th Century* (3 vols., 1911).

4. Courts in exile: Bourbons, Bonapartes and Orléans in London, from George III to Edward VII

Philip Mansel

The history of French royal exiles in London confirms the exceptional intimacy of the bonds between London and Paris. French princes repeatedly chose to reside in London, rather than Brussels, Vienna or Rome. Far from being 'natural and necessary enemies', as Jeremy Black complained in a 1990 book, or the Channel being, in the words of David Starkey, 'wider than the Atlantic', from the late eighteenth century until 1919 French and British elites, and London and Paris in particular, were 'inextricably entangled'. There was an 'Anglo-French moment', almost as important as the 'Anglo-Dutch moment' in the seventeenth century.

London and Paris were the only cities in western Europe which shared proximity, a wealthy and cultivated nobility and commercial class, and status as royal capitals. They were bound to attract each other. Each became the natural model for, alternative to and refuge from the other. London provided the fascination of a parliamentary monarchy, a dynamic economy and a less rigorous (until the 1880s) censorship; Paris had the arts. France, the historian of English Francophilia Robin Eagles has written, was 'everywhere' in England, in food, manners, dress, entertainment and, especially, language. French was the second language of educated England, as of educated Europe.[1] Members of his cabinet had addressed George I in French. Horace Walpole, Edward Gibbon and William Beckford (and later Algernon Swinburne and Oscar Wilde) wrote in French as well as English.

The shuttle between London and Paris, interrupted by the Reformation, had resumed with the arrival in London in 1625 of Henrietta Maria and her enormous household and unpopular Catholic chapel.[2] Her illegitimate half-brother the duc de Vendôme, the duchesse de Chevreuse and others took refuge in London from Cardinal Richelieu's regime in Paris. Thirty years later the comte de Gramont enjoyed London and the court of Charles II so

---

[1] R. Eagles, *Francophilia in English Society* (2000), pp. 1, 9, 42, 48, 63, 67, 94.
[2] P. Cyprien de Gamaches, *Mémoires de la Mission des Capucins de la province de Paris près la reine d'Angleterre* (Paris, 1881), *passim*. I am grateful for this reference to Professor Edward Chaney.

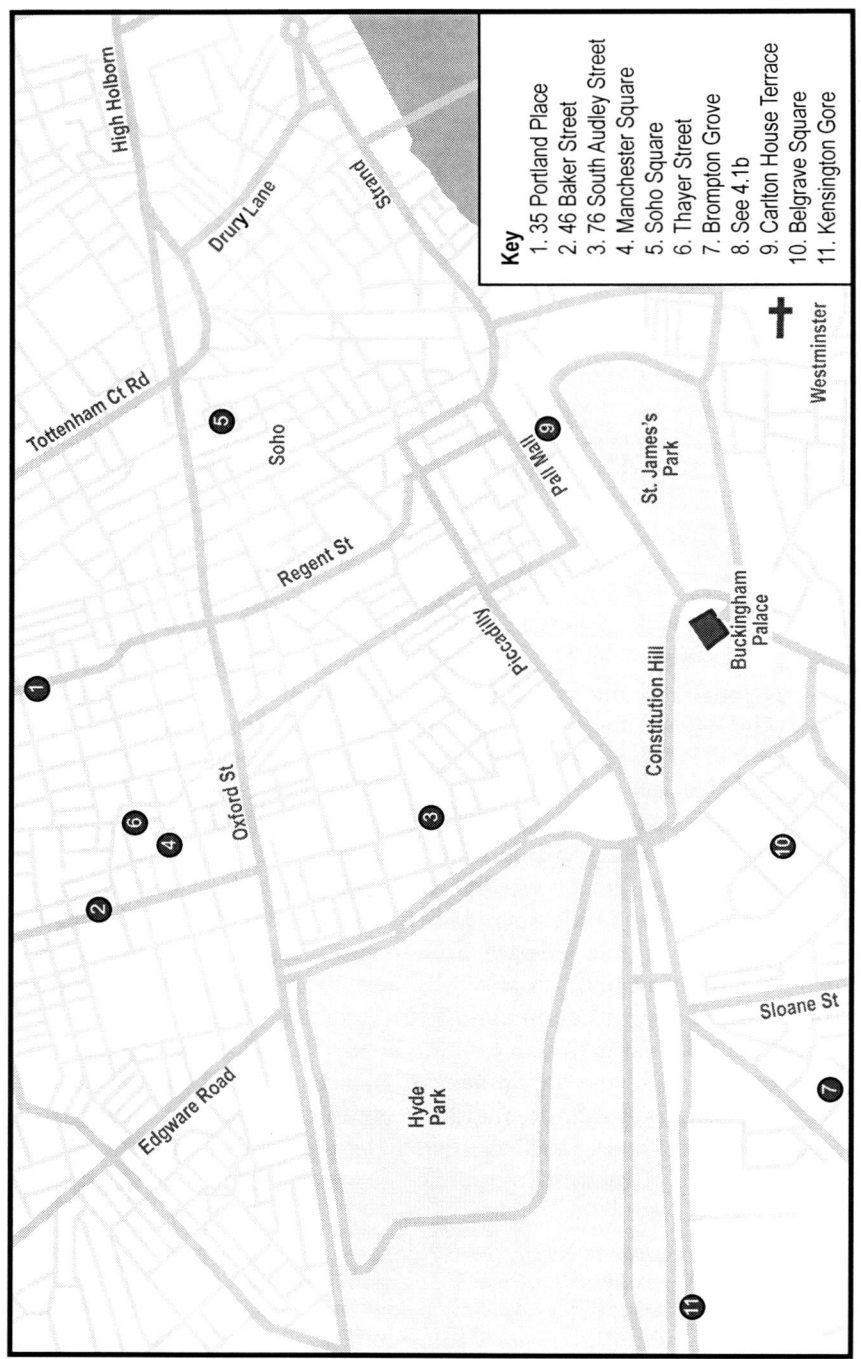

Map 4.1a. Places mentioned in the text (Base map: London c.1850)

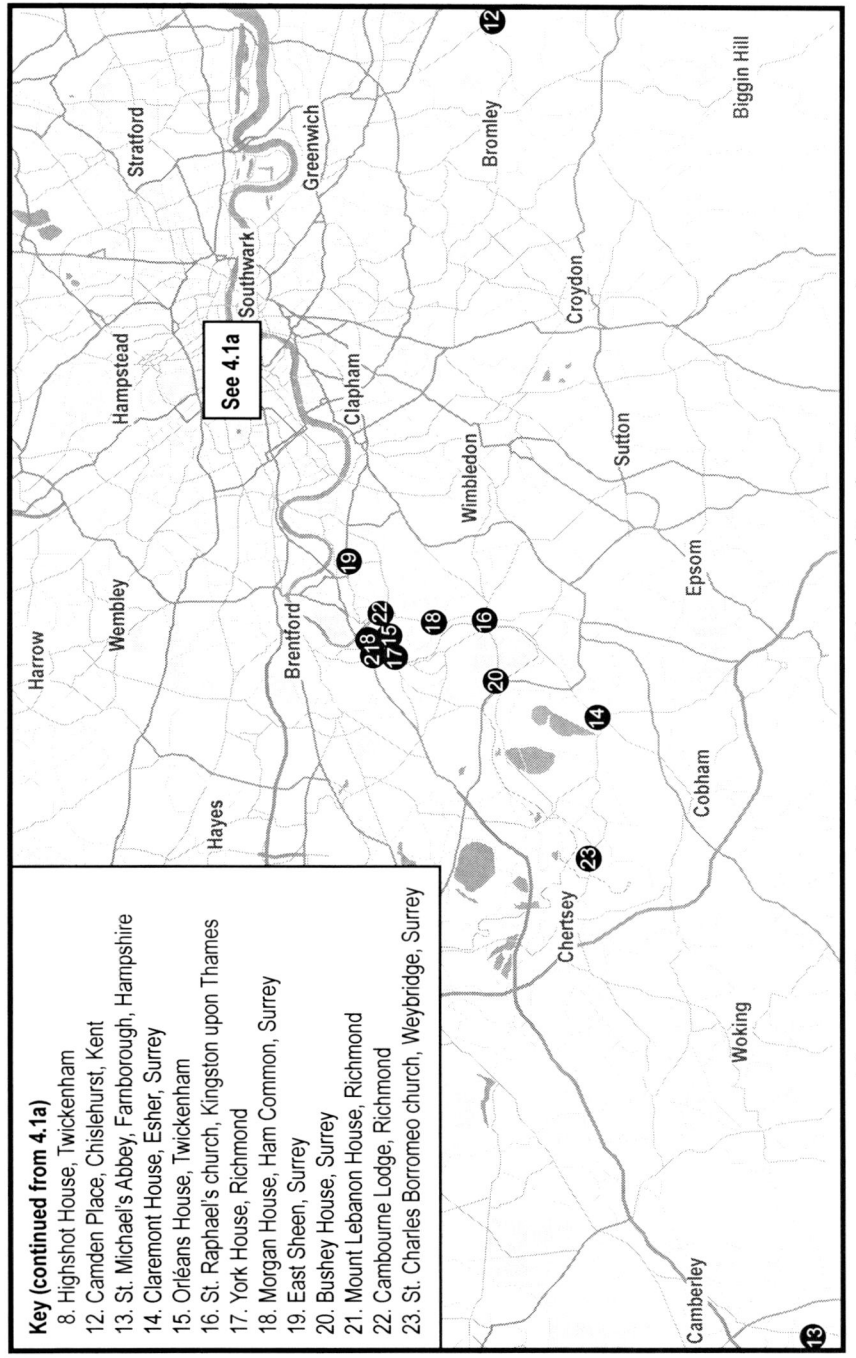

Key (continued from 4.1a)
8. Highshot House, Twickenham
12. Camden Place, Chislehurst, Kent
13. St. Michael's Abbey, Farnborough, Hampshire
14. Claremont House, Esher, Surrey
15. Orléans House, Twickenham
16. St. Raphael's church, Kingston upon Thames
17. York House, Richmond
18. Morgan House, Ham Common, Surrey
19. East Sheen, Surrey
20. Bushey House, Surrey
21. Mount Lebanon House, Richmond
22. Cambourne Lodge, Richmond
23. St. Charles Borromeo church, Weybridge, Surrey

Map 4.1b. Places mentioned in the text outside central London (Base map: 2013)

much that he could hardly believe he had left France.[3] Other Frenchmen, such as the writer Charles de St.-Evremond in 1661, and Voltaire in 1726–8, also moved to London. By 1780 it was increasingly attractive to French people. It was the largest, richest and most modern city in Europe; it provided relative freedom; the journey took only thirty hours.

Philippe Egalité: the search for pleasure

Pleasure and freedom attracted the first French prince to live in London. Louis-Philippe Joseph d'Orléans, duc de Chartres, was so Anglophile that in 1779, although France and Britain were fighting the War of American Independence, he had imported an English orphan called Nancy Syms (later known as 'la belle Pamela', wife of Lord Edward Fitzgerald, leader of the Irish rebellion of 1798) to Paris to help teach his children English. As the war ended, he looked for what he called, in a letter to his agent Nathaniel Forth, 'a pied à terre which I want to have in London where I can arrive from Paris whenever it suits me and where I will not have to render an account of my conduct to anybody'. In 1782 he rented 35 Portland Place for 350 louis a year: London was the only city outside France in which a French prince had a residence.

Soon he was visiting London as easily as if he was arriving at one of his country estates, sometimes for as little as two weeks, choosing women 'selon les fantaisies du moment' ('according to the whims of the moment'), going to the races and visiting Brighton.[4] He often dined with the prince of Wales, a Francophile who employed French cooks and craftsmen at Carlton House, of whom Chartres's grandson would write 'I have never heard a foreigner speak such good French'.[5] Chartres was an 'enlightened' prince, who admired the House of Commons and considered, like many Frenchmen, that the British government represented 'the will of all' – a view more revealing of his opposition to French absolutism than of his grasp of British politics. London was popular with a growing number of Frenchmen, including visitors such as the duc de Fitzjames, the marquis de Conflans and the comte d'Avaray; Jean-Paul Marat (who worked there as a doctor and writer for a number of years); and the comte de Calonne, Louis XVI's finance minister, who took refuge there in August 1787, after his dismissal from office in April, to avoid prosecution in France.[6]

---

[3] A. Hamilton, *Count Gramont at the Court of Charles II*, ed. and trans. N. Deakin (1962), p. 10.

[4] A. Britsch, *La Jeunesse de Philippe Egalité* (Paris, 1926), pp. 393, 395, 399, 401.

[5] F.-P. duc d'Orléans, *Souvenirs 1810–30* (Geneva, 1993), p. 136.

[6] Letter of French ambassador, 20 May 1783 (E. Lever, *Philippe Egalité* (Paris, 1996), p. 213); R. Lacour-Gayet, *Calonne: financier, réformateur, contre-révolutionnaire, 1734–1802* (Paris, 1963), p. 247.

Chartres seemed as much at home at Brooks's as Charles James Fox. He soon acquired in London the same reputation as in Paris. In 1783 the prince of Wales, no prude, called him 'a great beast' and complained of the round of entertainments caused by the duke's 'large party of French, both men and women'. His face was so red that it was said he should have been called the duke of Burgundy. Nevertheless, in 1785 the prince commissioned his portrait for Carlton House, from Sir Joshua Reynolds.[7]

'Philippe Egalité', as the duc d'Orléans (his title since his father's death in 1785) was often called, returned to London for the last time in October 1789–July 1790. After his flagrant support for the Revolutions of July and October 1789, the French government sent him on an official mission, as it wanted him out of Paris. The French ambassador, the comte de La Luzerne, reported to the foreign minister: 'the conduct of the Duc d'Orléans is as feeble in London as in Paris. Wine, horses, women, gambling and Madame de Buffon [his principal mistress] appear to be his sole occupations'. He was said to be drunk every night.[8] He was executed in Paris in 1793, devoured by the Revolution he had encouraged. However, some of his possessions continued to move to London. The Orléans collection of pictures, the finest private collection in Europe, which he had sold to pay his debts, was re-sold in London between 1793 and 1799:[9] thanks to the French Revolution, the centre of the European art market had moved to the capital of Great Britain.[10]

---

[7] Lever, *Philippe Egalité*, pp. 214–15; Wales to duke of York, 27 May 1783 (*The Correspondence of George, Prince of Wales 1770–1812*, ed. A. Aspinall (8 vols., 1963), i. 107 and n.).

[8] Lever, *Philippe Egalité*, p. 384; letter of 21 May 1790 (R. Heron de Villefosse, *L'Anti-Versailles, ou, le Palais-Royal de Philippe Egalité* (Paris, 1974), p. 253).

[9] J. Stourton and C. Sebag-Montefiore, *The British as Art Collectors, from the Tudors to the Present* (2012), pp. 154–5.

[10] The Wallace Collection (in Hertford House, Manchester Square, London W1), 'is a national museum which displays the works of art collected in the eighteenth and nineteenth centuries by the first four Marquesses of Hertford and Sir Richard Wallace, the son of the 4th Marquess and a French mother. It was bequeathed to the British nation by Sir Richard's widow, Lady Wallace, in 1897' (Wallace Collection website). Because of the successive collectors' residence in and appreciation of France, and the opportunities for collecting provided especially by the break-up of many continental collections during the French Revolution and the Napoleonic wars, the focus of the Wallace Collection is on French paintings, furniture and gilt bronzes, Sèvres and other French porcelain, and French objets d'art. In particular, the 4th marquess of Hertford, 'like his father … was attracted by the superb craftsmanship of eighteenth-century France, but he acquired a wider range of objects and on a far larger scale. He bought pictures by Jean-Antoine Watteau, Jean-Baptiste Greuze, François Boucher and Jean-Honoré Fragonard; many fine pieces of Sèvres porcelain; furniture by the greatest French cabinet-makers such as Antoine Gaudreau and Jean-Henri Riesener, as well as miniatures, gold boxes, tapestries and sculpture' (website, with first names added).

The comte d'Artois and the Bourbons: royal refugees

Pleasure had first attracted Orléans to London; seventeen years later politics brought his cousin, Louis XVI's reactionary youngest brother the comte d'Artois. The expansion of the French Republic after 1794 alarmed the British government more than the reign of terror after 1792. It began to believe in the restoration of the Bourbons as the best guarantee of the peace of Europe, and was rich enough to grant them and other French émigrés pensions. There was a geopolitical motive. The Bourbons were prepared to give up French conquests, including the key strategic area of the southern Netherlands and the great port of Antwerp, possession of which by France – as by Germany in 1914–18 – was believed to threaten British security.

In August 1799 the comte d'Artois arrived from Edinburgh – having made an arrangement with the creditors who had confined him to the protected precinct of Holyrood House – for consultations with the British government. The foreign secretary Lord Grenville, anti-Bourbon in 1793, by 1799 believed: 'Europe can never be restored to tranquillity but by the restoration of the monarchy in France'. Pitt himself declared in Parliament in January 1800: 'The restoration of the French monarchy … I consider as a most desirable object because I think it would afford the strongest and best security to this country and to Europe' – although it was never a sine qua non of peace.[11]

Artois settled at 46 Baker Street with a small household and a pension of £6,000 a year. In London he rediscovered friends whom he had known at Versailles before 1789. The Whig leaders the duke and duchess of Devonshire, for example, held a breakfast in his honour at their villa at Chiswick on 7 July 1800. The duke's mistress Lady Elizabeth Foster wrote in her diary:

> I was very much struck with his manner and deportment. He neither seeks nor avoids talking on public affairs and even of the misfortunes of his family and country, but when he does, it is with feeling for the past, patience and firmness in the present moment, some hope for the future, without violence or resentment against the present rulers of France. It is impossible to see him and not to feel both interest and admiration for him. The Duke attended him to his carriage and marked his civility to the exiled Prince beyond what he had done to the Prince of Wales.[12]

[11] P. Mackesy, *Statesmen at War: the Strategy of Overthrow 1798–9* (1974), p. 69; Sir C. Webster, *The Foreign Policy of Castlereagh* (2 vols., 1925–31), i. 234; cf. J. Ehrman, *The Younger Pitt: the Consuming Struggle* (Palo Alto, Calif., 1996), pp. 223, 230, 344n., 347.

[12] Norwich, Norfolk Record Office, Fellowes MSS., Lady Elizabeth Foster diary, 7 July 1800.

Other English friends whom Artois visited included the duke of Portland, Lady Salisbury and Lady Harrington. Madame de Boigne, one of many émigrés who spoke and felt both French and English, disapproved of Artois's politics but found his manners, at Lady Harrington's, so noble that, beside him, the prince of Wales seemed to be his caricature.[13]

In accordance with his royal rank, and his official status as a British protégé, until his return to France in 1814 Artois held a regular levée in his residence (he moved from 46 Baker Street to 76 South Audley Street in 1805) for émigrés and English friends.[14] He attended the small French Catholic chapel in Marylebone at what was then called Little King Street (later Carlton Street, demolished in 1978), one of eight French Catholic chapels established in London. Built by émigrés themselves, it had been consecrated by the archbishop of Aix, assisted by sixteen bishops, on 15 March 1799.[15]

In London Artois – despite appearing to English friends to be a 'dear, good-natured man'[16] – also plotted against Bonaparte. Even after most émigrés returned to France during the peace of Amiens in 1802, some remained in London and provided him with a pool of followers. From London he helped to organize assassination attempts on Bonaparte by Georges Cadoudal, the Polignac brothers and others, in 1800–2 and 1803–4.[17] Later he received and corresponded with the foreign secretary George Canning and his successor the Marquess Wellesley. Although no French Bourbon was allowed by the British government to fight in the Peninsular War, on 1 September 1808 Canning wrote: 'I am at Your Royal Highness's disposal, either tomorrow or Saturday, at any hour tomorrow and at any hour from twelve to five on Saturday which may best suit Your Royal Highness's convenience'.[18]

London remained the capital of French royalist propaganda, as it would be of Gaullist propaganda in 1940–4. Works first published in London,

---

[13] Comtesse de Boigne, *Mémoires de la Comtesse de Boigne* (2 vols., 1998), i. 132.

[14] Cf. AN, 224 AP IV, journal du comte de Broval, 28 Jan. 1812, 2 Nov. 1813; C. Knight, *Autobiography* (2 vols., 1863), i. 238.

[15] J. Yeowell, *The French Chapel Royal in London: a Brief History of the Chapel of St Louis, Carton Street, St Marylebone* (1958), *passim*.

[16] Letter to Lady G. Morpeth, 11 Oct. 1811 (Lady Granville, *Letters of Harriet Countess Granville 1810–45* (2 vols., 1894), i. 22). The same writer, however, also called him 'so made up of noise, thoughtlessness and nonsense that it is no wonder that compassion does not occur to me … when I hear of the miseries of French royalty' (letter of 7 Nov. 1808 to Countess Spencer (*Hary-O: the Letters of Lady Harriet Cavendish 1796–1809*, ed. G. L. Gower and I. Palmer (1940), p. 285)).

[17] V. W. Beach, *Charles X of France: his Life and Times* (Boulder, Colo., 1971), p. 112.

[18] Canning and Artois sometimes corresponded four or six times a month (see Leeds, West Yorkshire Archives, Harewood papers, Canning archives, HAR\GC\56, *passim*).

such as *Journal de ce qui s'est passé à la tour du Temple pendant la captivité de Louis XVI* (1798) by Jean-Baptiste Cléry, and *Dernières années du règne et de la vie de Louis XVI* (1806) by François Hue, went through many editions, both in French and English. The list of over 1,200 subscribers to the first edition of Cléry's book, printed in French in London, was headed by THE KING, THE QUEEN (so printed) and sixteen members of the British royal family. Newspapers such as the *Courrier de Londres* (1776–1826), the *Courrier d'Angleterre* (1805–1815) and *L'Ambigu* (1802–18), written by royalists like the comte de Montlosier, Pierre-Victor Malouet, Jean-Gabriel Peltier and others, were also published in London, and distributed in Europe.[19] The coteries of émigré writers and conspirators in London were sometimes called 'la république de Manchester', owing to their many disputes, and residence near Manchester Square.[20] The principal émigré publisher and bookseller, with an office in Soho Square, was a former Benedictine called A. B. Dulau: he helped to inspire François-René de Chateaubriand to write *Le Génie du Christianisme*.[21] London also contained at least two émigré painters, who painted the Bourbons and their followers in exile: Henri Pierre Danloux, who returned to Paris in 1801;[22] and François Huet Villiers, who became 'Miniature-Painter to Their Royal Highnesses the Duke and Duchess of York' in 1804, and stayed in London until his death in 1813.

The lure of British pensions, and Britain's safety from French invasions, soon drew more Bourbons to London. Artois's second son the duc de Berri arrived in 1802, after the dissolution in Russia of the army commanded by his cousin the prince de Condé, in which he had been serving. He too led a London life, living beside his father in Thayer Street and in Brompton Grove (now Ovington Square) with a mistress called Amy Brown, buying prints and pictures, and drawing pictures of himself in a carriage escorted by liveried footmen. His two illegitimate daughters by Amy Brown were baptized at the French chapel. He later called England, echoing Philippe Egalité twenty years earlier, 'that good country where one can think at one's ease and where I have been so happy'.[23]

---

[19] S. Burrows, *French Exile Journalism and European Politics 1792–1814* (2000), *passim*.

[20] Colonel de Guilhermy, *Papiers d'un émigré* (1886), pp. 154, 269.

[21] An 1812 book catalogue states: 'Families, Schools and Gentlemen applying to A. B. Dulau and Co. may be supplied with the best Masters of the dead and living languages'. The firm continued until the Second World War.

[22] Baron R. Portalis, *Le Peintre H.-P. Danloux et son journal durant l'émigration* (1910).

[23] Boigne, *Mémoires*, i. 131; M. Weiner, *The French Exiles 1789–1815* (1960), p. 175; A. Castelot, *Le Duc de Berri et son double mariage* (Paris, 1950), pp. 43, 61; P. Mansel, *Paris between Empires 1814–1852* (2001), p. 151.

In 1802 the prince de Condé himself arrived in London, where his son the duc de Bourbon had been living since 1796. Having early removed his fortune from France, he was able to live surrounded by French servants, in the Palladian mansion of Wanstead (now demolished) in Essex. 'His household is maintained and organized marvellously, it is still the household of a prince: it has dignity', wrote a royalist, Madame de Lage, in 1804.[24]

London's role as capital of French royalism was confirmed by the process of reconciliation between Artois and the sons of Philippe Egalité, Louis-Philippe, duc d'Orléans, and his brothers the duc de Montpensier and the comte de Beaujolais, who after 1789 had been Jacobins and after 1792 Republicans. They had arrived in England in January 1800. Artois insisted that Orléans's letter offering 'the homage of our fidelity and our devotion' to the head of the family, the exiled Louis XVIII, and expressing regret for 'culpable measures into which I was seduced', dated 13 February 1800, be at once shown not only to senior émigrés but also to the Russian ambassador and British ministers. Only *after* Orléans had written his submission to Louis XVIII did he receive a British pension, the honour of presentation to George III and Queen Charlotte, and the opportunity to meet, at dinner in Artois's house, Lord Grenville and the Austrian, Russian and Neapolitan ambassadors.[25] The Bourbons held the keys to Europe.

In June 1800 Orléans and his brothers rented Highshot House in Twickenham (now destroyed), thus beginning their family's long love-affair with this London suburb, which lasted until the death there of Orléans's descendant ex-king Manuel of Portugal in 1932. London, a British pension, and the exaltation of the struggle against the French Republic and Empire, weakened the boundaries of nationality. Far from being a patriot who refused to fight against his fatherland, as he later claimed, in London Louis-Philippe became half-British, and wholly counter-revolutionary. He called France 'a nation rotten internally and externally'; its government was a 'disgusting edifice'. He constantly proclaimed in letters to Canning his desire to fight for England against France: 'no one has more at heart than I the health and prosperity of England'. Until after the Hundred Days he would send copies of his letters to Louis XVIII to the British foreign secretary.[26]

Finally, Louis XVIII himself arrived from Russia in England in November 1807. His motives were: poverty; fear of Alexander I's pro-Napoleonic policies after the Treaty of Tilsit; and desire for direct discussions with the

---

[24] Letter of 20 Apr. 1804 (Madame de Reinach-Foussemagne, *Une Fidèle: la marquise de Lage de Volude, 1764–1842* (Paris, 1908), p. 235).

[25] E. Daudet, 'Une reconciliation de famille en 1800', *Revue des deux mondes*, xxix (16 Sept. 1905), 284–319, at pp. 293–5.

[26] G. Antonetti, *Louis-Philippe* (Paris, 1994), p. 347, 21 Aug. 1802, pp. 348, 373, 480.

British government and control over Artois and the French royalists in London.[27] He wrote to Canning that 'the salvation of Europe' should come from the 'union of George III and Louis XVIII', and to Wellesley that the interests of France and England were 'inseparable'.[28]

Orléans, however, considered him 'beyond all bearing' for not following the instructions of the British government to go to Edinburgh. In his turn Louis XVIII condemned Orléans for being 'tout à fait anglais' ('totally English'). The following year, partly owing to such disputes, Orléans left for Sicily.[29] Louis XVIII was obliged to live, first at Gosfield in Essex, then at Hartwell near Aylesbury. He failed to obtain formal recognition as king of France, the right to live in or near London, or the chance to meet British ministers. British governments did not want to compromise the possibility of making peace with Napoleon. He was, however, awarded a pension of £16,000 a year.[30] (In 1811 French royalists, including refugees from uprisings in Toulon and Corsica, were receiving a total of £154,752 a year from the British government, of which £45,500 went to members of the Bourbon dynasty.[31])

Funerals advertised London's role as the capital of French royalism. Requiem Masses were held in the French chapel for Condé's grandson the duc d'Enghien, kidnapped and shot on Bonaparte's orders in 1804 (partly in retaliation for the assassination attempts organized from London by Artois); and in 1807 for Louis-Philippe's brother the duc de Montpensier, and for the last confessor of Louis XVI the Abbé Edgeworth. On 26 November 1810 the exiled 'Queen of France' Marie-Josephine of Savoy, who had been living with her husband at Hartwell, was buried in the Henry VII chapel in Westminster Abbey (where Montpensier had been buried three years earlier). There was a five-hour service in the French chapel. The funeral oration (printed by R. Juigne and sold by Bernard Dulau at his shop in Soho Square) was preached by the Abbé de Bouvens: *Oraison funèbre de la très haute, très puissante et très excellente princesse, Marie-Josephine-Louise de Savoie, reine de France et de Navarre.* The service was attended by eleven French bishops and four ambassadors: of Spain, Portugal, Sardinia and Sicily.[32]

[27] P. Mansel, *Louis XVIII* (2005 edn.), pp. 137–9.

[28] P. Mansel, 'From exile to the throne: the Europeanization of Louis XVIII', in *Monarchy and Exile: the Politics of Legitimacy from Marie de Médicis to Wilhelm II*, ed. P. Mansel and T. Riotte (2011), pp. 181–213, at pp. 193, 200.

[29] AN, 300AP (Archives de la Maison de France) II 16, Orléans to Beaujolais, 21, 26 Dec. 1807; Antonetti, *Louis-Philippe*, p. 326.

[30] Mansel, *Louis XVIII*, p. 139.

[31] Enclosed in a note of Spencer Perceval to the regent, 13 May 1811 (Aspinall, *Correspondence of George, Prince of Wales*, vii. 344).

[32] See also the note on French Catholics in London at the end of the previous chapter.

The procession taking the coffin from the French chapel to Westminster Abbey revealed the Bourbons' popularity in London. It consisted of the hearse, drawn by six horses; two carriages for the queen's household; chevaliers de St. Louis and soldiers of the French royal gardes-du-corps on foot; 'four mourning coaches' containing the French princes; and ten coaches for 'the Foreign Nobility and ambassadors'. As a sign of respect the procession was followed by the state coaches of the prince of Wales and all his brothers; of the marquess of Buckingham and Marquess Wellesley; of the prime minister Spencer Perceval 'and all the ministers'; and of 'several English noblemen and gentlemen'.[33] In the abbey the choirs of the Chapel Royal, the abbey and St. Paul's Cathedral sang hymns. A total of 300 émigrés attended the service. Despite the cold and rain 'the populace without were very numerous'.[34]

Until the end of the nineteenth century one factor connecting all French royal exiles was, as this French royal funeral in a British royal chapel confirms, the friendship of the British royal family. Already in 1808 the prince of Wales had visited Louis XVIII at Wanstead House in Essex, gone down on one knee and sworn 'to restore him to the throne of his ancestors'.[35] This was his personal policy, which he never abandoned.

Seven months after the queen's funeral, on 19 June 1811, Louis XVIII and his family were the guests of honour at the fête for 3,000 in Carlton House by which the prince inaugurated his Regency. Louis XVIII had not only broken the ban on visiting London, he was given a military escort to go from South Audley Street, where he was staying, to Carlton House. The new regent welcomed him, in a room hung with fleurs de lis tapestries and a portrait of Louis XV, with the words – dynamite for an exile – 'Ici Votre Majesté est roi de France' ('here, Your Majesty is king of France'). The British government addressed him as 'M. le comte de l'Isle'; at court, however, he maintained his royal rank.[36]

As the presence of all the ministers' and all the princes' carriages at the funeral in 1810 showed, the Bourbons remained a British project. In 1811 Lord Fitzwilliam dedicated to Louis XVIII a pamphlet, in French, comparing Protestantism and Catholicism, saying 'it suffices not that your Majesty should be restored to France – it is necessary that France should

[33] *The Gentleman's Magazine*, lxxx (Nov. 1810), 502.

[34] AN, 224 AP IV, journal du comte de Broval, 27 Nov. 1810.

[35] Fellowes MSS., Lady Elizabeth Foster diary, 20 Oct. 1808, 5 Sept. 1818.

[36] Mansel, *Louis XVIII*, pp. 168–70; letter of 22 June 1811 to Mrs. Jackson (*The Bath Archives: a Further Selection from the Diaries and Letters of Sir George Jackson*, ed. Mrs G. Jackson (2 vols., 1873), i. 271); cf. F. Baron de Geramb, *Lettre à Sophie sur la fête donnée par le prince régent pour célébrer l'anniversaire de la naissance du Roi* (1811), *passim*.

be restored to your Majesty'.[37] Napoleon's defeat in Russia increased the Bourbons' chances. In London on 19 December 1812 and in early 1813, at secret meetings unknown to British historians, Louis XVIII's principal adviser the comte de Blacas promised the foreign secretary Lord Castlereagh that the king would support 'the present order of things'. (The meetings were kept secret to prevent denunciations of war-mongering by the government's enemies in Parliament, and the alienation of Britain's allies Russia, Prussia and Austria.) Louis XVIII had already begun to moderate his counter-revolutionary policies in 1800–5; but the British government pushed him further in this direction.

Declarations were the king's principal means of influencing French opinion and in the declaration of Hartwell of 1 March 1813, written with Castlereagh's help, he repeated the moderation of his 1805 declaration. It promised union, happiness, peace and 'repose'; the maintenance of 'le Code dit Napoleon' except in matters of religion, and of 'administrative and judicial bodies'; and guaranteed 'the freedom of the people'. Thereafter the British government and its agents abroad – without telling Britain's allies – provided the king with the financial means to print the declaration and to have it distributed by what Blacas called 'devoted servants who can inform the French of the king's intentions and the king of the dispositions of the interior'.[38]

The Entente Cordiale between Britain and France began in London. Already in August 1813 the British government suggested a Bourbon restoration.[39] As allied armies approached France's frontiers, and agents arrived with news of royalist activity, Artois had several meetings with Liverpool. According to his 'most secret' memorandum of 4 January, Liverpool 'urged the advantage of delay'. He demanded an 'actual rising' or the allies' consent. For once in his life relying on public opinion, Artois threatened to appeal to 'the whole world' if the British government would not give him and his sons passports to leave the country. Honour obliged them to answer 'the wishes of the French People'. At first Liverpool refused. On 17 January, however, due either to royal pressure, or to the course of the campaign in France, Liverpool accompanied the regent to call on Artois in South Audley Street.[40] On 22 January he and his sons Angoulême (who had

---

[37] R. Fitzwilliam, *Letters of Atticus, or Protestantism and Catholicism Considered in their Comparative Influence on Society* (1826 edn.), p. xiv.

[38] TNA, FO 27/91, note of 19 Dec. 1812; AN, 37 AP 1, Blacas to Bonnay, 17 March 1813; Archives privées, Louis XVIII to Blacas, 9, 19, 21 Feb. 1813.

[39] Webster, *Castlereagh*, i. 234.

[40] Liverpool to Castlereagh, 29, 30 Dec. 1813, 20 Jan. 1814 (Webster, *Castlereagh*, i. 510, 511, 516); BL, Additional MS. 38364 fos. 206–14, 'most secret' memorandum by Liverpool, 4 Jan.

been living at Hartwell with his uncle) and Berri set sail for the continent with British passports. They too, like Louis XVIII, had become more moderate on British soil.

On 25 January 1814, breaking British constitutional proprieties in the presence of Lord Liverpool (in order to demonstrate his ministers' approval), the regent summoned Count Lieven, the Russian ambassador, to Carlton House. He informed Lieven that peace with Napoleon – which Britain's allies were still considering – would only be a breathing space. His entire life was 'a series of bad faith, atrocity and ambition'. In the interests of European peace a restoration of the Bourbons, in whom the regent personally took 'a strong interest', should be proposed to the French nation.[41]

On this issue public opinion agreed with the regent: it was called 'insane' and 'nearly unanimous' in its opposition to peace with Napoleon.[42] The Bourbons' popularity came from their association with peace. On 24 March the royalist agent the comte de La Barthe, arriving with news of the declaration of the city of Bordeaux in favour of the Bourbons on 12 March 1814 – sparked by the arrival of the duc d'Angoulême and British and Portuguese troops – was escorted by a crowd to 10 Downing Street with shouts of: 'Bourbons for ever! God bless the Bourbons! No peace with Boney, with the invader!'[43]

London's enthusiasm for the Bourbons reached its zenith in April. On 7 April Louis XVIII was proclaimed in Paris. On 12 April the comte d'Artois made his official entry into the city; the only foreigners with him, as a sign of gratitude for British hospitality, were Lord Castlereagh and his mission.[44] In one moment, according to the marquis de La Maisonfort, author of a best-selling pro-Bourbon pamphlet printed in London, *Tableau de l'Europe* (1813), England was covered in white cockades; even the hackney coachmen in London wore them. A popular tune was called 'The white cockade'.[45]

At 3.00 p.m. on 20 April, after an attack of gout had immobilized him at Hartwell, Louis XVIII received a triumphant welcome in London. Sitting with the duchesse d'Angoulême, the prince de Condé and the regent in the regent's state coach, followed by a procession of carriages of British and French court officials, they were escorted from Stanmore, where the regent had gone to welcome the king, by the Royal Horse Guards, volunteers and

1814; Fellowes MSS., Lady Elizabeth Foster diary, 17 Jan. 1814.

[41] BL, Add. MS. 47245 fo. 107, Lieven to Nesselrode, 14/26 Jan. 1814 (secret).

[42] Webster, *Castlereagh*, i. 237–8 and n.

[43] L. de Contenson, 'Un agent royaliste en 1814', *Revue de Paris*, 15 July 1910, p. 320.

[44] C. Dupuis, *Le Ministère de Talleyrand en 1814* (2 vols., 1919), i. 221n.

[45] L. D. D. La Maisonfort, *Mémoires d'un agent royaliste: sous la révolution, l'empire et la restauration, 1763–1827* (Paris, 1998), p. 222.

Figure 4.1. Edward Bird, 'The departure of Louis XVIII from
Dover, 24 April 1814'. Private collection, detail.
The king is embracing the prince regent, whose friendship, hospitality and support had helped
lead to his restoration, before sailing to France on the British royal yacht, *The Royal Sovereign*.

nobles on horseback. All the British troops and noblemen wore French white cockades.[46] 'One mass of carriages', filled with spectators, stretched from Kilburn down Edgware Road and Park Lane to Piccadilly. They had been waiting four hours before the king arrived at about 4.00 p.m. White flags flew from every roof. Roofs, balconies and windows were filled with

[46] BL, Add. MS. 35160 fos 1–5, George Nayler, York Herald, 'An Account of the Entrance of His Most Christian Majesty Louis XVIII King of France and Navarre into London on 20 April 1814', 1814.

spectators.[47] As the procession reached Grillion's Hotel, 7 Albemarle Street, the crowd cheered; ladies waved handkerchiefs. Louis XVIII entered the hotel on the regent's arm.[48]

In the hotel ball room, in the presence of 150 French and English nobles, all the foreign ambassadors and the British cabinet, the regent offered his congratulations, in French: 'the triumph and joy with which Your Majesty will be received in your own capital can scarcely exceed the joy and satisfaction with which Your Majesty's restoration to the throne of his ancestors had been received in the capital of the whole British empire … May your Majesty long reign in peace, happiness and honour!' Louis XVIII expressed his 'gratitude and delight' and admiration for Britain: 'May its greatness and happiness be eternal!' Then, assisted by the prince de Condé and the duc de Bourbon, he invested the regent with his own Cross of the Order of the Holy Spirit, taken from his breast.[49]

For the next two days the charm offensive continued. Clearly the king and the regent were trying to inaugurate an era of peace between the two nations. At individual presentations, according to the writer Fanny Burney (wife of the émigré chevalier d'Arblay) 'the English, by express command of his Majesty, had always the preference and always took place of the French'.[50] At a special chapter in Carlton House on 21 April, Louis XVIII was invested by the regent with the Order of the Garter. The Corporation of the City of London, after offering its congratulations, expressed the hope that France and England would remain so 'indissolubly allied by the relations of amity and concord as to ensure and perpetuate to both, and to Europe at large, uninterrupted Peace and Repose'. Louis XVIII replied in English: 'neither myself nor my Family will ever forget the Asylum afforded us, nor the Stand which has been made against Tyranny by England, whose powerful aid has enabled my people to speak freely their sentiments of loyalty'. In a speech after dinner at Carlton House on 22 April 1814, he attributed 'the restoration of our house on the throne of its ancestors', after divine providence, 'to the counsels of Your Royal Highness, to this glorious country and to the steadfastness of its inhabitants'. On 23 April, having bidden a last farewell to the regent after dinner on board the royal yacht *The Royal Sovereign*, he sailed for France from Dover, with a loan of £100,000 from the British government to pay for his journey – preceded or followed by most of the

[47] Alexander d'Arblay to Monsieur d'Arblay, 22 April 1814 (F. Burney, *The Journals and Letters of Fanny Burney (Madame D'Arblay)* (8 vols., 1978), vii. 318).

[48] French exiles in London chose the best hotels: Grillion's Hotel was a direct ancestor of the Connaught Hotel, the London home of many Free French in 1940–4.

[49] *The European Magazine*, i (1814), 384–5.

[50] Journal, 22 Apr. 1814 (Burney, *Journals and Letters*, viii. 309).

French émigrés in London.[51] Lord Liverpool commented, on Louis XVIII's reception in London: ' I never saw so much enthusiasm in my life on any occasion'.[52]

The Bourbons left London physically, but not mentally. From the moment the king returned to Paris, British visitors could count on a warm welcome at court. Louis XVIII also blew them kisses in the street. Anglophilia became a factor in French politics. Reports of the king's pro-British speeches in London, and frequent consultations in Paris with the British ambassador the duke of Wellington, lost him some of his initial popularity.[53] Nevertheless, both Louis XVIII and Charles X (as Artois became on his brother's death in 1824) practised a pro-British foreign policy, remarkable in a country which had been fighting Britain for the last twenty years. At Navarino in 1827 the French and British navies co-operated for the first time since the reign of Louis XIV. A club dedicated to union between the two nations, called the Cercle de l'Union, was founded in Paris in 1828, under royal patronage, on the model of London clubs.[54]

Even after the restoration of their dynasty in Paris, however, London continued to attract some French princes. While 'all the world' was said to be in Paris, in 1815–17 Orléans rented a house later known as Orléans House, in 'dear old Twick', to show his disapproval of Louis XVIII's ultra-royalist ministry in Paris. Since he had recovered his fortune in France, it was grander than Highshot House, with a garden on the Thames. His wife, Marie-Amélie of Naples, found that London's lack of monuments made it more like a large village than one of the first cities in Europe, but praised what she called the tranquillity of Twickenham, 'far from the world and its intrigues'.[55] In reality her husband continued his own intrigues, printing *Extrait de mon journal du mois de mars 1815, à Twickenham de l'imprimerie de G. White*, which defends his own conduct and condemns Louis XVIII's.[56] Seven months after the king had appointed a more moderate ministry, on 9 April 1817, the Orléans left, needing ten carriages to convey them and their households back to Paris.[57]

[51] BL, Add. MS. 35160 fos 6–7; Mansel, *Paris between Empires*, p. 54.

[52] Liverpool to Castlereagh, 26 Apr. 1814 (Webster, *Castlereagh*, i. 538).

[53] Mansel, *Paris between Empires*, pp. 54, 58–9.

[54] Mansel, *Paris between Empires*, p. 157.

[55] Marie-Amélie, *Journal de Marie-Amélie, reine des Français, 1800–66* (1981 edn.), p. 215, 25 March 1815, p. 218, p. 227, 31 Dec. 1815.

[56] L.-P. d'Orléans, *Extrait de mon journal du mois de mars 1815* (Twickenham, 1816).

[57] T. H. R. Cashmore, *The Orléans Family in Twickenham 1800–1932* (2nd edn., Richmond, 1989), p. 6.

The son of the prince de Condé, the duc de Bourbon, 'enslaved' by his English mistress Sophie Dawes, refused his father's pleas to return to Paris and stayed in London until Condé's death in 1818.[58] Orléans and Bourbon were not exiles, but French princes who, for political or personal reasons, preferred (like Philippe Egalité in 1782–90) London to Paris.[59]

After he ascended the throne in 1830, Louis-Philippe continued his cousins' Anglophile policies. It was said that an English accent was enough to ensure a welcome at court. He continued to consult the British ambassador on policy. His refusal to go to war against Britain in 1840 lost him popularity in France and may have contributed to his overthrow in 1848.[60]

Louis-Napoléon and the Bonapartes: imperial pretenders

Some Bonapartes, like their enemies the Bourbons, also became Londoners and Anglophiles in this period. Despite their leadership of France's war against Britain in 1803–14 and 1815, the Bonapartes in London show a pattern of liberty, fraternity, opportunity – and love affairs – similar to the Bourbons and Orléans. London weakened national boundaries for Louis-Napoléon as well as for Louis XVIII and Louis-Philippe.

Joseph Bonaparte, Lucien Bonaparte and Achille Murat arrived in London in 1831, sensing the weakness of the July Monarchy in France. The first two stayed until 1837 and sometimes attended the French chapel (which in 1823 the French ambassador Prince Jules de Polignac had raised to the status of a royal chapel under the grand almoner of France). Louis-Napoléon, the future Napoleon III, came in 1831 and returned in 1838. After 1838 his uncles and father lived as exiles in Florence or Rome, far from the public gaze. In London, a convenient observation post for France, and a symbol of modernity, Louis-Napoléon lived as a dynastic pretender. He felt safer there than in his previous residence, Switzerland, which had expelled him at the request of the French government in 1837.[61] He entertained notables like Benjamin Disraeli and Edward Bulwer Lytton in a house he leased in Carlton House Terrace, and went to see French plays performed at the St. James's theatre. He admired the moral and material conquests of England and planned to unite France and England through their interests.

At the same time he was planning a Bonaparte restoration. His political programme, and determination to reduce pauperism, were outlined in his own *Des Idées Napoléoniennes* (1839) and in *Lettres de Londres* (1840), written

---

[58] Mansel, *Paris between Empires*, p. 151.
[59] Marie-Amélie, *Journal*, pp. 232–3, 17 July 1817, p. 241, 8 Apr. 1817.
[60] Mansel, *Paris between Empires*, pp. 269, 364.
[61] A. Dansette, *Louis-Napoléon à la conquête du pouvoir* (Paris, 1961), p. 137.

by his follower the duc de Persigny: a propaganda work which stresses his ideas, the 'seductive distinction' of his manners, and the number of his British friends.[62] It was with rifles and uniforms bought in London that he sailed in 1840 to launch a doomed coup at Boulogne. Thus London was a spring-board for Bonapartist plots in 1838–40, as it had been for royalist plots in 1799–1814.[63]

In 1843–4 London was also used as a political base by the legitimist pretender the comte de Chambord, grandson of Charles X (the former comte d'Artois). Renting a house in Belgrave Square, he then toured the factories of the Midlands as well as a large number of sympathetic country houses. About 2,000 French royalists, including the aged Chateaubriand, came to acclaim him in London and to hear him promise to defend 'les libertés nationales'.[64]

Louis-Napoléon lived in London again, after his escape from prison in France, in 1846–8. He visited the Anglo-French salon of Lady Blessington and the comte d'Orsay in Kensington Gore, went to parties and country houses, joined the Army and Navy Club and acted as a special constable during Chartist scares in 1848.[65] It was from London that he left for Paris on 24 September 1848, partly financed by Miss Howard, a beautiful English courtesan with whom he had been living in Berkeley Street.[66] He took with him plans for modernizing Paris, in part inspired by his years in London.

After the proclamation of the Empire in 1852, his Anglophilia helped to create the Crimean alliance which united Britain and France in war against Russia in 1854–6. His state visit to London and Windsor during that war, in April 1855, was a triumph, with more ovations than Louis XVIII had received in April 1814. In a speech in English to the Corporation of London in the Guildhall on 19 April, asserting the 'sentiments of sympathy and esteem' which he retained since his exile in London, Napoleon III said he represented 'a nation whose interests are today everywhere identical with your own (immense cheering) ... England and France are naturally united on all the great questions of politics and of human progress which agitate the world ... I see in the moral as in the political world for our two nations but one course and one end (loud cheers)'. When they went to the opera, Queen Victoria wrote in her journal: 'never did I see such crowds at night, all in the highest good humour ... cheering and pressing near the carriage'.[67]

---

[62] See, e.g., J. Barnes, *Lettres de Londres* (Paris, 1840), p. 53.
[63] I. Guest, *Napoleon III in England* (1952), pp. 20, 49, 56, 65, 75, 155.
[64] D. de Montplaisir, *Le Comte de Chambord, dernier roi de France* (Paris, 2008), pp. 203–4.
[65] Dansette, *Louis-Napoléon*, pp. 140, 214; Guest, *Napoleon III*, p. 67.
[66] S. A. Maurois, *Miss Howard and the Emperor* (1957), pp. 42–3, 46.
[67] Guest, *Napoleon III*, pp. 124, 126.

In March 1871 he returned to England in very different circumstances, after six months as a prisoner following defeat in the Franco-Prussian War. He insisted on living in England, rather than Switzerland or Italy, because of its freedom. Despite relative poverty, the grandest of all French exiled courts in England gathered around him at Camden Place in Chislehurst (then in Kent, now in south-east London), where the Empress Eugénie and their son the prince imperial had been residing since September 1870. It included his grand chamberlain the duc de Bassano, his cousins the duc and duchesse de Mouchy and the ex-minister Eugène Rouher (who founded a Bonapartist newspaper, *La Situation*, in London), as well as aides-de-camp, chamberlains and about twenty-five servants.[68]

Queen Victoria had come to like Napoleon III for his 'constant kindness', and for being a 'faithful ally'. She visited Chislehurst several times: 'the poor Empress looked so lovely in her simple black', she wrote in her diary. There were other English and French visitors after Sunday Mass. In 1872 there was a New Year reception.[69] From Chislehurst the emperor directed the Bonapartist party and press in France until his death in January 1873.[70] During the lying-in-state there was a 'great and pressing crowd at the gates'. His funeral at St. Mary's church on 15 January was a Franco-British occasion, attended by about 30,000 people, from both countries, including senators, marshals Canrobert and Leboeuf, workers, members of the Bonaparte dynasty and the prince of Wales. The British lord chamberlain Lord Sydney and the French grand chamberlain the duc de Bassano were both in attendance. The prince imperial was 'vociferously cheered along the line of route', by cries of 'Vive l'Empéreur!' 'Vive Napoléon IV!' 'Vive la France!' and 'Vive l'Angleterre!'[71] For *The Graphic* it was proof that 'imperialism is still a living creed': 'tout peut se rétablir' ('everything can be re-established').[72]

The prince imperial – 'Napoleon IV' – held rallies at Chislehurst, on St. Napoleon's Day, 15 August, and on his eighteenth birthday on 16 March 1874. Thousands came. Chislehurst briefly resembled a suburb of Paris.[73] He studied at King's College London and the Royal Military Academy Woolwich, and made speeches praising 'the friendship which now united England and France'.

---

[68] L. Girard, *Napoléon III* (Paris, 1986), p. 497; R. Schnerb, *Rouher et le Second Empire* (Paris, 1949), p. 287; H. Kurtz, *The Empress Eugénie, 1826–1920* (1964), pp. 255, 256.

[69] Guest, *Napoleon III*, pp. 167, 173, 177; Kurtz, *Empress Eugénie*, p. 275.

[70] See, e.g., the letters of 10 June and 6 Aug. 1871 to Eugène Rouher about forthcoming elections, sold by Nouveau Drouot, 6 March 1987.

[71] *Illustrated London News*, 25 Jan. 1873, pp. 81, 88, 90.

[72] Girard, *Napoléon III*, p. 501; *The Graphic*, 25 Jan. 1873.

[73] Kurtz, *Empress Eugénie*, p. 280.

Anglophilia, however, helped to kill him. Driven by accusations that his father had been a coward, and by a desire for military fame, he volunteered for the British army, writing 'I could not be satisfied to remain aloof from the fatigues and perils of that army in which I have so many comrades'. He was killed on 20 June 1879 in the first Zulu War.[74]

His funeral at Chislehurst on 12 July was the last ceremony of the Second Empire. The Bonaparte family, 'the great officers of the Imperial Crown' and many other court officials were in attendance. Many British came, because of his popularity and his tragic death fighting in the British army. Queen Victoria herself attended – an honour she extended to few of her own subjects – as did senior army officers, 200 cadets of the Royal Artillery, the prince of Wales and the crown prince of Sweden. Thirty-two special trains ran, bringing about 30,000 people in all, according to the *Illustrated London News*.[75] In her letter of condolence the queen told the empress that her son was 'loved and respected by all'.[76] His heirs, his cousins Prince Napoleon and Prince Victor Napoleon, were not. Bonapartism as a political force was finished.

Two monuments to the last Napoleons survive in England. One is St. Michael's Abbey, Farnborough, a grandiose domed basilica in 'flamboyant' French neo-gothic, decorated with Bonaparte bees and eagles and housing the tombs of Napoleon III, his wife and son. The basilica and adjoining monastery were erected by Gabriel Destailleur on the orders of the Empress Eugénie beside Farnborough Hill, her residence from 1883. The abbey's construction had been the motive for her move from Chislehurst, where she lacked space and local support: proximity to Windsor must have been another attraction. Until her own funeral there in 1920, in the presence of George V and Queen Mary, and the king and queen of Spain, she made Farnborough Abbey a living museum of the First and Second Empires, filled with Napoleonic portraits, sculpture and memorabilia. Her household was French, but her servants (around thirty in all) mainly English. Annual memorial Masses in honour of Napoleon I, Napoleon III, the empress and their son are said there by the Benedictine monks to this day.[77] The second monument is the memorial effigy of the prince imperial, erected at the suggestion of Queen Victoria in St. George's chapel, Windsor – another

[74] Kurtz, *Empress Eugénie*, p. 298; A. Filon, *Memoirs of the Prince Imperial, 1856–79* (1913), pp. 111, 165, 167.

[75] *Illustrated London News*, 16 July 1879, p. 27.

[76] Kurtz, *Empress Eugénie*, pp. 310–12.

[77] A. McQueen, *Empress Eugénie and the Arts: Politics and Visual Culture in the 19th Century* (Farnham, 2011), pp. 296–307; and W. Smith, *The Empress Eugénie and Farnborough* (Winchester, 2001), *passim*.

sign, like Montpensier's tomb in Westminster Abbey, of the friendship between the French and British monarchies.[78]

The House of Orléans: permanent exiles

After 1789–90, 1800–8 and 1815–17, London was again the residence of the Orléans, from 1848 to 1871 and 1886 to 1906. Four Coburg-Orléans marriages – a shared programme of constitutional monarchy embodied in the Quadruple Alliance of 1834 – and exchanges of visits in the 1840s, had made the Orléans and the British royal family cousins, allies and friends. Naturally Louis-Philippe and his family chose England as their refuge after the revolution of 1848 in France. As 'comte de Neuilly', he asked the queen for the hospitality he had once enjoyed as duc d'Orléans.[79]

The queen lent Louis-Philippe and his wife Claremont House in Surrey, the large Palladian mansion which had been bought for Princess Charlotte and Prince Leopold on their marriage in 1816. Visits between the two royal families were frequent.[80] Soon Claremont, like Hartwell during the residence of Louis XVIII, was full from the cellars to the attic. The king's youngest son the duc d'Aumale described the Orléans as 'fort calmes, fort tristes, fort pauvres' ('very calm, very sad, and very poor').[81] Although the king gave up hope of return to France, saying that all respect had died there, he was visited by many French politicians including the duc de Broglie, François Guizot and Narcisse-Achille de Salvandy.[82] There were painful discussions with his sons over the revolution of 1848. They blamed it on their father's refusal to reform. He complained: 'Qu'ai je fait pour être si dépopularisé?' ('What have I done to become so unpopular?').[83] On 20 July 1850 he attended the first communion of his grandson and heir, the comte de Paris, in the French chapel royal in London. He died on 26 August. His funeral, organized by his aides-de-camp and family at the Catholic church of St. Charles Borromeo, Weybridge, was attended by about 200 people including the ambassadors of Portugal, Naples, Spain and Brazil, and some of his favourite artists like Eugène Lami and Ary Scheffer.[84]

---

[78] Kurtz, *Empress Eugénie*, pp. 323–4, 354.

[79] For the queen's sympathy, see extracts from her diary for Feb. and March 1848, in J. Duhamel, *Louis-Philippe et la première entente cordiale* (Paris, 1951), pp. 347–58.

[80] See the letters in *The Letters of Queen Victoria: a Selection from Her Majesty's Correspondence between the Years 1837 and 1861*, ed. A. C. Benson and Viscount Esher (3 vols., 1908), ii. 160–5.

[81] Aumale to Cuvillier-Fleury, 30 June 1848, Atthalin to Mme. Atthalin, March 1850 (A. Teyssier, *Les Enfants de Louis-Philippe et la France* (Paris, 2006), pp. 195, 202).

[82] Antonetti, *Louis-Philippe*, p. 933.

[83] Marie-Amélie, *Journal*, p. 545.

[84] D. Paoli, *Fortunes et infortunes des princes d'Orléans* (Paris, 2006), pp. 32, 54.

Thereafter the widowed Queen Marie-Amélie continued to live at Claremont, a guest of the queen, with members of her family; they founded the Claremont Harriers for hunting. Devoted courtiers such as Raoul de Montmorency, Anatole de Montesquieu and Comtesse Mollien came from France. She disliked what she called the 'atmosphère lourde et énervante' ('heavy and irritating atmosphere') of England, and spent much of her time writing letters.[85]

The rest of her family and their households settled nearby in Richmond and Twickenham. They became the court suburb of the Orléans, as Chislehurst would be of the Bonapartes. East Sheen and later Bushey House near Hampton Court, again lent by Queen Victoria, were used by the duc and duchesse de Nemours; Mount Lebanon House in Richmond by the prince and princesse de Joinville; and the widowed duchesse d'Orléans lived in Cambourne Lodge in Richmond. All were accompanied by French servants and courtiers.[86] In time the housheolds became less French. According to the 1861 census only one of the duc d'Aumale's twenty-three servants was English; in 1871 he had eight English servants. Rosa Lewis, later famous as owner of the Cavendish Hotel, began as a kitchenmaid in the household of Aumale's nephew the comte de Paris.[87]

Aumale was the richest of the Orléans princes, thanks to the intrigues of his father and Sophie Dawes, who had combined to persuade the duc de Bourbon to leave Aumale most of his fortune. In 1852 he bought Orléans House, where his parents had lived in 1815–17. He gave fêtes there to benefit the French Société de Bienfaisance of London, and until his death in 1897 was president of the Twickenham Rowing Club. A celebrated bibliophile, he began to collect in London some of the treasures now on display in France in his château of Chantilly, including the *Très riches heures du duc de Berri* and the 'Orléans Madonna' by Raphael.[88] One purpose was to assert the grandeur of his dynasty and remind the outside world of its existence. He added a library and picture gallery to Orléans House and also subsidized sympathetic newspapers in France. For him, however, as he wrote, 'nothing can replace the absent fatherland'.[89]

Most of the Orléans spent every evening together, in one of their houses in Richmond or at Claremont, in 'une intimité complète' ('complete

[85] M. A. Trognon, *Vie de Marie-Amélie* (Paris, 1871), pp. 342, 348, 368.

[86] Paoli, *Fortunes et infortunes*, p. 97; R. Bazin, *Le Duc de Nemours* (Paris, 1903), pp. 313, 330, 336, 376, 335; and see Cashmore, *Orléans Family, passim*.

[87] Cashmore, *Orleans Family*, pp. 12, 23.

[88] 'Orléans House: a history' (2008) <http://www.richmond.gov.uk/home/leisure_and_culture/arts/orleans_house_gallery/orleans_house_-_a_history.htm> [accessed 6 Nov. 2012].

[89] R. Cazelles, *Le Duc d'Aumale* (Paris, 1984), p. 289.

intimacy').[90] Perhaps because of the unpopularity of their father's Anglophilia in France, the rise of exclusive nationalism after 1850, or the self-sufficiency of large families, they lived in a French ghetto: 'Claremont was entirely French', wrote one of their courtiers. They did not interact with the English as easily as the Bourbons, the Bonapartes or Louis-Philippe himself. Aumale's neighbour, adviser and friend was a political hostess – 'dearest Frances' – Lady Waldegrave, chatelaine of Strawberry Hill. She helped to win him support in the London press.[91] However, she admired Napoleon III and the prince imperial, in part for their love of England: 'the Orléans princes have never had the pluck to take the same line', she complained in 1879.[92]

Marriages and funerals, for which hundreds specially crossed the Channel, helped the Orléans to remind France of their existence. The duchesse d'Orléans's sons the duc de Chartres and the comte de Paris were married – in both cases to first cousins, daughters of the prince de Joinville and the duc de Montpensier – in St. Raphael's church, Kingston, in 1863 and 1864 respectively: Marie-Amélie was cheered by spectators at the latter wedding, which was also attended by the prince and princess of Wales.[93] Thereafter, to the delight of the local tradesmen, the young couples settled in Morgan House, Ham and York House, Richmond (now Richmond Chamber of Commerce, the only Orléans residence in the borough which has not been demolished), respectively. On 24 August 1864 – the day before the feast of St. Louis – the comte and comtesse de Paris made a grand entry into their new residence: the vicar read an address of welcome. There were flags, music, cheering school-children, games, illuminations and fireworks.[94]

The funeral of Marie-Amélie on 3 April 1866 was far better attended than that of Louis-Philippe in 1850 – a sign of the respect which she inspired and of her close relationship to the royal families of Europe. Like that of Marie-Josephine in 1810, it was an act of defiance against the regime in Paris. It was attended by the general staff of Orleanism – Adolphe Thiers, Guizot, Charles de Rémusat and Tanneguy Duchâtel in the same carriage; the marquis d'Harcourt, the comte d'Haussonville, the journalists Saint-Marc Girardin and Lucien-Anatole Prevost-Paradol – as well as by her

[90] Marquise d'Harcourt, *Madame la duchesse d'Orléans* (Paris, 1859), p. 200.

[91] O. W. Hewett, *Strawberry Fair: a Biography of Frances, Countess Waldegrave 1821–79* (1956), pp. 236, 250.

[92] Hewett, *Strawberry Fair*, pp. 257, 265.

[93] Marquis de Flers, *Le Comte de Paris* (Paris, 1889), pp. 120, 123; <http://www.richmond. gov.uk/local_history_french_royal_residencies.pdf> [accessed 6 Nov. 2012]; Marie-Amélie, *Journal*, p. 579.

[94] Cashmore, *Orléans Family*, p. 20.

Figure 4.2. 'The chapelle ardente of Marie Amelie in Claremont House, Surrey, April 1866'. *Illustrated London News*, 14 April 1866, private collection.

Queen Marie-Amélie had lived in Claremont House as a guest of Queen Victoria, since her flight from France in 1848. From basement to attic the house was filled with her relations and courtiers.

grandson the king of the Belgians, the prince of Wales, her own family, and the ambassadors or ministers of Austria, Prussia, Bavaria, Belgium, Italy, Portugal, Saxony, Spain, Brazil and Mexico. A total of 150 carriages followed the procession, which was watched by all of Esher. The queen was buried in the dress she had worn when fleeing France in 1848.[95]

The Orléans returned to France when the laws of exile were repealed by Thiers's government in 1871. Incredibly, they were passing through the corridor connecting Dover station and the Lord Warden Hotel, on 20 March, at exactly the moment that the ex-Emperor Napoleon III arrived there from his prison in Germany. The Empress Eugénie curtsied. The men passed by without a word, merely raising their hats.[96] One exiled French court was going to London; another was leaving it. Aumale and Nemours, however, may have kept properties in England – not sure if they would have to return.[97]

Particularly after the deaths of the prince imperial in 1879 and of the legitimist claimant the comte de Chambord in 1883, the chances of the comte de Paris, whom French monarchists called Philippe VII, increased. He seemed moderate and reliable; the Third Republic appeared unstable and divided. In the elections of 1885 the right did well. On 14 May 1886 in the Hôtel de Matignon, rue de Varenne, he gave a lavish reception for 4,000 people – ambassadors, nobles and 'the elite of the world of science, the arts, literature and the magistrature', in honour of the wedding of his daughter Amélie to the duke of Braganza, heir to the throne of Portugal.

Republican authorities were offended. They had not been invited: moreover their carriages could not get through the streets to reach the Chamber of Deputies in time for a parliamentary debate. *Le Temps* claimed that there were two governments in France, republican and royalist: 'the pretender acting openly as a king has constituted around himself a veritable court'. A law was passed on 11 June exiling all heads of dynasties claiming the throne of France.[98]

The comte and comtesse de Paris returned to Twickenham, where (since they had sold York House, assuming they would not need it again) they lived in Sheen House and in Stowe in Buckinghamshire. The London region now contained two rival French courts: the Empress Eugénie in Farnborough and the comte de Paris in Twickenham. In Sheen House, Paris, although often accused of being weak, cosmopolitan and over-gentlemanly, frequently received men come to discuss French politics; in

[95] *The Golden Era*, 20 May 1866; *Illustrated London News*, 7 Apr. 1866, p. 331.
[96] Guest, *Napoleon III*, p. 174.
[97] Cashmore, *Orléans Family*, p. 15.
[98] Flers, *Comte de Paris*, pp. 289, 295, 297.

Figure 4.3: 'The funeral procession of Queen Marie Amelie, April 1866'. *Illustrated London News*, 14 April 1866, private collection. The queen's funeral was attended by the prince of Wales, the queen's grandson the king of the Belgians, other royal relations, ambassadors and Orleanists who had come especially from France to show support for the exiled dynasty. She was buried in the Catholic chapel of St. Charles Borromeo at Weybridge. After 1871 her remains were taken to France, where she is buried with Louis-Philippe in a marble tomb in the Orléans mausoleum at Dreux.

1887 the marquis de Breteuil described him as 'overwhelmed with visits and does not have the time to be bored or even to suffer from exile'.[99] The elegant Charles Swann, in Proust's *A la recherche du temps perdu*, has 'letters from Twickenham' in his pocket.

Another marriage, between Paris's next daughter Hélène and the son of the prince of Wales, the duke of Clarence, was favoured by Queen Victoria, still a family friend, but prevented by religion. As inflexible on faith as his cousin Chambord had been on the flag, Paris refused to let his daughter convert to Protestantism.[100]

Paris died at Stowe on 8 September 1894 and was buried in the church of St. Charles Borromeo, Weybridge. It was the last but one of the grandiose French dynastic funerals in England: Marie-Josephine in 1810; Louis-Philippe in 1850; Marie-Amélie in 1866; Napoleon III in 1873; the prince imperial in 1879 (the last would be the Empress Eugénie in 1920). Since he was the last serious pretender to the French throne, it can be said that, while Bonapartism had been buried at Chislehurst, royalism was buried in Weybridge.[101] One commentator, J. E. C. Bodley, who criticized his 'incapacity to touch the imagination of the people of France', called his death an event of 'complete insignificance'.[102]

After the funeral, however, his son, the duc d'Orléans, born in Twickenham in 1867, received 1,000 French royalists at the Grosvenor Hotel Victoria (since it was the station for Paris) – one of the last French royalist rallies in London. He held another at York House in Twickenham in January 1900. Princess Hélène married the duke of Aosta in St. Raphael's, Kingston on 25 June 1895; her sister Isabelle married a cousin, the duc de Guise, in 1899.

Orléans was rich, right-wing and unhappily married to an archduchess. Increasingly restless, he moved between England, Sicily and Belgium. Moreover, his pro-Boer attitude during the Boer War lost him many English friends. In 1906 he sold York House to a Parsee millionaire. Brussels became the headquarters of the House of Orléans, until the next comte de Paris returned to France, after the laws of exile were repealed, in 1950.[103]

[99] Marquis de Breteuil, *La Haute Société: journal secret 1886–9* (Paris, 1979), p. 123, 19 June 1887; cf. p. 361, 11 May 1888.

[100] Paoli, *Fortunes et infortunes*, pp. 295, 300.

[101] There were few royal mourners and little space devoted to it in the *Illustrated London News*, 15 Sept. 1894, p. 336.

[102] J. E. C. Bodley, *France* (2 vols., 1898), ii. 332, 347.

[103] Cashmore, *Orléans Family*, p. 23; Paoli, *Fortunes et infortunes*, pp. 295, 314, 318; E. Mension-Rigau, *L'Ami du prince: journal inédit d'Alfred de Gramont 1892–1915* (Paris, 2011), pp. 25, 98.

Figure 4.4. Case with volumes on the Galeries Historiques de
Versailles, reproducing pictures in the museum established there
in 1837 by Louis-Philippe (photo © Christie's and Co.).

These books were given to the Travellers Club in 1859, by Louis-Philippe's grandson the comte
de Paris, and his uncles the duc de Nemours, the prince de Joinville and the duc d'Aumale,
who lived in exile in Twickenham from 1848 to 1871. The last three had been elected honorary
members in 1849 'upon expulsion from France'; the first was appointed a visitor in 1858. At
the height of the Second Empire, such a present served to remind members of the Travellers
Club of the Orléans princes' existence. The Travellers Club's other prominent French members
included the comte d'Orsay, Talleyrand, Thiers and, elected in 1871, in their turn, as honorary
members on expulsion from France, Napoleon III, the prince imperial and the duc de Persigny.

In conclusion the exiled French courts in London were important
both for Franco-British relations and for French politics. They show that,
contrary to traditional narratives of hereditary enmity, Francophilia could
be as widespread in England as Francophobia. The large attendance at the
principal French royal and imperial funerals in London, and the ovations
given by Londoners to Louis XVIII in 1814 and to Napoleon III in 1855,
showed that French monarchs could be extremely popular in Britain.

Anglophilia, for its part, could be as characteristic of France as Anglophobia. All three dynasties remained Anglophiles in France. They initiated the pro-British foreign policies of the Restoration, the July Monarchy and the Second Empire. London and Paris were never closer than in the years between 1814 and 1870.

London was an incubator of French monarchies as well as Franco-British alliances. For almost a century London, as a capital of French royalism, Orleanism or Bonapartism, was as much part of French politics as it is today, as the seventh largest French city, with 100,000 French voters. National frontiers were porous. For many Frenchmen, due to their country's revolutions, Paris represented instability, London legitimacy — and lucidity. Its proximity, modernity and freedom made London a better observation post and spring-board than Vienna, residence of Napoleon's son the duc de Reichstadt in 1815–32, or Frohsdorf, the Austrian castle where the comte de Chambord lived.

Their years in London helped to modernize French pretenders and to ensure that, in 1814, 1848 and 1871, they were welcomed back in France. As their ceremonies and rallies in London suggest, the king or emperor 'over the water', could appear a plausible political alternative to a vulnerable regime in Paris. Indeed, French pretenders in London were often more realistic about French interests and French diplomacy than the government in Paris.[104] Exiles can be more lucid than men in power.

All three dynasties failed. However, all three had had more followers than would, at the beginning of his London years, the next French leader to establish his headquarters there — namely General de Gaulle.

[104] See, e.g., Bazin, *Duc de Nemours*, p. 442, for Nemours's expressions of horror at the folly of the French government in 1870, playing with the blood and future of France; or Louis-Napoléon's concern, in London before 1848, for the living conditions of French workers compared to Louis-Philippe's indifference; or, before 1814, Louis XVIII's frequently expressed desire for peace and European reconciliation.

5. The French in London during the 1830s: multidimensional occupancy

Máire Cross

Introduction

There is a long tradition of French political writers who, having visited London, then published their impressions of either the political system or the climate, or of both, Montesquieu and Voltaire being notable examples from the eighteenth century. Their remarks depended on a range of factors – personal tastes, experience as a visitor, knowledge gleaned from encounters in London, and strength of feeling about political, economic and social developments in France as well as in Britain. Much less attention has been paid to the French attitudes to encounters with their compatriots: much more common is the French interpretation of the British. As many previous studies have demonstrated, cross-national writers used their specific knowledge of their own home nation as a point of reference to offer a critique of the host country, with varying differences of opinion – Anglophile, Francophile, Anglophobic and Francophobic.[1] This chapter will address for the first time the question of how the subject of the French in London occurred in writers' accounts during the July Monarchy, a rather neglected era in comparative studies of Britain and France, but no less significant for our understanding of the French presence in London at that time. We shall see that the writers selected each reflect developments in France as well as events in London according to their individual standpoint. Yet they also reflect a multiple occupancy of London, simultaneously extending the boundaries of their knowledge as travellers beyond their real and imagined 'natural' home – in this case outside the French national space – but all the while interacting with what they find in London, including with other French citizens. Their residence in London reinforced their French identity as individuals while contributing generally to spreading knowledge of the city. Using the examples of Jules Michelet (1798–1874),

---

[1] For the French socialists' critique (including that of Flora Tristan) of England, 'the mother country of modern industrialism and capitalism where "unfettered individualism" found its fullest expression, and not in France', see K. W. Swart, '"Individualism" in the mid-19th century (1826–60)', *Journal of the History of Ideas*, xxiii (1962), 77–90, at p. 81. See also *La France et l'Angleterre au XIXe siècle*, ed. S. Aprile and F. Bensimon (Paris, 2006).

Map 5.1. Places mentioned in the text (Base map: 2013)

Key
1. Waterloo Road
2. The Crystal Palace

Alexis de Tocqueville (1805–59) and Flora Tristan (1803–44), I will suggest that their inclusion of their impressions of other French citizens is part of their physical and intellectual occupancy of London.

French writers visiting London have been analysed in many other genres of scholarship, of which three are of relevance to this investigation: urban studies, comparative studies of Britain and France, and the literature of travel writing. In the first instance, in a study of how cities were interpreted in the nineteenth century, a distinction is made between the approaches of ideologues towards London:

> Evaluations of urban society in Britain both reflected and helped to define foreign ideological orientations. Liberals tended to look on British cities favourably ... The rising strength of socialism on the European continent added a noticeably more radical flavor to the discussion of British towns by Frenchmen and Germans than was to be found in the writings of their British contemporaries.[2]

According to Lees, the July Monarchy was a particularly intense moment of scrutiny of London and Britain from the continent:

> After the 1840s, continental writers showed diminished interest in British society ... Frenchmen and Germans had flocked to Britain for over two decades in large part because they saw there not only promise but also problems, and as the difficulties stemming from the early phases of the industrial revolution abated so too did the desire among foreigners to make sense of the British experience ... As France and Germany started to compete with Britain in the race to industrialize, writers in these countries became increasingly concerned with their own urban societies.[3]

Since of the three French writers under consideration here – Michelet, Tocqueville and Tristan – the last-named is the one who wrote extensively about the phenomenal urban change in London, it is not surprising to find her included by Lees, who offers a useful outline of what London constituted as a geographical entity for her:

> At the very start ... she indicated her critical intentions by emphasizing the enormous contrasts presented by the major geographical subdivisions of the metropolis: the commercial 'City', the aristocratic West End, and the vast territories to the northeast and the south inhabited by often impoverished workers ... The rest of the work offered a series of impressions of London life, ranging from the slums of St. Giles to the race tracks at Ascot.[4]

---

[2] A. Lees, *Cities Perceived: Urban and American Thought, 1820–1940* (Manchester, 1985), pp. 58–60.

[3] Lees, *Cities Perceived*, pp. 68–9.

[4] Lees, *Cities Perceived*, pp. 61–2.

This brief analysis is found wanting, however, from a gender perspective. In spite of his continual reference to any French writer as 'Frenchman' throughout his study, Lees cites Tristan without referring once to the gender insight of her writing. His brief inclusion of Tristan concluded (without substantiating his claim) that her book had had some considerable success. The fact is, as Bédarida asserted, evidence of its impact has yet to come to light on the London side of the Channel, although it was published simultaneously in both countries in 1840.[5] Reactions to Tristan as a French visitor in Britain are equally difficult to detect, although there had been references to her as the author of *Peregrinations of a Pariah* in the London and regional press at the time of the trial of her husband, André Chazal, for the attempted murder of his wife in September 1838, most of the accounts taken second hand from the *Gazette des tribunaux*.[6] Under the heading, 'Life in London', one provincial newspaper quoted an extract from *Promenades dans Londres*, obliquely reporting at second hand the extract by Flora Tristan on 'Splashing Houses' in London from her sketch on 'les Puffs anglais', finishing with her comment: '"We give," says the writer, "the example above cited to show that in England, that classic land of hypocrisy, there is nothing neglected to give effect to their pretensions to importance, and to usurp confidence"'.[7]

In the second genre, comparative studies of Britain and France, the July Monarchy seems to be almost passed over; the strong moments of Franco-British relations being the Revolution of 1789 and the 1914–18 war. In one study, the nineteenth century is quite overlooked, with a jump from Waterloo to the crises over colonial expansion around Fashoda.[8] In addition, considering that the capital city was (and still is) often the only place visited or mentioned in accounts by excursionists in the early nineteenth century, it is surprising how eclipsed London becomes in accounts of the functioning of 'English' society.[9] Yet as we shall see, the 1830s saw an increase in traffic to and from the continent, with important developments

---

[5] For a more detailed account of the circumstances of its publication, see M. Cross, 'Cross-Channel reflections on Flora Tristan's *Promenades dans Londres*', in *Regards croisés sur la Grande-Bretagne: textes rassemblés à la mémoire de François Poirier*, ed. M. Parsons and F. Bensimon (*Revue française de civilisation britannique*, hors série, forthcoming).

[6] See *The Examiner*, 10 Apr. 1838; *Freeman's Journal*, 17, 22 Sept. 1838; *Champion and Weekly Herald*, 23 Sept. 1838; *Morning Post*, 4, 10 Feb. 1839; *Essex Standard*, 12 Sept. 1839.

[7] *Essex Standard*, 9 Dec. 1842; *West Kent Guardian*, 10 Dec. 1842.

[8] Aprile and Bensimon, *La France et l'Angleterre*, p. 6.

[9] 'England' and 'London' are highly ambiguous geographical terms, used interchangeably, as are the 'French revolutions' of 1789, 1830 and 1848. For a discussion of the imprecision and persistence of the French use of *Angleterre*/'England' as a political and geographical term, see Aprile and Bensimon's introduction to *La France et l'Angleterre*, p. 8.

of mass tourism, added to which visits from France to England in the nineteenth century are punctuated by political crises in France (1830, 1848–52, 1870–1) and stimulated, as our examples are, by curiosity about the 'English phenomenon' of industrialization. We shall see that the London of the period of the July Monarchy, as a capital city, was a space where the transmission of cultural differences was facilitated, and where stereotypes of the French endured and were retransmitted. Taking examples of individual French visitors' opinions of other French people in London we can enrich and nuance our understanding of the transmission and use of stereotypes. I suggest that this evidence expresses a doubly important national presence of the French in London: 'There can be a more nuanced study of utilization and representation of the other which sees beyond stereotypes of rejection or commemoration'.[10]

Of course, we are using individual trajectories, the momentary appearance of which in London is described even more briefly, and the impressions of which are largely anecdotal. Yet, as Aprile and Bensimon state:

> the accounts of writers or diplomats, men and women, told as individual trajectories, also reveal group mobility … these [examples] as such are only some of the many threads woven between the two countries … but their impact and meaning often go beyond the case of the individual concerned.[11]

Within the third genre, of the travelogue in literature, Flora Tristan's *Promenades dans Londres* is very much in the shadow of her better-known work on Peru, *Pérégrinations d'une paria*.[12] One author considers Flora Tristan as a woman who moves back into the past, in contrast to Tocqueville, whom he sees as a man who moves towards the future.[13] We shall see that Tristan was fully aware of the implications for the future after being in London.

---

[10] 'Hormis cette déclinaison des stéréotypes, il est de regard plus nuancés, des usages et de représentations de l'autre qui échappent au rejet ou même à la célébration' (Aprile and Bensimon, *La France et l'Angleterre*, p. 15). All translations are by Máire Cross unless otherwise stated.

[11] 'ce sont les trajectoires individuelles qui disent aussi la mobilité des hommes et des représentations à travers la vie d'écrivains ou de diplomates, d'hommes et de femmes … ces [exemples] ne sont, par nature, que quelques-uns des innombrables fils tissés entre les deux pays … Mais leur portée et leur signification dépassent souvent les cas individuels dont il est question' (Aprile and Bensimon, *La France et l'Angleterre*, pp. 16–17).

[12] For a literature-based study of Flora Tristan as female traveller in Peru, see C. Nesci, *Le Flâneur et les flâneuses: les femmes et la ville romantique* (Grenoble, 2007). In contrast, the absence of any women in a recent study of travel in 19th-century French literature is baffling, if not unacceptable (*Le Voyage et la mémoire au XIXe siècle*, ed. S. Moussa and S. Venayre (Paris, 2007)).

[13] O. Ette, *Literature on the Move*, trans. K. Vester (Amsterdam and New York, 2003), pp. 23, 58.

Figure 5.1. Flora Tristan.

This chapter also examines the cross-political attitudes of French visitors to London: Michelet, Tocqueville and Tristan did not move in the same political circles, but the sum of their presence enshrines French politics across political boundaries: 'The intention is for matters and people who never would nor could be associated otherwise, to be considered together'.[14]

Ideologies are not the only focus for the French in London; they were interested in their physical surroundings. To situate this study of being French in the London of the 1830s within current research on the link

---

[14] 'Il s'agit ... de mettre sous la même bannière des objets et des sujets qui n'auraient jamais pu ou dû se côtoyer' (Aprile and Bensimon, *La France et l'Angleterre*, p. 15).

between places and ideas, I refer to Ralph Kingston's recent assessment of the work of historians in the past ten years who have 'celebrated history's rediscovery of space and place'.[15] He asks whether bricks and mortar matter, or if space is just another 'language game'.[16] The spatial turn was necessary, he suggests, because of the missing element in the analysis of 'cultural historians [who] have been less interested in the uses of physical artefacts'.[17] I argue that cultural history alone is not sufficient to contain the experience of the French in London in the mid nineteenth century. The opinions of French visitors were informed as much by bricks and mortar as they were by people and ideas: they occupied London as writers with a specific social, economic, cultural and political background, commenting on their experiences according to their gender and circumstances of travel. Their expression of their French identity is clear, as they constantly referred as individual writers to a larger group through their adherence to a French singularity. Finally, and not least, the French writing on, and presence in, London also affirm the city's identity as a space where things happen. As such, an analysis of the historical identity of the city of London is an important dimension. What kind of a place was the London of the 1830s?

London in the 1830s

The July Monarchy was noteworthy for several developments relevant to the French in London. On one side of the Channel, the industrial might of Britain and urban improvement had put London in the lead as a cosmopolitan city; it attracted commercial activity and had an open-door policy to visitors seeking to discover the essence of the London success. Added to the interest in industrial Britain, the political upheavals that began and ended the July Monarchy, and political turmoil elsewhere on the continent, had resulted in the growth of traffic to London, where political exiles proliferated.[18] The 1830s saw the dawn of the new railway age, but it was also the time of the fastest stagecoach travel to and from the continent. If Britain was in the lead for industrial growth, the July Monarchy is known as an era of advances in political ideology in France, with the development of liberalism, socialism and feminism; London was by extension an important venue for these thinkers to try out their ideas. A microcosm of France's political life made up this French presence.

---

[15] R. Kingston, 'Mind over matter? History and the spatial turn', *Cultural and Social History*, vii (2010), 111–21, at p. 111.

[16] Kingston, 'Mind over matter?', p. 112.

[17] Kingston, 'Mind over matter?', p. 112.

[18] See *Exiles from European Revolutions: Refugees in Mid-Victorian England*, ed. S Freitag (Oxford, 2003).

While recent scholarship in cultural history has concentrated on literary and artistic expressions of the nature of London as a city (in particular the works of the canonical Dickens, Balzac and Flaubert), the voices of political commentators are of equal interest. As with the range of literary and cultural production, London inspired a wide number of French political and professional opinions: liberals, socialists, academics, diplomats, journalists and exiles. Furthermore, comparisons were constantly being made with Paris.[19] By the mid nineteenth century, if London's reputation as a world city had spread, it was because French visitors had played no small part in the construction of its identity.

There is no doubting the significance of London and its capacity for absorbing large numbers of visitors and for enabling them to stay and work, the trend accelerating to a peak in mid century when 'nearly forty per cent of all Londoners had been born elsewhere'.[20] Yet there were ways in which northern cities were of greater novelty interest, as they were the scene of railway expansion.[21] Politically London in the 1830s was eclipsed, as major events in radical politics and industrial expansion had shifted the focus from the city. Unlike Paris, the new phenomena of mass meetings and mass demonstrations, of which both French and British governments were so fearful, were also outside the capital.[22]

Jules Michelet

Michelet did not limit his stay to London or to England. The extracts from his journal during his trip of 1834 have been published only recently as *Voyages en Angleterre*, but include descriptions of northern France on his journey via Calais, Dover and Kent to London, where he stayed from 9 to 13 August, going on from there to Warwick, Newport, Bangor, Dublin, Belfast, Glasgow, Edinburgh, York, Manchester and Liverpool, and back to London before returning to Paris, all within a month from 5 August to 6 September. His account is dominated by his impressions of stagecoach travel, fellow passengers, bad weather, the beauty of the countryside, the historic contents of cathedrals and castles, and the dirt and poverty of the

---

[19] See, for instance, 'Paris and London, capitals of the 19th century', ed. D. Arnold, T. Rem and H. Waahlberg, special issue of *Synergies, Royaume-Uni et Irlande* (2010).

[20] F. Sheppard, 'London and the nation in the 19th century: the Prothero lecture', *Transactions of the Royal Historical Society*, 5th ser., xxxv (1985), 51–74.

[21] See Sheppard, 'London and the nation', p. 55.

[22] For a discussion on the role of Daniel O'Connell, admired and cited by Flora Tristan for holding 'monster' meetings, in the emergence of the crowd in Irish politics, see L. Colantonio, 'Mobilisation nationale, souveraineté populaire et normalisations en Irlande (années 1820–40)', *Revue d'histoire du XIXe siècle*, xli (2011), 53–69.

crowds in Dublin. While in London, Michelet encountered prominent Frenchmen, including the elder statesman and diplomat Talleyrand, and reported their conversations. The portrayal of political and economic differences between the two countries was of paramount interest for Michelet but the conversations reveal a further dimension to the French multiple occupancy of political space in London, one of different political experience and perspectives between generations, between a man who had had a long career in politics and an aspiring historian whose equally long career was ahead of him:

> At Mr de Talleyrand's for dinner at seven … After dinner Mr de Van de Veyer spoke of the important Lords' debate of the previous evening on the question of motherhood and poverty. The bishop of London, forceful and harsh, in favour of toughness; the bishop of Exeter mild and insinuating, spoke of weakness and human nature. In reality, English women fare badly from inheritance laws and are devoid of business resources, giving them more than one excuse for their moral weaknesses when they find themselves destitute and abandoned. This country is the most ideal in the whole world for Mr de Talleyrand. He is so English he makes those of us who are attached to France tremble.[23]

Michelet gave no indication about how he succeeded in gaining an invitation to dinner, but related with alarm Talleyrand's opinion that the likelihood of social unrest in Britain was remote, and that France could be spared industrialization, which was bad for national morale, and concentrate instead on developing its agricultural economy:

> There is nothing stirring. Inequality does not shock here; it is inherent in the customs. The younger son wants the eldest to inherit everything. The only poverty-stricken are the Irish; their destitution is caused solely by their addiction to gin … The big worker processions, the associations etc., are of no significance … The effect of industry is to weaken national morals. France should be agricultural.[24]

[23] 'Chez M. de Talleyrand, dîner à sept heures … Après le dîner, M. de Van de Veyer parle de l'importante discussion qui a eu lieu la veille à la Chambre des Lords, sur la question de la maternité dans le paupérisme. L'évêque de Londres fort et rude, pour la sévérité; l'évêque d'Exeter, doux et insinuant, en faveur de la faiblesse et de la nature. Dans la réalité, la femme anglaise, maltraitée par la loi de succession, étrangère aux ressources du commerce, a souvent quelque excuse de ses faiblesses dans une position malheureuse et délaissée. Ce pays-ci est l'idéal du monde pour M. de Talleyrand. Il est Anglais, à nous faire frémir, nous autres qui tenons encore à la France' (J. Michelet, *Voyages en Angleterre*, introduction by J.-F. Durand (Arles, 2005), pp. 35–6).

[24] 'Rien ne remue. L'inégalité ne choque pas ici; elle est dans les mœurs. Le cadet veut que l'aîné ait tout. Il n'y a ici, d'autre misérable que des Irlandais; leur abattement tient uniquement à l'usage du genièvre … Les grandes processions des ouvriers, les associations,

Michelet claims that Talleyrand listened more carefully to him after his objections:

> We left it there. He showed me much more consideration after this conversation. Doubtless he felt inwardly that my counter-argument was serious. If Britain becomes increasingly industrial, other countries which become increasingly specialized in agricultural production would become more and more confined, restricted in their output, dependent.[25]

Like so many visiting Britain, Michelet's awareness of the power of the industrialization process there led him to reflect on the future for France and its possible failure to industrialize. He shared his opinions on worker conditions and on class relations with a senior diplomat from Belgium: 'His opinion about this country is exactly the same as mine. Even despite the mix that the strength of trade has brought, England is synonymous with exclusion'.[26] If Michelet was anxious about exclusion he was also concerned about the increasing disparity between rich and poor, which he believed was exacerbated by the growth of cities. After his tour of Britain and Ireland he continued to write on the subject, comparing England unfavourably to France.[27]

Alexis de Tocqueville
In contrast to Michelet, the liberal Tocqueville displayed an admiration for the ability of the English aristocracy to adjust better than their counterparts

---

etc., n'ont rien de sérieux … L'industrie ne fait qu'affaiblir la moralité nationale. Il faut que la France soit agricole' (Michelet, *Voyages en Angleterre*, pp. 36–7).

[25] 'Nous en sommes restés là. Il m'a témoigné beaucoup plus d'égards après cette conversation. Sans doute, il sentait intérieurement que les objections étaient sérieuses. L'Angleterre deviendrait de plus en plus industrieuse, les autres pays de plus en plus agricoles dans la spécialité de leur principale production naturelle, c'est-à-dire de plus en plus bornés, limités, dépendants' (Michelet, *Voyages en Angleterre*, pp. 36–7).

[26] 'Son avis est exactement le mien sur ce pays-ci. Le synonyme de l'Angleterre, malgré le mélange même qu'amène par force le commerce, c'est: exclusion' (Michelet, *Voyages en Angleterre*, p. 38).

[27] For a discussion of Michelet's perspective on the 'English model' of industrialization compared to that of Buret, see F. Vatin, 'Modèle et contre-modèle anglais de Jean-Baptiste Say à Eugène Buret: révolution industrielle et question sociale (1815–40)', in Aprile and Bensimon, *La France et l'Angleterre*, pp. 69–88. The conclusion ends: 'Obnubilés par la question du paupérisme industriel, qui traduisait leur défense d'un mode productif ancien contre le spectre de la fabrique, les observateurs français de l'Angleterre semblent ainsi avoir été incapables de percevoir dans les années 1830–1840, les prémices d'une transformation en profondeur du statut économique, social et politique de la classe ouvrière britannique qui s'affirmera dans la seconde moitié du siècle' (Vatin, 'Modèle', p. 88). Tristan's analysis of the workers in London was different again, as she recognized the growth of the new class. Vatin does not include her in his discussion.

in France, and for the reasonable nature of English radicals compared to the French. Arriving in England first in 1833 on a family visit as the husband of Mary Mottley, by the time of his second visit in the summer of 1835 he was a famous author: his *Democracy in America* had been published and translated. Like Michelet he expressed great misgivings about civil unrest. Interestingly, both authors were prompted to write about the treatment of women, revealing their views of gender relations of their time. Tocqueville linked his opinion of French social matters to a parliamentary enquiry in London. He was dubious about the proposed freedom to bring a paternity suit: he considered that the lack of it in France could be a suitable brake on woman's moral behaviour:

> Illegitimate children. 3 September 1833. Enquiry of paternity. For a long time I held the view that the French law forbidding this favoured bad morals. Now I am of a diametrically opposite opinion. Good morals in a people depend almost always on the women and not on the men. One can never stop men attacking. The point is therefore to make things so that they will be resisted ... All the laws which make the position of a woman who falls more comfortable are therefore eminently immoral; for example laws such as ours relating to foundlings. Further, the law which permits enquiry of paternity, might well serve to restrain the men, but it greatly diminishes the strength of resistance among the women, which must be avoided at all costs. Any people which permits the enquiry of paternity is forced to believe the woman on oath, for how else can a fact of this nature be proved? The woman thus has an infallible way of diminishing the consequences of her error and even has a way of making it profitable. Thus in England a girl of the people who has illegitimate children generally marries more easily than a chaste girl.[28]

Tocqueville showed some more awareness of grass-roots movements than Talleyrand but admired the English radicals as they were in favour of consensual non-violent means, they respected property and religious beliefs and they were well read. On the other hand:

> The most characteristic trait of the French Radical is a wish to use the power of some to secure the happiness of the greatest number, and his most important means of government is material force and contempt for the law ... The French Radical has the greatest mistrust for property; and, ready to violate it in practice, he attacks it in theory ... One of the principal characteristics of the French Radical Party is the flaunting not only of anti-Christian opinions, but also of the most anti-social philosophical ideas ... The French Radical is almost always very poor, often boorish, and still more presumptuous, and profoundly

---

[28] A. de Tocqueville, 'Illegitimate children', 3 Sept. 1833 (*Journeys to England & Ireland (1833 & 1835)*, ed. J. P. Mayer, trans. G. Lawrence and K. P. Mayer (1958), pp. 62–3).

ignorant of political science, who understands nothing but the use of force, and deals in empty words and superficial generalisations. In brief, at present I think that an enlightened man, of good sense and good will, would be a Radical in England. I have never met those three qualities together in a French Radical.[29]

Comparison of the political conversations of French observers from very different political perspectives brings out the diversity of opinions and the opportunities that London afforded. In the first case Michelet is entertained in the home of France's most senior diplomat: in the second, Tocqueville is consulted in Westminster about parliamentary reform. Michelet and Tocqueville both referred briefly in passing to the French context of women, poverty and public morality; in neither case was women's emancipation their priority, although the effect of poverty on women was highly visible to these visitors.

Flora Tristan

Women's emancipation and London's slums were of particular interest to our third example, one of London's most singular visitors of the July Monarchy, Flora Tristan. Unlike Michelet and Tocqueville, who left brief traces of their impressions of London within other works that were published posthumously, Tristan made London the central theme of what was to be one of her major and most innovative works: *Promenades dans Londres*. While her knowledge of London was not always accurate, she wrote it specifically as a visitor and as a writer, desirous of confirming her position as a Frenchwoman who had already gained literary success and, as we have seen earlier, notoriety. Her London study subsequently secured her recognition as an original thinker among socialists. In her previous travel account as an unhappily married woman seeking her inheritance from her father's Spanish-Peruvian family and entering the literary profession, she had stressed her position as an outcast.[30] Others who have examined her originality as a female writer have emphasized equally that she overcame her lack of status by vaunting her identity as a pariah in a patriarchal society.[31] Her study of London reveals quite a different side to her self-portrayal: this time because her different national perspective equipped her with an intellectual authority which she shared with her contemporary compatriots, such as knowledge of the history of relations between Britain and France, the legacy

[29] Tocqueville, 'Radical', 29 May 1835 (*Journeys to England*, pp. 86–7).

[30] D. Nord, 'The female pariah: Flora Tristan and the paradox of homelessness', in *Home and its Dislocations in 19th-Century France*, ed. S. Nash (New York, 1993), pp. 215–30.

[31] C. Nesci, 'Flora Tristan's urban odyssey: notes on the missing flâneuse and her city', *Journal of Urban History*, xxvii (2001), 709–22.

of the French Revolution and potential for further political upheaval, and the body of literature that had already been published by French authors on social conditions in Britain. For this reason a brief comparison with impressions left by Michelet and Tocqueville is of use for us to contextualize her interest in London as part of a body of French thinking.

Promenades dans Londres contains specific references to the French in London as well as indirect references, revealing many dimensions to their occupancy of the 'monster city' as Flora Tristan called it. We shall see how she achieved this by using the 'bricks and mortar' of London, thereby creating her own space in French politics. She expresses her national identity within her political reaction to the layout of the city of London, but in spite of her close scrutiny her observations are fragmented; she strategically distances herself from French viewpoints as well as British ones, yet she also aligns herself with other French writers in her study of London. In other words, her multiple occupancy manifests both union with and fragmentation from the other foreigners present within London. As a result it is difficult to categorize her study of London, as can be seen in the limited extent to which her work on the city has been read, as a survey of urban change, a feminist political tract and as a travelogue. Tristan creates ambiguity and opacity around the spaces she occupies by shifting viewpoints and turning ideas on their heads.

Expanding the French presence in social surveys of London

One set of French people that Tristan made visible in her study was that of writers – Eugène Buret, Gustave de Beaumont and Alexandre Parent-Duchâtelet being notable examples – who, like the legislators discussed by Michelet and Tocqueville, were troubled by the corruption of public morals.[32] She too was perturbed: 'In London every class of society is rotten to the core. In the child, vice precedes experience; in the old man it outlives potency. Not one family has escaped the taint of the diseases associated with debauchery'.[33] But she claimed to be even more outraged by the indifference with which London treated some of its inhabitants, and identified certain

---

[32] F. Tristan, *Promenades dans Londres, ou l'aristocratie et les prolétaires anglais*, ed. F. Bédarida (Paris, 1978), p. 135. Bédarida's 1978 edition provides very useful historical details from studies of poverty by Tristan's contemporaries – works by doctors as well as political economists – to which she would have had access. Of the two translations, *Flora Tristan's London Journal 1840* (trans. D. Palmer and G. Pincetl, 1980) and *The London Journal of Flora Tristan, 1842* (trans. J. Hawkes, 1982), Hawkes's 1842 version is mainly used here, as it is the 1842 edition that Bédarida annotated.

[33] 'A Londres, toutes les classes sont profondément corrompues: dans l'enfance, le vice devance l'âge; dans la vieillesse il survit à des sens éteints, et les maladies de la débauche ont pénétré dans toutes les familles' (Tristan, *Promenades*, p. 134 (Hawkes translation, p. 88)).

categories particularly worthy of pity: 'In the monster city there is no compassion for the victims of vice: the fate of the prostitute inspires no more pity than that of the Irishman, the Jew, the worker or the beggar'.[34]

She was not simply concerned with condemning moral decadence. By drawing attention to the outcast who had no place in London she was creating ample occupancy for herself, going beyond her role as a visitor and in doing so defining her remit of a writer who was taking on an impossible task: 'My pen refuses to describe the depths of depravity and perversion to which men sink when they are surfeited with material pleasures, when they live only through their senses and their souls are dead, their hearts withered, their minds a desert'.[35]

If Tristan saw herself as included among French authors who had already contributed to the growing trend for sociological surveys, she was also conscious of her status as a temporary occupant of London; she had to negotiate her way past national prejudice to claim a position of authority as a foreign resident to speak out on what was considered to be a rather delicate and inappropriate matter for a foreigner and a woman, prostitution:

> National vanity makes us want the country where Providence ordained our birth to reign supreme. This malevolent disposition towards other nations, the bitter fruit of past conflicts, constitutes the greatest obstacle to progress and often prevents us from acknowledging the causes of the evils which the foreign visitor calls to our attention. Then the old hatred revives, and we challenge him to furnish proof for phenomena as obvious as a Thames fog! All nations have a common interest, but as yet only a few enlightened individuals understand this, so the foreigner who dares to criticise is taken for an enemy who slanders us.[36]

Anticipating the possible suspicion and antagonism that her study would produce, Tristan used her knowledge of French and English writers,

---

[34] 'Dans la ville monstre, on est sans commisération pour les victimes du vice; le sort de la fille publique n'inspire pas plus de pitié que celui de l'Irlandais, du Juif, du prolétaire et du mendiant' (Tristan, *Promenades*, p. 134 (Hawkes translation, p. 89)).

[35] 'La plume se refuse à tracer les égarements, les turpitudes dans lesquelles se laissent entraîner les hommes blasés, qui n'ont que des sens et dont l'âme est inerte, le cœur flétri, l'esprit sans culture' (Tristan, *Promenades*, p. 134 (Hawkes translation, p. 88)).

[36] 'L'amour-propre national, qui nous porte à désirer que le pays où la Providence nous a fait naître prime toute la terre, cette disposition malveillante envers les autres nations, fruit amer des luttes passées et qui forme le plus grand obstacle au progrès, nous empêche souvent de reconnaître les causes des maux que l'étranger nous signale; l'esprit de haine se réveille alors, et nous le sommons de fournir des preuves pour des faits aussi manifestes que les brouillards de la Tamise; car l'unité de l'intérêt des nations n'étant encore conçue que par un petit nombre de personnes avancées, l'étranger qui ne nous approuve pas est pris pour un ennemi qui nous injurie' (Tristan, *Promenades*, p. 135 (Hawkes translation, p. 89)).

acquired in London, to back up her study of what she considered to be the worst form of exploitation, particularly exacerbated in the capital: 'Prostitution is found everywhere, but in London it is so widespread that it seems like an omnivorous monster'.[37] In this manner, there is a French dimension added even when discussing those who are London's social outcasts, but who are the object of French interest: 'In London a prostitute has no right to anything but the hospital, and then only of there is an *empty* bed for her' (Tristan's emphasis).[38] The location of the social outcasts that Tristan describes here was as distant as could be from French diplomats' conversations in Talleyrand's dining-room, but her cross-referencing of French fellow writers anchors her firmly among the French intelligentsia in London.

Approaches to London

Promenades dans Londres was not the only publication by Tristan resulting from her knowledge of London. Already in 1837 she had succeeded in getting into print two short articles on her observations of the city in the *Revue de Paris*. Describing the inauspicious approach to London, in 1837 Tristan conveyed a sense of disorientation at the openness, and disappointment in London's architecture:

> I had arrived almost before I noticed: I had thought that wide avenues and great monuments appropriately scaled for a capital would announce our proximity to London ages before arriving. I was really astonished to get there by bare narrow lanes and to find myself in the city when I thought I was still going through one of the villages along the way. The indistinct boundaries of a city bereft of ramparts are a disappointment. I knew that I was going to visit an open city, but who would have guessed the extent to which the outskirts of London are indistinguishable from the most humble of villages?[39]

---

[37] 'La prostitution existe partout, mais à Londres elle est un fait si immense qu'on la voit comme un monstre qui doit tout engloutir' (Tristan, *Promenades*, p. 135 (Hawkes translation, p. 89)).

[38] 'A Londres, la prostituée n'a droit qu'à l'hôpital, et encore quand il s'y trouve une place *non occupée*' (Tristan, *Promenades*, p. 135 (Hawkes translation, p. 89)).

[39] 'Je suis arrivée presque sans m'en douter: je me figurais que Londres me serait annoncé de loin par des avenues, des monumens [sic] en rapport avec ses proportions colossales et la hauteur de sa fortune. J'ai été très étonnée d'y arriver par des chemins nus, étroits, et de me trouver dans la ville lorsque je croyais traverser encore un des villages de la route. Les limites indécises des villes privées d'enceinte préparent au voyageur de pareilles déceptions. Je savais que je me rendais dans une ville ouverte; mais qui eût pensé que les approches de Londres ne se distingueraient pas de celles du plus humble des villages?' ('Lettres à un architecte anglais', *Revue de Paris* (1837), i. 37, 134–9; ii. 38, 280–95, 135).

Here she was writing for fellow French visitors, curious to see the new phenomenon of the fastest growing urban powerhouse sprawl.[40] A city of opportunity, the scale of the city and its consequences is the first striking feature, but its boundaries are unclear and distances are enormous:

> London, the centre of capital and business for the British Empire, constantly attracts new inhabitants; but the resulting advantages for industry are offset by the disadvantages caused by vast distances: the city is several cities in one and it has grown too large for people to keep in touch or to get to know one another. How can one maintain close relations with one's father, daughter, sister, friends when, in order to pay an hour's call, one must spend three hours and eight or ten francs in cab fares to make the trip?[41]

At first sight it is a city of darkness:

> the docks, the huge wharves and warehouses which cover twenty-eight acres of land; the domes, towers and buildings looming out of the fog in fantastic shapes; the monumental chimneys belching their black smoke to the heavens to proclaim the existence of a host of mighty industries; these confused images and vague sensations press almost unendurably upon the troubled soul.[42]

And of dazzling light:

> But it is especially at night that London should be seen; then, in the magic light of millions of gas-lamps, London is superb! Its broad streets stretch to infinity; its shops are resplendent with every masterpiece that human ingenuity can devise; its multitudes of men pass ceaselessly to and fro. To see all this for the first time is an intoxicating experience.[43]

---

[40] In the 19th century London became the home of political refugees and the 'barometer for the whole of Europe', and 'in the spring of 1829 there was an abrupt increase in the numbers of French in London' (P. Ackroyd, *London: the Biography* (2000), p. 705).

[41] 'Londres, centre des capitaux et des affaires de l'Empire britannique, attire incessamment de nouveaux habitants; mais les avantages que, sous ce rapport, il offre à l'industrie sont balancés par les inconvénients qui résultent de l'énormité des distances: cette ville est la réunion de plusieurs villes; son étendue est devenue trop grande pour qu'on puisse se fréquenter ou se connaître. Comment entretenir des relations suivies avec son père, sa fille, sa sœur, ses amis, quand, pour aller leur faire une visite d'une heure, il faut en employer trois pour le trajet et dépenser huit ou dix francs de voiture?' (Tristan, *Promenades*, pp. 67–8 (Palmer translation, p. 3)).

[42] 'les docks, immenses entrepôts ou magasins qui occupent vingt-huit acres de terrain; ces dômes, ces clochers, ces édifices auxquels les vapeurs donnent des formes bizarres; ces cheminées monumentales qui lancent au ciel leur noire fumée et annoncent l'existence des grandes usines; l'apparence indécise des objets qui vous entourent: toute cette confusion d'images et de sensations trouble l'âme – elle en est comme anéantie' (Tristan, *Promenades*, p. 66 (Hawkes translation, p. 17)).

[43] 'Mais c'est le soir surtout qu'il faut voir Londres! Londres, aux magiques clartés de millions de lampes qu'alimente le gaz, est resplendissant! Ses rues larges, qui se prolongent

Recognizing it as the most beautiful city in the world Tristan, as a foreigner, was nevertheless intent on uncovering what lay behind appearances of grandeur:

> no foreigner can fail to be entranced when he first enters the British capital. But I must warn you that the spell fades like a fantastic vision, a dream in the night; the foreigner soon recovers his senses and opens his eyes to the arid egotism and gross materialism which lurk behind that ideal world.[44]

Generalizations and stereotypes

Flora Tristan saw London as a very separate spatial entity, governed principally but not uniquely by a climate that created types of people: 'There is so great a difference between the climate of England, of London particularly, and that of countries on the continent in the same latitudes, that before I could talk about Londoners and their characteristics, I had to work out which aspects they owed to their climate'.[45] Her negative opinions about London and Londoners, conveyed throughout her short chapters, are well known and often commented upon.[46] Just as she was influenced by her overall opinion of London as an enormous physical space, a monster city, Tristan's basis of comparison was another city and another people – Paris and its citizens, by far superior in her eyes:

> Now it is not my intention to analyse the many and diverse factors which modify human individuality, or to examine the part played by climate, education, diet, customs, religion, government, profession, wealth, poverty, history in making one nation serious, arrogant and heroic, and another convivial, cultured and fond of pleasure; in making Parisians lively, gregarious, frank and brave, and

---

à l'infini; ses boutiques, où des flots de lumière font briller de mille couleurs la multitude des chefs-d'œuvre que l'industrie humaine enfante; ce monde d'hommes et de femmes qui passent et repassent autour de vous: tout cela produit, la première fois, un effet enivrant!' (Tristan, *Promenades*, p. 66 (Hawkes translation, p. 17)).

[44] 'il n'est point d'étranger qui ne soit fasciné en entrant dans la métropole britannique; mais, je me hâte de le dire, cette fascination s'évanouit comme la vision fantastique, comme le songe de la nuit; l'étranger revient bientôt de son enchantement: du monde idéal il tombe dans tout ce que l'égoïsme a de plus aride et l'existence de plus matériel' (Tristan, *Promenades*, p. 67 (Hawkes translation, p. 17)).

[45] 'Il existe une si grande différence entre le climat de l'Angleterre, de Londres particulièrement, et celui des pays du continent situés sous les mêmes parallèles que, désirant parler du caractère des Londoniens, j'ai dû remarquer les effets qui sont propres à leur climat' (Tristan, *Promenades*, p. 74 (Hawkes translation, p. 24)).

[46] See, for instance, Jeremy Jennings's summary of the observations of Flora Tristan in his *Revolution and the Republic: a History of Political Thought in France since the 18th Century* (Oxford, 2011), pp. 151, 194.

Londoners grave, unsociable, suspicious and timid, fleeing like rabbits before policemen armed with truncheons.[47]

Tristan did convey to her readers her awareness of the limitations of her study, caused by the enormity of the city of London but equally by the extent of her investigation: 'For such a study the life of not just one but several German philosophers would be too short'.[48] She admitted the danger of generalizations: in her chapter on the character of Londoners, immediately preceding that of foreigners in London, she wrote: 'I shall therefore confine myself to a rough sketch of the general character of the Londoner, and I make no claim that it holds good for everybody'.[49] Even so, she wrote about the French in categories, as we shall see. Her inclusion of prostitution, giving a feminist dimension, has also been examined by scholars, but her comments on the French in London reveal another aspect to her feminism and to her bias. She is equally severe about the French scoundrels and rogues, of whom Napoleon was the greatest.

Her authority as a writer derived from her claim to convey her 'first' impressions of London as an unbiased 'outsider'. Her ability to convey to readers a unique account relied on that stance of novelty, an artificial one since she had already been to London on more than one occasion and in more than one role, details of which are obscured by her silence, like the swirling fog of London to which she compared the murkiness of prostitution. She dated her visits and increasing familiarity with her subject by indicating a progressive change for the worse in the city:

> I have made four visits to England in recent years to study the manners and morals of its people. In 1826 I found the country very rich. In 1831 it was considerably less so, and I saw marked signs of unrest. In 1835 the middle classes were feeling the strain as well as the workers. In 1839 I returned to find the

---

[47] 'Je n'ai point l'intention d'analyser les nombreuses et les diverses influences qui modifient l'individualité humaine, d'examiner le degré d'action que peuvent avoir le climat, l'éducation, la nourriture, les mœurs, la religion, le gouvernement, les professions, la richesse, la misère, les événements de la vie qui font que tel peuple est grave, enflé d'héroïsme et d'orgueil, et tel autre bouffon, passionné pour les arts et les jouissances de la vie; qui rendent les Parisiens gais, communicatifs, francs et braves, et les Londoniens sérieux, insociables, défiants et craintifs, fuyants comme des lièvres devant des *policemen* armés d'un petit bâton' (Tristan, *Promenades*, pp. 74–5 (Hawkes translation, p. 24–5)).

[48] 'Ce serait là une longue étude à laquelle la vie de plusieurs philosophes allemands ne suffirait pas' (Tristan, *Promenades*, p. 75 (Hawkes translation, p. 25)).

[49] 'Je me bornerai donc à esquisser à grands traits le caractère général des habitants de Londres, sans prétendre à l'universalité du type' (Tristan, *Promenades*, p. 75 (Hawkes translation, p. 25)).

people of London sunk in deepest poverty; disaffection and discontent were rife at every level of society.[50]

She indicated her awareness of the manner in which the French formed a dominant presence among the crowds of foreigners arriving:

> I am told that more than fifteen thousand Frenchmen live in London, to say nothing of all the Germans and Italians. Recent events have brought an influx of Spaniards and Poles as well, though I cannot be sure how many there are … it is worthy of remark that the English call all foreigners *Frenchmen* no matter what their country of origin [Tristan's emphasis].[51]

Tristan's categories of the French in London

If her figures were imprecise, Tristan knew what attracted incomers: exile, work or tourism. She categorized them by their moral worth, distinguishing above all between the honest and dishonest. On the one hand, foreigners of all classes engaged in business transactions, confident of their role in contributing to the bustling activity of the metropolis, and earned their living by the sweat of their brow:

> With the exception of refugees, all these foreigners are here *on business*; among them are numerous craftsmen in various trades, honest folk working hard to maintain their families; then there are wholesale and retail merchants, teachers dedicated to their profession, theatrical performers, doctors, members of the diplomatic corps, and lastly a floating population of travellers who stay in the country no more than a month or two. As for those who *settle down* … even the most touchy Englishman could never question their *respectability*, so they enjoy the esteem which is their due; the same is true of tourists, whose reason for being in England is plain for all to see.[52]

---

[50] 'Quatre fois j'ai visité l'Angleterre, toujours dans le but d'étudier ses mœurs et son esprit. En 1826 je la trouvai très-riche. En 1831, elle était beaucoup moins, et de plus je la vis très-inquiète. En 1835, la gêne commençait à se faire sentir dans la classe moyenne aussi bien que parmi les ouvriers. En 1839, je rencontrai à Londres une misère profonde dans le peuple; l'irritation était extrême, le mécontentement général' (Tristan, *Promenades*, p. 61 (Hawkes translation, p. 12)).

[51] 'On m'a assuré que plus de quinze mille Français habitent Londres; les Allemands et les Italiens y sont aussi en grand nombre; depuis les derniers événements, les Espagnols et les Polonais y affluent: il me serait impossible de préciser le chiffre de chacune de ces émigrations … il est à remarquer que jamais, en Angleterre, le peuple n'a désigné l'étranger, de quelque partie du continent qu'il fût, que par l'épithète de *Français (Frenchman)* [Tristan's emphasis]' (Tristan, *Promenades*, pp. 78–9 (Hawkes translation, p. 29)). Bédarida adds that, according to the only available census figures which date from 1851, the number of foreigners indicated by Tristan was much lower than the reality.

[52] 'A l'exception des réfugiés, tous ces étrangers sont venus *pour affaires*: parmi eux se trouvent un grand nombre d'ouvriers de divers métiers, honnêtes gens qui travaillent

While there is no specific mention of the French among the honest foreigners, Tristan is amused to uncover how the less honest took liberties with being French in London and tricked the English:

> It is droll to see a commercial traveller, a hairdresser, or some other totally uneducated person sign one of the noblest names of France with such ease and aplomb that one would think he had been *born* the Chevalier de Choiseul or the Vicomte de Montmorency ... The mania for titles has now reached such a pitch in London that *kept women* and even *prostitutes* use them *as a ladder to fortune*; these ladies insist on being addressed as Madame la marquise de —, Madame la baronne de —, Madame la comtesse de —, and so on; they do not scruple to use the coat-of-arms of their adopted family ... Naturally in a country where *appearance is everything*, a prostitute got up in all the trappings of the nobility is bound to make her mark – and sometimes makes her fortune into the bargain ... Nobody but the English could be taken in by such *humbug!*[53]

Tristan reported that courtesans were among those with false French titles from among whom the French police recruited spies to report on French activities in London, another form of French occupancy of the city associated with exiles and the subject of other chapters in this volume. Tristan's national prejudices were what Bédarida terms her 'patriotisme de gauche', and contrasted with her universalist aspirations, in the name of which she claimed that she wished to enlighten John Bull about foreigners in London:

> I wanted the English to know us better, not to be taken in by appearances, but to learn how to distinguish the well-informed man from the charlatan,

---

laborieusement pour nourrir leur famille; puis ce sont des négociants faisant le commerce en gros ou en détail, des artistes attachés aux théâtres, des professeurs voués à l'enseignement, des médecins, le corps diplomatique, et enfin une masse flottante de voyageurs qui ne séjournent dans le pays qu'un mois ou deux. Quant à ceux qui sont *établis* ... l'Anglais le plus ombrageux ne saurait élever aucun doute sur leur *respectabilité*, ils jouissent donc de l'estime qui leur est due; il en est de même des voyageurs dont le séjour en Angleterre est motivé aux yeux de tous' (Tristan, *Promenades*, p. 79 (Hawkes translation, p. 30)).

[53] 'Il est plaisant de voir un commis voyageur, un garçon coiffeur, ou tout autre individu sans la moindre éducation, signer les plus beaux noms de France avec un aplomb et une aisance qui peuvent faire croire qu'il s'est toujours appelé le *chevalier de Choiseul* ou le *vicomte de Montmorency* ... Enfin à Londres, la manie des titres est poussée si loin que les *femmes entretenues*, et mêmes les *filles publiques* s'en servent comme *moyens de succès*: ces dames se font appeler Madame la marquise de ***, Madame la baronne de ***, Madame la comtesse de ***; elles font usage, sans façon, des armes de la famille dont elles ont pris le nom et le titre ... On conçoit que dans un pays ou *l'apparence est tout* une prostituée, ainsi affublée de l'enveloppe aristocratique, doit jouer un certain rôle ... et parfois faire fortune ... Il n'y a qu'un Anglais au monde pour croire à de pareilles *blagues*! [Tristan's emphasis]' (Tristan, *Promenades*, p. 80 (Hawkes translation, pp. 30–1)).

the nobleman from the impostor, the duke from his valet and the duchess from her maid. I would like *John Bull* to give up his absurd recriminations and stop venting his wrath on an entire nation when he has nobody to blame but *himself!*[54]

Tristan had reserved her most caustic remarks for a particular set of French rogues in her 1840 edition, but in that of 1842 reduced the passage to a footnote referring to the abortive coup by Louis-Napoléon when he tried to land in Boulogne and invade France:

> In the first edition of my book this chapter was much longer; in it I mentioned Prince Louis-Napoleon Bonaparte and his retinue. My readers will recall that in 1840, M Louis Bonaparte was in London posing as the *Pretender*; he had himself addressed as '*Your Highness*' and had a *court*; in a word, he set up as a celebrity and made himself ridiculous … The farcical episode which took place at Boulogne three weeks after the publication of my book, proved that I was right in my judgement of this aspirant to royalty and the crowd of sycophants who encouraged his folly because they were making a living from it.[55]

Travel and French history in bricks and mortar

A London place name served as an important reference point for Tristan's interpretation of another Napoleon. Ironically, Waterloo Road was the area that Tristan visited where prostitutes plied their trade, but it was in the context of the 1815 battle that defeated France's despot that Tristan linked the London place name Waterloo, and all that it evoked, to the French:

> The word *Waterloo* appears all over London: bridges, streets, public squares and monuments bear its name; it is given to ships of the Royal Navy and the merchant fleet, the big shops adopt it as their sign, and manufacturers name their latest fabrics after it, so that this one word has become, so to speak, the *coat of arms* of England, its heraldic device, the symbol of its renown. Everybody understands that Waterloo is the greatest feat of arms that England has ever

[54] 'J'ai désiré apprendre aux Anglais à nous connaître; à ne pas être *dupes* de grossières apparences; à distinguer le savant du charlatan, l'homme véritablement noble de l'intriguant, le duc de son valet, la duchesse de sa soubrette. Je voudrais que *John Bull* n'exhalât jamais de ces plaintes absurdes, et que, dans son irritation, il n'injuriât pas toute la nation, lorsqu'il ne doit s'en prendre qu'à *lui-même*' (Tristan, *Promenades*, p. 83 (Hawkes translation, p. 34)).

[55] 'Dans la première édition ce chapitre avait beaucoup plus d'étendue. J'y parlais du prince Louis-Napoléon Bonaparte et de son entourage. On se rappelle que M. Louis Bonaparte, en 1840, se posait à Londres comme un *prétendant*; il se faisait appeler *Altesse*, avait une *cour*; en un mot, il tranchait du personnage et jouait un rôle ridicule … La burlesque équipée de Boulogne, qui eut lieu vingt jours après la publication de mon ouvrage, prouva que j'avais bien jugé cet aspirant à la royauté et cette foule de gens qui flattaient sa folie parce qu'ils en vivaient' (Tristan, *Promenades*, p. 83 (Hawkes translation, p. 35)).

been called upon to accomplish, and that it alone represents her past power and sums up her entire glory.[56]

In a curious digression into French history Flora Tristan poses a counter-argument to the interpretation of Waterloo, suggesting that it was a blow for freedom as important as the taking of the Bastille or the July Revolution of 1830. The battle was a forbidden subject, associated in its immediate aftermath with the enemies of the 1814 Restoration monarchy, but somehow, as the memory of military defeat had waned as peace became the norm between France and Britain, it was less feared by the July Monarchy when it began to appear as a symbol of a glorious defeat, one associated with the republican notion of the nation at war to defend liberty: 'The essential question about the Battle of Waterloo is this: why and how did its historical meaning become inverted from the 1830s through depiction in literary works, engravings and paintings? How did a decisive defeat become transformed into a quasi-victory?'[57]

The railways
In her French-inspired explanation, as a French visitor, of the social problems and poverty that caused prostitution in London; in her description of the miserable nondescript outskirts that greeted the French visitor in the approach to magnificent modern London; in her mockery of French *poseurs* using titles; and in her interpretation of French history insisting that Wellington was a hero for France, Flora Tristan turned ideas on their heads and assumed a unique and somewhat quirky position hovering between contempt and admiration for the capital. By way of conclusion I shall briefly refer to her most insightful reflections, which occur in a chapter entitled 'Les tribulations de Londres'. Almost as an aside Tristan introduces a spatial dimension that would affect the future of the cultural aspect of French occupancy of London: the increasing ease of cross-Channel links.

---

[56] 'Le mot *Waterloo* paraît à Londres en tous lieux; les ponts, les rues, les places publiques et les monuments portent ce nom; il est donné aux vaisseaux de l'Etat, aux paquebots du commerce; les grands magasins le prennent pour enseigne, les fabricants l'appliquent à leurs étoffes nouvelles, enfin ce mot est devenu, pour ainsi dire, l'*écu* de l'Angleterre, son signe héraldique, le symbole de sa renommée. Tous comprennent que Waterloo est le plus grand fait auquel l'Angleterre a été appelée à concourir, que ce fait à lui seul représente sa puissance passée et résume sa gloire!' (Tristan, *Promenades*, p. 217 (Hawkes translation, p. 188)).

[57] 'La question que l'on peut se poser à propos de la bataille de Waterloo est plutôt celle-ci: pourquoi et comment assiste-t-on à partir des années 1830, à travers les représentations (écrites, gravées, peintes) de la bataille, à une inversion du sens de l'histoire? ... Pourquoi la défaite éclatante de Waterloo se transforme-t-elle peu à peu en une quasi-victoire?' (E. de Waresquiel, *L'Histoire à rebrousse-poil: les élites, la Restauration, la Révolution* (Paris, 2005), p. 173).

She identified the dawn of the railway age as a momentous moment for civilization:

> The railways from Paris to Calais and from Dover to London could enhance the well-being of our two peoples in moral as well as material respects. Oh! the railways, the railways! In them I see the means whereby every base attempt to prevent the growth of union and brotherhood will be utterly confounded. Let people unite and share their thoughts: let them exchange their various talents as they now exchange material goods, and quarrels between nations will become impossible.[58]

With this theme Tristan returns to the attraction of London for the French. She was back on track in her recognition of London as a city of progress: railways were the future for European peace and harmony; the railway becomes a vehicle of commonality, a space of sharing and dialogue that would reinforce the power of the people.

Promenades dans Londres ran to three editions, with the author adding a new preface to each one. By 1842 her preface was directed away from those interested in the description of London, to French workers. Her experience of London had confirmed her aspirations to turn to activism. *Promenades dans Londres* had become a political treatise. However, although there has been very little written on its impact on the subsequent presence of the French in London, one reference I have uncovered indicates that after her death her text became a reference book for those intending to travel from France for reasons other than political. Circulation traces of Flora Tristan's London publication in the French press show that it became classified as a travel book, since during the period under consideration in this chapter the increased opportunity for travel had brought with it the spread of publications about journeying to London. She saw the growth of two trends that attracted the French to London. An example of the difference of attitudes among the French to the city is to be found in the following review, which refers to other reading material from Anglophobic French authors by way of contrast to the more Anglophile one under consideration here, *Promenades sentimentales dans Londres et le Palais de Cristal*.

Promenades dans Londres is mentioned as biased reading material for those interested in visiting London as excursionists:

[58] 'Les chemins de fer de Paris à Calais et de Douvres à Londres seraient féconds en résultats avantageux au bien-être des deux peuples, à leur avancement moral autant que matériel. Des chemins de fer! des chemins de fer! Voilà les moyens d'union, de confraternité, contre lesquels viendront expirer de honteux efforts! Que les peuples se mêlent, se communiquent leurs pensées; qu'ils fassent échange de talents comme de choses, et les querelles entre nations deviendront impossibles' (Tristan, *Promenades*, p. 290 (Hawkes translation, p. 274)).

The Crystal Palace has attracted a good number of journalists to England to report on the marvels of the Universal Exhibition, providing a whole new series of travel accounts. Our tourists have discovered Great Britain just as Alexandre Dumas had previously discovered the Mediterranean. Some took advantage of this ideal opportunity to yet again set upon perfidious Albion 'our everlasting enemy'. Before leaving Paris they had already taken the precaution of rereading the blistering diatribe of M. Capo de Feuillide on Ireland, Flora Tristan's *London Journal* ... then had set off full of indignation ... In vain did our neighbours give them the best welcome possible; in vain did they overwhelm them with thoughtfulness and kindness: it was a waste of effort![59]

In Tristan's case, her visit to London was a formative moment in her development; she arrived as a writer and she left as an activist, determined to take up the cause of a workers' union. London was a place of opportunity to explore notions of equality and liberty. A woman found a political space for herself and at the same time contributed to the profile of the French in London. *Promenades dans Londres* has never been studied alongside the work of other French political writers as a testimony of the presence of the French in London. Her study of London gave her an opportunity to speak of French affairs beyond the city limits; she reserved her strongest critique for Louis-Napoléon and his uncle, and turned Waterloo into a victory against despotism, one made possible by the British troops at Waterloo. Yet her opinion of Londoners betrays her view of the superiority of the French political system, and the ability of the French to resist oppression in spite of defeat as a legacy of the French Revolution. Her highly politicized feminist, socialist and national views add a fragmented but multiple dimension to being French in London.

Conclusion

Comments of French writers in London offer insights into the strength of their identity as French out of France, in addition to their assessment

---

[59] 'Le Palais de Cristal, en attirant en Angleterre un bon nombre de journalistes chargés de rendre compte des merveilles de l'Exposition universelle, nous a valu toute une série de nouvelles impressions de voyage. Nos touristes improvisés ont découvert la Grande-Bretagne comme M. Alexandre Dumas découvrit naguère la Méditerranée. Quelques-uns ont profité de cette bonne occasion pour tomber une fois de plus à bras raccourcis sur la perfide Albion « notre éternelle ennemie. » Avant de quitter Paris, ils avaient pris la précaution de relire les tirades fulgurantes de M. Capo de Feuillide sur l'Irlande, les *Promenades dans Londres* de Mme Flora Tristan ... puis ils étaient partis le cœur plein d'indignation ... Vainement nos voisins leur faisaient-ils le meilleur accueil possible; vainement les accablaient-ils d'attentions et de prévenances: c'était peine perdue!' (G. de Molinari, book review in *Revue mensuelle d'économie politique et des questions agricoles, manufacturées et commerciales*, xxx, 10ᵉ année (Sept.–Dec. 1851), 286).

of London from the outside. The texts studied reveal more than multiple attitudes in political ideologies. London during the July Monarchy offered a space for a generation of aspiring writers and activists who were intent on making a career from their writing, through occupying a position as French citizens in London, with their own notions of liberty and equality, but using the experience to push their career further in France. Michelet, Tocqueville and Tristan knew they were part of the French presence in London, which was in turn part of the phenomenon of greater movement of populations across the Channel, itself an inevitable part of progress and unity among nations. The writers were the conduit for transmitting ideas, but bricks and mortar were used in the construction of the railway line that is now so crucial to linking London to the French. Flora Tristan could well say: 'Des chemins de fer! Des chemins de fer!' ('Railways! Railways!')

6. Introductory exposition: French republicans and communists in exile to 1848

Fabrice Bensimon

It is well known that the periods following the 1851 *coup d'état* and the 1871 Paris Commune were marked by flows of thousands of republican and socialist exiles to Britain, and to London in particular.[1] However, under the July Monarchy (1830–48), lesser flows – of not more than a few dozen refugees – preceded these. In this brief introduction, the main features of this republican and communist exile from France to London are sketched out. Their social history has yet to be written, but their political groupings offer some clues to their activity.

1815–30
The royalist émigrés of the period of the French Revolution and the Napoleonic wars are not under consideration here; probably between 20,000 and 25,000 of them stayed in Britain. Neither are the Bonapartists, who, like Louis-Napoléon Bonaparte, spent several years in Britain between 1815 and 1848.[2]

In the 1820s, the Carbonari exiled from France mostly went to Spain.[3] As for the regicides who had rallied to Napoleon, they were banished from France by the law of 12 January 1816, and went to Brussels. A few men forced into exile went to Britain following the Restoration and came back following the 1825 amnesty or the fall of Charles X in 1830. They were under surveillance by the French authorities, who feared their return to France under cover names.[4] One example was Pierre-Daniel Martin-Maillefer, a

---

[1] See the following chapter by T. C. Jones and R. Tombs, '*Quarante-huitards* and Communards in London, 1848–80'.

[2] See ch. 4 above, for a discussion of royalist émigrés.

[3] The Carbonari were a loosely-grouped revolutionary secret society originating in Italy.

[4] See, e.g., Archives départementales de la Somme, 4M 1317, transfuges français réfugiés en Angleterre, 1824, letter from the Ministry of the Interior, Police Section, to the prefect of the Somme, Amiens, 4 Oct. 1824: 'J'ai appelé votre attention particulière sur les transfuges français réfugiés en Angleterre. Le signalement des plus marquants vous ont été transmis: ceux de plusieurs autres qui ont été condamnés à diverses peines se trouvent portés sur les feuilles imprimées. Cependant, j'ai la certitude que les plus dangereux de ces transfuges pénètrent

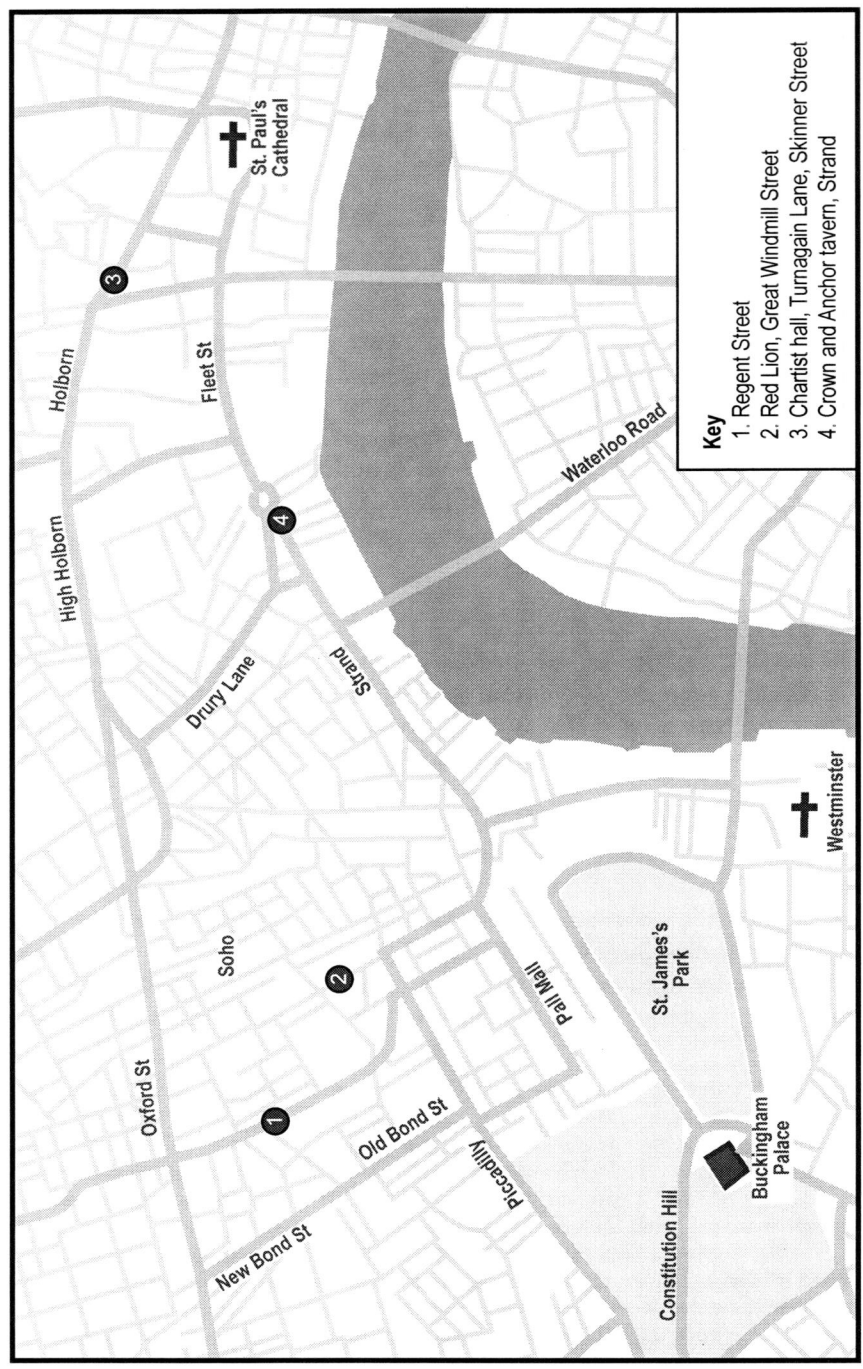

Key

1. Regent Street
2. Red Lion, Great Windmill Street
3. Chartist hall, Turnagain Lane, Skinner Street
4. Crown and Anchor tavern, Strand

Map 6.1. Places mentioned in the text (Base map: London c.1850)

political *proscrit* following his involvement in a conspiracy in Lyon: he had gone to London in 1824, before heading to Latin America, where he met Simón Bolívar. Another was Nicolas Thiéry, who first went to England in 1822 following his involvement in secret societies. He settled in London and became a successful footwear manufacturer and dealer in Regent Street. Later on, he employed several *proscrits*. He was to be involved in the Société Démocratique Française (SDF) founded in 1835 and in the Union Socialiste in 1852 (see below).[5] But all in all, there were very few republican exiles in London.

The July Monarchy (1830–48)

Under the July Monarchy, London was one of the rare places where political exiles could go and stay without being expelled. No foreigner was known to have been expelled from Britain between 1823 and 1905, for reasons that have been well studied by Bernard Porter: Britain was powerful enough to resist political pressure from continental powers, and there was a public attachment to political liberties that could be exploited by foreigners.[6] On various occasions, some individuals and small groups went to Britain to escape from prison or prosecution. These stays were often short-term and did not involve large flows of people. Sources on these stays are sketchy, and mostly produced by the exiles themselves: newspaper articles, memoirs and autobiographical texts, all of which can be partly misleading.[7]

From Etienne Cabet …

One of the first such exiles was Etienne Cabet (1788–1856). Cabet was one of the leading republicans under the July Monarchy and one of the founders of utopian communism in France.[8] In February 1833 he had become the

---

fréquemment en France avec la seule préoccupation de prendre des noms supposés, pour y venir lieu de nouvelles intrigues' ('I have called your attention in particular to the French fugitives who have taken refuge in England. Details of the most notable ones have been passed on to you: those of several others who have been given various sentences are given on the printed sheets. However, I am certain that the most dangerous of these fugitives enter France frequently with the sole objective of taking assumed names in order to devise fresh plots').

[5] Cf. I. Prothero, 'Chartists and political refugees', in *Exiles from European Revolutions: Refugees in Mid-Victorian England*, ed. S. Freitag (Oxford, 2003), p. 216.

[6] B. Porter, *The Refugee Question in Mid-Victorian Politics* (Cambridge, 1979).

[7] See also ch. 5 above, for further discussion of exiles during the July Monarchy.

[8] The most complete work on Etienne Cabet is François Fourn's unpublished dissertation, *Etienne Cabet (1788–1856): une propagande républicaine* (2 vols., Paris, 1996; Lille, 1998). See also F. Fourn, 'Etienne Cabet', in *Le Maitron: dictionnaire biographique. Mouvement ouvrier. Mouvement social* (43 vols., Paris, 1964–93), i. This paragraph is based on Fourn's research. See also C. H. Johnson, *Utopian Communism in France: Cabet and the Icarians, 1839–51* (Ithaca, NY, 1974).

secretary of a Parisian society, the Association Libre pour l'Education du Peuple, which soon became a type of republican working-class party, with thousands of subscribers and attendees at the evening classes it organized. He then created a newspaper, *Le Populaire*, which by 15 October 1833 was selling 27,000 copies per issue, that is, more than the total number of copies of political papers published in Paris at this time. The regime could not let this organized protest thrive. And in March 1834, after being tried and sentenced to two years in jail for articles he had published in *Le Populaire*, Cabet had his sentence commuted to five years in exile. He left France for Brussels and then for London, where he stayed until April 1839. In later autobiographical works, he presented this exile as a sacrifice for the democratic cause; he also argued that his banishment had been an opportunity to study, think about the history of the century and find solutions to the distress of workers; that is when, he said, he became converted to communism. He was initially isolated and depressed and his wife Denise Lesage and daughter Céline later joined him.

In 1835, republican fugitives also came to London. Among those who escaped from the Sainte-Pélagie prison in Paris on 13 July 1835 was republican Godefroy Cavaignac (1800–45). A republican in the Carbonari tradition, Cavaignac had been part of various secret societies under the Restoration and the July Monarchy. Following his escape, he went to Belgium and then to London, where he was involved in the creation of the Société Démocratique Française. He kept on writing for the *National* and the *Journal du peuple*, two republican papers. He left London for Algeria in 1840 and went back to Paris in 1841. Armand Marrast (1801–52), a future member of the 1848 provisional government, had also fled to London, where he married Miss Fitz-Clarence, the daughter of the duke of Clarence, and sent articles to the *National*.

... to the Société Démocratique Française

Following the failure of the uprising organized by French secret societies in Paris on 12 and 13 May 1839 and the repression that ensued, more republicans fled to Britain. Several were involved in what was probably the largest and most long-lasting of the French groups of exiles in London, the Société Démocratique Française. This communist group of followers of François-Noël Babeuf is not well known. A prominent figure among them was Camille Berrier-Fontaine (sometimes spelt Berryer-Fontaine; 1804–82). A former secretary of the central committee of the republican Société des Droits de l'Homme, he had also escaped from Sainte-Pélagie jail on 12 July 1835 and went to Belgium and then London, where he worked as a doctor and was politically active. He became Cabet's friend, and was involved in the creation of the SDF, which he led from 1840 to 1844. Some of its members can be identified – Jean Juin (called Juin d'Allas, alias Jean Michelot; b. 1797), Jacques Chilmann, Napoléon Lebon (b. 1807), Jean-Jacques Vignerte (1806–70) and Joseph Guinard (1789–1879) – although not all of them stayed in London during the whole of its existence: Guinard was back in France in 1845, although he returned to London in 1846, Vignerte went to Brazil, and so on. The SDF largely debated British Chartism and what could be learnt from it, with a view to an uprising in Paris. For instance, in September 1840 it published in London a small booklet entitled *Rapport sur les mesures à prendre et les moyens à employer pour mettre la France dans une voie révolutionnaire, le lendemain d'une insurrection victorieuse effectuée en son sein*, with eighteen questions on a republican revolution.[9] It was clear from the answers that the SDF was neo-Babouvist, that is, inspired by Babeuf's egalitarianism. The booklet was circulated in France by secret societies and was republished in 1841 by the July Monarchy following an assault against the king on 15 October 1840 – the purpose of the regime being to prove that the republicans were communists in disguise.[10] The SDF had also sent an address to the 1839 Chartist convention, with an internationalist message in the mode of the Thomas Paine: 'Democrats of Great Britain! Our two countries were [for] many years rivals … We desire with all our hearts, the intimate union of the nations – the most civilized in the world – the result of which would be liberty. We wish for the universal brotherhood of the people'.[11]

The SDF met on Mondays in the Red Lion, in Great Windmill Street. Arthur Lehning, who has researched this little-known organization, posits that it was related to a German group, Deutscher Arbeiterbildungsverein (the German Association for the Education of Workers), which also met at

---

[9] *Rapport sur les mesures à prendre et les moyens à employer pour mettre la France dans une voie révolutionnaire, le lendemain d'une insurrection victorieuse effectuée en son sein, lu à la Société démocratique française, à Londres, dans la séance du 18 novembre 1839; les diverses conclusions de ce rapport ont été adoptées après discussion par la Société démocratique française, le 14 septembre* ('Report on the measures to be taken and the means to be employed to set France on the path to revolution, following a successful uprising, read to the Democratic French Society at London in the session of 18 Nov. 1839; the various conclusions of this report were adopted after discussion by the Democratic French Society, 14 Sept.') (1840).

[10] A. L. G. Girod de l'Ain, *Cour des pairs. Attentat du 15 octobre 1840. Rapport fait à la cour* (Paris, 1841) (the *Rapport* is reproduced at pp. 77–95). See F. Fourn, 'Les brochures socialistes et communistes en France entre 1840 et 1844', *Cahiers d'histoire. Revue d'histoire critique*, xc–xci <http://chrhc.revues.org/index1455.html> (2003; online 1 Jan. 2006) [accessed 21 Nov. 2011].

[11] *The Charter*, 28 July 1839, p. 428, quoted in H. Weisser, *British Working-Class Movements and Europe* (Manchester, 1975), p. 86.

the Red Lion.[12] He suggests that in 1847 the SDF merged with the German group; it is known that in 1843 the leaders of Arbeiterbildungsverein belonged to the French communist organization. In February 1840 it had helped Carl Schapper to found the Deutsche Demokratische Gesellschaft, which became the Communistischer Arbeiter-Bildungs-Verein (Communist Association for the Education of Workers), which also met in the Red Lion and continued to exist in London until 1914.

In London, where he said he became a 'communist', Etienne Cabet had met future Chartist leader Peter Murray McDouall (1814–54). McDouall left Britain in order to avoid arrest and renewed imprisonment, and took refuge in Paris between 1842 and 1844. Although his activities in France are not well known, we do know that he was then in contact with French communists, and with Cabet in particular.[13] Cabet had returned to France in April 1839 and in 1840 he published his *Voyage en Icarie*, one of the first formulations of his communist ideal. In 1843, McDouall wrote in Cabet's paper *Le Populaire*, explaining why he subscribed to Cabet's ideal, and supporting the communists during the trial of members of a so-called communist plot in Toulouse.[14] McDouall wanted to, and possibly did, translate Cabet's book into English. No copy of the *Adventures of William Carisdale in Icaria* has survived, but the author of the translation was stated to be Peter McDouall, 'at the author's especial request'.[15] In his publications, Cabet himself spoke of the '8 million Chartists … who were communists', and he had English followers who created an Icarian committee for England in the mid 1840s.[16] When McDouall returned to London in 1844, he had contacts with French refugees, and a republican meeting took place in September 1844 to celebrate the 1792 First French Republic. This 'banquet' – a device used by republicans in France to escape the 1834 ban on meetings of more than twenty people – was chaired by McDouall.[17]

---

[12] A. Lehning, *From Buonarotti to Bakunin: Studies in International Socialism* (Leiden, 1970).

[13] On P. Murray McDouall, see 'The "people's advocate": Peter Murray McDouall (1814–54)', in O. R. Ashton and P. A. Pickering, *Friends of the People: Uneasy Radicals in the Age of the Chartists* (2002), pp. 7–28; and D. Goodway, 'M'Douall [McDouall], Peter Murray (c.1814–1854)', *ODNB*.

[14] *Le Populaire*, 19 Aug. 1843, p. 106.

[15] The book was advertised as published by Hetherington in 1845, e.g. in *Morning Star, or Herald of Progression*, i (17 May 1845), 19. This was the journal of the Tropical Emigration Society, of which Chartist Thomas Powell was secretary. The advert appeared only once. I owe this reference to Malcolm Chase.

[16] E. Cabet, *Etat de la question sociale en Angleterre, en Ecosse, en Irlande et en France* (Paris, 1843), pp. 18–25; Ashton and Pickering, *Friends*, p. 17; W. H. Armytage, *Heavens Below: Utopian Experiments in England 1560–1960* (1961), pp. 205–7.

[17] Prothero, 'Chartists and political refugees', p. 217.

Cabet and the SDF were in touch, but they soon disagreed. In the spring of 1844, Cabet submitted his plans for the foundation of a small community in Paris to the SDF.[18] They discussed his letter on 6 May 1844 and Berrier-Fontaine replied to Cabet that it was not a good idea. This highlighted an ongoing debate among socialists and communists in the 1840s, where Fourierism and Owenism were influential: should they try to set up model communities, such as those which Robert Owen and Charles Fourier had already attempted, but which had failed in several instances; or should they try instead to convince large masses, in order to overthrow despots and parasites? Cabet now believed in the first option, while the SDF, as far as its definite stance on the issue is known, stuck to the latter.

The Fraternal Democrats

Some integration of the republican refugees among British radicals came in 1845, with the establishment of the Fraternal Democrats. It seems that, thanks to Friedrich Engels (1820–95), who was in contact with German and French exiles in London, they met Ernest Jones (1819–69) and Julian Harney (1817–97), whom Engels had encountered in Leeds.[19] Both Jones and Harney were among the Chartist leaders with internationalist beliefs. Harney was probably at the origin of the meeting of reportedly 'more than one thousand' that was held on 22 September 1845 in the Chartist Hall (1 Turnagain Lane, Skinner Street) to commemorate the establishment of the First French Republic, with some British, German, French, Italian, Polish and Swiss members. It was chaired by Chartist Thomas Cooper and the main speaker was Harney. Berrier-Fontaine spoke for the French.[20] Toasts were proposed to Young Europe, to Thomas Paine, to the 'fallen Democrats of all countries', to those of England, Scotland and Ireland, and to deported Chartists; democratic songs in all languages were sung. The meeting brought home the idea that fraternization between nations was only possible through a union of working men, the proletariat alone being capable of such action. A French police informer lamented:

in the various toasts that were proposed, the most impious and extravagant doctrines were developed and exalted. Robespierre and Marat were praised

[18] *Le Populaire*, 2 May 1844; Lehning, *Buonarotti to Bakunin*, p. 131.

[19] See J. Grandjonc, M. Cordillot and J. Risacher, 'Camille-Louis Berrier-Fontaine', in *Le Maitron: dictionnaire biographique* <http://maitron-en-ligne.univ-paris1.fr/spip.php?article26380&id_mot=23> [accessed 28 Aug. 2012]; see, e.g., his letters in *The Harney Papers*, ed. F. Gees Black and R. Métivier Black (Assen, 1969).

[20] See extensive report on the meeting by Engels, *Rheinische Jahrbücher zur gesellschaftlischen Reform 1846*, repr. in K. Marx and F. Engels, *Collected Works*, ed. R. Dixon (50 vols., 1975–2005), v. 3–14; *The Northern Star*, no. 411, 27 Sept. 1845.

in fulsome terms, *yet reproached for having fought their enemies with too much gentleness.* Toasts were drunk to *revolution, to the death of Kings,* and the opinion was expressed that the great European movement should begin with France, etc.[21]

The result of the meeting was the formation of the Fraternal Democrats, who met regularly on anniversaries of revolutionary events and discussed important events in manifestos or at meetings until February 1848.[22] Marx and Engels were involved in this organization, whose story is better known than that of the SDF, because it was larger, published several booklets, and had its meetings reported in the Chartist and German radical newspapers; and also because the French police had a well-placed informer, presumably Jean Juin, known as Michelot.[23] One of the important activities of the Fraternal Democrats was to try to agitate on the Polish question – a key question for radicals in the period 1830–70. Following the crushing of the Cracow uprising, the Fraternal Democrats organized a meeting in the Crown and Anchor tavern on the Strand, on 25 March 1846. According to the report sent to Guizot,[24] the room was full, with 3,000 workers attending. The French and the Germans did not speak, so as to avoid the accusation that the meeting was not wholly English. Part of the French police report read:

> M Guizot and Louis-Philippe were presented above all as denouncers of the Polish Revolution and its implacable enemies … thunderous imprecations, death threats, repeated twenty times over in this crowd. Many speakers did not speak but mooed, bellowed, or roared, which aroused among the audience similar vociferations, so that you would think it was a gathering of demons or at least of people possessed by them. It was in the English style.[25]

[21] 'On a, dans les différents toasts qui ont été portés, développé et exalté les doctrines les plus impies et les plus extravagantes. On a fait l'éloge le plus pompeux de Robespierre et de Marat, *mais cependant en leur reprochant d'avoir combattu leurs ennemis avec trop de mollesse.* On a bu *au renversement, à la mort des Rois,* en exprimant l'opinion que le grand mouvement Européen devrait commencer par la France, etc.' (AN, P, Fonds Guizot, 42 AP 57, rapport du préfet de police à Guizot, 10 Nov. 1845; cited in J. Grandjonc, 'Les émigrés allemands sous la monarchie de Juillet. Documents de surveillance policière 1833–février 1848', in *Cahiers d'études germaniques* (Aix-en-Provence, 1972), p. 194).

[22] Lehning, *Buonarotti to Bakunin,* p. 164.

[23] This was assumed by Jacques Grandjonc, who researched the German political refugees in the 1830s and 1840s (see J. Grandjonc, 'Juin Jean, Augustin, dit Juin D'Allas, dit Michelot J.-A. J. D.', in *Le Maitron: dictionnaire biographique* <http://maitron-en-ligne.univ-paris1.fr/spip.php?article32911> [accessed 28 Aug. 2012]; and also Grandjonc, 'Les émigrés allemands', pp. 115–249).

[24] François Guizot was at that point Louis-Philippe's minister for foreign affairs.

[25] 'M. Guizot et Louis Philippe ont surtout été présentés comme les dénonciateurs de la Révolution Polonaise et ses ennemis implacables … tonnerre d'imprécations, de menaces

The Fraternal Democrats continued to be active until the eve of the 1848 revolutions, with regular meetings and several publications.[26] For instance, they opposed the possibility of war with the United States over the Oregon question in 1846, and advocated the gathering of a Congress of Nations to settle international disputes.[27] In particular, in September 1847, they issued a manifesto which was published in the *Northern Star*, *La Réforme* and possibly other newspapers. They asserted democratic as well as internationalist principles, with the idea of international fraternization among workers. When the 1848 revolutions broke out, the continental members returned to their native countries and the Fraternal Democrats ceased to exist. It seems that the Chartist George Julian Harney briefly revived them in 1851.[28] More importantly, the Fraternal Democrats are often considered as one of the ancestors of the International Association (1855–9) and above all of the International Working Men's Association (1864–72). And while the French refugees of 1848, 1849 and 1851 were far more numerous than and different from those of the 1830–48 period, some Chartists, like Harney, represented a link between both groups.

---

de mort, renouvelées vingt fois dans cette foule. Plusieurs de ces orateurs ne parlaient pas, ils mugissaient, beuglaient, rugissaient, ce qui excitait parmi les gens du peuple des vociférations analogues, capables de faire croire à un rassemblement de démons ou au moins d'énergumènes. C'est dans le genre anglais' (AN, P, Fonds Guizot, 42 AP 57, rapport transmis par le préfet de police à Guizot, 26 March 1846; cited in Grandjonc, 'Les émigrés allemands', p. 209).

[26] *Address of the Fraternal Democrats Assembling in London to the Working Classes of Great Britain and the United States* (4 July 1846); *The Democratic Committee for Poland's Regeneration, to the People of Great Britain and Ireland* (7 Dec. 1846); *The Fraternal Democrats (Assembling in London) to the Democracy of Europe* (7 Dec. 1846); *Address of the Fraternal Democrats Assembling in London, to the Members of the National Diet of Switzerland* (13 Dec. 1847); *Principles and Rules of the Society of Fraternal Democrats* (undated).

[27] *Address of the Fraternal Democrats* (4 July 1846).

[28] See in particular TNA, HO 45/4332, a tract dated 22 Sept. 1851, entitled *The Fraternal Democrats to the People of Great Britain and Ireland*, signed by John Pettie (52 College Place, Camden-town, London), Edward Swift and G. Julian Harney.

7. The French left in exile: *Quarante-huitards* and Communards in London, 1848–80

Thomas C. Jones and Robert Tombs

Political defeat in France and political asylum in London

For over thirty years in the latter half of the nineteenth century, London was home to hundreds, and at times thousands, of French revolutionary, republican and socialist exiles. These refugees were drawn from across two generations and were associated with periods of intense political instability in France. During their time in London, they had a significant impact on the life of the city, transforming several of its neighbourhoods into essentially French enclaves, infused themselves into certain sectors of London's economy, blended into particular social milieux, and greatly affected the shape and trajectory of political radicalism in the capital.

The first generation of exiles during the period under study consisted of supporters of the French revolution of February 1848, the Second Republic founded that year, and members of the left-wing *démocrate-socialiste*, or *démoc-soc*, political party, an alliance of radical republicans and socialists. These refugees came to Britain in several waves, with the first arriving in the summer of 1848. In June that year, the closure of the 'national workshops', a work programme for the unemployed, sparked an uprising across much of Paris. This rebellion was bloodily stamped out and many of the rebels fled France, arriving in London shortly after the fighting ceased. The violence of these 'June Days' quickly led to a search for scapegoats, and France's increasingly conservative constituent assembly stripped Louis Blanc, a noted socialist, prominent figure in the February revolution and member of the republic's provisional government, and Marc Caussidière, head of Paris's provisional police force during the revolution, of their parliamentary immunity. Both men fled to London before they could be convicted of inciting the uprising. A year later, in the spring of 1849, Louis-Napoléon Bonaparte, who had been elected president of the Republic in December 1848, curried favour with French Catholics by sending the army to Rome to crush the revolutionary government there and restore the pope (Pius IX) to his temporal throne. Incensed, Alexandre Ledru-Rollin, a leader of the 1848 revolution and head of the *démoc-soc* party, moved for Bonaparte's impeachment and organized a protest for 13 June. The authorities responded

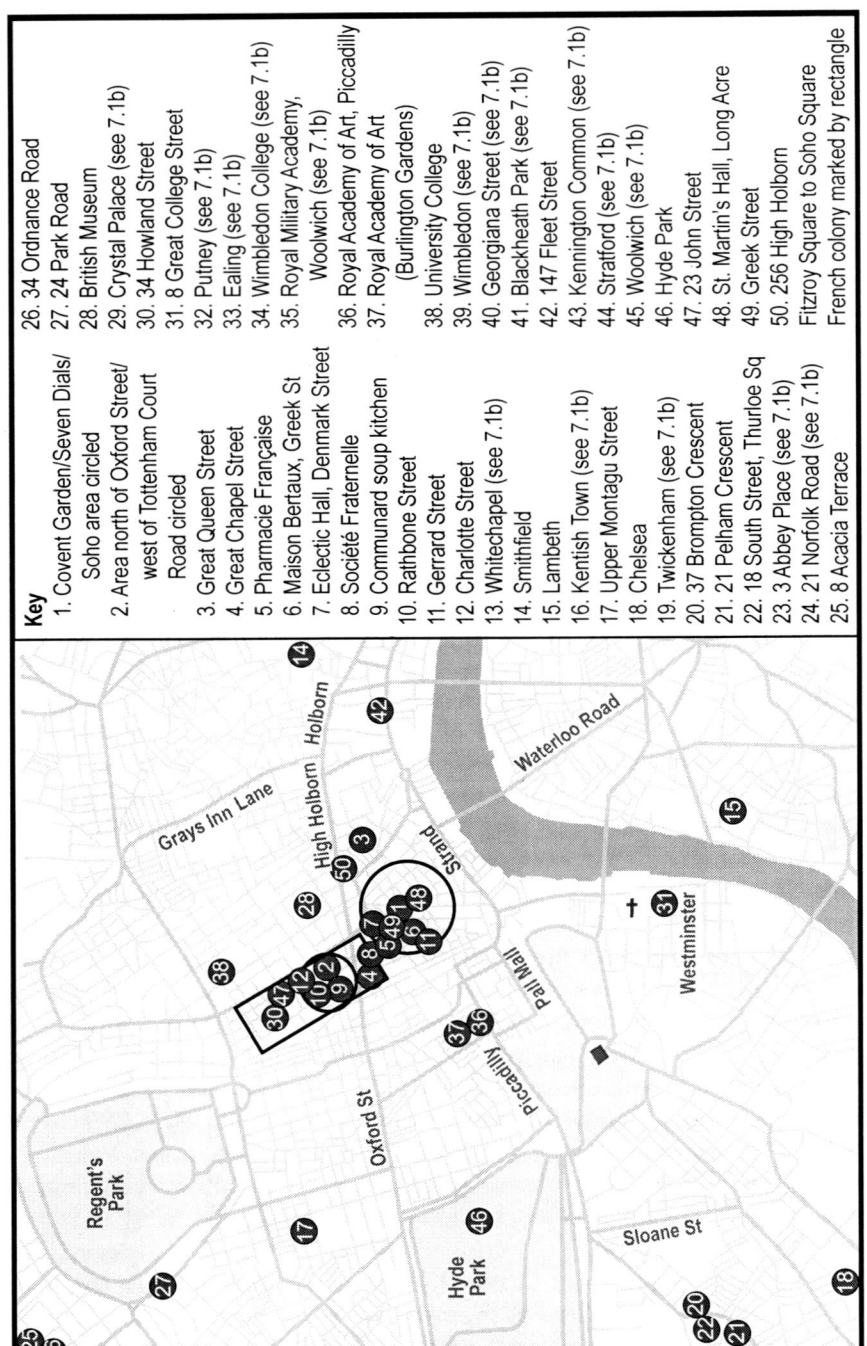

Key
1. Covent Garden/Seven Dials/ Soho area circled
2. Area north of Oxford Street/ west of Tottenham Court Road circled
3. Great Queen Street
4. Great Chapel Street
5. Pharmacie Française
6. Maison Bertaux, Greek St
7. Eclectic Hall, Denmark Street
8. Société Fraternelle
9. Communard soup kitchen
10. Rathbone Street
11. Gerrard Street
12. Charlotte Street
13. Whitechapel (see 7.1b)
14. Smithfield
15. Lambeth
16. Kentish Town (see 7.1b)
17. Upper Montagu Street
18. Chelsea
19. Twickenham (see 7.1b)
20. 37 Brompton Crescent
21. 21 Pelham Crescent
22. 18 South Street, Thurloe Sq
23. 3 Abbey Place (see 7.1b)
24. 21 Norfolk Road (see 7.1b)
25. 8 Acacia Terrace
26. 34 Ordnance Road
27. 24 Park Road
28. British Museum
29. Crystal Palace (see 7.1b)
30. 34 Howland Street
31. 8 Great College Street
32. Putney (see 7.1b)
33. Ealing (see 7.1b)
34. Wimbledon College (see 7.1b)
35. Royal Military Academy, Woolwich (see 7.1b)
36. Royal Academy of Art, Piccadilly
37. Royal Academy of Art (Burlington Gardens)
38. University College
39. Wimbledon (see 7.1b)
40. Georgiana Street (see 7.1b)
41. Blackheath Park (see 7.1b)
42. 147 Fleet Street
43. Kennington Common (see 7.1b)
44. Stratford (see 7.1b)
45. Woolwich (see 7.1b)
46. Hyde Park
47. 23 John Street
48. St. Martin's Hall, Long Acre
49. Greek Street
50. 256 High Holborn
Fitzroy Square to Soho Square
French colony marked by rectangle

Map 7.1a. Places mentioned in the text (Base map: London c.1850)

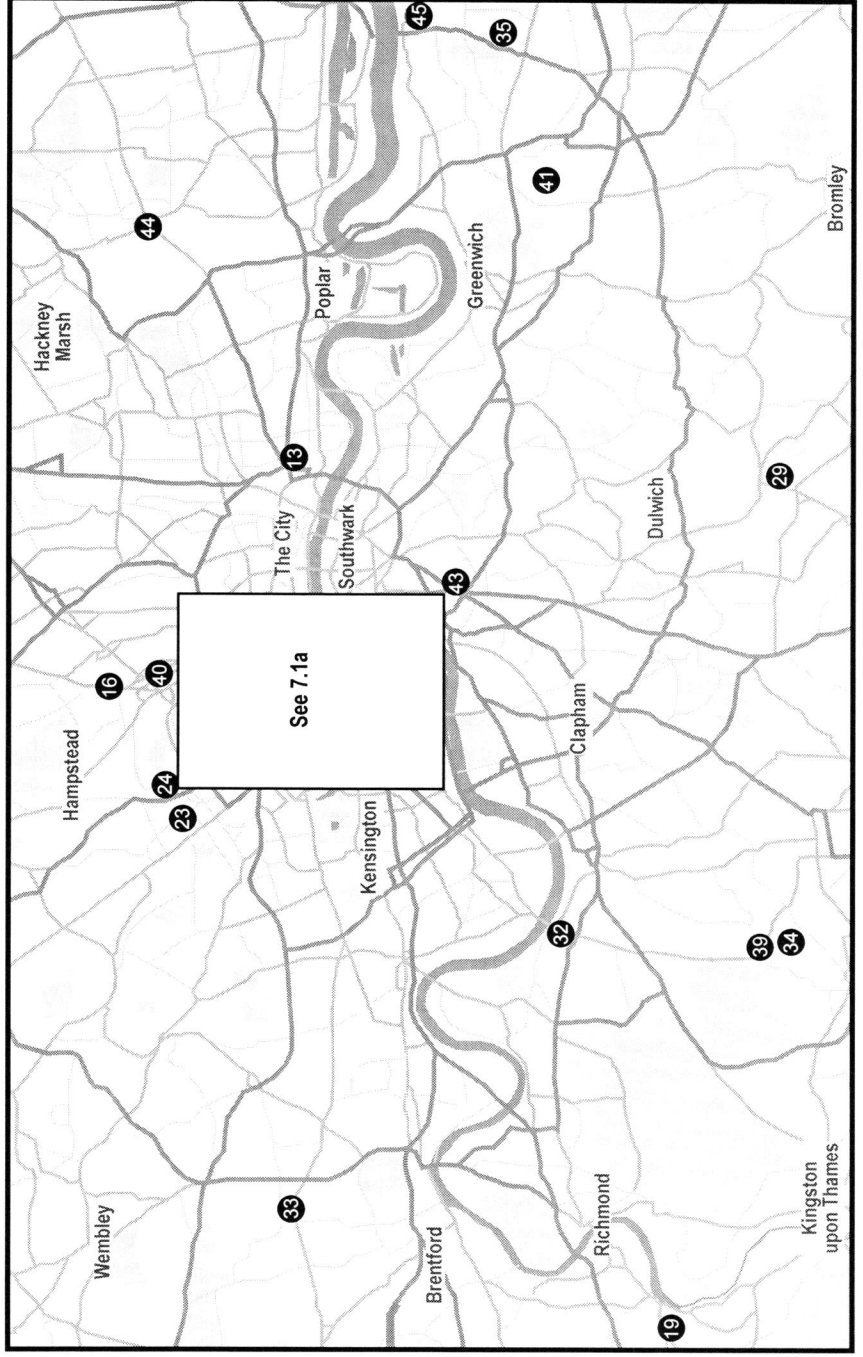

Map 7.1b. Places outside central London mentioned in the text (Base map: 2013)

by declaring a state of siege, suppressing leftist newspapers, and issuing arrest warrants. Ledru-Rollin, dozens of *démoc-soc* representatives and many of their followers quickly fled to London.

But by far the biggest wave of refugees arrived in the winter of 1851–2. On 2 December 1851, rather than step down after a single presidential term, as mandated by the constitution of 1848, President Bonaparte overthrew the Second Republic in a coup. Soldiers flooded the streets, the legislature was dissolved and many of Bonaparte's prominent *démoc-soc* opponents were arrested and expelled from the country. Armed resistance to the coup soon started in Paris and spread across France, particularly to areas of *démoc-soc* strength in the centre and south. The uprising, which involved nearly 100,000 people, was crushed and the Bonapartists instituted a harsh system of repression. Many rebels fled, while others were expelled, placed under house arrest or sent to penal colonies in Algeria and Cayenne. Some escaped these colonies and prisons and made their way into exile. Thus, in the months after the coup, thousands of French exiles joined their compatriots from 1848 and 1849 in London. Many others followed, preferring self-imposed exile to life under Bonaparte. For the purposes of this chapter, we will refer to this generation of exiles as *Quarante-huitards*, a term often used in the nineteenth century to signify their support for the revolution of 1848 and the republican regime that it established.

A new generation of refugees arrived in London in 1871. That year, the Paris Commune emerged in the aftermath of France's defeat in the Franco-Prussian War, when a monarchist-dominated National Assembly, based at Versailles, took a series of measures that seemed to be hostile to Paris and to threaten the new Third Republic. The Commune, popularly elected by the people of Paris and dominated by an amalgamation of radical republicans, Jacobins, socialists, Blanquists and anarchists, chased out the regular army, declared itself autonomous and promptly began running its own affairs. The government at Versailles could not countenance this and the regular army crushed the Commune's forces in May. Rebels were then executed en masse and, for years to come, the police hunted and arrested suspected Communards, who were tried by military courts. Fleeing abroad was often the only alternative to the firing squad, prison or transportation to the desolate penal colony in New Caledonia. Thousands of Communards therefore retraced the steps taken by the *Quarante-huitards* twenty years earlier.

Numerically, the refugee population in Britain was small but not insignificant. It peaked in 1852, in the aftermath of Bonaparte's coup, at around 4,500.[1] Most of these exiles, however, did not remain long, and

---

[1] Figure quoted in B. Porter, *The Refugee Question in Mid-Victorian Politics* (Cambridge, 1979), p. 16, n. 9.

from 1853 Britain's exile population stabilized at around 1,000, with 800 in London.[2] These numbers remained roughly constant until Bonaparte issued an amnesty in 1859, of which about half the refugees took advantage.[3] In the 1860s, a core of around 400 exiles remained, resolutely awaiting the end of the Second Empire. When this came in 1870, the majority returned to France, but a few decided to settle in London permanently. In 1871–2, roughly 1,500 adult male Communards took refuge in London, accompanied by at least 600 wives and 1,200 children.[4] As the 1870s wore on, probably a few hundred Communards left Britain, with a mini-exodus occurring after Belgium liberalized its asylum policies in 1874.[5] But the bulk of the Communards remained until a partial amnesty was issued in 1879, followed by a complete amnesty in 1880.

The nuclei of both cohorts initially consisted of young, though not overly youthful, men. Sylvie Aprile has posited that the typical French exile during the Second Empire was between thirty-five and fifty years old, while Paul Martinez has calculated that around three-quarters of the incoming Communards were in their twenties and thirties.[6] This, of course, changed as time went on and the refugees often returned to France after they had passed into middle age. Both groups were also largely male, despite the presence of a few famous female refugees like the socialist and feminist activist Jeanne Deroin and a number of wives and daughters of male exiles. Because many refugees had been prominent leaders and important functionaries of the Second Republic and Commune, professional politicians, civil servants, journalists, lawyers, doctors and, after 1871, National Guard officers were overrepresented in the exile populations.[7] Yet there were substantial numbers of working-class refugees in both generations. Thousands of ordinary people had risen up against Bonaparte in 1851 or resisted the Versailles government in 1871 and also required safe haven from the repression that followed defeat. Thus, as Charles Hugo noted, the more famous and prominent refugees were accompanied in their exile by a 'legion'.[8]

There was also a significant degree of personal overlap between the two groups of exiles. Indeed, a few prominent refugees were members of both.

---

[2] TNA, HO 45/4816, police report of 19 March 1853.

[3] S. Aprile, *Le Siècle des exilés: bannis et proscrits de 1789 à la Commune* (Paris, 2010), p. 124; A. Calman, *Ledru-Rollin après 1848 et les proscrits français en Angleterre* (Paris, 1921), p. 190.

[4] P. Martinez, 'Paris Communard refugees in London' (unpublished University of Sussex PhD thesis, 1981), p. 109.

[5] Martinez, 'Paris Communard refugees', p. 112.

[6] Aprile, *Siècle des exilés*, p. 112; Martinez, 'Paris Communard refugees', pp. 117–19.

[7] For the disproportionate number of professional men among both sets of exiles, see Aprile, *Siècle des exilés*, pp. 112, 260.

[8] C. Hugo, *Les Hommes de l'exil* (Paris, 1875), p. 162.

Some *Quarante-huitard* exiles, like Christophe Benoît, Alexandre Besson, Jean Baptiste Bocquet, Pierre Malardier, Félix Pyat and Pierre Vésinier, became involved in the Commune after returning to France, and were therefore forced to seek asylum in London once again in 1871.[9] Moreover, a number of Communards were the sons of earlier exiles. Thus, Camille Barrère, who as an infant had accompanied his exiled father Pierre to London in 1851, was obliged to return twenty years later as a refugee in his own right.[10] Similarly, Frédéric Cournet, a refugee from June 1848, was succeeded in exile by his son and namesake Frédéric Etienne Cournet in the 1870s.[11] And, as we will see, some of the *Quarante-huitards* who remained in Britain mingled significantly with their younger compatriots.

These refugees chose Britain as their asylum for several reasons. First, they were free to do so. Britain had no regular entrance restrictions in this period and anyone, regardless of national origin, could come to the country and stay indefinitely. Moreover, the few extradition treaties that Britain had with its neighbours intentionally excluded political offences. The Alien Act of 1848 did briefly allow ministers to remove foreign individuals deemed threatening to the state, but potential deportees could still make appeals to the Privy Council, and the act lapsed, having never been used, in 1850.[12] So throughout this period, the government had no legal means of barring or expelling the exiles.[13] Second, the exiles were able to continue their political activism in Britain. The country's free press and protections of speech meant that the exiles could issue manifestos and propaganda, while the right to free assembly allowed exile political associations to flourish. Indeed, the political latitude enjoyed by the exiles even extended, in practice if not in law, to assassination conspiracies. In 1858, when Felice Orsini, co-operating with French exiles in London, attempted to assassinate Napoleon III, the French government demanded that Britain clamp down on the refugee population. Yet Palmerston, the then prime minister, was unable to push through legislation transforming conspiracy to murder from a misdemeanour to a felony, and his ministry collapsed after the Commons censured the government's willingness to truckle to

---

[9] Aprile, *Siècle des exilés*, pp. 263–5; Martinez, 'Paris Communard refugees', pp. 75–7.

[10] For the Barrère family, see G. Ferragu, 'Anglophones, anglophiles, anglomanes?', in *La France et l'Angleterre au XIXᵉ siècle: échanges, représentations, comparaisons*, ed. S. Aprile and F. Bensimon (Paris, 2006), pp. 541–59.

[11] For the elder Cournet's experience in exile, see C. Hugo, *Les Hommes de l'exil*, ch. 2. For the younger, see Martinez, 'Paris Communard refugees', p. 495.

[12] B. Porter, 'The asylum of nations: Britain and the refugees of 1848', in Freitag, *Exiles from European Revolutions*, pp. 43–56, at p. 44.

[13] Porter, *Refugee Question*, pp. 143–4.

Bonaparte's demands.[14] The subsequent Derby government then charged one of Orsini's co-conspirators, Simon Bernard, with accessory to murder. Bernard was acquitted when the jury heeded his lawyer's advice to 'not pervert and wrest the law of England to please a foreign dictator!'[15] The exiles were therefore protected by a strain of patriotic libertarianism in Victorian Britain's political culture which made perceived or conspicuous concessions to foreign despotic governments nearly impossible. By 1871, this was so well known that the French government did not bother to request the extradition of even the most notorious Communards.[16]

This all contrasted sharply with other potential refuges, which tended to be small and to share borders with France. The French government was therefore able to pressure states like Belgium, Switzerland and Piedmont into passing restrictive legislation against the exiles.[17] Those hoping to remain politically active had little choice but to come to Britain. As John Sanders, the Metropolitan Police's main agent in charge of exile affairs, explained in 1852: 'They cannot reside in any other Country. The Governments of Belgium and Switzerland are ordering all those known in their respective Countries away, unless they obtain a special order from the Government, they then are placed under the surveillance of the Police. They prefer coming to England'.[18]

Within Britain, London was by far the most attractive refuge. Its huge size and economic importance meant that it offered better employment prospects than other British cities. Meanwhile, its physical proximity to France combined with its role as the centre of British politics, the press and the publishing industry made it an ideal base from which the exiles could continue their political activism. Finally, the pre-existing presence of a French exile community from 1848 meant that, for each successive wave of refugees, London was the logical first port of call. Newly arriving exiles could be sure that there they would find French-speaking company,

[14] Porter, *Refugee Question*, pp. 182–3.

[15] Quoted in G. J. Holyoake, *Sixty Years of an Agitator's Life* (2 vols., 1892), ii. 32–3. Records of the trial exist in the City of London, Corporation of London Record Office, item CLA/047/LJP/04/003.

[16] Martinez, 'Paris Communard refugees', p. 55.

[17] For examples, see J. B. Boichot, *Souvenirs d'un prisonnier du coup d'état sous le Second Empire* (Leipzig, 1867), pp. 5–6; M. Dessal, *Un Révolutionnaire Jacobin: Charles Delescluze, 1809–71* (Paris, 1952), p. 141; C. Lévy, 'Les proscrits de 2 décembre', in *Les Républicains sous le Second Empire*, ed. L. Hamlin (Paris, 1993), pp. 15–31, at p. 25; Martinez, 'Paris Communard refugees', p. 55; M. Nadaud, *Mémoires de Léonard*, ed. M. Agulhon (Bourganeuf, 1895; Paris, 1976), pp. 408–9; J. Tchernoff, *Le Parti Républicain au coup d'état et sous le Second Empire, d'après des documents et des souvenirs inédits* (Paris, 1906), p. 120.

[18] TNA, HO 45/4302, police report of 13 Feb. 1852.

political sympathizers, familiar faces and perhaps a helping hand. London was consequently an 'almost irresistible magnet for the refugees'.[19] The rest of this chapter will therefore examine the physical, socio-economic and political spaces that the exiles occupied while in London, as well the impacts that the city and refugees had on one another.

The exiles' London

Physically mapping the exiles' place in London is fairly straightforward. From 1848 to 1880, the great majority of them settled in a contiguous area stretching through Covent Garden, Seven Dials, Soho and, increasingly after 1871, the blocks just north of Oxford Street and west of Tottenham Court Road. These areas offered relatively inexpensive accommodation and so attracted the bulk of the poorest refugees and those left short of resources after their abrupt departures from France. Because it was the chief residence of the refugees, the area in and around Soho also became the centre of exile social and economic life. The exiles founded numerous businesses there, including a *Quarante-huitard* bookshop in Great Queen Street, the Hôtel de Progrès in Great Chapel Street, the Pharmacie Française in Greek Street, and the famous Communard patisserie, Maison Bertaux, also in Greek Street and still flourishing today.[20] Institutions of exile sociability were also based in these neighbourhoods, from the freemason Grand Loge des Philadelphes, housed in the Eclectic Hall in Denmark Street, to charitable organizations like the Société Fraternelle des Démocrates-Socialistes à Londres headquartered near Soho Square or the Communard soup kitchen in Newman Passage, just north of Oxford Street.[21] As the recognized centre of refugee life, Soho was usually the first stop for new exiles arriving in London. Thus, after Bonaparte's coup, the socialist schoolteacher Gustave Lefrançais sought out an exile-run tavern in Rathbone Street and the expelled *démoc-soc* legislators Pierre Malardier, Martin Nadaud and Victor Schoelcher spent their first night in London in a hotel in Gerrard Street. Similarly, after the crushing of the Commune, many Communards flocked to F. Lassassie's barber shop in Charlotte Street.[22]

---

[19] Porter, *Refugee Question*, p. 19.

[20] *L'Homme*, 10 and 24 Oct. 1855, p. 4 of both issues.

[21] A. Prescott, 'The cause of humanity: Charles Bradlaugh and freemasonry', *Ars Quatuor Coronatorum*, cxiii (2003), 15–64, at p. 30; Calman, *Ledru-Rollin*, p. 36; Martinez, 'Paris Communard refugees', p. 136.

[22] G. Lefrançais, *Souvenirs d'un révolutionnaire* (Brussels, 1903), pp. 190–1; Nadaud, *Mémoires*, p. 410; *La Correspondance de Victor Schoelcher*, ed. N. Schmidt (Paris, 1995), p. 156; Martinez, 'Paris Communard refugees', p. 77.

Of course, not every French exile in London lived in and around Soho. In the early 1850s, notable colonies of refugees sprang up in Whitechapel, Smithfield and Lambeth.[23] From 1871, a few dozen Blanquists, attracted by the presence of Karl Marx, gathered in Kentish Town. Yet disputes between some of these Communards and Marx, mostly over the breakdown of the International Working Men's Association, caused this colony to dissipate somewhat after 1873.[24] Some of the wealthier exiles also spread out into the leafier districts of west London. Blanc lived in Upper Montagu Street, just west of Baker Street, while Schoelcher maintained residences in both Chelsea and Twickenham, and, during his two decades of exile, Ledru-Rollin moved at least seven times between various addresses in Brompton and St. John's Wood.[25]

Exile reactions to London were extremely diverse. Some, and those that have attracted the most historical attention, were extremely harsh. In 1850, Ledru-Rollin published his *Decline of England*, where he condemned Britain's unconscionable levels of political and economic inequality and predicted the country's imminent internal collapse, warning that 'The barbarians for England are those hordes of men who raise their withered hands towards heaven, demanding bread'.[26] He dedicated a significant proportion of the book to highlighting the horrors of London slum life.[27] For material, he drew directly on Henry Mayhew's celebrated exposés of London poverty that were then appearing in the *Morning Chronicle* and would soon be collected into the famous book *London Labour and the London Poor* (1851). Ledru-Rollin's heavy reliance on Mayhew was derided by the British press, which wrote him off as an unoriginal sensationalizer of more nuanced sources.[28]

London was similarly pilloried by Jules Vallès, a former member of the Commune's ruling council and editor of its most important newspaper, *Le Cri du peuple*. In his 1876 *La Rue à Londres*, Vallès, like Flora Tristan and Ledru-Rollin before him, savaged almost every aspect of English life, from boys whistling in the street to the colour of the buildings. Although he deplored London's lack of facilities for illicit sex, he also lamented that English women were 'shocking' in their willingness to pet on park benches,

---

[23] Lefrançais, *Souvenirs*, p. 191.

[24] Martinez, 'Paris Communard refugees', pp. 146–7. For the International Working Men's Association and the exile community, see below.

[25] Hugo, *Les Hommes de l'exil*, p. 328; Schmidt, *Correspondance de Schoelcher*, pp. 40, 45; Calman, *Ledru-Rollin*, pp. 273–4.

[26] A. Ledru-Rollin, *The Decline of England*, trans. E. Churton (1850), p. 10.

[27] Ledru-Rollin, *Decline of England*, pp. 124–88.

[28] See, e.g., *The Times*, 6 June 1850, p. 4.

that the climate made them 'stupid' and 'frigid', and that, after their early twenties, they went off 'like game'. Worse still were the feminists; 'eccentrics', who in his view, were 'neither man nor woman'. He was appalled by the lack of class militancy among London workers, which set them apart from their French counterparts, a rift that encompassed 'the furious fog that resents the sun ... the duel between beer and wine!'[29]

More prosaic, or petty, complaints were also common among the exiles. As the Russian exile Alexander Herzen wryly noted:

> The Frenchman cannot forgive the English, in the first place, for not speaking French; in the second, for not understanding him when he calls Charing Cross Sharan-Kro, or Leicester Square Lesesstair-Skooar. Then his stomach cannot digest the English dinners consisting of two huge pieces of meat and fish, instead of five little helpings of various ragouts, fritures, salmis and so on. Then he can never resign himself to the 'slavery' of restaurants being closed on Sundays, and the people being *bored to the glory of God*, though the whole of France is bored to the glory of Bonaparte for seven days in the week.[30]

But this sort of familiar republican Anglophobia was not ubiquitous among the refugees. Schoelcher distanced himself from Ledru-Rollin, writing in the *Morning Advertiser* that 'to ally ... a whole party with this or that idea of one of its members, however honest or however eminent that member may be, is carrying solidarity much farther than is reasonable or than I can accept'.[31] Other refugees wrote glowing accounts of life in London. Alphonse Esquiros, a socialist author and *démoc-soc* legislator, marvelled at the city's technological and engineering feats, as well as the material benefits these bestowed upon Londoners of all classes:

> The inhabitant of London has already at his orders more railways than exist in any capital of the world, and he commands a network of electric wires ever ready to transmit his messages and wishes from one place to another for a few pence. To several railway stations drinking fountains are attached, which pour out for him gratis the purest and freshest water. All along the line he can purchase for a trifle newspapers, in which men dare to say everything.[32]

Rather than finding London overwhelming or alienating, Esquiros saw an exhilaratingly diverse city filled with opportunity: 'There is a species of

---

[29] J. Vallès, *La Rue à Londres*, ed. L. Scheler (Paris, 1950), pp. 2, 3, 7, 90–1, 164–8, 174–7, 184–5, 223.

[30] A. Herzen, *My Past and Thoughts: the Memoirs of Alexander Herzen*, trans. C. Garnett, rev. H. Higgens (4 vols., 1968), iii. 1048.

[31] *Morning Advertiser*, 30 Dec. 1853, p. 3.

[32] A. Esquiros, *The English at Home: Essays from the 'Revue des Deux Mondes'*, Third Series, trans. L. Wraxall (1863), pp. 369–70.

charm and dizziness in studying all the phases of human life, whose variety is inexhaustible'.[33]

Arthur Rimbaud, who had fled to London to avoid police enquiries into his tenuous connections with the Commune, was similarly effusive. He was 'delighted and astonished' by the 'energy', the 'tough' but 'healthy' life, the fog, which he likened to a 'setting sun seen through grey crêpe', and the drunkenness and vice, which made Paris seem provincial.[34] Several exiles also appreciated London's cultural and intellectual amenities. Schoelcher enjoyed 'tak[ing] in the very beautiful concerts which are both well composed and well executed'.[35] Nadaud used the British Museum's reading room to familiarize himself with British history and economic theory, knowledge on which he later drew to publish several books after his return to France.[36] Rimbaud, too, spent much time in the reading room, where he composed a poem which was published in the *Gentleman's Magazine*, and wrote the great work of Franglais, *Illuminations*. The Crystal Palace also attracted wide acclaim. Esquiros praised it as a wondrous temple of modern, secular knowledge.[37] Even Victor Hugo, who detested London and spent his exile in the Channel Islands, tersely recorded of one of his few trips to the metropolis: 'Crystal Palace, merveille. Tussaud, *humbug* (supercherie)'.[38]

The French colonization of these areas did not go unnoticed. Charles Dickens's *Household Words* referred to the area in and around Soho as a new Patmos, a reference to the Greek island where the apostle John was supposed to have been exiled:

> The Patmos of London I may describe as an island bounded by four squares; on the north by that of Soho, on the south by that of Leicester, on the east by the quadrangle of Lincoln's Inn Fields (for the purlieus of Long Acre and Seven Dials are all Patmos), and on the west by Golden Square.[39]

Although the refugees who populated London's 'great *champ d'asile*' were drawn from numerous European countries, the French denizens of these neighbourhoods were distinctive and unmistakeable.

---

[33] A. Esquiros, *The English at Home*, ed. and trans. L. Wraxall (2 vols., 1861), i. 116.

[34] G. Robb, *Rimbaud* (2000), pp. 184, 194.

[35] Victor Schoelcher to Ernest Legouvé (no date) (Schmidt, *Correspondance de Schoelcher*, p. 255).

[36] M. Nadaud, *Histoire des classes ouvrières en Angleterre* (Paris, 1873), pp. viii–ix.

[37] A. Esquiros, *Religious Life in England* (1867), pp. 196–7.

[38] *Lettres: Victor Hugo, Victor Schoelcher*, ed. J. Gaudon and S. Gaudon (Charenton-le-Pont, 1998), p. 184, n. 1.

[39] *Household Words*, 12 March 1853, p. 26.

Here are Frenchmen – ex-representatives of the people, ex-ministers, prefects and republican commissaries, Prolétaires, Fourierists, Phalansterians, disciples of Proudhon, Pierre le Roux [*sic*] and Cahagnet, professors of barricade building; men yet young, but two-thirds of whose lives have been spent in prison or in exile.[40]

These neighbourhoods had essentially become a European, and especially French, space. As the radical journalist Adolphe Smith recalled in 1909, 'the caricaturists inevitably associated the foreigner with Leicester Square, and it is in this neighbourhood that are still to be found the greatest number of foreign shops, restaurants, cafés, and hotels'.[41]

The exiles' social and economic life in London

Socially, the exiles occupied a number of niches in London. Economically, they were often able to continue their previous scholarly or artisanal pursuits, or found work by meeting London's brisk demand for French cooking, tailoring and language instruction, whether they had experience in those trades or not. Still, poverty was rife and, with it, demoralization and despair. To counteract these problems, the refugees constructed a vibrant miniature civil society for themselves in their Soho enclave. Yet they were not wholly insular, and many achieved high levels of social integration with particular segments of British society.

As we have seen, many exiles had been journalists and professional politicians. Some of these men of letters struggled to survive by the pen. Exile newspapers, with the notable exception of the Jersey-based *L'Homme*, usually folded fairly quickly, as did a planned French cultural centre in Bloomsbury.[42] Yet some did successfully make a living through scholarly pursuits. Blanc spent much of his exile completing his mammoth history of the French Revolution and was delighted that 'the *British Museum* contains upon the French Revolution many precious documents, many sources, of which no historian has yet availed himself'.[43] Schoelcher produced a biography, *The Life of Handel*, which met with considerable critical and commercial success.[44] Jean Philibert Berjeau, co-founder of the radical

---

[40] *Household Words*, 12 March 1853, pp. 25, 27.

[41] A. Smith, 'Political refugees', in *London in the 19th Century*, ed. W. Besant (1909), pp. 399–406, at p. 399.

[42] R. Tombs and I. Tombs, *That Sweet Enemy: the French and the British from the Sun King to the Present* (2006), p. 387.

[43] *Louis Blanc's Monthly Review* (Oct. 1849), p. 128.

[44] V. Schoelcher, *The Life of Handel*, trans. J. Lowe (1857); Schoelcher expressed satisfaction with the book's reception in a letter to Victor Hugo on 19 May 1857 (see Gaudon and Gaudon, *Lettres: Hugo, Schoelcher*, pp. 171–2).

Vraie république, authored and edited numerous texts and periodicals on bibliophilia. François Tafery, former publisher of the radical *L'Oeil du peuple* in the Vendée, set up a printing press in Islington.[45] Other scholarly-inclined exiles were invited to give lectures to London's various local literary societies, as when Nadaud lectured in Ealing on French and British history.[46] Blanc was contracted by the Marylebone Literary and Scientific Society to lecture on France in the eighteenth century and received the considerable sum of £25 per appearance for his efforts.[47]

Many exile artisans and manual labourers also continued in their old trades. Nadaud, who had been a mason before turning to politics, was hired to do building work at sites all over London and as far out as Foots Cray in Bexley, near Sidcup.[48] Benoît Desquesnes, a local *démoc-soc* leader from Valenciennes who had previously studied art and sculpture in Paris, received commissions not only to paint individual portraits, but to assist in the sculpting of the decorations for the Crystal Palace.[49] Similarly, the Communard sculptor Jules Dalou, who would later create the statue of the Triumph of the Republic in Paris's Place de la Nation, received a commission for the royal mausoleum at Frogmore in Windsor Park.[50] A number of Communard engineers, printers and ceramic makers were able successfully to start their own companies in London.[51]

In some trades, there was strong demand for French labour. The prestige of Parisian cooks, cobblers and tailors was particularly high, and many provincial exiles working in these sectors falsely claimed to hail from Paris, even if they had never before set foot in the capital.[52] Others decided to enter these trades for the first time after arriving in London. The former artist and cartoonist Georges (Labadie) Pilotelle or Pilotell, for example, became a successful ladies' dress designer and also a theatrical designer, memorably creating the costume for the 'super-aesthetical' poet Bunthorne in Gilbert and Sullivan's operetta *Patience*.[53] Caussidière became a wine merchant whose customers included the lieutenant-governor of Jersey.[54] Two members

[45] Prescott, 'The cause of humanity', p. 36.

[46] Nadaud, *Mémoires*, pp. 435–7.

[47] L. Loubère, *Louis Blanc: his Life and Contribution to the Rise of French Jacobin-Socialism* (Evanston, Ill., 1961), p. 127.

[48] Nadaud, *Mémoires*, p. 415.

[49] B. Desquesnes, *Esquisse autobiographique d'une victime du coup d'état du 2 décembre, 1851, crime et parjure de Louis Bonaparte* (Blackpool, 1888), p. 25.

[50] B. Tillier, *La Commune de Paris, révolution sans images?* (Seyssel, 2004), pp. 273–4.

[51] Martinez, 'Paris Communard refugees', p. 143.

[52] Lefrançais, *Souvenirs*, p. 192.

[53] Information kindly supplied to the authors by Mr. A. E. Bohannon, Pilotelle's grandson.

[54] TNA, HO 45/4547A, police reports of 26 and 28 Sept. 1852.

of the Commune's council, Auguste Serailler and Jules-Paul Johannard, engaged in the typically Parisian manufacture of artificial flowers.[55] French language lessons were also in high demand among London's 'well-bred English men and women' and many exiles became freelance language tutors.[56] The *Quarante-huitards*, arriving shortly after the European-wide disturbances of 1848, occasionally faced stiff competition in this sector from French domestic servants, who did not offend the political and aesthetic sensibilities of London's respectable classes: 'They often preferred these latter to the dreadful exiles, those enemies of order and religion and *wearing a full beard*'.[57] Fortunately for the exiles, these prejudices seem to have dissipated as the years passed and tutoring became one of the more reliable sources of income for refugees like Rimbaud and Paul Verlaine who offered their lucky customers 'LEÇONS de FRANÇAIS, en français – perfection, finesses'.[58]

A surprising number of exiles also secured posts in Britain's schools and universities. Nadaud began teaching French at a number of small private schools in Putney and Ealing in 1855, before transferring in 1858 to the preparatory military academy in Wimbledon, where he taught French and history until his return to France in 1870.[59] Pierre Barrère also taught at Wimbledon, before taking up a lecturing position at the Royal Military Academy at Woolwich.[60] Britain's military academies seem to have been particularly fertile ground for the exiles. When Barrère joined Woolwich, two of his fellow exiles, Esquiros and Joseph Savoye, were already employed as examiners.[61] They were succeeded in the 1870s and 1880s by General La Cécilia, Hector France and Pierre Barrère's son, Camille.[62] Sandhurst, meanwhile, employed first the *Quarante-huitard* Alfred Talandier and later the Communard Jules Andrieu.[63] Back in the heart of London, Dalou taught at the Royal Academy of Art, while Bocquet was hired by University College London twice, first as an exile during the Second Empire and again after fleeing the destruction of the Commune.[64]

[55] Martinez, 'Paris Communard refugees', p. 143.

[56] Porter, *Refugee Question*, p. 22.

[57] 'On préfère de beaucoup ces derniers aux affreux proscrits, ennemis de l'ordre et de la religion et *portant toute leur barbe*' (Lefrançais, *Souvenirs*, p. 193).

[58] Robb, *Rimbaud*, pp. 208–9.

[59] Nadaud, *Mémoires*, pp. 429–43.

[60] Ferragu, 'Anglophones', p. 545.

[61] Nadaud, *Mémoires*, p. 447.

[62] Martinez, 'Paris Communard refugees', pp. 139–40, 300, 512.

[63] S. Aprile '"Translations" politiques et culturelles: les proscrits français et Angleterre', *Genèses, sciences sociales et histoire*, xxxviii (2000), 33–55, at p. 36; Martinez, 'Paris Communard refugees', p. 301.

[64] Martinez, 'Paris Communard refugees', pp. 75, 477, 496.

Edouard Vaillant, one of the original agitators for the Commune and a member of its council, also found employment at UCL, where he taught medicine.

Yet many refugees were unable to procure work at all and accounts of extreme misery abound in exile memoirs.[65] Poverty caused many to abandon London altogether. By March 1853, only fifteen months after Bonaparte's coup, the Metropolitan Police estimated that some 3,000 refugees had already departed Britain's shores.[66] The bulk of these returned to France, their families and quietly apolitical (or, at best, clandestinely political) lives. They were able to do so either through the partial amnesties and commutations issued by Bonaparte in the early 1850s, because they had personally pleaded for clemency, or because they had voluntarily fled the chaos and violence of 1848–52 and had not been officially proscribed.[67] A smaller, but still sizeable number gave up on Europe entirely and went to start new lives in the United States. Some, like the Soho-based Breymond in 1852, asked the British state to assist their passage. 'I come in the name of several French political refugees, who, like myself, beg you to provide us the means of passing to America where we wish to use our hands; which is impossible for us here'.[68] The British government was willing to oblige, not least because the exiles' presence in London complicated its diplomatic relations with Bonaparte's regime.[69] It therefore discreetly provided exiles who asked for assistance with free, one-way passage to New York.[70] By 1858, approximately 1,500 French and other refugees had made their way to America at the British taxpayers' expense.[71] From about 1873, there was a similar decrease in London's Communard population, as refugees dispersed

[65] Some notable examples include Hugo, *Les Hommes de l'exil*, pp. 161–6; Lefrançais, *Souvenirs*, pp. 209–10; and Nadaud, *Mémoires*, p. 414. See also Martinez, 'Paris Communard refugees', pp. 57–61.

[66] TNA, HO 45/4816, police report of 19 March 1853.

[67] For examples, see Calman, *Ledru-Rollin*, p. 189; Lefrançais, *Souvenirs*, pp. 160–1, 223; V. Wright, 'The coup d'état of December 1851: repression and the limits to repression', in *Revolution and Reaction: 1848 and Second French Republic*, ed. R. Price (1975), pp. 303–33, at pp. 325–6.

[68] TNA, HO 45/4302, letter from Breymond, 3 Jan. 1852: 'Je viens au nom de plusieurs réfugiés politiques français, qui, ainsi que moi, se trouvent dans la misère, vous prier de nous faciliter les moyens de passer en Amérique où nous désirerions utiliser nos bras; ce qui nous est impossible ici'. The name may also be 'Breymoud', as his handwriting is somewhat difficult to decipher. Nothing further is known of him.

[69] The best account of the refugees' problematic role in Britain's diplomatic relations remains Porter, *Refugee Question*.

[70] Tickets were to be issued 'without public notice being taken' (see TNA, HO 45/4302, memorandum by 'G' (most likely Earl Granville) [n.d., 1852]).

[71] Porter, *Refugee Question*, p. 161.

to such destinations as the United States, South America, New Zealand and the Communard enclaves in Brussels and Switzerland.[72]

Physical deprivation, cultural disorientation and political defeat often bred demoralization. The Communard Poncerot (full name not known) coined the term 'l'exilité' to describe the unique sense of dislocated ennui that afflicted the exiles.[73] This was compounded by the fear of police spies, who came over in great numbers from France to monitor the exiles or to act as agents provocateurs.[74] Misery and mistrust could engender violent conflict, as when Emmanuel Barthélemy killed the elder Cournet in a duel in Egham in 1853.[75] Thus mutual assistance and solidarity were necessary to combat the deprivations of exile life. Refugees often assisted one another in securing or locating work. Blanc and Pierre Barrère, for example, alerted Nadaud to his first teaching opportunity, and it was the recommendation of Tristan Duché that secured posts for both Barrère and Nadaud at Wimbledon.[76] More directly, a number of Communard-run ceramics, engineering and printing concerns were staffed exclusively by refugees, and one musical instrument maker in Georgiana Street, Camden Town, employed at least fifteen other exiles.[77] But by far the most common form of exilic mutual assistance was charity for the indigent and unemployed. The most significant organization dedicated to these ends was the Société Fraternelle des Démocrates-Socialistes à Londres founded in 1850. This organization, which featured prominent refugees like Blanc, Caussidière, Charles Delescluze and Ledru-Rollin, raised numerous charitable subscriptions from British and French benefactors. Despite its successes in alleviating the worst exile misery, it was undermined by internal squabbles and was defunct by 1860.[78] In the first few years after 1871, similar efforts were undertaken by the Société des Refugiés de la Commune.[79] Meanwhile, exile organizations not specifically dedicated to charity also occasionally provided relief. The Philadelphes ran a free, French-language medical dispensary while the Imprimerie Universelle dedicated the proceeds of many of its publications to indigent exiles.[80] And,

---

[72] Martinez, 'Paris Communard refugees', p. 206.

[73] Martinez, 'Paris Communard refugees', p. 206.

[74] TNA, HO 45/4547A, police report of 19 Sept. 1853.

[75] Hugo, Les Hommes de l'exil, pp. 30–8.

[76] Ferragu, 'Anglophones', p. 545; Nadaud, Mémoires, pp. 429–30, 437–8.

[77] Martinez, 'Paris Communard refugees', pp. 142–3.

[78] The Société Fraternelle is mentioned in numerous sources, but a good comprehensive account appears in Calman, Ledru-Rollin, pp. 35–6, 70, 140–8. It may have re-emerged with the influx of Communards in 1871 (see Martinez, 'Paris Communard refugees', pp. 84, 99).

[79] Martinez, 'Paris Communard refugees', pp. 135ff.

[80] Prescott, 'The cause of humanity', p. 36; For examples of Imprimerie publications raising money for indigent exiles, see V. Hugo, Discours sur la tombe du citoyen Jean Bousquet,

in 1871–2, there was a general outpouring of charity from the remaining, and usually well-established, *Quarante-huitards* to the incoming wave of Communards.[81]

Such charitable ventures formed a central part of the refugees' vibrant, ad-hoc civil society. This included clubs like the Cercle d'Etudes Sociales which, from its headquarters in Francis Street, 'developed an ambitious programme of educational and discussion meetings which included English lessons, research into the causes and content of the Commune and the establishment of a newspaper reading room'.[82] Similar roles were taken on by the refugees' various freemason lodges. Elements of the exile press sought to 'preserve and tighten links between the exiles' and *L'Homme* therefore dedicated significant column-space to advertisements for exile businesses, services, products and events.[83] There were also attempts to educate the exiles' children. Jeanne Deroin, a former headmistress in Paris, opened a boarding school for 'daughters of fellow exiles' in 1861. A decade later, a new school for the Communards' children gained wide support in the refugee committee, including a £100 loan from La Cécilia. Unfortunately, both of these initiatives failed, the former because Deroin charged exceedingly low fees and the latter due to sadly typical squabbling among its administrators and benefactors.[84] More casually, exile social life was marked by a succession of banquets, tea parties, dances, raffles and various fundraising events for needy refugees. Funerals provided a grimmer impetus for sociability, and often included long processions and rousing eulogies urging exile solidarity.

British reactions to the exile community varied. The government, with a few notable exceptions like the Orsini affair, was usually content to leave the exiles more or less alone. The Metropolitan Police did set up a new 'foreign branch' to keep regular tabs on their activities, an illiberal first for the force.[85] But even here, the Met's chief undercover agent, the bearded and French-speaking Sanders, repeatedly informed his superiors that Britain had little to fear from the refugees.[86] In the wider public, a few feared and

---

proscrit, mort à Jersey. Prononcé le 20 avril 1853, au cimetière de Saint-Jean (Jersey, 1853); and V. Hugo, *Discours sur la tombe de la citoyenne Louise Julien, morte à Jersey. Prononcé le 26 juillet 1853, au cimetière de Saint-Jean* (Jersey, 1853).

[81] Martinez, 'Paris Communard refugees', pp. 76–7.

[82] Martinez, 'Paris Communard refugees', p. 220.

[83] S. Aprile, 'Voices of exile: French newspapers in England', in Freitag, *Exiles from European Revolutions*, pp. 149–63, at p. 152.

[84] P. Pilbeam, 'Deroin, Jeanne (1805–1894)', *ODNB*; Martinez, 'Paris Communard refugees', pp. 253–5.

[85] B. Porter, *Plots and Paranoia: a History of Political Espionage in Britain, 1790–1988* (1992), p. 92.

[86] TNA, HO 45/3518, police report of 1 Nov. 1851; HO 45/4302, police report of 13 Feb. 1852; HO 45/4816, police reports of 5 March and 8 Nov. 1853.

loathed the revolutionary aspect of the exiles' politics, including Thomas Macaulay who informed a friend that if he had been in charge of France, the suppression of the 'June Days' would have been far bloodier.[87] The great bulk of the established press took a more nuanced view. While *démoc-soc* politics were by no means popular with papers like *The Times*, their right to asylum was undeniable and it was a credit to Britain that it offered refuge to all, regardless of their politics.[88] Similarly, although *The Economist* abhorred the 'atrocities of the Commune's last acts', it recognized that those acts were political and therefore non-extraditable.[89]

The exiles also enjoyed more fulsome support. A few well-known exiles worked their way into London high society. Blanc, already relatively famous for his political writings when he arrived in London, 'did not hesitate to accept invitations to dine among the members of English high society. The cosmopolitanism of their dinner parties was an exhilarating pleasure, and he appeared at them, wrote Carlyle, "looking as neat as if he had just come out of a bandbox"'.[90] Esquiros, who spent much of his exile writing books and articles on British culture, was soon able to 'move freely in English literary and intellectual circles where he became acquainted with John Stuart Mill, Dickens, and Frederick Temple, then Headmaster of Rugby and subsequently Archbishop of Canterbury'.[91] Schoelcher frequented the liberal salons of John Chapman and Arethusa Gibson.[92] Dalou, who commented that the 'English welcome us with open arms', integrated into leading artistic circles and soon attracted commissions from wealthy benefactors.[93] After Frederic Harrison introduced him into London's leading literary circles, Camille Barrère began writing articles for the *Graphic, Echo, World* and *Fraser's Magazine*.[94]

The exiles also had political sympathizers from whom they received financial aid, assistance with the publication, dissemination and translation of their works, and positive press coverage. Some of this support came from

---

[87] F. Bensimon, 'The French exiles and the British', in Freitag, *Exiles from European Revolutions*, pp. 88–102, at p. 94.

[88] Porter, *Refugee Question*, p. 7.

[89] Quoted in M. Lenoir, 'Regards croisés: la représentation des nations dans la caricature, Allemagne, France, Royaume-Uni, 1870–1914' (unpublished University of Bourgogne M.A. dissertation, 2002), pp. 200–1.

[90] Loubère, *Louis Blanc*, p. 181.

[91] S. Beynon John, 'Alphonse Esquiros: a French political exile in Merthyr and Dowlais in 1864', *Merthyr Historian*, iii (1980), 112–23, at pp. 115–16.

[92] G. S. Haight, *George Eliot: a Biography* (Oxford, 1968), pp. 98–9; C. L. Cline, 'Disraeli and Thackeray', *Review of English Studies*, xix (1943), 404–8, at pp. 404–5.

[93] Martinez, 'Paris Communard refugees', pp. 299–300; Tillier, *Commune de Paris*, p. 188.

[94] Martinez, 'Paris Communard refugees', p. 300.

the intelligentsia. Blanc and J. S. Mill developed a close friendship and dined together often at Mill's home in Blackheath, discussing ideas and reviewing one another's work.[95] For Britain's small but influential school of Positivists, most notably E. S. Beesly, Richard Congreve and Harrison, the Commune represented an important theoretical and historical breakthrough of truly popular and direct self-government, the welcome incorporation of the working classes into political life, and a reassertion of local autonomy against an overweening centralized state.[96] They therefore became important patrons for the Communard refugees, for whom they ran an evening school in Francis Street and provided free English classes.[97] Harrison also raised multiple charitable sums and placed over 100 exiles in various forms of employment.[98] Radical politicians and MPs often provided similar assistance. Joseph Cowen used the international reach of his family's business to aid the exiles in their propaganda-smuggling operations, and he and Mill donated money to Simon Bernard's legal defence fund in 1858.[99] Similarly, the Communards' cause was defended in Parliament by MPs like Jacob Bright, Charles Dilke, A. J. Mundella and George Whalley.[100] Finally, as we will see in more detail below, the exiles developed close links to a number of radical British activists and elements of the popular press. Notable among these was George Jacob Holyoake who, from his 'Fleet Street House' at 147 Fleet Street, printed exile pamphlets, acted as one of the principal vendors of *L'Homme*, and sold portraits and busts both by and of the refugees.[101]

Exile activism and London as a transnational political space

With these contacts, the exiles were able to place themselves at a unique intersection on London's political map. As members of the French republican

[95] Bensimon, 'The French exiles', p. 96; J. Morley, *Recollections* (2 vols., 1917), i. 52; R. Reeves, *John Stuart Mill: Victorian Firebrand* (2007), pp. 241, 309. Some of their correspondence is published in J. S. Mill, *Collected Works of John Stuart Mill* (33 vols., Toronto, 1963–91), xiv–xvii. See also Blanc's affectionate obituary of Mill in L. Blanc, *Questions d'aujourd'hui et de demain* (5 vols., Paris, 1873–84), iii. 329–53.

[96] For a collection of Positivist, and other, defences of the Commune and Communards, see *The English Defence of the Commune*, ed. R. Harrison (1971).

[97] Smith, 'Political refugees', p. 401.

[98] Martinez, 'Paris Communard refugees', pp. 65–6.

[99] E. Rowland Jones, *The Life and Speeches of Joseph Cowen, M.P.* (1885), p. 16; Newcastle, Tyne and Wear Archives (hereafter TWA), Cowen collection, 634/A617, Alfred B. Richards to Joseph Cowen, 12 July 1858.

[100] Martinez, 'Paris Communard refugees', p. 55.

[101] M. Finn, *After Chartism: Class and Nation in English Radical Politics* (Cambridge, 1993), p. 118.

and socialist Left, new participants in Britain's domestic radical tradition, and founding members of the emerging pan-European internationalist movement, the refugees significantly contributed to London's emerging role as a transnational political space and international laboratory of ideas.

The *Quarante-huitards* used London as a base to continue their struggle against Bonaparte. Chief among the societies they formed to undermine the Second Empire were the Commune Révolutionnaire (CR), the Société de la Révolution (SR) and the Union Socialiste (US).[102] The CR and US were officially socialistic, while the SR adhered to a strictly non-socialist radical republicanism.[103] All three organizations issued propaganda and employed highly innovative strategies to smuggle material into France. Desquesnes recalled one operation in which busts of the French empress were manufactured in Britain and stuffed with seditious material before being exported to France.[104] The CR and SR also sent agents into France to build up the domestic resistance to Napoleon III. This latter strategy was risky and some prominent exiles, like Delescluze and Jean Baptiste Boichot, were captured and imprisoned on clandestine trips.[105] Nevertheless, the CR successfully established a number of cells across France.[106] These organizations peaked in the early and mid 1850s. Financial strains forced the US to fold in 1852, while the other two organizations seem to have lasted until the end of the decade.[107] By that point, and especially after the amnesty of 1859, declining numbers sapped the refugees' political momentum. Nevertheless, through the 1860s, a number of prominent and intransigent exiles, including Blanc, Esquiros, Nadaud, Pyat and Schoelcher remained in London, where they continued to issue individual critiques of Bonaparte's regime.

The Communards were less ambitious. Despite early, quixotic interest in resuscitating the Commune, their hopes were focused not on upending the Third Republic, but on receiving amnesty from it. After the republican electoral victories of 1876 made an amnesty seem possible, the Communards began a spirited campaign pleading their case to their political allies in France, including some former refugees like Blanc.[108] For the partisans of the

---

[102] Calman, *Ledru-Rollin*, p. 135; Boichot, *Souvenirs d'un prisonnier*, pp. 8–9; A. Müller Lehning, 'The International Association (1855–9)', *International Review for Social History*, iii (1938), 204, 207; *Leader*, 5 June 1852, p. 529.

[103] Lehning, 'International Association', p. 204; *Leader*, 12 June 1852, p. 557; Calman, *Ledru-Rollin*, p. 135.

[104] Desquesnes, *Esquisse autobiographique*, p. 22.

[105] Dessal, *Révolutionnaire jacobin*, p. 109; Boichot, *Souvenirs d'un prisonnier*, pp. 11–13.

[106] Lehning, 'International Association', p. 217.

[107] Lehning, 'International Association', p. 201; Calman, *Ledru-Rollin*, pp. 135–6.

[108] For the refugees' lengthy campaign for an amnesty, see Martinez, 'Paris Communard refugees', pp. 311–26. For a thorough account of the amnesty debate, see J. T. Joughin, *The*

Commune, whose revolt in 1871 had been less against the Third Republic per se than against its perceived betrayal by the Versailles government, an amnesty was sufficient for their reintegration into French political life. Many republicans of 1848, by contrast, could not abide an imperial regime and were determined to remain in London until Bonaparte's fall, hence their greater seditious activism and longer exile.

At the same time, a number of exiles became involved in, and decisively shaped, several of London's most iconic radical movements. Among these was Chartism, which, despite its anticlimactic Kennington Common demonstration in 1848, persisted into the 1850s, particularly in London under Ernest Jones. Blanc and Caussidière, for example, helped George Julian Harney to set up his *Democratic Review* newspaper in 1849, where he dedicated much space to favourable coverage of the exiles and translations of their works and speeches.[109] More extensively, the CR and Jones's International Committee (IC), set up to 'deal with international questions', began a campaign of official co-operation in 1855, holding joint events and issuing propaganda together.[110] Margot Finn has argued, somewhat controversially, that this contact infected London Chartism with an explicitly socialistic character, visible with individuals like Harney, whose *Democratic Review* was succeeded by the *Red Republican*.[111]

A number of other radical movements also attracted exile participation. Jules Lechevalier, a refugee from 1849, joined the co-operative efforts of Britain's Christian socialists, led by Charles Kingsley, John Malcolm Ludlow, Frederick Maurice and others. Lechevalier gave lectures in support of the cause across London and founded a Central Co-operative Agency to promote consumers' co-operatives. Disputes over the allocation of resources, however, led to a bitter falling out with figures like Ludlow, and Lechevalier abruptly returned to France in 1854.[112] In contrast to this theologically inspired push for social reform, other exiles established links to Britain's secularist movement. The *Quarante-huitard* Victor Le Lubez

---

Paris Commune in French Politics, 1871–80: the History of the Amnesty of 1880 (Baltimore, Md., 1955). For Blanc's role in the amnesty, see S. Aprile, 'Louis Blanc, un des pères fondateurs de la "vraie République"', in *Louis Blanc: un socialiste en république*, ed. F. Démier (Paris, 2005), pp. 171–81, at pp. 175–8; and Loubère, *Louis Blanc*, p. 228.

[109] Finn, *After Chartism*, p. 121. For examples, see the (monthly) issues of the *Democratic Review* between June 1849 and Aug. 1850.

[110] For an account of the IC, see Lehning, 'International Association', pp. 212–22.

[111] Finn, *After Chartism*, ch. 3 *passim*. For a rebuttal of this interpretation, see M. Taylor, *The Decline of British Radicalism, 1847–60* (Oxford, 1995), pp. 111–14.

[112] For his own account of these events, see J. Lechevalier, *Five Years in the Land of Refuge* (1854). For Ludlow's less than flattering view of Lechevalier, see J. M. Ludlow, *John Ludlow: the Autobiography of a Christian Socialist* (1981), pp. 186–7, 233–4.

joined a secularist organization in Stratford and became close with Charles Bradlaugh, president of the National Secular Society, where Le Lubez's rousing renditions of the Marseillaise were highly popular.[113] There was also a high degree of interchange between the secularists and the exiles' masonic lodges, which had dropped all references to deities and dedicated their work 'Au nom de la Raison de la Fraternité Universelle'.[114] Bradlaugh and Austin Holyoake joined the Philadelphes, and the lodge founded new branches in Woolwich and Stratford which attracted overwhelmingly freethinking British memberships.[115] The movement for franchise reform also drew in a number of exiles. In July 1866, Blanc attended the famous 'monster' demonstration in favour of reform in Hyde Park.[116] Joseph Collet, meanwhile, was a member of Bronterre O'Brien's National Reform League and dedicated much space in his English-language *Working Man* newspaper to covering and promoting the movement.[117] Le Lubez joined the famous Reform League, serving on its executive council between 1867 and the organization's official winding down in 1869.[118]

The aftermath of the 1867 Reform Act saw a burst of ultra-radical activity in London which drew in representatives of both refugee generations. The most famous of these was the Land and Labour League, an organization founded in 1869 that vigorously pushed for universal male suffrage, progressive taxation, free education, land nationalization and other radical causes.[119] Lassassie joined the league and occasionally addressed its 'Sir Robert Peel' branch.[120] Le Lubez was a founding member of its executive committee and occasionally acted as treasurer.[121] At the same time, Britain's republican movement was flourishing in London. One republican organization, the International Democratic Association (IDA), which counted Le Lubez

[113] Prescott, 'The cause of humanity', p. 57, n. 75; E. Royle, *Radicals, Secularists and Republicans: Popular Freethought in Britain, 1866–1915* (Manchester, 1980), pp. 140, 201.

[114] Prescott, 'The cause of humanity', p. 36.

[115] Prescott, 'The cause of humanity', pp. 30, 36.

[116] Louis Blanc to *Le Temps*, 24 July 1866, in L. Blanc, *Dix ans de l'histoire de l'Angleterre* (10 vols., Paris, 1879–81), vi. 261–6.

[117] S. Coltham, 'English working-class newspapers in 1867', *Victorian Studies*, xiii (1969), 159–80, at pp. 164, 173–5; R. Harrison, *Before the Socialists: Studies in Labour and Politics, 1861–81* (1965), p. 92.

[118] *Daily News*, 4 July 1867, p. 3; *Reynolds's Newspaper*, 10 Nov. 1867, p. 8 and 21 Feb. 1869, p. 5; 'Special meeting of the executive committee of the Reform League, 12 March 1869', in *The Era of the Reform League: Selected by Gustav Mayer*, ed. J. Breuilly, G. Niedhart and A. Taylor (Mannheim, 1995), p. 300.

[119] Harrison, *Before the Socialists*, pp. 216–17, 229.

[120] Martinez, 'Paris Communard refugees', p. 77.

[121] H. Collins and C. Abramsky, *Karl Marx and the British Labour Movement: Years of the First International* (1965), p. 165; Royle, p. 200; Harrison, *Before the Socialists*, p. 237.

among its members, warmly welcomed the advent of the Paris Commune, denounced the Versailles government and compared the Communards' plight to that of the *Quarante-huitards*: 'We recognize in you the pioneers of progress and the architects of a new and purer social state; whilst we regard your oppressors, the men of Versailles, as the worthy disciples of the Man of December, and as the cowardly and mercenary instruments of European despots'.[122] After the Commune collapsed, the IDA served as one of the main sources of British support for the Communard refugees.[123] Some of these latter, like Jacques Chilmann, head of the nineteenth *arrondissement*'s municipal council during the Commune, subsequently joined the ubiquitous Le Lubez in the IDA's successor organization, the Universal Republican League.[124]

Finally, the French refugees were crucial to London's emergence as the centre of a new, pan-European internationalism. This began in 1850, when Ledru-Rollin, together with an international group of prominent exiles in London, including the Pole Arnold Darasz, the Hungarian Lajos Kossuth, the Italian Giuseppe Mazzini and the German Arnold Ruge, formed the Comité Central Démocratique Européen.[125] These refugees were convinced that the revolutions of 1848 had failed because of a lack of international revolutionary co-ordination and proposed that collective action would reverse their defeats. Until its collapse in the late 1850s, the Comité utilized Ledru-Rollin's *Voix du proscrit* newspaper for propaganda, sent agents into Europe 'pour organiser l'opinion républicain' and, through its 'Shilling Subscription for European Freedom', raised money for the cause and provided a degree of leadership for Europe's scattered revolutionaries.[126] Another attempt at international political co-ordination occurred in 1856, when the CR, Jones's International Committee and a number of German and Polish refugees formed a new International Association (IA). Unlike the Comité, this organization was explicitly socialist, and hoped to establish a 'Universal Democratic and Social Republic'.[127] It was also explicitly feminist, and women such as Deroin addressed its meetings.[128]

---

[122] *Bee-Hive*, 22 Apr. 1871, p. 13.

[123] Martinez, 'Paris Communard refugees', pp. 25–6, 30, 35.

[124] Harrison, *Before the Socialists*, p. 237; Martinez, 'Paris Communard refugees', p. 491.

[125] Calman, *Ledru-Rollin*, pp. 95–6.

[126] On propaganda, see Dessal, *Revolutionnaire jacobin*, p. 153. For the point on agents, see Calman, *Ledru-Rollin*, p. 97. The subscription's announcement can be found in TWA, Cowen collection, 634/A151. For its cancellation, see Cowen's and Linton's notice of 23 Dec. 1852, repr. in the *English Republic* newspaper on 1 Jan. 1853, pp. 212–13. For the Comité's collapse, see Calman, *Ledru-Rollin*, p. 123.

[127] From the IA's statutes, quoted in Lehning, 'International Association', p. 263.

[128] Lehning, 'International Association', p. 228.

The IA was impressively active in the late 1850s, holding events like a celebration of the tenth anniversary of the 1848 revolutions in the John Street Scientific Institution, and running a quadrilingual newspaper, the *Bulletin de l'International*, from its headquarters in High Holborn.[129] Yet, as was so often the case with exile organizations, internal disputes over administration and doctrine, and the fear of police spies destroyed the IA's cohesiveness and by 1859 it collapsed.

London's most famous and influential organization of this type was the International Working Men's Association (IWMA). Founded in 1864 in St. Martin's Hall and headquartered first in Greek Street and then at 256 High Holborn, the IWMA embraced an internationally and ideologically diverse membership. Several French exiles were crucial to its early history. Bocquet and Le Lubez attended the inaugural meeting, Le Lubez helped to shape its organizational structure by successfully proposing a plan for 'a central commission in London representing all the affiliated national sections', and Collet's bilingual *International Courier* operated as the IWMA's semi-official newspaper until it folded in 1867. But the exiles, who hoped to use the IWMA to agitate against Bonaparte, soon clashed with other Internationalists, including Marx, who thought that a more circumspect approach would facilitate the International's expansion into French territory. This dispute ultimately caused a rift in the IWMA and most of the French refugees resigned from its official general council. Through their autonomous 'London French' branch, they continued to propagandize against Bonaparte, who responded by clamping down on the IWMA branches in France. The IWMA therefore severed all relations with the 'London French' branch, which remained active into the early 1870s and helped to give rise to the IDA and Universal Republican League.[130]

Meanwhile, in 1871, Marx authored *The Civil War in France*, a robust defence of the Commune and vitriolic denunciation of Versailles, on behalf of the IWMA's general council. The council also organized charitable relief for the incoming Communard refugees, several hundred of whom joined the organization after arriving in London, including Vaillant, who served as an important ideological ally for Marx in the organization.[131] During

---

[129] *Bulletin de l'Internationale*, 1 March 1858, p. 1; Lehning, 'International Association', pp. 227–8.

[130] International Working Men's Association: General Council, *The General Council of the First International: Minutes* (5 vols., Moscow, 1963–8), i. 443; general council meetings of 2 Oct. 1866 and 16 Apr. 1867, in *General Council: Minutes*, ii. 42, 111; general council meeting of 10 May 1870, in *General Council: Minutes*, iii. 236; Collins and Abramsky, *Karl Marx*, pp. 36–7, 101–4, 135–6, 195, 251, n. 1; Coltham, pp. 175–6.

[131] Martinez, 'Paris Communard refugees', pp. 161–2; Collins and Abramsky, *Karl Marx*,

the first year of their exile in London, the IWMA provided a focal point for Communard activity and the means by which many of them hoped to strike back at the Versailles government. Those hopes were, of course, disappointed and organizational disputes soon led some refugees to form an autonomous branch called the Section Française de 1871, which, like the 'London French' branch before it, was critical of the general council.[132] The IWMA itself soon self-destructed at its 1872 congress in The Hague. Despite these fissures, the International, which owed so much of its early vitality to the French exiles in London, became an inspiration to many future attempts to build pan-European political institutions.

Throughout the decades the exiles deliberately blended these different political traditions together. *Quarante-huitards* like Blanc and Schoelcher attempted to justify the revolution of 1848 to a British audience and to cast French socialist politics in a light acceptable to British liberals.[133] In the 1870s, Communards like Camille Barrère did much the same with their own actions and experiences during the Franco-Prussian War and the Commune.[134] Many exilic works were also translated rapidly into English by friends of the refugees like Holyoake, Harney and Lascelles Wraxall.[135] The refugees also attempted to transplant what was best about Britain into France's political discourse. Thus Nadaud, who had watched the construction of London's Tube with astonishment, campaigned long and vigorously for a Paris *métro*, which finally began construction in 1898, the year of his death.[136] Moreover, many exiles were cognizant of the debt they owed to Britain's asylum, assembly and press rights (even Vallès admitted that London had taught him 'what liberty is'), and wanted the Third Republic to enshrine these civil liberties into law.[137] Britain's labour movement was also deemed worthy of emulation. Talandier therefore translated texts on co-operatives and Nadaud wrote histories of Britain's workers' associations in order to inspire French workers.[138] More abstractly, but with huge

pp. 264, 267.
[132] For an exhaustive account of the Communard refugees and the IWMA, see Martinez, 'Paris Communard refugees', ch. 6.
[133] L. Blanc, *1848: Historical Revelations. Inscribed to Lord Normanby* (1858); *Louis Blanc's Monthly Review*, Nov. 1849, pp. 134–5; *The Times*, 10 Apr. 1852, p. 7.
[134] For his journalistic endeavours, see Ferragu, 'Anglophones', p. 553. For an example of an account of his time as a functionary during the Franco-Prussian War written for a British audience, see his 'Six Months of Prefecture under Gambetta', *Fraser's Magazine*, Nov. 1872, pp. 651–66.
[135] Wraxall translated Esquiros's *The English at Home*.
[136] Nadaud, *Mémoires*, pp. 515–16.
[137] L. Blanc, *Discours politiques (1847 à 1881)* (Paris, 1882), pp. 221, 401; Nadaud, *Histoire*, pp. 181–2; Vallès, *La Rue à Londres*, p. 250.
[138] Aprile, 'Translations', pp. 36, 49; Nadaud, *Histoire*; M. Nadaud, *Les Sociétés des ouvrières*

consequences for the political development of France, the returning Blanquist Communards who had fraternized with Marx in London played a major role in the introduction of Marxism into France.[139] And while the defeats of 1848–52 and 1871 genuinely spurred the French left to try to build a truly international politics, one of the main appeals of organizations like the Comité Central, the IA and the IWMA remained their potential to achieve political change in Paris. The exiles' involvement in and intermixing of these diverse political currents helped to make Victorian London a truly transnational ideological and political space, a role that it would maintain well into the twentieth century.

Legacies of the exile community in London

The exiles left a lasting mark on London. A number of them chose to remain in the city even after they had been amnestied. Wealthy refugees like Ledru-Rollin and Schoelcher maintained their London residences and spent their post-exile years hopping back and forth across the Channel.[140] Others remained on a more permanent basis. Deroin, who found Britain's political atmosphere more congenial to female participation than France's, stayed in London and moved among the city's feminist, radical and socialist circles until her death in 1894.[141] Hector France remained at his post at Woolwich until 1895, and the law practice opened by the Communard Lefèvre-Roncier stayed open for some time.[142] Other familiar exile establishments, like Lassassie's barber shop or the shop of the Communard greengrocer Victor Richard, remained open into the 1880s and 1890s.[143] Some, like Pilotelle, started families in London and settled down. This remnant of the exile population was large enough that there was still a recognized 'French colony' between Fitzroy and Soho Squares at least until the early twentieth century. This area therefore provided a familiar haven for later generations of French visitors to London, and the anarchist refugees of the 1890s were immediately drawn to it.[144] Moreover, as the century turned and the children of the refugees, many of them born in London, came of age, this 'colony' was increasingly assimilated and contributed to the Franco-British

---

(Paris, 1873).

[139] Martinez, 'Paris Communard refugees', p. 247.

[140] Calman, Ledru-Rollin, pp. 251–2, 274; Schmidt, Correspondance de Schoelcher, p. 312, n. 1.

[141] Aprile, 'Translations', p. 43; Pilbeam, 'Deroin'. For more on Deroin, see Máire Cross's contribution to this volume.

[142] Martinez, 'Paris Communard refugees', pp. 416, 512, 536.

[143] Martinez, 'Paris Communard refugees', p. 77, Aprile, Siècle des exilés, pp. 266, 271.

[144] Aprile, Siècle des exilés, pp. 266, 271. For the anarchist exiles, see Constance Bantman's chapter in this volume.

rapprochement at the turn of the twentieth century. When, for example, President Emile Loubet made a state visit to London in 1903 to cement the budding Entente Cordiale, he met the 'French colony' in London, some of whom told him proudly that they were 'children of political exiles' who had lived in 'this great country' for half a century.[145] No doubt among them were children, or grandchildren, of *Quarante-huitards* and Communards who had by then become pillars of London society and defenders of the growing cross-Channel friendship.

---

[145] Tombs and Tombs, 'That sweet enemy', p. 441.

8. 'Almost the only free city in the world': mapping out the French anarchist presence in London, late 1870s–1914

Constance Bantman

The French anarchists who stayed intermittently in London between the late 1870s and the First World War closed the chapter of cross-Channel revolutionary exile in the long nineteenth century. While Britain's anarchist movement was relatively weak, comrades from all over Europe fled to London from the late 1870s onwards, just as the movement was starting to gain ground. By the late 1880s, French circles counted a few dozen individuals, many of them hotheads who had fled France to avoid prosecution for their very radical views or illegal activities. As terrorism spread within anarchist circles in the early 1890s, with the doctrine of 'propaganda by the deed', France was swept by repression; voluntary departures and expulsions resulted in the arrival of about 500 French-speaking comrades in London by 1895. These anarchist 'compagnons', as they called themselves, were not the most numerous group in the capital – that accolade belonged to the Jewish anarchists living in the East End, followed by the Germans settled around what used to be the Middlesex Hospital in Mortimer Street, W1. The French were, however, regarded as the most vocal of these increasingly undesirable refugees and crystallized many of the public fears associated with anarchism. An amnesty allowed most of them to return to France in February 1895, and although its terms were not quite clear many seized this opportunity. Thereafter, in the less feverish climate of the late 1890s until the First World War, the French and international circles lived on, devoting themselves to educational activities based in clubs, study groups and schools, in addition to their militant endeavours, now increasingly focused on trade-union-based revolutionary syndicalism.

This chapter charts four decades of anarchist presence in London through the prisms of space and perception. As a result of its rich history of exile, London had by the end of the nineteenth century become a connotated space, a palimpsest. The most literate and educated anarchist exiles were certainly conscious of walking in the footsteps of illustrious refugees, as evidenced by regular references to the generations of revolutionaries who

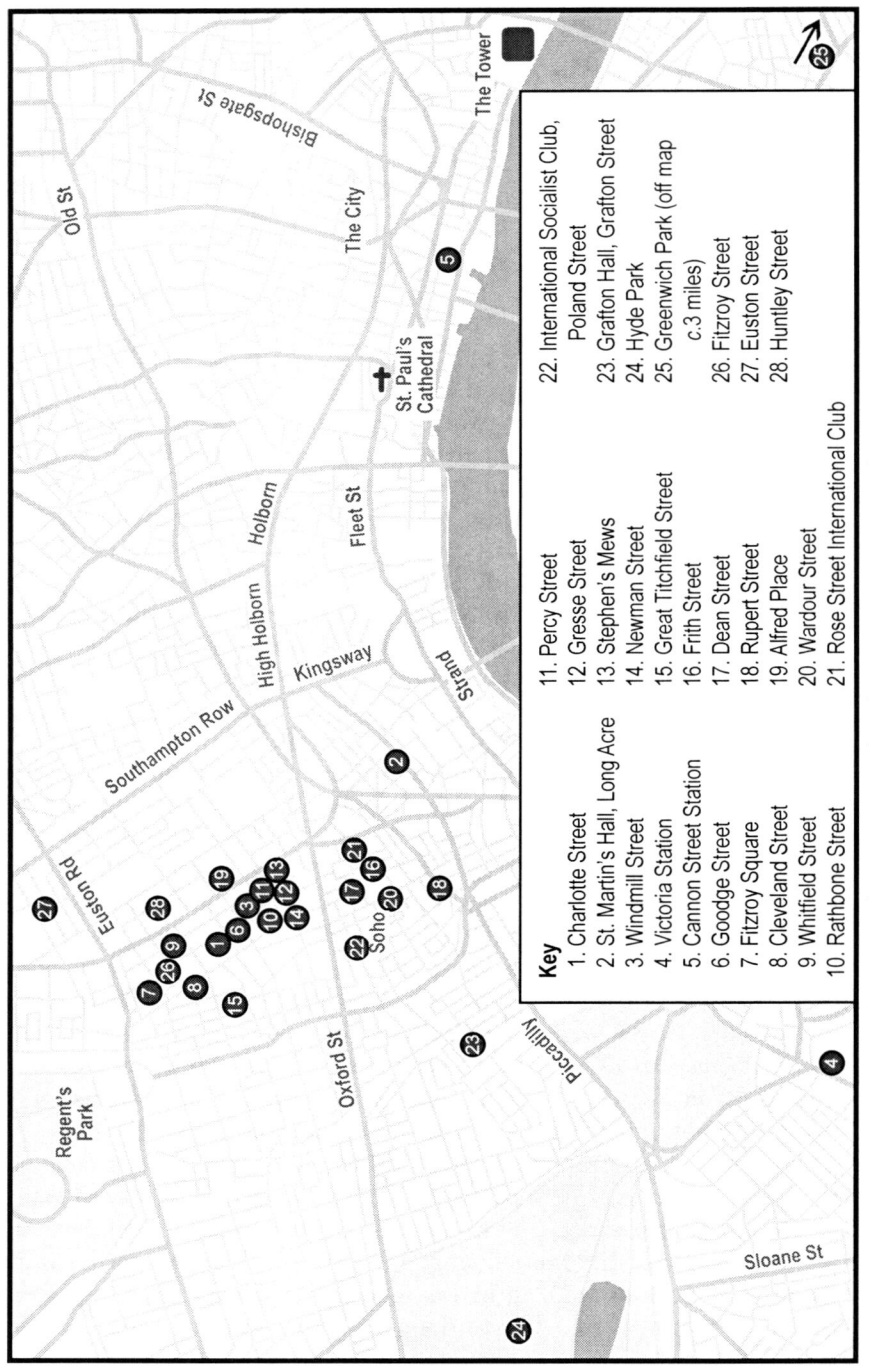

Key

1. Charlotte Street
2. St. Martin's Hall, Long Acre
3. Windmill Street
4. Victoria Station
5. Cannon Street Station
6. Goodge Street
7. Fitzroy Square
8. Cleveland Street
9. Whitfield Street
10. Rathbone Street
11. Percy Street
12. Gresse Street
13. Stephen's Mews
14. Newman Street
15. Great Titchfield Street
16. Frith Street
17. Dean Street
18. Rupert Street
19. Alfred Place
20. Wardour Street
21. Rose Street International Club
22. International Socialist Club, Poland Street
23. Grafton Hall, Grafton Street
24. Hyde Park
25. Greenwich Park (off map c.3 miles)
26. Fitzroy Street
27. Euston Street
28. Huntley Street

Map 8.1. Places mentioned in the text (Base map: London c.1910)

had preceded them in London. These nodded primarily to the post-1848 waves, as journalists noted, for instance, that the anarchists congregated in one of the rooms of St. Martin's Hall, where the International Working Men's Association had been set up in 1864, or inscribed themselves in the Communards' lineage: 'One street in the French quarter has conquered fame: it is Charlotte Street and, on this road, one house deserves the honours of history: it is that of Victor Richard, the faithful friend of Vallès and Séverine'.[1] This historical perspective also informed the eyes of beholders, although they were more likely to stress the different character of the anarchists, and especially the discontinuity with the previous, morally noble generations of exiles and the peak of French presence in London:

> How many French [in London]? A lot less than one may think. One should not assume that the streets of Soho and Fitzroy have regained since the recent explosions the very special character which they had after the Commune. A few rare French shop-fronts among the shop-fronts, a few vaguely familiar figures in Charlott-Street [sic] and in Wind-mill-Street [sic] and that's it.[2]

The importance of this historical lineage means that the London years of the French anarchists can be read both in continuity and in contrast with the preceding waves of revolutionary exile, including from the point of view of outside observers who constantly compared the anarchists with their illustrious predecessors. Their growing hostility and the polemics provoked by the anarchists' presence – suspected as well as seen – turned London into a contested space. The novelty that this presence represented must also be stressed, in order to convey the sense of puzzlement expressed by contemporaries – and by the exiles themselves – upon seeing or even just imagining these hundreds of individuals recreating an anarchist 'Petite France' in the streets of Soho and Fitzrovia. Their dismay stemmed from the fear of anarchist terrorism, because of the well-established reputation of the French as *dynamitards* or *bombistes*, but also from a culture shock, as these comrades were often described as quintessentially French artisans,

[1] 'Conférences anarchistes à Londres', *La Sociale*, 9 Aug. 1896. 'Une rue du quartier français a conquis la célébrité: c'est Charlotte Street et, dans cette rue, une maison a droit aux honneurs de l'histoire: c'est celle de Victor Richard, fidèle ami de Vallès et de Séverine' (C. Malato, *De la Commune à l'anarchie* (Paris, 1894), p. 276). All translations from French are by Constance Bantman, unless otherwise stated.
[2] 'Combien de Français là-bas? Infiniment moins qu'on ne le croit. Il ne faudrait pas supposer que les rues du Soho et de Fitzroy-Square ont retrouvé depuis les dernières explosions ce caractère tout particulier qu'elles avaient après la Commune. Quelques rares devantures françaises aux devantures des boutiques, quelques figures vaguement de connaissance dans Charlott-Street et dans Wind-mill-Street, et c'est tout' (*La Marseillaise*, 31 May 1892).

settling down in London in the heyday of the Victorian age. The written testimonies left by the French in London, as well as by the British observers of these groups, testify to the same impression of strangeness and otherness, often conveyed by a close attention to details revealing cultural differences and idiosyncrasies. This chapter emphasizes the physicality of this anarchist presence by examining different scales in turn, from the international level – why, of all places, did the anarchists settle in Britain? – to the very local, investigating anarchist public and private spaces.

The international level: England

Multiple factors took the French anarchists to London in the late 1870s, but their presence there was generally not a matter of choice. A handful of them were already in the capital, and were 'converted' to anarchism in the Communards' exilic circles. The Cercle d'Etudes Sociales de Londres set up in March 1880 was an important venue in this respect, although it was unambiguously republican and parliamentarian. But most of the anarchists arrived in London in the course of the 1880s and early 1890s, at a time when, under the impact of anarchist attacks, many Western countries closed their borders to foreign exiles, turning the United Kingdom into 'the only refuge for the rejected of Europe'.[3] The country was exceptional in that political asylum was an integral part of liberal traditions which were a key element of national pride and identity.[4] London remained comparatively immune to anarchist terrorist attacks throughout the nineteenth century – an exception which was both the cause and the consequence of its tolerance of anarchists. It was the target of Irish nationalist Fenian attacks between the 1860s and 1880s, but these seem to have had a minimal impact on the way anarchists were dealt with. Until 1902, the United States and Latin America (especially Argentina) were other possible destinations for the French companions, but for them as for previous exiles, Britain's proximity to France was a key factor in the decision to seek shelter there: 'There is America, of course: but apart from the fact that it is far from the centre of our operations, most of us cannot afford the journey'.[5]

Britain's treatment of the anarchists remained unique until 1905, when the first Aliens Act since 1826 was passed, putting an end to several decades of open-door policy. Until then, the country relied on an original model

---

[3] Hansard, *Parliamentary Debates*, 4th ser., iii (5 Apr. 1892), cols. 681–2; 'Aliens in London', *Hansard*, 4, cxiv (19 Nov. 1902), cols. 1357–8.

[4] B. Porter, *The Refugee Question in Mid-Victorian Politics* (Cambridge, 1979).

[5] Préfecture de Police de Paris Archives (hereafter APP), BA 1474, report by Etoile, dated 27 June 1882: 'Il y a bien l'Amérique: mais outre que c'est loin du centre de nos opérations, la plupart d'entre nous n'ont pas l'argent pour le voyage'.

of unrestricted immigration, whereby the control of potentially dangerous immigrants was implemented through the use of specific laws, notably the 1883 Explosive Substances Act which served to sentence several individuals suspected of terrorism in a few high-profile cases during the 1890s. The charge of incitement to murder was used to sentence the incendiary Prussian anarchist Johann Most in 1881. Very controversially, against the liberal dogma of political asylum, a few extraditions were granted by British courts, notably that of the French suspected terrorist Jean-Pierre François, known as 'Francis', in 1892. The use of provocateurs and intense police surveillance, both overt and covert, was pivotal to the country's control strategy, and remains a vexed question to this day.[6]

British authorities were faced with remonstrances in pursuing this course of action. These mainly came from a broad lobby centring on the Conservative party, with Lord Salisbury and Charles Darling, MP as chief spokespersons. Detractors of this anarchist asylum castigated the tolerance of continued immigration, especially when a terrorist attack occurred on the continent or was suspected in Britain; they were especially incensed during the 1892 Walsall case (a suspected bomb plot involving British, French and Italian comrades), throughout 1893, when 'propaganda by the deed' peaked on the continent, and in early 1894, following the Greenwich explosion accidentally provoked by the Frenchman Martial Bourdin near the Observatory, with no other victim than himself. The unfettered freedom of speech and meeting which the comrades enjoyed in London also caused great indignation. The conservative and penny press were vocal in their denunciation of anarchism and the risks to which it exposed Britain; *The Times* was especially supportive of the Conservative politicians who called for legislation to thwart the 'black peril'. Two main arguments were used in doing so. First, the dangers incurred by Britain in not adopting the same anti-anarchist measures as continental powers, especially with respect to freedom of expression and the publication of anarchist propaganda, and also the diplomatic tensions generated by this tolerance. *The Times* bemoaned:

> Mr Asquith thinks it expedient to permit such incitements to go unpunished, when merely printed and not spoken, lest a prosecution should give too much importance to a handful of fanatics. But when these doctrines are put in practice in Paris, in Marseilles, in Barcelona and in Madrid, we owe it to our neighbours and to ourselves to take care that they shall not be preached among us in impunity.[7]

[6] C. Bantman, *The French Anarchists in London: Exile and Transnationalism in the First Globalisation* (forthcoming Liverpool, 2013).
[7] 'The Anarchist Campaign against Society', *The Times*, 11 Dec. 1893.

The second argument – a recurring theme – was the difference between the anarchists and the exiles of yore (especially the Huguenots and the 1848 generation), even for the Liberal party which sought to uphold free circulation and the right of asylum and was therefore relatively inclined to defend the anarchists. Thus, in the words of Lord Asquith,

> When persons, instead of doing as political offenders in the strict sense of the word have been in the habit of doing, as the men of 1848 and 1867 did – instead of going out into the open field and meeting by force of arms the men to whom they were politically opposed – whets [sic] they resort to assassination and to dynamite, I say they are putting themselves as much outside the pale of political offenders as the man who in time of war goes and poisons the stream disentitles himself to be treated as a prisoner of war.[8]

Foreign pressures were also to be reckoned with, despite the suspicion that continental powers were rather pleased to be able to deport anarchists to Britain. Nonetheless, there were biting criticisms from the French conservative press, often playing on stereotypes, such as the alleged hypocrisy of the British: 'The British mind requires the paramount motive of self-interest. The trials of others do not affect it, but it is extremely sensible to its own', railed a French paper quoted by *The Times*, commenting on Lord Asquith's leniency towards anarchists, except when they seemed to pose a direct threat.[9] Diplomatic tensions arose over inter-police liaison and surveillance, but in the specific case of Anglo-French relations, no formal governmental pressure was exerted. In 1898, the French government briefly entertained the project of placing a *commissaire* in London to be exclusively in charge of anarchist surveillance, but gave up because this would be perceived as a violation of Britain's official liberalism.[10]

Despite their notable presence in the press and in political discourses, anti-anarchist views seem to have met with relatively little echo among the British population. This is especially manifest in comparison with the working-class support rallied by the critics of mass eastern-European Jewish immigration into London's East End, which could be heard from the mid 1880s onwards in the same conservative quarters. This support is evidenced by Trades Union Congress motions approving the idea of an Immigration Bill in 1892, 1894 and 1895, as well as the success of a xenophobic agitation group, the British Brothers League, in 1901–2. International disagreements over the control of anarchists came to a head with the 1898 and 1904 International

---

[8] *Hansard*, 4, viii (9 Feb. 1893), cols. 915–1012.
[9] *La Liberté*, cited in 'The Anarchist Conspiracy', *The Times*, 19 Feb. 1894.
[10] Paris, Ministère des Affaires Etrangères Archives, file 'Anarchistes, 1890–1906. Affaires diverses, police des étrangers, anarchistes', letter from Paul Cambon dated 10 Jan. 1900.

Anti-Anarchist conferences in Rome and St. Petersburg respectively, after which the overwhelming majority of the participants decided to strengthen their anti-anarchist legislation. Britain was the notable exception in refusing to do so, as well as France in 1904.[11] However, just a few years later, in 1905, an Aliens Act was passed, making entry into British territory more restricted for 'the insane, the diseased, the criminal, the putative public charge'. The rules concerning political asylum were also considerably tightened, with the anarchists in mind: asylum would only be granted 'to avoid prosecution or punishment on religious or political grounds or prosecution for an offence of a political character, or to avoid prosecution involving danger to life or limb on account of religious or political belief'.[12]

The anarchists had acted as a catalyst in the revision of Britain's liberal policy, but their impact must be understood in the broader context of the mass immigration of impoverished workers from eastern Europe and the growing national self-doubt which came together for the passing of the act. There were calls for the law to be made more stringent in 1911, following two highly publicized criminal cases involving Latvian 'anarchists'; however, it was only in 1914 that the outbreak of the war led to reinforced controls on new arrivals. By then, foreign spies rather than anarchists had become the authorities' main target.

In view of such tolerance – or at least indifference – in the face of anarchists, it is not surprising that Britain's liberalism was frequently commented on by the exiles, either approvingly or critically; it had been a running theme of cross-Channel exchanges and a cause of admiration for many continental refugees throughout the nineteenth century.[13] As exiles promoting radical views, the anarchists were indeed in an especially propitious position to assess the virtues of this ideology in practice. The few companions who commented on their British sojourn generally praised their hosts. The Franco-Italian writer, journalist and activist Charles Malato set out his views very clearly in the first page of his memoir, *Les Joyeusetés de l'exil*: 'O Albion's big metropolis, of you I shall not speak a bad word because, for three years, you gave me hospitality – if not a joyful one, at least wide and free, without any *concierge* and hardly any police'.[14] He was

---

[11] R. Bach Jensen, 'The International Anti-Anarchist Conference of 1898 and the origins of Interpol', *Journal of Contemporary History*, xvi (1981), 323–4.

[12] *Hansard*, 4, cxlix (17 July 1905), cols. 903–57.

[13] J. Garrigues, 'Un autre modèle pour la République: l'influence des Britanniques sur les libéraux français (1870–80)', in *La France et l'Angleterre au XIXe siècle*, ed. S. Aprile and F. Bensimon (Paris, 2006), pp. 177–88; M. Isabella, *Risorgimento in Exile: Italian Emigrés and the Liberal International in the Post-Napoleonic Era* (Oxford, 2009).

[14] 'O grande métropole d'Albion, de toi je ne veux point médire, car, pendant trois ans,

also quoted on the subject by the *Pall Mall Gazette*, declaring London to be 'almost the only free city in the world'.[15] Similarly, the Communard-turned-anarchist Louise Michel and the journalist Emile Pouget praised British tolerance – usually in contrast with France's unrelenting repression and police surveillance. Pouget repeatedly referred to the civil liberties which prevailed across the Channel; writing about a cab drivers' demonstration, he noted that 'in France, the troops would have been called on, and the police would have resorted to sabres and truncheons. In London – a country which is not a republic – the cabmen were left to demonstrate as they pleased'.[16]

However, the hypocrisy of so-called liberal Britain was also a sub-theme in the few memoirs of exile: the anarchist writer Zo d'Axa wrote some very bitter pages about his experiences in London. For him, 'Those revolutionaries who, on the credentials of traditional hospitality, come to London, are falling into a mousetrap … Expulsion is unheard of! True – but spying is constant. The refugees are followed, their addresses and occupations are investigated'.[17] It remains true that in terms of public liberties, there was a sharp contrast between British methods and France's very harsh treatment of anarchists, with the 'Wicked Laws' (*Lois Scélérates*) of 1892–3 – hence the paradox whereby monarchical Britain seemed to uphold republican values far better than France.

Lastly, when analysing the companions' half-hearted choice to live in Britain, the very notion of physical presence must be qualified, on at least two grounds. First, more than any previous generation of exiles, the London groups had significant transnational ties with France, Spain, Italy, the United States and beyond, and were an important hub in the global anarchist diaspora. Anarchist networks operated for the diffusion of propagandist material, of persons and, as a consequence, of political ideas. The greatest fear of many contemporaries was that these networks also sustained terrorist activities. The spy who wrote that 'London is the great centre of anarchy; it is in London that it lives in peace and sets about

---

tu m'as donné l'hospitalité, sinon gaie, du moins large et libre, avec absence de concierge et à peine de police!' (C. Malato, *Les Joyeusetés de l'exil* (1897; Paris, 1985), p. 5).

[15] 'The Foreign Anarchists in London', *Pall Mall Gazette*, 27 Apr. 1892.

[16] 'En France on aurait mobilisé la troupe, et la police aurait joué du sabre ou du casse-tête. A Londres, – pays pas républicanaille – on a laissé les colignons manifester à leur guise' (*La Sociale*, 9 June 1896).

[17] 'Les révolutionnaires qui, sur la foi de la traditionnelle hospitalité, viennent à Londres, tombent dans une souricière … L'expulsion est inconnue! Oui, mais l'espionnage est constant. On suit les réfugiés, on s'enquiert de leur adresse, de leurs occupations' (Z. d'Axa, *De Mazas à Jerusalem* (Paris, 1895), p. 90).

developing',[18] voiced the thoughts of many, and the press was instrumental in shaping these concerns. This idea of London as the centre of a global conspiracy was omnipresent: 'There is in London a central committee of international anarchy, and not only are orders sent from there, but also the money to implement all the decisions'.[19] London's place as the centre of the great anarchist conspiracy was also often denied, even by the movement's detractors: 'As for the statements, often repeated by English newspapers of standing and repute that London was – and is – the headquarters of the sect, the city whence the order for this or that deed went forth, no greater nonsense was ever written'.[20] However, such objections were ineffective in denting the idea that the city was the theatre of shady, threatening dealings. This interplay between the local and the transnational added an important dimension to the way the exiles were perceived, as it fed many fantasies about the international ramifications of the conspiracy allegedly led from London.

The notion of the physical presence of the anarchists in Britain was also made more complex by their almost complete lack of integration in their host society (examined below), as a result of which they appeared as a foreign body in the city. From the perspective of those observing the London groups from outside, the combination of national isolation with transnationalism conjured up an aura of mystery, as they seemed to be present yet elusive in London, while possibly entertaining some links all over the world: all the elements feeding a conspiratorial imagination were in place.

As a result of these suspicions, Britain and London as asylums were contested spaces. The anarchists were a catalyst and a political stake in the oscillation evidenced by British politicians between free trade and protectionism during this period, including in the area of migration. The polemics unleashed by their presence in London were made all the more acute by Britain's unique policy on asylum until the early years of the twentieth century, and by the refugees' overwhelming spatial concentration in the capital, and in particular in the areas of Soho and Fitzrovia.

The national level: heading for London

On 25 April 1892, with the approach of May Day, upon hearing of new expulsions from France, *The Times* lamented the fact that 'England will be a

---

[18] APP, BA 1509, unsigned report dated 6 Dec. 1893: 'Londres est le grand centre de l'anarchie; c'est à Londres qu'elle vit paisible et procède à son développement'.

[19] APP, BA 1509, report by Frouard dated 31 July 1894: 'Il existe à Londres un comité central de l'anarchie internationale et que non seulement les ordres partent de là, mais aussi l'argent nécessaire pour accomplir toutes les décisions'.

[20] E. Vizetelly, *The Anarchists* (1911), p. 71.

safer hiding-place, and London – to quote Johnson with a slight variation – will be the common shore of Paris and Berlin'.[21] Indeed, the great majority of comrades made their way to London from France, usually arriving via Victoria or Cannon Street stations. And from there they headed for the 'French quarter', in Soho and Fitzrovia. However, before homing in on the French quarter, it is worth following the divergent itineraries of the small minority of comrades who, for personal or socio-economic reasons, chose not to settle in the capital.

A handful of exiles lived briefly or permanently outside London. Scotland sheltered an important exile, Paul Reclus, who was the nephew of Elisée Reclus, one of the founding fathers of anarchist communism and a former London exile himself. Edinburgh was also visited by the sociologist Augustin Hamon, author of books on the psychology of soldiers and of a *Psychologie de l'anarchiste-socialiste*.[22] In both cases, personal connections and professional opportunities were determining factors in these geographical choices. It was probably the availability of work which took several comrades to large industrial cities such as Birmingham and Liverpool; the latter was also a port of call for those who hoped to travel on to North or Latin America. One spy's comments on a comrade's trip to Birmingham illustrate the combination of factors in individual mobility choices: he announced that the relatively well-known and active comrade Louis Grandidier, being subject to intense police surveillance in London, would 'soon go to Birmingham and stay with an Italian; there, he will be introduced to a French bookshop owner and they will look for a job for him'.[23] Gustave Mollet, originally from Roanne, stopped briefly in London before opting for Norwich, possibly because of the city's dynamic local movement. Mollet was one of the very few French comrades who stayed in Britain after 1895, appearing in the 1901 census under the name 'Mollett'. Brighton provided a hiding-place for comrade Constant Martin, whom the police were especially interested in arresting. Other locations in the south-east offered peaceful retreats to those who sought quiet and anonymity, starting with Peter Kropotkin in Bromley, with occasional visits to the seaside in Brighton and Eastbourne.[24] Similarly, Louise Michel moved to

---

[21] *The Times*, 25 Apr. 1892.

[22] Amsterdam, International Institute of Social History (hereafter IISH), Augustin Frédéric Adolphe Hamon papers, letter from Pouget to Hamon (not dated but probably Dec. 1894/Jan. 1895).

[23] APP, BA 1509, report by Z.6 dated 8 Dec. 1893: '[Grandidier] ira sous peu à Birmingham et descendra chez un Italien; de là, il sera présenté chez un libraire français où on doit lui chercher du travail'.

[24] Paris, Institut Français d'Histoire Sociale (hereafter IFHS), Grave correspondence,

Dulwich after leaving the hustle and bustle of the French quarter. Lucien Pemjean praised his provincial location of Alton (Hampshire) in a very bucolic fashion: 'This occupation, this countryside, this fresh air – all this novelty is so refreshing, restful and reinvigorating for me'.[25] In almost every case, a clear desire to distance oneself geographically and politically from London's disreputable circles was mentioned as a factor.

For indeed, London was the destination of choice for most of the refugees, and they were so concentrated in the capital that the word 'colonies' was frequently used to describe their groupings[26] – a term which denoted both geographical concentration and a sense of internal organization and isolation. Walking in the footsteps of the 1848 generation and the Communards, the anarchists settled down in Soho and Fitzrovia, in an area with a long-established tradition of hosting continental exiles and political radicals, which was known as 'the French quarter' and carried an aura of disrepute: 'a telling pout' thus appeared on the face of Malato's cab-driver when he was told where to take his passenger.[27] British and international onlookers were not the only ones to be somewhat put off by these anarchist colonies; there was a strong connection between the comrades' geographical localization and their political affiliations, so that most lived in the French quarter, but the elite (that is to say mainly the writers and journalists) of the exiles preferred to stay outside this area. This was the case for Malato, who eventually settled down in the suburb of Hampstead. Pouget was in Islington, and other comrades were reported to be in Camden.[28] The Italian activist Errico Malatesta lived in Islington, the veteran Gustave Brocher in Camberwell and Auguste Coulon in Balham. In this case, a marginal location most probably testified to a need for discretion, since Coulon was a spy and provocateur in the pay of the Metropolitan Police Special Branch. An interesting case is that of Victor Cails, one of the very few comrades who strove to meet the anarchist ideal of the *trimardeur*, that is to say the rootless wandering militant. His itinerary was more typical of a British working-

---

letters from Kropotkin dated 3 Sept. 1894, 14 and 22 Feb. 1912 (from Brighton), 3 July 1902 (from Eastbourne). Most of Kropotkin's other letters were written from Bromley.

[25] IISH, Zo d'Axa archive, letter from Lucien Pemjean dated 23 Sept. 1894, sent from 'Wey cottage, Alton (Hants)': 'Cette occupation, cette campagne, ce bon air, ces paisibles bêtes, tout ce nouveau me rafraîchit, me repose et me retrempe'.

[26] APP, BA 1509, report dated 23 Oct. 1894; IISH, Augustin Frédéric Adolphe Hamon papers, letter from Emile Pouget dated 15 Aug. 1894: 'D'Axa, Cipriani, Darien sont ici. La colonie augmente!' ('D'Axa, Cipriani, Darien are here. The colony is increasing!').

[27] Malato, *Joyeusetés de l'exil*, p. 6: 'une moue significative'.

[28] APP, BA 1510, report by Jarvis dated 8 Apr. 1896: 'Lemée demeure à Camden Town et fabrique des drogues pour les femmes' ('Lemée remains at Camden town and manufactures drugs for women').

class man than of a French anarchist, since he remained in Britain after the 1895 amnesty, and was employed in the very early years of the twentieth century in Millwall Docks and on the construction site of the Victoria and Albert Museum.[29]

The map of the anarchist colonies was therefore a political and socio-economic one. The comrades' overwhelming concentration in a few streets points to the paradox of their mobility, which occurred within a very restricted and already mapped-out space. This was not a voyage of cultural discovery; on the contrary, in most cases, installation followed a historical, linguistic and social logic. Nonetheless, there were divergent itineraries, which testify to the extent and diversity of the French presence in Britain and show a significant occurrence of French working-class travel even outside London, in a period usually associated with the rise of middle-class cross-Channel tourism.

The urban level
Charlotte Street and Goodge Street were the very heart of London's 'small anarchist Republic':[30]

> Since the beginning, Charlotte Street has been for the French exiled in London what the Agora was for the Greeks, the Forum for the Romans and [Paris's] boulevard de la Villette at one in the morning for the paladins of decadence: it is a constantly-open meeting place; it is, at the same time, a landmark … after 15 minutes, [I] had found Paris – Paris in London.[31]

The association with Fitzrovia was essential to the negative perception of the anarchists – and vice versa. By the end of the nineteenth century, the area already carried sordid connotations, and the anarchists added to its social hotchpotch. While some parts were affluent and middle-class, 'some inner and eastern areas of Fitzrovia attracted the political and artistic dissidents who were to give the area its specific character'.[32] In addition to Charlotte Street and Fitzroy Square, French anarchists could be found on both sides of Oxford Street. To the north, they lived in Cleveland Street, Whitfield

---

[29] IISH, Lucien Descaves collection, Louise Michel papers, letter from Victor Cails to Louise Michel dated 2 July 1903.

[30] 'Cette petite république anarchiste' (Malato, *Joyeusetés de l'exil*, p. 29).

[31] 'Charlotte Street … a, depuis son origine, été pour les Français proscrits à Londres, ce que fut l'Agora pour les Grecs, le Forum pour les Romains et le Boulevard de la Villette à une heure du matin, pour les paladins de la décadence: c'est un lieu, toujours ouvert, de réunion; c'est, en même temps, un point de repère … au bout d'un quart d'heure [j']avais retrouvé Paris, – Paris à Londres' (Malato, *Joyeusetés de l'exil*, pp. 6–7).

[32] M. Pentelow and M. Rowe, *Characters of Fitzrovia* (2001), p. 13.

Street, Goodge Street, Rathbone Street, Percy Street, Gresse Street, Stephen's Mews, Newman Street, Great Titchfield Street and Windmill Street. To the south, they lived mainly in Frith Street, Dean Street, Rupert Street, Alfred Place and Wardour Street.

This spatial concentration determined the reception of the anarchists; there was a strong visual element in the moral panic which they triggered. Many negative depictions of the anarchist colonies were variations on this theme of the threatening strangers in the city, and the press issued constant reminders – be they emphases or hints – of their presence in the heart of London. For instance, in December 1894, the sensationalist *Evening News* ran a series on London's anarchist groups, with the headline '8,000 Anarchists in London – where these enemies of society live in the great metropolis'. The French consistently attracted special attention because of their supposed extremism: 'Between Soho Square and Leicester Square are to be found a small group of the most dangerous anarchists in London, the mysterious and bloodthirsty Anonymat'.[33] The notion of the enemy secretly lurking within the community and plotting against it – a classic trope in conspiracy narratives[34] – occurred in several different forms. It can be seen in the suspicion that these undesirable guests were planning to attack key political landmarks in London:

> The Metropolitan police is said to have just uncovered a true anarchist conspiracy. The affiliates, numbering about 200, were planning to create an explosion, this week, at Westminster Palace, Saint-James (the residence of HM Queen Victoria), and Mr Gladstone's private residence.[35]

It was also latent in the repeated – and not always untrue – claim that London harboured foreign terrorists in hiding:

> We are increasingly certain that comrades Meunier and Francis are hiding in the club's vicinity. Indeed, the area could not fit them any better; very populous, frequented by the French Jews and also by London's most villainous individuals; they will be completely safe there.[36]

---

[33] '8,000 Anarchists in London', *Evening News*, 17 Dec. 1894, p. 2.

[34] R. Girardet, *Mythes et mythologies politiques* (Paris, 1986), pp. 25–62.

[35] 'La police londonienne vient de découvrir, paraît-il, le centre d'une véritable conspiration anarchiste. Les affiliés, au nombre de deux cents environ, se proposaient de faire sauter cette semaine, Westminster Palace (le Parlement), Saint-James, résidence de SM la reine Victoria et la demeure particulière de M. Gladstone' ('Les anarchistes à Londres', *La Cocarde*, 17 Feb. 1894).

[36] APP, BA 1508, report by Z.2 dated 11 Sept. 1892: 'On est de plus en plus certain que les compagnons Meunier et Francis sont cachés non loin du club. En effet le quartier est on ne peut mieux choisi; très populeux, fréquenté par les juifs français et surtout par tout ce qu'il y a de plus crapule dans Londres, ils s'y trouvent en parfait sécurité'.

The sense of danger evoked by the anarchists compounded the horror aroused by the vision of the modern, industrial city of which London was the epitome – dark, labyrinthine, potentially revolutionary.[37] All of these traits are dramatized in Joseph Conrad's fictionalized account of the Greenwich affair, *The Secret Agent*, which tellingly concludes with a sentence capturing this idea of the malevolent anarchists lurking within the community: 'He passed on unsuspected and deadly, like a pest in the street full of men'.[38]

Nonetheless, such discourses were more characteristic of the peak of the moral panic stirred by this anarchist presence, and fears ebbed in the late 1890s. Around 1894 already, at the climax of the terrorist period and of police surveillance in both France and London, spies remarked that the comrades were increasingly isolated and scattered:

> Since the Autonomie business [i.e., the police raid of the main anarchist club in February 1894, following the Greenwich explosion], the anarchists in refuge in London have spread here and there and only meet up very rarely in comparison to what used to be the case.[39]

This was, however, mainly an effect of the closure of their main haunt, the Autonomie Club; a decade later, there were far fewer French anarchists in London, but those who were still present in the capital tended to live in the same areas. By 1901, even spies dispelled rumours of anarchist agitation, and the notion of an anarchist quarter had pretty much disappeared: 'In fact, the movement has never been so calm. The groups which meet from time to time only do so for little unimportant chats. Most of those who attend the clubs only do so to be entertained with singing or dancing'.[40] By 1909, the time of nostalgia had come and verbal radicalism prevailed, replacing anarchist antics and public anxieties. Malatesta wrote of an old Italian comrade:

> There is nothing interesting here ... We live just as we used to 20 years ago, with the difference that there is even less of a movement than there used to

---

[37] C. Bantman, 'Anarchist scares in the late-Victorian city: an urban symptom?', in *Keeping the Lid On: Urban Eruptions and Social Control since the 19th Century*, ed. S. Finding, L. Barrow and F. Poirier (Newcastle, 2010), pp. 31–8.

[38] J. Conrad, *The Secret Agent* (1907; 1997), p. 229.

[39] APP, BA 1509, report by Léon dated 17 March 1894: 'Depuis l'affaire de l'Autonomie, les anarchistes réfugiés à Londres se sont dispersés un peu partout et ne se rencontrent que très rarement en comparaison de ce qui se passait autrefois'.

[40] APP, BA 435, report by Bornibus dated 6 Nov. 1901: 'Or, jamais le mouvement n'a été aussi calme. Les groups qui se réunissent de temps en temps ne le font que pour de petites causeries sans importance. La plupart de ceux qui fréquentent ces réunions sont de jeunes ouvriers qui ne vont dans les clubs que pour se distraire en chantant ou en dansant'.

be … Reava [most likely Rava] is still in London and he sells paintings … I sometimes bump into him; but every time a sovereign is killed, he comes to see us and rejoice with a bottle.[41]

The local level: anarchist haunts

What were the anarchist spaces in London? First and foremost, their clubs. The anarchist movement took off in London during and as a result of the golden age of 'Metropolitan clubland' radicalism,[42] and it is therefore hardly surprising that clubs appeared as the most congenial setting for anarchist exilic militancy; in France, by contrast, the comrades usually met in halls ('salles'). Given the centrality of clubs of all allegiances in Britain's political life, it may also be an effect of cultural mimicry which led the French and international comrades to set up their own clubs at an early date. The adoption of specifically 'English' features was even acknowledged by spies: 'The anarchists in London have an anarchist club much like English clubs. There is a buffet which is run by a stewart.[43] He serves drinks on Sundays and gives food to club members'.[44]

From the early 1880s onwards, French, British and other European comrades formed clubs where they could congregate and, more often than not, clash with one another, as exiles were legendarily wont to do. First came the Rose Street International Club (1881–2), dominated by German exiles and set up in the aftermath of the 1881 International Revolutionary Socialist Congress in London, which aimed to recreate the International Working Men's Association. Both the club and the association soon foundered, and the former was replaced with another international endeavour, the International Socialist Club of Poland Street: 'We have a beautiful club, with all the desirable commodities – large meeting rooms, billiard table etc', Brocher proudly wrote in November 1882.[45] The next international venture was the Stephen Mews Club in 1885, where the French had their

[41] IISH, Brocher archive, letter from Errico Malatesta to Victorine Brocher dated 27 Aug. 1909: 'Ici rien d'intéressant, à notre point de vue. Nous vivons toujours comme il y a vingt ans, avec la différence qu'il y a encore moins de mouvement qu'alors … Reava est toujours à Londres … Je le rencontre de temps en temps par hasard; mais toutes les fois qu'on tue un souverain, il vient nous voir pour se réjouir du fait en buvant une bouteille'.

[42] S. Shipley, *Club Life and Socialism in Mid-Victorian London* (1972), p. 21.

[43] The English word appears in the original quotation; the orthographic variation is correct in French.

[44] APP, BA 1508, report by Pépin dated 2 Aug. 1893: 'Les anarchistes à Londres ont un club anarchiste comme le sont les clubs anglais. Il s'y trouve un buffet qui est dirigé par un stewart. Celui-ci sert le dimanche des boissons et donne à manger aux membres du club'.

[45] IISH, Brocher archive, letter dated 29 Nov. 1882: 'Nous avons un beau club avec toutes les commodités désirables, grandes salles de réunion, billards etc.'

own section; the club was raided by the police that same year. Of all these meeting points, none was more famous – or rather infamous – than the Autonomie Club, an international gathering place where different meeting days were designated for each national section, and which doubled up as a soup kitchen and makeshift shelter for the most destitute companions. The club, originally set up in 1886 at 32 Charlotte Street and then relocated to 6 Windmill Street, catalysed all the myths and public fears associated with anarchism, and was believed to be the 'centre of the whole Anarchist organisation in the Metropolis'.[46] *The Times* casually described it as 'the headquarters' of London's 'dovecote of anarchists'.[47] Malato summarized its widely distorted public image:

> It was there, claimed reporters lacking inspiration and happy to speculate on bourgeois terrors for three pennies a line, that all the conspiracies meant to explode on the continent were plotted, that all the tragic resolutions were made, that dynamite, potassium chlorate, nitrobenzene, rack-a-rock and green powder were fabricated.[48]

By the time the club was raided by Chief Inspector Melville of the Special Branch of the Metropolitan Police and his men, in February 1894 following the Greenwich explosion, the club had become famous above all for 'being infested with the police spies of various governments'.[49] Even the most prolific and sensationalist writers on anarchism acknowledged then that it was 'doubtful whether these clubs were ever the hotbeds of conspiracy that has sometimes been represented',[50] but such stories certainly sold well.

These clubs were venues for propaganda, where national and international meetings took place, as well as commemorations of the Paris Commune on 18 March and, after 1887, of the six anarchists executed in Chicago on 11 November following their involvement in May Day protests. The clubs also hosted cultural activities which had a political dimension, such as talks, plays or concerts, often with a view to fundraising in defence of a specific cause. As early as 1884, when there were just a few dozen anarchists in London, one spy commented on a recent anarchist cultural evening: 'Of the concert, I will not say a word: it was weak beyond words. As for the fourth act of *Charlotte Corday*, it was performed by: Marillat as Danton,

[46] 'Anarchism in London', *The Graphic*, 24 Feb. 1894.
[47] 'The explosion in Greenwich Park', *The Times*, 17 Feb. 1894.
[48] 'Là … se tramaient tous les complots destines à exploser sur le continent, se prenaient toutes les résolutions tragiques, se fabriquaient la dynamite, le chlorate de potasse, la nitrobenzine, le rack-a-rock et la poudre verte' (Malato, *Joyeusetés de l'exil*, p. 57).
[49] 'Anarchist Conspiracies', *Western Mail*, 17 Feb. 1894.
[50] F. Dubois, *The Anarchist Peril*, trans. R. Derechef (1894), pp. 270–1.

Lucas as Robespierre, Raoux as Marat'.[51] Malato devoted a chapter of his London memoir to the performance in March 1893 of the play he had penned, *Mariage par la dynamite*, a 'one-act vaudeville', which copiously mocked the Paris police.[52]

Larger events bringing together all of the international groups took place in Grafton Hall, 55 Grafton Street. Other venues patronized with some regularity included the Athenaeum Hall, Liberty Hall (located out of the comrades' usual area, in Peckham Street in south-east London), as well as the occasional pub room or restaurant.[53] After the high tide of the French anarchist proscription in London, the political sociability of the exiles who stayed on was more diffuse, with no mention being made of regular meeting points.[54]

After the clubs, the street and a number of open spaces were the most important political spaces for the anarchists. Hyde Park was a favourite for May Day demonstrations, which became a militant ritual after 1890, provoking the sniggers of onlookers who found it difficult to regard anarchist manifestations as actual political events – in the same way as it was increasingly problematic to treat them as political refugees:

> In Hyde Park, as elsewhere, man is a gregarious animal. With the help of banners and music and speechifying, any number of species can be brought together. They come in their thousands to hear some glib-tongued fellow speak, and they would come just as readily for the amusement of seeing him hanged.[55]

The public nature of these events could also be a source of pride for some as it testified to the country's unique freedom of speech: 'In the great London Parks on every Sunday, streams of oratory are poured forth almost uninterruptedly from morning till dusk … Every variety of opinion is expressed, from the solemn exhortations of the Evangelist to the wild absurdities of the Anarchist'.[56]

Unsurprisingly, however, the street was an often disputed territory. Malato, in a vein reminiscent of Jules Vallès's *La Rue à Londres*, noted that London life was 'all interior … the cold street without benches is a

---

[51] APP, BA 435, report by Etoile dated 20 Nov. 1884: 'Du concert, on ne dira rien: il a été d'une faiblesse inénarrable. Quant au 4ème acte de "Charlotte Corday" il a été bien interprété par: Marillat dans le rôle de Danton; Lucas, dans celui de Robespierre; Raoux dans le rôle de Marat'.

[52] Malato, *Joyeusetés de l'exil*, pp. 94–103.

[53] APP, BA 1509, report by Cottance dated 19 Dec. 1894; APP, BA1509, report by Jarvis dated 3 July 1895.

[54] APP, BA 1509, report by Bourgeois dated 12 Feb. 1895.

[55] *The Times*, 25 Apr. 1892.

[56] 'The Forum of the Park', *The Graphic*, 10 Dec. 1887.

place which you only go through, and do not stop in'.[57] And yet, it was an important stage in the comrades' daily existence and political activities. Comrades met one another when strolling in the French quarter – a method, so to speak, adopted by the spies in charge of anarchist surveillance. One explained: 'All these individuals, you can believe it, are nowhere to be found in the refugees' quarter. We walk four times a day in Charlotte Street ... but we never meet them there'.[58] Indeed, the street was associated above all with the many *mouchards* or informers, both British and continental, constantly watching over the refugees in order to spot people and gather intelligence: 'The London police are currently pestering Lapie, exerting surveillance both day and night in front of his bookshop'.[59]

The streets of London also provided a stage for demonstrations, notably on the occasion of funerals, which were choice opportunities for anarchist professions of faith. When Mrs. Mowbray, the wife of the respected British companion Charles Mowbray, was buried in April 1892, the papers depicted 'a collection of crowds, consisting for the most part of very harmless people, in search of a little excitement as a set off to the tedium of everyday life'.[60] But, in February 1894, the funeral procession of the French comrade Martial Bourdin, killed in Greenwich Park by the detonation of the bomb he was carrying, was attacked by passers-by. It was repeatedly suggested that the attackers had been paid by the British police, in an attempt to stage public hostility to anarchism;[61] however that may be, the anarchists' public presence was increasingly resented, as evidenced by several debates in the House of Commons over their right to hold public demonstrations, which were started by Conservatives and opposed by Liberals in the name of freedom of speech.[62] However, both parties eventually agreed to censor the anarchists' public presence, notably during the very tense period of 'propaganda by the deed'.[63] This fear of public anarchist gatherings echoes the great panics triggered by the workers' strikes and unemployed demonstrations of 1886–9, in the West End (Bloody Sunday) and the London Docks. The

[57] Malato, *Joyeusetés de l'exil*, p. 15.
[58] APP, BA 1508, report by Z.6 dated 1 March 1893: 'Tous ces individus, croyez-le bien, ne se trouvent pas dans le quartier des réfugiés. On passe 4 fois par jours dans Charlotte Street et on voit fréquemment Richard, mais jamais on ne les y rencontre'.
[59] APP, BA 1508, report by Z.6 dated 7 July 1893: 'La police de Londres tracasse en ce moment le nommé Lapie devant la librairie duquel elle fait exercer une surveillance non seulement le jour mais encore dans la soirée'.
[60] *The Times*, 25 Apr. 1892.
[61] 'L'anarchie à Londres. Une interview du chef de la police anglaise', *L'Eclair*, 3 March 1894.
[62] *Hansard*, 4, xviii (14 Nov. 1893), cols. 874–5.
[63] *Hansard*, 4, xviii (28 Nov. 1893), cols. 1909–10.

fears associated with the sheer sight of the anarchists as a group must be understood in a broader context of social unrest, where agitation by the proletariat in the industrial metropolis was a cause of great concern and fear. The French origins of the companions, and therefore the immediate association in public minds with the revolution, certainly increased the sense of unease which they provoked.

Just off the street, and returning to the French quarter, two shops functioned as meeting points for the exiles and the spies watching over them. The first was the bookshop of Armand Lapie at 30 Goodge Street; the other was the grocery of Victor Richard, a former Communard who was supportive of anarchists without being one, located at 67 Charlotte Street. This last place was such an anarchist landmark that Malato advised future exiles in London to go straight there; interestingly, he also suggested that they pay a visit to William Morris, whose address Louise Michel would be able to provide.[64]

Schools and other educational settings were prime militant venues for the *compagnons*. The first school set up by anarchists in London was Louise Michel's Ecole Anarchiste Internationale, which opened in Fitzroy Street in 1890 and testified to the French comrades' lasting interest in pedagogical ventures. The school, whose short-lived existence ended with yet another bomb scandal involving the provocateur Coulon, emphasized the individual's integral development and bore the trace of the ideas of Mikhail Bakunin and the libertarian pedagogue Paul Robin. It caught the attention of the future leading educationalist Margaret McMillan, who later pioneered the socialist Sunday School movement.[65] In the pacified context of the early twentieth century, the French and other international exiles were increasingly interested in pedagogic and cultural activities, such as concerts, conferences and language classes.[66] February 1905 saw the inauguration of a Université Populaire set up by comrades of various nationalities in Euston Street.[67] This mirrored the development of similar initiatives in France at the same time, as part of the educational endeavours which followed the Dreyfus affair. The founders aimed 'to educate workers, by letting them see (through a free loan library, classes, conferences, etc.) a better future, based on a more scientific understanding of social life and by bringing them in the present the joys which knowledge brings'.[68] Theatrical performances were scheduled

[64] Malato, *Joyeusetés de l'exil*, pp. 166–7.

[65] M. McMillan, *The Life of Rachel McMillan* (1927), pp. 58–9.

[66] P. DiPaola, 'Italian anarchists in London (1870–1914)' (unpublished Goldsmiths, University of London PhD thesis, 2004), p. 226.

[67] APP, BA 1510, report by Bornibus dated 20 Feb. 1905; APP, BA 1510, report by Bornibus dated 3 March 1905.

[68] APP, BA 1510, prospectus 'Université Populaire de Londres'.

during the opening week, with plays by Georges Courteline and Octave Mirbeau;[69] there were also conferences on politics and evening classes in geometry, linguistics, English, physics and chemistry, mathematics, history and sociology. But the Université Populaire de Londres quickly collapsed, due to funding issues and dissensions between its German members, on the one hand, and French and Italian participants on the other.[70]

Given how difficult it was for the comrades to find and hold a job, their workplaces are hard to inventory. Most of the exiles were craftsmen and took on makeshift, often multiple activities to get by during their time abroad, frequently setting up shops in their own dwellings. A few of them had shops, such as Lapie's bookshop, where the spy Cottance (full name unknown) briefly ran a little toyshop/bazaar before he was exposed.[71] François Bourdin, a tailor and the brother of Martial Bourdin, worked 'in a small and dingy workshop in Great Titchfield Street'.[72] Several anarchists took on jobs in the traditionally French-oriented sectors of catering and teaching. Malato, Brocher and Michel were private tutors working in well-to-do families.[73] The hospitality sector, where Frenchness held a certain cachet, provided opportunities to some, including at the very chic Café Royal.[74] The brief *tour d'horizon* written by the informant Jarvis (full name unknown) testifies to the very casual, almost random nature of employment for the comrades: 'Lemée lives in Camden Town and makes drugs for women ... Ségot and Gouriot are going to set up a business as lantern-makers. Charpentier and Péroux are penniless'.[75] But the very precarious nature of employment meant that workplaces could be the street; comrade Bidault sold 'tie pins in the street, Oxford Street, mainly at the corner of Rat Bone Place [*sic*]'.[76] Anarchists were also frequently associated with prostitution. This was due to a widespread tendency to associate them with moral depravity, but also to the fact that Soho had been a pick-up place for French prostitutes for decades and, lastly, to the actual presence of a number of procurers among the comrades.

Private homes were, like work, characterized by precariousness. A degree of nomadism was the norm, because of financial difficulties, police

[69] *Les Temps Nouveaux*, 25 Apr. 1903.
[70] APP, BA 1510, report by Bornibus dated 24 Apr. 1905.
[71] APP, BA 1509, report by Lapeyre dated 14 Dec. 1894
[72] 'Anarchism in London', *The Graphic*, 24 Feb. 1894.
[73] Malato, *Joyeusetés de l'exil*, pp. 84–8
[74] APP, BA 1508, report by Y.3 dated 1 Dec. 1893.
[75] APP, BA 1510, report by Jarvis dated 8 Apr. 1896: 'Lemée demeure à Camden Town et fabrique des drogues pour les femmes ... Ségot et Gouriot vont s'établir fabricants de lanternes. Charpentier et Péroux sont à bout de ressources'.
[76] APP, BA 1508, report by Z.6 dated 15 June 1893: Bidault 'vend des épingles de cravates dans la rue, Oxford street, principalement au coin de Rat Bone Place [*sic*]'.

surveillance and the stigma attached to French migrants ('coming from France was a poor reference', Michel reminisced).[77] Most comrades lived in the furnished lodgings typical of the capital's poorer areas; in Soho and Fitzrovia,

> Only very well-off artisans could afford a house. Most rented rooms in a house that was subdivided. Better-off families might have two, or even three, rooms. Other labouring people could only afford temporary rooms in a common lodging house, where their neighbours might be prostitutes or criminals.[78]

Louise Michel first lived in Huntley Street in 'a small bedroom. A bed, next to the only window, a desk littered with books or writings'.[79] The house itself was one 'of blackened bricks, like the others'.[80] Pouget similarly lived 'in the top floor of a little house in a back street in Islington'.[81] Even when one found accommodation, instability remained the rule: 'Pouget cannot find anywhere to live and is sick of London', a spy reported back just before the editor of the *Père Peinard* returned to France.[82] The poorest comrades lived in the street (several died or caught very serious illnesses as a result of homelessness) or slept on the floor of the Autonomie Club.[83] Many made a stop in one of the houses run by Ernest Delebecque, at 28–30 Charlotte Street, where rooms could be rented out. Families were split into different houses, and sharing a room with other comrades (French or, quite often, Italian) was frequent.[84] Outside the French quarter and beyond London, accommodation was more spacious and affordable too; Lucien Pemjean thus prided himself on the three-bed cottage he could afford in Hampshire. However, most of the comrades lived in such dire conditions, and London was such an established destination for French exiles, that Louise Michel entertained for some time the project of an 'auberge des proscrits', a hostel or hotel for exiles, which was to be funded by a conference tour in the United States in 1895–6 but never saw the light of day.[85]

[77] 'C'était une mauvaise recommandation que de venir de France' (L. Michel, *Histoire de ma vie, deuxième et troisième parties. Londres 1904* (1904; Lyon, 2000), p. 135).

[78] Pentelow and Rowe, *Characters of Fitzrovia*, p. 15.

[79] IISH, Louise Michel collection, item 1050, 'Les anarchistes entre eux', about the London groups (1892): 'comme demeure, une petite chambre. Un lit, près de l'unique fenêtre un bureau couvert de livres ou d'écrits'.

[80] Malato, *Joyeusetés de l'exil*, p. 17.

[81] 'Anarchists in London', *Daily News*, 12 Aug. 1897.

[82] APP, BA1509, report by Satin dated 30 Nov. 1894: 'Pouget ne peut trouver à se loger et est dégouté de Londres'.

[83] Malato, *Joyeusetés de l'exil*, p. 29.

[84] APP, BA 1509, report by Satin dated 22 Sept. 1894; report by Z.6 dated 30 July 1894.

[85] 'Notes sur Louise Michel', *La Sociale*, 1 Dec. 1895.

Conclusion: liberty, equality, opportunity

During their time in London, did the anarchists enjoy the delights of 'liberty, equality and opportunity'? The theme of liberty was, of course, a recurring motif whenever debates on this anarchist asylum took place, as expressed through the topos that liberal England represented the values of the French Republic better than France itself. However, their extremely difficult material circumstances meant that no one among the French anarchists went as far as to claim that Britain was fairer from the perspective of its economic and social organization. Malato summed it all up with the untranslatable pun in the very first paragraph of his memoir: 'I disembarked in the big city which its inhabitants call London – *prononcez "l'on n'donne" et n'ajoutez rien* [pronounced 'one gives' and add 'nothing']'.[86] Although Louise Michel praised the infamous institution of the workhouse as evidence that 'England considered it a duty to look after those without bread or shelter',[87] most references to Britain's economic and social system confirmed the entrenched stereotype of a profoundly unequal order. Malato saw it embodied in London's houses – 'refined hedonism for some, sordid wretchedness for others'.[88] In their closed-off circles, torn apart by personal and political quarrels, the comrades did, however, experience some sense of brotherhood and solidarity, which also explains their proclivity to geographical concentration. Zo d'Axa encapsulated the comrades' isolated existence with a metaphor – with the inevitable, stereotypical references to insularity and racial opposition between Latin and northern European nations: 'Each English person strangely symbolises the country, these insulars representing as many unapproachable little islands where warm-hued plant sap does not rise'.[89]

The key term to describe the anarchist experience in London was in fact that of opportunity – paradoxical as this may seem for individuals and groups so isolated and forlorn. This was not professional opportunity, although a handful of exiles were able to create useful professional networks during their forced stay abroad. London afforded its French visitors a truly unique political opportunity, by allowing them to form contacts with

[86] 'Je débarquai dans cette grande ville que ses habitants appellent London' (Malato, *Joyeusetés de l'exil*, p. 5).

[87] 'L'Angleterre, elle, considère comme un devoir de s'occuper de ceux qui n'ont ni pain ni abri' (L. Michel, *Mémoires de Louise Michel écrits par elle-même* (Paris, 1886), p. 385).

[88] 'Jouissance raffinée chez les uns, misère sordide chez les autres' (Malato, *Joyeusetés de l'exil*, p. 24).

[89] 'Chaque Anglais symbolise étrangement le pays: ces insulaires figurant autant de petites îles inabordables où ne s'éveille point la sève des plantes aux tons chauds' (d'Axa, *De Mazas*, p. 77).

their international counterparts. The new direction of French anarchism towards revolutionary syndicalism after 1894 owed a lot to the personal contacts formed in London and the joint reflection possible in London's international meeting places. The networks formed in London thus allowed the French movement to survive at a time of heavy repression, and also to reinvent itself.[90]

[90] Bantman, *French Anarchists in London*.

9. Experiencing French cookery in nineteenth-century London

Valerie Mars

Introduction

This chapter discusses London's nineteenth-century French cookery and a little of its history before 1800. London's nineteenth-century French cooks were to be found in households, hotels, restaurants and, not least, in print. They were producing a cuisine transposed from one culture to another where they had to accommodate to a range of tastes and values differing from those of the cuisine's origin. The question is how French was London's French cuisine? Or was it sometimes something that might not have been recognized as French by the French and informed gastronomes? The aim is to locate the variety of French and French-style cuisine in this fast-changing city. How was this experienced by both French and English cooks and consumers, for French cookery was not always well understood? This problem was not particular to nineteenth-century London.

Predecessors: French cooks in London before 1800

For centuries French cooks had followed a long tradition of working for London's rich and powerful. The early modern period sees them at the Tudor and Stuart courts. Henry VIII's French cook is recorded as Pero Doulx who served at Hampton Court. Described as 'the French yeoman cook for the king's mouth', he was paid and clothed accordingly.[1] By Elizabeth I's reign, Harrison refers to 'the nobility whose cooks are for the most part musical-headed Frenchmen and strangers'.[2]

French influence continued in print with Robert May's *The Accomplisht Cook* in 1617.[3] He had, when ten years old in 1598, been sent to learn his

---

[1] *Letters and Papers Foreign and Domestic of the Reign of Henry VIII*, ed. S. J. Brewer (2nd edn., 1861–3), quoted in P. Brears, *All the King's Cooks: the Tudor Kitchens of Henry VIII at Hampton Court Palace* (1999), p. 113.

[2] *Harrison's Description of England in Shakspere's [sic] Youth. Being the second and third books of his Description of Britaine and Englande. Edited from the first two editions of Holinshed's Chronicle, 1577, 1587*, ed. F. J. Furnivall (3 vols., 1877–1909), i, *Extracts from Harrison's Chronology and from Foreign Writers on England*, bk. II, ch. 4, p. 144.

[3] Robert May, *The Accomplisht Cook, or the Art and Mystery of Cookery*, a facsimile of the 1685 edition, with foreword, introduction and glossary supplied by A. Davidson, M. Bell and T. Jaine (Totnes, 1994).

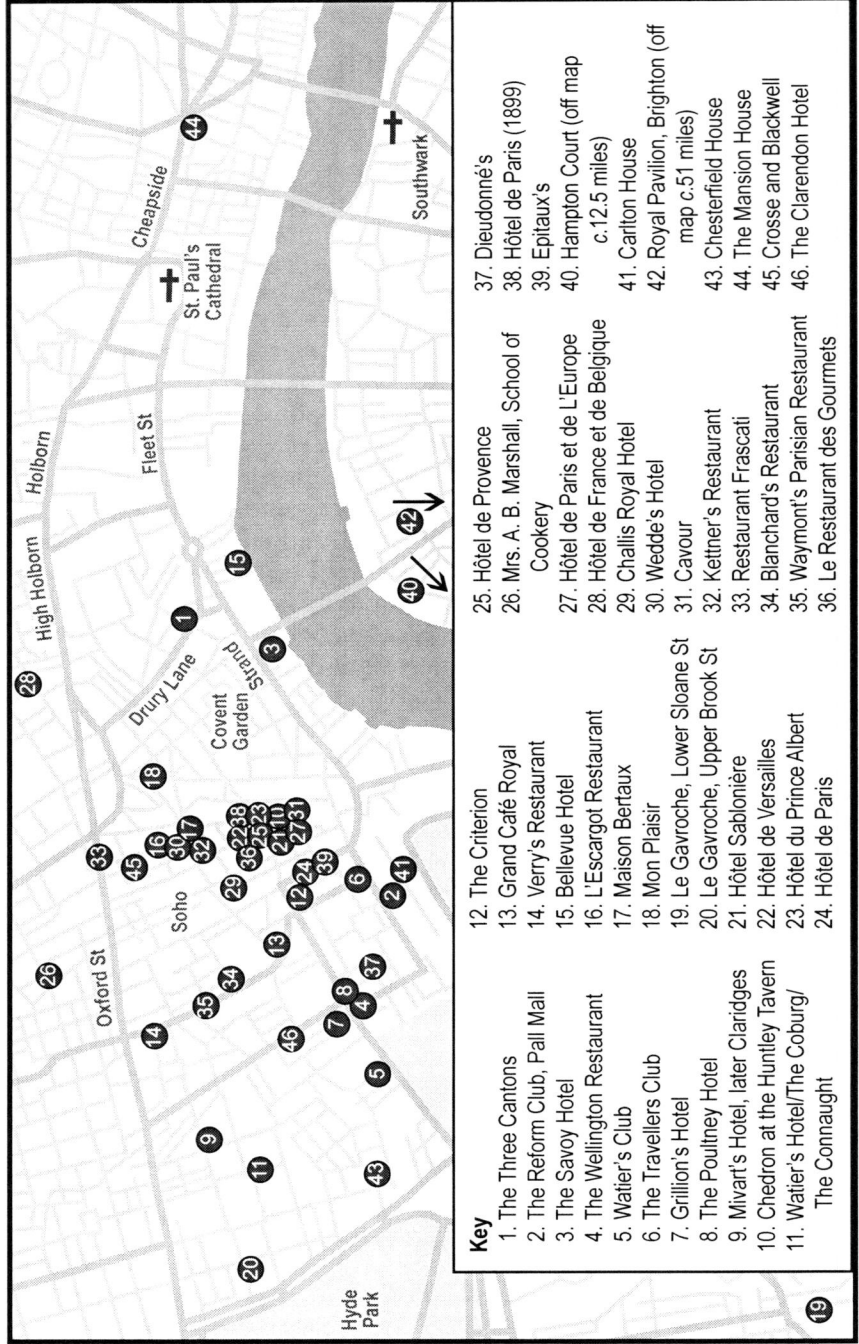

Key
1. The Three Cantons
2. The Reform Club, Pall Mall
3. The Savoy Hotel
4. The Wellington Restaurant
5. Watier's Club
6. The Travellers Club
7. Grillion's Hotel
8. The Poultney Hotel
9. Mivart's Hotel, later Claridges
10. Chedron at the Huntley Tavern
11. Watier's Hotel/The Coburg/
    The Connaught

12. The Criterion
13. Grand Café Royal
14. Verry's Restaurant
15. Bellevue Hotel
16. L'Escargot Restaurant
17. Maison Bertaux
18. Mon Plaisir
19. Le Gavroche, Lower Sloane St
20. Le Gavroche, Upper Brook St
21. Hôtel Sablonière
22. Hôtel de Versailles
23. Hôtel du Prince Albert
24. Hôtel de Paris

25. Hôtel de Provence
26. Mrs. A. B. Marshall, School of
    Cookery
27. Hôtel de Paris et de L'Europe
28. Hôtel de France et de Belgique
29. Challis Royal Hotel
30. Wedde's Hotel
31. Cavour
32. Kettner's Restaurant
33. Restaurant Frascati
34. Blanchard's Restaurant
35. Waymont's Parisian Restaurant
36. Le Restaurant des Gourmets

37. Dieudonné's
38. Hôtel de Paris (1899)
39. Epitaux's
40. Hampton Court (off map
    c.12.5 miles)
41. Carlton House
42. Royal Pavilion, Brighton (off
    map c.51 miles)
43. Chesterfield House
44. The Mansion House
45. Crosse and Blackwell
46. The Clarendon Hotel

Map 9.1. Places mentioned in the text (Base map: London c.1850)

218

trade for five years in the household of 'a noble peer', the first president of Paris.[4] John Murrell's *A New Booke of Cookerie* appeared shortly after in 1630, 'all set forth according to the now, new, English and French Fashion'.[5]

French culinary influence was found not only in the employment of French cooks but also in important cook books that were translated into English. French cuisine was set out in a new system of cookery: La Varenne's *Le Cuisinier François* was published in Paris in 1651 and 1652, followed by an English translation in 1653. The foundation stocks and sauces recorded by La Varennne were still the basis of French cuisine in the nineteenth century.

Major French works continued to be translated throughout the eighteenth century. In 1702 François Massialot's *Court and Country Cook* comprised translations of two books on cookery and confectionery.[6] There followed other fashionable French cookery books in translation such as Vincent La Chapelle's *The Modern Cook*, which appeared in three volumes in 1733, and was continued with a fourth edition in a single volume. The author had been chief cook to the earl of Chesterfield (1694–1773).[7] This was followed by a translation of Menon's fashionable *Les Soupers de la cour, ou, la cuisine reformée*.[8]

During the eighteenth century the importance of employing a French cook for many of London's elite households is shown in a letter written by the duke of Newcastle to Lord Albemarle, the British ambassador in Paris. In 1754 the duke had lost Monsieur Clouet, his French cook, to Albemarle (see Figure 9.1).[9] Feeling perhaps that an obligation was due to him, he wrote to Albemarle asking his help in finding a replacement. The duke's letter showed that he knew what he liked. His cook was to embody all the specialist skills that were undertaken by separately skilled cooks in France. Newcastle liked 'little *hors d'œuvre* or light *entrées*', 'plain simple dishes',[10] and

---

[4] May, *The Accomplisht Cook*, p. 13.

[5] John Murrell, *A New Booke of Cookerie Wherein is set forth the newest and most commendable Fashion for Dressing or Sowcing, eyther Flesh, Fish, or Fowle. Together with making all sorts of Iellyes … All set forth according to the now, new, English and French Fashion. Set forth by the observation of a Traueller. I. M.* [i.e., John Murrell] (1630), title page.

[6] François Massialot, *The Court and Country Cook* (1702), in translation (see V. Maclean, *A Short-Title Catalogue of Household and Cookery Books Published in the English Tongue 1701–1800* (1981), pp. 1–6).

[7] Vincent La Chapelle, *The Modern Cook* (1733) (see Maclean, *Short-Title Catalogue*, p. 85).

[8] Menon, *The art of modern cookery displayed. Consisting of the most approved methods of cookery, pastry, and confectionary of the present time* (translated from *Les Soupers de la cour, ou, la cuisine reformée*), trans. B. Cleremont (1767).

[9] R. Sedgwick, 'The duke of Newcastle's cook', *History Today*, v (1955), 309.

[10] Sedgwick, 'Duke of Newcastle's cook', p. 317.

Figure 9.1. The Duke N–le and his Cook, 1745. British Museum,
Prints and Drawings. Registration Number: 1849, 1003.27.

Caption: The duke of Newcastle with his French cook M. Clouet. The kitchen is equipped with charcoal stoves for French cookery.

he revealed a taste for what could be termed French mid century nouvelle cuisine that seemed to match well with contemporary English taste. He also asserted that he did not like 'strong soups' or 'disguised *entrées* and *entrements* [*sic*]'.[11] Disguise was a term used by the English to refer to the use of sauces as masking ingredients, and was a recurring theme. Signifying more than a preference but a patriotism, or more accurately a chauvinism, 'disguise' was equated with French 'deception' throughout the eighteenth and nineteenth centuries.

Of one recommended cook, Newcastle wrote:

> I own I like the man extremely, his temper and disposition. But I can't say that his qualities as a cook are quite what I wish … his *plats* don't seem to please here; and are not just what I like. They are generally composed of a variety of things, and are not the light dishes and clear sauces which Cloe excell'd in. They

[11] Sedgwick, 'Duke of Newcastle's cook', p. 311. The duke of Newcastle's French cook, M. de St. Clouet, was assisted by William Verral, who later wrote a cookery book to teach 'the whole and simple art of the most modern and best French Cookery' to his local Sussex gentry.

are unintelligible or *des grosses pièces, accommodées de leur façon. Les plats légers* are, I suppose, out of fashion. In short, it is not what carries authority with it and what would make people asham'd to disapprove.

Newcastle was not easily accommodated, and he wrote to Lord Albemarle yet again, in 1754, making a further request for renewed efforts in finding a skilled French cook from a great French household. In what appears to be a bout of hyperbolic exasperation, he asserts: 'This town swarms with them [French cooks] and there is scarce a young boy, or even a country gentleman, who has not his French cook'.[12]

This outburst certainly suggests that French cooks were plentiful but it is difficult to know the quality of their work or how far their cookery was adapted to English tastes. Newcastle could not find the ideal cook – even allowing that he needed a man with multiple skills[13] – or the correspondence with Albemarle would not have gone on for a year

A further indication of the status of male cooks, who were predominantly French, was that they earned wages well above those of female cooks. J. Jean Hecht gives examples: in 1795 a male cook was paid fifty-five to sixty guineas a year, a female cook a mere ten guineas.[14] These differentials continued throughout the nineteenth century.

Some of London's nineteenth-century French cooks and chefs[15]

Haute cuisine was experienced in London by French residents and travellers as well as native Londoners. French cooks were to be found not only in elite households but in the exclusive clubs of St. James's and the hotels and restaurants of Mayfair. Bourgeois French travellers and residents, along with native Londoners, were also catered for in French restaurants and hotels around Leicester Square and Soho. Baedeker and other guides to London offered services to suit a range of incomes and tastes.[16]

During the first half of the century visitors were more inclined to choose French hotels and restaurants, but as London became more cosmopolitan, French travellers appear to have ventured beyond exclusively French establishments. Similarly, as more Londoners began to visit and live in

[12] Sedgwick, 'Duke of Newcastle's cook', p. 314.

[13] The French guilds' rules forbade cooks trained in one skill to practise others in which they were not qualified. English rules allowed any trade to be followed after apprenticeship.

[14] J. J. Hecht, *The Domestic Servant Class in 18th Century England* (1956), pp. 142, 147.

[15] *Oxford English Dictionary* (2nd edn.), iii, gives T. Ingoldsby, *The Ingoldsby Legends* (1842), as the first literary reference to a chef. By 1860 Charles Dickens refers to both a chef and a menu in *All the Year Round*, lxxiv (1860), 567.

[16] K. Baedeker, *Londres suivi d'excursions dans l'Angleterre du Sud* (Coblenz, 1866); K. Baedeker, *Great Britain Handbook for Travellers* (1866) and (1894).

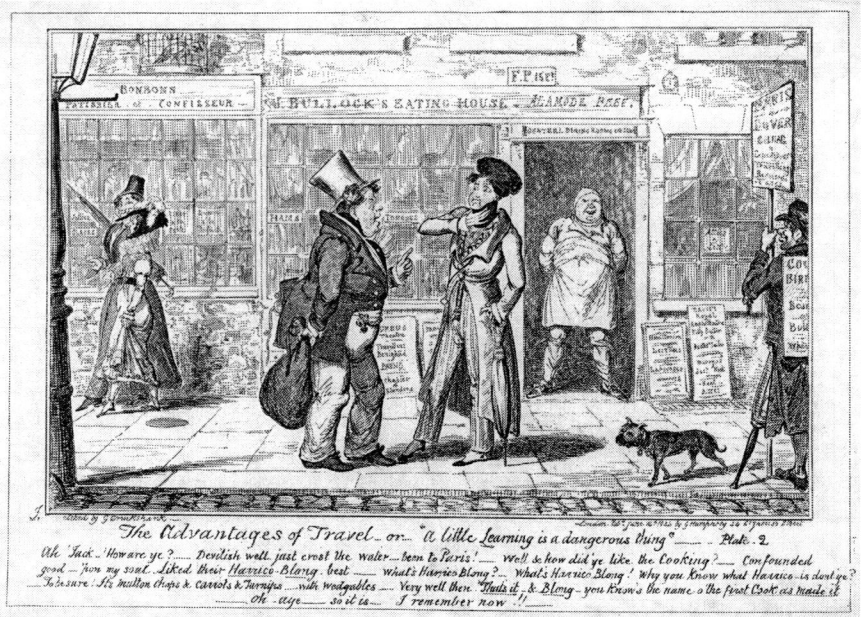

Figure 9.2. George Cruikshank 'The Advantages of Travel – or
– a little learning is a Dangerous Thing', 1824. British Museum,
Prints and Drawings. Registration Number: 1861, 1012.356.

Caption: A typical Alamode beef house

France they in turn brought back tastes for both *haute* and bourgeois cookery.

In culinary London not all that appeared French was as French as its attribution suggested. Beef, sold at traditional cooked meat shops and dining-rooms, and advertised as 'Alamode Beef', was not the French bourgeois dish *bœuf à la mode*. It had lost something in the translation. George Cruikshank's 1824 *The Advantages of Travel – or – a Little Learning is a Dangerous Thing* showed an extremely fashionable young man in a state of shock outside an alamode shop being addressed by another who wears the blue coat of the chauvinist Beefsteak Club. The latter's understanding of French dishes was demonstrably limited (see Figure 9.2).[17]

G. A. Sala similarly describes most of these shops in the 1850s and 1860s as offering an à la mode beef that 'with the exception of its bovine foundation,

---

[17] G. Cruikshank, *The Advantages of Travel – or – a Little Learning is a Dangerous Thing* (1824), repr. in *London Eats Out: 500 Years of Capital Dining* (1999), p. 68.

presented no culinary resemblance to that *bœuf à la mode* which is one of the standing dishes of the French *cuisine bourgeoise*. Sala, however, tells of visiting an exceptional à la mode shop with Alexis Soyer, the famous French chef. The Thirteen Cantons, in Blackmore Street, Drury Lane was where the alamode served was distinctive because of the 'remarkably luscious and tasty sauce, or rather soup with which it was accompanied'. After Jaquet the proprietor had retired he told Sala what his secret ingredient was: 'Morella mushroom powder, made from mushrooms gathered near London'. Sala believes this to be the common morel.[18]

Certain views of French cookery in England recur, such as Henri Misson's observation in 1650 that most of those who did not know France 'have very little idea of our tables'.[19] It is a view repeated in the nineteenth century, as here by Louis Eustache Ude: 'I have frequently met with young men who pretend to high birth and scientific knowledge, and who are yet unable to judge anything in cookery beyond boiled chicken and parsley and butter'. Yet Ude concludes that professional cooks will find 'some good judges that will advocate your cause, and perseverance in right principles will give a man of your profession the rank of an artist'.[20]

Joseph Florance, French cook to three generations of dukes of Buccleuch, tells the young duke in 1817: 'I should strongly advise that the master cook should wait at table when there is company, an epicure wishes to know what dishes are composed of'.[21] This also suggests that some of the duke's guests may have been somewhat less than familiar with French cookery.

Unfamiliarity with haute cuisine is not considered by Urbain Dubois. He did not work in London but could be read in translation. In 1872, Dubois's ideal French host (women were not considered arbiters of elite taste) is described as one who carefully selects a dinner and is addressed as the *amphytrion*,[22] a title unusual in England, in spite of an English penchant for classical allusion. This may reflect some of the uncertainty surrounding gourmet tendencies, suggesting that little social capital was to be gained in exhibiting a deep knowledge of haute cuisine.[23]

---

[18] G. A. Sala, *Things I have Seen and People I have Known* (2 vols., 2nd edn., 1894), ii. 202–5.

[19] M. [Henri de Valbourg] Misson (c.1650–12 Jan. 1722), *Memoirs and Observations in his Travels over England, With some Account of Scotland and Ireland, Disposed in Alphabetical Order*, trans. J. Ozell (1719), p. 316.

[20] L. E. Ude, *The French Cook: a System of Fashionable, Practical and Economical Cookery Adapted to the Use of English Families* (14th edn., 1841), p. xlv.

[21] A. French and G. Waterfield, 'Loyal servants', in G. Waterfield and A. French, with M. Craske, *Below Stairs: 400 Years of Servants' Portraits* (2003), pp. 57–75, at p. 75.

[22] U. Dubois, *Cosmopolitan Cookery* (1872), in translation.

[23] P. Bourdieu, *Distinction, a Social Critique of the Judgement of Taste*, trans. R. Nice (Cambridge, Mass., 1986), p. 114.

Views of nineteenth-century French cuisine are mainly offered by cooks whose London published works are augmented with menus and comment to assist the reader. Published opinions from diners and critics grew in number as travel to and from France increased after 1815. Throughout the nineteenth century the cachet of employing a French chef continued and is often described as having begun and concluded with two great French chefs: Antonin Carême (1783–1833) and Georges Auguste Escoffier (1847–1935).

French haute cuisine is essentially an evolving craft. Escoffier says that when updating old methods to satisfy 'modern demands', 'The fundamental principles of the science which we owe to Carême ... will last as long as cooking itself'.[24] There were those for whom there was no other cuisine which could compare with the French. The widely travelled Elim D'Avigdor wrote, with the unshakeable authority of the nineteenth-century epicure: 'French dinners cannot be compared with those of any other nation'.[25]

London's new and old money, as in the previous century, continued to offer French and French-trained cooks plenty of employment. Ude's *The French Cook; or the Art of Cookery developed in all its various braches* [sic] (1813–41) went through many editions with some improvements in its translations. Abraham Hayward, a noted epicure and critic, in *The Art of Dining* lists 'the most eminent cooks and *pâtissiers* of the present time in England', though they would for the most part only keep their reputations during the lifetime of their colleagues and maybe that of their diners.[26] With the exception of Jules Gouffé (1807–77), none of them wrote cookery books. Nearly all are French but Hayward only selects those employed by the aristocracy, excluding those who worked for other wealthy employers. Their pay was high, to match the status they had in their households – Ude was reputedly paid 300 guineas per annum by the earl of Sefton, followed by a pension of £100 per annum.[27]

These French cooks (or chefs as they were later known) would usually have worked in London during the social season, and for most of the rest of the year have been expected to return with their employers to their country estates. Similarly, from July 1816 to late 1817 Antonin Carême, employed by the prince regent, was obliged to travel between Carlton House in London and the Royal Pavilion in Brighton. His stay in England was brief. One of the reasons why Carême left his post so soon, Ian Kelly found, was the

[24] G. A. Escoffier, *A Guide to Modern Cookery* (1907; 5th impression, 1968), p. xii.
[25] E. D'Avigdor, *Dinners and Dishes* (1885), p. 199.
[26] A. Hayward, *The Art of Dining, or Gastronomy and Gastronomers* (1852; 1883 edn.), p. 77.
[27] Hayward, *Art of Dining*, p. 75.

constant travel between two places.[28] Carême's greater legacy is his published works, from which a number of recipes were translated into English.[29]

It can be argued that Carême's real influence in London was through Charles Elmé Francatelli (1805–76), who was described as 'advancing culinary art to unprecedented perfection in this country'.[30] He had worked for Carême in Paris and, almost as briefly as Carême, for the royal household. For two years, from 1841 to 1842, he was chief cook and maître d'hôtel to Queen Victoria. Francatelli also cooked for clubs and for the nobility. His works for upper- and upper-middle-class households are *The Modern Cook*, *The Cook's Guide* and *The Royal English and Foreign Confectioner*.[31] E. S. Dallas notes that Francatelli's 'great work', *The Modern Cook*, was in its twenty-third edition in 1877 'and of such authority that many of the best people swear by it'.[32]

Francatelli was also praised by Hayward, who described his dinners at Chesterfield House as being 'the admiration of the gastronomic world of London'.[33] His was an ideal interpretation of French haute cuisine and its influence is indicated in the French dishes chosen for the lord mayor of London's spectacular banquet to promote the 1851 Great Exhibition. For that occasion the caterers departed from the usual, mainly English bill of fare. The banquet's French dishes, although not exclusive to Francatelli, can be recreated from recipes in *The Modern Cook*.[34]

Hayward's lesser opinion of Francatelli's famous French contemporary, Alexis Soyer, derives from the fact that although 'his name has been a good deal before the public' and 'he is a very clever man, of inventive genius and inexhaustible resource … his execution is hardly on a par with his conception'.[35] Soyer's genius for publicity ensured that his reputation has

---

[28] I. Kelly, *Cooking for Kings: the Life of Antonin Carême, the First Celebrity Chef* (New York, 2003), pp. 121–53.

[29] M. A. Carême, *The Royal Parisian Pastrycook and Confectioner* ed. J. Porter (1834); M. A. Carême, *French Cookery Comprising l'art de la cuisine française; Le Patissier Royal; Le Cuisinier Parisien*, trans. W. Hall, etc. (1836).

[30] *Dictionary of National Biography*, ed. L. Stephen (1889), xx. 163.

[31] C. E. Francatelli, *The Modern Cook: a Practical Guide to the Culinary Art in All its Branches* (1845); *The Cook's Guide and Housekeeper's and Butler's Assistant* (1848); *The Royal English and Foreign Confectioner: a practical treatise on the art of confectionary in all its branches; comprising ornamental confectionary artistically developed. Also, the art of ice-making, and the arrangement and general economy of fashionable desserts* (1862).

[32] E. S. Dallas, *Kettner's Book of the Table* (1877; 1968 edn.), p. 3.

[33] Hayward, *Art of Dining*, pp. 75–7.

[34] V. Mars, 'North and south: two banquets given to promote the Great 1851 Exhibition', in *Celebration: Proceedings of the Oxford Symposium on Food and Cookery, 2011*, ed. M. McWilliams (Totnes, 2012), pp. 184–216.

[35] Hayward, *Art of Dining*, pp. 76–7.

lasted well beyond his lifetime, so that he continues to be promoted in biographies and articles. In his time he was the model for Mirabolant in Thackeray's *The History of Pendennis*[36] and was also satirized in *Punch*.[37] His early fame came as chef to the Reform Club, where he designed their innovative kitchens and to which he took visitors on tours. While there he gave several well-publicized dinners and banquets, as described by his secretaries.[38]

Soyer, like Francatelli, also wrote for the middle classes. He created *The Modern Housewife*, written as a series of letters from 'Hortense' at 'Bifrons Villa, St John's Wood', advising her friend Eloise, at her country cottage. In 1857, Soyer signed an indenture with Edmund Crosse and Thomas Blackwell, Italian warehousemen of Soho Square, to produce 'Soyer's Bottled Sauces'. The terms on which this was agreed included two years' advertising in the daily papers – worth £200.[39] Soyer's name was to be constantly before the public in print. If they could not employ a French chef, Soyer could add relish to their meals.

Chefs' works continued to be translated. Jules Gouffé, the son of a French pastry chef, was, at sixteen, recruited by Carême. His brother Alphonse, *pâtissier* to the queen, in 1868 translated and adapted Jules's *Le Livre de cuisine* as *The Royal Cookery Book*. The work is divided into two sections: 'Household cookery' and 'High class cookery'. Alphonse comments 'that he has endeavoured to adapt the recipes to the capabilities and requirements of English households', thus suggesting that English kitchens could not truly replicate French cookery.[40] Among the reasons were the different types of stoves and ranges.[41] Alphonse uses English where possible but 'all the terms belonging to that special culinary nomenclature which I have been compelled to adopt; although of French origin, most of these have now, by their constant recurrence, become household words in England'.[42]

By the end of the 1860s more dinners were being served *à la Russe*, requiring menu-cards that were usually written in French. More Londoners

[36] W. M. Thackeray, *The History of Pendennis* (2 vols., 1869 edn.), p. 261.

[37] *Punch*, e.g. vol. xix (July–Dec. 1850), 191.

[38] F. Volant and J. R. Warren, *Memoirs of Alexis Soyer* (1859; Rottingdean, 1985), 'Diner à la Sampayo', pp. 92–5; 'Dinner for 150 given by members of the Reform Club to Ibraham Pacha, 3 July 1846', pp. 87–9.

[39] Private collection, *Indenture*, 31 March 1857, between Alexis Soyer and Edmund Crosse and Thomas Blackwell.

[40] J. Gouffé, *Le Livre de cuisine*, trans. as *The Royal Cookery Book* by A. Gouffé (1868), pp. v–vi.

[41] V. Mars, 'Ordering dinner: Victorian celebratory domestic dining in London' (unpublished University of Leicester PhD thesis, 1997), pp. 147–56.

[42] 'Translator's preface', in Gouffé, *Royal Cookery Book*.

had by then spent time in France, but comprehension was by no means universal. Auguste Escoffier, when at the Grand Hôtel in Monte Carlo, found that à la carte menus were not understood by many of his English clients, who would ask the maître d'hôtel to order their meal. Later, at the Savoy, to solve this problem Escoffier composed *prix fixe* dinners for bookings involving four or more diners.[43]

Pleasing both French and English tastes

French cookery certainly held its place as the cuisine that could demonstrate luxury. Yet French haute cuisine was not always the exclusive choice. In print and in households both French and English cuisines would often be found together – as in Murrell's *New Book of Cookerie*, referred to above.[44] Misson had noted in 1698 that 'There are some noblemen that have both *French* and *English* cooks, and these eat much after the French manner'.[45]

During the nineteenth century English and French cuisine in the same establishment was still a familiar style. In 1860, Captain Gronow (1794–1865), remembered the cuisine of his youth at dinners he attended as 'wonderfully solid, hot and stimulating … The French or side dishes consisted of very mild but very abortive attempts at continental cooking'.[46] Throughout the period French haute cuisine was still both loved and hated. This was in part due to its political role in symbolizing recurrent views of all things French; but it was, at the same time, the cuisine of Europe's elites. Therefore, to please all who sat at table, two tastes needed to be accommodated. The lord mayor of London's banquet given on 15 June 1849[47] has just such a bill of fare.

French cuisine, therefore, did not supplant English cookery, which had its own admirers, including French cooks who worked in London, such as Ude. As a French cook working for English employers, he possibly flatters his English readers in writing 'cookery in England, when well done, is superior to that of any country in the world'.[48] Domestically and commercially the problem of pleasing both tastes was solved by offering both English and French dishes.

In Urbain Dubois and Emile Bernard's *La Cuisine Classique*, the two cuisines are put within the formal structure of separately styled services.

[43] A. Escoffier, *Memories of my Life*, trans. L. Escoffier (New York, 1997), p. 90.

[44] Murrell, *New Booke of Cookerie*, title page.

[45] Misson, *Memoirs and Observations*, p. 314.

[46] Capt. R. H. Gronow, *The Reminiscences and Recollections of Captain Gronow*, ed. J. Raymond (abridged version, 1964), pp. 45–6.

[47] Museum of London, Acc. No. 37, 146/20, Mansion House bill of fare.

[48] Ude, *French Cook*, p. xliii.

They describe two different menus: dinner *à la Française* and dinner *à l'Anglaise* are two separate styles, with only minor differences, such as *à l'Anglaise* serving turtle soup. The choice of cuisine reflected predominantly French or English taste, influencing the choice of service style. This was a way to differentiate between French- or English-biased cuisine among the cosmopolitan gourmet elite. *La Cuisine Classique* gives examples of both menus. Its *à l'Anglaise* menu for twelve conforms to a typically elaborate English dinner. To show the structures more clearly, I will give only the main ingredient of dishes, although a high degree of elaboration was incorporated into almost every one.[49]

The English dinner comprises, as a first service, two soups, one of which was mutton broth; two fish, salmon and haddock; two *relevés*, lamb and a chicken pie; and four *entrées*, chicken breasts, hare fillets, foie-gras and mutton cutlets. The second service begins with two roasts, ducklings and grouse; two *relevés*, a fondu and rice croquettes; plus six *entremêts*,[50] sole in aspic, young peas English style, orange jelly, peach pastries, plum pudding, artichoke bottoms and a 'scarlet' tongue on the sideboard.

The *à la Française* menu for twenty-two is selected, for the most part, from dishes that cater to French taste, which slightly alters the dinner's structure. Two soups are followed by hot *hors d'œuvre*, then by two *relevés*, salmon garnished with shrimps and English roast beef, and finally by four *entrées*. This is similar to the parallel section of the *à l'Anglaise* menu. The second service, like the English, begins with two roasts, turkey with foie-gras and barded quails, with two flancs (or side dishes), pâté de foie-gras and a basket of crayfish. *Entremêts* were again similar to those on the *à l'Anglaise* menu, with a *charlotte Parisienne* instead of plum pudding, but there are only four. These are followed by two more sweet dishes, a Neapolitan gateau and an orange *croquenbouche*, which are served as 'relevés de rôtis' that replace the roasts on the table.

Some restaurants also offered the same accommodation to divided tastes by providing both French and English cuisines. In an 1858 advertorial in *London at Dinner; or Where to Dine*,[51] the author notes that both English and French tastes were perfectly catered for at the Wellington Restaurant, 53 St. James's Street and 160 Piccadilly, where:

[49] U. Dubois and E. Bernard, *La Cuisine Classique* (Paris, 1856), pp. 8–9.

[50] 'Entremêts – or second-course side dishes – consist of four distinct sorts namely: – cold entrées, dressed vegetables, scalloped shell fish and lastly, of the infinitely-varied class of sweets' (C. E. Francatelli, in *The Cook's Guide and Housekeeper's and Butler's Assistant* (1861; 1884 edn.), p. 488).

[51] Anon. [Lord William Pitt Lennox], *London at Dinner, or, Where to Dine* (1858; Newton Abbot, 1969), advertisements, pp. 2–11.

the kitchens are two in number, each quite independent of the other. In one the English chef rules the roast [*sic*]; and in the other, one of the cleverest and most accomplished artistes that Paris can produce prepares, with the aid of his subs, 'petits diners', which the travelled English allow to excel the dinners served in the restaurants of the French capital.

The Wellington offers 'set dinners' between three and nine o'clock from 3*s* for six courses, to 8*s* for eight courses with more choice. All these menus are of their French dishes. At the same time the English kitchen lists joints and fish with favourite English sauces – typically boiled turbot with lobster sauce. There are also 'made dishes', the English equivalent of *entrées*. These include Soyer's famous recipe 'Cutlets Reform', as well as cutlets served with soubise (a white sauce with onion purée) or with tomato sauce, as well as the usual chops and rumpsteak. Also on these à la carte lists are 'soups', 'poultry and game', 'sweets' and 'sundries' that reflect traditional English taste.[52] Later, when Frederick Leal writes in the promotional booklet for the Restaurant Frascati in the 1890s, he makes a similar claim for their two main kitchens, English and Parisian.[53]

Learning to cook like the French bourgeoisie and offering recherché dinners

French bourgeois women were set as an example to counter the widely held genteel disdain of the English for contact with the cooking process. Much was written in England to dissuade this flight to gentility. As early as 1825 an anonymous physician's choice of dishes is directed especially to 'families hitherto unaccustomed to French cuisine'.[54] His was not an original work but an adapted translation of one of the most popular French cookery books *La Cuisinière de la campagne et de la ville; ou nouvelle cuisine économique*.[55]

Like all French cookery books the work begins with the proper way of making and using stocks. He names three basic stocks: 'Stock or first broth, consommé or jelly broth, blond or veal gravy'. There are essential instructions for cooking *pot-au-feu* in the French manner and explanations of how the beef 'answers three purposes: 1st, as a soup; 2ndly, as a dish of bouilli and vegetables; and 3rdly, for a reserve of stock'. Eliza Acton

---

[52] Anon. [Lennox], *London at Dinner*.

[53] Museum of London, Ephemera, L.75.52, F. Leal, *The Restaurant Frascati*, p. 19.

[54] Anon., *French Domestic Cookery, Combining economy with elegance adapted for the use of Families of Moderate fortune By an English Physician many years resident on the Continent* (1825), p. 1.

[55] M. L-EA [L.-E. Audot], *La Cuisinière de la campagne et de la ville, ou La Nouvelle Cuisine economique; précédée d'un traité sur les soins qu'exige une cave, et sur la dissection des viandes à table* (3rd edn, Paris, 1823).

(1799–1859) encouraged her readers to make soup, something that is 'so well understood in France'. She had spent a year in France as a young woman where she got to know French domestic cookery.

The Anonymous Physician makes clear that to cook in the French way a number of items must always be ready for use: 'dried herbs, preserved vegetables and fruits, bay leaves, onions, shallots, eggs, bacon and anchovies'.[56] This may have been unusual in middle-class Victorian kitchens, particularly those ruled from above-stairs, which were well known for the imposition of extreme economies.[57] Other writers followed Acton, such as Miss Crawford in her 1853 *French Cookery for English Families*.[58] The same appeal to adopt French cookery is continued by Percy Lindley who asks: 'Were the middle classes only but slightly acquainted with the domestic cookery of France, they would certainly live better and less expensively than at present'.[59] The Anonymous Physician told his readers that one of the advantages of French cookery was that it gave 'their dinners a genteel, and rather *recherché* appearance'.[60] In the aspiring and competitive circles of London's celebratory domestic dining, some of these French techniques offered a required elaboration.

While these new dinners were not quite replicating the work of elite French cooks, the dishes served needed a higher level of skill. Eliza Acton advises against her readers attempting a 'timbale';[61] it was not appropriate to their resources (see Figure 9.3). Like much of the professional French cook's repertoire, a timbale required technical expertise, an extensive *batterie de cuisine* and sufficient assistants. Both Thackeray and Dickens found these new dining circles a subject for satire. They attacked those who did not keep a French cook and therefore required caterers to provide extreme, *recherché* dinners, Dickens's 'Veneerings' being the ultimate arrivistes.[62] Satirical remarks were made about patties from pastry shops, items not easily cooked at home by the typical plain cook.

[56] Anon., *French Domestic Cookery*, p. 1.

[57] V. Mars and G. Mars, 'Fat in the Victorian kitchen: a medium for cooking, control, deviance, and crime', in *The Fat of the Land: Proceedings of the Oxford Symposium on Food and Cookery 2002*, ed. H. Walker (Bristol, 2003), pp. 216–36.

[58] Miss (F.) Crawford, *French Cookery for English Families* (1853).

[59] *English and French Cookery*, attributed to A. H. Wall, ed. P. Lindley in *The Housekeeper* series (*c*.1890), p. 16; see E. Driver, *A Bibliography of Cookery Books Published in Britain, 1875–1914* (Totnes, 1989), p. 634.

[60] Anon., *French Domestic Cookery*, p. 1.

[61] E. Acton, *Modern Cookery for Private Families* (1845; 5th impression, 1868). The figure is from a facsimile of the 1855 edition (1966), p. 390; Glossary, p. xxvi: 'Timbale – a sort of pie made in a mould'.

[62] C. Dickens, *Our Mutual Friend* (2 vols., 1860–2), i, ch. 2.

Figure 9.3. Timbale of lamb sweetbreads in shells, Fig. 97
from Urbain Dubois, *Cosmopolitan Cookery* (1869).

A timbale is an elaborate recipe that is produced by chefs. Mrs. Acton advises her readers
against attempting an imitation.

Arbiters of domestic taste warned against an aspiration to offer dinners
above the givers' means and rank. Such warnings are found throughout the
period. This one, from 1864, is by A. V. Kirwan who, like Hayward, was a
lawyer and who also wrote on gastronomy in *Host and Guest*:

> Why, however, it will be asked, should persons of a couple or three thousand a
> year give so pretentious and costly a dinner? Because everyone in England tries to
> ape the class two or three degrees above him in point of rank and fortune, in style
> of living, and manner of receiving his friends. Thus it is that a plain gentleman
> of moderate fortune, or a professional man making a couple of thousands a year,
> having dined with a peer of £50,000 a year in Grosvenor Square or Belgravia,
> seeks when he himself next gives a dinner to imitate the style of the marquis, earl
> or lord lieutenant of a county with whom he has come into social contact.[63]

This style not only displeased those who promoted French bourgeois cuisine
but also connected with an undercurrent of prejudice and male chauvinism
that was to continue throughout the century. Much chauvinist rhetoric had
traditionally cited dishes such as fricassée as 'disguised' and therefore as
an unacceptable French practice. Yet in spite of this, upper-middle-class
dinner cuisine remained a material expression of feminine separation from
contamination by the natural.[64] Service *à la Russe* removed the sight of
whole joints, in their natural animal form, from the table, since in this
service joints are carved on the sideboard.[65]

[63] A. V. Kirwan, *Host and Guest: about Dinners, Wines and Desserts* (1864), p. 76.
[64] M. Douglas, *Purity and Danger: an Analysis of Concepts of Pollution and Taboo* (1966).
[65] V. Mars, 'A la Russe: a new way of dining', in *Luncheon, Nuncheon and other Meals:
Eating with the Victorians*, ed. C. Anne Wilson (Stroud, 1994), pp. 117–44.

Houses for the nascent professional classes were built during the second half of the century in new suburbs such as Kensington. Their inhabitants were to create their own fashionable dinner-giving circles. These dinners, largely organized by women, began to acquire a more feminized aspect. Food had to be served in a style that concealed its natural form. Recipes for masking sauces and aspic jellies offered the desired effect. This trend was typically derided by the pseudonymous Fin-Bec who had lived in France and promoted a French style of domestic entertaining. As an arbiter of taste, Fin-Bec wrote of French bourgeois domestic entertaining offering well-cooked modest dinners that reflected the hosts' status. He gives a satirical view in his journal *Knife and Fork*: 'There is plenty of pretension in middle-class houses. The *entrées* do not lack. But preserve me from a Bayswater *filet aux olives*, a Kensington *Salmi*, or, above all, a suburban *Soubise*'.[66]

Marion Sambourne, with her husband Linley Sambourne, the *Punch* cartoonist, reflected this trend at the dinners they gave at their Kensington house. The dishes Marion most admired when dining in other houses within their circle almost always included labour-intensive arrangements of ingredients, usually diced or similarly cut up. She describes a Russian salad in her menu notebook. It is an arrangement within an aspic border of carrots, turnips, beetroot, new potatoes, olives, egg and anchovy, cut very fine and mixed with mayonnaise or sharp sauce. First seen at a dinner with their neighbours Mr. and Mrs. Marcus Stone on 21 March 1881, it appears later on one of her own menus.[67] A classic version can be found in Francatelli's *Cook's Guide*.[68] Other examples of this style are in the books of Mrs. Marshall,[69] Mrs. de Salis[70] and Madame Emilie Lebour-Fawcett.[71] All offer recipes for dinner-party cookery and all of these authors claim French experience. Only Madame Emilie Lebour-Fawcett is French and a Cordon Bleu.

With the introduction of service *à la Russe*,[72] the more fashionable dinners required menu-cards to be placed on the table. These were often written in

---

[66] Fin-Bec [pseud.], *Knife and Fork*, ed. W. Blanchard Jerrold, i (Sept.–Oct. 1871).

[67] Royal Borough of Kensington and Chelsea Library, M. Sambourne, *Menu Notebook* (c.1877–83).

[68] Francatelli, *Cook's Guide*, no. 374.

[69] Mrs. Marshall [Agnes B. Marshall (1855–1905)], *Mrs A. B. Marshall's Cookery Book* (Marshall's School of Cookery, c.1888). Variations and an enlarged edition were published at least until 1902.

[70] Mrs. de Salis [Harriet Anne de Salis], *Cookery à la Mode*; the first of a series, *Savouries à la Mode* (1886), with further books in the series brought together in *A la Mode Cookery* (1902).

[71] E. Lebour-Fawcett, *French Cookery for Ladies* (1890).

[72] *The Servants' Guide and Family Manual* (4th edn., 1835), 'Duties of a butler', p. 94. The earliest note of *à la Russe* being fashionable in London was for the 1829 season, but it may have been known in London from 1815.

French or 'menu French'. Mrs. Marshall gives all her recipe titles in both languages, as does Mme. Lebour-Fawcett and Mrs. de Salis.[73] Mrs. Marshall is the most entrepreneurial of these authors. She sold kitchen equipment and other aides to producing *recherché* dinners. She also gave classes for cooks and their mistresses where 'she initiated them into the mysteries of dainty dishes'.[74] Mme. Lebour-Fawcett, author of *French Cookery for Ladies*, lectured at her Kensington cookery school. She remarked on her pupils 'obtaining rapid and almost marvellous successes in a hitherto alien pursuit – successes which I own have surprised as much as they have gratified me'.[75]

These young women were not, however, always going to dine at each other's houses: restaurant dining became fashionable from the late 1880s.

Eating out: haute cuisine

Early in the nineteenth century French cooks could move from cooking for great houses to cooking in clubs and hotels. The prince regent is reputed to have asked his cook Jean-Baptiste Watier to open a dining club, with Madison, the prince's page, as manager, and Labourie, also from the prince's kitchen, as cook. Watier's Club opened in Bolton Street, Piccadilly in 1807. Captain Gronow, who knew Paris in 1816, was a member. He describes the dinners as exquisite: 'the best Parisian cooks could not beat Labourie'.[76] It closed in 1819, the same year that the Travellers Club was founded. Talleyrand became a member when he was ambassador to London.[77] On finding the food unacceptable he had the head chef, John Porter, study Antonin Carême's works.[78] Porter subsequently published a translation of Carême.

Lord Crewe's cook, Alexander Grillion, opened Grillion's Hotel in 1813 in Albemarle Street, which had a number of hotels catering for the aristocracy and royalty.[79] At 105 Piccadilly, a private mansion was opened as a hotel, the Pulteney, in 1814 by the French cook, Jean Escudier. Like Watier's it did not last long, closing by 1823. Louis Jacquier, the cook who had served Louis XVIII during his stay in England, opened the Clarendon Hotel in Old Bond Street in 1815. It was described as 'the only hotel in England where a man could eat a genuine French dinner'.[80] The price for this was £3–£4.

---

[73] She was alleged to be plain 'Mrs. Salis'.
[74] A. B. Marshall, *Mrs A. B. Marshall's Cookery Book* (1894 edn.), advertisements, p. 3.
[75] Lebour-Fawcett, *French Cookery for Ladies*, p. vi.
[76] Gronow, *Reminiscences and Recollections*, p. 60.
[77] Charles Maurice de Talleyrand-Périgord, 1er prince de Bénévent, 1754–1838, ambassador to the Court of St. James's, 1830–4.
[78] Kelly, *Cooking for Kings*, pp. 220–1.
[79] M. C. Borer, *The British Hotel through the Ages* (Guildford, 1972), p. 186.
[80] Borer, *British Hotel*, p. 188, does not give a source for the quotation.

Not all of these establishments were short-lived. In 1815 another French cook, Jacques Mivart, opened a hotel on the corner of Brook Street and Davies Street. John Tallis notes in 1851 that it accommodated royal and other grand foreign guests.[81] In 1854 he sold out to Mr. and Mrs. Claridge, and the hotel was rebuilt in 1898 and renamed Claridge's. In the previous year Watier's hotel was rebuilt as the Coburg, in Charles Street, and was later renamed the Connaught.[82] Charles Street became Carlos Place.

At this time grand hotels were being built that required the means to serve haute cuisine to large numbers of people. This involved organizing kitchen brigades together with the French system of *fonds de cuisine*, the foundation, stocks, sauces and mixtures first recorded by La Varenne. Auguste Escoffier reorganized this for a number of palatial hotels both in London and abroad. In London he worked at the Savoy from 1890 with L. Echenard, remaining there until 1897. He then moved to the newly built Carlton Hotel in 1899, where he stayed until 1920.

With entertaining in new restaurants and hotels becoming fashionable, Escoffier, encouraged by Urbain Dubois, started writing his *Guide culinaire* in 1898, which was published in its final form as *A Guide to Modern Cookery* in 1907. It was a systematic reorganization of the repertoire of haute cuisine. In it Escoffier continued to draw on the works of Carême, Dubois and Bernard. Eugène Herbodeau notes that he also included ideas from the fourteenth-century Viandier of Taillevent. It was designed to enable the smooth and systematic production of meals in great hotel kitchens.

At the Savoy and later at the Carlton, Escoffier offered lighter meals to serve a new clientele. This novel interpretation of the repertoire not only suited a more hectic age but was also made to please the 'respectable' women who could now dine out. Previously, dining out had been an almost exclusively male activity. Escoffier's pupils and literary executors, Eugène Herbodeau and Paul Thalamus, in their biography, tell of Escoffier dining with Mme. Duchêne, the wife of the manager of the Ritz. She asked him, 'What is the real secret of your art?' Escoffier replied, 'Madame, my success comes from the fact that my best dishes were created for ladies'. The authors list some of the period's most glamorous women, for whom Escoffier created dishes: Réjane, Rachel, Mary Carden, Adelina Patti, Yvette, Sarah Bernhardt and several others. The best known of these tribute dishes is Pêche Melba for Nellie Melba.[83] Escoffier's recipes, as might be expected, catered to current

---

[81] J. Tallis, *Tallis's Illustrated London in Commemoration of the Great Exhibition of All Nations in 1851* (2 vols., 1851), i. 190. For Jacques Mivart, see *The Epicure's Almanack: or Calendar of Good Living* (1815), p. 164.

[82] Tallis, *Illustrated London*, i. 189.

[83] E. Herbodeau and P. Thalamus, *Georges Auguste Escoffier* (1955), p. 41.

feminine tastes: salads, quail, poultry and many *entremêts* or sweet dishes. At the same time as men and women were dining together at these grand hotels, others were enjoying dining out à la carte at the Criterion's East Room or at Verrey's, as Lieutenant-Colonel Newnham-Davis, restaurant critic of the *Pall Mall Gazette*, did with two female guests.[84]

Bourgeois dining out around Leicester Square, '[une] place spécialemont fréquentée par les Français'[85]

In 1868 John Timbs depicts a cosmopolitan Leicester Square. He quotes Maitland's 1739 description of the parish of St. Anne's (Soho and Leicester Square) as so greatly abounding with the French, 'that it is an easy matter for a stranger to imagine himself in France'.[86] This description was still valid during much of the nineteenth century. It was repeated when Sala met Soyer and went to his rooms in Soho. He describes the area as 'a district that retains many of its Gallic attributes, but which in 1850, was almost as French as the Rue Montmartre'. He lists French *charcutiers*, restaurants, hotels and shops with more French trades on the upper floors. John Burnett gives the French immigrant population in and around Soho in the 1860s and 1870s as 8,000.[87]

Diners with less to spend could always find French bourgeois cookery in and around Leicester Square, the site of several French hotels. Tallis's 1851 guide book describes the square: 'On every side rise hotels with foreign names, kept by foreign landlords and marked *Restaurant.* Occasionally a label may be seen in the window with the inscription *Table d'hôte à cinque heures'*.[88] These dinners were served at a shared table to hotel guests of both sexes and to non-residents. The 1858 edition of *London at Dinner* recommends 'in Castle Street, Leicester Square, a very unpretending little house, "Rouget's," [which] gives English and French dishes capitally done. The soup Julienne is as good as is to be had in London'.[89] In 1816 Papworth describes it as a French house where 'a *table d'hôte* affords the lovers of French cookery and French conversation, an opportunity for gratification at a comparatively moderate charge'.[90]

[84] Lt.-Col. N. Newnham-Davis, *Dinners and Diners: Where and How to Dine in London* (1899), pp. 32, 151.

[85] Baedeker (1866), p. 8.

[86] J. Timbs, *Curiosities of London* (1868), p. 515.

[87] J. Burnett, *England Eats Out: a Social History of Eating Out in England from 1830 to the Present* (Harlow, 2004), p. 95.

[88] Tallis, *Illustrated London*, i. 99.

[89] G. A. Sala, *Things I have Seen and People I have Known* (2 vols., 1894), ii. 243–4.

[90] J. B. Papworth, *Select Views of London* (1816), p. 54.

In 1851, *London Made Easy* offered a list of French hotels in and around Leicester Square: Hôtel Sablonière et de Provence, at 17 and 18; in Leicester Place, Hôtel de Versailles (2), Hôtel du Prince Albert (11) and Hôtel de l'Europe (16). In the Haymarket, Hôtel de Paris (58) and the Café de l'Europe (9)[91] had originally been Epitaux's Restaurant. Nathaniel Newnham-Davis describes it as being in the Opera Colonnade and later in the Haymarket. He says that in early Victorian days it was one of the very few restaurants where good French cookery could be found.[92]

The longest-lived of these hotels was the Sablonière (1788–1867), whose original owner was Antoinetta La Sablonière. Mme. La Sablonière's management was followed by Louis Jacquier and a succession of others.[93] The 1866 edition of Karl Baedeker's *Londres* describes the Sablonière as a *maison française*, by then at 30 Leicester Square.[94]

These hotels and premises adapted and changed, but French ownership continued. In 1834 Domnique Deneulain opened a boarding house at 18 Leicester Square, and after some changes to the arrangement of buildings from 1845 to 1868, 17 and 18 became the Hôtel de Provence; then between 1869 and 1892, the Hôtel Sablonière et de Provence; and finally from 1893 until its closure in 1919 it reverted to being Hôtel Provence.[95] In 1879, it is listed as a place 'where a dinner may be had at moderate prices'.[96] Baedeker in 1866 advises the *table d'hôte* at five o'clock: 'It costs 4 shillings at Hôtel Sablonière, and at the opposite corner of the square, l'Hôtel Provence has the same proprietor and the same prices'.

Charles Dickens knew the Sablonière. In recounting a walk around the West End in 1851 in search of exotic tourists who might be visiting the Great Exhibition, he notes Leicester Square as no more foreign than usual: 'some delightfully mysterious gushes of French cookery were wafted upwards from the kitchens of the Sablonière'.[97] His son, Charles Dickens the younger, mentions Sablonière in his *Dictionary of London* as the 'Sablonière and Vargue's Hôtel de l'Europe'. These restaurants were not only for continental visitors:

> Artful seekers after surreptitious good dinners, who knew London well certainly had some foreign houses in the back settlements of Soho or of Leicester Square,

[91] A. Hall, *London Made Easy: Being a Compendium of the British Metropolis* (1851), p. 1.
[92] Newnham-Davis, *Dinners and Diners*, p. 218.
[93] *Survey of London*, xxxiii–xxxiv: *St. Anne Soho*, ed. F. H. W. Shepherd (1966), pp. 488–503.
[94] Baedeker, *Londres* (Coblenz, 1866), p. 8.
[95] Shepherd, *Survey of London*, pp. 488–503.
[96] C. Dickens the younger, *Dickens's Dictionary of London, 1879: an Unconventional Handbook* (1879; 1972 edn.), p. 224.
[97] C. Dickens, 'The foreign invasion', in *Household Words*, lxxxi (11 Oct. 1851), 62.

to which they pinned their faith, but the restaurant, as it has been for many years understood in Paris practically had no place in London … We have still no Café Riche or Café Anglais.[98]

He lists restaurants specializing in *table d'hôte* dinners. In Piccadilly, in the Criterion's West Room, there are French dinners at 5*s*. Other restaurants he notes may also have had a French *table d'hôte* but they are simply listed as offering *table d'hôte*, so these may be less than truly French.[99]

The 1894 edition of Baedeker's Guide still describes the Leicester Square area as 'Much frequented by French visitors' and lists the Hôtel de Paris et de l'Europe, Challis Royal Hotel and Wedde's Hotel.[100] In or near Leicester Square he notes there are French restaurants, some in recommended hotels, such as Wedde's and the Hôtel de Paris. The Cavour is listed as a hotel and café, with French cuisine and 'attendance'.

These hotels' frequently advertised attraction was food and accommodation at moderate prices, which was necessary as the exchange rate with sterling was not favourable to the French. An undated advertisement directed French visitors to the Hôtel de l'Europe that had been established in 1840 at 15 and 16 Leicester Place and promised '*un restaurant à la française*, offering a moderately priced dinner'.[101] It is listed as Vargue's Hôtel de l'Europe in 1879.

Not all visitors were well served. When Auguste-Jean-Baptiste Defauconpret, who visited London in 1816, was asked if he was going to stay at L'Hôtel Impérial de Saint Petersburg[102] as his intended lodgings were not ready, he instead stayed at the French restaurant Chédron, at the Huntley Tavern, where the owner 'fleeces like an Englishman'.[103]

In the last years of the century Lieutenant-Colonel Newnham-Davis reviews a wide range of restaurants with French chefs, offering truly French repertoires. He says that around the Cavour 'there has always been a savour of Bohemianism'. Newnham-Davis had known the Cavour and its proprietor M. Philippe for some time. This proprietor was his own maître d'hôtel (and grew his own herbs and vegetables in the orangery and garden). Newnham-Davis describes 'the *Poulet Sauté Portugaise*' as 'a triumph of bourgeois cookery', but he is not quite as satisfied with the rest of the dinner.[104]

---

[98] Dickens the younger, *Dictionary of London*, p. 224.

[99] Dickens the younger, *Dictionary of London*, p. 224.

[100] Baedeker, *Baedeker's London and its Environs* (9th rev. edn., 1894), p. 8.

[101] Museum of London, Ephemera collections: hotels, Acc. No. 375, Advertisement.

[102] 'L'Hôtel Impérial de Saint Petersburg' appears to be a pseudonym for an untraceable hotel.

[103] A.-J.-B. Defauconpret, *Six mois à Londres en 1816: suite de l'ouvrage ayant pour titre quinze jours à la fin de 1815* (Paris, 1817), ch. 1.

[104] Newnham-Davis, *Dinners and Diners*, ch. xxviii, pp. 128–31.

Newnham-Davis offers another of his discoveries, a place that his upper-middle-class readers may not have known, Le Restaurant des Gourmets in Lisle Street, which had a shabby exterior in a run-down location. He finds a truly French restaurant where the staff and most of the customers are French and he shares a table with three French greengrocers. His dinner costs a modest 2*s* 7*d*. For this he has a herring *hors d'œuvre*, bread, soup for 2*d* which he thinks is as good as that to be had for 2*s*. He thinks less of the turbot and capers, but praises the gigot haricot and the omelette that follows. He also has cheese, and a half of *vin ordinaire*. But as he does not think much of it, the proprietor shrugs and offers him instead a pint of claret that he had bought cheaply from M. Nicols of the Café Royal.[105]

Dining out, as an entertainment, had been an almost exclusively male activity until the late 1880s. Previously women could only respectably visit cafés and restaurants such as Verrey's in Regent Street. Blanchards at 1–7 Beak Street, Soho, established in 1862, forbade ladies after 5 p.m.,[106] though if a woman was staying alone in a hotel she might dine in a private sitting-room. Families could dine at the commensal *table d'hôte* in the French hotels. In the 1890s entertaining in restaurants gained in popularity. Those who could not afford to dine in the new grand hotels could have dinner and supper parties. They were now places for men and women to dine together, usually to enjoy French cuisine. Almost all the menus in *Dinners and Diners* are in French.

In 1899 Nathaniel Newnham-Davis's revues were collected as *Dinners and Diners: Where and How to Dine in London*, directed at the new clientele. He does not always describe a restaurant's customers but lets the reader take a clue from the particular guests he takes to each establishment. Newnham-Davis was well aware that many diners were unfamiliar with French cuisine. He advises them to compose a menu to suit their tastes and appetite from the à la carte selection with the help of a friendly maître d'hôtel.[107]

Apart from restaurants in hotels, the number of French-owned restaurants increased during the second half of the century and, of all of these, possibly the most well known and long-lasting was the Café Royal. Its predecessor had been opened in Glasshouse Street in 1865 by Daniel Nicolas Thévenon. He had previously fled Paris as a bankrupt wine merchant. With his wife Célestine Lacoste he opened a café-restaurant that was so successful that it expanded into several premises in Regent Street, where it became the Café Royal. Famous for its wine cellar and as a favourite meeting place for

---

[105] Newnham-Davis, *Dinners and Diners*, ch. xiv, pp. 65–8.
[106] Baedeker (1894), p. 8, and Dickens the younger, *Dictionary of London*, p. 224.
[107] Newnham-Davis, *Dinners and Diners*, foreword: 'The difficulties of dining' (n.p.).

Bohemian London,[108] it is ranked by Charles Dickens the younger in 1879 as being on a larger scale than the older Verrey's. He notes that 'At both these houses, people who know how to order their dinners will be thoroughly well served'.[109] Baedeker's 1894 edition stars Kettner's Restaurant du Pavillon as a French house, at 28–31 Church Street, Soho. Auguste Kettner had been chef to Napoleon III.

Conclusion

How French was London's French cuisine in the nineteenth century? The rich who employed French chefs continued to enjoy French haute cuisine as they had in the eighteenth century. Likewise, when they dined out they could eat at hotels that offered the same cuisine. Bourgeois French visitors could find familiar style and service at the French hotels and restaurants around Leicester Square. The rest of the scene appears to have been somewhat uneven. The basement kitchens of London's upper-middle-class houses do not appear to have become the new home of French bourgeois cookery. Instead French elaboration was used to add a much-desired *recherché* touch. Yet through the nineteenth century the influence of French cuisine steadily grew. The lord mayor of London no longer offered a predominantly English bill of fare but an *à la Russe* menu in French. New patterns of dining out gave both men and women new opportunities to eat a meal cooked by a French chef.

Some names remain familiar to us: L'Escargot, opened in 1894, where they reared their own snails in the cellar; Kettner's, referred to in Baedeker's 1894 edition; and Maison Bertaux, the patisserie in Greek Street, opened in 1871, said to have been founded by two Communards and still flourishing.

During most of the twentieth century, even through hard times, the place of French haute cuisine remained secure as the ideal cuisine for elite dining. A fashion for French menus continued until the 1950s, regardless of how little the dishes related to their titles. In the early 1960s, with a new bias towards youth and informality, inexpensive French cookery was to be enjoyed in the new bistros. A taste for French bourgeois cookery had been reintroduced in 1951 with Elizabeth David's *French Country Cooking*,[110] and as a result, more English households began to enjoy French bourgeois recipes than appears to have been the case following the publication of *French Domestic Cookery* in 1825.[111] Those who read *French Country Cooking*

---

[108] G. Deghy and K. Waterhouse, *Café Royal: 90 Years of Bohemia* (1955), pp. 17–35.

[109] Dickens the younger, *Dictionary of London*, p. 224.

[110] E. David, *French Country Cooking* (1951).

[111] Anon., *French Domestic Cookery*.

and its sequel, *French Provincial Cooking*,[112] cooked the recipes themselves, unlike their predecessors who asked their plain cooks to produce dishes from an unfamiliar repertoire.

From the second half of the twentieth century cuisines from around the world flourished in London. Today, in spite of London now offering a greater range of cuisines, an entry in Michelin's Red Guide[113] still gives the imprimatur of French culinary standards, and their prized rosettes continue to offer chefs the ultimate accolade. In this postmodern London, French cuisine and French influences still flourish. Bourgeois diners can still eat at Mon Plaisir in Monmouth Street just north of Leicester Square and haute cuisine still thrives in Mayfair at Le Gavroche in Upper Brook Street.

[112] E. David, *French Provincial Cooking* (1960).
[113] *Guide Michelin: Great Britain and Ireland* (2012).

10. The London French from the Belle Epoque to the end of the inter-war period (1880–1939)

Michel Rapoport

The years from 1880 to 1939, by the end of which time the Third French Republic had been in the hands of the republicans for sixty years, witnessed a series of events that affected the presence of French people in London. There was the amnesty of 14 July 1880, which enabled most of the Communards who had fled to London after 1871 to return home; the anarchist crisis of the 1890s, which drove several hundred anarchists in the opposite direction, to exile in London; the French Exhibition at Earl's Court in 1890; the signing of the Entente Cordiale in 1904, followed by the 1908 Franco-British Exhibition at Shepherd's Bush, attracting a flood of French tourists; the First World War and its aftermath, when politicians, government officials and army officers came to London for the many Anglo-French and international conferences, while some of its 'French colony' were called up and had to return to France; and finally, the Great Depression of the 1930s.

The French who were in London during those sixty years can be grouped into two broad categories, which would then, of course, need to be sub-divided more specifically. There were the French men and women who lived there permanently or for a long time, whether or not they worked, or were married to British subjects. These form what French and British authorities term London's 'French colony'. The second group would consist of 'temporary visitors', and can in turn be divided into two sub-groups: 'occasional' visitors staying, perhaps repeatedly, for not more than a month at a time; and 'tourists', coming to London for short stays of only a few days, usually for enjoyment.

London's 'French colony' – uncertain demographics
The task of reckoning the numbers of French in London during those years is an ambitious and necessarily somewhat arbitrary one. A census was taken every ten years from 1871 to 1921; the results of the 1931 census were lost in a fire in 1942, but Home Office statistics are available. However, despite the apparent precision of the census data, they provide only an approximate idea of the number of French living in Britain and London.

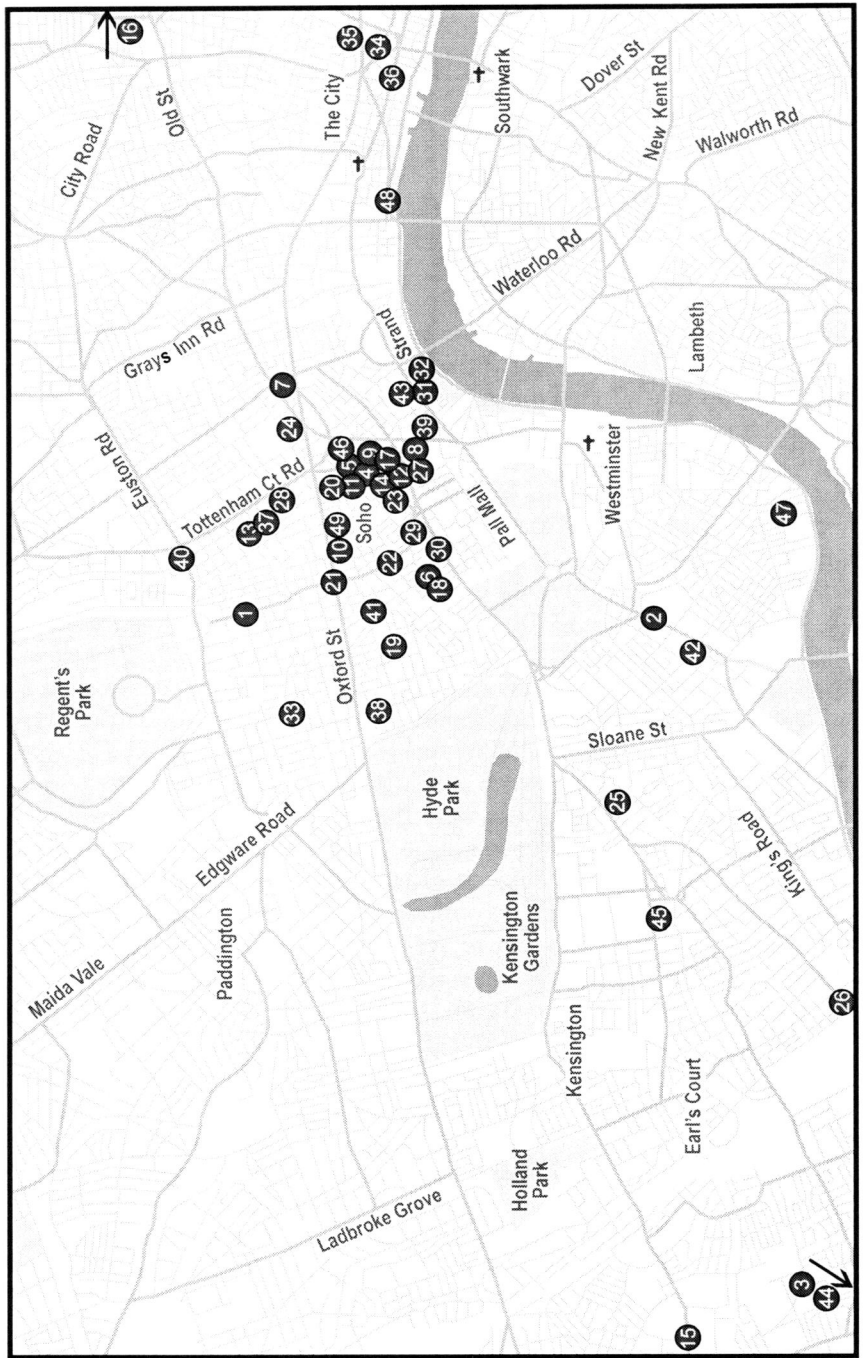

Map 10.1. Places mentioned in the text (Base map: London c.1910)

Key to Map 10.1

1. Portland Place
2. Grosvenor Hotel
3. Penn House, Weybridge (off map c.15.5 miles)
4. Greek Street
5. Old Compton Street
6. Alfred Duclos, Royal Arcade
7. De Bry's, New Oxford St/Southampton Row
8. F. Guibert, 10 Charing Cross Road
9. Launay-Benoist *réunis*, 55 Charing Cross Road
10. Ramillies Place
11. Frith Street
12. Lisle Street
13. Charlotte Street
14. Gerrard Street
15. F. N. Huber, King Street, Hammersmith
16. Abraham Adler, Tredegar Square, Bow (off map c.2.5 miles)
17. Louis Mahieu, Little Newport Street
18. Dover Street

19. Worth, Grosvenor Street
20. Charles Alias, Soho Square
21. Grands Magasins du Louvre de Paris, Oxford Circus
22. Galeries Lafayette, Regent Street
23. Shaftesbury Avenue
24. Museum Street
25. Beauchamp Place, Brompton Road
26. Fulham Road
27. Leicester Square
28. Hôtel Restaurant de la Tour Eiffel
29. Café Royal, Regent Street
30. Prince's Restaurant, Piccadilly
31. Hotel Cecil, Strand
32. Savoy Hotel, Strand
33. Baker Street
34. Crédit Lyonnais, Lombard Street
35. Comptoir National d'Escompte, Threadneedle Street

36. Crédit Immobilier, Cannon Street
37. Librairie Française, Goodge Street
38. J. Barrière and Co., Green Street
39. Hachette Bookshop, King William Street
40. Besson's, Euston Road
41. Goupil Gallery, New Bond Street
42. Elizabeth Street, Belgravia
43. Restaurant Boulestin, Southampton Street
44. Charterhouse School, Godalming (off map c.31 miles)
45. Cromwell Gardens
46. French Hospital, Shaftesbury Avenue
47. Société de Bienfaisance, St George's Square
48. French Chamber of Commerce, Queen Victoria Street
49. Ecole de l'Eglise Protestante Française, Noel Street

243

Table 10.1. French people living in Britain and London, 1871–1931

	1871	1881	1891	1901	1911	1921	1931
French people living in Britain	17,906	14,596	20,797	20,467	28,827	23,659	
French people living in London	10,719	8,251	12,834	?	17,856	?	9,684

The drop in numbers between 1871 and 1881 is partly explained by the effects of the amnesty of 1880. The rise between 1881 and 1891 is partly linked to the United Kingdom's position in the world economy at that time and its financial strength. The leap between 1901 and 1911 is mainly due to the change in Franco-British relations signalled by the Entente Cordiale, as well as to London's economic growth, which attracted businessmen, skilled workmen, and employees and managers of French companies and banks with offices in London. With the outbreak of war the French presence in London altered in composition and was reduced overall, since the members of French delegations and refugees who arrived were fewer in number than the Frenchmen called up to the army (around 3,000), who returned to France. The end of the war did not bring about a return to the previous situation; on the one hand, a significant number of members of the 'French colony' had been killed in the fighting (550 have been identified),[1] and on the other, some of the French who had been living in London decided to remain in France after the war. According to the French Consulate, not many more than 1,000 people presented the declaration claiming the payment offered to ex-combatants. Finally, the 1930s were marked by a net drop in numbers. The Great Depression had two effects here: first, a serious reduction in employment, meaning that many job opportunities for French people disappeared; and second, a more rigorous application of immigration laws.

Out of the total French population living in Britain, the percentage living in London varies between 48 and 55 per cent. In 1911 it was estimated at 47.9 per cent and in 1921 it was just over 50 per cent, that is, between 10,000 and 12,000 people. But these figures are in fact very imprecise, since a large number of French people in London were not included in the official statistics. In 1901 and again in 1902, *La Chronique de Londres* referred to a 'floating' population of around 30,000 in London, which would be 50 per cent more than the figure shown by the census.[2] Henri

[1] H. Goiran, *Les Français à Londres: étude historique, 1544–1933* (Pornic, 1935), p. 219.
[2] *La Chronique de Londres*, 21 Dec. 1901.

Goiran, in *Les Français à Londres*, suggests that the census figures should be increased by 35–40 per cent.[3] It is true that there is a question about the exact boundaries of London, so that figures would vary depending on whether one is speaking of Greater London, Outer and Inner London, or Inner London alone. Additionally, there is a certain number of people who do not figure in the census, either voluntarily – prostitutes and dropouts, for example, among others – or because they were simply overlooked. It should also be borne in mind that there were large inflows of French people in connection with notable events (the French Exhibition at Earl's Court in 1890 and the Franco-British Exhibition of 1908, which was linked to the Olympic Games; the 1901 Glasgow Exhibition; perhaps the Coronations and the Jubilee) whose numbers cannot be calculated, since statistics at ports of entry do not give the destination of immigrants and visitors. Moreover, the census figures may include those for Belgians and Swiss. Until 1914 the French colony in London was the third largest, after the German and Russian. After the First World War it was the largest, since many Germans considered undesirables had been forced to leave the United Kingdom, and the independence of Poland meant that the census no longer included Poles among the total for Russians.

The French colony included more women than men: in 1891 there were 10,994 women and 9,803 men; forty years later, in 1931, out of 9,684 French residents, there were 6,196 women and 3,488 men.[4] This imbalance may be partly attributed to the employment of Frenchwomen as governesses and tutors by aristocratic and upper-class London families. The general age of the French colony was young, though it did include elderly people, as witnessed by the assistance offered by charities to a certain number of impoverished widows over seventy and others.[5]

Who were the French in London? A socio-professional approach

During the nineteenth century London represented a safe haven for a certain number of French people. It is not surprising, then, despite the effects of successive legal amnesties, that the French colony included refugees and descendants of refugees. These formed a minority, however; their failure to return to France was due either to their succeeding in setting up in business

---

[3] Goiran, *Français à Londres*, p. 216.

[4] Data from the 1891 census. This item is not included as such in the 1891 and 1901 censuses. For 1931, see Goiran, *Français à Londres*.

[5] In some years *La Chronique de Londres* gave the names, ages and sometimes the former profession of beneficiaries. Thus the issue dated 28 Feb. 1903 gives as new recipients of Société de Bienfaisance pensions two dressmakers of 62 and 72 respectively, a teacher of 70, a painter of 82 and a laundress of 65.

in London, their fear of being unable to find a place in French society after long years of absence, or their advanced age. Sylvie Aprile recalls that in the 1890s only thirteen of the Paris Commune refugees remained.[6] They included Paul-Antoine Brunel, French teacher at the Naval College at Dartmouth; Albert Barrère, French teacher at Woolwich, author of a well-known dictionary of French slang and himself the son of an exile who had come to London in 1851, and brother of another Communard who had also been exiled to London, the future French ambassador to Rome, Camille Barrère; Victor Richard, whose grocery became a meeting place for French anarchists in the 1890s; the painter Constant de L'Aubinière; and the cartoonist Georges Pilotell who, having once been fashionable, ended his days in poverty. Some of the descendants of exiles of 1851 were extremely successful: Marius Duché, for instance, born in 1841, was brought to London by his father, a victim of the 2 December *coup d'état*. Marius took over and developed his father's business, took part in the founding of the French Chamber of Commerce in London in 1883, and was its president for many years.[7] There was also Albert Barrère, mentioned above. As for the anarchists, their generally brief stays in London precluded their setting up in business or the professions. Someone who did stay for longer was Louise Michel, who lived in London from 1890 to 1895, running, together with Charlotte Vauvelle, a school founded by the 'Liberal French Language Group' (Groupe Libertaire de Langue Française).[8]

Well-known figures who sought refuge in London briefly during the Third Republic were General Boulanger, who lived in an apartment at 51 Portland Place;[9] Henri de Rochefort; and Emile Zola. Zola came to London on 18 July 1898 to avoid going to prison, after receiving a one-year prison sentence in the French courts, confirmed by the Court of Appeal, following the publication of his article 'J'Accuse'. He lived in the Grosvenor Hotel for a while and then moved to a hotel in Weybridge, south-west of London, and afterwards a furnished apartment, Penn House, nearby.

---

[6] S. Aprile, *Le Siècle des exiles, bannis et proscrits de 1789 à la Commune* (Paris, 2010), pp. 271–2.

[7] These details come from the profile of Duché published in *La Chronique de Londres*, 21 Apr. 1900. Such profiles were published regularly and are an important source of information on people belonging to London's French colony about whom little or nothing would otherwise be known.

[8] For more on Louise Michel, see the chapter by Lane and Faucher.

[9] M. Quinton, *Le Journal de la Belle Meunière, le Général Boulanger et son amie, souvenirs vécus* (Clermont-Ferrand, 1895); Gaston Lapierre, in his article 'Boulangeries', published in *Le Moderniste*, 31 Aug. 1889, speaks of the 'contumax de Portland Place'; see also *The New York Times*, 23 Sept. 1889.

Because of the risk of arrest, Zola lived under several pseudonyms – Pascal, Beauchamp, Rogers and Richard. This did not prevent him from making brief trips to London, or from receiving numerous visitors, including his friend Georges Charpentier and his publisher Fasquelle in October 1898; Clemenceau at the beginning of January 1899; Octave Mirbeau in February; and especially several visits from his mistress Jeanne and her children, and from his wife Alexandrine; not forgetting his translator, Ernest Vizetelly. All in all, he was surrounded by a real support network from 18 July 1898 to 3 June 1899, the day when Fasquelle, Vizetelly and Zola shared a last London dinner together at the Queen's Hotel before his return to France.[10] During this period of enforced exile, Zola wrote *Fécondité*.

Apart from all these 'Londoners despite themselves', the French who lived in London during the period under study generally came because they were attracted by a very open labour market, with, in some cases, the prospect of professional and social success that would not have been possible for them in France. Others were sent by their families for training in commerce and finance or to improve their English, and then chose to remain in London. Still others worked in London as representatives or agents for their companies; and others again became Londoners by marriage. Nor should the staff of the French Embassy and Consulate be forgotten, and later, of the various French cultural institutions. The composition of this population changed and developed between 1880 and 1930.

---

[10] This was Zola's second stay in London. He had been there from 20 to 30 Sept. 1893, invited by the Institute of British Journalists to take part in their congress and that of the Authors' Club, whose president was Sir Frederick Pollock (he was also president of the Société des Gens de Lettres). That trip was organized by Léon Wolf, Ernest Vizetelly and Georges Petilleau, representing the Société des Gens de Lettres in England. During his stay Zola delivered a resounding speech at the Institute of British Journalists at Crystal Palace, underlining a fundamental difference between the English press and the French press: articles in the former were anonymous, those in the latter were signed. He also made his own Petilleau's suggestion of creating a parliamentary press 'International'. The speech was translated and quoted in the British press. On 28 Sept. he spoke at the Authors' Club dinner at the Metropole Hotel presided over by Oswald Crawford, attended by Oscar Wilde, Conan Doyle, Vizetelly and Petilleau. 'In England, where previously he had met with the greatest resistance, he has just been received like the *Imperator Litterarum*', declared Crawford. During this same visit he went to the British Museum, to the National Gallery to see the Turners (Zola was also an art critic) and to Westminster. He was guided round London by George Moore and discovered the poorer quarters, being able to 'cast a glance over the abject poverty and drunkenness in London', as Vizetelly wrote. For more on this visit, see *Mon cher maître, lettres d'Ernest Vizetelly á Emile Zola 1891–1902*, ed. D. E. Speirs and Y. Portebois (Montreal, 2002), pp. 107–13.

Table 10.2. Socio-professional categories of the French in England, 1881–1931

	1881	1891	1901	1931
Teachers	1,647	1,760	1,209	613
Students		717		1,049
Roman Catholic priests/sisters	388	407		796
Servants	1,592	2,190	2,997	595
Governesses, hired companions				616
Employees/Managers (companies/banks)				109
Commercial clerks/Commercial travellers	455	628	596	1,827
Merchants/Brokers	292	245		548
Cooks, out/domestic	566	819	867	879
Waiters			518	
Hairdressers/Wig-makers	126	153		182
Milliners/Dressmakers/Shirt-makers	648	831	1,014	
Tailors	144	214		
Artists/Musicians/Painters		342		319
Jewellers	160	119		
Seamen/Sailors	1,280	1,067	1,230	

Sources: Census figures for 1881, 1891 and 1901; and Home Office statistics

It is not possible to determine the exact numbers in London according to their profession, but we can guess that most of these French people lived and worked in London or its suburbs.

The Graphic, in an article of 16 December 1922 entitled 'French colony in London', noted that 'the principal activities of the French colony in London may be divided in four groups, i.e. commercial, educational, social and charitable'. During the debate on the Aliens Bill on 3 July 1905 Charles Hutchinson, Liberal MP for Rye, made a humorous reference to the French presence in London:

> Take the case of a man who came up to London for a night's pleasure … He went to a West End hotel where he was received by a cashier who was a Frenchman … He ordered his dinner from a French maître d'hôtel … and the food was cooked by a French chef. Afterwards he went outside, got into a motor car driven by a French chauffeur … he was accosted in one street by a French courtesan.[11]

[11] Hansard, *Parliamentary Debates*, 4th ser., cxlviii (3 July 1905).

These two references complement one another in a way; they are accurate, if somewhat summary, as is shown by the socio-professional statistics furnished by the censuses.

Commerce, labour and industry

These three spheres of action offered numerous opportunities for work, whether the commerce was wholesale or retail, or the labour skilled or unskilled. Certain sectors saw a particular concentration of French workers: food, dress, shoe-shops and shoe-repairs, and furniture.

While many French retail businesses were opened after the years 1850–70, the increase in numbers of the French colony and the buying-power of some of its members, together with the demands of a particular English clientele with a taste for French products, produced a sharp increase in businesses connected with food: French groceries, dairies and *charcuteries*, fine wine and champagne merchants, patisseries, and confectioners, all offered products imported from France or prepared according to French traditions. Among long-standing firms was the patisserie belonging to Bertaux, an exile from the Paris Commune, which stood at 28 Greek Street, Soho, from 1871. This shop rapidly became well known, and it was not the only one: close by, at 10 Old Compton Street, was the Maison Lombardy, while at 9 Church Street, off Shaftesbury Avenue, was Lemaire's 'Patisserie Parisienne'.[12] Confectioners and chocolate-makers were not lacking: in 1867 Alfred Duclos founded his shop at 2 Royal Arcade, off Old Bond Street, and from 1900 to 1910 this 'French Confectioner', supplier to the English aristocracy, had a regular advertisement in *La Chronique de Londres*, as did De Bry's, whose shop was close to Holborn, at 64 New Oxford Street and 45 Southampton Row. Delicatessens, specialist *charcuteries* and wine shops abounded in 'Petite France'. In Charing Cross Road, F. Guibert, fine wines and champagnes, was at no. 10, and at no. 55 was Launay-Benoist *réunis*, specialist *charcuterie* with a workshop in Ramillies Place. In Frith Street, Pierre de Loriol sold French wines next door to the Compagnie Française specializing in coffees. In Lisle Street, Fernand Robert had his 'Epicerie de Leicester Square' at no. 21, while at no. 3 Haizé sold French chickens. In Charlotte Street, F. Gasnier and E. Baudouin *successeur* had their 'Maison Française, charcuterie française, foies gras, vins fins'. Lovers of French veal and Pauillac lamb could obtain them from Cointat, French butcher at 15 Old Compton Street; those who preferred snails or frogs' legs could find

---

[12] *La Chronique de Londres*, with its advertisements, is one of the main sources of information on French commercial activity in London at this period. Church Street no longer exists under that name, but ran parallel with Shaftesbury Avenue from Greek Street down to Cambridge Circus.

them at L'Escargot, Greek Street, from 1894 onwards. Charles Bourdeau, who sold fruit and vegetables at 21 Gerrard Street, claimed the distinction of having a market-garden and orchards at Orléans that supplied his London business. Others set up shop further from the centre, such as F. N. Huber, merchant in wines and spirits, in King Street, Hammersmith.

Some of these traders played an important role within the French colony: M. L. Moussary was president of the Société des Confiseurs Français de Londres, La Bonbonnière. Only occasionally is it possible to trace the itinerary of these traders; Henri Ludovic Noël arrived in London in 1858, began by working in a French café-restaurant, and in 1860 opened a dairy selling butter and cheeses imported from France, and eggs. He then widened his range to include preserves and fine wines and started a jam factory with fruit imported from France; but his real claim to fame is that it was he who introduced camembert to England. In the area of flowers and fruit, Nestor Fauquemberge, who took over the firm started by his uncle A. Bisson in 1876, Albert Hernu and M. C. Franco supplied Covent Garden with produce imported daily from France.

The multitude of these retailers entailed the development of wholesale importers such as Abraham Adler, established in Tredegar Square, Bow, in the 1870s, and Louis Mahieu, a former chef, who had a wholesale business in Little Newport Street. There were also London branches of French wholesalers, such as Duchesne for champagne, and a network of their agents.

The French presence was also important in the sphere of clothing. Here there were two types of demand. France's reputation in the world of fashion was vast; high-society London ladies, plus the Frenchwomen in the elite of the French colony, were a major market. Ladies who went to balls and receptions during the London season either ordered dresses and hats from Paris, or obtained them at French shops in London, or else from the French fashion designers, dressmakers and milliners who worked there. One of the greatest firms of French haute couture in London was Paquin. The proprietor, Jeanne Paquin, in association with English partners, moved her headquarters from the shop in Rue de la Paix, Paris, to 39 Dover Street, London, in 1896. At the beginning of the twentieth century her London business employed 200 or 300 girls, almost all from Paris. In competition with Paquin's was Worth. This firm was founded in Rue de la Paix, Paris, by the Englishman Charles Frederic Worth, inventor of haute couture and supplier to empresses Eugénie and Elizabeth and European courts. In 1898, on the initiative of Gaston, one of the founder's sons, it opened a London branch at 50 Grosvenor Street. Until 1936, when it was sold by Jacques Worth, the founder's grandson, Worth was the symbol of French luxury in

London.[13] Charles Alias was another firm that built up a large clientele in the same sphere. Alias, a doctor's son, had come to London in the 1870s to sell leeches, but turned to theatre costumes; his shop in Soho Square also sold costumes to ladies for the fancy-dress balls held by the princess of Wales, the duchess of Devonshire and other aristocratic hostesses.[14] As for 'Paris goods', ladies could procure them in the London branch of the Grands Magasins du Louvre de Paris at Oxford Circus, or at Galeries Lafayette, which in 1920, before becoming well established in Regent Street, had been a commercial agent, centralizing orders and redistributing purchases to customers. Those in search of French underwear could buy it at the shop opened by Mme. Léoty at 26 Dover Street (a branch of the one at Place de la Madeleine, Paris), or at L. Bonvalet's 'maison parisienne' in Shaftesbury Avenue. French launderers, such as Mme. Delozanne's Blanchisserie Française at 40 Museum Street, and French dry-cleaners also had a good reputation and worked for a large customer base.

Less wealthy Englishwomen and Frenchwomen who were anxious to follow Paris fashions were another type of customer that kept French-owned clothing workshops and shops going. These were often on the borderline between businesses and crafts. Men's and women's clothing was supplied by G. Victor in Shaftesbury Avenue. The Deligny sisters in Beauchamp Place, off Brompton Road, produced blouses and skirts, and placed small advertisements in *La Chronique de Londres* for French fitters, bodice-makers and skirt-makers for their workshop. Bootmakers and shoemakers complete the picture: Nicolas Thierry had a shop in Regent Street for many years before going into shoemaking on an industrial scale. And finally, shoe-repairing seemed to be a French speciality in London. French skills and competence also explain the presence of numerous workmen and craftsmen such as cabinet-makers, carpet-makers, builders and electricians. It is impossible to give any estimate of their numbers.

As a centre of industry, London attracted engineers working for branches of French firms such as Saint-Gobain or Michelin, which opened in Sussex Place in 1905 and in 1911 moved to Michelin House at 11 Fulham Road, a prime example of French *art moderne*. Such people often went on to find employment for themselves in London, and some, in time, set up in business on their own account. Albert Sauvé, a graduate of the Ecole Centrale de Paris, arrived in London in 1868 and ten years later opened a machine workshop; Louis Percheron, a mechanical engineer, came to

[13] Another provider of French luxury goods in London was the firm Vuitton, specializing in bags and suitcases, which opened a branch in Oxford Street in the 1870s.
[14] *La Chronique de Londres*, 11 Nov. 1899.

London working for the Compagnie Française, and then set up as a maker of chocolate and sweet machines, equipping many businesses, notably the firm of Lipton's. Eugène Cocquerel, employed in a trading-house in London from 1859, started his own business in Croydon producing pendulums and decorative glass flowers, and became the only manufacturer of china wreaths for undertakers. Demand was so great that he opened a factory in Paris.[15]

Business and production, then, seemed to attract many French people. But variations and developments in this pattern need to be borne in mind. What was true of the 1880s no longer applied twenty years later. To take the example of French food businesses, still mainly based in Soho during the 1880s, a large number of them were French only in name, as Englishmen, Germans or Italians had taken over from the original French, keeping on the name of the firm as a way of attracting customers.

Services

The service sector was probably the largest provider of employment for French people over a wide range of jobs, with notable variations according to the period. In the years from 1890 to 1914, the largest group was that of domestic servants, most of whom were women; in 1911 this sector employed over 2,600 Frenchwomen. It is impossible to give figures for London alone, among other reasons because some employers only came to London for the season. Up until the First World War, families belonging to the aristocracy and gentry employed French governesses, paid companions, nurses, cooks and chauffeurs. Having the services of a 'Mademoiselle' was a mark of distinction. But between 1911 and 1931 this sector shrank by 60 per cent, as the upper classes ran into difficulties after the war, finding themselves obliged to sell London properties and reduce their lifestyle and number of servants.

Two other groups were of significant size: restaurateurs and hoteliers, and hairdressers. Restaurants and hotels employed over 1,250 people, two-thirds of them men. There was a strong demand for cooks, partly because of the reputation of French cooking, and partly because of the size of the French colony; and also for staff of all kinds in both hotels and restaurants. Additionally, these jobs in London offered good opportunities for success and promotion. French hotels and restaurants – whether or not they were run by French people – multiplied in Soho (Old Compton Street had the Hôtel Dieppe at no. 76, and the Restaurant des Nations at no. 40, run by M. Mulot, a former waiter), around Leicester Square (the Grand Hôtel de

---

[15] *La Chronique de Londres*, 19 May 1900 (Eugène Cocquerel) and 10 Feb. 1900 (Louis Percheron).

l'Europe whose restaurant was managed by Paul Courvoyer, and the Hôtel de la Paix run by Joseph Belot), and around Tottenham Court Road (Hôtel Restaurant de la Tour Eiffel). However, in 1933 Paul Morand noted that 'there are only two purely French restaurants left in Soho: L'Escargot and the Jardin des Gourmets run by General Gouraud's former chef'.[16]

The opening of large luxurious establishments made possible by the transformation of the Strand in the late nineteenth and early twentieth century, was a godsend for the French. Among the most famous hotels and restaurants, four in particular illustrate the French reputation in this field: the Café Royal, the Prince's Restaurant, the Hotel Cecil and the Savoy. The first two, because they were French establishments, the third because of the personality of its manager, Auguste Judah, and the last because of its chef, Auguste Escoffier.

The Café Royal, opened in Regent Street in 1865 by Daniel Nicolas Thévenon, was, between 1890 and 1920, the best wine-cellar in London, a 'club' for the French, the haunt of famous artists and writers including Aubrey Beardsley, James Whistler and Oscar Wilde, and the setting for some notorious scandals. The Prince's Restaurant, on Piccadilly, was founded by Gustave Fourault, who, after having been chef at the Bristol had been in charge of the Brelant Restaurant; on his death in 1906 the position was taken by Victor Benoist, who was at the same time supplier to Buckingham Palace and various ministries and embassies, providing catering for receptions, parties, balls and picnics. Auguste Judah served his apprenticeship in Paris kitchens and worked as a chef in London before becoming manager of the Hotel Cecil, 'the prized centre of all high society', where he took 'the genius of hospitality' to a fine art, personally presenting each of his noble guests with a bouquet of flowers as they left. As for the renowned Escoffier, 'the chef of kings and the king of chefs', after a career on the continent he arrived in London with César Ritz in 1890, working until 1897 at the head of the kitchens in the Savoy, and then, from 1899 until his retirement in 1921, at the Carlton. This inventive chef revolutionized kitchen management, organizing his underlings' work according to F. W. Taylor's principles of scientific management, and being personally present everywhere, from kitchen to dining-room. At the Savoy he invented the fixed-price menu, and offered a menu based on produce imported from France. In June 1911, still in London, he launched a magazine in French and English, *Le Carnet d'épicure*, where he published certain of his recipes. Of his pupils, Charles Habensreithinger from Alsace also worked in London. Other French chefs were employed by great families, such as Octave Lamare, who, starting in

---

[16] P. Morand, *Londres* (Paris, 1933), p. 193.

the kitchens of the duc d'Aumale, in 1867 entered the service of Countess Frances Waldegrave, and in 1900 became president of the Club Culinaire.

'Justine announces "The hairdresser is here" with all the portentous solemnity that the butler would say "Madam is served," and my lady closes up the paper at once to greet the Frenchman ... The hairdressing is soon over, the skilful fingers of the *coiffeur* have laid the locks of my lady in shining waves'.[17] Mrs. Aria's words recall the position held in London by French hairdressers and wig-makers, whose numbers increased throughout the period under study. They too came in response to the double demand, on the part of French people in London and of English high society. And they too included all kinds of hairdressers, from the simple *merlan*[18] to the great artist. What could there be in common between Auguste Derouette, in Charlotte Street, who was book-seller, stationer, newspaper-vendor and hairdresser, and Charles Klein of Baker Street? Klein had first worked for the hairdresser Jalabert in Paris, and arrived in London in 1873, where he opened a hairdressing salon. He invented electric hairdressing appliances, and developed his own hair treatment method. He was an active member of the French colony, organizing a fashion exhibition in 1897, holding many hairdressers' conferences, and becoming president of the Société du Progrès de la Coiffure, the Société d'Epargne de l'Espérance and the Anglo-French Piscatorial Society, as well as honorary member of other French societies in London.[19]

Another service, an illegal one, was prostitution.[20] The sex trade in the capital did not diminish and French prostitutes were well represented: their 'exoticism' enabled them to earn more than the others. Most of them plied their trade and lived in Soho and to the north of that area, either walking the streets or working in brothels. A minority, in the higher price-range, frequented more elegant parts such as Regent Street and Oxford Circus. In the 1930s they attracted more attention when their activities were controlled by gangs. Among the procurers were Marcel Vernon, who had

[17] Mrs. Aria, 'My lady's evening in London', in *Living London*, ed. G. R. Sims (3 vols., 1901), ii. 183.

[18] *Merlan*, literally 'whiting', French slang for the local barber.

[19] *La Chronique de Londres*, 30 March 1901.

[20] J. Laite, *Common Prostitutes and Ordinary Citizens: Commercial Sex in London 1885–1960* (2011), pp. 149–59; F. Linnane, *London the Wicked City: 1,000 Years of Vice in the Capital* (2003), p. 330; J. White, *London in the 19th Century* (2007), p. 312. With regard to French women, Morand notes that 'it is no longer French women who walk the streets in London; since the war, like everywhere else, it is young Polish-Jewish women. The Frenchmen trafficking their women, whose terribly spruce jackets used to adorn the cafés of Shaftesbury Avenue and Leicester Square, have found it hard to get anywhere in England for the past three years' (Morand, *Londres*, p. 195); an observation belied by the three works cited.

establishments in Soho, and Casimir Micheletti, a Frenchman of Italian parentage and a West End figure; he brought girls over from France either by promising them jobs in London, or by organizing false marriages for them with Englishmen to enable them to get into the country. Such was the case of Marthe Watts, who arrived in London in 1939 and was quickly taken in hand by the Italian Massini gang. Numbers of French prostitutes in London varied between 500 and 1,000; in the years 1884–6, of the 4,286 prostitutes arrested in the West End, 769 were French; fifty years later there were perhaps 500 of them. At the beginning of the twentieth century they also supplied the market for pornographic photographs.

The world of business

From 1870 onwards, because of its financial might and its role in the exchange markets, at least until the First World War, the City attracted the great French trading and savings banks. Crédit Lyonnais (in Lombard Street), Comptoir National d'Escompte (in Threadneedle Street), Crédit Immobilier (in Cannon Street), Société Générale, and Crédit Industriel et Commercial all had branches in London, employing mainly French staff. The same held true of the great trading houses (the more so because London was the great port of redistribution for tropical produce), shipping companies such as the Compagnie Générale Transatlantique, and some insurance companies such as Le Phénix de Paris. The managers and staff of these companies all took part in the activities of the French colony, some of them playing a major role. Jules Moyse, for instance, a bank employee, was assistant manager of the London branch of Crédit Lyonnais in 1875, and in 1882 became manager of the Banque Anglo-Etrangère in Lombard Street. He was president of two of the most important societies of the French colony, the Société Nationale Française and the Société Française de Bienfaisance.

Account should also be taken of all the young French people sent to London to be initiated into British business and financial practices, employed in English firms for one or two years. One such was young Jean Monnet, who had been placed with the Chaplins, a family of traders, from 1902 to 1904. In London again in 1911, this time to oversee the activity of his family cognac business, he took an agent and planned to open an office in London.[21] There were sufficient numbers of young French people for Leon Clerc, secretary to the French Chamber of Commerce in London, to found the Union Commerciale des Enfants de France in England in 1898, whose mission was to 'ensure solidarity among young

[21] E. Roussel, *Jean Monnet* (Paris, 1996), pp. 33–4, 38–9.

French people in employment in England'. It accomplished this to good effect, if we are to believe the letter written by G. Lamorel, a teacher at the Ecole de Commerce de Boulogne to *La Chronique de Londres* in November 1900: 'The need to place one of my sons in England, to gain his business training there ... brought me into contact with two institutions whose eminently useful and patriotic roles I had not hitherto suspected: I mean the Chambre de Commerce Française de Londres and the Union des Enfants de France'.

Booksellers, performers, and teachers

Booksellers, performers and teachers each contributed in their own way to the spread of French language and culture in London. French book- and newspaper-selling was a lively business. Hachette Bookshop, 'an intellectual link between the two countries' according to *La Chronique de Londres* of 24 September 1904, had been in King William Street since the mid 1860s. It was the leading seller of French books under the management of Henri Kleinan, and from 1911 onwards, under the management of Emile Rotival, of French newspapers. Other bookshops also had a significant customer base: Mme. Pirnay's Librairie Parisienne in Charlotte Street sold French and foreign newspapers, as did Charles Bachelet's Librairie Française in Goodge Street. J. Barrière and Co.'s bookshop, a 'corner of France' in Green Street, offered all the well-known French newspapers. La Librairie Cosmopolite, in Charlotte Street, had a reading-room with 5,000 French works, while the Librairie Universelle in Bloomsbury, and A La Civette in Old Compton Street both had lending-libraries.

Like the bookshops, French performers attracted by London had an important role to play. In the field of music, some French conductors were in the front rank. The best known was the composer André Messager, artistic and administrative director of the Royal Opera House, Covent Garden, from May 1901 to July 1906. Messager became an ambassador for French music in London, introducing to the public the contemporary composers Claude Debussy, Jules Massenet and Edmond Missa, whose one-act lyric drama *Maguelone* was performed on 21 July 1903; and inviting French conductors. Less well known but likewise active at this time were Léopold Wenzel, composer and conductor, recruited by the Empire Theatre, and Jules Rivière, doyen of London conductors, who, invited to London by Dion Boucicault, conducted the orchestras at the Adelphi and the Alhambra, and then Covent Garden promenade concerts. French singers included the soprano Hélène Michaëlis. A pupil of Jacques Offenbach's daughter, she arrived in England in 1886 and learned singing at the Guildhall School of Music;

Figure 10.1. Façade of Barrière's bookshop at 17 Green Street. Author's postcard collection.

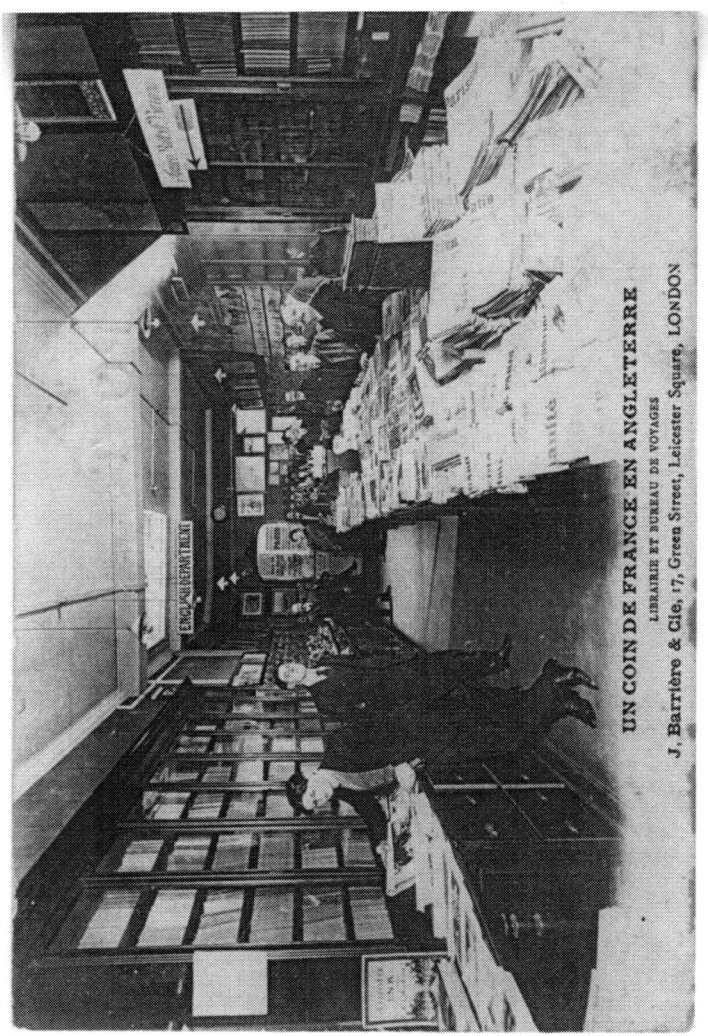

Figure 10.2. Interior of Barrière's bookshop. Author's postcard collection.

she was active in many aspects of the French colony such as dinners at the French Hospital and the Society of French Teachers.[22] Louise and Jeanne Douste, who had the privilege of singing at Buckingham Palace, gave piano and singing lessons. Léon Schlesinger founded the London French Musical Association to promote French works in England, organized concerts, gave lectures and held musical reviews.[23] French instrument-makers also set up in London and gained an international reputation: Besson's, founded in 1837, was in the Euston Road and by the end of the nineteenth century was employing 131 workers and producing around 100 brass instruments a week. In 1925 it was able to take over Quilter's, and it was still in business in 1939.

Painters and sculptors also swelled the ranks of the French colony. One of the painters was C.-A. de l'Aubinière, a pupil of Gérôme and Corot, who was exiled after the Paris Commune and worked in London from 1870 to 1880. In 1880 he and his wife Georgiana, who was a painter herself and the daughter of the painter John Steeple, held an exhibition of about forty paintings; Queen Victoria bought three of them. After a protracted stay in the United States and Canada, they returned to London around 1887 and organized an exhibition of French paintings, on behalf of the Société des Français Amis de l'Angleterre.[24] Faustin Betbeder, a well-known water-colour painter and cartoonist, arrived in London after 1870 and first worked for the *London Figaro*, then designed ballet and opera costumes for the Alhambra, the Lyceum and the Comic Opera. He was then recruited by the South Kensington Museum (now the Victoria and Albert Museum) to teach chromolithography techniques; he had a studio in Brixton where, with a large team, he executed a considerable number of commissions. Paris galleries opened branches in London hoping to profit from a possible market arising from their exhibitions: Paul Durand-Ruel, for instance, arriving in 1871, organized an Impressionist exhibition in 1882 and a retrospective Monet exhibition in 1905. In 1873 the art dealer Adolphe Goupil, father-in-law of the painter Gérôme and owner of the Galerie d'Art Parisienne, opened the Goupil Gallery, which from 1884 onwards stood in New Bond

---

[22] *La Chronique de Londres*, 13 May 1899. This newspaper frequently referred to Hélène Michaëlis between 1899 and 1901; it mentioned her marriage to Walter H. Freeman in May 1900, and published a eulogy after her premature death in Oct. 1901.

[23] *La Chronique de Londres*, 19 Aug. 1899. Schlesinger's articles in the *Chronique* seem to denote a certain reserve with regard to the new forms of musical composition. On 3 Dec. 1904, in a review of a concert conducted by Henry Wood who had included in the programme the *Prélude à l'après-midi d'un faune*, he noted: 'Interesting composition and fine, skilful orchestration. I doubt if the public will take to it'.

[24] After her husband's death, Georgiana, who enjoyed the favour of Queen Victoria, was given a post as artist at Kew Gardens.

Street, where visitors could view works by Vincent J. B. Chevillard and, in 1889, Claude Monet.[25]

Writers, poets and other literary figures did not come to London in such numbers, at least for long periods. However, the correspondents of major French newspapers should not be overlooked, as they gravitated around the French Embassy, British government circles and the literary scene. Paul Morand, the writer-diplomat, was by and large an exception in London. When he was appointed attaché at the French Embassy in 1913, he was not a stranger to the city. He had come there as a boy in 1903 and 1904, and as a student in 1908. In *Londres*, published in 1933, he provided a testimony on fashionable London life before the First World War: 'Every evening, I went to four or five balls, which lasted until the dawn, and I often walked down Piccadilly as the sun was rising over the Ritz'; then, during the war, 'in the theatres, Parisian-style revues featuring French actors draw packed audiences. In the absence of our chefs, who had gone to the front, *dinettes* and *luncheonettes* in Soho at little square tables in ridiculous little pseudo-French restaurants called "La Madelon" ... served by Italians'.[26]

The other exception was Marcel Boulestin, 'music critic, novelist, journalist, cookery-book publisher, and prince of gastronomes', with an immense reputation. Arriving in London in 1906, he opened an interior design shop at 15 Elizabeth Street, Belgravia, and then, in 1927, the Restaurant Boulestin in Southampton Street, Covent Garden, decorated by Albert Groult, with drawings by Jean-Emile Laboureur and Marie Laurencin and fabrics by Raoul Dufy on the walls. Morand was a frequent visitor to the restaurant during his 1932 stay in London. Among the correspondents of Paris newspapers some figures stand out: Robert Loyalty Cru, director of the Maison de l'Institut de France, university lecturer and correspondent of *Le Temps* in the 1930s;[27] and Jean Massip, teacher at the French Lycée, correspondent of *Le Petit Parisien* newspaper and president of the Foreign Press Association in London, who in July 1920 tried to launch a French gazette, *L'Entente*, which was quickly taken over by *La Chronique*

[25] The London branch was also a sales point and distribution centre throughout the United Kingdom for prints, photographs and photogravures of works he had bought; these reproductions were produced in France, in his studios at Asnières-sur-Seine.

[26] Morand, *Londres*, p. 52.

[27] Robert Loyalty Cru, born in 1884, graduated from the Ecole Normale Supérieure (ENS) in 1905 with a degree in English, and defended his doctoral thesis in 1913 on the topic of 'Diderot as a disciple of English thought'. He was attached to the British Expeditionary Force as an interpreter from 1914 to 1916, and from 1916 to 1919 worked at the London office of the Maison de la Presse. Afterwards he was appointed director and secretary of the Maison de l'Institut de France until his death in 1944 in the bombing which destroyed the Maison de l'Institut.

de Londres. As for Henry Davray, specialist in Anglo-French literary connections, with multiple networks in British circles, and founder, with his friend Edmund Gosse, of Entente Cordiale associations that formed the basis for the Anglo-French Society, he was correspondent from 1915 to 1925 of *Le Petit Journal*, and then from 1928 to 1929 of *Le Temps*. Coudurier de Chassagne was correspondent of *Le Figaro* from 1903 to 1919, and of *L'Illustration*, *Le Voltaire*, *La Politique* and *Coloniale*. André Géraud, better known under his pseudonym Pertinax, was correspondent of *L'Echo de Paris* from 1908 to 1914, and then again in the 1920s. He was taken on as a journalist by the *Daily Telegraph*, and it was Paul Cambon who initiated him into international politics.

However, the most active defenders of French language and culture were teachers, who formed a major group in the colony, numbering 505 men and 2,133 women in 1911. Distinctions need to be made here: on the one hand, there were young women, representing a significant proportion of Frenchwomen in employment. They came to London in search of work as primary-level teachers. They were much in demand; it is impossible now to know how qualified they were, though some claim they were less qualified than primary-level women teachers working in France.[28] But the need for moral guarantees led to the setting up of systems for reception, accommodation, placement and protection for them, as well as registration and monitoring. Between 1844 and the beginning of the twentieth century no fewer than four associations were created: Le Bon Accueil, the National Home, La Société Française des Institutrices and L'Association des Institutrices Françaises.

As well as these, there were secondary- and tertiary-level French teachers, a more heterogeneous group, primarily because of their origins. These teachers were faced with competition in French teaching from British people and even Germans.[29] For an exile, teaching their native tongue was a way of obtaining some income, and many of those who joined the French colony as language teachers at the end of the nineteenth century came from backgrounds that had nothing to do with teaching. Georges Petilleau worked in the secretariat of Ferdinand de Lesseps at the Compagnie du Canal de Suez, and went on to work as a journalist in Paris for *Le Nain Jaune*, *Le Figaro* and *Le Charivari*. After difficulties with the government,

[28] A. Thomas, 'A la conquête d'un statut professionnel: les enseignants de français en Angleterre et leurs associations (1880–1914)', *Documents pour l'histoire du français langue étrangère ou seconde*, xxxiii–xxxiv (2005), 214–26.

[29] In 1885 Charles Cassal complained about the large proportion of Swiss, Belgian, English, Italian, Polish, Russian and German nationals among the 2,500 teachers of French in London.

whom he had attacked in *La Fronde*, a newspaper he created in 1874, he settled in London. He obtained a BA and, in 1881, was recruited as head of the department of French language and literature at Charterhouse School. He translated and adapted a number of French authors for the benefit of his pupils, wrote *John Bull à l'école*, translated Elgar's *Sea Pictures* cycle, and, with Clémence Saunois, published *L'Entente Cordiale à la campagne* in 1918. He was a member of the Société des Gens de Lettres.[30] But beyond all this he was the founder, in 1881, of the Société Nationale des Professeurs de Français (SNPF), a powerful instrument for the spread of French, and organized its first congress.

Alfred P. Huguenet from Alsace graduated from the Ecole Spéciale Militaire de Saint-Cyr before becoming a teacher and also editor-in-chief of *La Chronique de Londres*. The defence of the French teaching profession, one of the reasons for the existence of the SNPF, led progressively both to a 'nationalization' and to a genuine professionalization, and to the recruiting of qualified secondary-level and university-level French teachers, by schools in London. One example was Bernard Minssen: he had a degree in arts and qualified as a university lecturer; he began by teaching in the *lycée* in Le Havre before coming to London and being recruited by Harrow, where he taught French. The status of these teachers in London society, whether British or that of the French colony, varied according to the kind of school in which they taught. Separate consideration should be given to French university professors who taught in London either at a university – Henri Lallemand was professor of French literature at University College; Denis Saurat[31] was director of the Institut Français du Royaume-Uni (IFRU) and professor of French at King's College – or, like the historian Paul Vaucher, at the London School of Economics.[32] Many of these, like Petilleau or Saurat, published scholarly works, translated, gave public lectures and joined in the London literary and social scene.

Finally, from 1910 onwards, the IFRU occupied an important place, both culturally and socially. Marie d'Orliac, a young Frenchwoman, wishing to make French writers, artists and intellectuals better known in England

---

[30] This explains his insistence on being present during Zola's 1893 visit (see above, n. 7).

[31] For more on Saurat, see the chapter by Martyn Cornick.

[32] Paul Vaucher (a former pupil of Elie Halévy and nephew of the founder of the Ecole des Sciences Politiques, the Anglophile Emile Boutmy), although a historian, was twice president of the SNPF, in 1925–6 and 1929–30. A specialist in Walpole, he taught modern French history at the University of London from 1922 onwards. At the London School of Economics he taught a course on French institutions. A notable number of Frenchmen worked at the LSE, either as professors (Paul Mantoux, followed by Paul Vaucher) or lecturers (Elie Halévy or Marc Bloch, for instance).

and to strengthen Anglo-French relations, suggested the idea of creating a University of French Humanities in London. Supported by influential figures such as Lord Askwith and the industrialist Emile Mond, her initiative brought about the inauguration, in Marble Arch House, of a new French institution, the IFRU, in 1911. In 1913 its status was fixed: it was a society run by an administrative council of twenty-one members, mostly British, with Lord Askwith as president. Between 1913 and 1919 it was financed by subscriptions and donations. As its activities expanded, the British government generously lent the IFRU a building in Cromwell Gardens. At the same time the universities of Paris and Lille became its sponsors, and in 1922 an accord was signed that altered its status. A Paris-Lille inter-university commission was created to work with the IFRU's administrative council in the areas of general administration and to promote the educational programmes of the University Section (Faculty of Arts and Lycée), distinct from the Social Section (public lectures). But as the administrative council remained the only body authorized to take financial decisions, British predominance was maintained. The inter-university commission proposed nominations for the Institute's director and staff, but the council's permission was necessary for their appointment. In 1922, beside Marie d'Orliac-Bohn, Emile Audra was appointed director; in 1924 he was replaced by Denis Saurat, who, because of his many years in the post, played a major role in the Institute's development.[33] It was Saurat who, from 1932 onwards, set in motion the construction of the new IFRU building in Queensberry Place, which was inaugurated in 1939, financed by the French government and the Université de Lille. The IFRU Faculty of Arts offered a course leading to an arts degree awarded by the universities of Lille and Paris; a course leading to the Certificate in French awarded by London University, where Saurat, who had a professorship and a doctorate, taught; and courses of university-level lectures.[34] In 1931 the Faculty of Arts had 423 students, 400 of whom were British. The Social Section had 369 people enrolled for its public courses; its talks and lectures, given by celebrities from the worlds of literature, arts and sciences, attracted quite as many people as the tea-parties it held once a week.[35] The list of the IFRU's patrons attests to the high regard in which

[33] Archives du Ministère des Affaires Etrangères (hereafter MAE), relations culturelles, S.S. 1945–59, 0-106-3, rapport de Vaucher conseiller culturel au ministre de l'education nationale en date du 24/11/1944.

[34] One of the professors at the French Institute was René Maheu. He graduated from the ENS in 1925 with a degree in philosophy, and was a friend of Jean-Paul Sartre and Simone de Beauvoir. He was a cultural attaché in London from 1936 to 1939. It was Denis Saurat who asked him to teach courses at the French Institute. He later became UNESCO's director general.

[35] Goiran, *Français à Londres*, p. 238.

it was held: Princess Mary, Lord Harewood and the president of France; the French ambassador was its honorary president, and its vice-presidents were the rectors of the universities of Paris and Lille and the French consul general. The French presidents did not fail to honour the IFRU with their presence on their official visits to London: Raymond Poincaré went there in May 1913 and again in January 1921, just before the inauguration of the Cromwell Road premises; Gaston Doumergue visited it in April 1927; and Albert Lebrun in February 1939 to inaugurate the Queensberry Place site.

As well as this new epicentre of French cultural influence, the eight London committees of the Alliance Française which had been created between 1903 and 1908, on the initiative of the SNPF, continued to bring conference speakers from France, starting with René Bazin. Professor Amédée Salmon and his daughter were the main driving forces behind this venture.

Structures and forms within London's French colony

Social contacts within London's French colony were based around all sorts of societies and associations. There were professional associations, sports clubs (such as the Jeunesse Cycliste, organizing bicycle races; and the Contre de Quarte for fencing) or spiritual organizations (three Masonic lodges, one of which, Hiram, affiliated to the Grand Orient de France, was not recognized by the English Grand Lodge, although the Loge de France and the Loge l'Entente Cordiale were). Some were long-standing but still active, such as the Société de Bienfaisance, founded in 1842, which was seen as 'the soul of the colony',[36] and whose directors figured among its elite; or the Club Culinaire Français, founded in 1845. Others were more recent, such as the London section of France Mutualiste, one of the societies of ex-servicemen which started in 1929 and also had VIPs as its directors. The 1880s were a key moment in the starting of French associations in London. The years 1880–3 saw the founding of three of the most important associations: in 1880, the Société Nationale Française, started by Emmanuel Cadiot in order to group together the various London French associations; in 1881, the Société Nationale des Professeurs de Français en Angleterre, the 'embassy for French thought'; and in 1883, the London French Chamber of Commerce. All these societies had the same aims: defending their profession and seeing that new arrivals found places; propagating French culture, each in their own field; and providing help to those in need. They were also an instrument of social control, defending the morality and cohesion of the group.

---

[36] Goiran, *Français à Londres*, p. 227.

Like English clubs, these societies were very selective in their recruitment of members. Normally, candidates for membership had to be sponsored by two existing members; strict criteria were applied. The SNPF required candidates for membership to be French. Criteria for morality were essential. The National Home for Women Primary School Teachers was an association founded in 1900 by the SNPF on the initiative of Alfred Huguenet, with Marie Lauraint as its first director, whose aim was to provide its residents with family life and ensure their protection. A primary-level woman teacher who applied to it for membership had to provide two character references and a third about her family. 'Competence, honesty, good manners' were the entrance criteria for the Société des Progrès de la Coiffure. The Chamber of Commerce had a special information office on the honesty and commercial situation of dealers and industrialists; when the question was raised, in 1904, of creating a 'Cercle Commercial Français', the proposers underlined that members would have to be 'of proven honesty'. As a result, membership of some societies was quite low. The London section of the SNPF had only about twenty members in 1901. Moreover, societies were basically masculine. One of the rare ones that accepted women, first as mere associates and later, from 1884, as members, was again the SNPF.[37] The only societies for women were the Société Française d'Institutrices, founded in 1894 by a female teacher who was an associate of the SNPF, and the Association des Institutrices Françaises, founded in 1903 by Marie Lauraint.

The defence of France's image and culture was of primordial importance for these associations. The SNPF claimed to represent 'French thought and culture in England', defend the recruitment of French nationals as French teachers, and maintain the pre-eminent position of French in foreign-language teaching in Britain. Under Petilleau it organized a major annual competition, with prizes, gold and silver medals from the French Ministère de l'Instruction Publique and the Alliance Française, and the Prix Hachette de Littérature,[38] awarded at a ceremony at the Guildhall in the presence of the lord mayor – proof of the audience reached by the SNPF, and the interest taken by the British in French teaching. The Société Culinaire

[37] See Thomas, 'A la conquête'.

[38] In 1900 the Hachette Bookshop in London, which published works by members of the SNPF, inaugurated a 'Prix Hachette de Littérature' as a prize in the Grand Concours de Langue et Littérature Françaises. This competition had been established in 1884, and its prizes were two gold medals (offered by the French Ministry of Public Instruction and Fine Arts); three silver medals (one from the ambassador, the other two from the Alliance Française); prints offered by the Galerie Lefevre; and works of art offered by Charterhouse School, Harrow School, Godalming School, M. Petilleau (president of the Comité des Professeurs), M. Testard (of the Alliance Français), M. Vasselier, the SNPF, and, from 1900, the Hachette Bookshop.

Française, besides the defence of its members' interests, and their jobs in London, established itself as the 'faithful and vigilant guardian of French culinary traditions'.

In certain areas there were rival societies; this was the case for primary-level women teachers, and also in the culinary sphere, where as well as the Club Culinaire Français there existed the Société Culinaire, the Club de l'Avenir Français founded in 1893 to help in finding jobs for young French people newly arrived in London, and the Société des Cuisiniers et Confiseurs. In 1932 the first two of these united into one, whose purpose remained that of 'maintaining the superiority of French culinary art' and defending the interests of the profession. Membership of these societies bestowed considerable importance on people, and some, like G. Petilleau or Marius Duché, became VIPs, invited as guests by the French ambassador and the lord mayor, given places at receptions held for official visits by the French president, etc.[39]

The life of these societies was organized around general assemblies, artistic and musical soirées, and especially dinners, banquets and annual balls – high points in their activities and the opportunity for honoured members of the French colony to meet one another, since it was the habit of each society to invite Embassy dignitaries, eminent members of other societies and British high-society figures. The banquets were punctuated by toasts proposed to the queen or king, the French president and distinguished guests, and by speeches, including one by the French ambassador if he was present. As for the balls, they were opportunities to dress up. Some societies were known for their soirées and balls: participants at the soirées of the Société des Progrès de la Coiffure were invited to come in 'historical, modern and fantasy hair-styles' and its balls were in fancy-dress. These festive occasions (the most important of which were the dinners of the Hôpital Français and the Chamber of Commerce in the presence of the French ambassador and the lord mayor) were certainly social events, but they were also fund-raising occasions for the charitable works of the French colony. The Société de Bienfaisance provided monetary help to French people in difficulties, contributed to the cost of returning to France, and paid annual pensions to five or six destitute elderly people. The Ligue de la Bonté was founded in 1901 by the SNPF. The Hôpital Français, founded in 1867 by Dr. Rimmel

---

[39] *Le Livre d'or de l'entente cordiale* (Bordeaux, 1908), contains the reports of the visits to London made by President Loubet (pp. 89–110), the members of the French Parliament (pp. 113–18), naval officers of the Escadre Française du Nord (pp. 171–80), the Paris town councillors (pp. 211–16), a delegation of members of French universities (pp. 192–4) and others. As well as an account of the receptions, the *Livre d'or* gives the welcoming speeches, speeches of thanks, names of some of the delegates, and photographs.

and Dr. Vintras, offered treatment free to French people in reduced circumstances or to foreigners who had no-one to look after them. From 1890, the hospital stood in Shaftesbury Avenue and underwent successive enlargements; doctors, surgeons and sisters treated over 16,000 in-patients between 1867 and 1904, and more than 23,000 between 1904 and 1930; nearly 364,000 out-patients between 1867 and 1904, and over 500,000 between 1904 and 1930.[40] In 1904 the British inspection of hospitals stated that 'the hospital is a model of what an institution of this kind should be, and leaves nothing to be desired'. Dr. Vintras had added to the hospital a convalescence and rest home at Brighton.

These societies faced two related problems: the absence of premises, and the absence of a federating organism. Apart from the Société de Bienfaisance, the National Home, which had a spacious residence in St. George's Square, and the French Chamber of Commerce, which occupied premises at 153 Queen Victoria Street, the rest were 'of no fixed address'. Repeated attempts were made from 1880 to the inter-war period to put in place a structure to act as a link between the various French societies in London, and as a rallying-point for French people in London. Cadiot founded the Société Nationale Française in 1880, with three sections: industrial and commercial; artistic; and scientific and literary (with Petilleau as its president). This, however, had no real effect, and neither did an attempted re-launch in July 1900. De Bry, Fauquemberge and others had set up La Vraie France the month before, but it too was a failure. In December 1901 Cambon, the only French ambassador to take an interest in the question, organized a meeting in view of the financial problems resulting from this lack of cohesion, which had assailed the Société de Bienfaisance, the convalescence home at Brighton and the National Home. He called for absolute harmony among the members of the colony, insisted that a central committee should be set up with the French consul general as president, supported by four sub-committees (commercial, financial, cultural and press), and told them to set to work.[41] The question came up again in 1908 and finally, in December 1913, a permanent committee for the colony was set in place, with Duché as its president, charged with ensuring proper discipline between the societies, representing them officially and defending French national traditions.

---

[40] *La Chronique de Londres*, 12 Nov. 1904, and Goiran, *Français à Londres*, pp. 231–2. In 1932 the hospital had 70 beds, an operating theatre, three consulting-rooms, an x-ray department and a laboratory. The nursing care was provided by Sacred Heart nuns trained at Versailles. During the First World War it was a department of the First London General Hospital and 30 beds were reserved for wounded British soldiers. The French Hospital, bought back in 1967, became the Shaftesbury Hospital. It was closed in 1992.

[41] *La Chronique de Londres*, 21 Dec. 1901.

A further question facing the colony was that of their children's schooling. Until 1915 the few schools available were only at primary level. The Ecole de l'Eglise Protestante Française in Wardour Street had three classes; it taught children of members of the Eglise Protestante Française, children of members of Protestant churches which held their services in French, and children who had at least one French parent and whose mother-tongue was French. As for the French schools in Leicester Square, which appear to be the only ones recognized and supported by the French Embassy, they were linked to the Catholic church Notre Dame de France, which was the colony's parish church. The girls' school was run first by Sacred Heart nuns and then, after 1892, by the Sisters of the Blessed Sacrament, and had 120 pupils in 1902. The boys' school was established in 1892, and run by Marist Brothers; in 1902 it had 100 pupils. There was a kindergarten for eighty children between the ages of three and seven. These schools were located in the district where many of the poorer members of the French colony still lived. They were insufficient to meet demand, and did not solve the problem of secondary education. From the beginning of the twentieth century, the colony's leaders were concerned that this lack of provision was leading the children to abandon their French nationality to be able to attend English schools. They aspired to create a school where 'generations of English and French children' could 'grow and be educated together, get to know each other and learn to appreciate each other'.[42] The First World War and the influx of French and Belgian refugees led to the opening, on 18 January 1915, of two French secondary schools, one for boys, with a Belgian university lecturer as headmaster, and one for girls, with Marie d'Orliac as headmistress. They were set up by the IFRU, thanks to gifts from Emile Mond. Seen as a patriotic effort, they offered free places to about 100 boys and about thirty girls, refugees from France and Belgium or children of French, Belgian or English soldiers who had gone to war. Until February 1919 they were located in two houses in Buckingham Palace Gardens lent by an individual, and afterwards in a collection of buildings lent by the British government in Cromwell Road. The teachers were all French, and were generally qualified university lecturers or secondary school teachers.

Between patriotism and Entente Cordiale

The French colony in London always stood aside from the political struggles and great crises that divided French life. Individual political opinions

---

[42] Y. Guyot, G. R. Sandoz, P. Bourgeois and J. Clarétie, *Exposition Franco-Britannique de Londres 1908, rapport général au Comité Français des Expositions à l'Etranger* (3 vols., Paris, 1913), ii. 420.

belonged in the private sphere, and were never expressed in public, either in the London French press or within the various societies. The only shared views that were strongly upheld in this colony were patriotism, forcefully expressed in the celebration of 14 July, and the defence of French language and culture and French interests, but never to the detriment of the Entente Cordiale. Hence the great deference towards the crown,[43] which was shown when the occasion arose, and especially at times when Franco-British relationships were strained – during the Fashoda crisis, the Transvaal affair, and above all, during the Boer wars, before 1914 and immediately after the First World War. The offensive caricatures of Queen Victoria by Léandre, among others, led the representatives of the French colony in London and the editors of *La Chronique de Londres* to assure the queen of their profound respect and to denounce the bad manners of certain French people in France. There were constant reminders of and references to the Franco-British Entente and the need to defend it, especially during the tensions of 1920–1.

The expression of these sentiments was particularly emphatic during the First World War. Within the French colony, the *union sacrée* was unquestioned. The mobilization of French people living in London and their departure for the continent was accomplished without difficulty. The French Red Cross, the London section of the Union des Femmes de France, whose president was Mme. Brasier de Thuy, and the church of Notre Dame de France all lent their support and provided material assistance to the families of the men called up, to refugees arriving from the northern parts of France, and to Belgian refugees as well.[44] The war did not lead to any slackening in the work of spreading French language and culture: the French Lycée and the Théâtre des Alliés, which put on French repertory, saw to that. The alliance between England and France brought to London members of the French army and French members and representatives of the many Franco-British commissions. Jean Monnet, back in London in July 1914, was, from 1915 onwards, the personal representative of Etienne Clémentel and a member of the Commission for the Distribution of Tonnage. Staying at the Ritz, he spent his evenings at the theatre.[45] Georges

---

[43] 'The French had the greatest reverence for Queen Victoria, and they entertain the same feeling towards the present King who, when Prince of Wales, gave to the French colony so many proofs of interest and a kindly patronage' wrote Paul Villars in 'French London', his contribution to Sims, *Living London* (ii. 138).

[44] *La Chronique de Londres*, 22 Aug. and 5 Sept. 1914. A committee for aid to families of French soldiers was set up with Duché as president. Mme. Brasier de Thuy was the wife of the London agent of a shipping company.

[45] See Roussel, *Jean Monnet*, pp. 45–82, on this period of the war.

Boris, who joined his brother Rolland, an adjutant to the French naval attaché, in London, was appointed to the French section of the Franco-British Commission for Supplies.[46]

The London French press also echoed the feelings of patriotism and support for the Entente Cordiale. The French colony in London had its own newspapers. There were not many of them and some were short-lived, but they were felt as a necessity. *La Chronique de Londres*, which considered itself the organ of the opinions of the French colony, lasted the longest. Founded in 1899 by Henri Didot, and having, for its editors-in-chief and then directors, A. P. Huguenet, professor of French and influential member of the SNPF, followed by A. Philibert, it appeared continuously until 1924, when it was swallowed up by *La Gazette de Grande Bretagne*, which ceased publication in 1932, hit by the Great Depression. These newspapers defended the Franco-British Entente Cordiale, constituted an organ of information and a link between the societies and people of the French colony in London, and defended French economic and cultural interests. Their target readership included French men and women who were in London more briefly. *La Chronique* appeared weekly, offering basically a chronicle of events in England, literary and arts reviews, portraits of members of the colony, news of French triumphs, a serial, information on the French societies in London, news of charitable and social events, a women's page from 1921 onwards, personal columns, and advertisements. It was not a vehicle for politics as such, but often for expressing gratitude towards Great Britain, as evidenced by this editorial of 29 December 1900: 'Next Tuesday *La Chronique* enters its third year ... Setting aside all political questions, all of the French residing in London owe a debt to the country which accords us such generous hospitality, and the payment of that debt of gratitude is for us a sweet duty'.[47]

Geographical sketch of the French colony in London

The French colony in London was an endogamous one. Eight out of ten marriages, as demonstrated by a systematic analysis of the wedding and marriage announcements published in *La Chronique de Londres* in the years between 1899 and 1924, were between French people; mixed marriages

---

[46] J. L. Crémieux-Brilhac, *Georges Boris, trente ans d'influence Blum, de Gaulle, Mendès France* (Paris, 2010), p. 26; in London, Boris shadowed General de Gaulle and kept in contact with 'Jacques Duchesne', the theatre producer-manager Michel Saint-Denis (see below, under 'French intellectuals and artists').

[47] At the end of Aug. 1914 the publication of a newspaper called *Le Cri de Londres* was announced, which aimed to deal with all aspects of the combat and appear until the end of the war.

tended to occur in the upper social strata. In the years 1880–90, the colony was essentially concentrated in the area of Soho and around Leicester Square, where the Protestant church, the Catholic church, the primary schools and, to begin with, the French Hospital, were all located. However, from the end of the 1890s the sociology of the colony changed; the upper middle classes increased in proportion, with a surge in activities linked to commerce and finance, and the development of cultural structures and education. This in its turn brought about a gradual move towards the more prosperous parts of London. The addresses of SNPF members in London at the beginning of the twentieth century are evidence of this movement: more than half lived in South Kensington, Hampstead, St. John's Wood and Harrow.[48] According to the 1911 census and the data from 1931, the French population of the Borough of Westminster, which includes Soho, went from 2,486 to 1,388, that of St. Pancras from 1,580 to 938, that of St. Marylebone from 1,197 to 678, and that of Kensington from 1,156 to 1,089.[49] Thus, in the general reduction of the French colony in London, Kensington maintained its numbers.

French visitors in London

London seems to have been for the French what Paris was for the English, a lover. Politicians and businessmen came to London in increasing numbers. The Entente Cordiale and then the First World War favoured contacts and exchanges; additionally, from the 1920s on, air travel meant that for these classes of people London was on Paris's doorstep: 'You come to London for lunch to sort out some question, and in the afternoon you go back to Paris without even having to change your dinner-time'.[50] They were not the only ones to flock to London: university researchers and students, writers, artists and scholars came to work and hold seminars, invited by institutions or members of their networks.

Official receptions

Official visits by delegations – parliamentarians, town councillors, university professors, army officers – all followed, with varying degrees of ceremoniousness, the model of the presidential visits. A president of France came to London on an official visit six times between 1903 and 1939: Emile Loubet in 1903, Armand Fallières in 1908 to inaugurate the Franco-British Exhibition, Poincaré in 1913 and 1921, Doumergue in 1927 and Lebrun in

---

[48] *La Chronique de Londres*, 5 Oct. 1901.
[49] N. Atkin, *The Forgotten French: Exiles in the British Isles, 1940–4* (Manchester, 2003), p. 190.
[50] Goiran, *Français à Londres*, p. 213.

Figure 10.3. President Loubet visits the Home des Institutrices
Françaises, 1903. Author's postcard collection.

1939. The standard components remained the same: reception by the king at Buckingham Palace or Windsor, with gala dinners and ball; visit to the Guildhall and reception by the lord mayor, lunch or dinner; receptions at the French Embassy – on the day of the president's arrival, a delegation from the French colony in London was presented to him (in 1903, to Loubet, by Marius Duché); official dinner given by the president to the king; evening at Covent Garden. Other visits were made to the French institutions in London: the Hôpital Français, the National Home for Women Primary School Teachers and, after 1910, the French Institute, with the conferring of decorations. In 1908 Fallières conferred the insignia of Officier de la Légion d'Honneur on Marius Duché and Paul Villars, correspondent of the newspaper *Journal des débats* and author of a piece on the French in *Living London* edited by George R. Sims; while Marie Lauraint was appointed Officier de l'Instruction Publique. Finally, the president attended a military review.

Delegations of parliamentarians were received by the sovereign either at Buckingham Palace or at Windsor, invited to a banquet at the House of Commons, given receptions by the lord mayor and lunches or dinners by liveried companies; visits to the great financial institutions were also organized (in July 1903 to the Baltic Exchange and Lloyd's). The seventy-one members of French universities who visited London from 4 to 8 June 1906 were given receptions by the king at Windsor, by the Foreign Office, the University of London and the French Embassy; they visited Kensington Palace, Westminster Abbey and Camberwell School. In 1905 the town councillors of Paris were given receptions by Edward VII, the London County Council and the lord mayor at Mansion House; they visited the headquarters of the Fire Brigade and the Barking Sewage Works. All these ceremonies were punctuated by speeches: by the king, the French president, the ambassador and officials (on 5 June 1906, during the visit of members of French universities, no fewer than forty speeches were given!).[51] Presidential visits and visits by French naval or army personnel were also accompanied by processions through London streets lined with crowds, in which the British mingled with the people of London's French colony.

French intellectuals and artists

From Ernest Renan, who came to London in 1884 to deliver the Hibbert Lectures, and Paul Verlaine, whose stay in London in November 1893, organized by William Rothenstein, Thomas Powell and Arthur Symons, was a failure, to Paul Morand and Paul Valéry, who both stayed in London

---

[51] *Livre d'or*, pp. 192–4.

many times, literary figures, artists, dramatists, university lecturers and students all made the journey to the capital, perhaps finding it a source of inspiration and networking, and helping to bring French cultural life to England. Particular figures illustrated this special relationship with London.

Between 1902 and 1934 Valéry Larbaud made about twelve visits to London, 'a city of people with unpolished shoes', but also 'the place in the world where I have been happiest', and one that 'fills me with courage and ardour', he noted.[52] These stays were times for research and working in the British Museum for Larbaud, a specialist in Chesterton and Walter Savage Landor and translator of Samuel Butler. They were also an opportunity for meetings: in July 1911 he met André Gide; together, on the initiative of Agnès Tobin, they went to visit Arthur Symons and Joseph Conrad; in September–October 1919, while doing research on Butler at the British Museum, he met H. F. Jones, his biographer.[53] During his stay in May–July 1921, he gave a lecture at the IFRU on the French Poets.[54] They were also days of affection, from the time of his 1912 stay with Gladys, his London 'ally'.[55] Of the five stays that Gide made in London, the one in December 1912 was the most fruitful in literary terms: he met Edmund Gosse, whom he had first encountered the year before, Edith Sichel and George Moore; he also revisited Conrad, whose translator he became.

Paul Valéry was also assiduous in his London visits. His first stay dates back to 1878, before his seventh birthday, and, he wrote, 'no other trace of that first contact with England now remains to me save an impression of extreme terror experienced in Tussaud's Museum'.[56] Despite this, by 1934 a further six London visits had followed. In 1922 he unveiled a plaque in memory of Verlaine and Arthur Rimbaud, gave a talk at Lady Colefax's, and spent a day with Conrad; the following year he gave a talk on Charles Baudelaire and Victor Hugo at the French Institute; in 1934, on 23 November he gave a lecture at King's College, on 24 November went to watch *Hamlet*, and on 26 November met Luigi Pirandello at the Italian Embassy.[57]

Another visitor, both a man of letters and a politician, was Georges Clemenceau, who came to London ten times between 1880 and June 1921. Clemenceau was shepherded into London's literary and political circles by Admiral Maxse, to whom he had been introduced by Louis Blanc in 1872,

[52] V. Larbaud, *Journal* (Paris, 2009), pp. 150, 599, 724.
[53] Larbaud, *Journal*, pp. 710–34.
[54] V. Larbaud, *Œuvres* (Paris, 1958,) p. li.
[55] Larbaud, *Journal*; Gladys is mentioned throughout the *Journal*.
[56] P. Valéry, *Œuvres* (2 vols., Paris, 1957), i. 13. Valéry and his parents went to stay with his aunt, Pauline de Rin.
[57] Valéry, *Œuvres*, i. 45, 46, 60.

and his daughters, to whom he was linked. His first visits were as much cultural as political in nature.[58] In 1884 Clemenceau, the radical, was invited into aristocratic English circles, met Lord Granville and other members of the nobility, and spoke at the Cobden Club. In January 1899 he paid a visit to Zola, the exile; in February 1900, on the initiative of Violet Maxse, he and Gustave Geoffroy met Claude Monet at the Savoy and went together to listen to the Minstrels at St. James's Hall, Piccadilly. In 1903 he met the socialist Henry Hyndman, later Clemenceau's biographer, and Rudyard Kipling.[59] From March 1918 to January 1920 Clemenceau came to London as president of the council and negotiator, either alone or in the company of Marshal Foch. During his last visit, on the way to Oxford to receive an honorary doctorate on 21 June, he stopped over in London, went to Claridge's, and met Churchill, the Steeds, the Kiplings, the Cecils, the Asquiths and, without any pleasure, Lloyd George.[60]

Of the artists, Claude Monet, a refugee after the Paris Commune, came back to London three more times, in September–October 1899, February–April 1900 and January–March 1901, to work on his series of views of London, some painted from his room at the Savoy, others from a room in St. Thomas's Hospital. Paintings of the Thames, Charing Cross Bridge, Westminster Bridge, views of the Houses of Parliament, Leicester Square by night, and Waterloo Bridge, in the light effects specific to London, were some of the fruits of these stays. In spring 1898 Henri Matisse came to study J. M. W. Turner's paintings and spent his honeymoon in London. He returned in 1922, having been commissioned by Sergei Diaghilev to design sets and costumes for Igor Stravinsky's ballet *Rossignol*.

Individual French actors such as Réjane,[61] Sacha Guitry and Yvonne Printemps achieved considerable successes on the London stage, but still more influential were the tours by theatre companies. These included: the Comédie Française, which came with Sarah Bernhardt[62] at the end of the nineteenth century, and after the First World War was asked by Aristide Briand to perform at Drury Lane on the *Journée du Combattant*, 31

---

[58] J. B. Duroselle, *Clemenceau* (Paris, 1988), p. 198.

[59] Duroselle, *Clemenceau*, pp. 404, 415.

[60] Duroselle, *Clemenceau*, p. 879.

[61] On 27 June 1894 she played the role of Catherine in V. Sardou and E. Moreau's *Madame Sans-Gêne* at the Gaiety Theatre; the theatre company was French and the piece had previously been performed on 27 Oct. 1893 at the Théâtre du Vaudeville, Paris (programme, private collection).

[62] Sarah Bernhardt was a familiar figure on the London stage. For example, on 11 Oct. 1913 she performed at a soirée to raise funds for the French Hospital; in 1896 she performed at Daly's Theatre (2 and 8 Cranbourn Street, Leicester Square) during the season of French theatre.

March 1921, when the king and queen were invited;[63] the Théâtre Libre de Copeau in 1891; and Michel Saint-Denis's Compagnie des Quinze, which performed in London several times between 1931 and 1934. The last two named introduced elements of experimental theatre to London. Michel Saint-Denis settled in London where, from 1935 to 1939, he directed the London Theatre Studio, a place of innovation and cultural exchange.[64]

Debussy visited London seven times between 1902 and 1914. In July 1902 he came in response to an invitation by André Messager; in 1903 he was sent by the literary periodical *Le Gil Blas* to report on Wagner's Ring cycle, conducted by Hans Richter at Covent Garden; in February 1908 he conducted the *Prélude à l'après-midi d'un faune* and *La Mer* to immense acclaim at Queen's Hall, Langham Place; a year later he returned to conduct *Nocturnes* and the *Prélude* again. In the 1908 season Edouard Colonne had the immense privilege of being the only foreigner to conduct at the Proms before the death of Henry Wood.[65]

Elie Halévy and Marc Bloch were two of the many university teachers who came to pursue their research at the University of London or the British Museum, to give lectures or attend conferences. Halévy was a philosopher specializing in Benthamite utilitarianism, and a historian, author of the *History of the English People in the Nineteenth Century*; his correspondence reveals his journeys and his network of London acquaintances. Starting with his first stay in 1892 he met Henry James, the Burne-Joneses, Jane Ellen Harrison, Miss Margot Tennant, the Sickerts, the publisher Unwin, and George Moore;[66] in 1898 he met the Sassoons; in 1902, Leslie Stephen; in 1919, Lord Haldane; in 1927, Eileen Power, whom he had previously met in Paris, and the Webbs; but one of the solid friendships he formed, this time in Cambridge, was with Bertrand Russell. His circle of contacts was wide and complex. Besides his research work, he met all these people at dinners,

[63] MAE, relations culturelles, série Z, carton 312, pièces 28 (dated 8 March 1921), 29, 31.

[64] M. Saint-Denis, *La Compagnie des Quinze: les cahiers* (Paris, 1931); J. B. Gourmel, 'Michel Saint-Denis, un homme de théâtre (1897–1971)' (unpublished Université Paris I-Panthéon Sorbonne MA dissertation, 2005). A nephew of Jacques Copeau, Michel Saint-Denis went by the name of Jacques Duchesne during the war and broadcast the programme 'Les Français parlent aux Français'. The London Theatre Studio trained many actors and directors including Peter Brook and Michael Redgrave.

[65] M. Rapoport, 'Debussy et les Proms', in *Actes du colloque Debussy*, ed. M. Chimenes (Paris, forthcoming 2013).

[66] E. Halévy, *Correspondance 1891–1937* (Paris, 1996), letter of Tuesday 1 Nov. to Ludovic Halévy, p. 87; for 1898, letter of Thursday 12 May to L. Halévy, p. 245; for 1902, note at p. 286; for 1919, letter of 16 March to Mme. Ludovic Halévy. Elie wrote very regularly to his father Ludovic, and after his father's death, to his mother. His interest in the socialist movement led to several meetings with the Webbs.

went out to the theatre at Covent Garden, frequented the Athenaeum and was invited to give lectures at the London School of Economics. His stays in London gave rise to observations on British politics as seen by a man who was close to the socialists, as well as on London life. On 8 May 1935 he wrote to Xavier Léon:

> I really did not want to go to this Jubilee procession. But *everyone* told me it was my duty to be there. I yielded, and do not regret it. It was very beautiful and at the same time very charming, very simple, very family-like … What is a king of England? It is England herself, adoring herself in an individual incarnation …[67]

His correspondence also records his migrations within London, from his first stay to his last, from the Family Hotel in Great Russell Street, where he stayed in 1892, to Gordon Street, where he stayed in the 1930s.

Marc Bloch's connection with London has become better known since the publication of F. O. Touati's book.[68] Bloch's researches on medieval history revolved around a comparison between France and England. Between the summer of 1921 and March 1939 he came to London four times, both for research and to give classes at the London School of Economics. Generally he stayed at the Maison de l'Institut de France, a foundation bequeathed to the Institute by Edmond de Rothschild in 1919 and intended to offer accommodation to researchers and members of universities in order to 'strengthen the intellectual links between France and England … to help create, between the two countries, a spiritual alliance in order to spread throughout the world the ideas of progress, justice and peace'.[69] But for Bloch, unlike Halévy, the most important encounters occurred less in London than in Cambridge or Oxford: Eileen Power, Michael Postan and F. M. Powicke.

Tourists

Finally, London, which Elie Halévy said 'is still the most extraordinary city in the world',[70] was a tourist destination: 'Saturday sees Victoria thronging with groups of Parisians, somewhat stunned to find themselves in a foreign country',[71] London being the epitome of exotic new surroundings. It would be impossible to calculate the numbers. H. Goiran estimates that the

---

[67] Halévy, *Correspondance*, p. 729. Xavier Léon was one of Halévy's oldest friends and the founder of the journal *Revue de métaphysique et de morale*.

[68] F. O. Touati, *Marc Bloch et l'Angleterre* (Paris, 2007).

[69] Touati, *Marc Bloch*, p. 72. Marc Bloch was one of the first guests of the Maison de l'Institut de France when he stayed there in the summer of 1921.

[70] Halévy, *Correspondance*, letter to Ludovic Halévy of 2 Feb. 1893, p. 116.

[71] Goiran, *Français à Londres*, p. 214.

number of French tourists increased year by year.[72] London was a strong attraction, but apart from special occasions like the great exhibitions,[73] when railway and boat companies offered reduced rates, it was basically the upper middle classes who crossed the Channel and headed for London.

Conclusion

At the beginning of the Second World War the components of London's French colony had undergone a change over the previous sixty years and now consisted largely of two groups. On the one hand, were those connected with business, represented by people like Pierre de Malglaive, London director of the Compagnie Générale Transatlantique, E. Bellanger, director of Cartier de Londres, Jacques Métadier, director of a pharmaceutical company, or T. J. Guéritte, former president of the French Chamber of Commerce. On the other hand, were people from the world of culture: Professor Paul Vaucher, Denis Saurat, Robert L. Cru and Michel Saint-Denis. The colony was structured around a number of institutions – cultural ones such as the Institut Français, the French schools and churches; economic ones like the French Chamber of Commerce; the many professional societies; and charitable institutions such as the French Hospital. Throughout this period the colony had maintained its cohesion despite the divisions that had shaken France. Those in charge of its various institutions had been energetic defenders of the Entente Cordiale, particularly at times of tension between England and France; they affirmed the colony's patriotism and its fidelity to France, but at the same time its respect and gratitude towards Great Britain and the king or queen.

The outbreak of war, and especially the collapse of France in May–June 1940, brought about a radical change in the features of the French colony in London. For the first time, its members had to make choices: whether to stand by the legal government of France in Vichy, or to rebel and join the partisans backing General de Gaulle or another resistance group, or to support England. Some returned to France, and others left London, while large numbers of French newcomers appeared there – officers, ordinary soldiers, civilians from every sphere of French society, and politicians,

---

[72] Goiran, *Français à Londres*, p. 214.

[73] The preparation of these great exhibitions, the Franco-British Exhibition of 1908 for instance, involved visits by French delegations of experts, government representatives, members of parliamentary commissions and chambers of commerce. Once the exhibition was under way, these same people would come back for the many events scheduled: the opening, banquets, receptions, etc. Account should also be taken of the hundreds of exhibitors, their employees and agents, who flocked to London for several weeks and who had to be accommodated.

often from opposing sides. Some of the French institutions in London, and particularly the Institut Français, became rallying-points for a section of London's French colony and the more recent arrivals. New French locations appeared in London and, between 1940 and 1944, new French institutions connected with the war were set up. French London in the 1940s was no longer the same as before the war either in its make-up or its geography. It was a new colony that was being born, with its own history.

Translated by Helena Scott

11. French cultural diplomacy in early twentieth-century London

Charlotte Faucher and Philippe Lane

France has long been engaged in very active cultural and scientific diplomacy, but state intervention is relatively recent and was embodied in the creation of different sections within the French Foreign Office, Quai d'Orsay, from 1910 onwards.[1] The absence of a government-planned foreign cultural policy did not prevent France from developing its international presence in the domains of culture, language, science and arts. In the *ancien régime*, French writers moved in diplomatic circles, as was the case with Joachim du Bellay who worked with his uncle in Rome, or Jean Jacques Rousseau who served as secretary for the Venice Embassy in 1743.[2]

Cultural diplomacy relies on networks of cultural co-operation services in embassies and cultural institutions, with numerous other operators including private and religious initiatives and transnational cultural transfers.[3] Therefore, cultural diplomacy must be comprehended in a broad sense and not solely as the product of a government's decision. Early twentieth-century London was no exception: most of the French cultural societies and associations were the result of individual or religious ventures and barely benefited from state funding; indeed, the multiple governments of the Third Republic did not have a specific external cultural policy. It was only after the First World War that both the Ministère de l'Instruction Publique et des Beaux Arts and the Ministère des Affaires Etrangères became aware of their impact on the projection of France abroad. After the Second World War, cultural diplomacy was mostly dealt with by the Quai d'Orsay.

This chapter explores the promotion of French language and culture in early twentieth-century London, a tendency which was in tune with the

---

[1] Ph. Lane, *Présence française dans le monde – l'action culturelle et scientifique* (Paris, 2011) and *French Scientific and Cultural Diplomacy* (Liverpool 2013).

[2] F. Roche and B. Pigniau, *Histoires de diplomatie culturelle des origines à 1995* (Paris, 1995), p. 9.

[3] See the conceptualization of cultural diplomacy suggested by P. Ory in the preface to *Entre rayonnement et réciprocité: contributions à l'histoire de la diplomatie culturelle*, ed. A. Dubosclard and others (Paris, 2002).

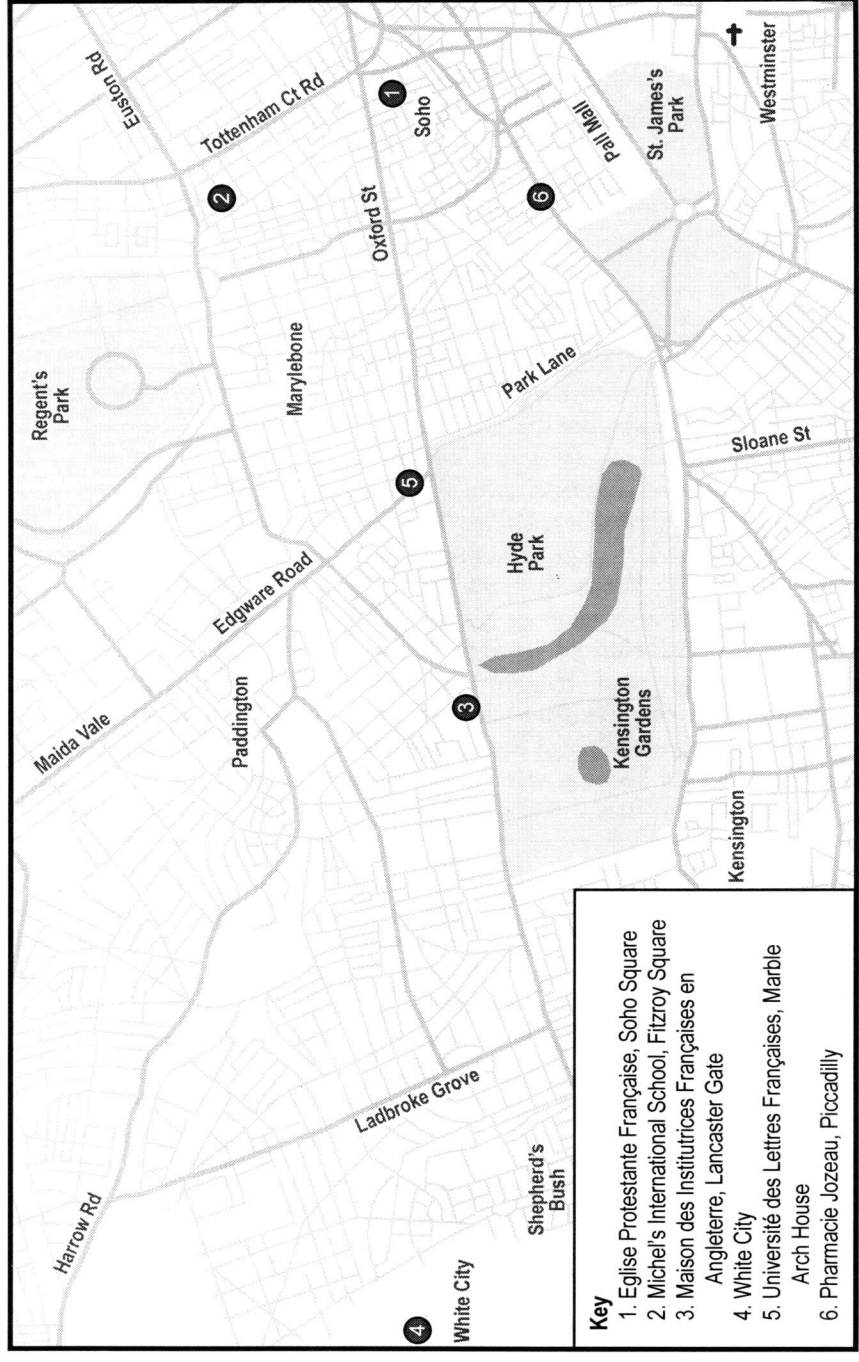

Key
1. Eglise Protestante Française, Soho Square
2. Michel's International School, Fitzroy Square
3. Maison des Institutrices Françaises en Angleterre, Lancaster Gate
4. White City
5. Université des Lettres Françaises, Marble Arch House
6. Pharmacie Jozeau, Piccadilly

Map 11.1. Places mentioned in the text (Base map: London c.1910)

dissemination of French throughout the world. Indeed, in addition to the existing religious congregations, societies such as the Alliance Française (1883) and the Mission Laïque Française (1905) were created at the turn of the century. These schemes were linked to the colonialist mentality of the time, an 'ideal civilisateur' which was used to assert France's power in the world. For example, the Alliance Française (AF) aimed, first, at spreading French in the French provinces (it had branches in almost all departments of the country), second, in France's colonies, and third, in the rest of the world.[4]

This chapter will first briefly outline the linguistic and cultural foreign policies of France from the late eighteenth to the early twentieth century. Then it will consider in more detail the dissemination of French culture through the French language and the role of French institutions in London from the late nineteenth century to 1914, concentrating mainly on the Institut Français du Royaume-Uni (IFRU), and examining the growing role of the state within this institution. It will trace a progressive shift in the IFRU's role, from cultural and linguistic to political.

Background
1789–1870: the nation and cultural activities
Albert Salon has shown that the French Revolution resulted in the 'nationalization'[5] of foreign cultural initiatives during the last decade of the eighteenth century when intellectual, diplomatic and military forces joined together to spread the new ideas of the Revolution. This almost evangelical sense of mission corresponded to the voluntarism of the spirit of the Enlightenment: it was a drive for the moral and intellectual perfecting of mankind. The belief in a never-ending progress of knowledge, as well as this strong desire to develop ideas in every sphere, belonged to the dominant philosophy of the eighteenth century.

There were other ways of spreading French culture and language outside the nation. François Roche and Bernard Pigniau consider that Napoleon Bonaparte's 1798 expedition to Egypt was the first embodiment of what is today described as cultural 'co-operation', as it included several scientists, engineers, intellectuals and artists who would contribute to the creation of Egyptology and to the cultural and scientific relations that followed.[6]

During the nineteenth century, cultural activities accompanied diplomacy. Culture, as well as other components such as religion or colonization, was

---

[4] M. Bruézière, *L'Alliance Française – histoire d'une institution* (Paris, 1983), p. 12.

[5] A. Salon, 'L'action culturelle de la France dans le monde: analyse critique' (unpublished Université Paris I, Panthéon-Sorbonne PhD thesis, 3 vols., 1981) (abridged version in A. Salon, *L'Action Culturelle de la France dans le monde* (Paris, 1983)).

[6] Roche and Pigniau, *Histoires*, p. 12.

seen as a way to promote *l'esprit français*.[7] The Quai d'Orsay negotiated the first cultural agreements, which were mainly concerned with intellectual and artistic property. Two years before the end of the Second Empire, the Galatasaray *lycée* was opened in Istanbul. It was a co-operative project between France and the Ottoman government which would educate on a non-confessional basis generations of French-speakers who would constitute the Turkish elite in subsequent decades.[8] Until the end of the nineteenth century, the learning of the French language was aimed at the upper classes.

1870–1914: the creation of the French cultural network in the world
In this period political events impacted on the running of the cultural networks of France. Britain, France, Germany, Italy and Russia were competing in the same areas, mainly Africa and the Orient, and each aimed to maintain or enhance their influence on the elites of other nations;[9] they kept watch over each other through their diplomatic and consular staffs. The linguistic rivalry, which was one aspect of contention between France, Germany or England, also happened outside Europe. Therefore, in 1881, the vast majority of the Quai's budget was directed to the Oeuvres d'Orient.[10] Egypt was a focal point of this competition. The Quai d'Orsay talked of a 'languages war' occurring in this area in 1891, and a note produced by Paul Deschanel, future president of France, displayed French administrators' awareness of the danger represented by English officials who had recently started to 'invade' the field of public education in Cairo, which had so far been a French monopoly. Seeing that some students might 'escape' from French domination, the French Foreign Office decided to pay teachers and opened l'Ecole de Droit du Caire.[11]

In Europe, the French language, which enjoyed prestige among the aristocracy and governing elite, began to lose some of its influence during this period. This can at least in part be explained by the rise of new nation-states such as Germany and Italy, which were often governed by individuals who had not received the classical education of the previous ruling elite and so had little or no knowledge of French.[12]

---

[7] J.-M. Guéhenno, 'Diplomatie culturelle: culture de France, culture d'Europe', *Politique Etrangère*, li (1986), 165–71.

[8] S. Akşin Somel, *Historical Dictionary of the Ottoman Empire* (Lanham, Md., 2003), p. 94.

[9] Roche and Pigniau, *Histoires*, p. 14.

[10] J.-M. Delaunay, *Des Palais en Espagne: l'Ecole des Hautes Etudes Hispaniques et la Casa de Velázquez au cœur des relations franco-espagnoles du XXe siècle (1898–1979)* (Madrid, 1994), p. 32.

[11] Roche and Pigniau, *Histoires*, pp. 14–22.

[12] S. Balous, *L'Action Culturelle de la France dans le monde* (Paris, 1970), p. 30.

The language war was also waged on the diplomatic field, as French diplomats defended the use of the French language in international organizations. Roche and Pigniau illustrate that in 1902, Jules Cambon, ambassador to Washington, realized that, in the conflict between the United States and Mexico, the Americans were trying to impose English as the working language at the International Court of Arbitration at The Hague.[13] Vigorous diplomatic action led by Théophile Delcassé, then minister of foreign affairs, convinced the Danish president of the court to recognize French as 'the universal language of law and diplomacy'. That situation prevailed until the Treaty of Versailles in 1919, when American president Woodrow Wilson insisted on its being expressed in both languages.

It was not until the first decades of the twentieth century that the Quai established a nascent cultural and linguistic policy specifically aimed at European countries. In order to co-ordinate the lecturers sent to work abroad, several bodies were created at the end of the 1900s. They embodied the beginning of France's foreign cultural policy in Europe. On 29 November 1907 the Comité Consultatif de l'Enseignement Français à l'Etranger was set up[14] and in 1910 the Office National des Universités et des Ecoles Françaises, a private association, was created. It was not a governmental body but was nevertheless backed by the Ministries of Foreign Affairs and Public Instruction.[15] In 1911, a Bureau des Ecoles et Œuvres Françaises à l'Etranger was created within the French Ministry of Foreign Affairs and was managed by two people.[16] This bureau was in charge of the co-ordination of information relating to the situation of educators and schools abroad, though in practice, teachers mainly dealt directly with the Embassy and consulates.

Alongside the policies set up by the Ministry of Foreign Affairs, there existed an active network of associations (either Paris-based or locally-based) which aimed at promoting French. A landmark event was the birth of the Alliance Française in 1883, created thanks to the initiative of French notables who wished to assemble 'friends of France' in foreign parts. In many countries, local committees were established, incorporated locally and linked to the AF in Paris. In 1890, for example, the Alliance Française of Melbourne was formed by Frenchmen and Australians. The AF was to develop throughout the twentieth century and had numerous committees

---

[13] Roche and Pigniau, *Histoires*, p. 22.

[14] Delaunay, *Des Palais en Espagne*, p. 49.

[15] B. Neveu, 'De l'instruction publique aux affaires étrangères: la politique culturelle extérieure de la France depuis 1910', *Commentaire*, xiii (1990), 351–4.

[16] A. Outrey, 'Histoire et principes de l'administration française des affaires étrangères', *Revue Française de Science politique*, iii (1953), 714–38.

in small provincial towns,[17] unlike the French institutes, which were only set up in important cities. The Mission Laïque Française was another association which focused on the creation of French schools outside Europe, opening a number of institutions in Salonica (1905), Ethiopia (1908), and Lebanon and Egypt (1909).

While the 1905 separation of church and state was detrimental to religious congregations within France, as the state withdrew its financial support, it was actually favourable for the dissemination of French language outside the Republic, as a few orders established themselves abroad, notably in Belgium and in the United Kingdom, to escape the French law.

Around 1910, the first French institutes were established in Florence (1907), Athens (1907), London (1910/13), Madrid (1910) and St. Petersburg (1911). In that respect, France was a pioneering country even though these cultural institutions did not directly emanate from the government and were either individual or semi-public ventures. State funding was available through several organizations, and notably the Pari Mutuel, a state betting organization similar to the Tote, managed by the Ministry of the Interior: in 1909 for example, it gave 20,000 francs to build the Institut Français in Madrid.[18] Some funding was also provided by the Colonial Office.

As a point of comparison, the British Council was founded only in 1934, though some British institutions existed independently, such as the Anglo-French Guild in Paris (1884), which was more akin to a university than a cultural association. The Deutsche Akademie was founded in 1925 and was to become the Goethe Institute in 1951. France was therefore a pioneering country in terms of cultural diplomacy.

French culture in London in the early twentieth century

In 1870–1914, there was a significant increase in the number of French nationals visiting or settling in London. There were about 10,000 French people living in the capital in 1911[19] and approximately 40,000 French people living in Britain.[20]

Relations between France and Britain were eased thanks to the 1904 Entente Cordiale, a convention and two declarations which settled their colonial disagreements. As John Keiger phrases it, 'it physically pushed

---

[17] F. Chaubet, *La Politique Culturelle Française et la diplomatie de la langue: l'Alliance Française, 1883–1940* (Paris, 2006).

[18] Delaunay, *Des Palais en Espagne*, p. 50.

[19] P. Gerbod, *Les Voyageurs Français à la découverte des Iles Britanniques du XVIIIème siècle à nos jours* (Paris, 1995), p. 134.

[20] Chaubet, *Politique Culturelle Française*, p. 111, table 9.

them apart by establishing respective spheres of influence in Siam and West Africa'. The most important point of this settlement was that France recognized Great Britain's position in Egypt, while the British did the same for France in Morocco. Interestingly enough, 'The agreements did not even contain a statement of general policy on friendlier relations'.[21] The Entente nevertheless provided fertile ground for future literary, intellectual and educational partnerships.

Various French societies were centralized in London: the Société Française de Bienfaisance (created 1842), the Société Nationale des Professeurs de Français en Angleterre (1881), the Union des Cuisiniers Pâtissiers Glaciers, the Société des Progrès de la Coiffure[22] and the Société Sportive Française de Londres[23] were among these. Some places were explicitly French, though not intended solely for the French community, such as the French Hospital (1867) the French Chamber of Commerce (1883), the Eglise Protestante Française (founded in 1550, and established in Soho Square since 1893) and the French Catholic chapels. There also existed societies aimed at promoting Franco-British relations which possessed branches in London, such as the Union Franco-Britannique du Tourisme. In terms of legal status, these societies did not come under France's 1901 law on associations but were governed by British law.[24]

French ambassadors in London played a key role in expanding intellectual relations between France and the United Kingdom. William Waddington (1883–93) was born in France but came from an Anglo-Scottish family and studied in France (Lycée St. Louis, Paris) and then at Trinity College, Cambridge. Waddington had been minister for public instruction (1873 and 1876–7), minister for foreign affairs (1877–9) and president of the council of ministers in 1879.[25] He has been largely overlooked by historians, but his political experiences, his nationality (he became French at the age of eighteen), his religious views (Protestant), his passion for archaeology and numismatics, and his election to the Académie des Inscriptions et Belles-

[21] J. Keiger, 'How the Entente Cordiale began', in *Cross-Channel Currents: 100 Years of the Entente Cordiale*, ed. R. Mayne, D. Johnson and R. Tombs (2004).

[22] La Courneuve, Archives du Ministère des Affaires Etrangères (hereafter AMAE), correspondance politique et commerciale, 1896–1918, Grande Bretagne, 161CPCOM/84, 'demandes de renseignements', letter from the French Consulate in London to the French minister of foreign affairs, 25 Nov. 1908. See also Rapoport's chapter, for further details of such French associations and societies.

[23] AMAE, 161CPCOM/82, 'Français à l'étranger'.

[24] AMAE, 161CPCOM/82, 'Français à l'étranger'.

[25] 'Waddington (William)', entry in *Dictionnaire des parlementaires français: notices biographiques sur les ministres, sénateurs et députés français de 1889 à 1940*, ed. J. Jolly (8 vols., Paris, 1960–77), viii. 3211.

Lettres in 1865[26] made him a central character in the furthering of Franco-British relations in all domains at the end of the nineteenth century. The same can be said of Paul Cambon, vice-president of the Alliance Française in 1883, French ambassador in London (1898–1920) and signatory of the 1904 Entente Cordiale, who was actively involved in the life of French cultural societies and schools in London.

Other protagonists of the propagation of French culture in London include teachers of French such as Marie d'Orliac, who established the Université des Lettres Françaises, or personalities like Max O'Rell, who was a journalist and lectured in Britain and in the USA, creating characters such as Jacques Bonhomme, the supposed embodiment of the Frenchman.[27]

The following pages try to identify how French cultural diplomacy was carried out in early twentieth-century London, the extent to which the French state was involved in this and, more generally, on whom cultural diplomacy relied. The emphasis will be on an elite culture, mostly developing in West London, though we are fully aware that this is but one facet of French culture in London at the time. More research needs to be done on popular culture and the French communities in North and East London in the first decades of the twentieth century.

The main component of France's 'soft power' in London: the teaching of French

The teaching of the French language was the core element of the dissemination of French culture in the early twentieth century, as it was thought that the best way to spread *l'esprit français* was through its language. In that respect, the emphasis on teaching in London was quite similar to other policies set up outside Europe by the government, individuals or religious communities.

The involvement of the state in the teaching of French began in the early twentieth century. Before that, it was carried out by religious communities, schools, live-in teachers or governesses and even internationalist ventures such as Louise Michel's International School, founded in 1892 in Fitzroy Square, near Euston,[28] whose aims were rooted in the socialist tradition, endeavouring to diminish French nationalist ideas.[29] The suggestion of a

---

[26] M. Mopin, 'Les trois vies de William Waddington', *Mémoire de la Fédération des Sociétés d'Histoire et d'Archéologie de l'Aisne*, xlvi (2001), 79–105.

[27] J. Verhoeven, *Jovial Bigotry: Max O'Rell and the Transnational Debate over Manners and Morals in 19th-Century France, Britain and the United States* (2012).

[28] BL, 'International school conducted by Louise Michel', *Prospectus* (1892).

[29] C. Bantman, *Anarchismes et anarchistes en France et en Grande-Bretagne, 1880–1914: échanges, représentations, transferts* (unpublished Université de Paris XIII-Villetaneuse PhD thesis, 2007).

lycée français appeared in the correspondence of Gabriel Hanoteau, minister of foreign affairs, as early as April 1897. This project was recommended by a member of the Société Nationale des Professeurs de Français en Angleterre and was viewed positively by the French Embassy in London: 'Such a school could have benefits in a country where there are no French institutions of the kind and where the organization of local teaching is in every respect different from what exists in France'.[30] Yet such an institution was not to be mentioned again until the early days of the First World War, when the Lycée Français was created within the Institut Français du Royaume-Uni.

As has been shown by Adèle Thomas, French nationals teaching their language in the United Kingdom were given a hard time in nineteenth-century Britain. Popular consciousness held that they taught long and tedious lessons and they were consequently largely undervalued by the British. This stereotype changed in their favour when they started to associate themselves, notably within the Société Nationale des Professeurs de Français en Angleterre in 1881. This society propagated the idea that not every French speaker could be a good teacher – as had previously been assumed in the case of refugees and migrants – and that only trained men and women should be allowed to teach the language.[31]

The quality of teaching therefore became a major concern in the first decades of the twentieth century – so much so that the French ambassador was frequently sent reports about the teaching of French in specific schools.[32] Stress was also laid on teaching quality and training at the Maison des Institutrices Françaises en Angleterre, under the patronage of Paul Cambon and the archbishops of Canterbury and Westminster. This institution was founded in 1897 and was located at 18 Lancaster Gate, Hyde Park, West London. It was inaugurated in 1903 by Princess Henry de Battenberg, the youngest child of Queen Victoria, and several upper-class and aristocratic ladies were present on that day. A few months later the French president, Emile Loubet, visited this Maison during his official visit to King Edward VII. In 1903, 168 female schoolteachers lived there, either on a long- or a short-term basis. It was within this home that the Association des Institutrices Françaises was created, also in 1903. The

[30] AMAE, 161CPCOM/81 'Français en Angleterre', letter from the French Embassy in London (political direction) to Monsieur Hanoteau, minister of foreign affairs, 28 Apr. 1897: 'Un établissement de cette nature pourrait rendre des services dans un pays où il n'existe aucune institution française de ce genre et où l'organisation de l'enseignement local est de tous points différents du régime français'.

[31] A. Thomas, 'Les professeurs de français en Angleterre', in *Cordiale Angleterre: regards trans-Manche à la Belle Epoque*, ed. F. Poirier (Paris, 2010).

[32] AMAE, 161CPCOM/ 82.

Maison, which did not solely accommodate French teachers, was part of the London Francophile network, organizing literary conferences or musical evenings for its residents and literary benefactors.[33] Some members of the board were involved in other French societies in London, such as Eugène Karminsky, director of the Crédit Lyonnais, who was treasurer of the Maison des Institutrices and was to occupy the same position within the Université des Lettres Françaises in 1910. The female teachers selected to live in the Maison had to meet certain requirements, notably related to their own education, which was expected to be 'superior', their morals, and the likelihood of their succeeding as French teachers.

It was only in the early years of the twentieth century that the French government involved itself in education policy abroad, setting up teaching exchanges with Germany, Austria and Britain and therefore operating a selection of the individuals meant to teach French outside France. In the summer of 1904, the Office d'Informations et d'Etude, whose role was to register French and foreign students wishing to be language assistants either in France or abroad, formalized a link with the Board of Education which had two similar offices, one for England and the other for Scotland.[34] This marked the beginning of an active co-operation between the two countries and improved teaching quality.

Outside the educational system, associations such as the Alliance Française provided French courses for children and adults as well as various cultural activities. The British Federation of the Alliance Française (BFAF) was a prominent society in early twentieth-century London and still exists today, mostly as a language centre.[35] The AF's first English committee was formed under the name of Comité Regional de Londres in 1885 in London. Its first president was Charles Cassal, a member of the 1849 legislative assembly of the Second Republic who had fled France in 1852 following Bonaparte's *coup d'état*. He subsequently ended his days in London, where he lectured in French at University College London.[36] It was only in 1908 at the Franco-British Exhibition at White City that the British Federation of the Alliance Française was officially formed, with the endorsement of Paul Cambon.[37]

---

[33] AMAE, Services des Œuvres Françaises à l'Etranger, 417QO/19, leaflet of the Maison des Institutrices Françaises en Angleterre.

[34] AMAE, 161CPCOM/47, letter from the Ministry of Public Instruction and Fine Arts to the minister of foreign affairs, 15 June 1904.

[35] The history of the British Federation of the Alliance Française is difficult to record as its archives are closed to the public, researchers included. It would be interesting to compare this institution with the Institut Français du Royaume-Uni, created a few decades later.

[36] 'Cassal (Hughes-Charles-Stanislas)', entry in *Dictionnaire des parlementaires français*, ed. A. Robert and G. Cougny (5 vols., Paris, 1889), i. 601.

[37] Website of the Alliance Française de Londres <http://www.alliancefrancaise.org.uk/m_history.htm> [accessed 8 June 2012].

The BFAF was a pioneering society in London in that it organized talks throughout the British Isles as well as school exchanges, bestowed prizes to pupils and teachers and ran a book-lending service. The main aim of the British Federation was to inform audiences of what was happening in France, culturally and socially, and conversely, to make sure that 'the French would learn to understand the English'.[38]

Several societies were affiliated to the BFAF, consequently encouraging its dynamism. Both the Societé Nationale Française à Londres and the Société Nationale des Professeurs de Français en Angleterre formed part of the regional committee of the British Isles. Similarly, following the 1904 Entente Cordiale, the Alliance Littéraire Scientifique et Artistique Franco-Anglaise joined the AF. The BFAF offered a large variety of lectures, a prominent feature in this kind of institution in the early twentieth century. What is more, it provides a typical example of London as the central point from where societies could spread out to the provinces, in Liverpool, Manchester, Glasgow, etc.

Finally, even though it was not their first priority, religious communities, such as the Catholic and Protestant churches, promoted the French language as well as a specific image of France through their activities, as the priests and ministers were French and delivered services in that language. Their ability to speak French was an essential requirement, as was made obvious after the death of M. Dégremont, the minister of the Protestant church in Soho Square in 1913. When looking for a successor, the Eglise Protestante Française demanded that the French Ministry of Foreign Affairs should intercede with the British ambassador in Paris in favour of the appointment of a French Protestant minister. This linguistic issue was linked to broader questions of the French Protestant church of London, and in particular its audience.[39]

Case study: the Université des Lettres Françaises (1910) – towards the creation of l'Institut Français du Royaume-Uni (1913)

The French Institute of London was created under the name of the Université des Lettres Françaises (ULF) by Marie d'Orliac in October 1910.[40] It acquired its current title on 30 September 1913, when the ULF registered under the Companies Act of 1908, and still exists today in Queensberry

---

[38] 'Les Français apprendraient à connaître les Anglais' (website of the Alliance Française de Londres <http://www.alliancefrancaise.org.uk/m_history.htm> [accessed 8 June 2012].

[39] AMAE, 161CPCOM/82, letter from the French Embassy in London to M. Pichon, minister of foreign affairs, 29 Aug. 1913.

[40] L. Auer, 'Marie d'Orliac, fondatrice de l'Institut Français du Royaume-Uni', available at the Institut Français du Royaume-Uni, 2012.

Place, South Kensington (West London). It has been a leading institution in the furthering of French culture, through lectures, language classes, a library and drama plays in the first part of the twentieth century.

First established at Marble Arch, the ULF was predominantly managed by women. Marie d'Orliac, aged nineteen, arrived in the UK in 1907 from Auvergne. She attended a summer school in Oxford[41] and then became a teacher at South Hampstead High School, North London. Marie d'Orliac had connections in British society and the London Francophile elite. Her venture notably received the moral and financial support of Lord and Lady Askwith, the former having been appointed at the Board of Trade by Lloyd George in 1907 and subsequently becoming chief industrial commissioner in 1911. Between 1911 and 1919 he chaired the fair wages advisory committee. Lady Askwith published two novels under the name of Ellen Graham and was active on several government committees.[42]

The French Embassy in London acknowledged the necessity and value of such a venture and Ambassador Paul Cambon became its patron. The ULF was officially accredited by the British authorities (London County Council and the Board of Trade) in 1911 and the French government became linked to the project in 1913, through the Université de Lille. That year, the ULF became an academic department of the Université de Lille, and it was then that it became the Institut Français du Royaume-Uni.

The creation of the Université des Lettres Françaises in London was a unique undertaking, differing from that of the British branch of the Alliance Française, which was backed by the flagship association in Paris. It also differed from the establishment of other French institutes abroad. That of Florence was opened in 1907 thanks to the work of Julien Lachaire, who founded it as an annexe to the University of Grenoble, at which he was a lecturer. His objective was for French students reading Italian at Grenoble to have a pied-à-terre where Italian people would come as well, thus participating in a cultural and linguistic exchange.[43] From the very first days, the French Institute in Florence was a branch of Grenoble University, and this was the case for the institutes in Madrid and St. Petersburg, which belonged respectively to the universities of Toulouse and Paris.[44] By contrast

[41] Interview with Cyril Kinsky (grandson of Marie d'Orliac) conducted by Charlotte Faucher on 13 March 2012.

[42] R. Lowe, 'Askwith, George Ranken, Baron Askwith (1861–1942)', *ODNB*.

[43] I. Renard, *L'Institut Français de Florence 1900–1920, un épisode des relations franco-italiennes au début du 20ème siècle* (Rome, 2001).

[44] See the map of French institutes created by French universities in J.-M. Delaunay, *Méfiance cordiale: les relations Franco-Espagnoles de la fin du XIXe siècle à la première guerre mondiale* (2 vols., Paris, 2010), i. 638.

the Université des Lettres Françaises was during its first three years an independent body which then became part of a French university.

Besides, unlike the French Institute in Florence, d'Orliac did not aim her Université at French people willing to stay in London, but rather designed it as 'the extension in Great Britain, especially among women and young girls, of "la vraie culture française" by giving them the opportunity of attending courses of good French lectures on various subjects, and hearing at the monthly meetings some of the best known Parisian lecturers'.[45] In its first year, the Université was highly gender divided. The live-in teachers were all women,[46] but most of the members of the executive committee were men, and, more strikingly, Marie d'Orliac was never director or president of the executive council. Women of influence were not present in the managing body of the ULF, but some (the duchesses of Somerset and Rutland, Madame la duchesse de Rohan, Madame Alphonse Daudet)[47] were part of the comité d'honneur.

Early newspaper articles insisted on the role of the ULF for the furthering of girls' and women's education. The *Evening Standard* published a long article a couple of weeks after the opening of d'Orliac's Université on 'the Anglo-French club for women' opened in the premises of the Université. This club was described both as 'cours de jeunes filles ... to girls who are at an age when the little intimate talks on literature, art, music, and feminine matters have all charm of novelty' as well as 'a social club' and a lecturing place for women of experience.[48] Another journalist, reporting on the Université as a whole, stated that 'Special lectures on the art of women, reserved for the feminine public, and historical lectures, intended more particularly for men, completed the programme'.[49] In its first years, the Université was a place which celebrated the best Frenchwomen of the period. For instance, the novelist Marcelle Tinayre gave a lecture on 'Women and friendship'.[50] Although she is now relatively forgotten, Tinayre was extremely popular in her time, as demonstrated by the long chapter devoted to her in Winifred Stephens's *French Novelists To-day* (second series), where she is described as 'French of the French'.[51] Her novel *La Maison du péché*, published in 1900,

---

[45] Archives of the South Hampstead High School, school magazine, 1910.

[46] 1911 UK census.

[47] Anon., 'French thought in London', *Morning Leader*, 11 Oct. 1910.

[48] Anon., 'The new cercle-social and literary rendezvous for French and English women', *Evening Standard*, 10 Oct. 1910.

[49] Archives of the Institut du Français du Royaume-Uni, 'French literature – University in London', [no date].

[50] Anon., '"Les Femmes et l'Amitié", Conference by Mme Marcelle Tinayre', *The Times*, 31 March 1911.

[51] W. Stephens, *French Novelists of To-day* (2nd ser., London and New York, 1908), p. 46.

was also highly praised by James Joyce. Among the other guest-lecturers was Mlle. Helène Miropolski, a twenty-four-year-old barrister from Paris.[52]

Louise Michel's aforementioned Université, the International School, relied on internationalist and socialist ideals, and was designed to cater for all classes; by contrast, d'Orliac's institution was much narrower in its aims. The Université des Lettres Françaises was an elite establishment which promoted a very restricted view of early twentieth-century French culture for 'ladies and girls of social position'.[53] Its location was in keeping with the audience that the Université wanted to attract: 'Marble Arch House, the home of the society, with its handsome rooms, spacious hall and staircases, and its atmosphere of social and intellectual Paris, is likely to become one of the most popular rendezvous during the coming winter'.[54]

In January 1913 the ULF started publishing *La Revue Française*, a short-lived monthly magazine of which only six issues appeared. It contained the programme of lectures and classes to be given at the institute, a portrait of a key personality in the life of the Université, book and drama reviews, extracts of novels, and exercises for the people taking the 'cours par correspondance'. There was a 'Femina' section devoted to women's fashion, and most advertisements targeted a female audience, either promoting hair salons or clothing shops where one could buy 'the latest Parisian creations'. French bookshops and pharmacies,[55] notably the Pharmacie Jozeau on Piccadilly, described as the pharmacy of the French Embassy and French Hospital, found their place in the commercial announcements.

The Université organized series of lectures on French literature, comparative literature, history, diction and drama, and 'arts de la femme'.[56] From spring 1913 it was divided into sections, namely the 'artistic and literary department', 'language classes and French institutions' and the 'commercial department'.[57]

Once the Université became the Institut Français du Royaume-Uni in 1913, the emphasis on women's education was to disappear in favour of the hosting of French academics and classes for Lille students and British people, thus becoming more similar to other French cultural institutes abroad. Nevertheless, it retained some features of the Université's internal

[52] Anon., 'French Portia in London, woman lawyer tells of her success, beautiful advocate' *Daily Express*, 7 Dec. 1911.

[53] Anon., 'Les Femmes et l'Amitié'.

[54] Anon., 'The new cercle-social'.

[55] *La Revue Française*, i (21 Jan. 1913).

[56] Nottinghamshire Archives, DD/H/178/161–55, Université des Lettres Françaises, Marble Arch House, London, programme of courses, 1911.

[57] 'Programme de l'Institut', *La Revue Française*, iv (25 Apr. 1913).

organization, notably the three main departments. In 1913, the Institut Français also spread geographically, opening branches in Liverpool, Manchester, Tunbridge Wells, Leeds, Bradford and Harrogate, and sending them lecturers and notable speakers, as the Alliance Française was also doing.

On the eve of the First World War, the Université des Lettres Françaises had transformed itself from an elitist society, primarily aimed at upper-class girls and women, into an Institut Français with roots in the Université de Lille which managed slightly to broaden its audience, through the *lycée* (1915) and its activities in the British provinces.

Cultural diplomacy through fairs and events in London

So far, cultural diplomacy has been examined as a phenomenon spread through institutions, societies and bi-national agreements mostly set up by the embassies. But it is also necessary to concentrate on specific events, as they illustrate the effort made to promote particular aspects and often resonate beyond the moment they occurred, bearing a strong 'memory value'[58] and affecting popular consciousness.

The first major Franco-British cultural event of the twentieth century was the Franco-British Exhibition in 1908,[59] which was a decisive step in showcasing the 'cordiality' of the 1904 Entente and was studied in depth for its centenary anniversary in 2008.[60] This exhibition, held in White City from May to October, strengthened the cultural and commercial ties between the two countries and was described in laudatory terms by contemporaries.[61] Its success was visible in the numbers of visitors: nearly 8.5 million people came to 'the Franco' as it was commonly named. There were in total twenty palaces and eight buildings, each of them devoted to specific themes such as education, science, arts, textile, etc.,[62] embodying a testament to the progression towards genuine Franco-British friendship. Martyn Cornick shows that this commercial and cultural event had strong political and

---

[58] This phrase is used to describe the 1908 Franco-British Exhibition by D. Kelly and T. Jackson, 'The Franco-British exhibition of 1908: legacies and memories 100 years on', in *Synergies Royaume-Uni et Irlande: 'regards sur l'entente culturelle'*, ii (2009), 11–23.

[59] M. Cornick, 'Putting the seal on the Entente: the Franco-British exhibition, London, May–October 1908', *Franco-British Studies*, xxxv (2004), 133–44.

[60] See *Synergies Royaume-Uni et Irlande: 'regards sur l'entente culturelle'*, ii (2009).

[61] M. Cornick, '"Sceller l'Entente": l'importance politique et internationale de l'exposition franco-britannique, Londres, 1908', in *L'Entente Cordiale: cent ans de relations culturelles franco-britanniques (1904–2004)*, ed. D. Cooper-Richet and M. Rapoport (Paris, 2006), pp. 245–60, at p. 245.

[62] M. Cornick, 'Sceller l'Entente', p. 250.

diplomatic significance.[63] The French president Armand Fallières and the minister of foreign affairs Stephen Pichon came to England in late May 1908 and were invited to Buckingham Palace, where they delivered speeches stressing the collaboration of the two peoples. Commentators of the time saw in this visit the hope for a strong Franco-British alliance which could hinder the progress of Germany, which was acting against the French interest in northern Africa. What was designed as a pleasure exhibition thus also served as a means to assert Franco-British ties, spreading the hope of a peaceful situation within the European countries.

On a larger scale, the British issued repeated invitations to the Musique de la Garde Républicaine, the military marching bands of the French Republican Guard. In 1905, one of the conditions laid down for the bands to play in Britain was that their performances should only occur during charitable events. That year, the French Ministry of War replied positively to the Entente Cordiale League, which was organizing a series of events to raise money aimed at supporting the poorest members of the French community in London and Britain. These events were part of the Queen's Fund for the unemployed.[64] This example demonstrates that cultural diplomacy was not always initiated from Paris, even when it involved symbols of the French Republic, as it was the Entente Cordiale League, based in London, which first contacted the Ministry of War (which proved slightly reluctant to release its musicians). The concerts, which finally took place in London at the end of February 1906, helped with the promotion of French patriotism, and manifested Franco-British friendship and French support after the sudden death of Edward Grey, British minister of foreign affairs, which had occurred earlier that month.[65]

The progressive engagement of the state in the field of cultural diplomacy

'Culture is another name for propaganda',[66] stated Marc Fumaroli in his controversial essay on state and culture *L'État Culturel: essai sur une religion moderne*, published in 1991. It seems that the state started to rely partly on an institutionalized form of cultural action for its external propaganda in the early years of the Third Republic, and the case of London provides fruitful insight into the creation of a French cultural diplomacy.

---

[63] M. Cornick, 'Sceller l'Entente', pp. 250ff.

[64] AMAE, 161CPCOM/81, letter from Paul Cambon to Maurice Rouvier, président du conseil, 13 Dec. 1905.

[65] AMAE, 161CPCOM/81, letter from J. E. Lyndall to the minister of foreign affairs, 22 Feb. 1906.

[66] M. Fumaroli, *L'Etat Culturel: essai sur une religion moderne* (Paris, 1991), p. 20.

In the late nineteenth century the French government, through its ambassadors in London, encouraged French societies in the capital which were promoting French civilization by granting them medals and making small donations of money or books.[67] The government also took part in cultural exchanges. In 1901 the gift of a Sèvres vase was offered to the British Museum, and the following year the French Ministry of War sent over books and letters to the British Museum, the Public Record Office and the Historical Manuscripts Commission. The French state controlled the image of France, for example hindering the lending of flags, weapons and trophies related to the 1871 Paris Commune for the 1901 London military exhibition, on the grounds that: 'It seems inappropriate in any case to present souvenirs of our last civil war amongst the collections exhibited in a foreign city'.[68] The First World War speeded up the definition of the image of France, as the state delineated its foreign cultural policy. It was in this context that it partly took over the Institut Français du Royaume-Uni via the Université de Lille. Beyond its cultural and linguistic functions, the IFRU became a clearly political forum from 1914 onwards and was to be the preferred site for French and British politicians to unveil the aims of their respective country's policies, and developments in Franco-British relations. The inauguration of the Lycée Français in March 1915 gave the French ambassador to Britain, Paul Cambon, the opportunity to express his hopes that it would become a permanent institution, thus enabling 'the spreading of French culture as distinct from German culture'.[69] This was the first time in the history of the French Institute that one of its sections was pointed out as instrumental in diminishing the prestige of German civilization (which, according to a Belgian newspaper, Cambon had described as 'odious').[70] Cambon was to take this anti-German rhetoric further at various events at the Lycée, stressing the differences between French, Belgian and British cultures, on the one hand, and German culture, on the other.

Propaganda became one of the main concerns within the French Foreign Office during the First World War. In 1914, la Maison de la Presse was created, including a propaganda service within which a section was dedicated to propaganda in the Allied countries. Building on the 1911 Bureau des Ecoles et Œuvres Françaises à l'Etranger, the Service des Œuvres Françaises à l'Etranger (SOFE) was created in 1920, partly to manage the

[67] AMAE, 161CPCOM/81.

[68] AMAE, 161CPCOM/81: '[i]l … parait peu convenable en tout cas, de faire figurer, parmi les collections exposées dans une ville étrangère, des souvenirs de notre dernière guerre civile'.

[69] Anon., 'New French schools in London', *Manchester Guardian*, 25 March 1915.

[70] Anon., *La Chronique*, 29 March 1915.

French institutes abroad and also because:

> Our literature and humanities, our arts, our industrial civilization, our ideas, have at all times had a strong attraction for foreign nations. Our universities, our schools abroad are truly centres of propaganda in favour of France. They are a weapon in the hands of our public powers. This is why the Ministry of Foreign Affairs and its agents abroad must direct and control initiatives, inspire and promote the diffusion of French thought and culture at all costs, with the conviction that it is one of the most efficient forms of action abroad.[71]

In the early nineteen-twenties, the creation of the SOFE therefore helped to establish the predominance of the Quai d'Orsay (over the Ministère de l'Instruction Publique et des Beaux Arts, and later the Ministère de la Culture) but did not prevent private initiatives from continuing to disseminate French culture abroad, which these bodies did all the more eagerly as they were in desperate need of money.

---

[71] 'Nos lettres, nos arts, notre civilisation industrielle, nos idées ont exercé de tout temps un puissant attrait sur les nations étrangères. Nos universités, nos écoles à l'étranger sont de véritables foyers de propagande en faveur de la France. Elles constituent une arme entre les mains de nos pouvoirs publics. C'est pourquoi le ministère des Affaires Etrangères et ses agents de l'extérieur doivent diriger et contrôler les initiatives, inspirer et favoriser à tout prix la pénétration intellectuelle française, avec la conviction qu'elle est une des formes les plus sûrement efficaces de notre action à l'étranger' (from a speech by the auditor of the budget at the Chambre des Députés, quoted in Roche and Pigniau, *Histoires*, p. 38).

Chapters 12–14: The French in Second World War London

Map 12.1 (on the following pages) refers to places mentioned in the text in chapters 12–14.

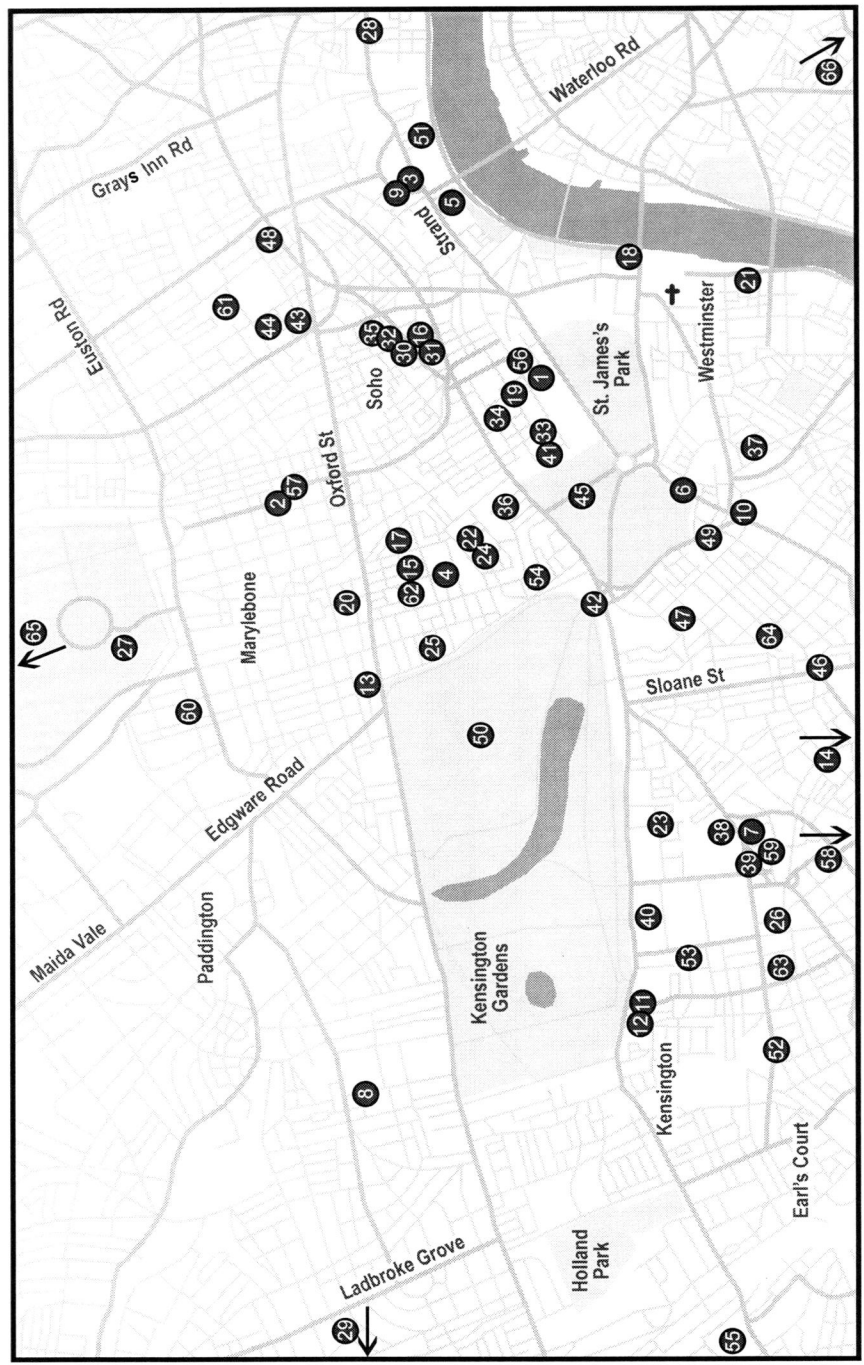

Map 12.1. Places mentioned in the text (Base map: London c.1930)

Key to Map 12.1

1. Headquarters of the Free French, 4 Carlton Gardens
2. BBC, Portland Place
3. BBC, Bush House, Strand
4. Connaught Hotel, 16 Carlos Place
5. Savoy Hotel, Strand
6. Rubens Hotel, 39 Buckingham Palace Road
7. Rembrandt Hotel, 11 Thurloe Place
8. Hyde Park Hotel, Leinster Square
9. Waldorf Hotel, Aldwych
10. Grosvenor Hotel, 101 Buckingham Palace Road
11. Hôtel de Vere, de Vere Gardens
12. Kensington Palace Hotel, de Vere Gardens
13. Mount Royal Hotel, Bryanston Street
14. Ashdown Park Hotel, Coulsdon (off map c.12 miles)
15. Savile Club, 69 Brook Street
16. Hôtel de Boulogne, Gerrard Street
17. Claridges, 49 Brook Street
18. St. Stephen's House, Victoria Embankment
19. French Intelligence Services, 3 St. James's Square
20. BCRA, 10 Duke Street
21. Free French Navy and the Français de Grande Bretagne Association, Westminster House, Dean Stanley Street
22. Free French Women's Barracks, 42 Hill Street
23. Free French Women's Barracks, Moncorvo House and Hackin House, Ennismore Gardens
24. Commissariat National de l'Intérieur, 19 Hill Street
25. Union des Français d'Outre Mer, 33 Upper Brook Street
26. Free French Air Force, French Institute, Queensberry Place
27. Bedford College, Regent's Park
28. Havas French Press Agency, 85 Fleet Street
29. Queen Charlotte's Hospital, Du Cane Road (off map c.1 mile)
30. Le Berlemont, 49 Dean Street
31. Chez Victor, 45 Wardour Street
32. Chez Rose, Frith Street
33. Prunier's, 72–73 St. James's Street
34. L'Ecu de France, Jermyn Street
35. L'Escargot, 48 Greek Street
36. Le Coq d'Or, Stratton Street
37. Westminster Cathedral
38. Brompton Oratory
39. 69 Cromwell Gardens
40. Royal Albert Hall
41. Le Petit Club Français, 13 St. James's Place
42. Allies' Club, Hyde Park Corner
43. YMCA, Great Russell Street
44. Bedford Square
45. Green Park

46. Sloane Square
47. Belgrave Square
48. Bloomsbury Square
49. Statue of Maréchal Foch, Lower Grosvenor Gardens
50. Hyde Park
51. King's College London, Strand
52. 33 Cromwell Road
53. Maison de l'Institut, Queen's Gate
54. 7–8 Seamore Place
55. Empire Hall
56. Athenaeum Club, Pall Mall
57. Queen's Hall, Langham Place
58. Royal Victoria Patriotic School, Wandsworth (London Reception Centre (LRC), off map c.2 miles)
59. *La France Libre*, Thurloe Street
60. Alliance Française, 1 Dorset Square
61. Senate House, University of London
62. 15 Grosvenor Square
63. 53 Stanhope Gardens
64. 108 Eaton Place
65. Frognal Rise, Hampstead (off map c.2 miles)
66. 41 Birchwood Road, Petts Wood (off map c.12.5 miles)

301

12. Mapping Free French London: places, spaces, traces

Debra Kelly

The arrival in London in June 1940 of the man who would become the leader of 'Free France' and who would be joined by a variety of French men and women who refused to accept Marshal Pétain's armistice with Germany, or who escaped military attack or incarceration by the Germans after the fall of France, created a very different kind of French presence in the British capital from that which can previously be identified, although it might be said to share some characteristics with French exiles and refugees from previous centuries. The continuing interest of both scholars and the public in wartime London is clear. The events organized in June 2010 to commemorate the seventieth anniversary of the arrival of de Gaulle, and the presence of the Free French in London during the war, attracted large audiences at the French Institute in South Kensington and considerable media interest in the UK and France, as did the visit by the then French president to Carlton Gardens, the BBC and the Chelsea Hospital.[1] Yet, while prominence is given by historians to the key figures and events of the period, knowledge of the ordinary men and women who joined de Gaulle, and indeed of those who chose to fight the Nazi Occupation of France while remaining wary of the Gaullist vision and ambitions, and of their everyday lives in London, is much more fragmentary, dispersed in memoirs, novels, public and private archives, and in some visual evidence.

The French presence in Second World War London, whether already resident or added to by the Free French – or the 'Fighting French', as sources of the period often refer to them – was complex, made up of people with very different backgrounds and origins, whether social, political, religious, generational or based on gender. The main aim of this chapter is to present

[1] I am grateful to the main organizers of the 70th anniversary conference 'L'Appel du 18 juin. La Flamme de la Résistance', 16–17 June 2010 – Rod Kedward, Matthew Cobb and Julian Jackson – for suggesting that I work on the idea of 'mapping Free French London' for a paper presented there. The conference was hosted by the French Institute in London, and some of the sessions and other details can be consulted online at <http://culturetheque.org. uk/la-flamme-de-la-resistance> [accessed 14 Jan. 2013].

diverse aspects of the London of the Free French, and to situate where those French citizens lived and worked, and what sort of traces (if any) they have left. It seeks, therefore, to bring together both well- and lesser-known personalities, places and events through a range of disparate sources. It is not a principal aim of this chapter to analyse in detail the 'who and why' of the members of the resident French community who either stayed in or left London, or of those French nationals who may have arrived to escape the German Occupation, or indeed to continue the fight against the Nazis while not necessarily joining the Gaullist camp, although there is necessarily reference to some of the complexities of this.

This study also provides a context for the stories of such ordinary French men and women as Gaston Eve (French born with an English father and French mother whose family returned to England in the 1930s and who left a reserved occupation in an arms factory to join the Free French); Maurice Vila (another young man of dual British and French nationality, called up by the French Consulate in London with instructions to proceed to France in February 1940, and who then spent two years trying to get back to London, passing through the Empress Hall refugee reception centre and the Royal Patriotic School in Wandsworth once there); Louis Delanchy (who spent time in a Spanish prison before reaching London); Barthélémy Borelly (who escaped from incarceration in Russia with the group of men known as 'the Russians' led by Captain Billotte); Jeanne Hart (née Ducruet, married to an Englishman, living in south-east London before the war, who worked as a telephonist at de Gaulle's headquarters); Mlle. Claire Toutain (British born of French parents with dual British/French nationality); and indeed British citizens such as Lesley Boyde (née Gerrard) from Douglas in the Isle of Man, who had spent time in France before the war, and who much preferred life in the French women volunteers' (Corps des Volontaires Françaises) barracks to the training in the British Auxiliary Territorial Service (ATS) (Figures 12.1 and 12.2).[2]

---

[2] See the war diary of Sgt. Gaston Eve: 'Arriving at 4 Carlton Gardens early morning I presented my French birth certificate and waited there over three days for the formalities. For the first time in my life I drank wine with my meals. I found myself very disorientated because I had an English upbringing and an English accent. Even though my speech was fluent it was lacking many words. The facilities for eating and sleeping at Carlton Gardens were very inadequate because there were so many there, a mixture of sailors, soldiers and aviators waiting to be posted. I had no military training whatever and so was submitted to much good humoured teasing' (<http://www.gastoneve.org.uk> [accessed 14 Jan. 2013]); IWM Documents 6470, private papers of M. Vila; IWM Documents 5267, Free French diary for 1942 (Jeanne Hart); IWM Documents 459, private papers of Miss C. E. Toutain; IWM Documents 270, private papers of Mrs. L. Boyde. The latter also gives an official document that lists all those women who were promoted to the grade of 'Aspirant' on

Figure 12.1. A head and shoulder portrait of a Free French soldier in uniform.
War Artists' Advisory Committee commission, Henry Lamb (MC) (RA),
1941, oil, height 508mm × width 406mm. Art.IWM, ART LD 888.

These men and women all joined the Free French Forces in some capacity, and their memories live on in archived papers and photographs, as do those of people who are better known through their published memoirs and official

24 July 1945: Lucienne Gerard; Annie Gayot; Denise Lacroix; Georgette Lafaille-Morfin; Suzanne Laurent-Reboul; Marthe Martin; Julie Noesen; Gisèle Orget; Marie-Antoinette Pary; Dominique Roy; Denise Sarrau – and Leslie [*sic*] Gerrard, out of alphabetical order, presumably since she is British. See also the stories of Louis Delanchy, Barthélémy Borelly and those of their other companions who appear in the same photograph at <http://www.francaislibres.fr> [accessed 14 Jan. 2013].

Figure 12.2. A member of the newly formed 'Corps Femina' [later the Corps des Volontaires Françaises], the equivalent of the British Auxiliary Territorial Service (ATS), on parade. IWM, KY 14981.

To aid in their training several of the ATS were sent to the Corps Femina. It consisted mainly of French women although some of its members were British-born wives of Frenchmen who were ineligible for the ATS.

photographs, from those close to de Gaulle (either in the long or short term) such as Jean-Louis Crémieux-Brilhac, Colonel Passy, André Gillois, Jean Pierre-Bloch and de Gaulle's 'National Committee' – René Pleven, Maurice Dejean, André Diethelm, René Cassin, Generals Gentilhomme and Valin, and Admirals Muselier and Thierry d'Argenlieu; to headquarters personnel such as Elisabeth de Miribel, who became de Gaulle's secretary until 1942; to those involved in the now celebrated French programmes

Figure 12.3. French officers and men escaped from German prison camps arrive in London to join de Gaulle giving the 'V' sign to a London policeman as they leave the railway station on arrival in London (10 September 1941). IWM, PL 6723B.

broadcast from the BBC, known by the names of Pierre Bourdan, Jean Marin and Jacques Duchesne, with Pierre Dac and Jean Oberlé;[3] to Tereska Torrès in her published diary and more infamous fictional account of 'life and love in the Free French Army', *Women's Barracks*; or in numerous historical accounts, such as those of the 127 inhabitants of the Breton Ile de Sein who arrived between 20 and 26 June 1940, or the group of men known as 'the Russians' ('Les Russes') who escaped incarceration first as German prisoners of war in 1940 and then from Russia once Stalin joined the Allies, arriving in London in September 1941 (Figure 12.3).[4]

[3] See the following chapter by Martyn Cornick, for more details.

[4] In addition to de Gaulle's memoirs, see, e.g., the memoirs of Jean-Louis Crémieux-Brilhac, *La France Libre: de l'Appel du 18 juin à la Libération* (Paris, 1996); Col. Passy, *Mémoires du chef des services secrets de la France libre* (Paris, 2000); J. Pierre-Bloch, *Londres capitale de la France Libre* (Paris, 1986); A. Gillois, *Histoire secrète des Français à Londres de 1940–4* (Paris, 1973); E. de Miribel, *La Liberté souffre violence* (Paris, 2010); J. Oberlé, *Jean Oberlé vous parle ...* (Paris, 1945), and also his *Images anglaises ou l'Angleterre occupé* (1943); T. Torrès, *Une Française Libre: journal 1939–45* (Paris, 2000) and *Women's Barracks* (1950; New York, 2005). See also the historical accounts of, e.g., P. Accoce, *Les Français à Londres 1940–1* (Paris, 1989); F. Broche, *L'Epopée de la France Libre 1940–6* (Paris, 2000); G.-M. Benamou, *Les Rebelles de l'an 40: les premiers Français racontent* (Paris, 2010); M. and J.-P. Cointet, *La*

The concept of 'mapping' is considered here integral to an analysis of the wartime French presence. Why such a 'mapping', then? The sources regarding sites associated with the Free French are frequently vague and sometimes contradictory, and this chapter adds some precision both to well-known and less well-known places and events that involved the activities of the Free French. It therefore assumes an underlying premise that one way to re-engage with the history of the Free French is through the physical and symbolic traces of their presence in London during the Second World War and since. It seeks to bring together the histories and stories of some of the places and spaces associated with the French during the war in order to 'map' their spatial and temporal presence there. This mapping documents, on the one hand, the 'real' spaces where high politics, military tactics and intelligence-gathering were discussed and, on the other, where the Free French lived and socialized. However, such a mapping in the case of the Free French necessarily also represents the 'imaginary' space of London as used to great effect in the creation of the idea of 'Free France' as simultaneously a reality and myth, and on which this chapter concludes.

Maps have, of course, always been used in the study of history, and are essential for the analysis of military and political history. Here, however, the aim is rather different. Currently, cultural geographers and cultural historians share many of the same preoccupations, and some of the same philosophical and political starting points. As the cultural geographer Doreen Massey has noted: 'The spatial ... is precisely one of the sources of the temporal ... One way of thinking about all this is to say that the spatial is integral to the production of history, and thus to the possibility of politics, just as the temporal is to geography'.[5] It is no coincidence that around the time of the extensive seventieth anniversary commemoration events of de Gaulle's arrival in London, an *Atlas de la France Libre* was published, or that the Fondation Charles de Gaulle created an iPhone application which offers, via some thirty places associated with de Gaulle, a discovery of key scenes of Free France in combat. These chronological and cartographic points of reference allow navigation across the Free French world, from London to Brazzaville, from Algiers to Paris, thereby allowing a (virtual) movement across time and space.

France Libre à Londres: renaissance d'un état (Brussels, 1990); H. Michel, *Histoire de la France Libre* (Paris, 1967); J.-L. Crémieux-Brilhac, *Ici Londres, 1940–4: les voix de la liberté* (5 vols., Paris, 1975); on 'Les Russes', see J.-L. Crémieux-Brilhac, *Prisonniers de la liberté: l'odyssée des 218 évadés par l'URSS, 1940–4* (Paris, 2004) and Fig 12.3.

[5] D. Massey, 'Politics and space/time', *New Left Review*, i, 196 (1992), 84.

Figure 12.4. French Embassy staff and families leaving London. IWM, PL 8856.

Members of the French Embassy, accompanied by the bulk of the French Mission which had been established in London since the war, leaving London on their way back to France to the French government headquarters at Vichy.

'A sober, well-behaved ... and law-abiding community':[6] the French in London on the eve of the Second World War

In order to provide a context for this 'mapping', it is clear from the preceding chapters that the French who arrived to join de Gaulle were arriving in a capital with a history of receiving a wide range of French nationals seeking either refuge or new opportunities, or a mixture of both. In a book that remains a reference point for primary sources and analysis concerned with the French population in the British Isles from 1940 to 1944, Nicholas Atkin observes that in the 1931 census there were around 30,000 French men and women in England (with two-thirds being women), and they were the third largest European group after the Poles and the Russians, both displaced

---

[6] P. Villars, 'The French', in *Living London*, ed. G. R. Sims (3 vols., 1901), ii. 133, quoted by N. Atkin, *The Forgotten French: Exiles in the British Isles, 1940–4* (Manchester and New York, 2003), p. 185.

by events in eastern Europe, with the Germans a close fourth. The overall figure for the French was roughly the same as in 1901 and 1911. The figure would drop by almost two-thirds by 1941, and those who did stay remained concentrated in London and the surrounding areas.

Although Atkin's perspective is different from that of this chapter, since his concern is with those French people who did not necessarily form part of London's 'Free French' and, indeed, one of his aims is to make clear the distinctions between other French exiles and the Free French, it is worth beginning with some aspects of his analysis which have resonance for the wider investigation into the history of the French in London in this book:

> Apart from General de Gaulle and his supporters, who have generated what one historian has described as an 'intimidating' literature, those French exiles who sheltered in Britain during the 'dark years' of 1940–44 have largely been forgotten by historians. Why this neglect? Part of the answer lies in the fact that the French in wartime Britain constituted a small, self-contained community, or rather communities, who left few traces of their existence, and who were all too eager to return to France, some seeking repatriation while the Germans still occupied their lands.[7] (Figure 12.4)

The reasons for this are varied and complex, and it is not the intention to cover them in detail here; suffice it to say that, for example, young men who were working in London had been called up to join the French forces before the débâcle of 1940, and two-thirds of the pre-war French community were female, no doubt deciding to re-join their families as war seemed imminent and was then declared; there was considerable financial and emotional distress caused to French families or families with French fathers when the men were called to France.[8] Later, cited in a final chapter that deals specifically with the 'tradition of exile' and what he terms the 'French colony' (as French historians do, and following the British and French authorities' terminology of the early twentieth century), one source for a description of the French in London during the period resonates still more with the overall history being undertaken in this book. In a 1901 three-volume conspectus of London life several chapters were devoted to immigrant communities (Greeks, Germans and Italians, among others) that had made London their home. In the pages on the French, the following observation was made:

---

[7] Atkin, *Forgotten French*, pp. 5–6.

[8] The wartime novels of Mrs. Robert Henrey (Madeleine Henrey, née Gal) detail some of these misfortunes. See further references and details in n. 42 below.

Figure 12.5. New recruits for All Free French Army. Volunteers being interviewed in the new recruiting office (17 September 1940). IWM, LN 11532.

Figure 12.6. French sailors, soldiers and merchantmen signing on at Olympia. IWM, TP 8304.

Recruiting for the Legion of French Volunteers who wish to serve with the Allied forces in progress at the London depot of the Legion at Olympia.

The French in London form a sober, well-behaved, industrious and law-abiding community. They give very little trouble to the police and law courts, and it is seldom that the name of a French resident obtains an unbelievable notoriety in the newspapers. There are about 21,000 French sojourners in England, and about 11,000 of them in the metropolis …. [they are] not to be found loafing in the neighbourhood of Leicester Square and Piccadilly Circus … They are to be found in City offices and warehouses, in workshops and studios, in West End establishments and shops, in schools and in private families.[9]

Looking forward down the decades towards the contemporary lives of French men and women in the British capital there is a sense that they can be considered very much the heirs of this community, as will be seen in the final chapter of this book.

Not the 'usual suspects':[10] Free French men and women

What, then, of the changes that occurred with the creation of the notion of the Free French around de Gaulle, and with the arrival of disparate individuals and groups who rallied to him in the British capital (Figures 12.5 and 12.6)? Although there do exist several rich memoirs of key figures of the Free French who were in London from 1940 onwards, those memoirs are usually more concerned with high politics and relations with other key personalities than with recording everyday living, and there is in fact very little about how the Free French settled in the British capital, just as it is difficult to find information about the French nationals who were already settled there:

While historians of Vichy have shown great creativity in developing new lines of enquiry, the one area where they have not displayed the same kind of imagination is in uncovering the life of exiles in Britain. Here, the concerns of scholars have unquestionably been extensive, but they have been very traditional, focusing largely on diplomacy and high politics, the sort of issues that de Gaulle himself tackles in his memoirs … Generals, admirals, politicians and professors thus dominate the history of France in Britain to the exclusion

---

[9] Villars, 'The French', p. 133, quoted in Atkin, *Forgotten French*, p. 185.

[10] The term 'the usual suspects' has become part of English usage, popularized in no small part by the success of the 1995 film starring Kevin Spacey and Gabriel Byrne which uses the term as its title. However, it can be traced to dialogue at the end of the 1942 film *Casablanca*, starring Humphrey Bogart and Ingrid Bergman, when Capt. Renault, the incarnation of Vichy corruption, vice and dissemblance, rather unexpectedly orders the rounding up of 'the usual suspects' to cover up Rick's shooting of the Nazi Maj. Strasser, allowing the Resistance leader Laszlo and his wife Ilsa to escape. Often thought of primarily as a love story, *Casablanca* was made as a propaganda film, a morale-booster put together quickly on a set in Hollywood, and rushed out in late November 1942.

Figure 12.7. Free French soldiers and sailors enjoy
a pint of beer in a London pub, 1940.

A young woman serves them their drinks. Official photograph, 'Allied Soldiers Like London And London Likes Them: Overseas Troops In England, 1940'. IWM, D1725, Ministry of Information, Second World War Official Collection.

of those other émigrés – the refugees, non-Gaullist soldiers, Vichyite officials and colonists, the 'forgotten French' – who also sought refuge here in 1940.[11]

In fact, this is also true of those predominantly young men and women who rallied to de Gaulle. Despite evident continued interest in the history of the Second World War, and the ongoing public and academic enthusiasm for the figures of de Gaulle and Churchill, together with some of the major figures around them – indeed the Fondation de la France Libre notes that de Gaulle's reputation as the leader of the Free French during the war has eclipsed that of his status as president of the Fifth Republic – the sources for the social and cultural history more generally of the French in Britain are often scarce, and this is true also for the war period. The French are largely absent in social histories of Britain during the Second World War, often relegated to the footnotes of accounts of wartime London, despite

11 Atkin, *Forgotten French*, p. 13.

the numbers and prominence of some of the 'Free French' who arrived there at various times and for various reasons, and hidden or only briefly referred to in most survey histories of London. An analysis and a mapping of the French in London in the Second World War therefore adds a further dimension to the notion of the presence of a French community that is at once both 'visible' (as various chapters in this book testify) and 'invisible' in accounts of the history of the capital.

One way to render this new 'visibility', then, is to attempt to map the various and varied places and spaces associated with the French in London during this period. Indeed the high political and military authorities of the Free French were also interested in those places frequented by their compatriots for all sorts of reasons (Figure 12.7). As Colonel Passy, the head of the French Intelligence Services, notes rather uncharitably, and in a depiction that differs from that of a sober, well-behaved French colony earlier in the century as observed above:

> A whole horde of French people who didn't have much else to do spent most of their time in London's bars. They became the echoes of the brilliant improvisations of Labarthe, and that's how the henchmen that Scotland Yard and MI5 ran in those places filled their police reports with this gossip.[12]

This is a revealing insight. One suspects that Passy (André Dewavrin), who writes elsewhere in the memoir that he is himself so very busy that he has no time for frequenting London's bars and restaurants, uses it to remind the reader of his own more high-minded calling to London. It also paints a striking picture of the importance of men like André Labarthe (the founder of the journal *La France Libre*, published from 1940 to 1946, which figures prominently in the subsequent chapter on Raymond Aron) and those who remained suspicious of de Gaulle while also being anti-Vichy. A man such as Labarthe made his presence felt in London, and indeed beyond. He figures in the wartime letters of Marie Touchard, living in Glasgow during the war and impressed by, although cautious of, Labarthe, who gave a talk on France since the Occupation at the Franco-Scottish Society. She writes on 16 February 1941:

> He [Labarthe] publishes a French review which has appeared in London for the last three months ... the review is much more interesting [than *La France*] ... He's a 38 year old man, with youthful looks and a friendly face, he spoke with a

[12] 'Toute une foule de Français qui n'avaient pas grand-chose à faire passaient le plus clair de leur temps dans les bars londoniens. Ils se firent les échos des brillantes improvisations de Labarthe, et c'est ainsi que les sbires que Scotland Yard et MI5 entretenaient dans ces endroits remplirent de ces *gossips* leurs rapports de police' (Passy, *Mémoires*, p. 74).

great deal of energy and emotion about the current situation that we all know about [in France]. He's a scientist who is writing journalism for the first time ... His review seeks to remind the 'Anglo-Saxon' public about all that is enduring in French art, science and letters.[13]

Passy's account also shows the high levels of mistrust between the British and French intelligence services which are so vividly documented in the memoirs of those from both nations, in archival evidence and in the ensuing histories of the period. Bars, restaurants and hotels were essential meeting-places in wartime London. Matthew Sweet brings into sharp focus the importance of the public and private spaces of the city's hotels and the lives of those who worked, socialized, sheltered from the bombing and carried out business of various types there:

> Instead of vanishing into history, London's grand hotels became more prominent in the cultural and political life of this country then ever before. They were the homes of Cabinet ministers and military leaders, plutocrats and aristocrats. At lunch tables and in smoking rooms, decisions were made that affected the progress of the war. Hotel apartments became the retreats of governments-in-exile, diplomatic missions and the deposed monarchies of occupied Europe ... Con-artists and swindlers, invigorated by the opportunities brought by war, hunted for victims among the potted palms ... Writers, poets, artists, musicians and prostitutes haunted bars and lobbies ... Spies and spymasters made rooms above Park Lane, Piccadilly, Brook Street and the Strand into thriving centres of espionage, using quiet suites for debriefings and interrogations, picking at the plasterwork for hidden microphones, and despatching agents of the secret state to loiter in the coffee lounges and listen for treachery. The Dorchester, the Savoy, the Ritz and Claridge's: each was a kind of Casablanca.[14]

To which we might add the Connaught, favoured lunch spot and temporary home of Charles de Gaulle, although he also enjoyed the Savoy.

---

[13] IWM 63/43/1, private papers of Miss M. L. Touchard: 'Il est l'éditeur d'une revue française publiée à Londres depuis trois mois ... la revue est beaucoup plus intéressante [que La France] ... C'est un homme de 38 ans, à l'allure jeune au visage sympathique, qui a parlé avec beaucoup d'élan et d'émotion de la situation actuelle telle que nous la connaissons tous ... C'est un scientifique qui pour la première fois fait du journalisme ... Sa revue veut rappeler au public anglo-saxon tout ce qui est français et impérissable dans l'ordre des arts, des sciences et des lettres'. Despite reservations concerning Labarthe, Marie Touchard undertook to co-ordinate the promotion of the review in Glasgow. She had been teaching French in a Glasgow commercial college since 1932; her twin brother, Pierre-Aimé Touchard, was a close friend of Emmanuel Mounier, the editor of Esprit and the review's theatre critic from 1933 to 1947.

[14] M. Sweet, West End Front: the Wartime Secrets of London's Grand Hotels (2011), pp. 12–13; as Sweet also observes: 'London's hotels supported a number of vigorous subcultures: aristocrats, journalists, actors, criminals, spies' (p. 195).

The number of hotels associated with the Free French is impressive. In addition to the Connaught and the Savoy (connected with de Gaulle and many others, notably Lord Bessborough's French Welfare organization), there were several others of note: Rubens Hotel; Rembrandt Hotel; Hyde Park Hotel (again all used by de Gaulle for meetings and/or accommodation); the Waldorf (Captain Rémy); Grosvenor Hotel (Muselier, but also many other people and events); Hôtel de Vere in de Vere Gardens (Jean Moulin was lodged there by British Secret Services); Kensington Palace Hotel (Pierre-Bloch was lodged there by British Secret Services); Mount Royal Hotel at Marble Arch (Pierre-Bloch among others stayed there); the Ashdown Park Hotel, Coulsdon (now the White Swan), the place where Joseph Kessel and Maurice Druon composed 'Le chant des partisans' (or perhaps that was at the Savile Club in London as others claim); and finally the less salubrious Hôtel de Boulogne in Lisle Street, Soho, which still has its name in mosaics in the doorway of the Chinese restaurant it now houses, and was frequented during the war by the armed forces of the Free French. Such hotels were, or (in the case of the Italians interned as enemy aliens) had been, staffed to a great extent by foreign nationals, including some very prominent French chefs and restaurateurs, as well as many ordinary French men and women (Figure 12.8). Passy was right to be wary of those who spent time in London's bars and hotels, for German and Vichy spies also haunted those places – as Sweet puts it: 'at Claridge's there were more spies than sommeliers' – and so did women like Mathilde Carré:

> Carré had been a leading Resistance co-ordinator in Paris – until November 1941, when, for a monthly fee of sixty thousand francs, she had agreed to switch her allegiance to the Nazis. In February 1942 she had travelled to London to make a report to her masters on the structure of the Special Operations Executive: her audacious plan was to become the mistress of Lord Selbourne, the government minister responsible for the organization. After reading reports of a conversation conducted over cocktails at Claridge's, some of Selbourne's colleagues were under the impression that she was on the point of succeeding.[15]

There were, then, fewer French people in London during the war, but they become, for a period, more visible than is usually the case. Who, then, were these 'Free French' who rallied to de Gaulle? Despite Passy's reservations concerning some of them, they were certainly not what *Casablanca's* Captain Renault would have termed the 'usual suspects' at odds with his

---

[15] M. Sweet, *West End Front*, p. 280. Carré was interned on 1 July 1942 at HMP Aylesbury in Buckinghamshire and later that month Stella Lonsdale, a notorious suspected Nazi double agent whose career is detailed by Sweet, was transferred there and put into a cell with Carré, since Stella could speak French (pp. 247–8).

Figure 12.8. Allied Aliens Register: French chefs sign on. IWM, NIX 237851.

French chefs from nearby restaurants snatch a few moments to register for service in an international labour force. Left to right: M. Gauthier of the Cantine, M. Le Bihan of the Cigale, M. Bailly of the Coquille and M. Jean Pages, proprietor of the three restaurants (June 1941).

own ideas of law and order. They were also not necessarily members of the French communities who were already living in London and in other places in Britain.[16] Many French people preferred either to leave for the United States or indeed remain in Britain without becoming members of the Free French, even if they did not necessarily support Vichy and its actions. As Elisabeth de Miribel, secretary to de Gaulle, wrote: 'In June 1940, London was not a place that one came to, but one from which one left'.[17]

Not everyone was convinced by de Gaulle and his notion of a 'Free France' that was not established on French soil. Jean Monnet, the president of the Committee for Franco-British Coordination, told de Gaulle that he did not believe that France could be rallied from London. Others, on all sides of the political spectrum and for varying reasons, were suspicious of

[16] For more detail, see Atkin, *Forgotten French*, and also S. Albertelli, *Atlas de la France Libre* (Paris, 2010), pp. 10–11.

[17] 'Londres, en juin 1940, n'était pas une ville où l'on arrivait, mais une ville d'où l'on partait' (quoted by Albertelli, *Atlas de la France Libre*, p. 10).

de Gaulle's intentions and ambitions, and his claims to 'incarnate' the true France, which went beyond the development of a military force.[18]

The identity of the Free French more generally is an area that is still contested and discussed among historians of the Resistance and of this period, but what is agreed on is that numbers are small, in total only between 52,000 and 55,000, with fluctuations during the course of the war – a fact that makes de Gaulle's claim to represent France all the more remarkable.

The work of Jean-François Muracciole is revealing on London's role and on other aspects of the Free French during the course of the war. While in 1940 close to 60 per cent of the Free French joined in Britain, by 1943 that had dropped to 10 per cent, with over 75 per cent engaging in North Africa.[19] The composition of the Free French is also interesting – and has consequences for the mapping here: they were in general not politically active, but from conservative right backgrounds; two-thirds did not have the right to vote before the war (soldiers, women, foreigners, minors) and were motivated by rejection of collaboration and attachment to de Gaulle. Within France, their origins are striking: 21 per cent came from Brittany, 15 per cent were Europeans in French colonies, and 16 per cent came from the Parisian region. The vast majority (70 per cent) of the Free French were already living outside France, either in the French empire (43 per cent) or in other countries (27 per cent).[20]

The social, professional and educational composition is even more striking: 83 per cent were young and urban (aged under thirty; and among them just over a third were younger than twenty-one, then the age of majority), with large numbers of school and university students. Another third were military personnel. There were comparatively few industrial and farm workers, even though these made up almost two-thirds of the French population. Over half of the Free French had the baccalauréat, and 20 per cent came from the Grandes Ecoles. Again, we may expect such a particular population to have an effect on any mapping of their presence in London.[21]

[18] E.g., diplomats such as Charles Corbin (French ambassador to London 1933 to June 1940) and Roger Cambon (the French chargé d'affaires); or Georges Gombault and Louis Levy for political reasons.

[19] Murraciole's statistics in *Les Français Libres: l'autre résistance* (Paris, 2009) are used in Albertelli's *Atlas de la France Libre*, p. 12; see also J.-F. Murraciole, *Histoire de la France Libre* (Paris, 1996).

[20] Albertelli, *Atlas*, pp. 14–15 (again based on Murraciole, *Les Français Libres*).

[21] Albertelli, *Atlas*, p. 16, 'Sociologie des Français Libres', with reference again to Murraciole, *Les Français Libres*.

Figure 12.9. General de Gaulle and his national committee
observe the five minutes 'stand still' in honour of Frenchmen
murdered by the Germans in France. IWM, SG 8155B.
Left to right: M. Maurice Dejean, M. André Diethelm, Admiral Emile Muselier, General de
Gaulle, Professor René Cassin, M. René Pleven, General Martial Valin (31 October 1941).

'Books that record great events do not explain how the ordinary people of a great city live during momentous days':[22] mapping Free French London

Taking a lead from the memoirs of key figures in the Free French around de
Gaulle (as with the extract of Passy's memoirs above) and also using other
sources such as novels of the period, archival material and a range of documents
and images, this chapter now focuses on the underpinning of the mapping
of Free French London, although the maps accompanying this chapter are
necessarily a work-in-progress as more details and sources come to light. The
maps represent both what can be termed 'political and military' and 'cultural
and social' Free French London, although such a divide is not clear-cut, since
much 'war business' was conducted outside the official places and spaces.

---

[22] R. Henrey, *The Incredible City* (1944), p. 148.

The maps include, to begin with, the obvious political/military locations: for example, de Gaulle's headquarters at St. Stephen's House, Victoria Embankment and then 4 Carlton Gardens (Jeanne Hart's commercially produced 'Free French diary' for 1944 gives her work address and phone number as 'Fighting French Headquarters, 4 Carlton Gardens, Whitehall 5444) (Figure 12.9); 3 St. James's Square and then 10 Duke Street, home to the French Intelligence Services (Bureau Central des Renseignements d'Action; BCRA); Westminster House, Dean Stanley Street, used by the Free French Navy (FNFL) and the Français de Grande Bretagne association; 42 Hill Street, Mayfair, the original Free French women's barracks until it was bombed in April 1941 and they moved to Moncorvo House, Ennismore Gardens in Kensington (Figure 12.10); 19 Hill Street, offices of the Commissariat National de l'Intérieur; 33 Upper Brook Street, which housed the Union des Français d'Outre Mer (UFOM), and where the newspaper *France* was printed in the basement; Queensberry Place, South Kensington, used by the Free French Air Force (FAFL) and home of the French Institute; the BBC in Portland Place and Bush House, and indeed Bedford College in Regent's Park, which housed the team of 'Les Français parlent aux Français' after their office near the BBC was bombed; and finally the French Press Agency at 85 Fleet Street.

The maps also include the better-known and less well-known cultural/social places the Free French frequented (such as Queen Charlotte's Hospital in Hammersmith, where Raymond and Lucie Aubrac's daughter was born), the many hotels (as previously noted), restaurants and bars in which they met, such as Soho's Le Berlemont (see below for more details), Chez Victor and Chez Rose, the grander Prunier's and L'Ecu de France, L'Escargot and Le Coq d'Or, and, in contrast, places of worship and remembrance such as Westminster Cathedral and the Brompton Oratory, as well as the French churches, which held Catholic services (sometimes in honour of those killed in France), in order to chart what was effectively a micro-society that moved into and around the existing city.

The overlaps and differences between those spaces and places and who frequented them and when is interesting in itself. The memoirs of key figures provide a valuable although limited source as, from time to time, there is a glimpse there of the visibility and effects of the Free French on the British capital – from the uniforms of the French Army, Navy and Air Force in Regent Street and Piccadilly as commented on in an article in *The Daily Mail* and noted by Crémieux-Brilhac, so that in August 1940 London resembled 'a French garrison town';[23] to the various places

---

[23] J.-L. Crémieux-Brilhac, *La France Libre*, p. 93; the article by Ward-Price appeared on 12 Aug. There are notes here of several favourable reports in the British press on the Free French recruits in, e.g., *Daily Express, Daily Telegraph, Manchester Guardian*.

Figure 12.10. Members of the newly formed French equivalent of the ATS, the Corps Femina, seen marching through a London street. IWM, KY 1704A.

(both political and social) where the Free French met; to the figure of de Gaulle himself walking from Carlton Gardens to lunch at the Connaught Hotel, as noted by a number of observers (Figure 12.11, Figure 12.12). Of course, 'Free France' covered many more territories right across the globe than London, and in military terms other countries were more important in the fight against Nazi Germany, especially those linked to France through its colonial empire, and notably French Equatorial Africa and Cameroon, which created a huge bloc for Free French Africa (AFL). Both Brazzaville, which had an important independent radio station (and which from 18 June 1943 was able to broadcast as far as France) and a training camp, and was situated in French (colonial) territory, and then Algiers, for which de Gaulle left London at the end of May 1943, also have the status of real and symbolic capitals of Free France. Nonetheless, the founding act of Free France and of the Free French took place in London on 18 June 1940 and London remained essential for connections to the Resistance in France. That founding act took place in a space that incarnates so many aspects of British culture to those both inside and outside the British Isles: the BBC.

Figure 12.11. A policeman gives directions to Free French soldiers and sailors, somewhere in London in 1940. Official photograph, 'Allied Soldiers Like London And London Likes Them: Overseas Troops In England, 1940'. IWM, D 1724, Ministry of Information Second World War Official Collection.

In the background a London Underground sign is just visible, and a car is parked alongside the troops.

BBC radio linked Britain to its empire, and to the world beyond that. The geography of historical events was not lost on de Gaulle in his famous 'Appeal', in which, as well as calling for the 'flame of French resistance' not to be extinguished, he also set the fall of France within its global dimensions, convinced that both the United States and the USSR would join the conflict. The photograph of de Gaulle at the microphone of the BBC on 18 June is iconic for the history of both the French and the British in the Second World War, and for any mapping of Free French London. De Gaulle would continue to make many of his most important interventions to rally the French to the cause of the continued fight of the Free French, and indeed continue to create the image and symbolic status of 'Free France' in well-chosen words and images, through the BBC. 'A new France' would emerge (29 November 1940) after the fight 'between lies and truth, darkness and light, evil and good' (18 April 1942), thanks to France's 'genius

Figure 12.12. Free French soldiers and sailors buying a copy of the *France* newspaper from a newsagent somewhere in London in 1940. Official photograph, 'Allied Soldiers Like London And London Likes Them: Overseas Troops In England, 1940'. IWM, D 1722, Ministry of Information Second World War Official Collection.

This newspaper enabled French troops in Britain to read about the war in their own language.

for renewing itself' (24 March 1942). Indeed it could be said that the first 'site' of the Free French in London was the figure of de Gaulle himself, a figure that incarnated both the physical and mythical elements that can be said to epitomize 'Free France':

> The romantic image of this lonely soldier, defying the menace of Nazism and the cowardice of Vichy, appealed to a nation that had few enough heroes at the height of the Blitz. His striking presence, and enormous height, was quickly noted in the streets of London … The general was a familiar sight in metropolitan life, and quickly became enmeshed in the British legend of a heroic and steadfast nation determined to resist the German onslaught at whatever cost.[24]

---

[24] Atkin, *Forgotten French*, p. 10.

Figure 12.13. General de Gaulle addressing a large gathering at
a meeting convened by Les Français de Grande Bretagne at the
Albert Hall, London (15 November 1941). IWM, LN 9020B.

Although Atkin's study, referred to above, and some of the chapters here
also show that the British population was not always quite so welcoming
to French 'exiles' of various sorts, British opinion apparently remained
generally favourable to the Free French and to de Gaulle, despite the fall of
France, and even when those involved in the high politics of the period were
suspicious of him, and actively or less obtrusively attempting to undermine
him.[25]

As far as more obvious geographical sites are concerned, the most
convincing are those that are corroborated by more than one source, or by
one detailed source (for example, 69 Cromwell Gardens, where Passy and
others lived) or that are particularly successfully brought to life when there
are one or more detailed descriptions and/or visual evidence available (for

---

[25] 41% claimed to be favourable to Free France in 1940–1, rising to 52% in 1941, and those
unfavourable to it dropped from 31% to 11% in the same period (Albertelli, *Atlas*, p. 34,
with reference also to the work of P. M. H. Bell, e.g. *France and Britain 1940–94: the Long
Separation* (1997)).

instance the large event at the Albert Hall, 15 November 1941, attended by de Gaulle and 4,000 members of the association of the Français de Grande Bretagne) (Figure 12.13).[26] Just one example of the difficulties of accuracy, however, is the case of the site of the well-known Petit Club Français. Its location is given variously as 'in St James'; 'behind Green Park Station'; 'in St James's Street'; 'near the Carlton Club'; and '4 St James's Place'. However, it is a shot of a membership card contained in Timothy Miller's 2010 documentary on the Free French in London that provides real visual evidence for the contemporary viewer – the Petit Club was housed in 13 St. James's Place.[27]

Of the other very prominent members of the Free French, the memoirs of Crémieux-Brilhac, as might be expected, contain precious insights into some of the everyday lives of the Free French, even if he is overall more preoccupied with the military and political history of this time and place:

> the routine of daily life developed. The French officer class, weekly tenants in service flats in South Kensington, got used to porridge for breakfast. Rallying points were associated with meals, the hubbub of the Navy and Air Force Canteen, where so many young men who were to die rubbed shoulders, and more select was the Allies Club, open to Allied officers in the grand house that had belonged to Wellington at the side of Hyde Park. When the bombings became less frequent in the autumn, people began to go to the French bistrots in Soho, the cheap and popular 'Berlemont' ... [28]

Crémieux-Brilhac goes on to mention L'Escargot, 'where the old waiters looked like provincial solicitors',[29] and Chez Rose, Prunier's (to which

---

[26] The 'Français de Grande Bretagne' was the self-appointed civil wing of the Free French (see, e.g., Atkin, *Forgotten French*, p. 45), not to be confused with the Fédération des Associations Françaises en Grande Bretagne, founded in 1942 and still flourishing today.

[27] The Petit Club Français was established by a Scottish woman, Alwyn Voghan. According to Pierre-Bloch, the British (intelligence services) mistrusted this club where people talked a lot, and where officers and men mingled (Pierre-Bloch, *Londres Capitale de la France Libre*, p. 141). The TV documentary reference is to T. Miller (dir.), *Libres Français de Londres 1940–4* (Cinétévé/ECPAD, 2010).

[28] 'la vie matérielle s'organise. Les cadres français, locataires à la semaine de *service flats* à South Kensington, s'habituent aux *breakfasts de porridge*. Les lieux de ralliement sont ceux des repas, le grand brouhaha de la cantine de la Marine et de l'Air, où se côtoient tant de jeunes que la mort allait emporter, et plus *select* l'Allies Club, ouvert à tous les officiers alliés dans l'hôtel particulier qui fut celui de Wellington, en bordure de Hyde Park. Quand les bombardements s'espacent à l'automne, on commence à fréquenter les bistrots français de Soho, le populaire et peu coûteux *Berlemont*' (Crémieux-Brilhac, *La France Libre*, pp. 227–8).

[29] 'dont les vieux serveurs français ressemblent à des notaires de province' (Crémieux-Brilhac, *La France Libre*, p. 228).

we will return), L'Ecu de France, Le Coq d'Or and (again) Le Petit Club Français; but often with imprecise locations for those that do and do not still exist. Investigations into them are nonetheless rewarding. To take the passing reference to the Berlemont as one example: this opens out onto the history of one of Soho's best-known pubs, today familiar as the French House in Dean Street, and provides fascinating detail for any cultural history of London in the twentieth century. The pub was bought in 1914 by the Belgian Victor Berlemont from a German forced to leave on the outbreak of the First World War. Berlemont had worked with the famous and influential French chef Escoffier at the Savoy, and was therefore a member of the French community in London that had worked in the restaurant and hotel trades for many decades. The name Berlemont gave it was the very English pub name of The York Minster, although the first-floor restaurant was commonly referred to by his name, as Crémieux-Brilhac does above; it was not re-named officially until 1984 under the ownership of his son, Gaston, a very well-known Soho figure of the mid to late twentieth century. A photograph of de Gaulle and Major General Spears still hangs above the bar, and a copy of the 'Appeal' on a wall; a myth endures that the 'Appeal' was written here. As a novel of the period notes:

> Arguing strategy and politics over a restaurant table had proved the salt of their *émigré* existence. They liked the atmosphere of Soho ... the French sailors leaning up against the lamp-posts ogling the girls, they found an echo of home at Berlemont's where aperitifs were served, continental fashion, and afterwards they would go to their favourite restaurants to be greeted amicably by the *patronne*.[30]

Among the other French restaurants mentioned by Crémieux-Brilhac, another favourite was the cheap and cheerful Chez Rose, loved for its (horse) steak-frites and appearing in other personal accounts such as the letters of the lively and sociable Lesley Boyde (Gerrard), who glosses it as 'a Belgian restaurant in Soho and frequented by the Free French'. The more dutiful Mlle. Toutain, another French woman volunteer, also frequents it: 'On Friday, Fifi (Thomas) and I go to Soho to eat horse steak and chips at our favourite restaurant'.[31] On a grander scale, the wartime history of the London branch of the famous Parisian restaurant Prunier's is well documented in the account of the grand-daughter of its founder,

---

[30] R. Henrey, *The Siege of London* (1946), p. 132. For more details of the novels of Robert Henrey, see n. 42 below.

[31] The IWM describes the letters (May 1944–March 1946) of Lesley Gerrard as 'light-hearted, somewhat flippant'; they give vivid descriptions of what it was to be a young woman in London during the war (see also IWM, private papers of Miss C. E. Toutain).

Madame Prunier (Simone Barnagaud-Prunier), on whose initiative the London Prunier's was established in early 1935 in St. James's Street.[32] Madame Prunier,[33] cut off from her family including her husband, kept the restaurant open throughout the war, despite bombing (the worst being on 16 April 1941, when considerable damage was done to the premises), meal prices fixed by the government, temporary necessary wage cuts, rationing, and her refusal ever to be involved in the black market (more easily indulged in by smaller restaurants with less high-profile clientele), even when offered assistance by a 'hero of Free France' known in the Resistance as Commander Langlais.[34] In Madame Prunier's account there is a wealth of detail concerning the origins of top London restaurants in the 1930s, the selection and recruitment of staff, and dealings with important agencies such as the fishmongers' firms of Billingsgate and the Ministry of Agriculture and Fisheries, and with advertising companies. She is able to deal with an established French solicitor in London, and Achille Serre set up a specialized laundry based on the Parisian system especially for Prunier's, and which became a large London cleaning firm. She also details the network of other French people working in London, such as M. Herbodeau, a pupil of Escoffier who became the proprietor of L'Ecu de France, then chef at the Carlton, and who gave Simone Prunier a list of suppliers. As war approached, the first and then regular visits of von Ribbentrop, a long-time client of Prunier's in Paris, were noted, as were the details of the Paris and London seasons of 1939; then on Sunday morning, 3 September:

> I went straight to St James's Street; the staff had gathered there too, and together we filled sandbags and erected barricades against bomb blast round the front of the restaurant. Those of the men who were French went off to the consulate to report for mobilization.

> The mobilization hit us hard. Three-quarters of the cooks were French, and all were called to the colours; my restaurant manager, Guyot, and my chef, Cochois, were both in their forties and fathers of families, but they, too, were ordered to leave at three days' notice … The previous day a new French chef, M. Cadier, had reported for duty; it was only later that I learned that he had missed the wedding of his son, who was one of those called up, so as not to let

---

[32] Mme. (Simone) Prunier, *La Maison: the History of Prunier's* (1957).

[33] I am most grateful to Hugo Dunn-Meynell (a former *Good Food Guide* critic) and Alice Wooledge Salmon, a chef formerly at the Connaught, for taking the time to tell me about restaurants in Soho in the 1940s and 1950s as remembered by Hugo in his youth, and also for his memories of Mme. Prunier and for recommending Prunier, *La Maison* to me as a reference.

[34] His real name was Claude Péri (Prunier, *La Maison*, pp. 265–6).

the Maison down. M. Cadier brought some of his team with him: older cooks had come out of retirement …[35]

Madame Prunier's view of the war through the prism of a great restaurant is a real insight into the London of the period. After Dunkirk: 'The uniforms of the men who came into Prunier's in St James's Street were sometimes a little creased, and their faces were sometimes more than a little worn … all the stories ended in retreat, always retreat';[36] the days of June 1940 'were humiliating for a French woman in London who has always been proud of her country. My English friends were kindness itself. They never reproached my country; they never even talked of the capitulation'.[37] She continues (ever the name-dropper):

> The refugees, of course, flocked to St James's Street. Pierre Cot, the former Radical Air Minister, appeared for lunch one day; then it was Geneviève Tabouis, the diplomatic correspondent who set up to know the secrets of all the chancelleries; when the final boats arrived from Bordeaux, some of their passengers came straight to my office.[38]

Simone Prunier heard de Gaulle's 'Appeal', and on 20 June, with the other 'Conseillers du Commerce Extérieur':[39]

> I voted for the sending of a letter to Mr. Churchill thanking him for his proposal of an Anglo-French Union and placing ourselves at his disposal. And naturally I joined the Société des Français de Grande Bretagne, as soon as it was formed in July to support de Gaulle. A few days before, a French friend had rung up to say that a hundred members of the French colony in London, all good Frenchmen, were being invited to meet the General at the Y.M.C.A. building in Great Russell Street. 'In principle, it's for men only, but you're a man in skirts', he said. There was a platform in the room where the hundred of us gathered; the General mounted it with a certain reluctance and made a stiff little speech. Then we filed up to shake hands with him, naming ourselves as we reached him.[40]

---

[35] Prunier, *La Maison*, pp. 254–5. I am grateful to Linda Cadier, whose husband is the grandson of the chef M. Cadier, for telling me something of his story. She confirms that Mme. Prunier's account is true: he missed his son's wedding (which incidentally was the first reported by the *Evening Standard* after war was declared). Adolphe 'Pépé' Cadier later served the war out in the Cotswolds as chef de cuisine for an officers' club.

[36] Prunier, *La Maison*, p. 257.

[37] Prunier, *La Maison*, p. 258.

[38] Prunier, *La Maison*, p. 258.

[39] In 1938, the French Ministry of Commerce gave Simone Prunier the honorific title of 'counsellor of foreign trade', a distinction granted to French tradesmen abroad on the recommendation of the commercial counsellor (*conseiller*) of the French Embassy to the country in which they worked. She was one of the first women to be nominated, and one of 12 women among 2,500 'counsellors' in the British section.

[40] Prunier, *La Maison*, p. 259.

A final eventful anecdote involves Maurice Rossi, the maître d'hôtel at Traktir, Prunier's sister restaurant in Paris, who had formed a group of some thirty or forty of his colleagues in the best restaurants in Paris with a plan to poison every German officer who came into their restaurants as soon as the Allied armies drew close to Paris. Later, he was put in touch with Rémy (Gilbert Renault) and joined his information network; Rossi turned up at Prunier's in London in autumn 1942. In her assessment, Madame Prunier writes:

> I do not think I should be boasting if I said that Prunier's in St James Street had become one of the favourite restaurants of the various European Resistance movements. General de Gaulle had been there, of course, so had André Diethelm, the Strasbourg professor of law, and André Philip, the Lyons socialist and Jacques Soustelle, the young anthropologist, who were all to serve as Ministers under him; Pierre Mendès-France had eaten there in the R.A.F. uniform he wore as a member of the Free French squadron, before he became a Minister.[41]

Other, less explicit, although connected, sources are rewarding, such as the little gems of novels (*A Village in Piccadilly* (1942), *The Incredible City* (1944) and *The Siege of London* (1946)) by Mrs. Robert Henrey, a Frenchwoman married to an Englishman who lived in Mayfair throughout the war, and who proves to be a vivid witness to life in London from 1940 onwards.[42] The first of this 'war' trilogy ends as the narrator notes: 'Officers in queer foreign uniforms were leaving Prunier's restaurant after lunch – reminding one sadly that Paris for the Englishman, was now thousands of miles away, and more difficult of access than the plains of Tibet'.[43] Earlier in the novel, the author writes of the Savoy in June 1940:

[41] Prunier, *La Maison*, pp. 273–4.

[42] As does her account of 1930s London, *The Foolish Decade* (1945), which is populated by a wide variety of London French, and clearly based on autobiographical material. Madeleine Henrey (1906–2004) wrote a number of autobiographically-based novels in English; her most widely read book is *The Little Madeleine* (1951). She was born into a poor family in Clichy, northern Paris; her father had been a miner and a First World War soldier and she and her seamstress mother moved to London after his death. They lived in Soho and she worked in a newsagents there, in a City silk merchant's office and then as a manicurist at the Savoy Hotel. She married one of her clients, Robert Henrey, an Etonian who became a journalist in 1928, and the marriage considerably elevated her social status. Another series of novels is based on their life at a house they bought in Normandy near Villers-sur-mer. Her nom de plume was Mrs. Robert Henrey, although the early novels sometimes appeared without the Mrs.; it was an acknowledgement of the close collaboration between husband and wife.

[43] R. Henrey, *A Village in Piccadilly* (1942), p. 163.

The restaurant overlooking the Thames and the Embankment remained open, but its normal atmosphere had gone. The city folk, who normally patronized it at lunchtime, spending their money lavishly on brandy and cigars, seemed to have faded away. In place of them, one met groups of Poles, Dutchmen, Belgians, Norwegians, and a few American newspapermen who had just crossed over from France. General de Gaulle, almost unknown as yet, held court at a large round table. French diplomats from the embassy and members of the various naval, military and economic missions who nearly all intended to obey the instructions of the Pétain government, kept as far from the new leader as possible, and even glared at him with undiplomatic rudeness. They intended to insist on their safe conduct home as soon as possible.[44]

The author cautions that there was no glamour about this international crowd, it was 'sombre and depressed'; in the big entrance hall, they moved about 'like ghosts, shattered and bewildered by the complete and utter wreckage of their homelands'.[45] As a Frenchwoman, she has (as in previous novels) a keen eye for her compatriots of all types. The main character in *A Village in Piccadilly* is a male English newspaper columnist (like the author's husband), and the veil of what is essentially fictionalized autobiography is a thin one:[46]

Passing through the foyer at about five o'clock one evening I saw a dozen shabby figures walking in Indian file into the reading room. What struck me first about them were their bent and lifeless backs. They looked as if they were being led to the gallows by a member of the Gestapo. I saw them sink limply into the settees. Soon their heads were close together as they talked and argued in low tones.

Suddenly I recognised familiar faces in this little crowd. Yes, indeed, they were France's most famous war and political correspondents, men and women whose names were known throughout the world, and whom I had met personally on every great international news-story during the last twenty years. But what an unbelievable change had come over them! The frail, white-haired woman was Geneviève Tabouis of the Paris *Œuvre*, whom the Nazis only a few days before had claimed to have captured. There was Elie Bois, gruff but dynamic, brave and honest editor-in-chief of the huge circulation *Petit Parisien*; 'Pertinax', considered by the Anglo-American press as an oracle; and Quilici of the Havas Agency, whose greatest coup had been to reveal and torpedo the Hoare-Laval plan ... They had caused governments to fall, and called their own Cabinet ministers by their Christian names ... Now they covered the greatest story of all; but the story was too big and had burned them up. They had no longer any

---

[44] Henrey, *Village in Piccadilly*, pp. 6–7.
[45] Henrey, *Village in Piccadilly*, p. 8.
[46] Madeleine Henrey's husband was a journalist (see above, n. 42).

papers in which to write what they had seen; they had no longer any country to call their own … They would soon have to leave the hotel, no longer having large expenses to draw upon. Many of them, like Mme Tabouis, planned to move into cheap lodgings until they could obtain permission to leave for New York.[47]

There is attention given to Soho's French colony, which

suffered immeasurable hardship. The men, who were mostly cooks, were called up in 1939, and only came back to this country in transit after Dunkirk. They were then sent back to France to continue a war which for them was soon to stop, but by then they were unable to return to their country of adoption, and their families in Soho starved for want of breadwinners.[48]

A number of French personalities populate the novels, either fleetingly in single encounters, or as recurring characters who provide a running thread throughout the narrative as the war progresses. For example, Charles Billecocq, the French consul, recalled by Vichy, in a small Georgian house almost facing the Consulate in Bedford Square, or the Paris industrialist calling himself 'Mr. James', with his story of how he managed to join the last French nationals being evacuated by a British ship.[49] The narrator lunches with Yvonne Salmon at de Gaulle's headquarters:[50]

The Free French occupied a modern building in old-fashioned and spacious Carlton Gardens, and Londoners who passed along this normally quiet backwater had become accustomed to seeing staff cars with French soldiers or sailors at the wheel, and the sentry marching back and forth below the tricolour above the entrance. The mess was at the top of the building, and through the wide windows one had a sweeping view over London … The officers were served by women volunteers with the Cross of Lorraine pinned to their breasts … There were strange, moving stories to be heard here – escapes from France in home-made aeroplanes, in fishing boats, even in barrels.[51]

---

[47] Henrey, *Village in Piccadilly*, pp. 8–12. The narrator also gives details of what happens to the Italian staff of London's hotels and restaurants and the tragedy of the *Arandora Star* (pp. 13–17), and (for example) the change in name from Quaglino's to the Meurice when Italy joined the war on the side of Germany.

[48] Henrey, *Village in Piccadilly*, p. 50.

[49] Henrey, *Village in Piccadilly*, pp. 21–2. Details are also given of Belgian refugees (pp. 32–6). The novel is also very evocative of the West End (whose places and people the author knows extremely well, living as she did in Shepherd's Market, W1) both during and after bombing in the Blitz, for example in a raid that set Christie's on fire (pp. 37–42).

[50] Yvonne Salmon was the general secretary of the Alliance Française de Londres, and an early biographer of de Gaulle (published in 1943).

[51] Henrey, *Village in Piccadilly*, p. 82. Mlle. Salmon reads out a letter from her younger brother in Brest, and other staff in the Free French HQ bring out theirs.

In *The Incredible City*, the ticket collector for the deck-chairs in Green Park is revealed as René Dijon, who when interviewed by the narrator turned out to be one of the most famous pastry-cooks in Europe, having worked with Escoffier and Mallet at the turn of the century, before going to the Grand Hotel in Folkestone, and now giving recipe advice to the ladies in the park, and attracting an increasing circle of friends to the 'drawing room in Green Park'.[52]

The (eventually tragic) story of Pierre Brossolette and his family runs through two of the novels. The identity of the red-haired Frenchwoman in her mid-thirties, first met in *The Incredible City* on a ship leaving Gibraltar and bound for England, is revealed in a short preface to the final book of the trilogy, *The Siege of London*, as the wife of Brossolette (Lavoisier in the novel) travelling with her son and daughter, her husband having taken another route to leave France. In the second volume of the trilogy, *The Incredible City*, the narrator is invited to a dinner party in Mme. Lavoisier's apartment at Grosvenor House where he meets her husband, preoccupied with the 'routine of life' and the schooling of his children in England after recounting the stories of friends left behind in France.[53] The narrator is invited to another dinner party by one of de Gaulle's staff officers in their new canteen in Lady Astor's house at the corner of St. James's Square: 'A large room with a balcony on the first floor had been transformed into a bar where people gathered before dinner, and there were always new arrivals to add interest to the general conversation'; there he also meets the French novelist Joseph Kessel (and co-writer of the French version of 'La chant des partisans', as previously noted). Mme. Lavoisier is also there and a further invitation is extended to her house near Sloane Square; her husband is there once again, this time just back from a three-month stay in Paris, with stories of police sweeps checking identity cards and rounding up forced labour.[54] Mme. Lavoisier's connection to the Free French movement in London provides many anecdotes, such as her having dinner in Belgrave Square with an 'important member of the Free French movement' who had been recording the principal events of the Free

[52] Henrey, *Incredible City*, pp. 100–3, p. 133.

[53] Henrey, *Incredible City*, pp. 31–6.

[54] Henrey, *Incredible City*, pp. 76–81. The first chapter of the final novel of the trilogy, *The Siege of London* (1946), reveals how Mme. Lavoisier, herself also highly educated, in pre-war days polished her husband's speeches and articles: 'This dual thinking, this co-operation of two active minds, was to achieve great results' (p. 3). Interestingly, with reference to an earlier chapter in this book on the royal exiles in London, Henrey makes an analogy between Brossolette on missions to and from France and the marquis de la Rivière, who made trips back to France on behalf of the exiled Bourbons in England a century and half before, with reference to the memoirs of Mme. Vigée Le Brun (Henrey, *Incredible City*, p. 101).

French ever since de Gaulle first came to England. The notes had been placed, for safety, in his bedroom; during the evening the house was bombed, leaving them suspended in mid-air.[55]

The journal of another woman, Tereska Torrès, also provides a wealth of detail.[56] The daughter of Polish Jews who had converted to Catholicism, Tereska and the family fled Paris at the outbreak of war. Separated from her parents, she arrived in London where she enlisted with the Free French forces and served as a secretary in the offices of de Gaulle. During the war she lived in the French women's barracks that became the setting for her thinly disguised autobiographical novel *Women's Barracks*. Written in French and translated into English by her husband, Meyer Levin, the American writer, it became a best-seller, although condemned in 1952 for its 'artful appeals to sensuality, immorality, filth, perversion and degeneracy' by the House Select Committee on Current Pornographic Materials.[57] Its 'sympathetic portrayal of lesbian relationships among women soldiers in the Free French forces during World War II sold millions of copies in the United States as a pulp paperback original'.[58] All of which also suggests that while memoirs written by the men who lived in London during the war occasionally name-check the places in which they lived, socialized or (more often) met to discuss high politics, it is the women who are the detailed chroniclers of everyday life, revealing more of both public and private spaces, and often just as much of the politics of the day, sometimes explicitly, sometimes obliquely.

The lively Lesley Gerrard, who worked in various posts in the women's section of the Free French Army, including in the pay office and in provisions, notes many of her rather good meals, served with wine, at Moncorvo House and later in Hackin House (named for one of their late women officers), both in Ennismore Gardens, Kensington (Figure 12.14). Gerrard delights in her 'French' status as she writes in June 1944 to her family in the Isle of Man: 'It's amazing what a difference the French uniform makes – it really gives you glamour! I got off with General Koenig's driver yesterday – quite unintentionally, I assure you!'[59] And the following year, after VE day on 21 May, she writes:

> One thing I noticed wherever we [including with male companions] went in the restaurants, with my being in French uniform, it was me the waiters consulted for the choice of dish, wines, etc. Everyone seems fond of, and strives

[55] Henrey, *Incredible City*, pp. 35–6.

[56] Torrès, *Une Française Libre*.

[57] Back cover of its re-publication in the series 'Femmes fatales: women write pulp' (New York, 2005); first published by Fawcett Publications (New York, 1950).

[58] T. Torrès, *Women's Barracks* (1950), foreword, p. xiv.

[59] IWM, private papers of Mrs. L. Boyde.

Figure 12.14. At dinner time, the Volontaires queue to get their meals. Cooking is done the French way, but the rations of food available per head are equal to those given in the British ATS. IWM, PLP 8418B.

to emulate the French somehow. Their opinions as regards food, etc are much respected. I have gained a good deal of assurance through this, and I'm glad.[60]

Even the more sceptical Miss Wrench, who had joined the Special Operations Executive's French section and was mistrustful of the French intelligence services during the war, enjoys the hospitality at a party in Bloomsbury Square (after D-Day and the Liberation of Paris) in October 1944, having temporarily joined their services and moved office to Dorset Square: 'There we were all addressed in laudatory terms by General Koenig, de Gaulle's second in command'. They were all promised a citation, which never materialized in her case: 'It could just have been an expression of high spirits for we all drank loads of champagne to the Liberation which had just been achieved'.[61] She does not say if General Koenig's driver was also there.

[60] IWM, private papers of Mrs. L. Boyde.
[61] IWM, private papers of Miss C. E. Wrench.

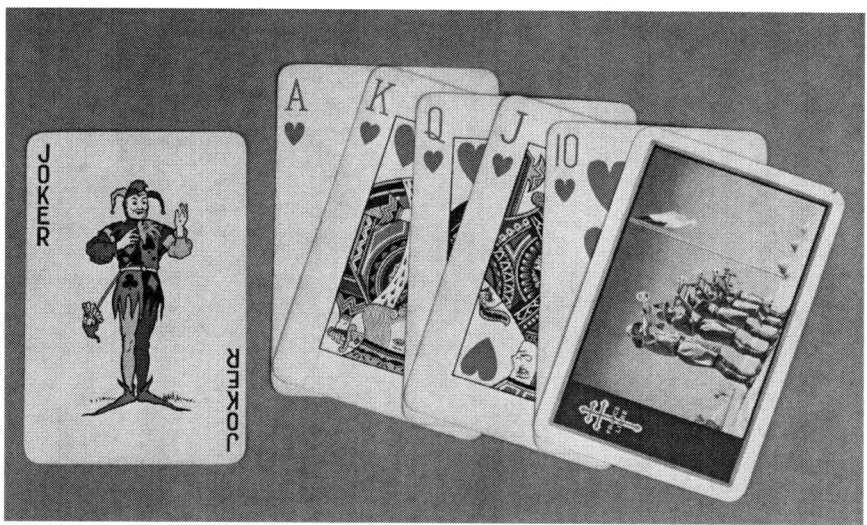

Figure 12.15. Pack of patriotic playing cards made in England during the Second World War by John Waddington Ltd. (Leeds and London). IWM, EPH 2500.

The pack loyally celebrates the contribution of the Free French military forces to the Allied war effort; the back of each card bears the Cross of Lorraine, the text 'France Libre' and an inspiring depiction of Free French soldiers.

As for the traces left by the Free French, as well as the institutional 'blue plaque' and the statue of de Gaulle in Carlton House Gardens, and the realities and myths of Soho's French House, these are also visible in consumer goods such as the packs of patriotic playing-cards made in England celebrating the contributions of the Free French Forces to the Allied war effort (examples held at the Imperial War Museum) (Figure 12.15); and the cleverly contrived headscarves made by a company called Jacqmar in Mayfair (British despite the 'Frenchified' name) with patterns made by repeated use of Free French symbols and first issued in 1941 (examples now in the collections of the Museum of London and the Imperial War Museum, London) (Figure 12.16). Photographic evidence celebrates both the people present at the Free French events and often ephemeral sites of the French presence such as rallies and meetings (Figures 12.17, 12.18), frequently addressed by de Gaulle, for example at the Albert Hall in November 1941; and symbolic moments that can often be matched with written accounts such as the 10 May parades for the French National Day for Joan of Arc. Mlle. Toutain writes of the latter event on 10 May 1941: 'Today the 10th, the Free French Troops parade in London. The flags and troops march through streets where smoke from

Figure 12.16. Free French Jacqmar scarf (cotton cloth L 86cm × W 86cm) showing a motif of envelopes addressed to various Free French units celebrating the role of the French fighting and merchant marine services, together with the Resistance. IWM, EPH 4553.

Jacqmar of London made propaganda scarves from 1940 to 1945. They were based in Mayfair and many were produced for the export market as well as for wartime sweethearts, especially in London. The design depicts envelopes addressed as follows: 'Escadrille Bretagne Front Russe URSS', 'Sergent Pilote, Fighting French Forces Ciel de Londres', 'Soldat Français citadelle de Bir Hacheim', 'Général de Gaulle La France Combattante Londres', 'Soldat Français, Free French Forces Mourzouk (Faire Suivre Koufre)', 'Français Front de la Résistance St Nazaire France', 'Caporal Marius 1ᵉ Division 8ᵉ Armée Libye', 'Editeur du Journal Libération France', 'Marin Français Sous Marin Le Rubis Bataille de l'Atlantique', 'Marin de la Marine Marchande Convoi de l'Atlantique', 'From Jacqmar London'.

Figure 12.17. Centre Syndical Français en Grande Bretagne (Trades Unions) celebrate the 150th anniversary of *The Marseillaise*, France's song of liberty. Speakers stand to attention during the playing of *The Marseillaise* (9 August 1942). IWM, AP 10935C.

bombed buildings still burning, makes a sad picture';[62] and she is present again on the afternoon of 15 November that year when 'everybody went to the Albert Hall where the General and Mr Diethelm made speeches. Some of the girls sold programmes'; and on 14 July 1942:

> Our troops march through London streets to the statue of Maréchal Foch, where General de Gaulle laid a wreath. The crowds in the street gave us a wonderful reception … In the evening, the band of the Fighting French Forces played in Hyde Park. French flags and coloured illuminated lamps were hung around the stand where the band played to make it look like streets in France on the 14th July (Figure 12.19).

---

[62] IWM, private papers of Miss Toutain; in one entry (1 Nov. 1941) she records her delight at de Gaulle visiting the women volunteers at Moncorvo House, where the General ate 'corned beef and chips, chocolate blancmange and coffee' and thanked them 'for a nice lunch!!!!' (her four exclamation marks).

Figure 12.18. Fighting French sale at Grosvenor House. Lord
Bessborough opened a two-day sale of work organized by
Les Français de Grande Bretagne. IWM, TP 737D.

The proceeds go to the association's Benevolent Fund. Two French girls in national costume
arranging the Libre Alsace and Lorraine stall (3 December 1942).

However, by 14 July 1945: 'As usual we have our march in honour of Bastille
Day. But there were not so many people watching the parade, the reason we
believe is the absence of General de Gaulle'.[63]

Traces may also be as ephemeral as the 'Chant des femmes de la France
Libre', referenced as Moncorvo House, 1942 and recorded by Mlle. Toutain:

[63] IWM, private papers of Miss Toutain. The Albert Hall was much used for meetings
of the Free French, as noted in her account, for example, 11 Nov. 1942 (when the whole of
France was now occupied); the Hall was filled with the Fighting French come to hear de
Gaulle; and M. Guéritte, president of the Association of the French in Great Britain, 'made
a speech to introduce various people to represent provinces of France'. On 4 Apr. 1945
Yehudi Menuhin gave a concert in aid of the Fighting French Forces, in the presence of de
Gaulle, who attended a big tea party given in his honour afterwards.

Figure 12.19. General Koenig at Fighting French Bastille Day ceremony. General Koenig, Fighting French supreme commander, laying the Fighting French wreath at the Marshal Foch statue, Victoria (14 July 1944). IWM, CP 11095E.

Partout dans la belle Angleterre
on les reçoit à bras ouverts, les Volontaires.
Bien que sans fusil sur l'épaule,
nous pensons avoir servi d'notre mieux de
Gaulle.
Que l'on soit conductrice, infirmière,
téléphoniste ou cuisinière,
qu'est-ce que ça peut faire?
Oui, nous les femmes de la France Libre
nous r'tournons à nos marmites
en disant, 'WE HAVE DONE OUR BIT'.

Everywhere in beautiful England
the volunteers are received with open arms.
Although with no rifles on our shoulders,
we think we've served De Gaulle to the
best of our ability.
Whether as driver, nurse,
telephonist or cook,
what does it matter?
Yes, we women of Free France
return to our pots and pans
saying, 'WE HAVE DONE OUR BIT'.

Figure 12.20. The Fighting French flag in the City. The Fighting French flag with St. Paul's Cathedral, where the bells were rung for half an hour today as a greeting to the Freedom of Paris (25 August 1944). IWM, FX 13250E.

Visibility and invisibility of Free French London: real and symbolic spaces

To conclude, while such a 'mapping' does document the 'real' spaces where high politics, military tactics and intelligence gathering were discussed, and where the Free French lived, ate and socialized, it must also necessarily represent an 'imaginary' space, since, as other commentators have noted for a long time after June 1940, Free France was just that. As Crémieux-Brilhac writes, the appeal to the imagination was one of the most important elements of de Gaulle's relationship to France:

> One of the most powerful resources of de Gaulle's relation with France was the appeal to the imagination. For Free France was simultaneously a reality and a myth, and he was the knowing artisan of both. In the creation of the myth,

the most effective instrument was the radio in London, the BBC. The mental war – a propaganda war, a war of words – ran parallel to the armed combat.[64]

Such a mapping in the case of the Free French, then, necessarily also represents the 'imaginary' space of London as used also to great effect in the creation of 'Free France'. This adds a further dimension to the notion of the 'visibility' and 'invisibility' of the French in London which was suggested above. Although the Free French were visible on the streets of wartime London, more visible than the French usually were, as testified by abundant photographic evidence, they still remain relatively hidden in its histories. Indeed, the symbolic may ultimately prove to be more essential in re-connecting us with the history of the Free French and their presence in London than what is left of their physical traces. The power of that imaginary place for the Free French, and indeed of London itself as the 'Capital of Hope', continues to exert its fascination in the cultural history of the Second World War (Figure 12.20).

---

[64] 'Un des ressorts les plus puissants de sa [de Gaulle] relation avec la France sera, en effet, l'appel à l'imaginaire. Car la France Libre a été à la fois une réalité et un mythe. Il a été l'artisan conscient de l'un et de l'autre. De la creation du mythe, l'instrument le plus efficace aura été la radio de Londres, la BBC. La guerre mentale – guerre de propaganda, guerre de mots – a doublé la guerre des armes' (Crémieux-Brilhac, *La France Libre*, p. 278).

13. 'The first bastion of the Resistance': the beginnings of the Free French in London, 1940–1

Martyn Cornick

> O France, your misfortune outrages my heart:
> I have said it before, and will never get tired
> Of repeating this cry that springs forth from my soul,
> Whoever does harm to my mother is vile.[1]

This chapter[2] begins by exploring the role of Denis Saurat at the French Institute in London on behalf of the Free French in the early months of the Second World War. Saurat, director of the Institute since 1924, and, since 1926, chair of French language and literature at King's College London, is a neglected and rather misunderstood figure. It will then examine how some of the French already in the capital, especially journalists, and those who arrived there after the defeat became engaged on behalf of Free France. The chapter also reviews some of the ways in which French culture was mobilized to advance the same cause, including the composition of a little-known but important special issue of the literary review *Aguedal*.

Saurat is one of the more important among the 'Forgotten French', to borrow the term used by Nicholas Atkin.[3] If he later became neglected, in the 1930s and 1940s he occupied an important place in Franco-British

---

[1] 'O France, ton malheur m'indigne et m'est sacré. / Je l'ai dit, et jamais je ne me lasserai / De le redire, et c'est le grand cri de mon âme, / Quiconque fait du mal à ma mère est infâme' (Victor Hugo, quoted by Denis Saurat, 19 June 1940).

[2] This study has drawn on the following unpublished sources: Institut Français du Royaume-Uni (IFRU), Denis Saurat Archive (hereafter DSA) (my thanks to Philippe Lane and the staff at IFRU for their help); interview with Stéphane and Christiane Hessel, Paris, 27 June 2012 (my sincere thanks to Clara Mure-Petitjean for her help in arranging the interview, to Stéphane and Christiane Hessel for their welcome, and to the research committee of the University of Birmingham for their financial support); I am grateful too to Patrick and Philippe Saurat for permission to read their grandfather's unpublished correspondence with Jean Paulhan, conserved at Abbaye d'Ardenne, Institut Mémoires de l'Edition Contemporaine (IMEC) Archive Centre.

[3] N. Atkin, *The Forgotten French: Exiles in the British Isles, 1940–4* (Manchester and New York, 2003).

cultural relations, as attested by Margaret Storm Jameson: 'Saurat was one of that handful of Frenchmen who have loved England. Loved it not blindly, as many Englishmen love France, but with a clear-sighted understanding of our faults and virtues. His passionate friendship with England did him lasting harm with his countrymen'. Saurat certainly was a multi-faceted creature: a capable administrator, a scholar, a 'mystical poet, a dreamer', a 'philosopher fascinated and a little repelled by the unconscious myth-making energies of the mind'. Jameson continues her portrait: 'He was not only bilingual, writing English as he wrote French, with ease, lucidity, wit, not only a scholarly critic of our literature, not only a poet in the tradition of English mystical poetry; he had an English heart living in what seemed complete amity with his mercurial French mind'.[4]

In addition to his official roles, after the outbreak of war in September and in the lead up to the Fall of France in June 1940, Saurat's Institute functioned as a rallying point for those French either already in the capital, or for those who succeeded in escaping Occupied France. Using his archives, as well as other, published, sources, this first section will sketch out Saurat's background, how the Institute came to be seen as a 'First Bastion of the Resistance', and how Saurat came to the aid of Charles de Gaulle on the latter's arrival in London.

Denis Saurat – from Toulouse to London

The initial focus of attention, then, is Denis Saurat, director of the French Institute in London. It is, of course, idle to speculate on how de Gaulle would have fared under different circumstances following his arrival in London in June 1940, but it is clear that Saurat, with access to a network of contacts among the established French 'colony' in London, as well as his contacts with figures in the British establishment, provided much ready support for de Gaulle.[5] Indeed, Paul Dupays, in one of the first volumes of his *Historical Chronicles* of the Second World War dating from 1951, opens his account on the 'Unassailable Island' (that is, Britain) with a reference to the:

> members of the London French 'colony', representing all classes and situations, [who] met on 9 July 1940, following the suggestion of Mr. Guéritte, former president of the French Chamber of Commerce in London, and pledged the active collaboration of French people residing in Britain to work hard for the British government. After a detailed examination of the situation, it

---

[4] M. S. Jameson, *Journey from the North: Autobiography of Storm Jameson* (2 vols., 1970), ii. 74.

[5] See especially Atkin, *Forgotten French*, ch. 5.

was decided to create a liaison committee between the French 'colony' and the government. The committee recognized the importance of the declaration made by Churchill whereby an English victory would lead to the liberation of France. The members of the provisional committee decided to renew their pledge to the British government to do their utmost to work together, as had been expressed by the permanent committee in its telegram of 20 June 1940.[6]

Denis Saurat was a member of this committee and had already been instrumental in enabling meetings and committee work to take place at the French Institute, in Queensberry Place, South Kensington, and at his residence at 33 Cromwell Road, opposite the Natural History Museum. During his many years in London prior to 1940, Saurat had constructed an extensive and rich cultural network, which included personal links with the prestigious monthly review, *La Nouvelle Revue française*, under the direction of Jean Paulhan. Indeed, it is significant that Paulhan, having fled south in the exodus from northern France in June 1940, and having already placed his faith in the British to stand up to Hitler, wrote to signal his appreciation of the presence of Frenchmen such as Saurat in London. Somehow, his letter got through to the British capital:

> If this letter reaches you, please, I implore you, let me have news of you and yours. The war has forced us all the way down to Carcassonne. We were trying to publish another issue of the *Nouvelle Revue française*, while still free, but our printers, one after the other, have been occupied … our sons are safe and sound. What has happened? Maybe one day we will be able to talk about it openly, without feeling too much sadness and shame. It will be explained by many reasons, and especially by those reasons which make us think about you, at this moment, with even more hope and friendship than usual.[7]

---

[6] See P. Dupays, *L'Île imprenable. Chronique historique, la Grande Bretagne juillet–août 1940* (Paris, n.d. [1950–1?]), p. 1. All translations are mine unless indicated otherwise: 'Les membres de la colonie française de Londres, représentant toutes les classes et situations, se réunissent le 9 juillet 1940, sur la proposition de M. Guéritte, ancien président de la Chambre de commerce pour apporter au gouvernement britannique la collaboration active des Français résidant en Grande-Bretagne. Après un examen minutieux de la situation, on décide de créer un comité de liaison entre la Colonie française et le gouvernement britannique. Le comité prend acte de la déclaration faite par Churchill signifiant que la victoire anglaise favorisera la libération de la France. Les membres du comité provisoire décident de renouveler au gouvernement britannique "l'assurance de collaboration totale" exprimée par le Comité permanent dans son télégramme du 20 juin 1940. Ils font aussitôt appel à tous les résidents français de la Grande Bretagne pour obtenir leur adhésion'.

[7] IFRU, DSA, unpublished letter from Jean Paulhan to Denis Saurat dated 14 Aug. 1940: 'Si ce mot vous parvient, donnez-moi, je vous prie, de vos nouvelles, et des nouvelle des vôtres. La guerre nous a repoussés jusque vers Carcassonne. Il s'agissait de publier encore une *NRF* libre, mais nos imprimeries, l'une après l'autre occupées … nos fils sont sains et

Because of the strong possibility that his letter might be opened or censored by the authorities, Paulhan is guarded in his comments, but it provides a clear enough early indication that the French were thinking of friends or acquaintances in London, and that they might ultimately work for a cause different from that prevailing in Occupied France.

We shall begin by outlining Denis Saurat's career as a scholar of English literature, teacher and cultural organizer.[8] He was born on 21 March 1890, in Toulouse. In 1894 the family moved to Trélon, in the Nord, where, between 1908 and 1911, Saurat enrolled as a student, first at the Ecole Normale d'Instituteurs (a teacher training school) in Douai, and then, specializing in English studies, in the Université de Lille. This would prove to be a happy coincidence as arrangements were being made in 1910 with the Université de Lille to found the French Institute in London.[9] Once he had graduated, Saurat took teaching posts in English at Valréas and Bourges. In the First World War, he was spared front-line service because of his myopia. After the war he took the examinations for the *agrégation d'anglais*, in which he was ranked first. Thus was his career launched. In 1920, he was granted a post as *professeur* in a Bordeaux *lycée*, and that year, based at the Sorbonne, he began his doctorate on the thought of the English poet John Milton. During these studies he built on his interests in metaphysics, esotericism and especially occultism. He believed he had discovered an influence of the Zohar, from the Kabbalah tradition, in certain passages of Milton's *Paradise Lost* and in Blake. Later debates in academic journals would take issue with these interpretations, but Saurat's influence in the inter-war period over studies on Milton, Blake and, in France, Victor Hugo, is undeniable. His doctoral studies resulted in his first book, *La Pensée de Milton*, published in 1920 by Alcan (Paris). In 1923, he was appointed professor of English at the Université de Bordeaux.

These achievements impressed those recruiting in 1924 for the directorship of the French Institute in London: Saurat would occupy the post there until 1945. His academic credentials, and knowledge of the English education system, again facilitated his appointment in 1926 as professor of French language and literature at King's College London, a post he retained until

---

saufs. Que s'est-il passé? Peut-être pourrons-nous quelque jour en parler librement, sans trop de tristesse ni de honte. Cela dépendra de bien des raisons et de celles en particulier qui me font songer à vous, en ce moment, avec un peu plus d'espoir et d'amitié encore que d'habitude'.

[8] For details of Saurat's career I have drawn principally on documents, CVs and manuscript and typewritten log sheets conserved in DSA, as well as the obituary in *The Times*, 10 June 1958.

[9] See the chapter in this volume by Charlotte Faucher and Philippe Lane.

1950. With his career as an academic now well established, in 1930 and 1932 he accepted posts of visiting assistant professor at Columbia University, in New York. He made return visits to Paris, where he would often meet with Jean Paulhan; their networks included the Education Ministry. Aged forty-four, his professional and cultural work was recognized by the award of Chevalier of the Légion d'Honneur.[10] The appointments to the French Institute and to King's College represent a considerable achievement, given the formidable workload accruing to a university departmental head, not to mention developing the skills and networks required to organize teaching, as well as a regular cultural programme at the Institute. Sometimes, of course, his dual role created fruitful connections for both organizations.

Emile Delavenay who, as well shall see, would play a leading role in the BBC's European Intelligence Department during the war, had lodgings for a while at the Maison of the Institute, and he records that Saurat recruited him to undertake conversation classes at King's College, as well as teaching at the Institute.[11] In regard to his cultural networking, Saurat's posts at King's and the Institute gave him the means (and the budgets) to invite high-profile speakers to London, showing just how vital was his contribution to maintaining French cultural life in the city. Among those whom Saurat invited were Paul Valéry, Georges Duhamel, André Maurois, Paul Morand, André Chamson, Henry de Montherlant, Jean Giraudoux, Jules Supervielle, Paul Eluard and Louis Aragon. In his correspondence with Paulhan he was not afraid to express his frank views. When Jules Romains was due to come to London in 1935, he wrote: 'Romains is really, really weak. He's coming in November and will have an enormous success'.[12] Finally, Saurat's pre-war interests in occultism and esotericism came to fruition in 1935 when, with Herbert Read, he co-edited A. R. Orage's *Selected Essays and Critical Writings*.[13] According to Saurat, Orage's review, *The New Age*, had been one of the liveliest intellectual forums in Britain between 1910 and 1914.

---

[10] It is a speculative point, but it is possible that his nomination for this honour was supported by Jean Paulhan, who was often consulted on such conferments by his friend Louis Planté, at the Education Ministry (see L. Planté, *Au 110 rue de Grenelle: souvenirs, scènes et aspects du Ministère de l'Instruction Publique-Education nationale (1920–44)* (Paris, 1967).

[11] E. Delavenay, *Témoignage: d'un village savoyard au village mondial* (Aix-en-Provence, 1992), pp. 92ff.

[12] Abbaye d'Ardenne, IMEC, Fonds Paulhan, unpublished letter from Denis Saurat to Jean Paulhan, dated 6 Sept. 1935: '[Romains:] C'est vraiment très très faible … Il vient en novembre et va avoir un succès énorme'. Delavenay bears witness too to Romains' boorish behaviour, in *Témoignage*, p. 92.

[13] See also, on the eccentric Russian occultist Gurdjieff, 'Visite à Gourdjieff', *La Nouvelle Revue française*, Nov. 1933, p. 686–98; 'Gourdjieff et Orage', *La Nouvelle Revue française*, June 1934, p. 1052.

Denis Saurat's war

Around the time of the Munich Accords in 1938, because he held semi-official status in London, Saurat told Paulhan he would have to cease his contributions to the *Nouvelle Revue française*. With the outbreak of war in September 1939, he strove to present the French point of view in a series of lectures and talks, some or all of which were broadcast on the BBC, and then published as pamphlets. These efforts were, of course, rapidly overtaken by events once the German assaults began on 10 May 1940. Around the time of Dunkirk, there was still talk in some circles in London of the possibilities of furthering an 'Intellectual Entente' between France and Britain:

> The first of a series of four articles by that recognized interpreter of England to France and of France to England M. Denis Saurat … will be published in our next issue June 22. *The articles will discuss the possibilities of a true entente cordiale in the intellectual sphere.* The first deals with religious differences and affinities as prelude to an examination of the other cultural fields in each country.[14]

His lectures and talks came out as brochures, under the titles *The Spirit of France* (Dent) and *French War Aims* (Methuen). Saurat also participated in a short-lived venture entitled the 'Post-War Bureau'.[15] This evidence reminds us that one must strive to retain a sense of historical perspective and not be too tempted to rush to judgement: no-one at the time could yet predict the outcome of the campaign as the Phoney War turned into the Battle of France.

When it did become clear in mid June 1940 that France was indeed heading toward defeat, and that Marshal Pétain was suing for an armistice, Saurat would rally to the cause of the newly arrived General. André Weil-Curiel, a liaison officer with the British Army during the Battle for France, was evacuated from Dunkirk in the first days of June 1940. Almost immediately after his arrival at Dover, he and his comrades were sent to Weymouth where a number of vessels were waiting to repatriate French troops to France. Everywhere along their route, English people were welcoming and generous towards them: this is an observation that recurs repeatedly in the memoirs of the Free French. Eventually, in the confusion, Weil-Curiel was sent to Tidworth camp, near Andover, where 'tens of thousands' of French troops were assembled, awaiting repatriation. However, Weil-Curiel and another comrade had written to Henri Hauck, an attaché at the French Embassy in London responsible for questions relating to work and the trades unions, and just before they were due to return to France, they received a counter-

---

[14] *Times Literary Supplement*, 15 June 1940, p. 291 (my emphasis).
[15] Letter to *The Times*, 6 May 1940, p. 9. The signatories were Norman Angell, David Astor, Ivor Churchill, Edward Hulton, Denis Saurat and John A. Hutton.

order inviting them to London. This would determine Weil-Curiel's future engagement in the Free French:

> Once in London, we went straight to the French Institute, 15 Queensberry Way, where we'd been told to go. Hauck ... brought us up to date. On his initiative, the head of French Information Services, [Paul-Louis] Bret, former Havas correspondent in London, had decided to recruit a number of Frenchmen who spoke English to stimulate the English war effort and aid to an imperilled France by means of radio talks, lectures and press articles. It was all too obvious that the mass of the public had no real appreciation of the gravity of the situation.[16]

Weil-Curiel went off to give lectures and talks in the city of Leeds. On his return, by mid June, the situation in France was deteriorating inexorably towards the 'capitulation', culminating in Pétain's broadcast on 17 June 1940 calling for a ceasefire. In the meantime, it had become clear that Hauck, Georges Boris, Emile Delavenay (whose name is misspelt by Weil-Curiel as Delavenai) and Captain Métadier, a doctor by training, a pharmacist by trade and a member of the permanent French colony in London, were all prepared to continue the fight. These men all gravitated around Saurat's French Institute. Weil-Curiel gives an insight into their resolve: 'Métadier approved my plan completely [to form a French National committee]. He realized the importance of our strategic position in this French Institute in London, *a parcel of French territory which could become the first bastion of the resistance*'.[17] At this crucial moment, the Institute represented a rallying point for these few, like-minded French in London: it was essential that it remain under their control so that the British had proof that they would ensure the 'continuity of France'. Despite being thoroughly 'downcast' by the terrible news from France, Saurat agreed to allow the Institute to be used in this way. Weil-Curiel, recalling the moment when 'pétainisme' manifested itself in some quarters of the London French community after the Marshal's broadcast, suggests that he and others were already convinced that the British would be the first to resist Hitler's eventual attempt to

---

[16] A. Weil-Curiel, *Le Jour se lève à Londres* (Paris, 1945), chs. 11, 12, quotation at pp. 170–1: 'Arrivés à Londres, nous allâmes immédiatement à l'Institut français, 15, Queensberry Way, où l'on nous avait dit de nous présenter. Hauck ... nous mit au fait de la situation. Sur sa proposition, le chef des Services Français d'Information, Bret, ancien correspondant d'Havas à Londres, avait décidé de recruter quelques Français connaissant l'anglais pour stimuler au moyen de discours à la radio, de conférences et, au besoin, d'articles de presse, l'effort de guerre et l'aide à la France en danger. Il n'était que trop évident que l'on ne se rendait pas compte dans le grand public de la gravité de la situation'.

[17] 'Métadier ... m'approuvait entièrement. Il sentait l'importance de notre position stratégique dans cet Institut français de Londres, parcelle de terre française qui pouvait devenir le premier bastion de la résistance' (Weil-Curiel, *Le Jour*, p. 203 (my italics)).

invade: 'Yet from this very moment I was ready to bet fifty-to-one that the British would only stop fighting when they had won or when they were no longer capable of doing so. Also, should our efforts fail to keep France in the war, we could still save our honour by fighting alongside the British'.[18]

De Gaulle spoke on the BBC the very next day, delivering what would be known as the 'Appel du 18 juin' but which, then, was labelled 'Rien n'est perdu' ('Nothing is lost').[19] The next day was an important one for the French in London: at 10.30am, Saurat hosted a meeting at his house in Cromwell Road, with 'Petit, Métadier, Hauck, Boris, Lord Ivor Churchill', where they resolved to 'rally to de Gaulle'; at 3.00pm, the permanent French Committee met ('Thémoins, Petit, Saurat', etc.), recording in the notes that they wished 'to continue the fight'; and at 10.30pm, with Métadier, Hauck and others, Saurat went to meet de Gaulle at 8 Seamore Place, to pledge the support of the Institute.[20] According to Storm Jameson, Saurat was 'fiercely devoted' to the General, pledging that he would do 'anything on earth for him'.[21]

De Gaulle would see him frequently over the next few weeks, as we shall see. Saurat found that he was even busier than usual. He delivered a programme of talks ('practically single-handed') at the Institute as there were few if no French speakers available: 'This effort was so appreciated by the public that the audience was approximately four times bigger than before the war; the Institute never closed, even during the summer months'.[22] It was recognized that maintaining the cultural effort was of crucial importance because, as many were to insist in the coming months, France was considered vital to the continuation of Western civilization. The day after meeting de Gaulle, Saurat and Yves Morvan (a journalist of long standing in London and already engaged at the BBC, better known as Jean Marin) performed a dialogue at 8.30 pm, on the 'Ici la France' programme – 'Reflect, and draw up your own account of the philosophical, intellectual and artistic wealth of the world, and see the share of France in all this. The gigantic share of France' – and Saurat mobilized Victor Hugo to launch

[18] 'Toutefois, j'étais prêt dès cet instant, à parier à cinquante contre un, que les Anglais ne cesseraient la lutte que quand ils seraient vainqueurs ou définitivement hors du combat. Et alors, au cas où nos efforts pour maintenir la France dans la guerre échoueraient, il nous resterait toujours la ressource de sauver l'honneur dans les rangs britanniques' (Weil-Curiel, *Le Jour*, p. 206).

[19] See *Discours et messages du Général de Gaulle* (1942), pp. 1–2.

[20] IFRU, DSA, typed and MS. log sheets.

[21] Jameson reports Saurat thus: 'Keep your eyes on him, he isn't only one man, he is France, my France. I'll do anything on earth for him. It rather looks as though no writer has had the sense to follow him to London' (Jameson, *Journey from the North*, p. 76).

[22] IFRU, DSA, extract from Saurat CV.

the cultural battle to safeguard French civilization.[23] Thus began a process which led eventually to the dropping by the RAF over France of what came to be known as French resistance poetry.[24]

Much has been written and continues to be written about de Gaulle's arrival in London, and about how different groups and individuals reacted to his presence there.[25] This is not the place to revisit these debates. Suffice it to say that in the first few months his presence and, above all, his words about keeping the 'flame of resistance' burning, are remembered in memoirs with deep affection. Most recall also the experience of the Free French recruitment centre at Olympia Hall, in west London, 'a ghastly, cavernous place', in the words of François Jacob, the future Nobel laureate, 'a sort of cross between the Saint-Lazare train station and the Samaritaine department store':

> Discussions went on without end. Always passionate. Sometimes violent ... Our principal theme was: What to join? What army? What branch? ... Rumor had it that General de Gaulle was forming a 'legion' of French volunteers ... A captain came to the Olympia to speak and explain what de Gaulle had in mind, what the Free French forces were to be. Not a legion, but an army ... regular troops with regular officers. Their goal: to return French units to the battlefields; to bring French territories into the war; to have France's part in the struggle against Germany and its allies recognized by foreign countries. The next day, we decided to join up ... I opted for the artillery.[26]

At Delville camp, part of the Aldershot army base, Jacob was recruited as a doctor: 'At this base in the English countryside were stationed the three

---

[23] IFRU, DSA, copy of BBC script, dated 20 June 1940: 'O France, ton malheur m'indigne et m'est sacré. / Je l'ai dit, et jamais je ne me lasserai / De le redire, et c'est le grand cri de mon âme, / Quiconque fait du mal à ma mère est infâme' (quoted from V. Hugo, *L'Art d'être grand-père*, xviii: *que les petits liront quand ils seront grands* (Paris, 1877).

[24] J. Bennett, *Aragon, Londres et la France libre* (Paris, 1998); T. Brooks, *British Propaganda to France, 1940–4: Machinery, Method and Message* (Edinburgh, 2007); and V. Holman, 'Airborne culture: propaganda leaflets dropped over France in the Second World War', in *Free Print and Non-Commercial Publishing since 1700*, ed. J. Raven (Aldershot, 2000), pp. 194–221.

[25] E.g., J.-L. Crémieux-Brilhac, *La France Libre: de l'appel du 18 juin à la Libération* (Paris, 1996), pp. 43–101; more recently, J.-L. Crémieux-Brilhac, *Georges Boris: trente ans d'influence. Blum, de Gaulle, Mendès France* (Paris, 2010), pp. 137–57. See also the more unconventional and very suggestive reading of the whole question in R. Belot, *La Résistance sans de Gaulle* (Paris, 2006).

[26] F. Jacob, *The statue within: an autobiography*, trans. F. Philip (1988), pp. 115–16. For Yves Guéna, Olympia represented the birthplace of Free France (*Le Temps des certitudes, 1940–69* (Paris, 1982), pp. 9–11), and Jean-Mathieu Boris remembers with emotion the spontaneous rendition of the Marseillaise there (see *Combattant de la France libre* (Paris, 2012), p. 45).

or four thousand men who, in July 1940, made up the Free French forces'. Jacob describes what de Gaulle meant for these raw recruits, cut off from family and news from France, in a passage that finds many echoes in other works:

> Most of us had never seen or heard the leader of the Free French … But we knew mainly the tract posted on the walls of London: 'France has lost a battle, but she has not lost the war'. And, then, there was the name 'de Gaulle', which rang like a challenge. A program … It was a very Gothic personage that I saw when … the general strode before the assembled troops … It was France itself standing erect in this corner of England. My spine tingled. A short speech by the general. An impressive figure … He spoke. He fulminated. He thundered against Pétain's government … He promised us fights, victories. *The* victory. [We had] the impression that de Gaulle was beyond any doubt the man for the situation. The impression that to make war, to participate in the reconquest of France, we had found the right address.[27]

Saurat's networks and his knowledge of London were immediately helpful to the Free French cause. When René Cassin arrived at the Institute on 28 June 1940, it was Saurat who recommended lodgings and arranged for volunteer 'conductrices' to drive him to see de Gaulle the next day.[28] His contacts afforded immediate access for de Gaulle and his supporters to the highest levels of the British establishment, for instance through Lord Ivor Churchill and Lord Askwith.[29] He was also a member of the Athenaeum Club. From 21 June 1940 he met with and accompanied de Gaulle frequently during these first weeks and months. One curious instance arose on 17 July, when, with de Gaulle present in the audience, Saurat delivered a talk at Queen's Hall designed to introduce the General to the public. Entitled 'Modern warfare and civilians', the main theme was that 'the British will not be "done in" … never will the heart of Great Britain forget France'; 'We will not reconquer France, we will invade Germany'. This was, of course, premature and politically unrealistic at a moment when the German Occupation was ever tightening its grip on France. Saurat's speech

---

[27] Jacob, *Statue Within*, pp. 118, 121–2.

[28] R. Cassin, *Les Hommes partis de rien* (Paris, 1987), pp. 71–2.

[29] Lord Ivor Churchill (1898–1956) was Winston Churchill's cousin, and an ardent Francophile. He also promoted the Amis des Volontaires Français (see Cassin, *Hommes partis de rien*, p. 179). Baron George Askwith (1861–1942) was a trade union negotiator and civil servant, and served as chairman of the Board of the French Institute (see H. Goiron, *Les Français à Londres* (Pornic, 1933), p. 239). Saurat's papers show that he and Askwith were close friends. Angela Mond, widow of the one of the principal benefactors of the Lycée Français, the eminent chemist Emile Mond (1865–1938), offered charitable donations to the French Institute (letters in DSA).

was, however, enthusiastically welcomed by the *Evening Standard*, whose reporter's interest was clearly piqued by the attitude of the 'Silent General'.[30] Yet this did not prevent the theme from being taken up by Georges Boris and developed into the very first book published on de Gaulle, *De Gaulle's France and the Key to the Coming Invasion of Germany*, by James Marlow, the nom de plume of journalist Richard Crawford. Mass-Observation was present at the talk, and recorded that the ovation lasted for 117 seconds, observing too that this was a 'surprisingly large gathering for such a meeting'. It was a rather embarrassed Saurat who returned to the podium to offer apologies for the General making no speech: 'he will speak after the victory'.[31] In the coming months, once de Gaulle's HQ became established in Carlton Gardens, changes were made which tended to side-line Saurat; he nevertheless travelled the length and breadth of the country, delivering lectures on behalf of the Free French, stressing the importance of French Africa and the future, post-war, role for France.[32] Indeed, between February and May 1941, Saurat was sent on an exploratory teaching mission to the Congo, Chad and the Cameroon, the result of which was another 'war pamphlet', *Watch over Africa* (Dent, 1941).[33] And as the numbers of French people arriving in London increased, Saurat continued the programme of talks at the Institute. Military and political speakers included Louis Marin, Félix Gouin, Henri Queuille, Vincent Auriol, Philippe Barrès, Generals Petit, Sicé and Valin, and Admiral Thierry d'Argenlieu.

In early July 1940, while accompanying Saurat to an appointment, de Gaulle requested him to 'do what I asked you last Friday [28 June]: we need a philosophy'.[34] The result was *Regeneration*, published in September 1940, with an introductory letter from de Gaulle in which he referred to Saurat as at once 'an analyst' and 'a synthesist'. 'There are two parts in the

---

[30] IFRU, DSA, press cutting, 'Silent General', *Evening Standard*, 18 July 1940.

[31] IFRU, DSA, log sheets and press cuttings; Mass-Observation report on France for July 1940, 'Lecture by Professor Saurat'. See also J. Marlow, *De Gaulle's France and the Key to the Coming Invasion of Germany* (1940); and Crémieux-Brilhac, *Georges Boris*, p. 109.

[32] E.g., IFRU, press cuttings in DSA, *Perthshire Constitutional*, 15 Oct. 1940; *The Scotsman*, 22 Oct. 1940; *Eastern Daily Press*, 18 Nov. 1940; *Dean Forest Mercury*, 22 Nov. 1940. See also 'France waits for another 14 July', *Daily Mail*, 14 July 1941. There is evidence to suggest that Saurat distanced himself from the De Gaulle camp because to him the General appeared too dictatorial and with René Cassin wished to transform the Institute against Saurat's wishes (see Atkin, *Forgotten French*, pp. 213–14, and V. Dupray, R. Lacombre and O. Poivre D'Arvor, *Londres sur Seine. Une histoire de l'Institut français du Royaume-Uni (1910–80)* (Paris, 1996)).

[33] An extract appeared in French: 'Attention au Tchad', *La France Libre*, ii (20 June 1941), 142–6.

[34] IFRU, DSA, foolscap MS. log sheet, [July 1940]: 'Faites ce que je vous ai dit vendredi: il nous faut une philosophie'.

human soul', began Saurat, 'a part of the soul which is clear and precise …
It is conscious of itself and resolute when at its best. This may be called the
Head'. But there was a much larger, chaotic, part of the soul 'best referred
to in the plural as the Masses'. He went on: 'The relationship between
the main parts, the head and the masses, is complicated and not clear'. In
what appears to be a reference to de Gaulle, Saurat noted that 'A new head
has been thrown up by the masses in an emergency'. There was a kind of
dialectic in play: the head was fed by the masses, but this head should not
be overpowered; at the same time, the masses should follow the head, all the
while remaining free and spontaneous. Saurat's philosophy for de Gaulle,
or, more accurately, for a restored Western civilization, arose more from a
restoration of religiosity than from practical politics: 'The spirit of man is
truly liberated for higher purposes than even those of mankind when this
true relationship of leadership to the masses within the soul is realized.
Then the soul is polarized and its energies flow in the direction of God'.[35]

Looking towards future 'Spiritual Reconstruction', Saurat assumed that,
as in the past, 'all civilizations have a religious basis'. Nazism and communism
were dominant because they resembled 'animated' and 'active' religions,
'whereas our religions are so tepid that they hardly stir at all'. Religion
and education had failed, so in future they would need to be properly
reconstituted. In the end, concluded Saurat, 'the problems of politics can
only be solved in the religious sphere; for God is the Chief really'. The
decadence of French (and Western, Judaeo-Christian) civilization would
only be arrested by a true return, in the post-war world, to religiosity.[36]
Saurat argued for reform of education after the war, not only in Germany,
but everywhere: 'Literature is education, it draws certain things out of the
human heart and spirit'.[37] It is not recorded what de Gaulle thought of this
text, which owes more to Saurat's interests in spiritualism than to political
philosophy.

After his return from his African mission, in September 1941 Saurat
hosted the seventeenth International Conference of PEN at the French
Institute. As Jennifer Birkett has shown, with Storm Jameson, Saurat was
central to the organization of this impressive conference; he participated
himself. Despite the windows of the Institute being blown out by bombs,
the conference went ahead. 'London had taken the place of Paris as a
cultural hive (alas, without cafés)', quipped Jameson; PEN representatives
from thirty-five countries attended, and the proceedings were published.

---

[35] D. Saurat, *Regeneration* (1940), pp. 7–9.
[36] Saurat, *Regeneration*, pp. 51, 52–62, 64.
[37] Saurat, *Regeneration*, p. 49.

André Labarthe laid much stress on the propaganda value of the conference, as it provided a striking example from a city 'in the front line of the battle' showing that 'the spirit remains free though the battle rages'.[38] For Storm Jameson, despite the Blitz and the thousands of civilians who were being 'assassinated' by the Luftwaffe, and despite London's 'ravaged streets', 'London had become the cultural centre of Free Europe'.[39] The conference defiantly showed that, against the odds, the Institute was keeping French and European culture alive in London when France and Europe were under the thrall of the Nazis; it also laid much stress on the importance of a new, European, organization of cultural politics after the war.

La France Libre *at the French Institute*
The most important cultural effort at the Institute on behalf of the French in London centred on the creation there of the journal *La France Libre*, under the direction of André Labarthe, with the tireless contributions of Raymond Aron.[40] Saurat's networks in educational and intellectual circles in London helped to expedite its creation, as shown by a circular letter sent to potentially interested parties in August 1940 and signed by various luminaries of British intellectual life, among them William Bragg, president of the Royal Society, Frederick Kenyon, secretary to the British Academy, Edwin Lutyens, president of the Royal Society of Arts, and J. B. Priestley. With France in German hands, there was now no opportunity for free expression. This clearly threw into relief the cultural, political and ultimately propaganda value behind the continuation and promotion of a 'free' French culture. Those few 'exiles' to have escaped to London, and who had intellectual interests, now needed to express themselves, and to do so they planned a 'periodical', *La France Libre*. Moreover, it would have 'intrinsic' value which scholars would 'relish', and there was cause for great confidence as there 'will be many able contributors'. Expressions of support and interest were to be addressed to 'Dr André Labarthe'.[41] The resulting issues of this review – the first one appeared on 15 November 1940 – do not disappoint. The magazine was read avidly by its French readers in London,

---

[38] Jameson, *Journey from the North*, p. 103; J. Birkett, *Margaret Storm Jameson* (Oxford, 2009), pp. 202–14; for Labarthe, see *Writers in Freedom*, ed. H. Ould (1942), pp. 38–43, at p. 38. Jacques Maritain's message from New York was also translated by Storm Jameson, and Saurat's intervention was recycled from *Regeneration* (*Writers in Freedom*, pp. 43–51).

[39] M. S. Jameson, 'Le 17ᶜᵐᵉ Congrès international des P.E.N.', *La France Libre*, ii (1941), 395–9, at p. 395).

[40] For Raymond Aron's role in this review, see the chapter by David Drake in this volume. See also Belot, *La Résistance sans de Gaulle*, pp. 52–60.

[41] IFRU, DSA, circular letter dated 'Aug. 1940'.

British university libraries readily subscribed, and on the review's first anniversary Winston Churchill wrote to congratulate Labarthe for keeping alive the flame of hope in Frenchmen for a future in which they would all be able to express themselves freely.[42] Later, *La France Libre* was also printed in a miniature edition for distribution by the RAF over France.[43]

La France Libre was dedicated to Franco-British amity, and sought to understand and explain the Allied defeat of June 1940. 'M. R.', in an article in the first issue, offered a close examination of the successive reactions in Britain to the 'capitulation'. A clear distinction should be made between the 'French people' and the 'Vichy government'. There were now plenty of eye-witness accounts to counter the view that French soldiers had been hopeless in battle. The British too were willing to admit their faults during the years of peace. Once again, the British recognized the need to fight towards victory to liberate France and to restore France to 'its true greatness'.[44] In the following article, which extolled 'French humanism' – again, seen as indispensable to European civilization – the novelist Ignace Legrand saw the inter-war period as a crisis of humanism; as soon as its 'corrupters', Hitler and Mussolini, were swept away, 'then our French humanism, for an instant obscured, will be reborn more alive and more glorious than ever'.[45] David Murray, the editor of the *Times Literary Supplement*, thought that Legrand's sentiment here 'might be taken as the motto of *La France Libre*'.[46]

Another writer to leave France for exile in London was Albert Cohen. He would carry out a mission representing the international Jewish Agency to various exiled governments in the English capital. He submitted a tribute to *La France Libre* in which, among other things, he celebrated the attitudes of the British towards France and of Londoners in the Blitz: 'Their French friend has given up the fight but they love her as before'. In fact, the English always took care to remember that 'France was betrayed, not traitorous'. 'This gentle people is strong', continued Cohen, and likened the British war effort to the biblical struggle between David and Goliath. In highly-charged, poetic and rhythmic prose, repeating the phrase 'Victoire de l'homme' ('Man triumphant'), Cohen paid tribute to Londoners' tenacity:

---

[42] Churchill Archive, CHAR 20/22 C, letter from W. S. Churchill to André Labarthe dated 29 Oct. 1941.

[43] Brooks, *British Propaganda to France*, p. 135.

[44] M. R., 'L'amitié franco-anglaise depuis la capitulation de juin 1940', *La France Libre*, i (15 Nov. 1940), 70–1.

[45] I. Legrand, 'L'humanisme français', *La France Libre*, i (15 Nov. 1940), 72–6: 'Alors notre humanisme français, un instant obscurci, renaîtra plus vivant, plus glorieux que jamais'.

[46] *Times Literary Supplement*, 30 Nov. 1940, p. 597.

Every night, for months on end, Londoners held firm, with no idle words, maintaining their daily routine. They would never mention freedom. They were defending it. Every night, there were noses torn off, eyes put out, jaws smashed, burials alive, and, worst of all, heads expecting death to fall on them. But every night there was calm and decency in every English head.[47]

Jean Vacher contributed a fascinating article, inspired by some important contemporary sources, to mark the second anniversary of the declaration of war. What was different now, in September 1941, was that in a world whose face had become distorted by hatred and violence, France was rising again, 'more radiant than ever', because of 'her martyrs' following the example set by the Battle of Britain, which had not merely saved the country from invasion, it had shown too that resistance could become a philosophy of existence.[48]

Finally, there is no doubting that the French Institute was truly in the front line during the Blitz, as it was damaged at various points during the war. In 1943, or during a 'baby Blitz' in 1944 (the sources vary), Robert Loyalty Cru, London correspondent of the Paris newspaper *Le Temps* and manager of the Maison de l'Institut at Queen's Gate, was killed outright by a bomb, along with all the inhabitants of the Maison. Despite having constructed a solid shelter in the garden, the building 'was smashed to bits'.[49] In a somewhat dubious play on words, Franck Bauer writes that 'poor Mr Cru [which means 'raw' in French] was cooked in his shelter'.[50] Later, Denis Saurat himself was severely injured by a V1 explosion at 33 Cromwell Road: 'During the air-raids a bomb brought his house down on him, dislocating his joints; he endured weeks of pain by coolly and subtly

---

[47] A. Cohen, 'Angleterre', *La France Libre*, ii (20 June 1941), 114–23, quotations at pp. 119–21 (collected in A. Cohen, *Écrits d'Angleterre* (Paris, 2002)): 'Leur amie française qui a renoncé à la lutte, ils l'aiment comme autrefois … Les Anglais savent ne jamais oublier que la France fut trahie et non traîtresse … Cette race douce est forte. Au mois de juin de l'année dernière, cette petite île … s'est trouvée seule. Vraiment David contre Goliath … Chaque nuit, pendant des mois, les hommes de Londres tenaient ferme, sans rhétorique, en toute quotidienneté. Ils ne parlaient jamais de la liberté. Ils la défendaient. Chaque nuit, il y avait des nez arrachés, des yeux crevés, des mâchoires fracassées, des enterrements vivants et, pire que tout, la tête qui attend la mort sur la tête. Mais chaque nuit, il y avait le calme et la décence dans chaque tête anglaise'.

[48] J. Vacher, 'Témoignages sur l'Angleterre en guerre', *La France Libre*, ii (15 Sept. 1941), 378–83. Vacher had been a member of the military mission in London before the war and chose to stay on in London (Delavenay, *Témoignage*, p. 228).

[49] Delavenay, *Témoignage*, pp. 90, 273; R. Mengin, *No Laurels for De Gaulle*, trans. J. Allen (1967), pp. 104–6, 134. Some of Robert Cru's pithy articles are collected in *Propos d'un Londonien* (Paris, 1936).

[50] 'le pauvre M. Cru fut cuit dans son abri' (F. Bauer, *40 à Londres: l'espion qui venait du jazz* (Paris, 2004), p. 303).

Figure 13.1. 33, Cromwell Road, after the V1 attack,
July 1944, IFRU, Denis Saurat Archive.

examining the nature of pain'. He was fortunate to escape with his life. Indeed, Saurat never fully recovered his health.[51]

London-French journalists fight the War of the Airwaves

At the end of the war, Georges Bidault, then French foreign minister and former Resistance leader, wrote a stirring tribute to the BBC to open the corporation's *Yearbook* for 1945.[52] He recalled that the French had been 'hurled living into the grave, [that] they had been walled up in a prison of silence where no friendly voice could ever reach them again'. In words echoing those of many who lived with the shock of defeat and Occupation, he described how those first days were dominated by fear, rumour and confusion. Bidault remembered that 'the law imposed by the occupying power would allow only submissive voices to be heard in France … voices soiled with vile ambitions'; France had been reduced to 'a hideous chattering of slaves'. However, inspired by de Gaulle's broadcast of 18 June 1940, and the daily offerings of the BBC French Service over the next four years, France was finally able to 'lift up the tombstone and from that time the voice of the BBC each day gave fresh impetus to the miracle of French resurrection'. He ended with a reminder of the call-sign-cum-title of the French Service: 'Ici Londres, les Français parlent aux Français'. This was the signal which, Bidault concluded, in the silence of the Occupation, 'when every mouth was gagged, helped the French to surmount and overcome the lies of the enemy. Largely thanks to you, our minds stayed free while our limbs were bound'.[53]

The BBC could never have fulfilled this extraordinary task without the unceasing efforts of many staff, who exploited the information they gleaned from the gradually increasing numbers of people who were arriving in London from France. The talents of the broadcasters themselves, the team of 'Les Français parlent aux Français', recruited by Cecilia Reeves and Darsie Gillie from July 1940 largely among French journalists already resident in London (and who did not wish to be repatriated), have been celebrated by historians, most recently in Crémieux-Brilhac's biography of Georges Boris, who spent much of the war engaged as a liaison officer between the Free French HQ at Carlton Gardens and the BBC.[54] Journalists

---

[51] Jameson, *Journey from the North*, pp. 74–5; IFRU, DSA, copies of Saurat CVs; *The Times*, 10 June 1958.

[52] Some of the material in this section is drawn from an unpublished paper entitled 'The BBC and French Resistance' prepared for the 70th anniversary of *L'Appel du 18 juin* conference, 16–17 June 2010, hosted by IFRU, and some of whose sessions may be consulted online at <http://culturetheque.org.uk> [accessed 14 January 2013].

[53] *BBC Yearbook 1945* (1945), pp. 12–14.

[54] Crémieux-Brilhac, *Georges Boris*, pt. 3; see also Crémieux-Brilhac, *La France Libre*, pp. 211–31.

Pierre Maillaud (better known as Pierre Bourdan) and Yves Morvan (Jean Marin) were the among the first, to be joined by theatre impresario Michel Saint-Denis, better known as Jacques Duchesne, and Maurice Schumann, who was responsible for the five-minute 'Honneur et Patrie' section linked with de Gaulle.[55] Others joined them, including Jean Oberlé, the humourist Pierre Dac and the jazz musician Franck Bauer, who was recruited in March 1941 for his amenable radio voice.[56] However, the BBC did not just make broadcasts. It was of vital importance in providing a reliable point of contact for the target audience, which in effect was the whole French population. Put succinctly, the BBC mediated the ideas and motivation necessary for awakening, encouraging and sustaining resistance in France. Alongside the Special Operations Executive (SOE), of course, over the months and years it slowly helped to transform vague notions of resistance into the more unified force it ultimately became.

Among the fraternity of French journalists in London who gravitated around Saurat's French Institute was Emile Delavenay, assistant director of the BBC's European Intelligence Department (EID).[57] A former student of the elite Ecole Normale Supérieure in Paris and Gonville and Caius College, Cambridge, specialist in the life and work of D. H. Lawrence, in the 1930s Delavenay worked in London at Havas, the French news agency, as well as carrying out diverse teaching duties, as we saw above. At Havas he developed an extensive network of contacts with other London-French journalists, such as the long-established Paul-Louis Bret, Paul-Henri Siriex and Jean Marin.[58] Stéphane Hessel remembers Delavenay (they were both former *normaliens*) as 'being a friend' and, alongside Saurat, as being 'incontestably one of the spokesmen for French culture in London'.[59] In 1939 Delavenay was recruited by the BBC and put to work on monitoring and, soon after, he joined the EID. Because of the recognized importance

[55] See C. Rimbaud, *Maurice Schumann: sa voix, son visage* (Paris, 2000), pp. 54–104.

[56] See, respectively, J. Oberlé, *'Jean Oberlé vous parle'* … (Paris, 1945); P. Dac, *Un Français Libre à Londres en guerre* (Paris, 1972); and Bauer, *40 à Londres*. See also T. Miller (dir.), *Libres Français de Londres 1940–4* (Cinétévé/ECPAD, 2010).

[57] See M. Cornick, 'The BBC and the propaganda war against Occupied France: the work of Emile Delavenay and the European Intelligence Department', *French History*, viii (1994), 316–54; and M. Cornick, '"Fraternity among listeners": the BBC and French Resistance', in *Vichy, Resistance, Liberation: New Perspectives on Wartime France*, ed. H. Diamond and S. Kitson (Oxford, 2005), pp. 101–13.

[58] P.-L. Bret, *Au feu des événements: mémoires d'un journaliste, Londres, Algers 1929–44* (Paris, 1959); P.-H. Siriex, *Souvenirs en vérité 1930–80: Oxford, Londres 1940, Afrique, Madagascar, Djibouti, Inde, URSS, Sibérie* (n.p., [1992]); and J. Marin, *Petit bois pour un grand feu* (Paris, 1994).

[59] Author interview with Stéphane and Christiane Hessel, Paris, 27 June 2012.

of France, Delavenay was eventually made assistant director. Along with Henri de Kérillis and Denis Saurat, on 19 June he called on de Gaulle.[60]

To carry out its task, the BBC relied on its EID to gather information. It produced interview reports for distribution, not only to programme planners and members of the BBC French Service, but also to higher echelons of wartime government, including the Ministry of Information and the Political Warfare Executive (PWE). When it was proposed later to streamline intelligence-gathering, the BBC, in the form of Ivone Kirkpatrick, Delavenay's superior, successfully resisted any merger with the PWE. The work of the EID was based on several sources of intelligence, the most important of which were daily digests from the BBC Monitoring Service and listener correspondence. A further component of this huge effort was added when, as we shall see, Delavenay and his staff interviewed a steady flow of refugees and returners from France. As regards the Monitoring Service, the Foreign Office had begun listening to Italian and German broadcasts in Arabic during the 1930s. With the increasing likelihood of war in Europe the BBC was asked to monitor European language broadcasts. This service was based at Evesham, in Worcestershire. According to one report, 'more than a million words in thirty languages are monitored each day from voice, morse [code] and other transmissions'.[61] Some 300,000 words were transcribed, with an average of at least 24,000 flashed by the Information Bureau, for news bulletins. For the analysis of foreign propaganda, the Service produced a Daily Digest reducing a huge and often highly repetitive mass to 100,000 words. This was published, fully indexed, in two sections, one of which was devoted solely to enemy transmissions. It was this Digest on which Delavenay's staff drew to produce the EID's intelligence reports, and it was also used extensively by Boris and Crémieux-Brilhac.[62] In 1943, the monitoring effort had become so large that it was moved to Caversham Park outside Reading, where the BBC written archives are now housed. There were around 1,000 people, mostly foreigners, working there.

Once people in France had had a chance to gauge the realities of the German Occupation, after November 1940 in particular, for those inclined towards dissidence, or resistance, a steady trickle of escapees began to arrive in London. The work of Delavenay's department in conducting over 500

---

[60] J. Lacouture, *De Gaulle* (3 vols., Paris, 1984), i. 373; and Crémieux-Brilhac, *La France Libre*, pp. 76–8.

[61] Information from *BBC Yearbook 1945*, pp. 50–3; and T. Hickman, *What did you do in the War, Auntie?* (1995), pp. 124–6.

[62] Crémieux-Brilhac, *Georges Boris*, pp. 120–9; and AN, 72AJ220, 'Témoignage de J.-L. Crémieux-Brilhac, Commissariat de l'Information', Jan. 1949. I thank Sébastien Albertelli for alerting me to this source.

interviews provides a fascinating insight into the background of their arrival, in addition to the invaluable information they were able to provide on social and listening conditions. The range of people interviewed is astonishing. Among them were personnel wishing to join the Free French armed forces; radio experts; returning English expatriates, including commercial representatives and a significant number of women; Irish priests; a Dutch writer; a Hungarian novelist; commercial travellers; journalists; Breton fishermen; and many political and Resistance personalities (including Pierre Mendès France, Henri Queuille and Fernard Grenier among the former, and Jean-Jacques Mayoux, Yvon Morandat and Raymond Aubrac among the latter). The year 1942 was the most productive, with 175 records; a further 141 and 131 were produced in 1943 and 1944 respectively.[63]

As was the case with most refugees arriving from Occupied Europe, when individuals or groups landed on British soil they were taken for screening to the London Reception Centre (LRC), based from January 1941 at the Royal Victoria Patriotic School (RVPS), in Wandsworth, south London. Some 33,000 'aliens' passed through the LRC.[64] Whether people arrived with valid papers or no papers at all, security officers interrogated refugees to check their stories. Some of the better connected were released after a few days; for others, whose stories needed more detailed verification, the wait could be 'months'. Because of his German background Stéphane Hessel spent at least four weeks there in April 1941, and remembers watching London burning in the distance while waiting for his credentials to be checked. Maurice Druon recalls the quiet efficiency of successive interrogation officers who crosschecked each refugee's story.[65] The writer Joseph Kessel has left a vivid portrait of 'Patriotic School', whose gothic exterior did nothing to allay the abiding sense of the bizarre to which it gave rise.[66] One or two came out only to 'face execution'. Yet the conditions were comfortable enough: the dormitory beds were 'excellent' and separated by curtains; there were bathrooms, soap, palatable food, a library and indoor and outdoor games facilities. This was a 'tower of Babel', yet a common cause – liberty, and the struggle against Nazi oppression – united the genuine refugees detained there. For Kessel, the RVPS was a 'no-man's-land between the past one

---

[63] Cornick, 'Fraternity among listeners'; and Delavenay, *Témoignage, passim.*

[64] O. Hoare, *Camp 020. MI5 and the Nazi Spies* (Richmond, 2000), pp. 16–17.

[65] M. Druon, *C'était ma guerre, ma France, et ma douleur: mémoires II* (Paris, 2010), pp. 157–60.

[66] J. Kessel, 'Patriotic School', *Bulletin de l'Association des Français Libres*, i (Dec. 1945), 18–19, also available at <http://www.france-libre.net/temoignages-documents/temoignages/patriotic-school.php> [accessed 22 July 2012]. Throughout, Kessel mistakenly writes 'Harmsworth' instead of Wandsworth.

had fled and an uncertain future'. The French were the most impatient
to be released and, while they waited, Kessel listened to dozens of their
individual adventures. One young sailor, detained on a French naval vessel
in Indochina, eventually escaped via China and India and, after his ship
was sunk in the Mediterranean, re-embarked for London at Malta: 'He
dreamed of leaving Patriotic School to serve on convoys'. Later in the war
there was a Free French-run office there. After rigorous questioning, with
the resulting information compiled on a large card index ('fichier'), resisters
were sent to Jean Pierre-Bloch, of the Bureau Central des Renseignements
d'Action (BCRA; the Gaullist secret service).[67] LRC log sheets were passed
to Delavenay's office, and refugees who were thought to be helpful for the
radio effort were given his address. Interviews were conducted in BBC
offices, either at Bedford College in Regent's Park, at Bush House, or in
hotel bars or restaurants. We shall return to the interviews shortly.

Very early in the war, British resolve and capacity for resistance had been
underlined by the writer Bernard Faÿ, reporting on a trip to London in
November 1939. Well before the Blitz ever became a reality, Faÿ concluded
his whimsical piece with the view that because of his 'positive qualities
and creative power', 'the Englishman carries within him an extraordinary
capacity for resistance'.[68] Once the German Occupation of France had
become established, British resolve in the face of the Battle of Britain,
the threatened invasion (Hitler's Operation 'Seelöwe') and then the Blitz
represented a potent sign of resistance. Thus it was the British who were the
first to be seen to resist the Germans. This became a key theme for the BBC,
and Churchill, in his broadcast in both French and English of 21 October
1940, used the bombing of London to bind Britain's lone destiny with that
of defeated France. Churchill's defiance of the Germans in this broadcast
made a deep impression on the French team at the BBC.[69] From the BBC's
point of view, the demonstrably simple fact of surviving the Battle of Britain
had already been more potent than the most sophisticated propaganda: the
message that Hitler could be and was being resisted within the island was

---

[67] J. Pierre-Bloch, *Londres, capitale de la France libre* (Paris, 1986), pp. 33ff. On the BCRA,
see S. Albertelli, *Les Services Secrets du Général de Gaulle* (Paris, 2009).

[68] B. Faÿ, 'Londres en guerre', *La Revue de Paris* (15 Dec. 1939), pp. 1107–15, at p. 1115: 'Pour
ma part, j'ai toujours goûté la qualité positive et la puissance créative … Aussi porte-t-il en
lui une force de résistance extraordinaire'. Under Vichy, Faÿ displaced Julien Cain, the Jewish
director of the Bibliothèque Nationale, and prosecuted a crusade against Freemasonry in
France. He has emerged from relative obscurity to become the subject of scholarly attention:
e.g., A. Compagnon, *Le Cas Bernard Faÿ* (Paris, 2009); and B. Will, *Unlikely Collaboration:
Gertrude Stein, Bernard Faÿ and the Vichy Dilemma* (New York, 2011).

[69] Bauer, *40 à Londres*, p. 331. For the impact of the Battle of Britain on public opinion,
see F. Bédarida, *La Bataille d'Angleterre* (Brussels, 1985), pp. 95–111.

being received and understood in France. Once the Blitz began in earnest in September 1940, persisting almost daily until May 1941, anyone arriving in London, as Stéphane Hessel explained, had to accept the danger of the bombing 'without moaning or complaining', and had to adopt, as it were, the legendary British 'flegme'. Such composure under duress was usually explained (as Faÿ had done) by reference to the British 'national character'. Pierre Bourdan, a seasoned observer of Londoners, noted that their 'patience arose from a daily rebirth of hope, one of the ingredients of British tenacity'. In one of the most striking passages in memoirs on the Blitz, Bourdan noted that for six months, with monotonous regularity, 'London lived its nights as a city on the front line, and during the days it worked, drew breath, took an hour off, went about its business, restored its public services and entertained its passers-by'.[70] Cassin felt similarly, though his own morale was severely sapped for a time in September to October 1940.[71] Jacques Soustelle remembered that while still in New York,

> Geneviève Tabouis had painted the darkest picture of England, exclaiming: 'My poor friend! What are you going to do over there [in London]'? For her, the island was open to the risk of invasion, or at the very least being pulverized by bombing; and Henri de Kérillis added: 'To leave America for London was sheer madness.'[72]

It is this bravery to which Pierre-Olivier Lapie refers in the opening pages of his memoirs, which are among the best available on the philosophical, even existential, implications of joining the Free French cause: the dilemma of whether to return to France, or whether to find exile in London in the Blitz, asked monumental questions of very ordinary men, he wrote, in whom the most intense heroism was revealed.[73]

One of Delavenay's earliest visitors was Maurice Halna du Fretay, whose spectacular arrival in London would make a deep and lasting impression

---

[70] P. Bourdan, *Carnet des jours d'attente (juin 40–juin 44)* (Paris, 1945), pp. 69, 72ff.: 'sa patience était faite d'un rajeunissement quotidien de son espoir, qui est un ressort de la ténacité britannique … Pendant ces six mois Londres vécut la nuit comme une cité en ligne, le jour, comme une ville qui travaille, respire, prend une heure de détente, vaque à ses occupations, entretient ses services publics, distrait ses promeneurs et même ses oisifs'. There is an even longer tribute by Bourdan to British wartime resolve in his *Perplexités et grandeur de l'Angleterre* (Paris, 1945), pp. 354–9.

[71] A. Prost and J. Winter, *René Cassin* (Paris, 2011), pp. 167–71.

[72] Author interview with S. Hessel; J. Soustelle, *Envers et contre tout* (2 vols., Paris, 1947), i. 29: 'Geneviève Tabouis m'avait dépeint l'Angleterre sous le jour le plus sombre: "Pauvre ami! qu'allez-vous faire là-bas!". Elle voyait l'île envahie ou, en tout cas, pilonnée sous les bombes; … de Kérillis aussi: "Quitter l'Amérique à cette époque pour aller à Londres, c'était folie"'.

[73] P.-O. Lapie, *Les Déserts de l'action* (Paris, 1946), pp. 9–11.

on the Free French exiles. In late November 1940, Lapie was introduced to du Fretay at Carlton Gardens. Aged only twenty, this young airman, who held a private pilot's licence, had decided to join the Free French by re-assembling the kit of a flimsy one-seater aircraft. On 15 November 1940, having waited for bad weather to help avoid detection, he took off from Ranléon, near Dinan, and landed just outside Dorchester, in Dorset. At first the British imprisoned him. Yet the arrival of this young man in London at last represented, wrote Lapie, 'the response of France' to their efforts. 'It meant that we had made contact, that we were not mistaken':

> Thus our efforts were not in vain: this was France's response, a response embodied by such an airy and so noble a person, who had arrived in such an unexpected and courageous manner that it made a much deeper impression on us than other recruits to the cause. Du Fretay became, for the English as well as for us, a symbolic figure, a young and promising hero … [74]

Du Fretay visited Delavenay who interviewed him for information about listening conditions (there was a ban already being widely defied), techniques to avoid the 'very strong' German jamming, and favourable reception of British propaganda leaflets. 'Everybody listens', was du Fretay's answer, when asked about BBC programmes: 'The radio is the chief source of information and the main moral support of the people of Brittany'; 'There is utter distrust of everything from French (German-controlled) sources, and complete confidence in the "French in London" [sic]'. Most interesting was early evidence of distrust in Pétain, whose status had hitherto been widely regarded in London as sacrosanct:

> This young man's uncle, a general and a senator, told him he was a fool to go to England to join the dissident and insubordinate de Gaulle. He told him that he ought to respect the orders of Marshal Pétain. The men of that generation … are impressed by Pétain; for them, he is above all the hero of Verdun. 'For us', says Corporal D., 'he is nothing of the sort. We have not known him as a hero, we only know his decadence.'[75]

---

[74] 'C'était le contact établi, l'assurance formelle que nous ne nous trompions pas … Notre effort n'était donc pas vain: voici la réponse de la France et matérialisée dans un personnage si aérien et si digne, venu d'une manière si inattendue et si audacieuse qu'elle frappait nos esprits bien plus que d'autres ralliements. Du Fretay devenait, et est resté pour les Anglais comme pour nous, un personnage symbolique, un jeune héros annonciateur' (Lapie, *Déserts de l'action*, pp. 61–2).

[75] Paris, Archive of the Institut d'Histoire du Temps Présent (IHTP), ARC 042, Fonds Emile Delavenay (hereafter Fonds Delavenay), 'Conversation at Broadcasting House with Air Corporal Duffretet [sic] of the Free French Air Force', report dated 29 Nov. 1940.

Everyone who met him was bowled over, reassured and enthused by du Fretay. The young pilot went for training with the RAF and was assigned to 607 Squadron. Tragically, though, on 19 August 1942 he was lost at sea returning from a mission providing air cover for the abortive Canadian attack on Dieppe.[76]

The primary function of these interviews was to gather as much information as possible about the effectiveness of BBC broadcasting. Almost all the reports carry data on wavelengths and jamming, and how listeners tried to avoid it. A radio engineer, M. Fua, who had fled Paris in June 1940 and who had lived around Pau until he left France on 7 February 1941, gave early confirmation that listening to the BBC was widespread in all the towns he had visited. He also confirmed that when jamming became too strong, listeners would fine-tune their dials, because there were fewer problems on short wave. This showed that people were following BBC broadcast advice:

> It was quite clear from his conversation that our transmissions … have priority over everything else in the French listener's mind. I asked [him] whether he would go so far as to say that the majority of French set owners listened to us. He considered his answer rather carefully and said, 'I would not say so. I would say *la totalité*'.[77]

When active resisters began to arrive in London, further evidence emerged confirming the effectiveness of the BBC line. In early 1942, Paulin Bertrand, alias 'Paul Simon', manager of the Paris-based clandestine newspaper *Valmy*, provided such proof. Founded in January 1941, fifty copies of *Valmy* had been produced on a child's printing outfit. It took one month to do so. By August 1941, its producers were roneo-printing 3,000 copies in four pages. Yet this was extremely dangerous and had to be halted during the winter. Significantly enough, Simon, in a broadcast interview with Jean Oberlé, confirmed that their primary motivation for this act of defiance against the 'now intolerable' German presence in Paris had been inspired very early on in the Occupation when 'we saw that the British were resisting'.[78] Simon confirmed that despite the dangers incurred in listening to heavily jammed radio broadcasts, many Parisians still took the risk. More importantly, people were organizing themselves into listening groups: 'Monsieur S. knew of a number of listening groups

---

[76] See the entry on du Fretay at <http://www.ordredelaliberation.fr/fr_compagnon/450.html> [accessed 2 Aug. 2012]; and Bauer, *40 à Londres*, p. 371.

[77] Fonds Delavenay, report dated 28 March 1941.

[78] Interview broadcast on 3 Feb. 1942, reproduced in *Ici Londres: les voix de la liberté 2, 8 décembre 1941–7 novembre 1942*, ed. J.-L. Crémieux-Brilhac (5 vols., Paris, 1975), ii. 45.

organized among people living in one block so that the curfew did not affect them and they could get back to their own flats after listening to the programme'. Furthermore, he confirmed that the V-campaign (drawing Vs on walls, etc.) had been 'invaluable in making it possible for all and sundry to show their spirit of resistance to the enemy'.[79] Group listening occurred in various forms: in major towns, listeners ran the risk of capture or denunciation. In more remote rural areas, where people were sure they would not be denounced, group listening took place more openly. Mrs. Cedar Paul, while near Grasse, received 'peasants' in her home, eager for news. She could listen in English to the BBC Home Service, which was not jammed, and paraphrase the news in French for her visitors.[80]

In the months leading to the desperately anticipated D-Day landings, Delavenay met more active political resisters. Among these was Raymond Aubrac, who came to London in February 1944. Delavenay caught up with him on 22 February, just before Aubrac's departure for Algiers. By this stage in the war, radios had become a precious commodity: it was 'impossible to get sets except "by stealing them". Valves are very scarce'. Aubrac was critical of aspects of the BBC's coverage. Worst of all was the 'war of nerves … you have played'. 'Talk about "Autumn Leaves" [an invasion codename] and similar promises' had completely 'upheaved' the lives of hundreds of French families. These had had two major effects: '1) to put Frenchmen "beside themselves" with irritation, 2) to create an anti-British mentality'. In these complaints Delavenay saw the necessity, post-war, for British and French to understand each other better. Yet despite the criticisms, 'A[ubrac] was full of praise of [sic] the BBC and said that in spite of the efficiency of the resistance organizations the latter were "pebbles" whereas the BBC was "the cement" which united the "pebbles in one solid block"'.[81]

This was high praise indeed, and pays tribute to the long and patient efforts of the BBC. The ever-increasing numbers of French arriving in London, as the war went on, spoke through the vector of the BBC and began to populate Bidault's very human 'miracle of French resurrection'. Sooner or later the 'fraternity of listeners' would resist the occupier more actively, and would look forward to the post-war period. Mainly through their French personnel, this was how the BBC helped the people of France to see beyond the darkness and repression of the Occupation.

---

[79] Fonds Delavenay, interview with Paul Simon, report dated 9 Feb. 1942. For the launch of the 'V-campaign', see the talk by Jacques Duchesne broadcast 22 March 1941 (Crémieux-Brilhac, *Ici Londres*, i. 204).

[80] Fonds Delavenay, interview with Mrs. Cedar Paul, report dated 5 Feb. 1942.

[81] Fonds Delavenay, interview with Raymond Aubrac, report dated 23 Feb. 1944.

Ignace Legrand and the 'Homage to France by … English writers'

Another Frenchman who sought exile in London, and who left an account of his escape and his reflections on his hosts, is the writer Ignace Legrand. Today he is almost entirely forgotten, whereas at that time he enjoyed a reputation as a relatively successful novelist, having been a contender for the Goncourt Prize in 1934 with *A sa lumière* (Gallimard). According to the few critics who have commented on his novels, he appears to have produced work not dissimilar to that of Jacques Chardonne, another purveyor of fictions presumed to offer insights into the psychological relationships between spouses, a subgenre which was something of an inter-war phenomenon, but which has long since fallen out of fashion. René Lalou, for instance, wrote that Legrand's fiction revealed the existence of a 'patrie intérieure', a kind of inner, or mental, homeland which governs our personality and determines couples' relationships.[82]

In his memoir *Nos amis les Anglais*, Legrand relates the circumstances surrounding his escape at the end of the *exode*, in June 1940. This text was destined for publication in a special issue of the French-language review, *Aguedal, revue des lettres françaises au Maroc*, based in Rabat, Morocco. In Rabat, *Aguedal* was managed by the writer Henri Bosco, the translations carried out by his wife Madeleine. There was another connection with Rabat. Legrand's brother, Edy, had lived there since at least the early 1930s and enjoyed a reputation as an artist.[83] Legrand's involvement in this venture shows that he did make his own contribution to an Anglo-French cultural mobilization demonstrating that despite the Anglophobic regime operating in Occupied France, the French and the British were still, at heart, close allies, sharing a common aim to protect the cause of liberty and the restoration of democracy in Europe. Accompanied by his wife and young daughter, Legrand left France in late June 1940 aboard HMS *Galatea*. This Royal Navy cruiser had, on 16 June, the eve of Pétain's call for a ceasefire, embarked the British ambassador to France, returning him safely to Plymouth, whereupon the ship returned to the Gironde estuary. At Le Verdon, HMS *Galatea* took the Legrands on board among one of the very last transports of refugees fleeing France; they arrived in Plymouth on 27 June 1940. Thus began an adventure which, he said, was 'one of the most important if not the capital event' of his life.[84] Storm Jameson recalls

---

[82] R. Lalou, *Histoire de la littérature française contemporaine, de 1870 à nos jours* (Paris, 1953), pp. 838–40.

[83] See *Vingt ans de peinture au Maroc, 1933–53 – Edy Legrand*, exhibition catalogue (Rabat, 1953).

[84] 'La découverte, la révélation de l'Angleterre et des Anglais a été un des plus grands événements de ma vie, peut-être son phénomène capital' (I. Legrand, *Nos amis les Anglais* (1944), p. 9).

that Legrand had been expecting 'to be made use of by his countrymen in London', yet added that 'they did not want him, and he was in depths of misery and poverty when D. L. Murray rescued him'.[85]

In London, Legrand was befriended by Storm Jameson, and as we have seen he contributed to the first issue of *La France Libre*. The special issue of *Aguedal* that he composed was dated December 1943 and entitled 'Homage to France by contemporary English writers'; the contents were 'unpublished texts written especially for *Aguedal*'.[86] There is insufficient space here to do full justice to this issue; we will devote a separate detailed study to it. Suffice it to say that Legrand – aided, one imagines, by Saurat and Jameson – assembled an impressive array of writers, twenty-three in all, including Charles Morgan, T. S. Eliot, the poet laureate John Masefield, E. M. Forster, Rosamond Lehmann, Raymond Mortimer, Irene Rathbone, Cecily Mackworth, Enid Starkie, David Murray, Basil Liddell-Hart and Douglas Goldring.

A prefatory note, presumably by Bosco, explained that Legrand's 'fine and long study of England' could not be included in the issue, and that it would be published later. It had become, by now, a familiar portrait: 'The English, in all classes of society, appear as uncomplicated, unselfconscious heroes, childishly naive. Moved by the misfortunes of others, they welcome exiles with a kind of discreet affection'.[87] In the messages included in the special issue, this affection shone through clearly. Charles Morgan was a popular author in the 1930s and had a considerable following in France, especially after the success of his novels *The Fountain* (1932) and *Sparkenbroke* (1936). During the war he worked at the Admiralty in naval intelligence, but continued writing. An article translated as 'Génie français' was published in France by Editions de Minuit, and he contributed 'L'Angleterre et les Français libres' to Aron and Labarthe's review.[88] He contributed his 'Ode à

---

[85] Jameson, *Journey from the North*, p. 114. D. L. Murray, editor of the *Times Literary Supplement*, was a successful novelist in his own right (see D. May, 'Murray, David Leslie (1888–1962)', *ODNB* <http://www.oxforddnb.com/view/article/68898> [accessed 24 July 2012]). René Cassin, however, briefly praised Legrand's efforts in a radio broadcast of 7 June 1941 (Cassin, *Les Hommes partis de rien*, p. 486).

[86] 'Hommage à la France des écrivains anglais contemporains', *Aguedal, revue des lettres françaises au Maroc*, vii (Dec. 1943). *Aguedal*, or *Agdal*, is derived from a Berber word for 'walled garden'.

[87] 'L'Anglais, de toutes les classes, y apparaît héroïque, presque à son insu, simple, bon enfant. Il s'émeut des misères d'autrui, et accueille, avec une sorte de tendresse discrète, les exilés ... C'est la flamme persistante de cette affection qui éclaire les messages que l'on va lire' (*Aguedal*, vii (Dec. 1943), 3).

[88] See C. Morgan, 'L'Angleterre et les Français libres', *La France Libre*, i (16 Dec. 1940), 114–15; and T. Hinchcliffe, 'Morgan, Charles Langbridge (1894–1958)', *ODNB*.

la France' (pp. 13–19), composed in September 1942, and which would be read on stage at the Comédie Française after the Liberation. For *Aguedal* Morgan sent a simple message, pleading exhaustion from his wartime duties: in all his writings, including his 'Ode', the message was simple, and needed no further explanation. Morgan felt a lifelong, deep love for France. Were France to be lost, then so would civilization.

T. S. Eliot's poem 'Little Gidding', written in 1942, during which time Eliot walked the streets of Kensington as an air-raid warden, was translated into French by André Gide and Madeleine Bosco. In his short message to Legrand, he insisted that it was one of the most important duties of writers to 'remind people that there were other values than those in politics and in struggles for power'. The 'literary periodical' was one of the most forceful ways of fulfilling this duty. Without referring by name to the *Criterion*, he himself had been engaged in this, especially through forging close friendships between French and English writers. He was waiting impatiently for this issue of *Aguedal* to inaugurate a happier future.[89] Rosamond Lehmann submitted a 'Letter to Jean Talva'. This was the pseudonym of her translator, Mme. Levêque. This moving letter laments the 'hard curtain of steel' that had come down between the two countries, preventing contact between them. Called upon by the BBC to broadcast to 'the women of France', she mused that 'Talva' would agree that 'we had all been responsible for our current suffering'. Then a letter arrived containing a single line in English, written, it turned out, before Lehmann's broadcast: 'With love and grief'. Lehmann's response, including her narration of a day in mid May 1943, ended 'With hope and faith'.[90] Raymond Mortimer was literary editor of the *New Statesman* and, in 1940–1, fulfilled a liaison role between the Ministry of Information and the BBC's French Service. In his message, he celebrated how much France had meant to cultured English people over the centuries. France and Britain shared 'a great intellectual tradition', and both execrated

---

[89] 'Nous devons rappeler aux hommes qu'il existe d'autres valeurs que celles de la politique et des luttes pour le pouvoir. Et pour accomplir de devoir, l'un des instruments le plus fort [*sic*] est le périodique littéraire … En ce qui concerne la maintenance de la culture européenne, j'ai toujours affirmé qu'une association et une amitié étroites entre les hommes de lettres français et anglais étaient d'une importance capitale. J'ai toujours lutté pour cette compréhension … j'attends avec impatience ce "Aguedal" comme l'oiseau annonciateur d'un printemps heureux' (T. S. Eliot, 'Little Gidding', *Aguedal*, vii (Dec. 1943), 17–23, and 'Message', *Aguedal*, vii (Dec. 1943), 27).

[90] 'Je pensai que, vous, ce que je voulais dire, vous le comprendriez: la faute, la responsabilité, incombaient à nous tous; à nous tous appartenait la souffrance … Puis quelques semaines plus tard, arriva une enveloppe. A l'intérieur, une seule feuille, mince; et, de votre écriture délicate une seule ligne en anglais: "With love and grief"' ('Lettre à Jean Talva', *Aguedal*, vii (Dec. 1943), 38–44).

the cult of the state and the leader, which amounted to nothing less than idolatry. Lacking fanaticism did not translate as decadence: 'the history of French as much as English resistance has already refuted this calumny'.[91]

The overall message behind this special issue was simple: at the turn of the year 1943, into 1944, the destinies of France and Britain were bound together as much as they had been in June 1940: by celebrating their common culture, whatever political differences there might be, by reaffirming their beliefs in the shared values of liberty and freedom from oppression, and by joining together in resistance, then the two countries were sure to prevail.

Conclusion

What emerged from preparing this chapter was the realization, and the surprise, that there is still so much to discover about the broad question of the French in London just before and during the Second World War. While it is difficult to agree fully with his contentions, Jean-François Muracciole argues that in French national memory the 'Français libres de Londres' have been squeezed out by Vichy, on the one hand, and the Resistance, on the other; that Vichy has in some sense 'taken revenge' over London.[92] As Robert Belot has written, and as we saw in several examples above, 'resistance is an intrinsically fractal phenomenon ... arising from a multitude of individual decisions which then gradually coalesce'.[93] So, considering the sheer numbers, the variety, the complexity of the 'Free French in London', these factors should give rise to further research. Denis Saurat's role deserves to be better understood: there is more that will be revealed from research into his archive. More light has been projected on to the central role played by the French Institute as a rallying-point in the first months of the war. And the deployment of the French journalists already in the capital, the refugees, the new arrivals, with their accumulated knowledge of conditions in Occupied France, made a considerable contribution to the anti-Axis war effort, understood in the broadest sense. I was struck by what Stéphane Hessel

---

[91] 'Les Français et les Anglais ont en commun une grande tradition intellectuelle ... Ils détestent le culte mystique de l'Etat et du Chef, ils y voient une idolâtrie à la fois perverse et ridicule ... Parce que nous manquons de fanatisme, on nous a taxés de décadence. L'histoire de la résistance tant française qu'anglaise a déjà réfuté cette calomnie' ('Ce qui est gravé dans notre cœur', *Aguedal*, vii (Dec. 1943), 45–4, at p. 47)

[92] 'Si les Français libres ne trouvent pas leur place dans la mémoire nationale, c'est certainement qu'ils sont écrasés entre le repoussoir pétainiste et l'astre résistant ... [I]l flotte comme une revanche posthume et mémorielle de Vichy sur Londres' (J.-F. Muracciole, *Les Français Libres: l'autre Résistance* (Paris, 2009), p. 362).

[93] 'Car la Résistance est un phénomène intrinsèquement fractal qui naît dans la dispersion, hors de tout plan d'ensemble, à partir d'une multitude de décisions individuelles qui vont tenter peu à peu de faire coagulation' (Belot, *La Résistance sans de Gaulle*, p. 12).

said in his interview: despite the fact that he was billeted initially with two fellow-recruits to the BCRA – one of whom was Tony Mella, the son of a London Frenchman – and in spite of the fact that their work kept them busy in the secret war with the enemy in France, they still felt that they had become Londoners, that they knew how to take the tube or a bus to Soho or King's Cross or to their favourite restaurants, and that they acquired a respectful fondness for shopkeepers and the 'bobbies on the beat'.[94] There is also a realization, finally, that the arrival in London of refugees from France did so much to help the BBC's monumental efforts in the radio war, because those refugees had understood the message that British resolve to stand firm against the odds was an example of resistance worth emulating. Culture – as a form of 'soft propaganda' – could continually be mobilized too, as shown by the 'Homage to France by ... English writers', compiled by a French novelist in exile.

Resistance – resisting violent oppression or occupation – if at first a fragmented or individualized phenomenon, may grow subsequently to mobilize outrage, outrage about acquired rights having been diminished or suppressed, about perceived or experienced persecution. It is salutary to remember that there is a historical continuum leading from the Free French who rallied to London in 1940 to the controversies and debates surrounding the publication of *Indignez-vous!* by one of the last survivors of that very cause ... Stéphane Hessel.[95]

[94] 'Dans Londres, n'est-ce pas, nous sommes devenus très vite de vrais londoniens, on savait comment fonctionne le métro, le bus, comment aller plus rapidement à Soho pour manger de la cuisine grecque. Ou aller plutôt vers Haymarket ou vers King's Cross. Donc, on devenait, je pense, des londoniens, on avait naturellement le respect de tous les anglais pour les policiers, pour les Bobbies' (author interview with Stéphane Hessel).

[95] See the sources listed at <http://fr.wikipedia.org/wiki/Indignez-vous_!> [accessed 10 Aug. 2012].

14. Raymond Aron and *La France Libre* (June 1940–September 1944)

David Drake

Introduction[1]

In the second half of the twentieth century Raymond Aron (1905–83) established a reputation in France and across the world as not only a sociologist but also as a philosopher, political scientist and journalist. His liberal, anti-Marxist outlook and measured clinical analyses were at odds with the values and polemical style of much of the writing of those contributing to the Marxist or *Marxisant* consensus which prevailed in the Paris intellectual milieu until the 1970s, a consensus which Aron famously criticized in *L'Opium des intellectuels*, published in 1955.[2] This work, and others including *Dix-huit leçons sur la société industrielle*[3] and *Démocratie et totalitarisme*,[4] are well known, and provide penetrating insights into Western society within the context of the Cold War. Students of cultural and intellectual history will also be acquainted with Aron's friendship with Jean-Paul Sartre, which lasted from their student days at the Ecole Normale Supérieure until 1947 when the two men found themselves on opposing sides of the Cold War ideological barricades.

What is less well known is the time Aron spent in London during the Second World War, and it is upon this four-year period that this chapter focuses. It explores what options Aron had in June 1940 and what led him to choose to go to London rather than to stay in France or seek a university post in the USA; it examines what his intentions were when he went to London and to what extent these were realized. It considers the nature of the London-based review *La France Libre*, with which Aron became intimately involved, his contribution to it, the nature of his relations with

---

[1] I would like to thank Iain Stewart for reading and commenting on an earlier draft of this chapter.

[2] R. Aron, *L'Opium des intellectuels* (Paris, 1955) (trans. in English as *The Opium of the Intellectuals* (1957)).

[3] R. Aron, *Dix-huit leçons sur la société industrielle* (Paris, 1963) (trans. in English as *Eighteen Lectures on Industrialised Society* (1970)).

[4] R. Aron, *Démocratie et totalitarisme* (Paris, 1965) (trans. in English as *Democracy and Totalitarianism* (1968)).

the leader of the Free French, General de Gaulle, and his entourage, and shows how Aron's time in London influenced decisions he took after his return to France in September 1944.

From the Phoney War to the armistice

After graduating from the Ecole Normale Supérieure, Aron had spent his military service in an army meteorological unit, so when he reported to a recruitment station in September 1939, it was with little surprise that he was directed to a meteorological station, this time on the Belgian frontier near Charleville. For Aron, like most of his fellow-conscripts, the next eight months lived up to the sobriquet 'the Phoney War'. France, like Britain, was at war but there was precious little fighting. This gave Sergeant Aron plenty of time for reading, reflecting and working on his study of Machiavelli, as well as contributing to a book on the history of socialism based on notes taken during lectures by Elie Halévy who had died two years previously. In May 1940 this tranquil, trouble-free existence was blown asunder as the German army launched its offensive. Aron's unit joined the mass of civilians and soldiers retreating southwards, and around 20 June he found himself near Bordeaux. He later recalled hearing the radio broadcast by Marshal Pétain on 17 June, in which the recently appointed head of government announced his hope of opening negotiations with the Germans in order to end the fighting. Aron later admitted to feeling shame, indignation, but also a sense of 'cowardly relief'.[5]

On his retreat to the south, Aron had become only too aware just how chaotic was the state of affairs prevailing in France and Pétain's speech made it clear that the French government was going to concede defeat. Aron now had to consider the options open to him. His wife Suzanne was staying with her parents some 250 kilometres away in Toulouse, and he managed to cadge a lift on a motorbike in order to discuss with her what he should do. When Aron had been mobilized he had been about to start teaching at the Université de Toulouse. One possibility, therefore, was to try to reach the USA where he could almost certainly secure a university post. Indeed, Aron's name was on a list of young university scholars 'as yet unknown internationally' who were marked down for potential 'rescue' by the Rockefeller Foundation.[6] This he ruled out, since he did not consider that the armistice, signed on 22 June, marked the end of the war, and he was determined to continue to play an active role opposing Nazism. So he had

---

[5] R. Aron, *Le Spectateur Engagé* (Paris, 1981), p. 77.

[6] E. Loyer, *Paris à New York: intellectuels et artistes français en exil (1940–7)* (Paris, 2005), pp. 48–9. My thanks to Iain Stewart for drawing my attention to this reference.

to choose whether to stay in France or to try to reach England. The future *résistant* Georges Canguilhem and others in Toulouse whom Aron met were vehemently opposed to the armistice and were bent on staying in France and resisting the Occupation. Aron took the view that Pétain would seek some sort of accommodation with Germany, and so the scope for action in France would be extremely limited. In addition, he realized that as a Jew it would be dangerous enough if he stayed, but as a Jew who had been in Germany from March 1930 to August 1933 during Hitler's rise to power and had penned articles warning of the dangers of National Socialism, he would be a marked man. He and his wife therefore agreed that he should try to reach London.

Aron's arrival in England

Accordingly Aron made his way to Saint-Jean-de-Luz and boarded the British liner the *Ettrick* which was transporting a Polish division to England. The *Ettrick* left on 24 June, and arrived in Plymouth two days later. From there Aron was taken to an army camp at Birkenhead where he joined some 20,000 Frenchmen, most of whom had been evacuated from northern France following the German offensive. A few days later the French at Birkenhead were given a choice between being returned to France, joining the troops who had rallied to de Gaulle or living as free citizens in Britain. Aron, still determined to play an active role in the war, opted to join de Gaulle's forces and, along with others who had made the same choice, was dispatched to the Empire Hall in west London, the newest of three halls comprising the Olympia exhibition complex. Olympia had been used during the First World War as a temporary civil prison camp for Germans and other 'undesirable aliens', and the Empire Hall (today Olympia 2) was requisitioned in June 1940 as a civil internment camp before being designated as the assembly point for those wanting to ally themselves with de Gaulle. After the Empire Hall, Aron joined the Free French forces at their camp in Aldershot, Berkshire, and was one of only 125 Frenchmen who marched through the streets of London in a 14 July parade attended by de Gaulle and King George VI.

In August, while still at Aldershot, Aron was contacted by one André Labarthe, who was about to launch a Free French monthly publication and was seeking possible contributors. Labarthe claimed to have read Aron's *Introduction à la philosophie de l'histoire*,[7] which was based on his

---

[7] R. Aron, *Introduction à la philosophie de l'histoire: essai sur les limites de l'objectivité historique* (Paris, 1938) (trans. in English as *Introduction to the Philosophy of History* (1961; repr. Westport, Conn., 1976).

doctoral thesis, and thought that Aron might well fit the bill. At the time when Labarthe was enticing Aron to participate in his publishing venture, Aron was preparing to participate in the war as a combatant. He had been undergoing military training and was set to join a combined British and Free French expeditionary force soon to be dispatched to Dakar, a French naval base in French West Africa (today Senegal) which had remained loyal to Vichy.

In September, just a few days before the Franco-British Expeditionary Force set off for Dakar, Aron was invited to the sixth floor of 4 Carlton Gardens, off Pall Mall, the HQ of the Free French in London. As part of Labarthe's charm offensive he had a meeting with Labarthe and two of his close associates, Mme. Marthe Lecoutre (real name Alta Kac)[8] and Stanislas Szymonzyk,[9] who urged him to stay and work on the new review. Aron was torn, since he realized that if he opted to work on the review he would almost certainly be ruling himself out of taking part in the fighting. After a few days of agonizing and, as he later said, for reasons that he himself did not fully comprehend, Aron agreed to become the deputy editor of the new review, of which Labarthe was the editor-in-chief.

Aron possibly realized that because of his age he might never find his place in the front line, but his decision to contribute to the struggle with the pen rather than the sword was one that haunted him for the rest of his life. He was never entirely sure that he had made the right choice. In 1981, two years before his death, he told Daniel Cordier, whom he had first met at Delville camp near Aldershot and who subsequently became secretary to Resistance leader Jean Moulin: 'I'm not as sure as you are about the choice I made during the war. I committed myself to take part in armed combat and I ended up in charge of a review. Was I right to stay there?'[10]

[8] See T. Cottour, '"Constellation" et Rencontre (1967–70): un malentendu fécond', in F. Vallotton, *Les Editions Rencontre, 1950–71* (Lausanne, 2004), pp. 137–74, at p. 138.

[9] Although this name is sometimes spelt 'Szymanczyk', it appears as 'Szymonzyk' in Aron's *Mémoires*, and, accordingly, in the English biography of Aron by Colquhoun (*Raymond Aron: the Philosopher in History 1905–55* (1986)) and the French one by Baverez (N. Baverez, *Raymond Aron* (Paris, 1993)). The name does not appear in *La France Libre* itself, as the Aron/Staro collaborative articles were published without a signature.

[10] 'Je ne suis pas aussi sûr que vous du choix que j'ai fait pendant la guerre. Je m'étais engagé pour combattre les armes à la main et j'ai échoué à la tête d'une revue. Ai-je eu raison d'y rester?' (D. Cordier, 'René Avord à Londres', in *Commentaire*, xxviii–xxix (Winter 1985), 26; a special issue of *Commentaire* entitled *Raymond Aron 1905–83: histoire et politique – textes, études et témoignages* (Paris, 1985)). All translations from French are the author's unless otherwise indicated.

Aron and the London Blitz

While in Aldershot in July the 'old sergeant', as Aron was known, had told Daniel Cordier, 'If Hitler doesn't land here and doesn't win this summer, he'll lose the war'.[11] From the autumn onwards, Aron's prognosis would be severely tested. On 4 September 1940, having failed to win the battle in the air over southern Britain, Hitler changed the tactics of the Luftwaffe air assault. Henceforth priority would be given to bombing raids on British cities, with London as the main target. From 7 September the city was bombed remorselessly by day and by night, and by the end of the year London had been attacked over 100 times. Aron's presence in London during the Blitz of 1940–1 assuaged somewhat his feelings of guilt at having left France – and his wife and daughter – to come to London to take up arms and then not having done so in the way he had originally intended: 'In the winter of '40–41 it was not embarrassing from a moral point of view to be in London because at that time we were being bombed whereas the French no longer were'.[12] He admitted that he never went down into the air-raid shelter, adding: 'I have never slept as well as I did during the Blitz … When, like me, you are a bad sleeper, it is because you are neurotic. When you are neurotic and there are calamitous things happening, you sleep better. So I slept better'.[13] However, during the 'baby Blitz' early in 1944, the Maison de l'Institut de France in Queen's Gate in Kensington, where Aron had lived in 1940, was hit by a bomb, killing Monsieur Cru the head of the Institute, Tobin the butler, and the housekeeper affectionately known as Mrs. Custard. Donald Monroe, a young war correspondent, was also killed, and Aron penned a short and moving obituary of the charming twenty-six year old with whom he had spent many a happy evening during the winter of 1940.[14] In 1944, the editorial offices of *La France Libre* were also bombed, and they relocated to nearby Thurloe Street; in the course of the war its printing presses were twice hit and destroyed during German air raids.

[11] 'Si Hitler ne débarque pas ici et n'est pas vainqueur cet été, il perdra la guerre' (D. Cordier, *Alias Caracalla* (Paris, 2009), p. 137).

[12] 'Dans l'hiver 40–41, ce n'était pas embarrassant, moralement, d'être à Londres parce qu'à ce moment-là on était bombardé alors que les Français ne l'étaient plus' (Aron, *Spectateur Engagé*, p. 84).

[13] 'Je n'ai jamais aussi bien dormi que sous le "blitz" … Quand on dort mal comme moi, c'est que l'on est névrosé. Quand on est névrosé et qu'il y a des événements catastrophiques, on dort mieux. Donc je dormais mieux' (Aron, *Spectateur Engagé*, p. 84).

[14] R. A., 'Donald Monroe', *La France Libre*, vii (15 March 1944), 327.

La France Libre, *'the true face of France and French culture'*[15]

It was in 1940, against the backdrop of the Blitz, that Aron, Labarthe and their associates began work on the review. It was originally going to be called *La Relève* (*The Relief*) but the name was changed to *La France Libre* (*Free France*) and its offices were in the Institut Français building in Queensberry Place, Kensington, West London. Labarthe would later claim that de Gaulle had taken the name of his movement from the title of the review. This needs to be taken with a pinch of salt. Labarthe was a rather odd fellow: Jacques Soustelle, then a member of de Gaulle's inner circle who would later, at the time of the Algerian War of Independence, become an implacable opponent, described Labarthe as 'a strange character – journalist, politician and scientist', adding that 'with him imagination won out easily over a taste for the truth'.[16] Labarthe was initially close to and admired by de Gaulle, who appointed him to be his director of armament and scientific research. However, Labarthe soon felt he was not sufficiently appreciated and resigned, making the review his main priority.

The first issue of *La France Libre* appeared on 15 November 1940 with 102 pages (17 cm × 23 cm), costing 2*s* and published by Hamish Hamilton, as were all subsequent issues, each of which carried a sub-heading *Liberté, Egalité, Fraternité*, followed, in the first issue, by an 1870 epigram from the philosopher Ernest Renan: 'France humiliated means the French spirit will be no more'.[17] Then came an unsigned rousing three-page appeal explaining that: 'This French review is for all French men and women. It is also for all those who love France'.[18] Despite what it called the sacrilege committed by the Germans in France, the review remained full of hope and promised to 'confront the invader with the spirit of resistance until our country is liberated'. To this end, *La France Libre* called on French men and women across the world to 'join with us and proclaim their loyalty to the national soul, that is to say to the values which were the pride of our country and remain its halo'.[19] The review was an immediate success, with the rapid sale

---

[15] Extract from advertisement inside back cover of Madeleine Gex Le Verrier, *Une Française dans la tourmente* (1942).

[16] 'une figure curieuse de journaliste, homme politique et savant'; 'l'imagination l'emportait de beaucoup chez lui sur le goût de la vérité' (J. Soustelle, *Envers et contre tout: de Londres à Alger (1940–2)* (Paris, 1947), p. 47).

[17] 'La France humiliée, vous n'aurez plus d'esprit français' (E. Renan, *La Réforme Intellectuelle et Morale* (Paris, 1875), p. 155).

[18] 'Cette revue française s'adresse à tous les Français. Elle s'adresse aussi à tous ceux qui aiment la France' (*La France Libre*, i (15 Nov. 1940), 3).

[19] 'opposer à l'envahisseur l'esprit de résistance jusqu'à la libération de notre patrie'; 's'unir à nous pour proclamer leur fidélité à l'âme nationale, c'est-à-dire aux valeurs qui furent l'honneur et restent l'auréole de notre pays' (*La France Libre*, i (15 Nov. 1940), 4–5).

of its 8,000 copies necessitating a second print-run of 10,000. By November 1943 its circulation had reached 40,000 (excluding an American edition in preparation in New York) and, according to *The Listener*, the number of subscribers eventually topped 76,000, making it the best-selling monthly in England.[20] However, according to Thierry Cottour, the sales of *La France Libre* at the Liberation were only 25,000.[21]

The initial issue contained the first of the regular monthly articles on military strategy inspired by Stanislas Szymonzyk, or 'Staro' as he was known, and written by Aron. A Pole from the southern frontier region of Cieszyn, and a former communist turned virulent anti-communist, Staro was an expert on the writings of von Clausewitz, whom he was always quoting. He had an outstanding knowledge of and an almost intuitive feel for military affairs, but a difficulty in articulating them; to complicate matters further, he spoke neither French nor English. He and Aron would lock themselves away for two or three hours, during which time both men would converse in German, with Aron teasing out Staro's wonderfully clear analyses of military operations. So insightful were the end results that the British War Office could not wait for the publication of these collaborative articles and would send over for the proofs.

In addition to the first Staro/Aron collaborative article, which Labarthe attributed to himself, the first issue contained two articles written by Aron alone. The first, 'La capitulation',[22] on the defeat of France, was unsigned; the second, 'Machiavellianism, doctrine of modern tyrannies',[23] was attributed to 'René Avord'. Aron hoped that by using this pseudonym he could ensure that his wife would continue to receive the payments made by the French authorities, since Aron had been officially declared missing in June 1940. He also hoped that using a pseudonym would lessen the chance of any reprisals by either Vichy or the Germans against his family. He took the name Avord from an air-base near Bruges and used it as his *nom de guerre* until his wife and daughter joined him in London in July 1943.

The heterogeneous nature of the content of the first issue, with its articles on military, scientific, economic, literary and political questions, set the tone for the ones that followed, as did the variety of national backgrounds of its readers and contributors. According to Aron, German bombing raids

---

[20] *The Listener* (18 Nov. 1943), p. 586; quoted by Colquhoun, *Raymond Aron*, p. 229.

[21] Cottour cites as his source AN, F.41/1167, 'Lettre de la direction de la presse à Mademoiselle [*sic*] Marthe Lecoutre', 7 March 1945 (see Cottour, '"Constellation"', n. 24, p. 167).

[22] Anon., 'La capitulation', *La France Libre*, i (15 Nov. 1940), 19–26.

[23] R. Avord, 'Le Machiavélisme, doctrines des tyrannies modernes', *La France Libre*, i (15 Nov. 1940), 45–54.

became rarer after the German invasion of Russia in June 1941. London had always been a cosmopolitan city, but its population was now swollen not only by French exiles but also by other nationals from countries such as Czechoslovakia, Poland, Belgium and the Netherlands invaded by Germany, who engaged in endless discussions about the issues confronting Europe:

> Life in London was noticeably different from ordinary London, because it was, for the first and last time, the capital of continental Europe. You would meet people from Czechoslovakia, Poland, Belgium, Holland, etc. There were endless discussions about all the problems facing Europe. There was a sort of European society within greater London.[24]

This view was echoed in an article in the September 1941 issue of *La France Libre*: 'London has become the cultural centre of free Europe ... There are moments when its English residents could – apart from the climate – think they were in Prague, Vienna, Warsaw, or Paris'.[25] Although dominated by contributions from French and British nationals, *La France Libre* also provided a platform for intellectual refugees from Occupied mainland Europe, and it enjoyed the support of leading figures from the resistance movements and governments-in-exile of these countries. The first anniversary issue of the review, for example, contained not only a warm message of support from de Gaulle and Winston Churchill, the latter praising French thought, culture and freedom, but also General Sikorski, head of the Polish government-in-exile, Dr. Edvard Beneš, his Czech counterpart, and E. N. van Kleffens, who had been appointed Dutch minister of foreign affairs in 1939 and subsequently became a member of the Dutch government-in-exile in London.[26] While the review remained steadfastly anti-Nazi, part of its appeal, as the British historian Richard Cobb told Aron decades later, was that it remained the only French intellectual presence and that it was not just propaganda.[27]

---

[24] 'La vie de Londres a été sensiblement différente du Londres ordinaire, parce que c'était, pour la première et la dernière fois, la capitale de l'Europe continentale. On rencontrait des Tchèques, des Polonais, des Belges, des Hollandais, etc. On discutait indéfiniment de tous les problèmes européens. Il y avait une espèce de société européenne à l'intérieur du grand Londres' (Aron, *Spectateur Engagé*, p. 94).

[25] 'Londres est devenue le centre culturel de la libre Europe ... Il y a des moments où ses habitants anglais pourraient se croire – climat à part – à Prague, à Vienne, à Varsovie, à Paris' (S. Jameson, 'Le 17ème congrès international des P.E.N.', *La France Libre*, ii (15 Sept. 1941), 395).

[26] *La France Libre*, iii (15 Nov. 1941), 2–17.

[27] Aron, *Spectateur Engagé*, p. 82.

La France Libre: *the voice of Anglo-French cultural solidarity*

Although *La France Libre* included contributions from non-French European anti-Nazis, the main focus of the review remained firmly centred on France and on promoting Anglo-French solidarity. While, on occasions, it carried articles which may strike the twenty-first-century reader as offering a somewhat sentimental and idealized picture of pre-war France, it needs to be remembered that many were written by French nationals in exile whose country was occupied by a foreign power aided and abetted by an indigenous government. It would not be surprising if many of the contributors needed to remind their readers (and themselves) of what France meant to them personally and of France's significant pre-war role in the world which, it was assumed, it would regain when the war was over and Germany was defeated. Among the eclectic range of French contributors were Georges Bernanos, Jules Romains, Joseph Kessel, Louis Aragon, Paul Eluard, Louis-Martin Chauffier and Romain Gary.

There were also contributions from British lovers and admirers of France and her people. Alexander Werth, the former correspondent of the *Manchester Guardian* and author of *The Destiny of France*, *France and Munich* and *The Last Days of Paris*, wrote a piece entitled 'Remember France' in which he expressed his love for the country, his confidence in its citizens and his solidarity with them in their suffering, calling on his readers not to forget or abandon France and its people.[28] Raymond Mortimer, the writer and literary critic who had lived in Paris in the 1920s, penned an article recalling his pre-war visits to France as a tourist when 'every year only increased my affection. And with good reason. It is almost beyond dispute that the French are the most intelligent, the most artistic, the most gifted in knowing how to live, of contemporary peoples'.[29] After eulogizing the various beauties of the French landscape, Mortimer concluded with a heartfelt expression of commiseration for those French men and women who were carrying on the fight in Britain and who were cut off from their *patrie*. One of their number, an unnamed officer in the Free French navy, gave a talk in November 1941 to the Oxford University French Club, the text of which appeared the following month in *La France Libre* under the title 'Missing France'.[30]

Within the British reminiscences on France, the theme of France being held prisoner recurs frequently. For example, Werth proclaimed: 'The youth

[28] A. Werth, 'Remember France', *La France Libre*, i (15 Nov. 1940), 27–33.
[29] 'chaque année n'a fait que rehausser mon affection. Et pour cause. Que les Français soient le plus intelligent, le plus artiste, le plus doué de savoir-vivre des peuples modernes ne se discute guère' (R. Mortimer, 'Souvenirs d'un touriste', *La France Libre*, iii (17 Apr. 1942), 471).
[30] Anon., 'Nostalgie de la France', *La France Libre*, iii (15 Dec. 1941), 124–32.

of France, these young French people whom the Lavals and Pétains of this world claim to have wanted to save by signing the armistice, are today prisoners of war';[31] while the politician and diplomat Harold Nicolson wrote: 'The body of France today is in chains'.[32] But a common theme running through the issues of *La France Libre* published during the war is the assumption that France will soon be free again. The political theorist Harold Laski concludes his article: 'So I think that the Vichy regime is a temporary, albeit tragic, episode in the history of France'.[33]

Both British and French contributors referred to France's civilizing mission, which it is expected it will reassume when the war is over. Henri Focillon, professor of the Collège de France and at Yale University, wrote: 'Working at the same time for itself and for the world, France is both a nation and a universal way of thinking'.[34] This is echoed by Charles Morgan, who asserted that, as far as he was concerned, 'France is an idea which is essential to civilization and that any victory which cut us off from her would be a defeat'.[35]

As if to illustrate the equation between France and civilization, the pages of *La France Libre* contain numerous articles by British intellectuals paying tribute to French figures and institutions related to their own specialisms. Thus, in the second issue, William Bragg, 1915 joint-winner (with his son) of the Nobel Prize for Physics, wrote one article praising the French scientist Paul Langevin[36] and contributed another in November 1941 protesting at Langevin's arrest and imprisonment in Paris.[37] This second article was one of a collection of short pieces introduced by British scientist Julian Huxley protesting at the arrest of Langevin and four other French scientists. When Bragg died in March 1942, Labarthe wrote an obituary, which appeared on the first page of the next issue of *La France Libre*, asserting that Bragg had

---

[31] 'La jeunesse de France, cette jeunesse française que les Laval et les Pétain prétendent avoir voulu sauver en signant l'armistice, – elle est aujourd'hui prisonnière de guerre' (Werth, 'Remember France', p. 29).

[32] 'Le corps de la France est aujourd'hui enchaîné' (H. Nicolson, 'Quelques mots sur la France', *La France Libre*, ii (17 July 1941), 190).

[33] 'Je crois donc que le régime de Vichy est un épisode temporaire, quoique tragique, de l'histoire de la France' (H. Laski, 'Réflexions sur l'avenir de la France', *La France Libre*, ii (15 Oct. 1941), 491).

[34] 'Travaillant à la fois pour elle-même et pour le monde, la France est une nation et elle est une pensée universelle' (H. Focillon, 'Fonction universelle de la France', *La France Libre*, ii (24 May 1941), 19).

[35] 'la France est une idée nécessaire à la civilisation, et que toute victoire qui nous séparerait d'elle serait une défaite' (C. Morgan, 'La France est une idée nécessaire à la civilisation', *La France Libre*, i (Apr. 1941), 503).

[36] W. Bragg, 'Paul Langevin', *La France Libre*, i (16 Dec. 1940), 103–4.

[37] W. Bragg, 'Paul Langevin', *La France Libre*, iii (15 Nov. 1941), 25–6.

told him shortly before his death 'When a country has given as much to the human sciences as yours, it is invulnerable'.[38] Here we have an example of a French exile using the words of a recently deceased British scientist to flag up France's particular contribution to science. Other articles paying tribute to France's cultural heritage include G. M. Trevelyan's tribute to fellow historian Elie Halévy, who had died in 1937 and whom he described as understanding England 'as well as we understand it ourselves, and in some respects better';[39] Desmond MacCarthy on Stendhal, who 'occupies a unique place in French literature';[40] Kenneth Clark on the Louvre; and in the 15 April 1944 issue of the review, Raymond Mortimer introducing a series of articles by British intellectuals under the general heading 'What France means to you'. Contributors to this included Vita Sackville-West, T. S. Eliot and Harold Laski, as well as the poet Kathleen Raine.[41]

La France Libre *and the French in London*

But it was not just one-way traffic. The artist Jean Oberlé was one of the first French refugees to reach London and was already there when de Gaulle made his historic broadcast on 18 June 1940. Oberlé was the originator of many Free French slogans, most famously the one denouncing Radio-Paris with the ditty 'Radio-Paris ment, Radio-Paris ment, Radio-Paris est allemand' ('Radio-Paris lies, Radio-Paris lies, Radio-Paris is German'), sung to the tune *La Cucaracha*. Beginning with the eighth issue of *La France Libre*, Oberlé contributed a series of articles entitled 'Images anglaises' comprising short snippets based on his observations of life in London and beyond. In his first contribution, Oberlé expressed his admiration for the calm demeanour, stoicism and sense of humour displayed by Londoners during the bombing raids and singled out the London cabbies as being possibly the most courageous of all.[42] In an article entitled 'Angleterre (1)', Albert Cohen recorded some of *his* impressions of London and its inhabitants. He wrote of 'the luxurious London underground' which made him yearn for his plebeian Paris métro with its dispensing machines selling bad but expensive Meunier chocolate, its smell of asphalt, gas and sweat, its carriages packed

---

[38] 'Quand un pays a autant donné que le vôtre pour la science humaine, il est invulnérable' (A. Labarthe, 'Sir William Bragg, OM, KBE, FRS', *La France Libre*, iii (17 Apr. 1942), 433).

[39] 'aussi bien que nous la comprenons nous-mêmes et, à certains égards, mieux' (G. M. Trevelyan, 'Elie Halévy 1870–1937', *La France Libre*, v (16 Nov. 1942), 9–10).

[40] 'occupe dans la littérature française une place unique' (D. MacCarthy, 'Stendhal', *La France Libre*, iv (15 May 1942), 19).

[41] R. Mortimer, 'What France means to you 1', *La France Libre*, vii (15 Apr. 1944), 401–8; 'What France means to you 2', *La France Libre*, viii (15 May 1944), 5–10; 'What France means to you 3', *La France Libre*, viii (15 June 1944), 94–9.

[42] J. Oberlé, 'Images anglaises', *La France Libre*, ii (20 June 1941), 172.

with under-nourished but cheerful crowds. Cohen found the Londoners in his tube carriage respectful and respectable: everyone sitting in dignified silence, reading their newspaper in a fug of tobacco and the smell of anti-septic soap.[43] Another contribution by Oberlé included his thoughts on an exhibition of French painting at the National Gallery, which, he found, was moving for the French visitor but also for *les Anglais* who loved France.[44]

Despite all the expressions of support for France and the frequent references to Franco-British solidarity and friendship, both French and British contributors acknowledged that tensions remained. Charles Morgan, for example, admitted that a mutual suspicion persisted between many French and British people which was deeply rooted in history and which the events of 1940 had done nothing to alleviate.[45] Here he was presumably thinking of the many French people who felt abandoned when the British army retreated to England after Dunkirk and those who could not understand why the British had attacked and destroyed part of the French fleet at Mers-el-Kébir, Algeria, killing over 1,000 French sailors. For their part, many British people believed that in June 1940, the French army collapsed without putting up much of a fight, and the Vichy government's shameful capitulation was compounded by a betrayal of Britain when it signed the armistice agreement with Germany. In April 1940, three months after Morgan's article appeared, Harold Nicolson was decrying the anti-French feeling, which he summarized as 'Never Trust a Froggy', and appealed to British readers not to be critical of the French. Admitting that the Vichy government was doing everything it could to help Britain's enemies, Nicolson said it was not surprising that many British people were tempted to blame the French en bloc and say that every country got the government it deserved. He, for his part, affirmed: 'The French people who are, and will always be, one of the best, the most decent and honest in the world, never deserved the Vichy government'.[46]

Aron's contribution to La France Libre

Although the flamboyant and volatile André Labarthe was very much the public face of *La France Libre*, it was Raymond Aron who was the mainstay of the review. Not only was Aron the de facto editor-in-chief, he

---

[43] A. Cohen, 'Angleterre (1)', *La France Libre*, ii (20 June 1941), 117.

[44] J. Oberlé, 'A propos de l'exposition française à la National Gallery', *La France Libre*, v (15 Jan. 1943), 212–14.

[45] Morgan, 'La France est une idée nécessaire', pp. 503–12.

[46] 'Le peuple français qui est, et sera toujours, l'un des meilleurs, l'un des plus braves et des plus honnêtes de ce monde n'a jamais mérité le gouvernement de Vichy' (Nicolson, 'Quelques mots', p. 190).

also contributed more articles to the review than anybody else. As Robert Colquhoun has noted: 'In only two of the fifty-nine monthly issues of the review which came out between November 1940 and September 1945 – the period for which Aron wrote for *La France Libre* – did no article of his appear. He habitually wrote two, and occasionally three, pieces for each number, totalling well over a hundred articles, editorials and book reviews in just under five years'.[47] This did not include the collaborative military analyses written with Staro.

Many of Aron's articles signed René Avord were philosophical in both style and content, as, for example, 'The origins of French thought'[48] or 'On political freedom'.[49] In the former, Aron considered a recently published work by Léon Brunschvicg in which the French philosopher reviewed Descartes's and Pascal's readings of Montaigne; the second contained Aron's reflections on Montesquieu and Rousseau. Through the Avord articles, Aron was helping to keep French culture and its intellectual tradition alive in exile in London, and aiming to show how French philosophical thought was still relevant to the world of the early 1940s. Other René Avord articles, written in the same somewhat academic style, fulfilled the same purpose but had a more explicit politico-sociological flavour, as, for example, 'Totalitarian strategy and the future of the democracies'[50] or 'Tyranny and the contempt for humanity'.[51]

Aron's other regular contributions to the review, unsigned and appearing under the heading *Chroniques de France* ('French chronicles'), were in some ways more ambitious than the René Avord articles. The aim of the *Chroniques*, Aron would later write, was 'to help readers, most of them foreign, to understand the events which were reported by the [French] daily press in a rather confused or sensational manner'.[52] Aron relied mainly on the French newspapers in the 'Free' Zone which, although heavily censored by the Vichy government, remained a valuable source of information, enabling him, for example, to paint a picture of everyday life in France,[53]

[47] Colquhoun, *Raymond Aron*, p. 225.

[48] R. Avord, 'Aux sources de la pensée française', *La France Libre*, iv (15 Oct. 1942), 441–8.

[49] R. Avord, 'De la liberté politique', *La France Libre*, iii (16 March 1942), 374–83.

[50] R. Avord, 'La stratégie totalitaire et l'avenir des démocraties', *La France Libre*, iv (15 May 1942), 29–37.

[51] R. Avord, 'Tyrannie et mépris des hommes', *La France Libre*, iii (16 Feb. 1942), 291–300.

[52] 'd'aider des lecteurs, en majorité étrangers, à comprendre des événements que les journaux quotidiens rapportaient de manière plus ou moins confuse ou sensationnelle' (R. Aron, 'Préface', in R. Aron, *Chroniques de guerre: la France libre 1940–4*' (Paris, 1990), p. 25).

[53] See, e.g., R. Aron, 'Problèmes de ravitaillement', *La France Libre*, v (15 Dec. 1942), 152–7.

analyse the French economy[54] and explain the nature of, and internal power struggles within, the Vichy government.[55] Looking back on his writings Aron said, with typical modesty, 'my analyses were not that wide of the mark given the information I had at my disposal'.[56] Indeed, reading them nearly eighty years later the reader is struck by the perspicacity and incisiveness of Aron's analyses. When comparing the *Chroniques* with the Avord articles one is also struck by the difference in style. If the Avord articles bear the familiar hallmarks of the somewhat dense, intense and often abstract style of exposition dear to French *universitaires*, the *Chroniques*, while rigorous and penetrating in their treatment of the subject, reveal Aron developing a journalistic style of writing, using his considerable intellect to drive the analysis but expressing his views in a way that is accessible to a wider public.

One feature of life in France that is almost totally absent from Aron's *Chroniques* is the anti-Semitic policies of the Vichy government and the German occupying forces. Aron later expressed his regret that he had not written more on this topic and especially on the anti-Jewish laws promulgated by Vichy, the exhibition 'Les Juifs en France' ('The Jews in France') and, above all, the 'Rafle du Vel' d'Hiv'[57] in Paris in July 1942.[58] During an interview, after considerable soul-searching, he offered three explanations for his quasi-total silence. First, there was a convention among the French in London that one mentioned the anti-Semitic measures as little as possible. Second, as a Jew, Aron was deeply affected by the fact that these measures were taken by his fellow Frenchmen, and his reluctance to write about them was, he said, 'a sort of reflex of emotional self-protection on my part to enable me to think as little as possible about what some French people were doing to the Jews'.[59] Third, influenced by the fact that a constant theme of Nazi propaganda was that the Jews were the cause of the war, he did not want to appear to be prioritizing the plight of Jews.

---

[54] See, e.g., R. Aron, 'Finances de défaite', *La France Libre*, iii (15 Dec. 1941), 162–9; R. Aron, 'Prix et salaires en France', *La France Libre*, iii (17 Apr. 1942), 498–503.

[55] See, e.g., 'Le nouveau régime: les hommes et les idées', *La France Libre*, i (Jan. 1941), 288–99; 'La désagrégation du regime de Vichy', *La France Libre*, v (15 Jan. 1943), 215–22.

[56] 'mes analyses n'étaient pas tellement fausses étant donné les informations dont je disposais' (Aron, *Spectateur Engagé*, p. 96).

[57] The round-up of over 13,000 Jews by the French police in Paris in July 1942. Those rounded up were initially held in the 'Vel' d'Hiv' (Vélodrome d'Hiver, or winter cycle track), a Paris stadium used for bicycle races.

[58] 'Pourquoi seulement trois passages d'un paragraphe ou deux sur le statut des Juifs ou la rafle du Vél' d'Hiv?' (Aron, in R. Aron, *Mémoires: 50 ans de réflexion politique* (Paris, 1983), p. 174).

[59] 'une espèce de précaution émotionnelle pour moi-même de songer le moins possible à ce que certains Français faisaient aux Juifs' (Aron, *Spectateur Engagé*, p. 101).

Aron, La France Libre *and de Gaulle*

Although *La France Libre* was too eclectic to be considered an orthodox Gaullist publication by de Gaulle and his immediate entourage, the General was initially very supportive and provided financial backing for the review. The fourth issue (February 1941) contained a glowing two-page letter of appreciation from de Gaulle, addressed to Labarthe, in which he wrote that *La France Libre*, described as 'your excellent review', 'will be one of the important elements in the success of our cause'.[60] However, relations between de Gaulle and the review became seriously strained after Labarthe distanced himself from the General and aligned himself with Vice-Admiral Emile Muselier, commander-in-chief of the Free French naval forces until sacked by de Gaulle in 1942. Labarthe and Muselier, described by one of Aron's biographers as 'tireless conspirators and a constant thorn in the flesh of de Gaulle and his closest associates',[61] finally left London for North Africa where they aligned themselves with de Gaulle's rival, General Giraud. Thus, largely as a result of Labarthe's wheeling and dealing, *La France Libre* came to be seen by de Gaulle and his entourage as a centre of anti-Gaullist dissent in London, and by 1943 de Gaulle believed the review was openly backing Giraud. However, the readers of *La France Libre* in France, Belgium, the Netherlands and Greece who obtained small-format, clandestine editions of the review thanks to regular drops made by the RAF, thought the publication was the semi-official voice of Gaullism.

Although Aron tried to keep out of the anti-de Gaulle intrigues engineered by Muselier and Labarthe, he later admitted that, because of his working relationship with Labarthe, he had been implicated in them to a certain extent.[62] But there were other reasons why Aron was viewed with suspicion by de Gaulle and his close supporters.

Initially, although Aron enjoyed cordial relations with de Gaulle, he never tried to become one of *le général*'s intimate circle.[63] In the very early days of the review, de Gaulle had read Aron and Staro's first article before it was published, putting 'B' (for 'bien') against the sections that he particularly liked – although Aron later added somewhat ruefully that he never got a 'TB' ('très bien'). Leaving aside questions of temperament, there were significant political differences between Aron and de Gaulle which meant that their relations would remain, at best, distant.

---

[60] 'sera l'un des éléments importants du succès de notre cause' (C. de Gaulle, 'Maintenir notre pays dans la guerre', *La France Libre*, i (Feb. 1941), 310).

[61] See Colquhoun, *Raymond Aron*, p. 219.

[62] Aron, *Spectateur Engagé*, p. 85.

[63] Aron, *Spectateur Engagé*, p. 85.

Up until November 1942, when any pretence that Vichy was a sovereign government was dispelled by the Occupation of the whole of France, there existed fundamental differences between the London Free French and Aron over how the Vichy government should be treated in the radio broadcasts from London. De Gaulle insisted that the Vichy government was illegal, while Aron, on the other hand, according to Daniel Cordier, did not, although this did not prevent Aron from publishing articles by jurist René Cassin in two consecutive issues of *La France Libre* making the case for the illegality of the Vichy government.[64] Nor, according to Cordier, did Aron believe that Pétain and his government had acted dishonourably by signing the armistice. Where de Gaulle sought to condemn Vichy, Aron typically tried to *understand* it in order to analyse it.[65] In Aron's view, every effort should be made to win over members of the Vichy government who were, in his opinion, dupes rather than villains. The Gaullists' relentless and uncompromising anti-Vichy propaganda ran the risk, Aron believed, of alienating them and thus being counter-productive: 'Until November 1942, I believed de Gaulle was wrong in making it more difficult for the Vichyites to come over to the right side'.[66] It should be noted that while Aron may have been isolated in London for taking this position, he was by no means alone. In October, while the British government was exploring the possibility of contacts with the Vichy government, it made unsuccessful attempts to persuade de Gaulle to desist from attacking Pétain. There were also some listeners to the BBC Free French radio programmes who were unhappy about the anti-Pétain content of the broadcasts.[67] Nonetheless, the differences between Aron's and the Gaullist perception of Vichy, coupled with Aron's perceived association with Labarthe and Muselier, resulted in his being viewed with considerable suspicion by those close to de Gaulle, and he remained something of an outsider in Free French circles in London.

Another point of difference between Aron and the inner circle of the Free French that reinforced Aron's relative isolation was his opposition to the Gaullist movement turning itself into a government while there was still a possibility that Vichy would establish itself as a government-in-exile in North Africa: 'I was sure that there would be a landing in North Africa …

---

[64] R. Cassin, 'Coup d'état', *La France Libre*, i (16 Dec. 1940), 162–76; R. Cassin, 'Coup d'état', *La France Libre*, i (Jan. 1941), 252–63.

[65] Cordier, 'René Avord à Londres', pp. 23–4. Aron makes similar observations in his memoirs (see Aron, *Memoires*) and in Aron, *Spectateur Engagé*.

[66] 'Jusqu'à novembre 1942 je croyais que de Gaulle avait tort de rendre plus difficile aux vichystes de passer du bon côté' (A. Gillois, *Histoire secrète des Français à Londres de 1940 à 1944* (Paris, 1973), p. 99).

[67] A. Luneau, *Radio-Londres 1940–4* (Paris, 2005), p. 94.

For as long as the situation in North Africa remained unresolved, the Vichy government had to be given a chance and premature claims [sc. by de Gaulle and his associates] to be the legitimate government should not be made'.[68] Aron's opposition to the violently anti-Vichy tone of Gaullist propaganda was probably the main reason for his refusal to make any overtly political BBC broadcasts to France.

Aron also harboured reservations about de Gaulle's style of leadership and his political intentions. This was evident in two articles that he published in *La France Libre* in 1943 which further reinforced suspicions among de Gaulle's circle that Aron was an anti-Gaullist. The first, entitled 'Long live the Republic',[69] appeared in June, a few weeks after the agreement that there should be a joint de Gaulle-Giraud leadership of the Comité Français de Libération Nationale (CFLN) in Algeria. Aron welcomed the perspective of unity, but enraged the Gaullist camp by writing that it was imperative to remember that in Algiers, 'Unity was established not around a man and a myth but on ideas',[70] adding that building unity in this way represented a choice between 'the re-establishment of a parliamentary republic' and 'a personal adventure'.[71] And just to reinforce the point he added that 'France has paid too dearly for its experiences of personal power'.[72] Two months later, by which time de Gaulle had outmanoeuvred Giraud to become the sole president of the CFLN, came the publication of an article by Aron entitled 'The shadow of the Bonapartes,[73] in which he returned to the theme of the dangers of personal power. Although Aron did not mention de Gaulle by name, he later admitted that it was him he had in mind when he examined the rise to power of Louis-Napoléon Bonaparte, the self-proclaimed man of providence who returned to Paris from London.[74] Aron completed the article with an analysis of events after Bonaparte's return and an examination of the links between Bonapartism and fascism.

After the marginalization of Giraud in Algeria, Labarthe moved to the USA where he founded an anti-Gaullist monthly called *Tricolor*. Aron

---

[68] 'J'étais persuadé qu'il y aurait un débarquement en Afrique du Nord … Aussi longtemps que le sort de l'Afrique du Nord n'était pas réglé, il fallait laisser une chance au gouvernement de Vichy et pas revendiquer trop tôt la légitimité' (Gillois, *Histoire secrète*, p. 99).

[69] R. A., 'Vive la République', *La France Libre*, vi (15 June 1943), 81–4.

[70] 'L'unité s'est faite non autour d'un homme et d'un mythe mais sur des idées' (R. A., 'Vive la République', p. 81).

[71] 'le rétablissement d'une république parlementaire' and 'l'aventure personnelle' (R. A., 'Vive la République', p. 82).

[72] 'la France a payé trop cher les expériences de pouvoirs personnels' (R. A., 'Vive la République', p. 82).

[73] R. Aron, 'L'ombre des Bonaparte', *La France Libre*, vi (16 Aug. 1943), 280–8.

[74] Aron, *Mémoires*, p. 185.

remained in London, where he was joined in July 1943 by his wife and daughter and, according to his autobiography, the family lived together for a while in a flat in Cromwell Gate. When the Arons' second daughter was born in June 1944, mother and daughters moved to Hertfordshire while Aron remained in London, now living, again according to his autobiography, in Queensberry Gate.[75] He returned to France in September 1944 and continued to contribute to *La France Libre* until September 1945. The last issue of the review was published in 1947.[76]

As well as making a crucial contribution to keeping the spirit of French democratic politics and culture alive during the war years, this period also marked a new personal departure for Aron which would be a vital part of his public profile for the rest of his life. In 1940, he was an aspiring academic who had written three monographs and numerous articles for learned reviews.[77] After his return to France, Aron turned down a university chair in Bordeaux. Bitten by the political bug, as he put it, he chose instead to remain in Paris and, drawing on the time spent in London, very soon confirmed the reputation as a respected political analyst that he had started to forge in London. Besides continuing to contribute to *La France Libre* until 1945, he wrote for a number of publications including the left-of-centre newspaper *Combat* before joining *Le Figaro* in 1947, where he remained for the next thirty years. In parallel with his journalistic activities he taught at the prestigious Ecole Nationale d'Administration and at the Institut d'Etudes Politiques, before taking up the post of professor of sociology at the Sorbonne in 1955.

The post-war period saw something of a reconciliation between Aron and de Gaulle. Aron agreed with de Gaulle's critique of the post-Liberation Fourth Republic, and about the same time as he started working at *Le Figaro*, he joined de Gaulle's Rassemblement du Peuple Français (RPF). However, he never quite managed to shake off his reputation, born in London, of being an opponent of de Gaulle. In 1991, eight years after Aron's death, Maurice Schumann, a former member of de Gaulle's Free French entourage in London, was still describing the stance of *La France Libre* as 'scandalous', citing in particular Aron's article 'L'ombre des Bonaparte'.[78]

---

[75] Aron, *Mémoires*, p. 235. Neither 'Cromwell Gate' nor 'Queensberry Gate' can be identified; it is very possible that Aron, writing years later, may have misremembered the street names.

[76] Colquhoun states that the last issue was no. 75, a special issue on the Low Countries, published in 1947 (Colquhoun, *Raymond Aron*, p. 237). Cottour states that no. 74, dated Dec. 1946–Jan. 1947, was the last issue (Cottour, "Constellation", n. 26, p. 167). I have been unable to clarify this point.

[77] For a complete list of Aron's pre-war writings see Colquhoun, *Raymond Aron*, pp. 500–5.

[78] Quoted in J. F. Sirinelli, *Deux Intellectuels dans le siècle, Sartre et Aron* (Paris, 1995), p. 165.

15. From the 16ème to South Ken? A study of the contemporary French population in London

Saskia Huc-Hepher and Helen Drake[1]

> To be French is to love France like a mother, to respect
> her like a father and to cherish her like a child.[2]

Introduction

If French identity can be defined as above, why is it that thousands of
French citizens, in the prime of their lives, are choosing to leave France
behind them in favour of London? Is this close relationship with the 'la
mère patrie' the initial trigger? Comparable to teenagers rebelling against
parents as a natural developmental process, have today's French come
to London in search of freedom, adventure and immersion in another
culture, another language, no longer seeking refuge, as in historical waves
of cross-Channel migration from the Huguenots to the post-Revolution
aristocracy and the Free French, but rather personal independence and
opportunity?

According to the Maison des Français de l'Etranger (MFE), on 31 December
2010 there were 108,999 French nationals registered at the French Consulate
in London. However, the Maison itself estimates that the true number of
French people living in and around London is more than double that figure,
at 250,000,[3] while the French Embassy moots a far higher amount, closer to
the 400,000 mark,[4] making the British capital France's 'fifth' or 'sixth' largest

---

[1] Photographs in this chapter courtesy of S. B. Huc-Hepher.

[2] 'Etre français c'est aimer la France comme une mère, la respecter comme un père, et
la chérir comme son enfant' (Amel, Stéphanie, Karim, Carla, Vito, Yanis – Extract from
responses to the question 'Pour vous, qu'est-ce qu'être français' in the Grand Débat sur
l'Identité Nationale, 4 Jan. 2010).

[3] See <http://www.mfe.org/index.php/Portails-Pays/Royaume-Uni> [accessed 28 Oct.
2012].

[4] See article in *The Independent*, 15 Nov. 2010 <http://www.independent.co.uk/news/
uk/this-britain/bienvenue-frances-expats-get-their-own-radio-station-2134199.html>; or *Le
Monde*, available via the Association des Membres de l'Ordre des Palmes Académiques
website <http://amopagb.org/Pages/articlelemonde.pdf> or <http://www.bbc.co.uk/news/
magazine-18234930> [all accessed 28 Oct. 2012].

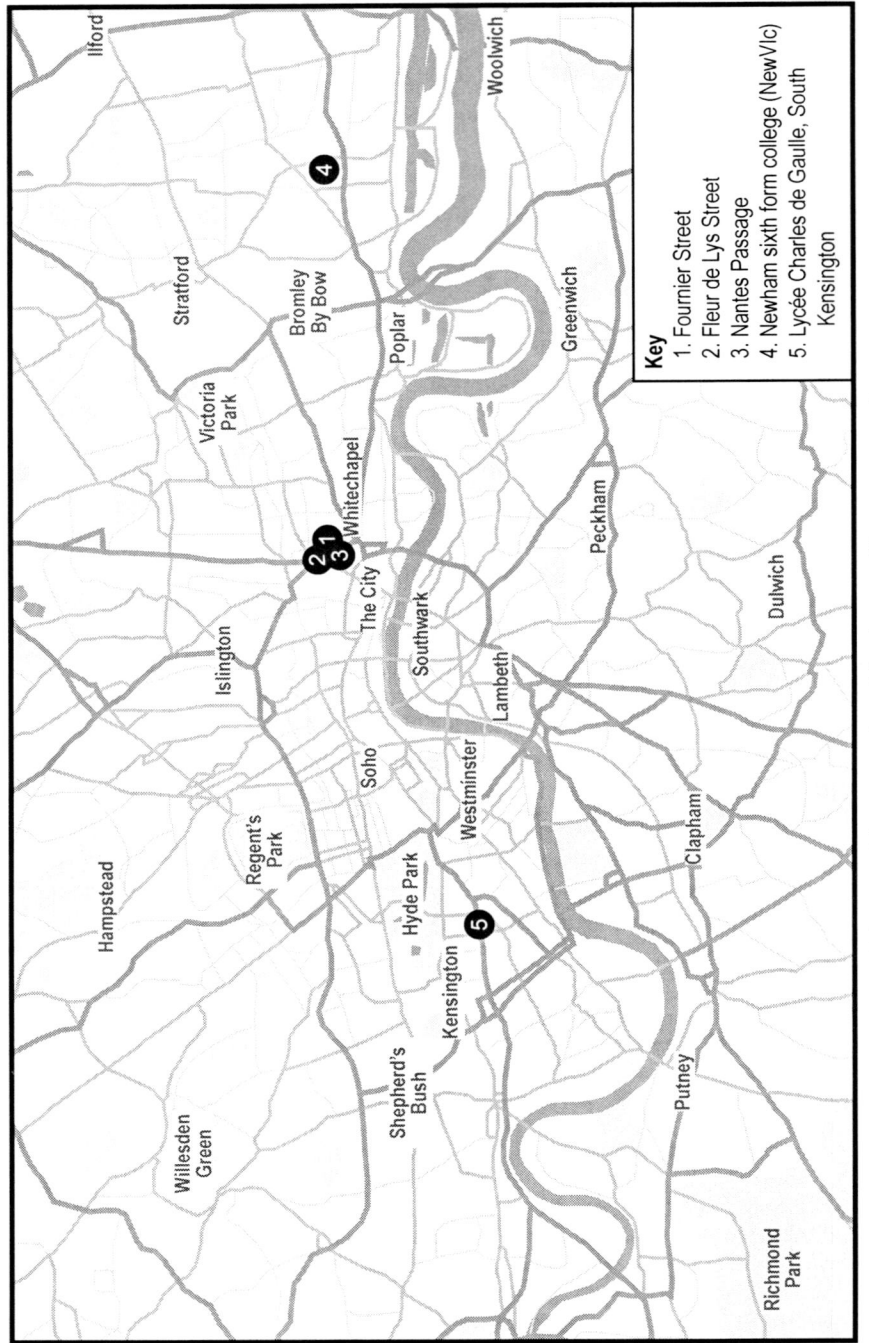

Map 15.1. Places mentioned in the text (Base map: 2013)

Key
1. Fournier Street
2. Fleur de Lys Street
3. Nantes Passage
4. Newham sixth form college (NewVIc)
5. Lycée Charles de Gaulle, South Kensington

city in population terms[5] (depending on the source). The MFE cites the twenty-five to forty age bracket as being the most represented among those registered at the French Consulate; in contrast, in Ewan Ledain's survey of young arrivals passing through the Centre Charles Péguy, and subsequently declining to register at the Consulate,[6] the eighteen to twenty-five age bracket was found to be the largest. This means that the under-twenty-fives are almost certainly under-represented in the official figures: they are 'the Forgotten of St Pancras'.[7] When we consider the number of French adults allocated a National Insurance number upon entry to the UK between 2002 and 2011, the figures are indeed striking. According to the Department for Work and Pensions official statistics,[8] France has been the only European nation to appear consistently in the 'top ten' year-on-year since 2002, with a peak in 2008–9 when allocations to individuals originally from France accounted for 24,010, placing France almost in joint third position with the Slovak Republic (24,090), after Poland and India. In fact, on the basis of NI number assignations, two other nations alone, worldwide, appear to have matched this consistency, in terms of the pattern of emigration to the UK, and they were – unsurprisingly, given Britain's colonial history – India and Pakistan. These NI figures demonstrate (contrary to Tzeng's evidence on the basis of Office of National Statistics (ONS) population estimates that Ireland is the 'largest group of foreigners from western European EU countries')[9] that the consistency of French migration to the UK is not equalled by movement from Ireland, Poland or any other EU country, including the A8 (recent Eastern European EU member states). The lowest influx was in 2003–4, when the total number nevertheless remained significant, at 13,130. It is worth noting that the 2008–9 peak referred to above took place during and immediately after the global financial crisis

[5] This popular media comparison is misleading, however, as it is based on the respective populations of the French city centres only (or 'communautés urbaines' proper), to the exclusion of greater numbers of inhabitants living in the adjoining suburban districts.

[6] A. Favell, 'London as Eurocity: French free movers in the economic capital of Europe', in *The Human Face of Global Mobility*, ed. M. P. Smith and A. Favell (New Brunswick, 2006), pp. 247–74.

[7] E. Ledain, 'Les Oubliés de St Pancras' survey, Consulat Général de France à Londres/Centre Charles Péguy (2010).

[8] Department for Work and Pensions, 'National Insurance number allocations to adult overseas nationals entering the UK: summary tables – latest quarterly data to December 2011, annual figures to March 2011' (2011), available at <http://statistics.dwp.gov.uk/asd/asd1/niall/index.php?page=nino_allocation> [accessed 28 Oct. 2012].

[9] R. Tzeng, 'International middle class migration and mobility: French nationals working in the UK' (Institute for the Study of European Transformations (ISET) working paper no. 18), p. 12, available at <http://www.londonmet.ac.uk/fms/MRSite/Research/iset/Working%20Paper%20Series/WP18%20R%20Tzeng.pdf> [accessed 11 Aug. 2011].

which, far from discouraging the cross-Channel migratory wave, as some analysts predicted, appears instead to have contributed to it, London no doubt enticing jobless young French men and women with its flexible, if fickle, labour market to a greater degree than in times of plenty.[10] That said, assessing the number of people simultaneously returning to France is a feat in itself, as return migrants are a notoriously elusive cohort the world over: 'There are no global estimates on the scale of return migration, although most experts believe that it is substantial'[11] and, confirming the empirical evidence provided by the interviewees, it 'is often the case that migrants go home to retire, having spent their working lives abroad. While they may take home money and experiences, they are not economically active themselves upon return'.[12] This grey area of return migration again casts doubt over the reliability and durability of the official statistics on the number of French people in London at any given time.

However, the 2011 UK census should shed new light on the French population of London, given that, for the first time in British censorial history, it included a set of questions pertaining to nationality, identity and languages other than English spoken by respondents. Indeed, scrutiny of the latest Annual School Census showing the distribution of different languages spoken in all London's state schools, published in August 2011, is revealing in both quantitative and demographic terms.[13] While offering only a partial picture of the true numbers, in that they represent British state schools only, the findings are nonetheless useful. Overall, they indicate a greater number of French speakers in inner London (1.7 per cent) than outer London (0.9 per cent), with the exception of the City of London, where a decidedly unambiguous 0.0 per cent was recorded. The more telling figures are perhaps those that offer a comparative representation of the number of pupils recorded as having French as their main language in Greater London as a whole: with a total of 11,680 pupils, more children speak French at home

---

[10] For confirmation that in the current 'double dip' recession the French are still flocking to London, see BBC News article 'London, France's 6th biggest city' by Lucy Ash, published 30 May 2012 at <http://www.bbc.co.uk/news/magazine-18234930> [accessed 26 July 2012]; or *London Evening Standard* article 'Pippa Middleton's Paristocrats are coming to London' by Joshi Herrmann, published 10 May 2012 at <http://www.standard.co.uk/lifestyle/london-life/pippa-middletons-paristocrats-are-coming-to-london-7733404.html> [accessed 26 July 2012].

[11] K. Koser, *International Migration: a Very Short Introduction* (Oxford, 2007), p. 21.

[12] Koser, *International Migration*, p. 51.

[13] Institute for Education, Centre for Analysis of Social Exclusion (LSE), and London Borough of Newham, 'Languages spoken by pupils, borough and MSOA' (2011) <http://data.london.gov.uk/datastore/package/languages-spoken-pupils-borough-msoa> [accessed 26 July 2012].

(1.2 per cent) than Spanish (0.8 per cent), Portuguese (1.1 per cent), Polish (1.0 per cent), Greek or Italian (both 0.3 per cent). Another perspective on the figure is that it constitutes twice as many as those who speak Chinese at home, and yet the Chinese community presence by far exceeds that of France in the collective host imagination and in local cultural practice, as Jacqueline, a French-Canadian HR manager of forty-two who lives in Nunhead, south London, pointed out during her interview:

> The Chinese community ... is far smaller than the French community, but far more visible. Everyone knows when the Chinese New Year is, not just in Leicester Square, but all over the city; my local library in Bromley dedicated a week of activities to the Chinese New Year, and the same can be said for lots of other communities. Maybe the French are more integrated, [so] their influence is relatively 'quiet'.[14]

Despite this comparatively discreet presence, there is little doubt that the London French make a positive contribution to the capital. In macro-economic terms, France has been the UK's primary outside investor 'since 2003, with 12.9 billion euros (about 19.3 billion pounds) invested, which represents 34.7 per cent of the total amount of the French outgoing Foreign Direct Investment',[15] and a dizzying 'over 2,900 companies [constituting] the French business community in London'.[16] Bearing a close resemblance to the cultural and commercial contributions of bygone generations of French Londoners, dating as far back as the Huguenots and beyond, the more tangible manifestations of the London French presence include at least thirty-two French schools;[17] 'an extensive range of fine French eating establishments to meet all budgets, from homely Parisian-style bistros to glamorous and exclusive restaurants [including ten] Michelin starred restaurants';[18] several French bookshops (from Clapham to South

---

[14] 'La communauté chinoise ... est bien plus petite que la communauté française, mais elle est bien plus visible. Tout le monde sait quand est la nouvelle année chinoise, pas seulement à Leicester Square, mais partout dans la ville; ma bibliothèque de Bromley a passé une semaine d'activités pour le nouvel an chinois, et c'est vrai aussi de bien d'autres communautés. Les Français sont peut-être plus intégrés, [du coup] le rayonnement [de leur présence] est relativement "peu bruyant"'.

[15] G. Bellion, 'French business in the UK – a survey' (Université de Franche-Comté/The Relocation Bureau MSc dissertation, Besançon/High Wycombe, 2005).

[16] Think London report 'French community in London' (2007), p. 2, available at <http://www.thinklondon.com/downloads/london_communities/europe_france/CommunityreportFranceAWlowres.pdf> [accessed 28 Oct. 2012].

[17] Seventeen French and bilingual (French/English) full-time weekday schools, from pre-school up to secondary level, and 15 part-time, often Saturday-morning, French schools, scattered all over Greater London.

[18] Think London report, p. 4.

Kensington); numerous French medical centres, such as Medicare Français, La Maison Médicale or the Cabinet Dentaire Français dental practice (there is even a dedicated French veterinary doctor for monolingual quadrupeds!); regular French markets (from Bromley to Wembley) and myriad neighbourhood delicatessens (such as *Le Tour de France* in Streatham or *Mimosa* in Herne Hill, which sits opposite a bicycle retailer named *Bon Vélo*); French estate and recruitment agencies; cultural and entertainment bodies such as the Institut Français and its Ciné Lumière, the French Music Bureau and the Maison du Languedoc-Rousillon in the West End, which stages an annual southern French festival every year in Cavendish Square; as well as various 'houses of worship, from the Synagogue Française de Londres in North London, to the *Eglise Protestante Française* in Soho and the *Eglise Notre Dame de France* near Charing Cross'.[19] And this is by no means an exhaustive list. Indeed, a cursory glance at the advertisements in French community publications, such as *Ici Londres*, reveals a plethora of French businesses, retailers, services, educational institutions, medics and associations, as well as regular community social gatherings, such as the London French Wednesday[20] or the burlesque Soirée Pompette.[21] The French in London also have their own alternative record labels, such as Brownswood Recordings or Thrills and Beats Records, their own underground online publishing house, Les Editions de Londres, their own theatre company, Tamise en Scène, and a dedicated digital radio station, French Radio London (FRL), launched in November 2010.[22]

Mindful of the gap between such realities, and the unreliability of statistics, our analysis is based on an unprecedentedly systematic and in-depth empirical study of today's London French conducted by Huc-Hepher between 2009 and 2011, with additional material derived from an earlier and smaller pilot study conducted by Drake in the summer of 2008, both studies based on extensive secondary analysis. The main study in particular comprised a mix of methods, all designed to elicit both information and observations from our respondents, and to contextualize these within the literatures of contemporary Franco-British mobility and migration. The field work in this case consisted of 200 questionnaires; twenty one-to-one, non-random interviews; and two focus groups of six and seven participants

---

[19] Think London report, p. 4.

[20] <http://www.facebook.com/pages/London-French-Wednesday/6244556445> [accessed 26 July 2012].

[21] <http://soireepompette.blogspot.co.uk> [accessed 26 July 2012].

[22] See <http://www.tunecore.com/music/thrillsandbeatsrecords> or (forthcoming) <http://thrillsandbeatsrecords.com>; <http://www.gillespetersonworldwide.com/brownswood-recordings>; and <http://www.editionsdelondres.com> [all accessed 2 Aug. 2012].

respectively. The desk work was characterized by its extensive search for web-based resources relevant to our enquiry. For its part, the 2008 pilot study comprised thirty one-to-one interviews conducted on the basis of a semi-structured questionnaire. In the following section, we set out further details of this primary research, and make some preliminary remarks about the demographics of our population and the issues that their study raises in terms of the motivations, experiences and observations of our respondents.

Questions of method, motivations and demography

> Jacqueline: 'I came to learn English, to get my Cambridge Certificate'.
> Arthur: 'It looks good to have London on your CV; that was my plan'.
> Moses: 'Everything's easier in England: I found a job the day I got here'.
> Bruno: 'English culture was why I came in the first place ... I liked English music, pop, etc., "Brit culture", the image it represents in France ... You feel like there's lots to do here and there's always something interesting going on, an exhibition, a concert... You can't really get bored in a city like London'.[23]

In the case of the main study, and in an initial, pilot phase, Huc-Hepher distributed 200 questionnaires to parents from the Grenadine French Saturday School in Blackheath, either in person at the school gates, and/or by email; the overall response rate was low, at 10 per cent. Subsequently, in the study's second phase, Huc-Hepher conducted twenty interviews with a separate sample constructed to represent the community's diversity in terms of age, gender, ethnicity, social status, occupation, sexuality, geographical provenance and adopted London neighbourhood.[24] Personal (hi)stories were discussed in depth, with the average interview lasting one and a half hours, in an attempt to understand the mechanisms at play in this latest wave of French migration to the British capital. Together with the interviews, and in order to gain insight into the perceptions of a younger segment of London's French population, two focus groups were subsequently conducted in two very different schools, socio-economically and geographically speaking. The ages of those participating in the focus groups ranged between sixteen and eighteen years, and they came from a variety of backgrounds. The first focus

[23] Jacqueline: 'Je suis venue pour avoir mon Cambridge Certificate, pour apprendre l'anglais'; Arthur: 'C'est bien d'avoir Londres sur le CV, c'était ça mon idée'; Moses: 'Tout est plus facile en Angleterre: j'ai trouvé du travail le premier jour'; Bruno: 'Je suis venu au départ pour la culture anglaise ... J'aimais bien la musique anglaise, pop, etc., la "British culture", l'image qu'elle représente en France ... On a l'impression de pouvoir faire beaucoup de choses ici et qu'il y a toujours quelque chose d'intéressant qui se passe, une exposition, un concert; on ne peut pas vraiment s'ennuyer dans une ville comme Londres'.

[24] For a complete list of interviewee profiles, including geographical residency particulars, see the Appendix to this chapter.

group (Focus Group 1) took place in a state-funded sixth-form college in Newham (NewVIc), one of London's most deprived areas to the east of the city, with one of the highest migrant populations in the UK: according to the ONS,[25] 76.4 per cent of all children in Newham were born to non-UK mothers in 2010, the highest proportion of all local authorities in England and Wales. The group of seven francophone youngsters taking part were all from ethnic minorities, holders (or sons/daughters of holders) of French passports (including France's Overseas Departments and Territories) and, as such, this cohort was in stark contrast to the sample of teenagers in the second focus group (Focus Group 2). The latter comprised six students of the same age attending the over-subscribed Lycée Charles de Gaulle – a semi-independent, means-tested fee-paying school, subsidized by the French state, providing both bilingual education and the French national curriculum. The school is in South Kensington, one of London's most affluent districts in the fashionable, francophone and Francophile west of the capital. One of the students participating in the French Lycée focus group was of Moroccan heritage, but the remaining participants were of French/European origin and from socio-economically privileged backgrounds. Initially, by way of introduction to the field of research, and with the aim of providing some 'hard', 'objective'[26] data for subsequent analysis, the students completed a brief, user-friendly questionnaire.

The final form of primary research used in the main study was an analysis of a selection of online resources. Not only were national statistics and official online data scrutinized, but also less conventional material, such as that contained in French-speaking London community blogs and online reference sites, e-magazines and e-newspapers. These sources proved a rich stream of unadulterated and apparently unselfconscious evidence. Finally, and by way of comparison here, Drake's study was conducted on the eve of the global financial crisis that was to strike in autumn 2008. Between May and July of that year, she conducted twenty-six face-to-face interviews with young French workers employed across London in franchises of the French baker and patisserie company *Paul*. All interviewees were aged between

[25] Office of National Statistics, 'Births in England and Wales by parents' country of birth' (2010), available at <http://www.ons.gov.uk/ons/rel/vsob1/parents--country-of-birth--england-and-wales/2010/births-in-england-and-wales-by-parents--country-of-birth--2010.html> [last accessed 26 July 2012].

[26] Like the initial survey conducted, these questionnaires had the advantage over the interviews of allowing the respondents to answer freely, without perceived pressure or prejudice from the interviewer or peers. The same can be said of the choice of language: French. This resulted in the participants responding spontaneously and impartially, without fear of offence or inaccuracy, which may not have been the case had the oral investigations been carried out in English.

twenty-two and twenty-five years, almost all were working full time, and over a third had been in post for over a year at the time of interview, with one or two having risen to the role of 'team leader'. Virtually all had completed at most three years of higher education, and were either from the Paris *banlieues* or from France's regional towns and cities.[27]

Our desk research had already established that, broadly speaking, the French community in London is thought to be divisible into two principal groups: the middle-class, highly-skilled, highly-educated and highly-sought-after (euro)City (euro)stars;[28] and Ledain's young 'Oubliés de St Pancras', seen above, seeking language skills, a new lifestyle, perhaps a new self and, above all, employment. However, this standard dichotomous distinction between, on the one hand, the more mature and highly-skilled (Mulholland and Ryan's 'highly-skilled French professionals')[29] and, on the other, the younger, low-skilled[30] faction of the French diaspora is over-simplistic. Indeed, our studies suggest common motivations and experiences across our respondents: both camps came initially and superficially in search of flexible, fluid employment opportunities and English language acquisition, coupled with a quest for the (multi)cultural liveliness that London is thought to embody. Furthermore, most, if not all, take on jobs that local inhabitants fail to fill, both in the high-end fields of finance or insurance *and* the low-end sectors of childcare or hospitality, and both are typically welcomed by host employers.

Christian Roudaut[31] attempts to grapple with this over-simplification by defining a third group of French Londoner which he refers to as 'Français escargots' ('snail French'), but which migration specialists might prefer to term 'inter-corporate transferees (ICTs)',[32] and who were also present in our populations. These are expatriates proper, often from the diplomatic or administrative corps, who, as the mollusc metaphor implies, carry their native culture and lifestyles firmly on their backs, in an autochthonic transposition to the host city, rather than attempting to assimilate into their

---

[27] See <http://www.francobritishcouncil.org.uk/data/files/reports/drake.pdf>, for the full study, in French [accessed 28 Oct. 2012].

[28] A. Favell, *Eurostars and Eurocities: Free Movement and Mobility in an Integrating Europe* (Oxford, 2008).

[29] J. Mulholland and L. Ryan, 'French capital: a study of French highly skilled migrants in London's financial and business sectors – a report on preliminary observations' (Middlesex University, ESRC RES-000-22-4240, Dec. 2011).

[30] This definition is in itself somewhat of a fallacy, as many of the young French movers employed in unskilled tertiary-sector posts are technically over-qualified, contentedly there for the culturo-linguistic benefits in kind rather than job satisfaction or capital gain.

[31] C. Roudaut, *France, je t'aime je te quitte* (Paris, 2009).

[32] Koser, *International Migration*, p. 18.

new-found socio-cultural context, as would their aptly termed 'chameleon' counterparts ('caméléons' in Roudaut's terminology). We note, furthermore, that in 2010[33] Roudaut drew attention to a fourth category, which could be termed the ethnic-minority French migrant group. Anecdotal and observational evidence – be it from university seminars, Grenadine exchanges or bustling Brixton streets – would suggest that it constitutes a considerable proportion of the French community in London, but one that fails to feature in official statistics, despite its more visible presence than that of its 'Français de souche' ('ancestral French') counterparts or white 'European phenotype', to use Block's terminology.[34]

At the same time, the statistics are revealing in relation to the neighbourhoods they represent, which may offer an indication by proxy of the ethnicity of the London French. Contrary to popular belief, it transpires that the most French-speaking borough is not Kensington and Chelsea (with a considerable 2.6 per cent share nonetheless), but Lambeth, the latter having a 2.9 per cent proportion of French-speakers among its schoolchildren (in keeping with other deprived areas such as Hackney and Lewisham, each with 2.1 per cent), whereas a mere 0.8 per cent and 1.4 per cent were attributed to Ealing and Greenwich respectively – areas often (mis)perceived as having high concentrations of French expatriates. On the basis of these figures and the demographic zones to which they correspond (that is, densely-populated boroughs with a proportion of ethnic minorities which far exceeds the national average), it is not unreasonable to assume that in addition to the 'Français de souche', or French nationals proper, they also include a significant number of French-speaking ethnic minorities of ex-colonial descent. The observations made during the Newham focus group session support this theory, and our overall evidence suggests that, rather than conforming to the 'South Ken expat' stereotype, the majority of the London French replicate the 'French' presence across the globe, in all its complexity and diversity. In this light, how do 'our' French define and identify themselves, in terms of the republican principles of the France that they have left behind?

Liberté *vs* fraternité: *identity, belonging and transformation of the self*

Charles: 'I think the emphasis is clearly placed on equality in France, I'd go as far as to say it's almost a form of egalitarianism, trying to make everyone

---

[33] In an interview with the news channel France24 on 23 Apr. 2010, available at <http://www.france24.com/fr/20100423-2010-04-22-2246-wb-fr-entretien> [accessed 29 July 2012].

[34] D. Block, *Multilingual Identities in a Global City: London Stories* (Basingstoke, 2006), p. 208.

fit into the same mould. In England, the emphasis is really on liberty, and expressing difference freely'.

Miranda: 'I feel 100 per cent integrated [here]. 80 per cent of me belongs here, but I am still French deep down'.

Sarah: 'I feel like I'm a Londoner, but not English'.

Sadia: 'I don't feel like an immigrant. "Immigration", there's a movement that goes with it'.

Questionnaire respondent: '"Immigration" refers to other people'.

Brigitte: 'I didn't want to come to England to meet France'.

Séverine: 'London's changed me. I think I'm more resourceful now; I've become more entrepreneurial'.[35]

To complement our discussion of the demography of today's London French thus far, we refer to the self-identification of our population: do they see themselves as belonging explicitly to any of the groups mentioned above? How, exactly, do they define themselves? And how do they rationalize their departure to London, and the company that they keep in their London lives? We found in our field work that each member of the French community experiences and embodies their existence 'abroad', in London, in a highly individual, highly subjective way, and that there is no single rule that can be attributed to the London French identity, rather endless exceptions thereto. The sole existential trait uniting most of them, however, is a clear impression of being a Londoner, which perhaps explains why the overwhelming majority do not feel a need to be part of the French community in London, as they have an underlying sense of belonging to a broader, richer community: they are Londoners, and themselves meliorated by being so. As Charles eloquently puts it: 'You have an identity somewhere that is enriched by living abroad ... You know yourself better ... because you've got something to compare yourself with. But if you're still in the amniotic fluid, you don't spend your whole time questioning yourself'.[36]

---

[35] Charles: 'Je pense qu'en France l'accent est nettement mis sur l'égalité, je dirais même presque l'égalitarisme, de faire en sorte que tout le monde soit logé à la même enseigne. En Angleterre, l'accent est vraiment mis sur la liberté, et l'expression de la différence'; Sarah: 'Je me sens londonienne, mais pas anglaise'; Miranda: 'Je me sens 100% intégrée [ici]. J'appartiens à ici à 80%, mais je suis quand même française dans le fond'; Sadia: 'Je me sens pas immigrée. "L'immigration", il y a un mouvement qui va avec'; Questionnaire respondent: '"L'immigration", c'est les autres'; Brigitte: 'J'avais pas envie d'être venue à Londres pour rencontrer la France'; Séverine: 'Londres m'a changée. Je suis peut-être plus débrouillarde; j'ai développé un tempérament plus entrepreneur'.

[36] 'Justement on a quelque part une identité qui est enrichie du fait de vivre à l'étranger ... On se connaît mieux ... puisqu'on a un élément de comparaison, alors que lorsqu'on baigne dans le liquide amniotique, on ne passe pas tout son temps à se questionner'.

From 'aliens',[37] to 'strangers',[38] to 'foreigners',[39] the London French have always been labelled in accordance with the historical times. Today's London French, by way of comparison, and especially those constituting Roudaut's 'Français-escargots', are more likely to define themselves as expats than immigrants. Indeed, the very notion of being categorized as an 'immigrant' was often met by our respondents with a combination of hostility, incomprehension and astonishment. The idea that purely by virtue of their conforming to the dictionary definition of an immigrant,[40] that is, a person who has undergone 'the process of immigrating; settling in a foreign country',[41] they could be regarded as such was a revelation, and a concept to which many of the interviewees could not relate. Instead, most of our respondents identified themselves in relation to an 'imagined community',[42] usually 'London' or 'Europe' (meaning the European Union), less often 'England' or even 'the UK'. For example, and in keeping with the vast majority of interviews and in addition to her European self-identification, twenty-eight-year-old doctoral student Miranda reveals a vivid sense of belonging to London – 'I feel like a Londoner, yeah, totally'[43] – but the somewhat tortuous overall account of her internalization of identity appears, like that of many of the other informants, to arrive at its conclusion by default, the 'immigrant', 'migrant' and 'expat' tags all failing to correspond to her selfhood for varying reasons.

Furthermore, all of our interviewees (in the main study) have, without exception, made a deliberate choice to divorce themselves from French community ties at some point in their London sojourn, if not permanently, despite the community's clear physical presence. Fifty-two-year-old urban designer and architecture lecturer Antoine, originally from Marseilles, now calls Archway home and has lived in London for twenty-two years; in his

---

[37] J. Clark and C. Ross, *London: the Illustrated History* (2011), pp. 77, 270.

[38] As in 'stranger churches' (see A. Pettegree, *Foreign Protestant Communities in 16th-Century London* (Oxford, 1986)).

[39] As the Foreign and Protestants Naturalization Act of 1708 testifies (see J. Noorthouck, *A New History of London - Including Westminster and Southwark* (1773), available at British History Online <http://www.british-history.ac.uk/report.aspx?compid=46735> [accessed 25 Sept. 2011]).

[40] These in themselves vary considerably: the *Collins English Dictionary* stipulates a strict temporal and temporary dimension ('a person who has been settled in a country of which he is not a native for less than ten years'), while the *Cambridge Dictionary Online* includes an entirely contrary notion of longevity and intent ('a person who has come to a different country in order to live there permanently').

[41] *Chambers 21st Century Dictionary* (1999).

[42] B. Anderson, *Imagined Communities* (1983; 2006).

[43] 'Je me sens londonienne, oui, carrément'.

Figure 15.1. 2012 Président Bankside Bastille Day Festival:
perceptions of being 'French in London'.

words: 'I have avoided the French community from the beginning … that was a conscious decision … I haven't seen the benefit; I cannot see how I could contribute, or what it could do for me'. In many cases, this resolve originally appears to have been instigated by a desire to learn the English language through immersion technique – the academic approach learnt at school in France for ten years having failed them – and in an attempt to achieve full integration within the adopted society.

There was also a tendency for interviewees to spurn inclusion within a French association or club – of which London has many[44] – as it was often felt that it would involve becoming part of a French clique, inevitably resulting in anti-British discourse, voicing hackneyed objections to local services (trains were singled out here) and cultural practices (such as having to buy rounds in a pub, and having to go to the pub to have a social life in the first place) etc., perceived by many as being unfruitful and unnecessary. This rejection of compatriot associations, commonplace among our interviewees, was echoed by one of the teachers interviewed by David Block in the framework of his six-year, longitudinal study of French

---

[44] By way of example, the Fédération des Associations Françaises en Grande-Bretagne, founded, significantly, in 1942, brings together over 70 separate organizations, and there are many more in London which are not members of the FAFGB.

foreign language teachers in London.[45] Nancy explained: 'Every time I meet French people who are teaching, they are complaining, they are frustrated people. So I think we are frustrated people living in another country. We keep criticizing England, but we are bitter about France, because [it] did not do anything for us'.[46] However, when friendships with fellow French men and women grow organically, it is a different matter entirely, and if befriending host residents proves an insurmountable challenge, our French turn to their compatriots. Indeed, Sadia's situation became so desperate that she resorted to placing an advertisement in a local newspaper in search of kinship with a French Londoner: 'It was a nightmare trying to make friends here for years … the people are nice enough, but they're a bit closed up. It takes them a long time to trust you and open up. You really have to work at it; two years later they'll invite you over for a coffee!'[47] Relationships with fellow nationals with whom one shares a common sociocultural heritage, including food and wine, are unconscious or instinctive, and all the more effortless for it. This was a phenomenon communicated by the majority of those interviewed for this study, whose networks of friends were generally composed of French nationals or other non-British migrants, despite not deliberately seeking them out.

A possible reason for the community's default inter-French friendships and resistance to organized associations with French social and/or professional assemblages is that the French in London remain attached to and part of France by virtue of its very closeness, and therefore neither feel a necessity to integrate into host culture nor to form a distinct, homogeneous community apart from it. This is a notion confirmed by Bellion: 'The cohesion of the French expatriates is weak. They do not feel the need to meet each other, maybe because of the geographical proximity of France'.[48] Respondents in the *Paul* UK study cited similar factors in their decisions to move: 'London is easy to get to', stated Sophie Le F, a twenty-year-old.[49]

As with previous generations of London French exiles, living in the capital was found to have a transformative effect, sometimes profound, on the identities and behaviour of those interviewed. Most felt that they had undergone modifications to their personalities or behaviour which they

---

[45] D. Block, 'French foreign-language teachers in London', in Block, *Multilingual Identities*, pp. 107–35.

[46] Block, 'French foreign-language teachers', p. 121.

[47] 'Ici, j'ai galéré pour faire des amis pendant des années … les gens sont sympa, mais ils sont un peu renfermés. Il leur faut beaucoup de temps pour avoir confiance, pour s'ouvrir. Il faut vraiment s'investir; deux ans plus tard ils t'invitent prendre un café!'

[48] G. Bellion, 'French business in the UK'.

[49] 'Londres est pratique d'accès'.

perceived to be a positive and liberating experience. One recurrent and intriguing theme was developing a less volatile temperament since living in London, or placing a greater emphasis on courtesy and good manners. Hotel manager Arthur, on the lower socio-professional echelons of London society, highlighted a discrepancy between his experiences of working life in Paris (disrespected) and London (treated with courtesy): 'my family says "you've changed: you're calmer; you think more" – and that's the positive side of having lived here. I think I'm a little bit English now'.[50] Further accounts of courtesy ranged from the almost mythological queuing at the bus-stop, to moving to one side on the escalator in order to leave the other free for more pressed or energetic commuters, not forgetting both the unexpected applying of the highway code manifested by drivers stopping at zebra crossings, and the unspoken highway code of allowing oncoming vehicles to pass before oneself. This 'pleasure in giving' ('plaisir d'offrir') positive host trait, remarked upon and, more often than not, adopted by the French Londoners interviewed in both their working and private lives, is nevertheless surprising when considered in the context of the egocentric, individualistic society also purporting to be the London norm.

Some felt, however, that the speed and pressure of life in the megacity had in turn made them less patient, more frenzied, as Bruno from Bordeaux testified. Despite feeling 'a bit freer here than in France',[51] one of the major drawbacks of London life was for him a sense of claustrophobia resulting from the sheer scale of the conurbation and the geographical boundaries of the isle itself: 'from time to time I feel a bit hemmed in here because it's hard to leave London, and go and see something else; it takes so long to get out of London that it makes you think twice before doing anything at all outside the city. And that feeling is heightened by the fact that we're on an island'.[52] Whereas Brice perceived this urban energy positively, as integral to London's liberating force: 'Now that I've experienced something else, a big city and so on, I think I'd soon feel cramped [in Carcassonne]'.[53] As if in a curious reversal of physical reality, his personal reality was defined by a greater sense of space, openness and freedom in the buzzing hive of activity

---

[50] 'Ma famille dit "tu as vâchement changé; tu es plus calme; tu penses plus" – et ça c'est le côté positif d'avoir vécu ici. Je pense que je suis un petit peu anglais maintenant'.

[51] 'un peu plus libre ici qu'en France'.

[52] 'J'ai l'impression de temps en temps d'être un peu enfermé ici parce qu'on a des difficultés pour quitter Londres, pour aller voir autre chose, parce que ça prend tellement de temps pour sortir de Londres, déjà, qu'on hésite à faire quoi que ce soit en dehors de la ville. Et cette sensation est accentuée par le fait qu'on est sur une île'.

[53] 'Maintenant que j'ai connu autre chose, une grande ville, etcétéra, je pense que je me sentirais très vite à l'étroit [à Carcassonne]'.

that is overpopulated London than in the topographically broader open spaces of south-west France. This is evidence, therefore, of both positive and negative forms of change and individual positioning within the megacity.

Do our London French experience other forms of liberation from their former selves? Perhaps serving to counterbalance the London individualistic status quo were other transformative effects of a more spiritual or cultural nature. Thirty-two-year-old, Franco-Algerian Sadia, for instance, embraced Christianity while in London, much to the astonishment and disapproval of her 'friends' in France; and one of the teenagers taking part in the focus group in Newham expressed in appreciative terms the freedom to become more devout in his practice of the Muslim faith, which he gratefully believed had prevented him from embodying the typical French media representation of the 'urban delinquent' ('délinquant banlieusard') he thought he would otherwise have become had he remained in Paris. Self-realization also came in the shape of cultural experiments; by way of example, Brice reported taking on an entirely different persona under the cover of the city's darkness, being a financial/IT consultant by day and an actor by night, performing with the Tamise en Scène[54] theatre company; while Séverine developed her entrepreneurial skills, and Bruno took up amateur photography.

Others found themselves becoming – perhaps despite themselves – 'Anglo-Saxon', that term used consistently and derogatively in French political culture. Being 'liberal' in this sense is perceived by some of our respondents to be one of the most powerful, singular attractions of London, whether it be the individual's right to dress as they wish ('you can wear whatever you like here, no-one will bat an eyelid',[55] comment from Focus Group 2); to listen to the music they choose (Miranda: 'the type of music I listen to is really weird; they call it "doom". It's very instrumental, experimental music – sludge');[56] to engage in nocturnal pursuits which dispel any preconceptions based on their day jobs (including the 'am-dram' pastime mentioned above and even pole-dancing); or simply to break away from the mould that (French) society has assigned them ('in Paris, you have to stick to the model',[57] Focus Group 2). Séverine, the lawyer from Nunhead, illustrated this point having noticed a Franco-English variation regarding attitudes to eccentricity: 'I think you have more options in England, more options in London; eccentricity is still allowed and respected … You can

[54] See <http://www.tamiseenscene.com/pages/la-compagnie/vocation.html> [accessed 12 Oct. 2011].

[55] 'Ici, on peut s'habiller comme on veut; personne ne regardera'.

[56] 'Le genre de musique que j'écoute, c'est vraiment spécial, c'est ce qu'on appelle "doom". C'est la musique très instrumentale, expérimentale, sludge'.

[57] 'à Paris, il faut suivre le modèle'.

Figure 15.2. 2012 Président Bankside Bastille Day Festival: French Londoners strengthen intracultural ties over a game of café-culture 'babyfoot'.

be upper-middle-class in England without having to conform to one single mode of thought, lifestyle, etc.'[58]

These varied manifestations of civil liberties, of Londoners' indifference towards difference, ultimately of individual freedom, simultaneously permit, even encourage, the unconditional generation of personal income, and, equally importantly, the aspiration to achieve it: the Anglo-Saxon stereotype par excellence. This is a fundamental contrast to France, where the accepted attitude in the face of socio-economic success is reportedly either one of contempt or, more commonly, undisguised envy, and where manifestations of such success are habitually met with rancour, causing those in positions of relative wealth to feel obliged to conceal it, together with any efforts to hold it as an objective: '[Londoners] have quite a healthy attitude towards money. What I like here is that people are quite positive, and not jealous'[59] (Laura). These attitudes led some of the interviewees to alter their political stance in London, as Charles openly acknowledged: 'Often at

---

[58] 'Je trouve qu'on a plus d'options en Angleterre, plus d'options à Londres, l'excentricité est encore admise et respectée … Je pense qu'on peut être bourgeois en Angleterre et ne pas se conformer à un seul modèle de pensée, de vie, etc.'

[59] '[les Londoniens], ils ont une façon de vivre cet argent qui est plutôt saine. Ce que j'aime bien ici c'est que les gens sont assez positifs, et pas jaloux'.

dinner parties with my friends [in France], I've practically been verbally abused. They'd swear at me, telling me I'd started thinking like a Blairite, that I'd become a liberal, and I'd say "no, I've become a pragmatist"'.[60] His interpretation of British liberalism is not restricted to market economics and free enterprise, although he does acknowledge these aspects, but it also incorporates freedom of thought, a sentiment that was echoed by Séverine: 'I think I've become less anxious, more tolerant ... more inquisitive'.[61] Cordier makes a pertinent comparison in this respect, which is representative of the divergence in attitudes towards socio-professional mobility on either side of the Channel, stating in his essay that 'One of the good things about job ads in the UK is that the salaries are shown, even for top managerial positions, which almost never happens in France [where] money is a taboo subject'.[62] It would appear that neither earning nor spending money, and subsequently flaunting its fruits, is taboo in London, a point borne out in Bellion's thesis: 'British people spend more money on shoes, clothes and accessories than the other Europeans'.[63]

Another justification for the aforementioned endemic obligation to conceal one's wealth in France, as a preventative measure against others' green-eyed disapproval, could lie in the country's Catholic tradition. Despite it seemingly being at odds with the nation's current, proactive, institutional secularism, several of the interviewees spontaneously referred to Catholicism's power to stifle success or at least any manifestations thereof. Indeed, the notion that material wealth should initiate a shameful sense of guilt, bringing with it only ignoble, short-lived, earthly pleasures, is one that is tacitly corroborated by Cordier, who writes 'there's nothing shameful about earning a good living [in London]',[64] and explicitly by forty-eight-year-old Chantal, who believes Catholicism to be deeply embedded in the French *vox populi*: 'actually in the Catholic religion you mustn't say what you have, you must never show it; no nice cars; as soon as you begin to show it, there's a huge amount of envy'.[65]

---

[60] 'Moi, souvent, j'ai été injurié presque, en me sortant des gros mots, pendant des repas avec mes amis [en France], en me disant que mes idées étaient devenues Blairistes, que j'étais devenu libéral, et moi je dis "non, je suis devenu pragmatique"'.

[61] 'je pense que je suis devenue moins anxieuse, plus tolérante ... plus curieuse'.

[62] 'L'une des bonnes choses avec les offres d'emploi au Royaume-Uni, est que les salaires sont mentionnés dans les annonces, même pour les postes de haut dirigeant, ce qui n'est quasiment pas le cas en France [où] l'argent est un sujet tabou'.

[63] Bellion, 'French business in the UK', p. 15.

[64] 'bien gagner sa vie n'a rien de honteux [à Londres]' (V. Cordier, *Enfin un boulot! Ou le parcours d'un jeune chômeur à Londres* (2005), p. 134).

[65] 'effectivement, dans la religion catholique il ne faut pas dire ce qu'on a, il ne faut jamais montrer, ne pas avoir de belles voitures, dès qu'on le montre un peu, il y a énormément d'envie'.

One respondent even claimed that, based on her own experience, there was a higher proportion of Catholic families among the French in London than in France: 'When we first moved here, we were surprised by the number of Catholic French expats … They go to mass, and get baptised and make their first communion: something I hadn't come across before and hadn't seen among my friends [in Paris]'[66] (Laura). In what is perhaps a manifestation of the same phenomenon, Bellion describes the above-average size of families emigrating to London, stating that, on the basis of French Consulate statistics, 58 per cent of families moving to the UK 'are three children families, 25.5 per cent are four children families, 8.6 per cent are five children families, 2.2 per cent are six children families, 0.6 per cent of them are seven children families, and the 0.5 per cent left represent families with eight to twelve [children]'.[67] Perhaps, then, it is precisely France's vehement secularist agenda that is causing its practising Catholics and Muslims (in the case, for example, of Focus Group 1) to seek religious freedom in London, just as, in an ironic twist of fate, their Protestant Huguenot forefathers sought refuge from the Catholics within London's walls several centuries earlier?

Given our findings, is it not justified to hypothesize that, contrary to popular and personal belief, many of the London French effectively correspond to the 'immigrant' epithet far more faithfully than might initially meet the eye? In *Migration Theory: Talking Across Disciplines*, Chiswick says that 'immigrants are … described as fleeing the poverty, repression, and claustrophobia of the place where they were born and raised, and sometimes as being attracted or pulled by the magnet of the wealth ("streets lined with gold"), opportunities, freedom, and anonymity of where they settle'.[68] While not escaping from the same sort of poverty as immigrants from developing nations, many of the London French did, as has been discussed, originally come to the city in search of employment, opportunity and freedom, and many also came to break loose from the ideological shackles that confined them in France, thereby conforming with uncanny exactitude to the experts' definition of the typical 'immigrant'. However incompatible the label may seem, as the London French tend to be considered more as long-term tourists than economic, labour, ideological or even lifestyle immigrants by the host population (and indeed by themselves,

---

[66] 'Quand on est arrivé ici, on a été étonné par le nombre de Français expatriés qui sont très catholiques … Ils vont à la messe et en font leur baptême, leur communion: quelque chose que je ne connaissais pas, et que je ne voyais pas dans mes amis'.

[67] Bellion, 'French business in the UK', p. 9.

[68] B. Chiswick, 'Are immigrants favorably self-selected?', *Migration Theory: Talking Across Disciplines*, ed. C. Brettel and J. Hollifield (2000; 2008), pp. 61–76, at p. 64.

as Laura appreciatively revealed when describing 'that feeling of being slightly on holiday all the time [in London]'),[69] the following illustrations of the underlying causes that ultimately triggered their first migratory steps should serve to quell any doubts.

Egalité: *escaping racism, xenophobia, sexism and homophobia*

> Miranda: 'Racism is more visible in France, it's really one side against the other … there's a lot of fighting between both camps'.
> Paulette: 'People don't see my colour in London'.
> Moses: 'Professionally speaking, in France people are generally categorised in terms of their status depending on their age, gender, that kind of thing, sometimes even their ethnic origin. In England, I didn't experience that; it's people's skills, attributes and strengths [that count]. You see people working their way up and getting promotions, and I know it doesn't happen quite like that in France'.
> Charles: 'In France, there's a tolerance of intolerance that is shameful'.
> Chantal: 'As soon as English couples have their first child, the man babysits one day in the week so that the woman can go out with her girlfriends, and another day, she'll stay in so that he can go out. That never happens in France'.[70]

In addition to personal and pecuniary motivations, a common cause for the French migratory wave, evidenced through both studies as well as web research, was *exile*, not an enforced banishment from their native land, as might be the case for a refugee, but a self-imposed flight. Despite their apparent diversity, the majority of those taking part in the study were linked by a shared – though not necessarily conscious – desire to escape a certain phenomenon in France. Whether they were fleeing racism, homophobia, xenophobia, sexism, conservatism, elitism or 'lookism', the realization that they had effectively been escaping a form of prejudice in France materialized, in a number of cases, as the interviews progressed.

---

[69] 'cette sensation d'être toujours un peu en vacances [à Londres]'.

[70] Miranda: 'En France, le racisme est plus visible, c'est vraiment les uns contre les autres … il y a vraiment beaucoup de combat entre tous les deux'; Paulette: 'À Londres on ne voit pas ma couleur'; Moses: 'Au niveau professionnel, en France, on est plutôt basé sur des statuts attribués par rapport à l'âge, par rapport au sexe, ce genre de choses, parfois même à l'origine. J'ai expérimenté en Angleterre que c'est pas ça; c'est plutôt les compétences, les qualités, les valeurs de la personne [qui comptent]. On voit les personnes qui montent en grade ou qui obtiennent des promotions, et je sais que ce n'est pas exactement comme ça en France'; Charles: 'En France, il y a une tolérance vis-à-vis de l'intolérance qui est coupable'; Chantal: 'Dès que les Anglais ont leur premier enfant, l'homme "babysit" un jour dans la semaine pour que la femme puisse sortir avec ses copines, et un autre jour, c'est la femme qui le fait pour l'homme. Ça, en France, on ne l'a jamais'.

While not all were the direct victims of such discrimination – some were, however, for whom it constituted an explicit motivation for leaving in the first place – many of them quite simply felt trapped by the country's narrow-mindedness and were keen to sample a fresh way of life: more tolerance, more equality.

First, the generally obscured yet reportedly endemic racism of France was referred to by a number of the interviewees, for whom it constituted a driving force for leaving the *patrie*. Arthur was unambivalent in his account of the degrading treatment to which he was subjected when he initially emigrated to Paris from his native La Réunion: 'It was hard for me in Paris because of racism. At work, people treated you as if you were a slave; it really wasn't easy'.[71] A comparable overt expression of racism in the workplace was recounted by an evidently non-Caucasian blog commentator: 'Time and again in France I was reminded that being from East Asia was a handicap. For that matter, do you ever see a single Oriental artist in any of the performing arts there, whether it be theatre, music or film?'[72] The harshness of the language employed is no doubt an impulsive re-articulation of the harshness with which each was treated when they lived in France. In a similar vein, Miranda, a young, *white* French female, perhaps surprisingly, also identified racism as a deciding factor for international migration: 'In Paris, society is really split in two – it's terrible. I think people live in a more unified way in England'.[73] She went on to explain how it was this racial antagonism at the core of French society, in Paris and the provinces, that compelled her to leave, no longer able to bear the tyrannical burden it posed for her. The tone of her discourse was lexically violent, with notions of physical confrontation peppering the language, such as 'combat' and 'fight' ('bagarre'), irrespective of the fact that in this case she was not the victim, rather a priori 'on the side' of the perpetrator, albeit against her will. This was evidently a position she was not comfortable assuming and which subsequently caused her to choose London as a permanent abode.

Leading on from undisguised racism is the notion of xenophobia, and this was another reason why London 'attracts many French people suffocated by

[71] 'À Paris c'était dur pour moi; j'ai eu des problèmes de racisme. Au travail on vous traitait comme si vous étiez un esclave; c'est vrai que ce n'était pas évident'.

[72] 'En France, j'ai souvent compris que pour un chanteur, le fait d'être asiatique était un "handicap". D'ailleurs, voit-on un seul artiste asiatique dans le milieu, que ce soit le théâtre, la musique ou le cinéma?', comment uploaded to the 'French in London' blog by 'An', 12 May 2009, 12:19, at <http://www.frenchinlondon.com/blog-francais-londres/2009/05/irreconciliables-francais-de-france-et-de-letranger/> [accessed 5 Oct. 2011].

[73] 'A Paris, il y a vraiment une division de la société qui est terrible; en Angleterre je pense que les gens vivent plus d'une manière homogène'.

the social mores of Paris'.[74] Since xenophobia is defined as an 'intense or irrational dislike or fear of people from other countries',[75] several of the interviewees can justifiably be said to have been subjected, in France, to xenophobic treatment which had tangible repercussions on their personal, but primarily their professional lives. Paulette, a thirty-five-year-old, black – or 'Black Other (French)', as she denotes herself on UK forms – international logistics manager and mother of two, came to London in search of more equitable employment opportunities given the discrimination to which she had fallen victim in the French workplace: 'I found it very, very hard to find a job in France … – and I'm talking specifically about discrimination. It was such a waste of my academic qualifications and my time going from one futile training course to the next'.[76] In France, since neither her extensive qualifications – holder of a French BSc equivalent and a BA in business studies – nor her immediately discernible ambition were sufficient to secure her a job which reflected these desirable attributes, following in her exiled sisters' footsteps, she took the courageous decision, almost despite herself, to test the UK labour market. There, she hoped that employers would not instil in her a confidence-crushing sense of being socially and professionally out of her depth, as they had in Paris: 'I was really made to feel I shouldn't be there'.[77] Like many of the interviewees, Paulette felt that the London labour market was a meritocratic one (confirmed by the initial findings from Mulholland and Ryan's research),[78] with the emphasis placed purely on knowledge, skills and performance. As a result, she describes herself as being 'completely fulfilled in [her] work'[79] and intends never to return to France. While a somewhat categorical and definitive decision, it is one that was informed by her experiences on the ground in Paris and London, as well as by non-moving friends who have remained in France.

Unfortunately, xenophobia of this kind is not isolated, and is spoken of by other interviewees and authors, such as Hamid Senni,[80] who dedicated an entire literary work, *De la Cité à la City*, to his personal professional pathway,

---

[74] M. Deen and A. Katz, 'French making themselves at home in London', *New York Times*, 5 Feb. 2008, available at <http://www.nytimes.com/2008/01/25/style/25ihtafrench.1.9495133.html> [accessed Sept. 2011].

[75] *Oxford Dictionaries Online* <http://oxforddictionaries.com/definition/xenophobia> [accessed 28 Oct. 2012].

[76] 'J'avais beaucoup, beaucoup de mal à trouver du travail en France … – et là, je parle vraiment vis-à-vis de la discrimination. Avec mon bagage académique, c'était un gâchis de rester là à traîner à perdre mon temps, faire des formations aussi futiles l'une que l'autre'.

[77] 'on m'a vraiment fait sentir que je n'étais pas à ma place'.

[78] See Mulholland and Ryan, 'French capital'.

[79] 'complètement épanouie dans [son] travail'.

[80] H. Senni, *De la Cité à la City* (Paris, 2007).

from growing up in the ghettoized suburbs of Paris to ultimately becoming the owner of a successful business in London, and the arduous journey in between. One sentence captures the frustrations expressed throughout the book with particular clarity and mirrors some of the accounts expressed by other interviewees with telling precision:

> In London I am Hamid the Frenchman, to whom people give the means to succeed, who is judged purely on his achievements. I do not want go back to being Hamid the North-African low-life from the hood, who has to prove himself on a daily basis and make the most of the tiny concessions people are willing to make for him.[81]

For others, homophobia appeared to be a key motivation for emigrating and, like Senni and Paulette, not envisaging a permanent return to France. Robert, a qualified teacher of French as a foreign language, who now lectures in higher education, is a forty-year-old, white, homosexual male, born and raised in a village in northern France, who had also lived in larger cities, such as Lille, before deciding to make his cross-Channel move. He came to Newcastle for his PGCE teaching qualification seventeen years ago, later migrating south to join his then common-law partner and now husband, Adrian, in London, where they now own a flat in East Dulwich. He recounted that the reason for his desertion of France was threefold, but recognized that escaping small-minded mis- and pre-conceptions regarding homosexuality, on a macro, societal level and a micro, personal level, constituted a primary contributing factor: 'well I left France because of that [my sexuality] … I had friends at uni who turned their backs on me when they found out I was gay; but that's never happened here; I don't feel that burden'.[82] His sexuality in France was experienced as a burden, a heavy load that weighed him down in all spheres of life, and one that was immediately lightened upon migrating to the UK. In Robert's case, flight was key in informing his decision, the discourse being entirely devoid of references to economic or employment motivations, unlike the aforementioned victims of xenophobia whose prejudicial treatment in France directly impacted their position, or inclusion, in the labour market, rendering occupational opportunity a simultaneous beacon. The prospect of return migration remains slim for Robert, just as it was rejected by Paulette, neither of

---

[81] 'A Londres je suis Hamid le Français, celui à qui l'on donne les moyens de réussir, que l'on juge uniquement sur ses résultats. Je n'ai pas envie de redevenir Hamid le Beur de la cité qui doit faire tous les jours ses preuves et se réjouir du peu que l'on veut bien lui concéder'.

[82] 'déjà, j'ai quitté la France à cause de ça [ma sexualité] … j'ai eu des amis qui m'ont tourné le dos à la fac quand ils ont appris que j'étais gay; alors qu'ici, jamais; je ne ressens pas cette lourdeur'.

them wishing to expose themselves to systemic discrimination on anything other than a visiting basis. Robert was, and evidently remains, an 'alien', 'stranger' and 'outsider' in his *native* country. In a paradoxical inversion of the traditional model, in which the immigrant is the 'alien' in the eyes of the host, Robert leads an inconspicuous existence in his capacity as immigrant, taking on 'alien' selfhood when returning to the motherland. Migrating to London freed him from the stigmatization linked to his homosexuality and allowed him fully, yet indiscriminately, to embrace his true identity without fear of victimization (in his fifteen years in London, only once has he fallen victim to 'a comment to do with my sexuality' – 'une remarque par rapport à ma sexualité'). London provides a setting in which Robert, together with the significant number of other French homosexual migrants in the capital,[83] can 'fit in', not to a distinct gay community as such, but to the established, heterosexual community, which is a significant distinction as it emphasizes the sense of self-portrayed belonging. In the interview, Robert made a point of verbalizing the fact that most of his friends were heterosexual and that he had become good friends with the heterosexual families that lived in his gentrified East Dulwich street, 'even' being on Christmas-card terms with his *Catholic* neighbours. Although Robert could not be considered a gay activist, there is little doubt that belonging to a predominantly 'straight' street has contributed to his sense of well-being, unlike in France, where his difference continually ricochets back at him through the reactions of others, be they friends, family, colleagues or strangers.

An additional trigger for cross-Channel migration was the experience of sexism, also touched upon by a number of the interviewees, and dealt with in some detail by historian and journalist – and French Londoner in her own right – Agnès Poirier.[84] It cannot be denied that gender attitudes and behaviour differ on either side of the Channel. Although some British women might succumb to the heavy-handed but romantically-versed 'French touch',[85] and their male counterparts may envy it,[85] so too has many a French woman tried to escape the tacit institutionalized sexism, or 'sexisme ordinaire' as it is dubbed by the Association des Femmes Journalistes;[86] the kind of deep-rooted sexism that is almost integral to inter-gender social codes in France, as Poirier openly affirms, but which can be experienced as retrograde and oppressive by women who have chosen to move to London. In practice, however, Frenchwomen are better paid than their English

---

[83] See <http://www.lepetitjournal.com> June 2012 [accessed June 2012].

[84] A. Poirier, *Le Modèle Anglais une illusion française* (Paris, 2007).

[85] Poirier, *Le Modèle Anglais*, p. 82.

[86] Quoted by J. Lambert, 'L'imaginaire du corps féminin freine la parité dans les médias', *Esprit*, 12 Oct. 2009.

counterparts and better represented in managerial, and now political, positions, as President Hollande's unprecedently paritarian government demonstrates. There seems, in France, to be a divorce between the equitable institutional reality concerning gender and the sexism perceived on the ground. In London, the opposite phenomenon could be said to exist; it is difficult to judge which form of discrimination is more offensive.

Related to sexism is the idea of what we are calling 'lookism', pinpointed by a number of the interviewees, and perhaps summarized most concisely by Chantal when she explained how, in France, she felt judged by the way she dressed. This represented a view common to several participants that the way people look physically affects how others categorize and prejudge them; this is true of biological factors including age, height and weight, but also of dress codes and deliberate bodily manipulations, such as piercing and tattoos. Many of the interviewees commented on the freedom they felt when dressing in London in comparison to the far more conservative and uniform (ironically, as they do not have an imposed uniform at school, rather a self-imposed, neutral 'jeans & T-shirt' one) dress codes of France, which seem to be, whether at the chic or the shabby end of the spectrum, overly regimented and conformist for the French in London. Our most telling story here concerned Miranda, who, legs adorned with an array of tattoos, and bodily parts pierced with decorative gems, appeared to make a self-conscious decision to rebel ostensibly against the French stereotypical ideal 'look', thus confirming Valentine's assertion that body modification is a lasting articulation of self-identity and those who practise it do so either 'to express individuality [or] as a group marker'.[87]

Our second example of lookism concerns forty-one-year-old singer-songwriter Laura's sartorial transformation, even liberation, and subsequent informed manipulation of national dress codes, deliberately playing to domestic stereotypes, and having gained greater sensitivity of gaze since living in London. She described how she dresses differently according to whether she is performing in the UK (London) or France: the 'girly', frilly French look appeals in the former; the low-key denim norm is a requisite in the latter. Laura expressed a rare awareness of the subtle codes that differentiate her audiences and their attitudes to her. She was not, however, prepared potentially to lose any face by donning the same 'frou-frou' attire in France, since the prospect of prejudice or ridicule on the part of the audience would inhibit such a brash break with convention. In France, therefore, she plays it safe, satisfies the opposite stereotype, and abides by the unspoken diktat of casual denim. It seems, nevertheless, that the new-found confidence

---

[87] G. Valentine, *Social Geographies: Space and Society* (Harlow, 2001), p. 37.

which she ascribed to living in London is becoming an intrinsic trait of her character, and one she is now tentatively taking back across the Channel, beginning with her blue-varnished nails. Laura now has a greater sense of indifference to the judgemental gaze of her Parisian audience, apparently taking pleasure in embracing her new, non-conservative 'look'. She perceives it to be a liberating experience that, to some extent, simultaneously also allows her to embody the so-called British eccentricity that Poirier, in an interview with the *New York Times*, discerningly summarized thus: '"Paris is the epitome of perfection and elegance," she said, "London of imperfection and eccentricity."'[88]

Opportunité? *Education, confidence and the new self*

> Sarah: '[At school in London], there's a lot more interaction, a lot of groupwork, it's not always the teacher explaining something. Pupils do a lot of teamwork and individual research, and everything's very lively and engaging'.
> Laura: 'In French schools, the discourse is far more "could do better" and so on. Whereas in English schools, it's always "well done, brilliant"; there's a lot more focus on oral work and on joining in; there's a lot more encouragement … In the French education system, we are all equal, so you're not allowed to say that some children find it easier than others; everyone has to do the same lesson, which means that the brightest kids are bored stiff and so are the weakest ones … That's what you get from the French system of equal opportunities and equality among individuals'.
> Catherine: 'You are more likely to make your way up quickly [in London]; not everything is based on which school you went to'.[89]

In London, where difference is purportedly met with assent, empathy or apathy, and where eccentricity, or simply otherness, is found by our respondents to be respected not denigrated, a positive cognitive self-representation is (re) born among French migrants, and the 'post-traumatic' repair process is set in motion, ultimately bringing with it a regained sense of self-respect. In Laura's

---

[88] Deen and Katz, 'French at home in London'.

[89] Sarah: '[A l'école à Londres], il y a beaucoup plus d'intéraction, beaucoup de groupes, c'est pas toujours le professeur qui explique quelque chose. Il y a beaucoup de travail entre élèves, de recherche personnelle, et puis ils rendent tout vivant'; Laura: 'Dans l'école française, le discours c'est beaucoup plus "peut mieux faire", etc. Alors qu'en l'école anglaise, c'est toujours "well done, brilliant"; beaucoup plus sur la prise de parole, sur la participation; beaucoup plus d'encouragement … Dans l'école française, on est tous égaux donc, on n'a pas le droit de dire qu'il y a des enfants qui arrivent mieux que d'autres; on fait le même cours pour tout le monde de sorte que ceux qui sont très forts se font chier et ceux qui sont très faibles aussi … C'est le résultat du système français de l'égalité des chances et de l'égalité de qui on est'; Catherine: 'On a plus de chance pour progresser vite [à Londres]; tout n'est pas basé sur l'école qu'on a faite'.

case, we saw that living in London liberated her sufficiently and instilled in her a sense of self-worth that gave her the opportunity to realize her suppressed ambition to become a singer-songwriter, rather than managing the performers she had formerly craved to emulate: 'I felt a lot freer to put myself forward as a performer here than in France ... To begin with it was difficult considering myself as a performer, probably because of my education and upbringing'.[90]

A key word in Laura's account is 'éducation' – upbringing/education. She saw the difficulty she encountered when trying to marry her internalized self-identity (her inner performer) with her external corporate representation (her outward managerial image, considered a more 'natural' evolution from the Paris stock-exchange trader she had previously been), as a function of her upbringing and academic education. Indeed, France's systemic tendency to value academic qualifications and disparage artistic qualities – in the workplace and at school – was cited time and again by our respondents, as was the education system's infamous achievement of ridding gregarious young children of any confidence they had once had before entering the 'usine' ('factory', Focus Group 2). Beginning at nursery and primary school, the British system was described as being more 'ludique' (user-friendly and fun) and generally a more positive and nurturing environment in which to learn than the French education system, where 'there's a lot more aggression, from teachers and students alike'[91] (Marie). This was not an isolated opinion; mothers of young children with experience of both the French and English early-years' education systems made analogous observations. For instance, Laura, who has three children, each of whom is following a different educational pathway in London (one attends an independent English secondary school, another the French Wix primary school and the third an English state primary school, Honeywell, with a strong French influence), echoed both the antagonism and lack of authority alluded to by Marie: 'the teachers feel like they're constantly under attack, and the parents feel like no-one ever listens to them'.[92] She described the French teachers' detrimental over-compensation for their authority deficiency: 'they're always giving orders, whereas in English classes, the children are very calm, it's all very peaceful and the teachers never shout'.[93] She also

---

[90] 'en étant ici je me suis sentie beaucoup plus libre ... de me présenter comme artiste qu'en France ... C'était d'abord difficile pour moi, pour des raisons d'éducation sans doute, de me considérer comme une artiste'.

[91] 'il y a beaucoup plus d'agressivité, autant chez les professeurs que les élèves'.

[92] 'les profs ont l'impression qu'on les attaque tout le temps; les parents, eux, ont l'impression qu'on ne les écoute jamais'.

[93] 'ils sont toujours en train de donner des ordres, alors que dans les classes anglaises, les enfants sont très calmes, il n'y a pas du tout de bazar, mais les maîtresses ne crient jamais'.

noted the lack of enthusiasm on the part of the teaching staff at the French school: 'at the Wix school, there's a heaviness to the atmosphere, you can feel the depression, whereas at Honeywell, all the staff seem to be having a whale of a time, they're really happy'.[94] She therefore believed the British system to be confidence-building and engaging, inspiring pupils to learn rather than reprimanding them if they do not. In short, the emphasis is on success and achievement, whereas French teaching aims to obtain results through a reverse approach, driving students towards their goals through humiliation and failure, as she explained: 'They are much more positive [in London], and geared towards enjoyment; in France, it's a lot more about punishment and frustration'.[95] Similarly, in the UK, a greater emphasis is said to be placed on 'learning through doing ... In France, there is too much thinking about doing, more than doing and then thinking about it', as Antoine wittily recounted in relation to higher education, but which Sarah claimed to begin at pre-primary level: 'I prefer the English education system for now. Children get to join in more than in French schools. I think the focus is on "engaging the children" rather than gorging them with information'.[96]

This overwhelming positivity among the interviewees regarding British pedagogics was more than a little surprising given that the French model is often lauded in British political and media discourses, as is the stereotypical French intellectual *homme de la rue* or 'man in the street', who has 'an interest in discussion for the sake of it' (Antoine) and a level of general knowledge that is generally far superior to his British counterparts, 'who couldn't locate China or Russia on the map at all' because 'they specialise very early, probably too early' (Moses).[97]

Likewise, spontaneously, unanimously and separately from each other, both focus groups of teenagers referred to education being either the main advantage of living in London, in the case of Focus Group 1 (comprising students attending the British state sixth-form college in Newham), or the main disadvantage, in the case of Focus Group 2, who were denoting the French Lycée itself (which they all attended), therefore coming to the same,

---

[94] 'à Wix, il y a cette espèce de poids, on sent le côté déprimé, alors qu'à Honeywell, vous y allez le matin, tous les profs ont l'air de s'éclater, ils sont hyper heureux'.

[95] 'Ils sont beaucoup plus positifs [à Londres], et dans le plaisir; en France on est beaucoup plus sur la punition et la frustration'.

[96] 'J'aime mieux pour l'instant [l'école anglaise que française]. Je trouve que c'est beaucoup plus participatif. Je pense qu'ils mettent l'accent sur "intéresser les enfants" plutôt que leur bourrer le crâne'.

[97] 'qui ne savaient pas du tout où situer la Chine ou la Russie sur une carte' because 'ils se spécialisent tôt, voire trop tôt'.

Figure 15.3. 2012 Président Bankside Bastille Day Festival
allows individual expressions of French history.

albeit reversed, conclusion. Indeed, despite their diametrically opposed socio-economic backgrounds and the divergent school pathways taken by the members of each group, both cohorts were unexpectedly concordant in their opinions on education, and both once again reiterated the comments made by the interviewees. The themes of punishment and an overly academic, 'hands-off' approach were cited by Focus Group 1: 'There's less punishment here than in France', where 'it was always written, written, written work, and there was a lot less practical work';[98] while Focus Group 2 criticized the attitudes of staff at the French Lycée in London and the emphasis placed predominantly on marks and qualifications. Although the

---

[98] 'Ici, il y a moins de punition qu'en France' where 'c'était l'écrit, l'écrit, l'écrit, et il y avait moins de pratique'.

students taking part in Focus Group 2 conceded that the Lycée was pleasant on a social level, the pedagogical rigidity and prosaicness, together with the haughtiness of staff, outweighed that singular advantage, causing a number of students to turn to the English alternative for GCSEs, A levels or the International Baccalaureate, and university courses, of which both Laura and Chantal had first-hand experience. Two out of Chantal's three children had opted for an independent Kent boarding school over the Lycée for their final years at school, while the third is set to go to Harrow, the archetypal English public school, next year. Likewise, one participant in Focus Group 2 expressed his intention to attend an English school (City of London School), and his downright rejection of the French higher education route: 'I am not going back to France [for my higher education], no way'.[99] In each case, and at all levels of the education system, from early years to higher education, it is the value placed on creative, practical and sporting pursuits that attracts the children (and their parents).

It is telling, however, that all the English schools to which they refer are high-fee-paying schools at the acme of the country's educational pyramid; only a select few will be able to access such schools, and even fewer will be in a financial position to pay the fees (in the region of £30,000 per annum for boarding places). These examples of French children in London from affluent backgrounds preferring English teaching – in privately-funded schools – could be perceived as non-representative of the francophone migrant picture as a whole. However, somewhat unexpectedly, and perhaps as a testament to their own naivety, the students involved in Focus Group 1 in Newham were also in favour of the English education system, in this instance specifically the state-run system. They were not opposed to its two-tiered (independent versus state-run) structure, believing it to be fair and ultimately a matter of personal choice, apparently unaware of the likelihood of means taking precedence over preference, and bearing no grudge against the inequity of the situation. Indeed, rather than resentment, they all expressed a feeling of gratitude that the English education system would not only offer them greater opportunities once on the labour market, but equip them to deal with such opportunities when they presented themselves, thereby reiterating the assertions made above. One student from Focus Group 1 stated: 'there are more opportunities here than in France ... you can get all kinds of different jobs with your qualifications ... you'll have more opportunities than in France'.[100]

---

[99] 'Je ne vais pas retourner en France [pour les études supérieures], no way'.

[100] 'il y a plus d'opportunités ici qu'en France ... les différentes places que tu peux avoir avec tes diplômes ... tu auras plus d'opportunités qu'en France'.

This is an impression reinforced by fifty-three-year-old Catherine who now lives in Bordeaux and whose experience of the British workplace dates back to the 1980s: 'When I was at university in France, it was very, very academic; with a degree in English, the only way to get a job would be to take the competitive State teaching exams. Going to England opened other doors for me that I may never have had at all if I'd stayed in France'.[101] Similarly, Laura believes that the English system's emphasis on oral, as opposed to written skills, improves applicants' chances of filling the positions on offer: 'the English are a lot better at oral skills because of their education, so they are far more at ease when speaking publicly'.[102] She feels that the English system instils confidence and aptitude in presentational skills, yet acknowledges that a French education, as draconian as the students might find it, provides essential competence in analysis and maths, ironically two key attributes London employers find highly attractive. Indeed, almost every interviewee referred to their skillsets speaking more loudly than their qualifications in a recruitment context, unlike in France, where employers suffer from the chronic condition Roudaut amusingly terms 'diplomitis' ('diplômite', 2009), hence closing door after door on applicants deemed insufficiently or inappropriately qualified for the job in question. Less defensibly still, this elitist recruitment approach also rejects those who possess the qualifications, but do not correspond to the 'expected' profile, as seen above, or lack the all-important 'connections', either in the workplace or via the Grandes Ecoles to which access is often denied, as it is itself often reliant on socio-professional connectedness and having previously attended the 'right' *lycée*; and so the vicious circle continues.

Consequently, it is logical for those who seek a more vibrant education system that leads on to present opportunities in a more open and adaptable workplace, in which 'everything is negotiable', unlike in France where 'everything is more certain, but less flexible' (Antoine), to choose London as their city of destination, finally free from the crippling preconceptions that haunted them in the superficially *douce France*, and try their luck in the city which is 'the exact opposite of what [they're] used to: brutal, fierce, unforgiving and yet magnificent, quick-witted and spirited'.[103] Keen to experience a different life, in a multicultural metropolis where they too

---

[101] 'Quand j'ai fait mes études en France, c'était très, très académique; avec une licence d'anglais, on aurait pu uniquement présenter des concours d'enseignement pour trouver du travail. Le fait que je suis allée en Angleterre m'a ouvert d'autres portes que peut-être je n'aurais pas du tout eues si j'étais restée en France'.

[102] 'les Anglais sont beaucoup plus performants à l'oral, de par cette éducation, et donc ils prennent la parole très facilement'.

[103] Poirier, quoted in Deen and Katz, 'French at home in London'.

are different, but where they can live this difference either as a personal asset, like Laura who enjoys her exoticism and exploits it creatively for her singing career ('I stand out from the crowd ... people notice I'm different straight away ... It's very nice to feel exotic. Actually, it's precisely because I'm different here that I was able to launch my singing career');[104] or on a more altruistic level, like Paulette, who despite appreciating her ethnic invisibility in London, considered her contribution to the city to be precisely her difference, of being first and foremost a Frenchwoman in an English society, rather than a black woman in a white one, as she had been in France.

Conclusion

The demographic complexities of the London French discussed at the beginning of this chapter mean that it would be over-simplistic and inaccurate to label them all as the *16ème arrondissement* diplomatic expat stereotype, although there is evidently a phenomenon where a population grows around a French educational institution – which probably led to the initial stereotype. That is, South Kensington is home to the Lycée Charles de Gaulle (and the French diplomatic corps), hence the undeniable 'Little Paris' effect. But we have discovered that there is also a considerable number of French people now living in Clapham since the Wix school opened in 2006, and in Greenwich/Blackheath with its Saturday school, Grenadine; and the same process of demographic transformation is taking place, as we write, in Kentish Town, where France's latest state-run *collège* was opened in 2011. Younger French migrants are opting for edgier (and more affordable) areas of London that could not be geographically or socially further from South Kensington, and so the East End too is seeing a French influx. Just as London's French are not all living in the neighbourhoods thought to be traditionally French, neither do they all come from bourgeois quarters of Paris. The population involved in our studies came from all over France, north, south, east and west, urban and rural, right-wing and left-wing regions, wealthy and deprived areas, and are inhabiting equally diverse and unexpected districts of the capital, some of which are notably the same places inhabited by previous generations of French immigrants: current French 'hotspots', such as Brick Lane in the East End and Richmond in the west, are areas occupied by their Huguenot forefathers 400 years previously. There is even evidence to suggest that some of the London French population is now seeping beyond the borders of Greater London,

---

[104] 'je ne suis pas noyée dans la masse ... je suis tout de suite différente ... Se sentir exotique, c'est très agréable. En fait, c'est en étant différente ici que j'ai pu me lancer dans la chanson'.

moving to the leafier towns and cities of the south-east, such as Guildford, Oxford and Canterbury. In the same way that it is impossible to designate a single geographical area of origin and destination to the London French, it is equally difficult to classify them socio-economically, professionally and ethnically. Our study attempted to provide an overview of opinions among a broad sample of London's similarly broad French community, who often presented a surprisingly narrow and united set of perspectives. Perhaps it is precisely this unity in diversity that epitomizes London and appeals to our French neighbours whose domestic, dogmatic search for equality and liberty seems to be failing.

London as a place of refuge, liberty and opportunity draws the French; it seems always to have done so and continues to fulfil that role. As we have seen, many of the French interviewed were at once attracted to London's liberating call and escaping France's petrified prestige. The professional value of the English language, the multicultural melting pot that is London, its green spaces and garden-backed houses, its proximity to France and its youth/pop culture are what ultimately make it score more highly than other potential destinations, such as Berlin or New York; together with a pinch of *eccentricité à l'anglaise*. And what London offers in terms of openness – spaces and minds – is ultimately what prevents many of the French from returning to France, as typified by Laura's words: 'London: it's greenery – it's trees, flowers and parks; it's the joy English people get from being in their parks. It's not like that in France: in Parisian parks you're not allowed to walk on the grass. You go to the park to sit on a bench and look at the flowers; absolutely no ball-playing allowed!'[105]

Together with language and career opportunities, the pull for younger migrants is evidently London's 'cool Britannia' image, the vibrant music and recreational scene which has attracted them in such numbers that it has culminated in its own term: 'les années Londres'. This phrase, coined by the French media to refer to 'gap years' spent in the capital, is itself a testament to the commonplaceness of the phenomenon and is not devoid of its own 'cool' connotations. Possibly what people did not anticipate, and what that phrase overlooks, is that many of the young migrants who intended to come for a year or two – to learn the language, escape their parents and make the most of London's liberated, liberal and liberating atmosphere – have ended up making London their permanent home (significantly a word absent from the French language).

---

[105] 'Londres, c'est la verdure – les arbres et les fleurs, les parcs; le bonheur qu'ont les Anglais à vivre dans leurs parcs. En France, ce n'est pas pareil, dans les parcs à Paris on n'a pas le droit de marcher sur l'herbe. On sort s'asseoir sur un banc pour regarder les fleurs; surtout pas le droit de jouer au ballon!'

Figure 15.4. Visual evidence of the diversity of the London French demographic: this graffiti is at the base of a tower block on the soon-to-be-demolished, notorious Aylesbury Estate, south-east London.

Thus, we have seen how the identity of French Londoners has changed over the course of their time in the capital and how their self-perceptions have evolved. Simultaneously, the French presence in London has altered the identity of the capital itself, both historically and presently. Today (as in previous waves of cross-Channel migration), there is a visible French presence in London areas with high concentrations of French inhabitants: quality French bakers, butchers, restaurants, cafés, bookshops and fashion boutiques have become habitual features of the cityscape, thereby making a socio-cultural and economic, as well as a visual, contribution to the capital and transforming the local environment. There are also less transparent, but equally ubiquitous, visible markers of the French presence, from its vast corporations to its downtrodden council-estate dwellers. The EDF logo adorns vans and billboards all over Greater London and beyond (whether the majority of the local population is aware of what the acronym designates – Electricité de France – is another matter), while the JC Decaux advertising trademark decks thousands of bus-stops and phone-boxes across the capital which, according to their website, '90 per cent of Londoners see'.[106] At the other end of the socio-economic spectrum, the French 'copier coller' ('copy and paste') gargantuan graffiti tag decorates buildings and railway embankments in the Elephant and Castle area, exposing a very different London French face. What links both representations is their presence at street level and their codification: while 90 per cent of Londoners might well see them, far fewer would be able to read into them and extrapolate their hidden messages about the London French.

Just as today's French inhabit many of the physical spaces once occupied by their predecessors, so they curiously step into the professional footprints of their forefathers, often taking the same career paths as previous waves of French migrants in London over the centuries. The French journalists, chefs, entrepreneurs, artists and teachers who dwell in the city currently are – possibly unwittingly – following a tradition handed down by the Free French journalists, Victorian chefs, Huguenot tradesmen, Impressionist painters and the aristocracy's French tutors who settled in the city before them. The French language heard on the terrestrial waves of French Radio London echoes that on the airwaves of the BBC during the Second World War, as does the title of the community's most widely distributed London French magazine, *Ici Londres*.

As well as mapping out the contemporary French presence in London, this chapter has attempted to demonstrate that, in a somewhat ironic twist, it is the very French republican motto of 'Liberté' and 'Egalité', in addition to the more obvious 'Opportunité', that the French are seeking in London, frustrated by the insufficiency of all three in France. 'Fraternité', however, is not developed in this chapter, precisely because the French community in London does not perceive itself as a single, bonded entity. No sense of brotherhood among the London French was conveyed in the interviews or surveys; all acknowledged the existence of a French community, but associated it with the 'others', the South Ken elite, and did not feel that they were a part of that closed community; nor were they keen to access it. It seems that many 'community' events are attended (and even orchestrated, in the case of the Bankside Bastille Festival, for example) by English Francophiles rather than French francophones. The London French are a group of diverse individuals keen to assert their individuality, but equally keen for it to go unnoticed in the urban mass that is London's population.

London French veteran, eighty-year-old Suzanne, explained in iconographic terms why London attracts and will doubtless continue to

---

[106] See POSTAR, available via <http://www.jcdecaux.co.uk/products/streettalk> [accessed 25 July 2012].

Figure 15.5. The London Eye, originally sponsored by
British Airways, and now sponsored by EDF.

attract a constant flow of French movers on a quest for freedom, equality
and opportunity. Referring to a symbol she thought fitting of the capital,
the London Eye, she mused: 'The London Eye: it can be seen from far below
and seen from far away. And it changes, it evolves, but it turns on itself,
whereas London never turns on itself, it evolves. The Big Wheel revolves,
London evolves'.[107] Since Suzanne made that comparison, sponsorship for
the London Eye has been taken over from British Airways by ... EDF.

---

[107] 'La grande roue; ca tourne, ça peut être regardée de très bas, et regardée de très loin. Et
puis ça change, ça évolue, mais ça tourne sur elle-même, tandis que Londres ne tourne pas
sur elle-même, ça évolue. La grande roue elle tourne, Londres elle évolue'.

Appendix: interviewee and focus group profiles

INTERVIEWEE PROFILES

Interview 1: Head chef in City; thirty-seven-year-old white male; originally from Bordeaux, now in south-east London, SE27. Lived in London: nineteen years [alias Bruno].

Interview 2: Human resources, EC3; forty-two-year-old white female; Franco-Canadian; lives in Bromley. Lived in London: nineteen years [alias Jacqueline].

Interview 3: Head of investment risk framework, EC2; thirty-seven-year-old white female; originally from Lyon, now in Greenwich. Lived in London: ten years [alias Sarah].

Interview 4: Hotel food and beverage manager; thirty-four-year-old non-white male; originally from La Réunion, now in Docklands. Lived in London: eleven years [alias Arthur].

Interview 5: UK foreign correspondent; thirty-four-year-old white male; originally from Brittany, now in Crystal Palace and Oxford. Lived in London: eleven years [alias Charles].

Interview 6: Urban designer/architecture lecturer; fifty-two-year-old white male; originally from Marseilles, now in Archway. Lived in London: twenty-two years [alias Antoine].

Interview 7: Retired import-export administrator; sixty-three-year-old white female; now based in Aix-en-Provence but lived in Wandsworth forty years ago [alias Marie].

Interview 8: French graduate/PGCE student; thirty-two-year-old female; Franco-Algerian; originally from Paris, now in Beckenham. Lived in London: twelve years [alias Sadia].

Interview 9: Financial/IT consultant and amateur actor; thirty-three-year-old white male; originally from Carcassonne, now in Tower Hamlets. Lived in London: fourteen years [alias Brice].

Interview 10: Surgeon in inner-city NHS hospital; fifty-two-year-old white male; originally from eastern France, now in Richmond. Lived in London: five years [alias François].

Interview 11: Post-doctoral molecular neuroscientist; thirty-five-year-old white female; originally from Lyon, now in Bethnal Green. Lived in London: three years [alias Brigitte].

Interview 12: Commerce/export representative; twenty-four-year-old black male (Senegalese heritage); now lives in Paris suburbs where originally from, but lived in London (Dartford/Abbey Wood, south London; Leighton, east London; then Arsenal, north London) for two years [alias Moses].

Interview 13: English as a foreign language teacher; fifty-three-year-old white female; now based in Bordeaux, but lived in London (South Woodford, north-east London for three years, then Acton for two years) for five years in the 1980s [alias Catherine].

Interview 14: French as a foreign language lecturer; forty-year-old white homosexual male; originally from the north of France, now in East Dulwich. Lived in London: seventeen years [alias Robert].

Interview 15: Retired teacher from Lycée Français Charles de Gaulle and writer; eighty-year-old white female; originally from Dijon, now in Holland Park. Lived in London: forty-seven years (first school exchange visit in 1948) [alias Suzanne].

Interview 16: Singer-songwriter; forty-one-year-old white female; originally from Paris, now in Clapham. Lived in London: five years [alias Laura].

Interview 17: Housewife, formerly in marketing; forty-eight-year-old white female; originally from Paris, now in Kensington. Lived in London: twenty-two years [alias Chantal].

Interview 18: International logistics manager; thirty-five-year-old black female; originally from Normandy, now in Chiswick. Lived in London: eight years [alias Paulette].

Interview 19: Doctoral linguistics student; twenty-eight-year-old white female; originally from a small village in the Aube region (north-east France), now in Brick Lane. Lived in London: ten years [alias Miranda].

Interview 20: Lawyer; fifty-year-old white female; originally from Paris, now in Nunhead. Lived in London: twenty-six years [alias Séverine].

FOCUS GROUPS

Focus Group 1: Seven students from Newham Sixth Form College (NewVIc), Prince Regent Lane, London E13; non-white (mainly of sub-Saharan African and Asian descent); male and female participants, all aged sixteen to eighteen.

FOCUS GROUP 2: Six students from Lycée Français Charles de Gaulle, South Kensington; predominantly white males, one female of North African origin, all aged sixteen to eighteen.

Conclusion: a temporal and spatial mapping of the French in London

Debra Kelly

This book has provided a history of the social, cultural, political and – to some extent – economic presence of the French in London, and explored the many ways in which this presence has contributed to the life of the British capital city. Within a dual historical and contemporary focus, the varied exchanges that have characterized the relationship between French 'exile', 'migrant', 'visitor' (any term used to describe those various French citizens who took up residence in London at different times, and for different lengths of time, is fraught with caveats) and host city have been discussed. As has been seen, the British capital has often provided a place of refuge and/or opportunity to very different French men and women from across the political spectrum, of differing religious and social beliefs, and from different social classes. Successive chapters have analysed in detail some of the well-known and less well-known stories in the history of these varied French citizens; from monarchs and aristocrats to revolutionaries, and on to today's high profile sportsmen and business people together with their several hundred thousand lesser known compatriots.[1]

Many French artists and writers have also been previously vividly brought to life in, for example, David Arkell's vignettes of Stéphane Mallarmé in Piccadilly, both Emile Zola and Camille Pissarro in Crystal Palace and Upper Norwood, Paul Verlaine and Arthur Rimbaud in Camden Town, Jules Vallès in Fitzrovia, James Tissot in St. John's Wood, Paul Valéry in Bloomsbury and the City, Guillaume Apollinaire in Clapham, and more.[2] Some stayed for a short time, others for longer than intended, some never

---

[1] Several contemporary French people have high public/media profiles in the UK for different reasons. Examples range from Arsène Wenger as the manager of Arsenal, Thierry Henry and several other French and francophone football players, to P.-Y. Gerbeau, nicknamed 'the Gerbil' by the British press at the time of the ill-fated Millennium Dome project (now the O2 in Docklands); the chef Raymond Blanc; the fashion designer Nicole Farhi; and the list could go on.

[2] D. Arkell, *Ententes Cordiales: the French in London and Other Adventures* (1989). Others included are: Villiers de l'Isle-Adam, Alphonse Daudet, Alain-Fournier, Marcel Schwob, Valery Larbaud, Louis Hémon, Céline, Jean de Boschère, Maurice Sachs, Simone Weil and Michel Butor.

departing and becoming part of the fabric of the city, and almost all leaving a legacy of some kind: the Huguenots, the French Revolution émigrés and later monarchist exiles often living in some considerable comfort, the various exile communities during the nineteenth century usually living in rather less comfort, the small but varied French communities operating in different spheres of the capital's life in the early twentieth century and the inter-war period, the complex histories of the Free French in the Second World War, and the increasingly numerous and diverse French and francophone contemporary residents of the capital.

Throughout these chapters, knowledge that we already have on the French in London is sometimes reinforced, and sometimes modified, with long-standing perceptions sometimes challenged. For example, Elizabeth Randall's work (further developed by the detailed examples provided by Paul Boucher and Tessa Murdoch) shows the ways in which the French bring skills and knowledge – in printing, silk and luxury goods, medicine, sculpture, silver- and goldsmithing, clock-making, tailoring, music and dance, engineering, teaching and translation, as craftsmen, artists and intellectuals, financiers – to London, but also shows that Protestant immigration at the time was not always for religious purposes, and already many claimed to have come to London to seek a new living and opportunities. Máire Cross shows how exiles who found London a less welcoming place nonetheless interacted with both their hosts and other French citizens, reinforcing a French identity while spreading knowledge (not always flattering or positive) of London. Importantly for a comparison with today's London French, she also shows how French visitors played a part in the construction of London's identity as a world city. Furthermore, the significance of London as an important and clearly defined political space for the French is added to that of a place of refuge (although that is also, of course, political) and of economic opportunity. The 'multiple dimensions' of being French in London in earlier centuries become more and more apparent, and in a way that resonates with the contemporary London French experience. Thomas Jones and Robert Tombs's work reinforces London as a centre of politics, the press and publishing, with the capital city and its refugees having an impact on each other in these domains; but political exiles established businesses and institutions too, while some exiled artisans and labourers also continued their old trades. In nineteenth-century London there was strong demand for French labour in some of these trades, including cooks, cobblers and tailors and also, again like the Huguenots before them, as designers and for language instruction, and (for example) as wine merchants.

As a counterpoint to those settling into trades and business, Constance Bantman stresses the strangeness and 'otherness' of the political exiles; for the anarchists there was an almost complete lack of integration into the host society, and strikingly they 'appeared as a foreign body in the city'. Life for many French refugees and exiles in the city was very hard; London and Londoners were unappealing, and their experiences and their accounts (where they exist) were sometimes harsh and negative. The terrible poverty in which many lived gave rise to another enduring feature of French life in London today: charitable ventures that also generated around them important social activities.[3]

Michel Rapoport however, focuses on the numbers of French citizens who participated in and contributed more successfully to London's economic growth in the late nineteenth and early twentieth centuries. There are again striking comparisons with today's French population – statistics difficult to obtain because of numbers not being included in official documentation; a largely young population; and the attractions of an open labour market and of a level of professional and social success seen as not possible in France. Four groups are identified in the 'French colony' which would be recognizable today and, as the previous chapters show, are identifiable since the settlement of the Huguenots: commercial, educational, social and charitable, with the French working in food – and Valerie Mars's chapter discusses the many facets (myths and realities) of the development of French cuisine in London which again endure to this day – and fashion, and as workmen, craftsmen and engineers; in the City of London (including young people being sent to London to be trained in British business and financial practices), in the service industry, as performers of various kinds, as booksellers, as painters and sculptors, and as teachers. It was in the nineteenth century that the importance of the French associations and societies in London begins to crystallize, another important aspect of French life in London for many professional people right up until today. The Federation of French Associations in Great Britain (founded in 1942) still thrives and is emblematic of a certain kind of French community in London, with close links to the French Embassy and to established professional associations, businesses and cultural groups, many with historic roots in London.[4]

---

[3] With reference to today's London, see the work and research commissioned in 2010 by the French Consulate 'The Forgotten of St Pancras' ('Les Oubliés de St Pancras'), referenced in the final chapter here, a testament to the continuing difficulties of some young French people arriving in the capital today; as is the Centre Charles Péguy, a French non-profit-making association in Shoreditch, established in 1954, which helps those struggling to find work and somewhere to live.

[4] Fédération des Associations Françaises de Grande Bretagne (FAFGB), established in 1942. Its categories of associations include Alumni and Parents; Cultural (e.g., the Alliance Française, Drama Groups); Leisure (including a Bridge Group); Regional (e.g., for those from the Auvergne, Alsace, Corsica); Professional (e.g., the Chamber of Commerce,

The problems faced by these predecessors would also be recognized by contemporary French Londoners, not least the issue of schooling their children, as is evident in the final chapter, but here again attitudes and experiences are not necessarily those that might be expected. There is, then, continuity in the pre-war French colony that can be seen to have its roots in seventeenth- and eighteenth-century ways of adapting to London (although these necessarily evolved down the centuries with the successive needs and desires of very different French exiles, refugees and economic migrants), a continuity that is still perceptible in contemporary London. There is however, one important rupture in the middle of the twentieth century:

> At the beginning of the Second World War the components of London's French colony had undergone a change over the previous sixty years and now consisted largely of two groups. On the one hand, were those connected with business … On the other hand, were people from the world of culture … The colony was structured around a number of institutions – cultural ones such as the Institut Français, the French schools and churches; economic ones like the French Chamber of Commerce; the many professional societies; and charitable institutions such as the French Hospital.[5]

Essentially, such an analysis suggests that there was cohesion in the colony, despite the many divisions that France had endured during this period, but the outbreak of war, and especially the collapse of France in May–June 1940, brought about a radical change in the French colony in London. The chapters by Debra Kelly, Martyn Cornick and David Drake analyse some of those changes. French citizens of all classes and professions were forced to choose whether to support the legal government of France in Vichy; to support the continuing British resistance to Nazi Germany; to put their families first in the face of likely attack on London, and return to their kin in France, from whom they risked being separated for an unknown length of time; or perhaps to join the partisans backing General de Gaulle or another resistance group. Many returned to France, while different types of French people arrived in London – officers, ordinary soldiers, civilians from every sphere of French society, and politicians, often from opposing sides. It was a period of rupture in every sense, and 'Free French London', except for a few remaining traces from the popular (Soho restaurants) to the official (de Gaulle's statue and the plaque in Carlton Gardens), would

---

Franco-British Lawyers, London Expat Entrepreneurs Group); Charitable Institutions; Sport; Health; Culinary; Education; Military; and Religious (both Protestant and Catholic churches in London). A number of Franco-British societies also belong.

  [5] See the conclusion here to Michel Rapoport's chapter.

be less recognizable, for all its temporary visibility in the host city, to the contemporary London French than the French colony before the war, even though certain businesses endured.

Throughout this history of the French in London considerable new research has therefore been presented, and areas where comparatively more research already existed (for example, work on the Huguenots and on various nineteenth-century exiles) have been re-evaluated within the larger context provided by this first continuous history. Current cultural, political, media, economic, academic and public interest (considered in more detail below) in the contemporary French presence in London is situated for the first time in a comprehensive historical contextualization of the presence of various French communities from the seventeenth century to the present day. Several broad areas of interest become apparent: the traffic of social, political and cultural ideas between France and London; the interchange of skilled workers between London and France and its effects; the traffic of technological knowledge and design ideas; ideas about French superiority in (for example) fashion, gastronomy and luxury goods; French visitors to London and London's image in France; and both commercial and cultural exchanges on a number of levels.

The fundamental questions that have been asked, either implicitly or explicitly, are numerous, and the answers vary in intriguing and important ways across the centuries. Who are the French nationals who come to London? When do they arrive? Why at that particular time? Why is London chosen as a destination? Where did and do the French live in London? Why that area, that street, that house? Has this remained the same, or evolved over the centuries, and why or why not for certain places? How do the French live in the capital? If they work, why do they work in that particular trade, profession, place? How do they build and develop their networks? How did and do the French in London act as a community? Is there indeed something that can be termed a French community (or communities) in London? Do the French in London consider themselves to be a community? Do other London citizens consider the French to be a community? If so why, and if not why not? Has this varied at different times and in different places? What are the other perceptions of Londoners by the French who have lived there at various times? What kinds of contributions do the French make socially, culturally and/or politically both to French community(ies) in London and to the host city? What has been and is their impact? Whether short-lived or longer term, like the lengths of stay of these French residents, what are the legacies that they have left? Successive chapters, each in their own way, answer these questions, and the first 'big picture' has emerged of how the French have made use of the liberty – sometimes the equality, sometimes the fraternity (left out of the book's title …) – and the opportunity afforded by London.

The narrative structure used has been that of a chronological mapping, intersected by a number of themes traced across the centuries and across the spaces and places of London: exile and refuge; politics; gastronomy; fashion; art, literature and music; leisure and pleasure; survival, opportunity and entrepreneurship; but above all, place and space. This 'picture' has also been given visual form in the series of maps created for each chapter as, collectively, the authors' analyses map those places in the capital most frequented and settled by the French, and the effects on those places across the centuries. From Hampstead in the north to Spitalfields in the east, from Soho in the centre to South Kensington in the south-west, and beyond, the physical traces of the French presence in London are many and varied, and are manifest in diverse places and institutions from the religious to the political, via the educational to the commercial. Mapping the places frequented and settled by the French, and the effects on those places across the centuries, facilitates an analysis of patterns of the London French according to class, gender, places of origin, historical period, and political and religious affiliation, leading to a further layer of conceptual considerations.

First, there is the question of the 'visibility' and 'invisibility' of the French during various historical periods. A partial answer to one of the fundamental questions listed earlier is that at certain times there has been a recognizable French community (or communities) in London, but not at others. The issue of the present day is particularly complex and it is clear that there is much more work to do on these aspects of charting and understanding more of the French presence. A further aspect of this book is that of making connections between the lives of contemporary French residents and their historical predecessors (whether seeking refuge or new opportunities), thereby giving further depth and significance to contemporary experience.

Second, on a more conceptual level, the transformation of places and spaces by the French presence in London has been considered: what are the lasting traces of this presence in diverse places and institutions from the religious to the political, from the educational to the creative to the commercial? Again, throughout the various chapters, these traces are apparent in the areas of London settled by the French, or in the institutions or professions with which they engaged, developed their ideas, and earned their living. As for the present day: how can contemporary traces of the large French presence (and this would need to include both real and virtual presences in the digital age) best be documented and analysed?[6]

Third, the preservation of values and/or identities by various categories of French exiles/migrants (for example on a religious or political level – Huguenots, monarchists, republicans) has been discussed; what difference did London make historically to these groups? It is clear that at various times, London offered a place to re-group, to re-evaluate strategies, to review relationships with France. How are French values and identities preserved by today's French migrants? What sorts of values and identities are important, and why? Finally, what are the old perceptions and new realities of the historical and contemporary French presence both for the French and for other Londoners, and indeed for French Londoners?

The point of tracing of links between where and how we find the French in London is certainly not to reinforce stereotypes, nor to 'essentialize' them in categories when there are clearly complex individual motives at work, even when these individuals are caught up in historical and political events. Quite the opposite. However, this first history clearly points to patterns among these complex sets of cultural and socio-economic interactions between already assimilated populations living in London, and French subjects or citizens arriving (both from France and from French overseas territories) in the capital over several centuries. These apparently simplistic 'categorizations' therefore reflect trends over time towards the clustering of French Londoners in certain trades and professions, from booksellers, luxury goods manufacturers and sellers, cooks and restaurateurs, and teachers, to financiers and entrepreneurs. However, further historical and contemporary research will no doubt disturb and revise such starting points, removing any risk of a unified or deterministic approach to historical and cultural analysis. Certainly in today's London, the younger generation of French and francophone residents present ever more and ever-evolving facets of what it is to live and work in the British capital. A search for understanding and meaning both in representations of the French in London (from within and from outside those communities) and in their experiences, motives, practices, organization and contributions, is necessarily an ongoing interpretive task, and one that analyses cultural change over time. The approach taken here as a starting point therefore analyses cultural exchange and transformation at the site of the encounter between French and British cultures, in a London that is itself constantly changing.

---

[6] Saskia Huc-Hepher, the co-author of the final chapter, is also the curator (working with the British Library) of the 'London French special collection' in the UK Web Archive, which documents the online presence of the contemporary London French.

This book ends by providing insights into the contemporary French presence by assessing the motives and lives of a cross section of French, and French-speaking, people seeking new opportunities in London in the late twentieth and early twenty-first centuries. This final attention to the present day marks the book out as a timely history on a number of levels. In the contemporary social context, the French Consulate estimates that between 300,000 and 400,000 French citizens reside in the UK, with the majority choosing to live and work in London and the south-east. The numbers are large enough for Nicolas Sarkozy to urge 'France's Children' to return home, in a highly mediatized campaign speech made in London in January 2007, marking the first time that a French presidential candidate campaigned in Britain, and highlighting what he called 'the intelligence, imagination and passion for work and desire for success' that the French have brought to London and that 'Paris needs so much'. Both the French and British press commented a great deal on the trip.[7] The Sarkozy visit to London and the appeal to French citizens living outside France also highlighted an element of the ambiguous attitudes that the French state holds with regard to those who choose to live and work outside France, and of political reforms in France from 2008 onwards, as is discussed in more detail below.

A further contemporary manifestation of the contribution made by the French to London was the establishment in 2007 of the 'Français of the Year Award', which celebrates the achievements of prominent French men and women in, for example, business, sport, fashion, the arts and gastronomy. Voted for by French citizens residing in London, recipients have included Arsenal manager Arsène Wenger, captain of the French rugby team and London Wasps player Raphaël Ibañez, fashion designer Nicole Farhi, actress Eva Green, writer Marc Levy, chefs Hélène Darroze and Raymond Blanc, business tycoon Vincent de Rivaz (EDF) and financier Yoël Zaoui (Goldman Sachs).[8] These well-known personalities serve as an identifiable reminder of the myriad living and working patterns of many thousands of their compatriots and of their historical predecessors in the capital, and have prompted headlines over the last five years or so in London's *Evening Standard* such as 'Zut alors! The French Are Taking Over' (1 November

---

[7] See, e.g., 'Sarkozy drague les expatriés', available at <http://www.lexpress.fr/actualite/politique/sarkozy-drague-les-expatries> [accessed 2 Nov. 2012]. The press also reported that a crowd of around 1,000 were unable enter the conference hall in Old Billingsgate Market, which was already full.

[8] The award was created in 2007 by Laurent Feniou, an investment banker with Rothschild who had then lived in London for 13 years; he was also president of the Association Grandes Ecoles City Circle. In the inaugural year some 3,500 French people in London took part in the voting. In 2011, the awards were taken up by the Chez Gérard restaurant group.

2007) and 'The French Invasion' (2 March 2011). Other media reports from both sides of the Channel focus on the contribution to business: 'La City est (un peu) française' ('The City is (a little) French', *Le Point*, 3 January 2008); 'Ces Français qu'on s'arrache à la City' ('The Frenchmen who are fought over in the City', *La Tribune*, 6 February, 2008; including subheadings on 'The Three Musketeers of Goldman Sachs' and asking 'Are they lost forever?'); 'Le roi des fusion-acquisitions en Europe couronné par la City' ('The king of mergers and acquisitions in Europe crowned by the City', on Moroccan-born banker Yoël Zaoui, *La Tribune*, 27 November 2008). There are also surveys of the more general image of prominent French people in London, often recycling (sometimes in an interesting way) old stereotypes and resonant images and worth quoting in some detail to show the types of discourse used: 'Election des meilleurs "Frenchies" de l'année à Londres' ('Election of the best Frenchies of the Year in London', *Le Figaro*, 27 November 2008); 'Ici Londres, les Français parlent aux Français' (*Les Echos*, using the 'London Calling' signal and the title of the programmes broadcast from London to Occupied France during the Second World War); 'Des lauriers pour les exilés français de Londres' ('Laurels for the French exiles in London', *Le Figaro*, 1 November 2007); 'French making themselves at home in London' (*International Herald Tribune*, 25 January 2008); 'Paris-on-Thames' (*The Economist*, 24 February 2011; the same heading had been used in the *Financial Times*, 12 July 2008); 'The Accidental Englishman, France's Other Ambassador' (*The Independent*, 2 November 2007 on the writer Marc Levy); 'New awards to toast London's French quarter' (*Evening Standard*, 13 July 2007); 'Expats vote on the crème de la crème of French in London' (*Evening Standard*, 11 July 2008); 'Les Français sont arrivés, successful French immigrants', (*The Independent*, 4 July 2008; the term 'émigrés' is also used in the headlining paragraph); 'French expats vote for their London crème de la crème' (*Evening Standard*, 10 July 2009); and 'London's French Foreign Legion Shuns Sarkozy Plea to Come Home' (Bloomberg.com, 17 January 2008).

The national events organized to commemorate the seventieth anniversary (June 2010) of the arrival of de Gaulle in London in June 1940, and the presence of the Free French in London during the war, attracted large audiences at the French Institute and considerable media interest in the UK and France, as did the visit by the French president to Carlton Gardens, the BBC and the Chelsea Hospital; and the event was used for a key moment in new developments in Franco-British military strategy, as discussed further below. In a further contemporary manifestation of the French presence in the British capital (but also of British interest in 'things French'), in November 2010 potential audience numbers were sufficient to see the successful establishment of a commercial French-language radio station, French Radio London (FRL). Broadcast on Digital Audio Broadcasting (DAB) reaching the area bordered by the M25 and online, twenty-four hours a day, FRL, 'the French Voice of London', hit its first year targets after just five months, with its success attributed to its mix of music and other programming including interviews, reviews, interactive debates on topical issues, news of events in London, etc. Its current commercial partners are diverse, but often also reflect strong French business interests in London and the UK: Renault UK, EDF, Eurostar, Cityjet, Nicolas Wine Merchants, the hotel and restaurant group Relais and Chateaux, the French Chamber of Commerce, and also other media corporations – France 24 and TV5 Monde.[9] FRL was notably featured in the opening sequence of BBC2's *This is Britain* series presented by Andrew Marr, which aimed to reveal unexpected trends and facts about Britain – 'a country we only think we know' according to the programme-makers – at the time of the 2011 census. The facts that there are up to 400,000 French people living in Britain, and that London is said to be the fifth (or sixth) biggest 'French' city, were chosen to headline the 'unexpected stories and strange twists' in Britain's story promised by Marr, and those figures also found their way into the British press. An additional irony in Franco-British relations revealed by the figures was pointed out by *The Telegraph*: 'This [the current numbers of French residents] is apparently the case, despite the fact that the original 1801 census was partly intended to discover whether or not we had enough men fit enough to fight Napoleon'.[10] It is the 2011 census which should finally be able to provide the evidence for these suspected numbers.

There continues to be sporadic media interest in the London French as one or other element of the phenomenon attracts the interest of journalists. Radio 4's May 2012 radio programme on the 'French East End' noted that today's London French community is racially and culturally diverse and has grown far beyond the bourgeois confines of 'Frog Valley' in 'well-heeled South Kensington'. The East End's 'French connections' were explored from the seventeenth century, when French Protestants settled in Spitalfields (represented today by the Denis Severs' House museum and in street names such as Fournier Street, Fleur de Lys Street and Nantes Passage), to the present, for example in a large sixth-form college in Newham with a considerable number of francophone pupils from former French overseas departments or colonies such as Réunion, Guadeloupe and

---

[9] Previous partners have ranged from luxury holiday resorts company ClubMed, to World First Foreign Exchange (its first sponsor), to the Barbican.

[10] P. Smith, review of *This is Britain*, in *The Telegraph*, 25 March 2011.

Algeria, and providing a contrast with the Lycée Charles de Gaulle in South Kensington.[11] The Radio 4 programme also featured Hackney and a group of young French designers, artists and digital media specialists working there.[12] In June 2012, the *Sunday Times Magazine* ran an eight-page cover story feature entitled 'Londres calling, why 400,000 French people are colonising the capital', complete with a Transport for London poster with often witty French names given to London's tube stations from 'Parc de la Reine' in the north-east and 'Mornington Croissant' in the north-west, to the renamed 'Gare de Napoléon' replacing Waterloo.[13] The opinions of the interviewees echo many of those in the final chapter here – the attractions of free enterprise, less racism, Britain as more meritocratic and less socially hierarchical, London having a more creative atmosphere.[14]

At the time of final preparation of this book, a further spate of headlines concerning the French in London was generated around the 2012 French elections. Even before the May 2012 French presidential election took place there was press speculation about how London might vote, provoked partly around the Socialist presidential candidate François Hollande's London visit in February 2012. The high-profile visit to London aimed also to boost his international profile, but the fact that London has become a crucial campaign destination for candidates in the French presidential race was also noted, and the echoes of Sarkozy's 2007 campaign urging expats to return home were not missed. The visit took place in an atmosphere of tension for a number of reasons: David Cameron's 'good luck' message to Sarkozy at a Paris summit earlier that month, and then the British government's refusal to sign up to the new EU treaty; Hollande's desire for more rules for the financial markets; and the recent announcement in France of his plans for a 75 per cent tax bracket on annual earnings above one million euros. Hollande's visit began with lunch with the Labour leader Ed Miliband and the shadow cabinet at Westminster, while Cameron refused to see him, putting the decision down to protocol, with the British prime minister not wishing to meet French presidential candidates during an election period. Cameron went on to compound antagonism to Hollande at the G20 summit in June 2012 by promising to 'lay out the red carpet' for French

---

[11] Therefore the same historical spread as this book. The same Newham College was also previously visited for the research in the final chapter here and a focus group carried out with students there.

[12] L. Ash, 'The French East End', BBC Radio 4, 30 May 2012; see also <http://www.bbc.co.uk/programmes/b01j5nw4> [accessed 30 May 2012].

[13] *Sunday Times Magazine* cover, 10 June 2012; image also used here as book cover.

[14] A. Turner, 'Vive la différence. Lower taxes, more creativity and innovation, less racism. Why the French are taking a fancy to London', *Sunday Times Magazine*, 10 June 2012.

businesses and entrepreneurs wishing to move to Britain when the top marginal tax rate in France was increased.[15]

In the run-up to the elections, it was already being noted that the traditional right leanings of London's expat community may be challenged by younger, less wealthy and more diverse French residents in the capital. At the time Axelle Lemaire, the Socialist party's Northern Europe candidate in the June legislative elections, based in London, presciently analysed changes in the London French, saying that the French community is 'more diverse' than often thought; she went on to win the new seat (discussed further below).[16] Other political analyses concur with this evolution over the last ten to fifteen years, with London's French residents diversifying from those primarily in diplomacy and business circles to less wealthy people working in services, public services and education, and students attracted by British universities.[17] A month later, in the 2012 French legislative elections, eleven new deputies were elected, representing newly-created constituencies for the French expatriate community across the world, and ending in unexpected results, especially for the right-wing Union pour un Mouvement Populaire (UMP) that initiated the legislation.[18]

---

[15] See, e.g., A. Chrisafis, 'French presidential forerunner makes campaign stop in London', *The Guardian*, 29 Feb. 2012; A. Chrisafis, 'François Hollande seeks to reassure UK and City of London', *The Guardian*, 14 Feb. 2012; G. Parker, 'Cameron avoids French Socialist candidate', *Financial Times*, 27 Feb. 2012, available at <http://www.ft.com/cms/s/0/a7b4eb14-6155-11e1-8a8e-00144feabdc0.html> [accessed 2 Nov. 2012]; G. Rachman, 'The tactless Mr Cameron and the Eurozone blame game', *Financial Times*, 19 June 2012, available at <http://blogs.ft.con/the-world/2012/06/the-tactless-mr-cameron-the-eurozone-blame-game> [accessed 2 Nov. 2012].

[16] L. Davies, 'French elections: how will London vote?', *The Guardian*, 13 Apr. 2012, available at <http://www.guardian.co.uk/world/2012/apr/13/french-elections-how-london-vote> [accessed 16 Apr. 2012].

[17] L. Davies, news blog, 'The French in London: bienvenue, François Hollande?', 29 Feb. 2012, available at <http://www.guardian.co.uk/world/2012/feb/french-london-francois-hollande> [accessed 16 Apr. 2012]. The random people interviewed for the blog ranged from a number of staunch Sarkozy voters, to those planning to vote for Hollande, to those who voted Sarkozy last time and were planning to change because of disappointment with him. Philippe Marlière kept an election diary on the French presidential election at <http://www.opendemocracy.net/philippe-marli%C3%A8re/marli%C3%A8re-across-la-manche-diary-of-2012-french-presidential-election> [accessed 16 Apr. 2012]. He also gave an informal snapshot on his own experience of voting in the newly established Kentish Town bi-lingual French-English school, where, standing in a long queue for a couple of hours, he saw the diverse social make-up of French voters; he notes that Hollande won in that area but Sarkozy won in South Kensington, reflecting the 'two worlds' of official France and newer arrivals (informal interview with Debra Kelly, London, 12 Sept. 2012).

[18] The right-wing UMP expected to create a number of safe seats for its own party 'because expatriate voters have, since extra-territorial voting was introduced in 1981,

French public discourse also reveals ambivalence about describing its expatriates, using terms such as 'The French settled outside France' ('Les Français établis hors de France'), as employed in the constitution, and two terms that can be translated as the 'French abroad', but reveal a subtle difference in the relationship to France: 'Les Français *de* l'étranger' (with a greater sense of attachment to the country of residence) and 'Les Français *à* l'étranger' (with a sense of continued greater attachment to France).[19] The Northern European constituency – which includes Denmark, Estonia, Ireland, Iceland, Latvia, Lithuania, Norway, the UK and Sweden – is dominated by the French population in the UK – and within the UK, London (the French Consulate recorded around 123,000 French citizens registered for the elections, far outstripping the next highest number of almost 9,000 in Ireland; Estonia recorded 182).[20] All of the main parties chose candidates based in London, and of the twenty official candidates for the seat, nine were based in London, and another three in other regions of the UK. Unsurprisingly, for the British press the deputy for Northern

---

always given massive support to the right. Yet although this trend was maintained for the presidential election, the outcome was unexpectedly reversed for the legislative elections, when only 3 of the 11 new seats were won by the UMP' (S. Collard, 'The expatriate vote in the French presidential and legislative elections of 2012: a case of unintended consequences', *Parliamentary Affairs*, vi (2013), 213–33, at p. 213). The initiative was taken by the then newly-elected President Sarkozy to fulfil an electoral pledge to French voters abroad who, for a long time, had demanded better political representation. Part of his campaign message, first in London in Jan. 2007 (as previously referred to) and then in March 2007 in a written message, targeted the French outside France, urging them to return home by saying that the France they had left because of its outmoded systems and obstacles to innovation was changing and needed their energy and initiative (see again Collard, 'The expatriate vote', for a very detailed analysis of the context in which the reforms came into existence and of the unexpected results and their significance; see also P. Marlière, 'A quoi vont servir les députés des Français de l'étranger?', available at <http://www.lemonde.fr/idees/article/2012/07/10/a-quoi-vont-servir-les-deputes-des-francais-de-l-etranger_1730960_3232.html> [accessed 13 Sept. 2012]. One of his main arguments is that it is difficult to see how the French abroad can place demands on the government as many do not pay taxes in France).

[19] See Collard, 'The expatriate vote', again, as above. She also notes that the only official use of the word 'expatrié' is in the title of the Senate's dedicated website <http://www.expatries.senat.fr> [accessed 13 Sept. 2012]. The same conversation was held with the editors of this book by members of the French diplomatic service around whether to use 'Les Français de/à Londres' for the French version of the 'French in London' or of the 'London French' when this book project and its further research were conceived. Compare also the beginning of this conclusion and the caveats around the ways to describe the French 'exiles', 'migrants', 'visitors' who took up residence in London at different times and for different lengths of time.

[20] See, e.g., the BBC news item, D. Finnerty, 'Why are the French getting an MP for London?', available at <http://www.bbc.co.uk/news/uk-17893296> [accessed 11 Sept. 2012].

Europe immediately became the 'MP for South Kensington': 'French to elect first "Kensington MP"' (*The Independent*, 31 May 2012); 'France elects left-wing Parti Socialiste candidate in so-called "MP for South Kensington" seat' (*The Independent*, 18 June 2012). Axelle Lemaire of the Socialist party won the first round vote by a clear margin, and went on to win the second round with 54.76 per cent of the vote, followed by the UMP's Emmanuelle Savarit with 45.24 per cent (turnout was around 18,000, just 20 per cent).[21]

More visibility, then, for the French presence in London, but one that serves also to show how far from these perceptions of the French in London those citizens have, in all senses, travelled. Across the spaces and places of London, the sites of the London French, real and virtual, continue to evolve. Is there something 'different' about French migration in the capital? Are they an 'a-typical' group of migrants, even when compared with other European migrants historically and in contemporary society? More work needs to be done on comparative analyses before these question can be answered. If, since the beginning of the eighteenth century, it has been argued that French immigrants came to exchange their poverty for English prosperity, the opposite argument that immigrants enrich the country has also endured, and the French have been admired for doing so much to help themselves once arrived in London.[22]

Perhaps the continued shared fascination is due to the observation that the French and British are not so different, while appearing to be very much so. As Kirsty Carpenter writes here of the French exiles during the Revolution: 'they provided the British with a living example of deep-rooted similarities between their two cultures that were in many ways more powerful and persuasive than the superficial differences suggested by dress and language'. Despite continued and persistent French-baiting in certain sectors of the British press and of the political classes, the late twentieth and early twenty-first centuries may represent another 'Anglo-French moment', as defined by Philip Mansel here for the period from the late eighteenth century to the end of the First World War. Then, as now, London plays a role in French politics, and London continues to offer 'proximity, modernity and freedom' as suggested by Mansel for the earlier historical period. Although the picture may be more complex, the research carried out by Saskia Huc-Hepher and Helen Drake in the final chapter certainly echoes in places those positive perceptions, and the image of a stultifying social and economic atmosphere

---

[21] See, e.g., 'Législatives: tous les résultats des Français de l'étranger', *Le Nouvel Observateur*, 4 June 2012; 'Resultats du 2ème tour dans la 3ème circonscription – Europe du Nord', *Le Monde*, 17 June 2012.

[22] See the first chapter here; reference to the *Rights and Liberties of Englishmen Asserted* (1701) and *England's Interest and Improvement* (1663).

in France is a recurring one both in the testimonials here, and in media and other discourses both in France and in the UK. Discrimination in France against various minority groups, or because of education and social status, may be real or perceived; but it is real to those who experience it, and a common thread runs through many of the motivations and experiences of those French (and francophone) people who come to London.

But, of course, London is no utopia and all may not be as it seems. To take just one example, consider an area of long-established French expertise and innovation, gastronomy and the restaurant business: seen by food critics and other food professionals as having fallen behind London in culinary terms,[23] Paris is nonetheless currently witnessing a renewed, young restaurant scene.[24] And although French labour laws and the bureaucracy which London French entrepreneurs complain about and are pleased to leave behind are a reality, setting up a business in Paris can be cheaper. The traffic between London and Paris runs both ways: 'I can't imagine we could have opened [even in East London] for less than half a million; here [in Paris] we did it for £150k. Our rent is expensive by Parisian standards, but cheap for London. We'd love to do something in London, but we'd need serious investment', says a young British chef who has travelled in the other direction and moved to Paris.[25] There is much more to say about this two-way traffic, again through a historical and contemporary lens, and further comparative study would be revealing.

As Huc-Hepher and Drake note, the French in London very often remain attached to, and indeed part of, France, by virtue of its proximity. It is questionable, therefore, whether they feel a real necessity to integrate into the host culture (although some do), or to form a 'distinct, homogeneous community apart from it'. The notion of a French community or communities in London remains nebulous, and at the very least in evolution. Perhaps instead it is rather a fluid community (or communities) with French residents in London trying on and using their various French and Londoner identities at different times and in different ways, and it is important to note that while French citizens quite often readily accept that they feel like 'Londoners', they do not admit to feeling English (although

---

[23] The Francophile American journalist Michael Steinberger's *Au Revoir to All That: Food, Wine and the End of France* (2009) provided arguments linking the decline in gastronomic prowess to that of France's political and economic status.

[24] Especially in 'bistronomie', a move away from classic haute cuisine towards a more experimental type of cooking, offered in more relaxed surroundings and at more affordable prices.

[25] Michael Greenwold, a British chef in Paris, co-owner of the 'Roseval' restaurant in the 20th *arrondissement*; 'Bistronomie Paris', *The Independent on Sunday Magazine*, 7 Oct. 2012.

the identification with being a Londoner is also true of many other migrants to the capital, including UK citizens born outside it). On the micro, individual level London seems to have a transformative effect on French identities and behaviours, as the final chapter also notes, and the city is still seen as offering space, openness and freedom. On the macro, national level there has been increased Franco-British co-operation on various levels in recent years, despite continuing tensions in the European debate.

One of the most obvious examples of this is in the area of military co-operation. London and Paris signed British-French security treaties in November 2010 and began to implement many of the military capability development issues contained in the Permanent Structured Co-operation (PESCO) protocol in the Treaty of Lisbon (2009) on a bilateral basis, such as the creation of multinational forces; harmonization of their military needs by pooling and specializing capabilities; co-operation on training and logistics; enhancing their forces' interoperability and deployability, and so on. London and Paris also agreed on the development of a new Combined Joint Expeditionary Force and the sharing of aircraft carriers. They also intend to co-operate on training and support for A400M military transport aircraft; joint development of technologies regarding submarine systems; aligning plans in maritime mine counter-measures to enhance interoperability; and military satellite communications and the possible French use of British spare capacities in the field of air-to-air refuelling. Furthermore, they agreed to work together on a new equipment programme of unmanned air systems, as well as a more efficient defence industry.[26]

In 2010, the British press widely reported this 'landmark defence alliance', ranging from military operations on land, sea and in the air to nuclear weapons.[27] In 2011, Britain and France worked together in Libya, supporting the opposition fighters against Colonel Gaddafi's regime, with British and French special forces sent in on the ground. In January 2013, as this book was being prepared for publication, Britain supported the French mission to drive Islamist militants from its former colony, Mali. Britain supplied transporter and reconnaissance aircraft to the French and expressed its willingness to send troops to assist logistics, intelligence and

[26] B. Németh, 'PESCO and British-French military co-operation', in *European Geostrategy*, ed. J. Rogers and L. Simon, 14 Feb. 2012, available at <http://europeangeostrategy. ideasoneurope.eu/2012/02/14/pesco-and-british-french-military-co-operation> [accessed 5 Nov. 2012].

[27] See, e.g., K. Sengupta, 'Anglo-French deal re-writes military history', *The Independent*, 2 Nov. 2010, available at <http://www.independent.co.uk/news/uk/politics/anglofrench-deal-rewrites-military-history-2122617.html> [accessed 5 Nov. 2012].

surveillance, without engaging in combat.[28] During these periods and since, French diplomatic teams in London have repeatedly stressed the importance of this close military alliance.

The importance of French approaches to diplomacy, especially cultural diplomacy and what is now termed 'soft power', is documented here by Charlotte Faucher and Philippe Lane,[29] and the continuing evidence of this was also very apparent in, for example, the 2010 de Gaulle anniversary (already discussed), and previously in 2004 for the centenary of the Entente Cordiale. With the 500th anniversary of Agincourt and the 200th anniversary of Waterloo approaching in 2015, perhaps a more fully rounded counter-discourse of Anglo-French co-operation and of long-established and enduring cultural, social and economic exchanges may yet emerge to challenge old perceptions with new realities, and with London providing a site of evidence.[30]

[28] See, e.g., *The Guardian*, 29 Jan. 2013.

[29] See also Ph. Lane, *Présence française dans le monde: l'action culturelle et scientifique* (2011); published in English as *French Scientific and Cultural Diplomacy* (Liverpool, 2013).

[30] For thoughtful histories of Franco-British relations, see, e.g., I. Tombs and R. Tombs, *That Sweet Enemy: the French and the British from the Sun King to the Present* (2006), which tells the story of the relationship between the French and the British over more than three centuries and whose authors believe that 'this relationship is unique in the modern world, not only for its duration and the breadth of its cultural, economic and political ramifications, but also for its global consequences' (p. 686). Robert Gibson, in *Best of Enemies: Anglo-French Relations since the Norman Conquest* (Exeter, 1995; 2nd edn. 2004, re-published for the centenary of the Entente Cordiale, and updated to include the Second Gulf War), says: 'no two other countries have a heritage that has been enriched over so long a period of time as England and France. And no two countries have made so powerful and protracted an impact as these two have upon the lives of one another. Over a span of almost a thousand years, no nation has had so many dealings with the English as the French' (p. 304). Diana Cooper-Richet and Michel Rapoport, in *L'Entente Cordiale: cent ans de relations culturelles franco-britaniniques, 1904–2004* (Paris, 2006), state: 'Derision and undisguised admiration rub shoulders, revealing the ambiguity of relations between the two countries. This ambivalence is no doubt what best characterises the ties that unite these two great nations in the areas studied here' (p. 390) (Dérision et admiration non déguisée se côtoient montrant, par là même, l'ambigüité des relations entre les deux pays. Cette ambivalence est sans doute ce qui caractérise le mieux les liens qui unissent ces deux grandes nations dans les domaines étudiés).

Index

Lightning Source UK Ltd.
Milton Keynes UK
UKOW031947230613

212643UK00002B/51/P